TOP TRUMPS®

FIGHTER
AIRCRAFT

This book is officially licensed by Winning Moves UK Ltd, owners of the Top Trumps registered trademark.

Peter March has asserted his right to be identified as the author of this book.

British Library Cataloguing-in-Publication Data:
A catalogue record for this book is available from the British Library

ISBN 1 84425 398 8

Library of Congress catalog card no. 2006928057

Published by Haynes Publishing,
Sparkford, Yeovil, Somerset BA22 7JJ, UK
Tel: 01963 442030 Fax: 01963 440001
Int. tel: +44 1963 442030 Int. fax: +44 1963 440001
Email: sales@haynes.co.uk
Website: www.haynes.co.uk

Haynes North America, Inc.,
861 Lawrence Drive, Newbury Park
California 91320, USA

Printed and bound in Great Britain by
J. H. Haynes & Co. Ltd, Sparkford

Photographic credits:

All except front cover main image: PRM Aviation Collection
Front cover main image © Eurofighter GmbH

The Author

Peter March is one of the UK's leading aviation experts. He has written for and edited several leading aviation magazines, and has more than 100 books on military and civil aviation to his credit.

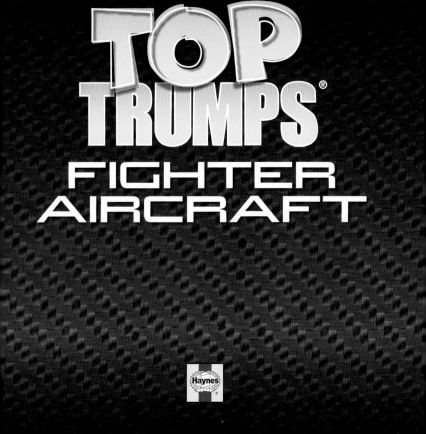

TOP TRUMPS

FIGHTER AIRCRAFT

Haynes

Contents

About
Top Trumps

It's now more than 30 years since Britain's kids first caught the Top Trumps craze. The game remained hugely popular until the 1990s, when it slowly drifted into obscurity. Then, in 1999, UK games company Winning Moves discovered it, bought it, dusted it down, gave it a thorough makeover and introduced it to a whole new generation. And so the Top Trumps legend continues.

Nowadays, there are Top Trumps titles for just about everyone, with subjects about animals, cars, ships, aircraft and all the great films and TV shows. Top Trumps is now even more popular than before. In Britain, a pack of Top Trumps is bought every six seconds! And it's not just British children who love the game. Children in Australasia, the Far East, the Middle East, all over Europe and in North America can buy Top Trumps at their local shops.

Today you can even play the game on the internet, interactive DVD, your games console and even your mobile phone.

You've played the game...

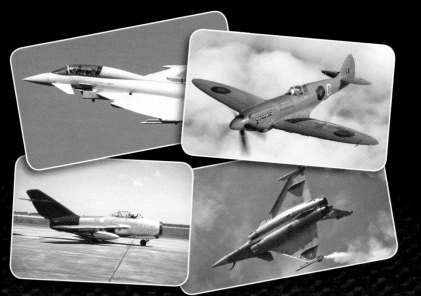

Now read the book!

Haynes Publishing and Top Trumps have teamed up to bring
you this exciting new Top Trumps book, in which you will find
even more pictures, details and statistics.

Top Trumps: Fighter Aircraft features 45 of the world's
most awesome fighter planes, from the Supermarine Spitfire
of WW2 to the Eurofighter Typhoon of today. Packed with
fascinating facts, stunning photographs and all the vital
statistics, this is the essential pocket guide. And if you're
lucky enough to spot any of these aircraft, then at the back
of the book we've provided space for you to record when and
where you saw them.

Look out for other Top Trumps books from Haynes Publishing
– even more facts, even more fun!

British Aerospace
Sea Harrier

Single-seat, single turbofan vertical/short take-off and landing naval multi-role fighter

British Aerospace
Sea Harrier

Single-seat, single turbofan vertical/short take-off and landing naval multi-role fighter

Developed from the RAF's Harrier jump-jet, the Sea Harrier FRS1 first equipped the Royal Navy's new aircraft carriers in the early 1980s. The 'FRS' (Fighter, Reconnaissance, Strike) showed that the Sea Harrier was intended for the interception of large low-performance Soviet aircraft shadowing the battle group or convoy on NATO exercises. It had an excellent 'Blue Fox' forward-looking radar. The Falklands War in 1982 proved the V/STOL fighter's value. During the conflict Sea Harriers flew 1,126 combat missions and 15 Argentinian aircraft were shot down for no loss in combat. In the late 1980s the original FRS1s were upgraded to FRS2 (renamed 'Fighter Attack' FA2 in 1994), together with some new-build examples. In the 1990s they were used on Combat Air Patrols in the Balkans and later Sierra Leone. Joint Force Harrier was set up in 2000 to have RAF and RN Harriers working together. The Sea Harrier was retired on 28 March 2006 with the RN squadrons re-equipping with Harrier GR7As at RAF Cottesmore.

Statistics

Sea Harrier FA2

Engines	One Rolls-Royce Pegasus 104/106 vectored thrust turbofan
Power	21,500lb thrust
Span	7.70m (25ft 3in)
Length	14.17m (46ft 6in)
Height	3.71m (12ft 2in)
Max weight	9,843kg (21,699lb)
Top	734mph (1,185km/h)
Ceiling	15,545m (51,000ft)
Max range	970km (602 miles)
Crew	One
Weapons	AIM-120, AIM-9 Sidewinder missiles 30mm Aden cannon
First flown	September 1979
Into service	31 March 1980
Out of service	28 March 2006

Bell P-39
Airacobra
Single-seat, single piston-engined fighter

Bell P-39
Airacobra
Single-seat, single piston-engined fighter

One of the first fighter aircraft to be equipped with a tricycle undercarriage, the Bell Airacobra first flew in 1939. When introduced it was unique in having an aft-mounted engine driving a tractor propeller, via a five-foot extension shaft between the pilot's legs. It had heavy armament, including a 37mm cannon firing through the propeller hub. A total of 9,558 P-39s was built, with over half (4,952) going to the Soviet Union under the Lend-Lease scheme. The Russians found it a very reliable and effective addition for the Red Air Force. In April 1942, large numbers were sent to the Pacific theatre of operations, where they helped contain the Japanese until something more effective was available. The US Army Air Force used the Airacobra in the Middle East but none were based in England during the Second World War. Many of the top Soviet aces flew the Airacobra and it was probably more damaging to the Germans over Russia than anywhere else.

Statistics

P-39Q Airacobra

Engine	One Allison V-1710-17 piston engine
Power	1,325hp
Span	10.36m (34ft 0in)
Length	9.19m (30ft 2in)
Height	3.63m (11ft 10¾in)
Max weight	4,104kg (9,048lb)
Top speed	612km/h (380mph)
Ceiling	10,668m (35,000ft)
Max range	724km (450 miles)
Crew	One
Weapons	37mm cannon, machine guns
First flew	25 November 1939
Into service	January 1941
Out of service	1944

Boeing (McDonnell Douglas)
F-15 Eagle

Twin turbofan, single-seat air superiority fighter

Boeing (McDonnell Douglas)
F-15 Eagle
Twin turbofan, single-seat air superiority fighter

The F-15 Eagle was designed as an air superiority fighter and interceptor
to replace the F-4 Phantom. It has two engines, very advanced avionics
and features large area wings. The Eagle's aerodynamic design was very
advanced by the standards of the day. F-15s were widely deployed in
Europe during the Cold War. When based in Alaska, they helped protect
North America from a Soviet attack over the Arctic. Israeli Air Force Eagles
made their operational debut claiming five Syrian Air Force MiG-21s.
During the 1991 Gulf War (Operation Desert Storm) 48 Eagles made the
longest non-stop fighter deployment in history, being airborne for up to
17 hours flying from the US to Dhahran. In its career the F-15 has scored
over 100 victories for no losses. More than 1,600 F-15s have been built,
mainly for the US Air Force and they are in service with the Israeli,
Japanese and Saudi Arabian air arms.

F-15C Eagle

Engines	Two Pratt & Whitney F100-PW-220 turbofans
Power	14,670lb thrust (dry); 23,830lb thrust (with afterburning)
Span	13.05m (42ft 9¾in)
Length	19.43m (63ft 9in)
Height	5.63m (18ft 5½in)
Max weight	30,845kg (68,000lb)
Top speed	2,655km/h (1,650mph)
Ceiling	18,288m (60,000ft)
Max range	5,745km (3,570 miles)
Crew	One
Weapons	M61A1 20m cannon; AIM-9, AIM-7 missiles
First flown	27 July 1972
Entered service	January 1976

Curtiss P-40
Warhawk

Single-seat, single piston-engined fighter

Curtiss P-40
Warhawk

Single-seat, single piston-engined fighter

The Curtiss P-40 was built in large numbers during the Second World War. The first version was the Tomahawk, a development of the long line of Hawk fighters. Powered by an Allison liquid-cooled in-line engine, the P-40 became a standard fighter with the US Army Air Force pursuit squadrons in the late 1930s. The Kittyhawk was a further development extensively used in the Middle and Far East by the Commonwealth air forces. In American service its first operational mission was during the Japanese attack on Pearl Harbor in December 1941. At first the ability of the P-40 was strictly limited by its Allison engine, so this was replaced by a British Rolls-Royce Merlin engine. The Warhawk made its mark in China where the American Volunteer Group, named the Flying Tigers, flew with distinction against the Japanese from 1942. The Soviet Union received 2,397 P-40s under Lend-Lease. By 1944 its performance had been overtaken by newer types.

P-40F-5 Warhawk

Engine	One Packard-built V-1650-1 Merlin piston engine
Power	1,300hp
Span	11.38m (37ft 3½in)
Length	10.16m (33ft 3¼in)
Height	3.76m (12ft 3½in)
Max weight	3,855kg (8,499lb)
Top speed	586km/h (364mph)
Ceiling	11,582m (38,000ft)
Max range	1,207km (750 miles)
Crew	One
Weapons	0.50 machine guns
First flew	14 October 1938
Into service	May 1939
Out of service	1944

Dassault
Mirage III

Single turbojet, single-seat multi-role fighter

Dassault
Mirage III
Single turbojet, single-seat multi-role fighter

The delta-winged Mirage III was produced in larger numbers than
any other European jet fighter. It was the first French aircraft to reach
twice the speed of sound in level flight in October 1958. The aircraft's
capability resulted in the French Armée de l'Air ordering the new fighter
in substantial numbers. Foreign air forces were also attracted, especially
Israel (where it was named Kafir) and South Africa (Cheetah). Some of
the Israeli examples were passed to the Argentine Air Force and were
used against Britain in the Falklands War of 1982. The type gave many air
forces their first fighters capable of flying at Mach 2 (twice the speed of
sound). It was also built under licence in Switzerland and Australia. In the
Arab–Israeli wars of 1967 and 1973, the Israeli Mirage IIIs outclassed the
Arab-flown MiGs. Many upgraded examples are still flying with smaller air
arms around the world.

Mirage III

Engine	**One SNECMA Atar 9K-50 turbojet**
Power	**11,023lb thrust (dry); 15,873lb thrust (with afterburning)**
Span	**8.20m (26ft 11½in)**
Length	**15.56m (51ft ¾in)**
Height	**4.50m (14ft 9in)**
Max weight	**14,000kg (32,407lb)**
Top speed	**2,338 km/h (1,453mph)**
Ceiling	**17,983m (59,000ft)**
Max range	**1,315km (817 miles)**
Crew	**One**
Weapons	**30mm cannon; Matra, Magic, Sidewinder missiles**
First flew	**17 November 1956**
Into service	**July 1961**

Dassault
Mirage 2000
Single turbofan, single-seat multi-role fighter

Dassault
Mirage 2000
Single turbofan, single-seat multi-role fighter

The Mirage 2000 was designed to replace the swept-wing Mirage F1.
Dassault went back to the previous delta wing shape of the Mirage III. This
high-lift wing gives greatly improved manoeuvrability from its
fly-by-wire controls. The Mirage 2000 has been the primary combat
aircraft with the French Armée de l'Air from the mid-1980s as an
interceptor and air superiority fighter. It has a very modern cockpit and
sophisticated navigation equipment and it can operate in all weathers.
Excellent acceleration, high speed and a high rate of climb, together with
good manoeuvrability have made it a successful export for the French
company to eight countries, including a number to the Republic of China
in the mid-1990s. The fighter was flown by the French in the Gulf War of
1991 and was used as part of the United Nations peacekeeping force over
Bosnia and Kosovo in the 1990s.

Mirage 2000C

Engine	One SNECMA M53-P2 afterburning turbofan
Power	14,462lb thrust (dry) and 21,384lb thrust with afterburner
Span	9.13m (30ft 0in)
Length	14.36m (47ft 1¼in)
Height	5.20m (17ft ¾in)
Max weight	17,000kg (37,478lb)
Top speed	2,338 km/h (1,453mph)
Ceiling	18,000m (59,055ft)
Max range	1,850km (1,150 miles)
Crew	One (C, E, R,-5 variants)
Weapons	30mm DEFA 554 cannon; MATRA Magic 2, MATRA Mica Super 530D missiles
First flown	10 March 1978
Into service	April 1983

Dassault
Mirage F1
Single turbojet, single-seat multi-role fighter

Dassault
Mirage F1
Single turbojet, single-seat multi-role fighter

Although most of the Mirage aircraft built by Dassault had delta-shaped wings the Mirage F1 fighter had swept-wings and conventional tail surfaces. It was a successor to the Mirage III. The F1 has an impressive rate of climb. Short take-off and landings are helped by the wing's high-lift system of leading-edge 'droops'. The fighter's radar enables the pilot to intercept targets at all levels, including very low level. With equipment and avionics upgrades it will remain in service into the next decade. The F1 has been exported to seven countries. In addition it has been built under licence in South Africa. Production ceased in 1990 after a total of 731 had been delivered. Twenty F1B tandem-seat trainers were later built to equip the Operational Evaluation Unit. During Operation Desert Storm in the first Gulf War, the Mirage was used by the French over Iraq. In the mid- and late-1990s the Mirage F1 also saw action in Bosnia and Kosovo in the Balkans.

Statistics

Mirage F1C

Engines	One SNECMA Atar 9K-50 turbojet
Power	11,025lb thrust(dry), 15,785lb thrust (with afterburning)
Span	8.40m (27ft 7in)
Length	15.30m (50ft 2in)
Height	4.50m (14ft 9in)
Max weight	16,200kg (35,715lb)
Top speed	2,335km/h (1,453mph)
Ceiling	19,999m (65,615ft)
Max range	600km (375 miles)
Crew	One (two F1B)
Weapons	30mm DEFA 553 cannon; AIM-9 Sidewinder, Magic missiles
First flown	23 December 1966
Into service	December 1973

Dassault
RaFale

Twin turbofan, single-seat multi-role fighter

Dassault
RaFale

Twin turbofan, single-seat multi-role fighter

In 1985 France withdrew from the European Fighter Aircraft project
(which led to the Eurofighter Typhoon) as it had decided to build a
smaller fighter. Both the French Air Force and Navy were interested in the
Rafale, which was originally called the ACX. Designed as a replacement
for the French Air Force Jaguars and Mirage F1s, and the Navy's Super
Etendards, it will eventually supersede the Mirage 2000. The Rafale is a
fifth-generation delta-winged aircraft with active foreplanes (or canards)
and some 'stealth' features. It has a high content of composite materials
in its construction and has digital fly-by-wire flight control systems. With
the use of the latest technology it is capable of outstanding performance
on multiple air-to-air targets, and it will form the main part of France's
defence force. In Navy service it is operational on France's latest aircraft
carrier, Charles de Gaulle.

Rafale D

Engines	Two SNECMA M88-3 turbofans
Power	10,950lb thrust (dry), 16,861lb thrust (with afterburning)
Span	10.90m (35ft 9in)
Length	15.27m (50ft 1in)
Height	5.34m (17ft 6in)
Max weight	21,500kg (47,400lb)
Top speed	2,125km/h (1,317mph)
Ceiling	16,764m (55,000ft)
Max range	1,760km (1,094 miles)
Crew	One
Weapons	30mm GIAT/DEFA 791B cannon; Matra Mica missiles
First flown	4 July 1986
Into service	June 2001

De Havilland
Mosquito

Twin piston-engined, two-seat day and night fighter

De Havilland
Mosquito

Twin piston-engined, two-seat day and night fighter

The multi-role Mosquito, powered by two Rolls-Royce Merlin engines, was one of the outstanding allied aircraft of the Second World War. It had a very clean, streamlined fuselage and a high power-to-weight ratio. Because of its wooden construction and performance, it was given the name 'Wooden Wonder'. The role of the Mosquito as a night fighter was important to the RAF, its radar equipment being progressively upgraded and the last (an NF 38) was produced in 1950. Fighter Command's most famous Mosquito mission was the attack on the Amiens jail in France in February 1944. This allowed 258 French Resistance prisoners to escape. To combat high-flying Luftwaffe bombers in 1942, the Mosquito fighter was adapted to operate at very high altitudes. With its excellent radar it was also used for long-range escort of RAF bomber formations attacking Germany at night in the later stages of the war.

Mosquito NF30

Engines	**Two Rolls-Royce Merlin 113 piston engines**
Power	**1,690hp**
Span	**16.51m (54ft 1¾in)**
Length	**12.64m (41ft 5in)**
Height	**4.65m (15ft 3in)**
Max weight	**9,789kg (21,575lb)**
Top speed	**544km/h (338mph)**
Ceiling	**11,278m (37,000ft)**
Max range	**1,899km (1,180 miles)**
Crew	**Two**
Weapons	**20mm cannon; 0.303in machine guns**
First flew	**15 March 1941**
Into service	**March 1942**
Out of service	**15 December 1955**

De Havilland
Vampire

Single turbojet, single-seat fighter

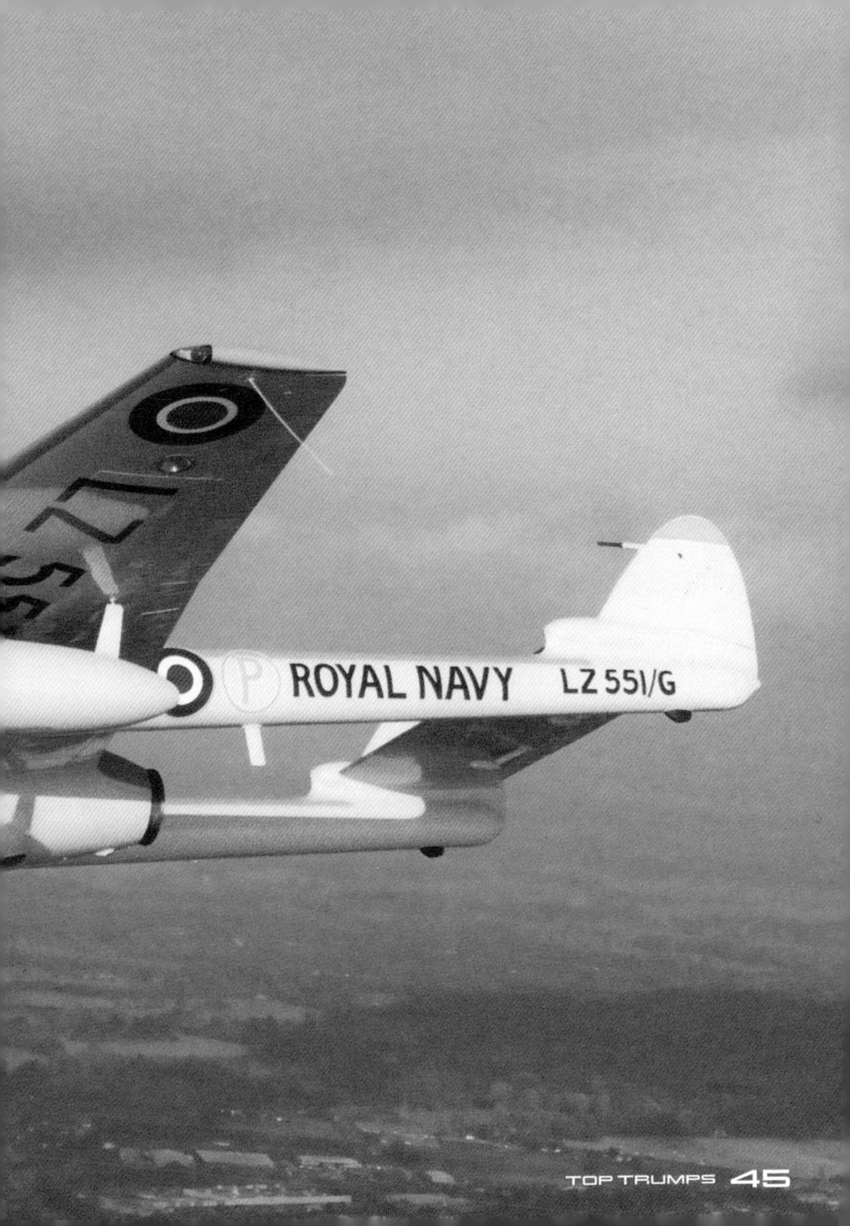
ROYAL NAVY
LZ551/G

De Havilland
Vampire
Single turbojet, single-seat fighter

The DH Vampire was the second jet fighter to be designed for the RAF and followed the Meteor into service. Like the Mosquito the fuselage was mainly made from plywood and balsa wood, and had a twin-boom design to accommodate the jet engine's exhaust. It arrived too late to see action in the Second World War, but entered RAF squadrons in early 1946. In the immediate post-war period, Vampires of RAF Fighter Command and the Royal Auxiliary Air Force played a key role in the first-line defence of the UK. They also had widespread use overseas with the RAF's Middle East and Far East Air Forces. A navalised Vampire made the world's first carrier deck landing by a jet aircraft. Two-seat Vampire night fighters also provided valuable service until replaced by Venoms and Meteors. Vampires were manufactured under licence in France, Italy and Switzerland.

Vampire FIII

Engine	One de Havilland Goblin II turbojet
Power	3,100lb thrust
Span	12.20m (40ft 0in)
Length	9.37m (30ft 7½in)
Height	1.91m (6ft 3in)
Max weight	5,520kg (12,170lb)
Top speed	845km/h (531mph)
Ceiling	12,192m (40,000ft)
Max range	1,843km (1,145 miles)
Crew	One
Weapons	20mm cannon
First flown	20 September 1943
Into service	1946
Out of service	1969

English Electric
Lightning
Twin turbojet, single-seat fighter interceptor

English Electric
Lightning
Twin turbojet, single-seat fighter interceptor

The English Electric (later British Aircraft Corporation) Lightning was the first British single-seat production jet fighter to achieve supersonic speed in level flight. It had an unusual engine layout with the jets being one above the other and had steeply swept razor-sharp wings. When it entered service it more than doubled the top speed and rate of climb of the RAF's Hunters. The Lightning was also the first fighter with an integrated weapon system. The advanced radar allowed the pilot to search above and below the horizon. Having very short range because of very high fuel consumption, the Lightning was one of the first fighters capable of being refuelled in flight. The last of the RAF's long line of classic single-seat fighters, it remained in service for over 20 years. RAF air defence squadrons replaced it with two-seat Phantoms and Tornado F3s from the mid-1980s.

Lightning F6

Engine	**Two Rolls-Royce Avon 301 turbojets**
Power	**13,000lb thrust (dry); 16,300lb thrust (with afterburning)**
Span	**10.61m (34ft 9½in)**
Length	**16.84m (55ft 3in)**
Height	**5.97m (19ft 7in)**
Max weight	**18,117kg (39,941lb)**
Top speed	**2,414 km/h (1,500mph)**
Ceiling	**19,685m (60,000ft plus)**
Max range	**Endurance 1.1 hours**
Crew	**One**
Weapons	**30mm cannon; Firestreak missiles**
First flew	**4 April 1957**
Into service	**October 1959**
Out of service	**1988**

Eurofighter
Typhoon

Twin-turbofan, single-seat multi-role combat aircraft

Eurofighter
Typhoon
Twin turbofan, single-seat multi-role combat aircraft

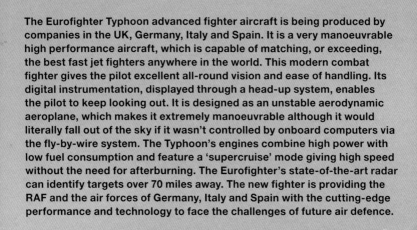

The Eurofighter Typhoon advanced fighter aircraft is being produced by companies in the UK, Germany, Italy and Spain. It is a very manoeuvrable high performance aircraft, which is capable of matching, or exceeding, the best fast jet fighters anywhere in the world. This modern combat fighter gives the pilot excellent all-round vision and ease of handling. Its digital instrumentation, displayed through a head-up system, enables the pilot to keep looking out. It is designed as an unstable aerodynamic aeroplane, which makes it extremely manoeuvrable although it would literally fall out of the sky if it wasn't controlled by onboard computers via the fly-by-wire system. The Typhoon's engines combine high power with low fuel consumption and feature a 'supercruise' mode giving high speed without the need for afterburning. The Eurofighter's state-of-the-art radar can identify targets over 70 miles away. The new fighter is providing the RAF and the air forces of Germany, Italy and Spain with the cutting-edge performance and technology to face the challenges of future air defence.

Statistics

Typhoon F2

Engines	Two Eurojet EJ200 afterburning turbofans
Power	20,227lb thrust with afterburner
Span	10.95m (36ft 0in)
Length	15.96m (52ft 5in)
Height	5.28m (17ft 4in)
Max weight	21,000kg (46,297lb)
Top Speed	2,125km/h (1,324mph)
Ceiling	16,764m (55,000ft)
Max range	3,705km (2,300 miles)
Crew	One
Weapons	BVRAAM, ASRAAM, AIM-9L Sidewinder missiles
First flown	27 March 1994
Into service	April 2006

Gloster
Meteor
Twin-turbojet, single-seat fighter

Gloster
Meteor

Twin-turbojet, single-seat fighter

In 1943, the Gloster Meteor was the first British interceptor jet fighter to fly. It became the first jet-engined aircraft to enter full production for operational service with any air force in the world and served for over a decade as the RAF's main fighter aircraft. Early Meteor Is were in action in the summer of 1944 when they claimed their first kills against the German V-1 flying bombs. Britain's prestige was considerably enhanced when a Meteor F4 established a new World Air Speed Record in September 1946 with a speed of 616mph. After the war the Meteor F8 was the RAF's standard day fighter with front-line squadrons until replaced by the Hawker Hunter. It also equipped many of the Royal Auxiliary Air Force Squadrons until they were disbanded. The two-seat Meteor NF11, with radar in its extended nose, was the first twin-jet night fighter to operate with the RAF.

Statistics

Meteor F8

Engines	**Two Rolls-Royce Derwent 8 turbojets**
Power	**3,500lb thrust**
Span	**11.32m (37ft 1¼in)**
Length	**13.59m (44ft 7in)**
Height	**3.96m (13ft 0in)**
Max weight	**7,122kg (15,701lb)**
Top speed	**962km/h (598mph)**
Ceiling	**13,564m (44,500ft)**
Max range	**966km (600 miles)**
Crew	**One**
Weapons	**20mm cannon**
First flown	**5 March 1943**
Into service	**12 July 1944**
Out of service	**1977**

Grumman
Bearcat

Single piston-engined, single-seat naval fighter

Grumman
Bearcat

Single piston-engined, single-seat naval fighter

The Bearcat was designed for the US Navy as a shipboard interceptor fighter. It was the last of a line of single piston-engined carrier-based fighters, which Grumman started in 1931. The fighter had to be capable of operating from aircraft carriers of all sizes and have excellent manoeuvrability, good low-level performance and a high rate of climb. To provide this it had the largest possible engine in the smallest and lightest airframe. Production was started only six months after the first flight of the prototype. The end of the Second World War came just before the Bearcat became operational, but a total of 1,266 were built. By the time production ended, Bearcats were serving with 24 US Navy squadrons, but all had been withdrawn by 1953. Some were supplied to the air forces of Thailand and North and South Vietnam. It was also used operationally by the French Air Force in Indo-China.

F8F-1 Bearcat

Engine	One Pratt & Whitney R-2800-34W piston engine
Power	2,750hp
Span	13.06m (42ft 9½in)
Length	10.24m (33ft 7¼in)
Height	3.99m (13ft 10¾in)
Max weight	5,799kg (12,786lb)
Top speed	681km/h (423mph)
Ceiling	11,704m (38,400ft)
Max range	1,754km (1,090 miles)
Crew	One
Weapons	0.50in machine guns
First flown	30 November 1943
Into service	January 1945
Out of service	1953

Grumman
F-14 Tomcat

Twin-turbofan, two-seat long-range fighter interceptor

Grumman
F-14 Tomcat

Twin-turbofan, two-seat long-range fighter interceptor

In the late 1960s the US Navy needed a new long-range interceptor to protect its large aircraft carriers from Soviet bombers. When the F-14 Tomcat made its first flight in 1970 it was the most technologically advanced fighter ever built. Because of its unique wings that moved automatically forward and backward during flight, the Tomcat was very manoeuvrable. Carrying a battery of deadly missiles, and a radar system able to track 24 targets at the same time and fire at six of them, it proved to be an outstanding interceptor. Tomcats will always be remembered for their starring role in the hit movie *Top Gun*, in which Tom Cruise played 'Maverick', a pilot training at Miramar, California, the US Navy's elite combat school. The last F-14s were retired from the US fleet in April 2006 and all had been withdrawn by September, having been replaced by FA-18 Super Hornets.

F-14B Tomcat

Engines	Two General Electric F100-GE-400 afterburning turbofans
Power	23,000lb thrust with afterburner
Span	19.54m (64ft 1½in) wings spread
Length	19.10m (62ft 8in)
Height	4.88m (16ft 0in)
Max weight	33,724kg (74,349lb)
Top speed	1,997km/h (1,241mph) plus
Ceiling	16,154m (53,000ft) plus
Max range	2,965km (1,840 miles)
Crew	Two
Weapons	M61A1 Vulcan cannon; AIM-9M Sidewinders, AIM-54C Phoenix, AIM-7M Sparrow missiles
First flown	21 December 1970
Into service	October 1972
Out of service	September 2006

Grumman
Wildcat

Single piston-engined, single-seat naval fighter

Grumman
Wildcat

Single piston-engined, single-seat naval fighter

The US Navy operated biplane fighters in the 1930s. The dumpy Wildcat all-metal monoplane was a carrier fighter when little else modern was available and became one of the most effective and successful carrier-borne fighters. To survive the harsh environment of carrier operations, naval fighters like the Wildcat had to be very rugged. Particularly effective in operating from the US Navy's small escort carriers, F4Fs remained in service throughout the Second World War. The Wildcat never outperformed the Japanese Zero, but in the battles of the Coral Sea, Midway and Guadalcanal of 1942 it was very significant. Over 300 F4Fs with folding wings were supplied to the Fleet Air Arm in Britain where it was named the Martlet. During Operation Torch it saw action with the US Navy in North Africa in the autumn of 1942. The FM-2 Wildcat was a later version, with a higher performance engine and bigger fin and rudder to improve directional stability. A total of 7,815 Wildcats was built.

Wildcat F4F-4

Engines	One Pratt & Whitney Twin Wasp R-1830-9 piston engine
Power	1,000hp
Span	11.6m (38ft ¾in)
Length	8.5m (27ft 10¼in)
Height	3.6m (11ft 7½in)
Max weight	3,974kg (8,761lb)
Top speed	512km/h (318mph)
Ceiling	10,973m (35,000ft)
Max range	1,448km (900 miles)
Crew	One
Weapons	0.50in machine guns
First flown	2 September 1937
Into service	February 1940
Out of service	1945

Hawker
Hunter
Single-seat, single-turbojet fighter

30 Jahre
Patrouille Suisse
J-4021

30

Hawker
Hunter

Single-seat, single-turbojet fighter

The graceful swept-wing Hunter was one of Britain's most successful post-war military aircraft. Hunters had equipped all of the RAF's day fighter squadrons based in Europe by 1958 and eventually the service received over 1,000 Hunters. The Mk 6 had a much improved Avon engine and had an impressive rate of climb, but it was only supersonic in a shallow dive. With a better performance at altitude, the Hunter was able to hold its own with most contemporary fighters. The arrival of the Lightning in RAF service spelt the end of the Hunter as an interceptor. The last Fighter Command F6 was withdrawn from front-line service in 1963. With great success in the export field, the Hunter was flown by 20 foreign air arms. In addition a further seven countries built it under licence. It saw active service with the Indian Air Force during the conflicts with Pakistan in 1965 and 1971, and in Jordan in the Arab Wars.

Hunter F6

Engine	One Rolls-Royce Avon RA28 Mk207 turbojet
Power	10,150lb thrust
Span	10.26m (33ft 8in)
Length	13.98m (45ft 10½in)
Height	4.02m (13ft 2in)
Max weight	8,051kg (17,750lb)
Top speed	1,150km/h (710mph)
Ceiling	15,240m (50,000ft)
Max range	2,567km (1,595 miles)
Crew	One
Weapons	30mm Aden cannon
First flown	20 July 1951
Into service	July 1954
Out of service	1994

Hawker
Hurricane

Single piston-engined, single-seat fighter

COOLANT

Hawker
Hurricane
Single piston-engined, single-seat fighter

Hawker Aircraft was convinced that only a monoplane could significantly improve fighter performance in the mid-1930s. The new Hurricane had a retractable undercarriage, flaps and an enclosed cockpit, all novel features for that time. Rolls-Royce had a new 1,000hp aero engine (the Merlin) under development that would enable the Hurricane to reach over 300mph. It was also the first fighter to have eight machine guns in the wings. At the outbreak of the Second World War in September 1939, 16 front-line RAF squadrons had Hurricane Is. The type was important in the air war over France in 1939–40, but it was in the Battle of Britain in the summer of 1940 that it became truly famous. Hurricane pilots shot down more German aircraft than the total destroyed by all other defences combined. It was the main RAF night fighter until the arrival of the Beaufighter, and the Sea Hurricane was used as a carrier fighter by the Fleet Air Arm.

Hurricane IIC

Engine	One Rolls-Royce Merlin XX piston engine
Power	1,300hp
Span	12.19m (40ft 0in)
Length	9.83m (32ft 3in)
Height	4.04m (13ft 3in)
Max weight	3,648kg (8,044lb)
Top speed	526km/h (327mph)
Ceiling	10,973m (35,600ft)
Max range	1,481km (920 miles)
Crew	One
Weapons	20mm cannon
First flown	6 November 1935
Into service	October 1937
Out of service	1951

Hawker
Sea Fury

Single piston-engined, single-seat naval fighter

Hawker
Sea Fury

Single piston-engined, single-seat naval fighter

Hawker originally designed the Fury, powered by the new powerful Bristol Centaurus radial engine, for the RAF in 1944. The Royal Navy was more interested. The Sea Fury, the last and fastest British piston-engined fighter, was one of the few British types that saw service in the Korean War in the early 1950s. They operated from four RN aircraft carriers and were credited with shooting down several North Korean MiG-15 jet fighters. It was the last piston-engined fighter in the Fleet Air Arm, but in 1953 was replaced by the jet-engined Sea Hawk. Some Sea Furies continued to fly with RN Volunteer Reserve squadrons until 1957. A total of 55 'Furies' (a land-based version of the Sea Fury) was exported as fighters to Iraq in the early 1950s. There were exports to six other countries, including Australia. A further 25 were built by Fokker in the Netherlands. In recent years retired Sea Furies have been used for air-racing in the USA, and have starred in many air displays.

Sea Fury FB11

Engine	**One Bristol Centaurus 18 piston engine**
Power	**2,550hp**
Span	**11.69m (38ft 4¾in)**
Length	**10.56m (34ft 8in)**
Height	**4.84m (15ft 10in)**
Max weight	**6,645kg (14,650lb)**
Top speed	**740km/h (460mph)**
Ceiling	**10,973m (36,000ft)**
Max range	**1,126km (700 miles)**
Crew	**One**
Weapons	**20mm cannon**
First flown	**21 February 1945**
Into service	**March 1947**
Out of service	**1957**

Hawker
Sea Hawk
Single-seat, single-turbojet naval fighter

WV908

WV908

ROYAL NAVY

Hawker
Sea Hawk
Single-seat, single-turbojet naval fighter

Originally designed as a land-based interceptor, the Sea Hawk was the last straight-winged Hawker fighter. It had an unusual layout with the jet intakes being in the roots of the leading-edge of the wings. The gases then left by ducts either side of the trailing edge roots. When Hawker started Hunter production, most of the Sea Hawks were built by Armstrong Whitworth Aircraft. Entering service with the Fleet Air Arm in 1951, it was the standard fighter for the next nine years. During the Suez campaign of 1956, Sea Hawks, along with Sea Venoms, provided fighter escorts for the RAF transport aircraft. Sea Hawks were exported to the Australian, Canadian, Indian, Netherlands and West German navies. Indian Navy Sea Hawks saw combat action in the Pakistan War of 1971. They were retired by the Royal Navy in 1960, but continued in India until 1983.

Sea Hawk FGA6

Engine	**One Rolls-Royce Nene 103 turbojet**
Power	**5,200lb thrust**
Span	**11.89m (39ft 0in)**
Length	**12.09m (39ft 8in)**
Height	**2.64m (8ft 8in)**
Max weight	**7,327kg (16,153lb)**
Top speed	**964km/h (599mph)**
Ceiling	**13,106m (43,000ft)**
Max range	**772km (480 miles)**
Crew	**One**
Weapons	**20mm cannon**
First flown	**3 September 1948**
Into service	**November 1951**
Out of service	**May 1983**

Lockheed Martin
F-16 Fighting Falcon

Single-seat, single-turbofan multi-role fighter

Lockheed Martin

F-16 Fighting Falcon

Single-seat, single-turbofan multi-role fighter

Originally designed as a relatively simple and lightweight air-combat fighter, the F-16 Fighting Falcon is able to fly in all weathers. The US Air Force has a large number of F-16s in service and several NATO countries selected it to replace the Starfighter. The single most distinctive feature is the location of the air intake directly below the cockpit. The pilot has excellent visibility being high up on the nose. A side-stick controller is fitted instead of the conventional centre-mounted control column, and operates through a fly-by-wire system. In the late 1980s second generation versions appeared and have been exported to many countries, bringing the total produced to over 4,500. This versatile fighter was in action with the US Air Force in Operation Desert Storm in 1991 and flew more sorties than any other aircraft. Throughout the 1990s they were based in Italy to help NATO countries keep the peace in the Balkans. They have since been operational in Iraq and Afghanistan.

Statistics

F-16C Fighting Falcon

Engine	One Pratt & Whitney F100-PW-100 turbofan
Power	29,588lb thrust (with afterburner)
Span	10.0m (32ft 9¾in)
Length	15.03m (49ft 4in)
Height	5.09m (16ft 8½in)
Max weight	19,187kg (42,000lb)
Top speed	2,145km/h (1,333mph)
Ceiling	In excess of 15,240m (50,000ft)
Max range	1,252km (780 miles)
Crew	One
Weapons	Vulcan M61A1 20mm cannon, AIM-9 Sidewinder, Rafael Python 3/4, AIM-7 and AIM120 missiles
First flown	14 December 1982
Into service	19 July 1984

Lockheed
P-38 Lightning

Twin piston-engined, single-seat fighter

Lockheed
P-38 Lightning

Twin piston-engined, single-seat fighter

The Lightning was one of an outstanding trio of 'pursuit' fighters produced by the USA during the Second World War, and it was the only one to remain in production throughout the entire war period. The P-38 was designed with a radical twin-engined, twin-boom layout. This was because there was no engine then available to meet the performance demands of a single engine layout. Therefore the nose was free to hold heavy armament. When the P-38 appeared it was the first fighter in the world to have a tricycle (nosewheel) undercarriage. Lightnings were in constant action in Europe and from England it was operated as a long-range escort for US Army Air Force heavy bombers attacking Germany in daylight. The Germans called it 'the fork-tailed devil'. By late 1944 the P-38 equipped 101 American squadrons. With its long range it was also used to its full potential in the Pacific area. Total production of all variants was 10,037.

P-38J Lightning

Engines	Two Allison V-89/ 1710-89/91 piston engines
Power	1,425hp
Span	15.85m (52ft 0in)
Length	11.53m (37ft 10in)
Height	3.00m (9ft 10in)
Max weight	9,798kg (21,600lb)
Top speed	579km/h (360mph)
Ceiling	13,411m (44,000ft)
Max range	3,637km (2,260 miles)
Crew	One
Weapons	20mm cannon; 0.50in machine guns
First flown	11 February 1939
Into service	June 1941
Out of service	1946

Lockheed Martin
F-22 Raptor

Twin-turbofan, single-seat air superiority fighter

Lockheed Martin
F-22 Raptor

Twin-turbofan, single-seat air superiority fighter

The US Air Force's F-22A is currently the world's most advanced fighter in service. Constructed mainly from composites and titanium alloys, the Raptor was designed to be capable of 'supercruising' – sustaining supersonic speed without using afterburners. This allows the advanced air superiority fighter to cruise at very high speeds, without a high fuel consumption, through hostile airspace. The Raptor's design uses the latest 'stealth' technology and is the world's first operational stealthy air defence fighter. To an opposing radar the large Raptor looks tiny, due to a careful blend of curves and straight edges which minimises radar reflectively. It has thrust-vectoring (the pilot can move the jet exhaust nozzles by as much as 20 degrees) to make it turn much quicker and improve its overall manoeuvrability. Its avionics were designed to enable a single pilot to undertake missions which normally require a two-man crew. The first USAF operational squadron was formed in 2005.

Statistics

F-22A Raptor

Engines	Two Pratt & Whitney F119-PW-100 turbofans with thrust vectoring
Power	35,000lb thrust
Span	13.56m (44ft 6in)
Length	18.92m (62ft 1in)
Height	5.02m (16ft 5in)
Max weight	27,216kg (60,000lb)
Top speed	1,482km/h (921mph)
Ceiling	Over 18,288m (60,000ft)
Max range	n/a
Crew	One
Weapons	20mm cannon; AIM-9 Sidewinders, AIM-120 missiles
First flown	7 September 1997
Into service	2005

Lockheed F-104
Starfighter

Single-turbojet, single-seat air defence/attack fighter

Lockheed F-104
Starfighter

Single-turbojet, single-seat air defence/attack fighter

The high-performance F-104 was designed by Lockheed based on
suggestions from pilots who flew in the Korean War. It was a lightweight
air superiority fighter with very small thin wings that were not swept. Able
to reach twice the speed of sound in level flight, the Starfighter was the
first operational fighter to achieve this. At one time the F-104 held both the
World Air Speed and Altitude Records. Less than one third of the F-104s
were built for the US Air Force, the majority being flown by NATO air arms,
especially West Germany, Denmark and Italy. A total of 843 Starfighters
were built by four companies in Europe and more
were produced in Canada. Unfortunately,
operational losses were very high, mainly because
pilots were not accustomed to such a powerful and
demanding aircraft. For a while it was called the 'widow maker' in
Germany. The Italians were the last to operate the F-104, nearly 50 years
after its first flight.

Statistics

F-104S Starfighter

Engine	One General Electric J79-GE-19 turbojet
Power	11,870lb thrust (dry): 17,900lb thrust (with afterburner)
Span	6.68m (21ft 11in)
Length	16.69m (54ft 9in)
Height	4.11m (13ft 6in)
Max weight	14,060kg (30,996lb)
Top speed	2,333km/h (1,450mph)
Ceiling	17,678m (58,000ft)
Max range	1,274km (775 miles)
Crew	One
Weapons	Selenia Aspide radar-guided and Raytheon AIM-9L Sidewinder infra-red homing missiles
First flown	28 February 1954
Into service	26 January 1958
Out of service	2003

McDonnell Douglas
F-4 Phantom II

Twin-turbojet, two-seat multi-role fighter

McDonnell Douglas
F-4 Phantom II

Twin-turbojet, two-seat multi-role fighter

One of the world's greatest combat aircraft, and capable of twice the speed of sound, the Phantom excelled in the air-superiority and interceptor roles. In the early 1960s it took the World Air Speed Record flying at 902mph, a record that stood for 16 years. Large numbers were delivered to the US Air Force and US Navy, and to many air arms around the world. Its design resulted from experience gained in air-to-air engagements over North Vietnam. The F-4E was the most numerous of all variants. The British government ordered its first F-4K Phantoms for the Royal Navy to serve as fighters on board HMS Ark Royal. This was followed by 185 for the RAF, first as fighter bombers, then as dedicated interceptor fighters for home defence. They were later replaced by Tornados. While no longer the primary fighter of any air force, the Phantom is still in use with a number of air arms, including Germany, Greece and Turkey.

F-4E Phantom II

Engines	**Two General Electric J79-GE-17A turbojets**
Power	**11,810lb thrust (dry): 17,900lb thrust (with afterburner)**
Span	**11.71m (38ft 4¾in)**
Length	**19.20m (63ft 0in)**
Height	**5.02m (16ft 5½in)**
Max weight	**28,030kg (61,795lb)**
Top speed	**2,390km/h (1,485mph)**
Ceiling	**18,974m (62,250ft)**
Range	**1,145km (712 miles)**
Crew	**Two**
Weapons	**Vulcan M61A1 20mm cannon; AIM-9 Sidewinder and AIM-7 Sparrow missiles**
First flown	**27 May 1958**
Into service	**December 1960**

Messerschmitt
BF.109

Single piston-engined, single-seat fighter

Messerschmitt
BF.109

Single piston-engined, single-seat fighter

The Messerschmitt 109 was the German Luftwaffe's main fighter throughout the Second World War. The fighter entered service just in time to be used in the Spanish Civil War in the late 1930s. It was produced in large numbers over a long period. The 'Me 109' is best remembered for huge numbers of dog fights with RAF Spitfires and Hurricanes, at high altitude over London, during the Battle of Britain. A total of 610 Luftwaffe 109s were lost at this time. It was flown by the majority of German aces and scored more kills than any other Luftwaffe fighter. The Bf.109 proved adaptable enough to accept new engines and weapons with minimum modifications. Though suffering heavy losses, the Messerschmitts wreaked havoc (especially with its cannon armament) on Allied bombers. Its main drawback was its lack of combat range and a very narrow undercarriage making it tricky to land. The last 109s were the post-war Rolls-Royce Merlin-engined Buchons flown by the Spanish Air Force until 1967.

Bf.109G-6

Engine	One Daimler-Benz DB 605A-1 piston engine
Power	1,475hp
Span	9.92m (32ft 6½in)
Length	9.03m (29ft 7½in)
Height	2.50m (8ft 2½in)
Max weight	3,400kg (7,496lb)
Top speed	621km/h (386mph)
Ceiling	10,500m (34,450ft)
Max range	998km (620 miles)
Crew	One
Weapons	20mm MG151 cannon; 7.9mm machine guns
First flown	29 May 1935
Into service	March 1937
Out of service	Late-1960s

Mikoyan–Gurevich
MiG–15 'Fagot'

Single-turbojet, single-seat fighter

Mikoyan-Gurevich
MiG-15 'Fagot'

Single-turbojet, single-seat fighter

The MiG-15 was the USSR's first operational jet fighter. It was also its first swept-wing aircraft. Built in large numbers, it became the Warsaw Pact countries' standard fighter and was also built in Czechoslovakia and Poland. The jet fighter was made possible by Britain's gift of examples of Rolls-Royce jet engines to the Russians in 1945. They were far more advanced than Russian engines and were immediately copied and improved. The MiG-15 was first encountered in battle during the Korean War, flown by Chinese pilots. The MiGs forced American bombers to operate at night. With its light weight it could out-climb any other fighter at that time, and reach 16,000ft in two-and-a-half minutes. Over 3,000 were built and exported to 17 countries, including China and Cuba. A handful are still in use with third-world countries, nearly 60 years after it first flew. Serviceability is now poor, with spare parts increasingly hard to obtain.

Statistics

MiG-15

Engine	One Klimov RD-45F turbojet
Power	5,004lb thrust
Span	10.08m (33ft 1in)
Length	10.11m (33ft 2in)
Height	3.39m (11ft 2in)
Max weight	5,400kg (11,905lb)
Top speed	1,049km/h (652mph)
Ceiling	14,825m (48,640ft)
Max Range	1,174km (730 miles)
Crew	One
Weapons	23mm and 37mm cannon
First flown	30 December 1947
Into service	8 October 1948

Mikoyan–Gurevich
MiG–21 'Fishbed'

Single-turbojet, single-seat fighter

Mikoyan-Gurevich
MiG-21 'Fishbed'

Single-turbojet, single-seat fighter

First developed as a high performance lightweight fighter, the MiG-21 was produced in very large numbers for the Russian Air Force. It was exported to many communist countries around the world. With small delta wings, this second generation fighter received constant upgrading, including more sophisticated radar, improved engines and weapons. This eventually resulted in an outstanding combat aircraft. About 12,500 MiG-21s were produced including those built in Czechoslovakia and India, while China produced a large number as the J-7. MiG-21s were sold to Arab countries who used them against the Israeli Air Force in the 1973 Arab–Israeli War. At least 21 air arms were known still to be operating the MiG-21 at the turn of the Century. It has more recently been upgraded by Israeli Aircraft Industries for the Romanian Air Force where it is in service as the MiG-21 Lancer.

MiG-21PFM 'Fishbed-F'

Engine	**One Tumanskii R-25-300 turbojet**
Power	**9,038lb thrust (dry); 15,653lb thrust (with afterburner)**
Span	**7.15m (23ft 5¾in)**
Length	**15.76m (51ft 8½in) with probe**
Height	**4.12m (13ft 6½in)**
Max Weight	**9,080kg (20,018lb)**
Top speed	**2,125km/h (1,320mph)**
Ceiling	**17,495m (57,400ft)**
Max range	**740km (460 miles)**
Crew	**One**
Weapons	**K-13 (R3S) missiles**
First flew	**16 June 1955**
Into service	**1960**

Mikoyan–Gurevich
MiG–23 'Flogger'

Single-turbojet, single-seat fighter interceptor

Mikoyan-Gurevich
MiG-23 'Flogger'
Single-turbojet, single-seat fighter interceptor

The MiG-23 air superiority fighter was very different from previous MiG designs. Instead of a nose intake it had twin intakes attached to the fuselage sides. This freed the nose so that a large radar scanner could be fitted. The most distinctive feature of the MiG-23 is its shoulder-mounted variable geometry wing. It was the first swing-wing fighter to go into service anywhere in the world. The three wing sweep positions gave it excellent performance at high speed and good handling qualities at low speed. Exported to many communist countries, it was also built in India for the Indian Air Force. Production continued for nearly three decades and some 4,000 examples were built. At the end of the Cold War the US Air Force acquired some ex-Egyptian Air Force examples, which were used for realistic air combat training of American and NATO pilots. It remains in service with a number of third world countries today.

MiG-23ML 'Flogger-G'

Engine	One Khachaturov R-27F2M-300 turbojet
Power	15,212lb thrust (dry); 22,046lb thrust (with afterburner)
Span	7.78m (25ft 6½in) swept; 13.96m (45ft 9¾in) spread
Length	15.65m (51ft 3¾in)
Height	4.82m (15ft 9¾in)
Max weight	17,800kg (39,242lb)
Top speed	2,500km/h (1,553mph)
Ceiling	18,500m (60,695ft)
Max range	3,162km (1,212 miles)
Crew	One
Weapons	Twin-barrel 23mm cannon; R23R missiles
First flown	10 June 1967
Into service	1969

Mikoyan
MiG-29 'Fulcrum'

Twin-turbofan, single-seat multi-role fighter

Mikoyan
MiG-29 'Fulcrum'

Twin-turbofan, single-seat multi-role fighter

The MiG-29 was designed
in the mid-1970s to replace
the MiG-21, MiG-23, Su-7 and
Su-17 to counter the American F-15
Eagle. Approximately 900 MiG-29s of all
versions were built for service with Soviet forces
and many continue in use today. In addition about 400 were
exported to 'friendly' states. It has a mid-wing mounting, with
wide leading edge root extensions, large twin fins and widely spaced
engines. It features a blended, high-lift, low-drag wing and forebody and
composites are widely used. To allow the aircraft to operate from forward
airfields, the low-mounted engine intakes are fitted with large doors that
close on start-up and taxying. While they are closed air is drawn through
spring-loaded louvres in the top of the wing roots. Various upgrades of the
MiG-29 have resulted in the MiG-29M and MiG-29OVT with swivelling jet
exhausts to give outstanding combat manoeuvrability.

Statistics

MiG-29S 'Fulcrum-C'

Engines	Two Klimov/Sarkisov RD-33 turbofans
Power	11,110lb thrust (dry); 18,300lb thrust (afterburning)
Span	11.36m (37ft 3¼in)
Length	17.32m (56ft 10in) including probe
Height	4.73m (15ft 6¼in)
Max weight	19,700kg (43,430lb)
Top speed	2,445km/h (1,520mph)
Ceiling	18,001m (59,060ft)
Max range	2,900km (1,800 miles)
Crew	One
Weapons	GSh-301 cannon; Aphid, Archer, or Alamo-A missiles
First flown	6 October 1977
Into service	1983

Mitsubishi

A6M2 Zero

Single piston-engined, single-seat fighter

Mitsubishi
A6M2 Zero
Single piston-engined, single-seat fighter

The original Zero-Sen was the standard carrier-borne fighter in the Japanese Navy when Pearl Harbor was attacked in December 1941. This brought the USA into the Second World War. Designed as a carrier aircraft it was required to have long range. Throughout the Pacific War the Zero was developed and improved to keep it in the front line. Its performance was enhanced, but it did not have self-sealing fuel tanks or armour protection for the pilot. Despite its growing air superiority in the Pacific, few Allied pilots cared to prejudge the outcome of combat with the Zero. But after the Battle of Midway in mid-1942, when many Japanese carriers were sunk, the Zero came up against a new generation of US Navy and Marines fighters. It was later refitted with a higher-powered engine, which gave it a closer performance to Allied fighters. Towards the end of the war many Zeros were converted for suicide (kamikaze) attacks and inflicted heavy damage to Allied shipping. Total production was 10,938.

Statistics

A6M2 *Zero-Sen*

Engine	One Nakajima Sakae 12 piston engine
Power	950hp
Span	12.00m (39ft 4½in)
Length	9.06m (29ft 8¾in)
Height	3.05m (10ft 0in)
Max weight	2,410kg (5,313lb)
Top speed	533km/h (331mph)
Ceiling	10,299m (33,790ft)
Max range	3,105km (1,930 miles)
Crew	One
Weapons	20mm Type 99 Mk 1 cannon; 7.7mm Type 97 machine guns
First flown	1 April 1939
Into service	July 1940
Out of service	August 1945

EII-102

North American
P-51 Mustang
Single piston-engined, single-seat fighter

North American
P-51 Mustang

Single piston-engined, single-seat fighter

Originally designed and built for the RAF at the start of the Second World War, the P-51 Mustang powered by an Allison engine was not successful. When it was re-engined with the American-built Rolls-Royce Packard Merlin engine and a four-bladed propeller, the P-51 was transformed into the finest US fighter of the war. It had sleek lines and was one of the first fighters to have a special laminar-flow wing design that gave it high speed and long-range. With extra tanks fitted, the P-51 could escort US Flying Fortress bombers deep into Germany and engage the Luftwaffe fighters. Like the Spitfire, the P-51 helped win the war in Europe. Over 300 were built in Australia and flew in the Pacific theatre. Some 40 US Army Air Force fighter groups and 31 RAF squadrons operated the type. It continued in US Air Force service through the Korean War in 1951–53 and was flown by the Israeli Air Force in the 1956 war.

P-51D Mustang

Engine	One Packard-built Merlin V-1650-7 piston engine
Power	1,450hp
Span	11.28m (37ft 0in)
Length	9.83m (32ft 3in)
Height	4.16m (13ft 8in)
Max weight	5,493kg (12,000lb)
Top speed	703km/h (437mph)
Ceiling	12,775m (41,900ft)
Max range	2,655km (1,650 miles)
Crew	One
Weapons	0.50in machine guns
First flew	26 October 1940
Into service	November 1941
Out of service	1963

North American
F-86 Sabre

Single turbojet, single-seat jet fighter

North American
F-86 Sabre

Single turbojet, single-seat jet fighter

The first swept-wing jet fighter to enter production, the Sabre entered service with the US Air Force in 1949. With a wing-sweep of 35 degrees its design benefited from information on German research undertaken during the Second World War. Supersonic in a shallow dive, the F-86 was the first transonic fighter to be flown by Western air arms. In the Korean War, US Air Force Sabres were the only fighters capable of matching the Russian MiG-15 jet fighter's performance. The RAF ordered 460 Sabres that were built under licence by Canadair in Canada. They replaced Meteor F8s with RAF fighter squadrons. This was a critical period when East–West relations were most tense. By mid-1956 all the Sabres in Germany had been replaced by Hawker Hunters. A US Navy version was known as the FJ-2 Fury. Sabres were also flown by Australian, Canadian and the West German air forces. Some were later passed on to Italy and Greece. Total number of Sabres built was over 9,500 in six main versions, including the all-weather/night fighter.

Statistics

F-86F Sabre

Engine	One General Electric J47-GE-27 turbojet
Power	5,190lb thrust
Span	11.92m (39ft 1½in)
Length	11.44m (37ft 6½in)
Height	4.49m (14ft 9in)
Max weight	6,894kg (15,198lb)
Top speed	1,091km/h (678mph)
Ceiling	19,690m (54,600ft)
Max range	1,490km (926 miles)
Crew	One
Weapons	0.50 machine guns
First flown	1 October 1947
Into service	1949
Out of service	1969

North American
F-100 Super Sabre

Single-turbojet, single-seat fighter

The F-100 was the World's first supersonic combat aircraft capable of exceeding the speed of sound in level flight. It replaced the F-86 Sabre with the US Air Force as an air superiority fighter. Many saw combat during the Vietnam War between 1966 and 1971 and served in Europe during the Cold War period of the late 1950/60s. In 1953, the F-100 set a new World Air Speed Record of 755mph. A total of 2,039 was built, and they were supplied to France, Denmark, Taiwan and Turkey under the Military Assistance Programme, some serving until the mid-1980s. When retired from US Air Force service in 1972, some were passed to Air National Guard units and F-100s remained operational until 1980. In the 1980s, a total of 340 Super Sabres were selected for conversions as drones (QF-100) for use in air defence exercises and missile tests. QF-100s could be flown in piloted or pilotless mode and many were destroyed in the air.

F-100D Super Sabre

Engine	One Pratt & Whitney J-57-21/21A turbojet
Power	10,200lb thrust (dry); 16,00lb thrust (with afterburning)
Span	11.82m (38ft 9½in)
Length	14.44m (47ft 4½in)
Height	4.94m (16ft 2½in)
Max weight	13,085kg (28,847lb)
Top speed	1,434km/h (891mph)
Ceiling	13,716m (45,000ft)
Max range	859km (534 miles)
Crew	One
Weapons	20mm cannon
First flown	25 May 1953
Into service	October 1955
Out of service	1985

63000

FW-000

R FORCE

Northrop
F-5E Tiger II
Twin-turbojet, single-seat light fighter

Northrop
F-5E Tiger II
Twin-turbojet, single-seat light fighter

In 1969, the US Air Force sought the development of a new lightweight fighter. Northrop offered an improved version of its successful F-5 Freedom Fighter. This improved F-5E had more powerful engines, an updated cockpit and improved air-to-air missile firing system. First flown in August 1972, over 1,000 Tiger IIs were produced by Northrop. It was also assembled in South Korea, Switzerland and Taiwan. Although few F-5Es were bought by the US Air Force, it was in service with 20 foreign air arms by the mid-1980s. Though it lacked an all-weather capability, the Tiger II was relatively cheap, easy to operate, robust and agile. It was also used as a successful aggressor aircraft for 'dissimilar' air combat training with the US Navy. This provided a realistic enemy for US (and some friendly foreign nationals) pilot training in aerial combat skills. Updates are continuing which should see the type still in service around the world until 2012.

F-5E Tiger II

Engines	Two General Electric J85-GE-21 turbojets
Power	3,500lb thrust (dry); 5,000lb thrust (with afterburner)
Span	8.13m (26ft 8in)
Length	14.45m (47ft 4¾in) including probe
Height	4.08m (13ft 4½in)
Max weight	11,187kg (24,664lb)
Max speed	1,700km/h (1,056mph)
Ceiling	15,240m (50,500ft)
Max range	1,405km (875 miles)
Crew	One
Weapons	20mm cannon; AIM-9 Sidewinder missiles
First flown	11 August 1972
Into service	1973

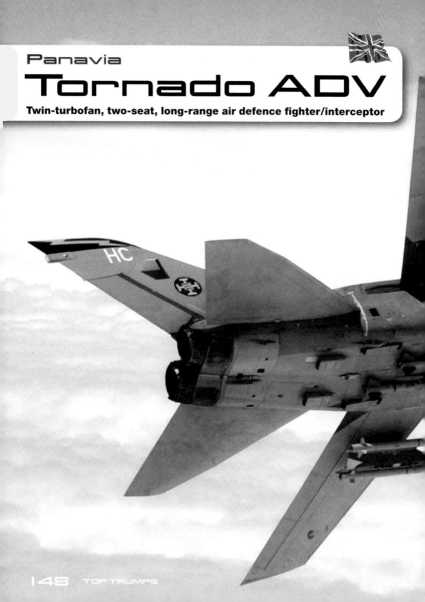

Panavia
Tornado ADV

Twin-turbofan, two-seat, long-range air defence fighter/interceptor

Panavia
Tornado ADV

Twin-turbofan, two-seat, long-range air defence fighter/interceptor

Originally known as the MRCA (Multi-Role Combat Aircraft) the Tornado evolved into two main versions, Interdiction Strike (IDS) and Air Defence Variant (ADV). The later fighter came into full service with the RAF in 1986, to replace Lightnings and F-4 Phantoms. It was the RAF's first variable-geometry (swing-wing) aircraft. The fighter F3 was urgently required in the closing stages of the Cold War period to counter newer Soviet types entering British airspace. Operational requirements demanded an interceptor for undertaking combat air patrols (CAPs) in all weathers – some 350 miles from base, beyond the range of land-based radars. A total of 144 Tornado F3s were delivered to the RAF. They first saw operational service in Operation Desert Storm, the 1991 Gulf War. Subsequent operations were participation in Operation Deny Flight, patrolling/policing the no-fly zones over Bosnia, in support of United Nations directives. Some RAF F3s were flown by the Italian Air Force, awaiting the delivery of Typhoons.

Statistics

Tornado F3

Engines	Two Turbo Union RB199-34R Mk104 afterburning turbofans
Power	9,100lb thrust (dry); 16,520lb thrust (with afterburning)
Span	13.91m (45ft 7½in) minimum sweep; 8.60m (28ft 2½in) maximum sweep
Length	18.68m (61ft 3½in)
Height	5.95m (19ft 6¼in)
Max weight	27,986kg (61,700lb)
Top speed	2,338km/h (1,453mph)
Ceiling	above 21,343m (70,000ft)
Max range	1,852km (1,151 miles)
Crew	Two
Weapons	IKMA-Mauser 27mm Mauser Cannon; BAe Skyflash, AIM 120 active radar, AIM 9L Sidewinder missiles
First flown	27 October 1979
Into service	1984

Republic P-47
Thunderbolt

Single piston-engined, single-seat fighter

Republic P-47
Thunderbolt

Single piston-engined, single-seat fighter

The P-47 Thunderbolt, popularly known as the 'Jug', was built in larger numbers than any other American fighter. Extremely fast and very tough, it was powered by a large turbocharged engine, and on its entry into service in 1942 it was one of the most advanced fighters in the world. It was also a stable gun platform and four machine guns were fitted to each wing. With external long-range fuel tanks, the P-47 could escort bombers deep into Germany (even to Berlin), going the whole way on most missions. On the return journey it became common practice to use unused ammunition shooting up targets of opportunity on the ground. The RAF received 825 Thunderbolts, which were mainly used in Burma. A total of 15,683 Thunderbolts was built. The European claim was 3,752 aircraft destroyed in air combat and an additional 3,315 on the ground.

P-47D Thunderbolt

Engine	One Pratt & Whitney R-2800-21 Double Wasp piston engine
Power	2,000hp
Span	12.44m (40ft 9¾in)
Length	11.02m (36ft 1¾in)
Height	4.31m (14ft 1¾in)
Max weight	7,938kg (17,500lb)
Top speed	584km/h (363mph)
Ceiling	9,144m (30,000ft)
Max range	2,897km (1,850 miles)
Crew	One
Weapons	0.50in machine guns
First flew	6 May 1941
Into service	March 1942
Out of service	1950

Saab 35
Draken

Single turbojet, single-seat supersonic fighter/interceptor

Saab 35
Draken

Single turbojet, single-seat supersonic fighter/interceptor

Designed in the early 1950s, the unusual Draken was a very agile supersonic fighter with a short take-off and landing capability. It was powered by a licence-built Rolls-Royce Avon engine with afterburner. A distinctive double-delta wing shape, the addition of a tailwheel and a braking parachute helped the fighter to operate from roads as well as airfield runways. The structure was largely conventional apart from the wing configuration, which was fitted with powered controls for each movable surface. Entering service with the Swedish Air Force in 1959, the Draken was the main interceptor fighter until the mid-1980s. Production ended in 1977 when 612 had been built. 66 aircraft were up-graded with increased power, better avionics and missile systems, and remained in service until the Gripen was fully operational. Other Drakens were sold to Denmark, Finland and Austria, the last being withdrawn by the Austrian Air Force in 2005.

J35F Draken

Engine	One Volvo Flygmotor RM6C turbojet with afterburner
Power	12,790lb thrust (dry); 17,650lb thrust (with afterburner)
Span	9.42m (30ft 11in)
Length	15.34m (50ft 4in)
Height	3.89m (12ft 9in)
Max weight	11,000kg (24,250lb)
Top speed	2,125km/h (1,320mph)
Ceiling	19,812m (65,600ft)
Max range	2,750km (1,709 miles)
Crew	One
Weapons	30mm ADEN M/55 cannon; Falcon missiles
First flown	25 October 1955
Into service	March 1960
Out of service	2005

Saab JAS39
Gripen

Single turbofan, single-seat all-weather interceptor fighter

Saab JAS39
Gripen

Single turbofan, single-seat all-weather interceptor fighter

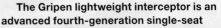

The Gripen lightweight interceptor is an advanced fourth-generation single-seat multi-role fighter. It was built to replace the Swedish Air Force's Viggens and remaining Drakens. It is a delta-winged aircraft with tailplane-shaped foreplanes, also known as 'canards', fitted to the front fuselage. The control surfaces can also be used as air-brakes to slow down after landing. A third of its construction is from composite materials and it has fly-by-wire controls. The engine, a licence-built American General Electric, enables the Gripen to reach twice the speed of sound. As with previous Saab designs, the Gripen is required to operate from dispersed sites, using ordinary roads. An onboard auxiliary power unit is installed for use when operating away from base. With the help of BAE Systems, Saab has received export orders for the Gripen from the South African, Czech Republic and Hungarian Air Forces.

JAS39A Gripen

Engine	One General Electric Volvo Flygmotor RM12 turbofan
Power	12,250lb thrust (dry); 18,100lb thrust (with afterburning)
Span	8.40m (27ft 6¾in)
Length	14.10m (46ft 3in)
Height	4.50m (14ft 9in)
Max weight	13,000kg (28,660lb)
Top speed	2,126km/h (1,321mph)
Max range	800km (497 miles)
Crew	One
Weapons	27mm Mauser BK27 cannon; AIM-120, Maverick and AIM-9L Sidewinder missiles
First flown	9 December 1988
Into service	8 June 1993

Saab 37

Viggen

Single turbofan, single-seat multi-role fighter

Saab 37
Viggen
Single turbofan, single-seat multi-role fighter

The Viggen 'Thunderbolt' had the
unusual delta wing and canard
planform with flaps on trailing edges
of both. As with most modern Swedish
designs, it had a short take-off and landing
capability, which enabled it to operate from
hard strips, such as concealed roads hidden
in Sweden's wooded landscape. A very strong
undercarriage and reverse thrust was fitted to the
engine to help shorten landings. The tail fin folded to
allow operations from underground hangars. The design incorporated
many honeycomb panels, which made the aircraft lighter, and the one-
piece wrap-round windscreen was specially strengthened to survive bird
strike at high speed. Although production stopped in 1990, after 330 had
been built, the Viggen was upgraded. Fitted with new computer systems
to provide integrated attack, fighter and reconnaissance capability,
ten squadrons continued to operate it until finally replaced by Gripens
in 2005.

JA37 Viggen

Engine	One Volvo Flygmotor RM8B turbofan with afterburner
Power	16,600lb thrust (dry); 28,110lb thrust (with afterburner)
Span	10.60m (34ft 9¼in)
Length	16.40m (53ft 9¾in)
Height	5.90m (19ft 4¼in)
Max weight	20,500kg (45,194lb)
Top speed	2,126km/h (1,321mph)
Ceiling	18,288m (60,000ft)
Max range	2,000km (1,243 miles)
Crew	One
Weapons	30mm cannon; Sky Flash and AIM-9L Sidewinder missiles
First flown	8 February 1967
Into service	June 1971
Out of service	2005

Sukhoi
Su-27 'Flanker'

Twin-turbofan, single-seat long-range air superiority multi-role fighter

Sukhoi
Su-27 'Flanker'

Twin-turbofan, single-seat long-range air superiority multi-role fighter

One of the major successes of the Russian aerospace industry, the Su-27 was designed as an all-weather interceptor and long-range bomber escort in the late 1970s. 'Flankers' serve with the Russian armed forces and the Ukraine, Belarus and Uzbekistan Air Forces. More recently they have been delivered to China, Egypt, India, Syria and Vietnam and it remains in production. The Su-27 features a powerful look-down/shoot down and track-while-scan radar. With fly-by-wire controls it is extremely manoeuvrable for its size and power. It has sufficient internal fuel to give it long range, but has a retractable inflight-refuelling probe. 'Flankers' were introduced during the Cold War to be capable of intercepting low-flying NATO attack aircraft and high-level bombers. They also had to secure Russia's enormous borders, provide air cover for naval forces and had to be able to meet agile fighters, like the F-15, on equal terms.

Su-27P 'Flanker-B'

Engine	Two Saturn/Lyulka AL-31F afterburning turbofans
Power	17,857lb thrust (dry): 27,569lb thrust (with afterburner)
Span	14.70m (48ft 3in)
Length	21.94m (72ft 0in)
Height	5.93m (19ft 6in)
Max weight	33,000kg (72,750lb)
Top speed	2,150km/h (1,336mph)
Ceiling	18,000m (59,055ft)
Max range	3,650km (2,287 miles)
Crew	One
Weapons	Single-barrel 30mm GSh-301 cannon; Alamo-A/B/C/D, Archer and Aphid missiles
First flown	20 April 1981
Into service	December 1984

Sukhoi
Su-30M/MK
Twin-turbofan, two-seat multi-role fighter

Sukhoi
Su-30M/MK

Twin-turbofan, two-seat multi-role fighter

The Su-30M is a multi-role fighter, which was developed from the very successful Su-27, to keep up with the performance of the American F-15E Eagle. It is fitted with advanced avionics and features thrust-vectoring (initially developed for the Su-35/Su-37), which swivels the thrust plus or minus 15 degrees, and is controlled by fly-by-wire systems. With the addition of foreplanes (canards) it has improved combat capability and manoeuvrability. Production has been slow due to funding constraints, but Sukhoi has continued to develop the aircraft with new navigation equipment and avionics adding to its air-to-ground capability. The Su-30M has been marketed overseas as the 'MK' with some success. It has been supplied to the Indian Air Force since 2003 and will continue in production in India until 2017. A total of 62, without canards and thrust vectoring capability, have been delivered to China.

Su-30MK

Engines	Two Saturn/Lyulka AL-37FP turbofans
Power	16,755lb thrust (dry); 27,557lb thrust (with afterburning)
Span	14.70m (48ft 2¾in)
Length	23.34m (76ft 6¼in) without probe
Height	6.36m (20ft 10¼in)
Max weight	34,000kg (74,957lb)
Top speed	2,500km/h (1,553mph)
Ceiling	17,800m (58,400ft)
Max range	3,000km (1,865 miles)
Crew	Two
Weapons	30mm GSH-301 cannon; Alamo, Acrid, Aphid, Archer and Adder missiles
First flown	1 July 1997
Into service	1999

Supermarine

SpitFire

Single piston-engined, single-seat fighter

Supermarine
SpitFire
Single piston-engined, single-seat fighter

The Spitfire is unquestionably the most famous British piston-engined fighter ever built. It was designed by Reginald Mitchell, based on the successful Schneider Trophy racing seaplanes of 1929/31. First flown in March 1936, the new Rolls-Royce Merlin engined fighter was fast, well-armed and very manoeuvrable. Entering service in August 1938 Spitfires flew on every operational front in the Second World War. It will be particularly remembered for its part in the Battle of Britain in 1940. Flying alongside Fighter Command Hurricanes, the Spitfire took on the Luftwaffe's Messerschmitt 109s in daily combat over south-east England. Through the war years the fighter was improved with more powerful engines, giving greater speed, and increased armament. A total of 22,768 Spitfires and Seafires in 33 different marks had been built when production stopped in 1949. The last operational flight was made by an RAF Spitfire XIX in Malaya on 1 April 1954.

Statistics

Spitfire F.IX

Engine	One Rolls-Royce Merlin 61 or 63 piston engine
Power	1,565hp
Span	11.23m (36ft 10in)
Length	9.45m (31ft ½in)
Height	3.56m (11ft 8in)
Max weight	3,402kg (7,500lb)
Top speed	657km/h (408mph)
Ceiling	13,106m (43,000ft)
Max range	698km (434 miles)
Crew	One
Weapons	20mm cannon; 0.303in machine guns
First flown	5 March 1936
Into service	August 1938
Out of service	1954

Vought F4U
Corsair

Single piston-engined, single-seat naval fighter

Vought F4U
Corsair
Single piston-engined, single-seat naval fighter

530

The Corsair, with its bent 'gull' wing was
the first carrier aircraft that could outfly the best
of the Japanese fighters. First flown in 1940, the F4U with its large radial
engine was one of the first US Navy monoplanes. It had a 'cranked' wing
so that a large diameter propeller could be fitted. When first in service the
Corsair was used by land-based US Marine Corps squadrons. The British
Fleet Air Arm, which received 2,012 examples, found the fighter was a
good carrier aircraft. This changed the view of the US Navy. It became
the premier air combat aircraft in the Pacific and the Japanese called it
'The Whistling Death'. Overall it had a combat record of 2,140 confirmed
victories in air battle – for the loss of only 189 Corsairs in action. Unlike
most other US piston-engined fighters, the F4U was also used extensively
during the Korean War of 1952/53. In the 1950s the French Navy flew 94
Corsairs operationally in Indo-China. A total of 12,571 Corsairs had been
built when production ceased in 1952.

F4U-1A Corsair

Engine	One Pratt & Whitney R-2800-8W Double Wasp piston engine
Power	2,250hp
Span	12.49m (40ft 11¾in)
Length	9.99m (32ft 9½in)
Height	4.58m (15ft ¼in)
Max weight	6,280kg (13,846lb)
Top speed	631km/h (392mph)
Ceiling	11,247m (36,900ft)
Max range	2,514km (1,562 miles)
Crew	One
Weapons	0.50in machine guns
First flown	29 May 1940
Entered service	June 1941
Out of service	Mid-1950s

Vought F-8
Crusader

Single turbojet, single-seat naval fighter

Vought F-8
Crusader
Single turbojet, single-seat naval fighter

When the single-seat F-8 Crusader entered service it was the first carrier-based aircraft that could fly faster than the speed of sound. The F-8 was dedicated to the air defence of the carrier and its strike aircraft and the Crusader featured an unusual variable-incidence wing to lower the nose on approach to landing. The raised centre section of the wing also acted as a speed brake to reduce speed further. Its air-to-air missiles were all carried on the fuselage sides with none on the wings. The Crusader made its combat debut in August 1964 at the start of the Vietnam War, and was used by both US Navy and Marine detachments. It was even used as a 'dogfighter' and shot down 18 MiGs. By 1972 it was being phased out by the US Navy and some were sold to the Philippine Air Force, who operated them until 1986. 40 were exported to France and flown from the Navy carriers. These were operational until 2002, when they were replaced by the Rafale.

F-8U Crusader

Engine	**One Pratt & Whitney J57-P-20A turbojet**
Power	**10,000lb thrust (dry); 18,000lb thrust (with afterburner)**
Span	**10.87m (35ft 8in)**
Length	**16.53m (54ft 3in)**
Height	**4.80m (15ft 9in)**
Max weight	**13,154kg (29,000lb)**
Top speed	**1,976km/h (1,228mph)**
Ceiling	**178,983m (59,000ft)**
Max range	**2,795km (1,735 miles)**
Crew	**One**
Weapons	**20mm cannon; AIM-9 Sidewinder missiles**
First flew	**25 March 1955**
Into service	**March 1957**
Out of service	**2002**

Checklist

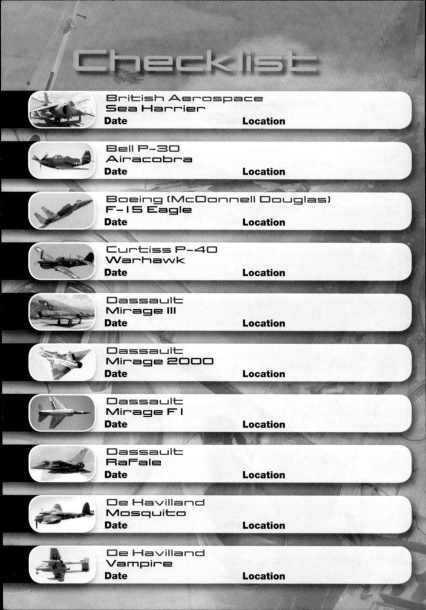

British Aerospace Sea Harrier
Date   Location

Bell P-30 Airacobra
Date   Location

Boeing (McDonnell Douglas) F-15 Eagle
Date   Location

Curtiss P-40 Warhawk
Date   Location

Dassault Mirage III
Date   Location

Dassault Mirage 2000
Date   Location

Dassault Mirage F1
Date   Location

Dassault RaFale
Date   Location

De Havilland Mosquito
Date   Location

De Havilland Vampire
Date   Location

English Electric Lightning
Date **Location**

EuroFighter Typhoon
Date **Location**

Gloster Meteor
Date **Location**

Grumman Bearcat
Date **Location**

Grumman F-14 Tomcat
Date **Location**

Grumman Wildcat
Date **Location**

Hawker Hunter
Date **Location**

Hawker Hurricane
Date **Location**

Hawker Sea Fury
Date **Location**

Hawker Sea Hawk
Date **Location**

Lockheed Martin F-16 Fighting Falcon
Date **Location**

	Lockheed **P-38 Lightning** **Date**	**Location**
	Lockheed Martin **F-22 Raptor** **Date**	**Location**
	Lockheed F-104 **Starfighter** **Date**	**Location**
	McDonnell Douglas **F-4 Phantom II** **Date**	**Location**
	Messerschmitt **BF.109** **Date**	**Location**
	Mikoyan-Gurevich **MiG-15 'Fagot'** **Date**	**Location**
	Mikoyan-Gurevich **MiG-21 'Fishbed'** **Date**	**Location**
	Mikoyan-Gurevich **MiG-23 'Flogger'** **Date**	**Location**
	Mikoyan **MiG-29 'Fulcrum'** **Date**	**Location**
	Mitsubishi **A6M2 Zero** **Date**	**Location**
	North American **P-51 Mustang** **Date**	**Location**
	North American **F-86 Sabre** **Date**	**Location**

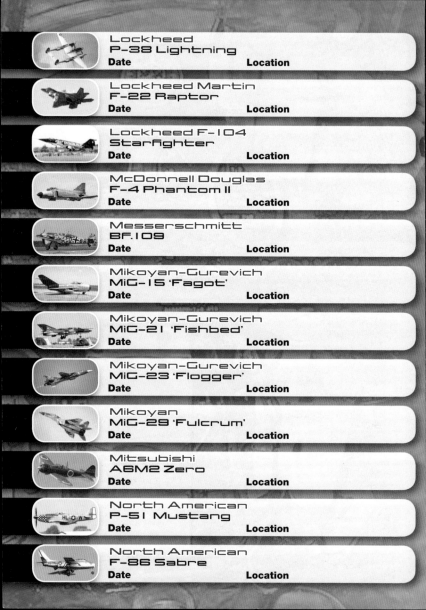

North American
F-100 Super Sabre
Date　　　　　　　**Location**

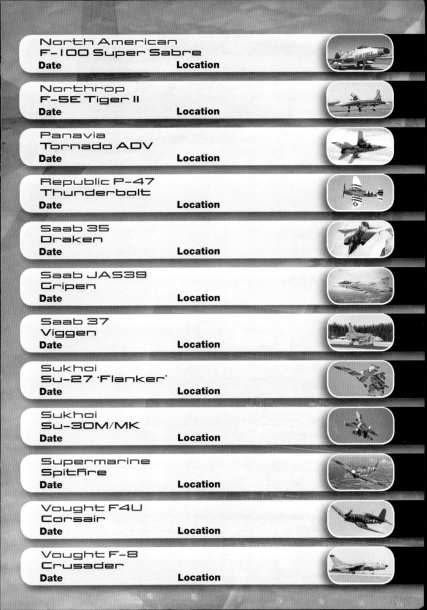

Northrop
F-5E Tiger II
Date　　　　　　　**Location**

Panavia
Tornado ADV
Date　　　　　　　**Location**

Republic P-47
Thunderbolt
Date　　　　　　　**Location**

Saab 35
Draken
Date　　　　　　　**Location**

Saab JAS39
Gripen
Date　　　　　　　**Location**

Saab 37
Viggen
Date　　　　　　　**Location**

Sukhoi
Su-27 'Flanker'
Date　　　　　　　**Location**

Sukhoi
Su-30M/MK
Date　　　　　　　**Location**

Supermarine
Spitfire
Date　　　　　　　**Location**

Vought F4U
Corsair
Date　　　　　　　**Location**

Vought F-8
Crusader
Date　　　　　　　**Location**

W. B. YEATS
SELECTED PLAYS

W. B. Yeats

SELECTED PLAYS

Edited

with an Introduction and Notes

by

A. NORMAN JEFFARES

Professor of English Literature
University of Leeds

LONDON

MACMILLAN & CO LTD

1964

PRINTED IN GREAT BRITAIN

CONTENTS

CONTENTS

INTRODUCTION

WE think of Yeats primarily as a poet, yet throughout his life
he devoted much of his energy to writing plays and for many
years his time was taken up as Manager of the Abbey Theatre
with 'theatre business, management of men'. The second
(posthumous) edition of his *Collected Plays* (1952), though it
does not include all his published dramatic work,[1] contains
over seven hundred pages of text, and this gives some indication of the scope of his dramatic work.

Yeats began to write play after play in imitation of Spenser
and Shelley in his teens. His father, who exercised a strong influence over him at this period of his life, used to read aloud
the most dramatic passages of whatever play or poem was at
the time engaging his capacity for acute, original, speculative
appreciation. His son read his own lines aloud as he wrote
them; as he did not understand prosody, he discovered that, in
order to create some common music for his lines, he needed a
listener, an audience. He developed a habit of acting what he
wrote and spoke. Indeed, when he left the High School and
joined the School of Art in Dublin he sometimes adopted an
artificial stride, seeing himself as a kind of Hamlet seeking for
heroic self-possession as he was torn by inner struggles.

His concern in drama was largely with the heroic. His early
plays were romantic and mournful, preoccupied with loneliness and beauty. *The Island of Statues* of 1885,[2] for instance,
though cast in dramatic form, was a romantic poem with little

---

[1] For details of some unpublished MSS. see G. B. Saul, *Prolegomena
to the Study of Yeats's Plays* (1958), pp. 99–100.

[2] Included in *The Dublin University Review*, April, May, June, and
July 1885.

dramatic content. About 1886, under the influence of John O'Leary and his own developing nationalism, he had decided to write out of his emotions; he had come to believe a new kind of Irish literature was needed. As he began to explore through translations a new world of Gaelic literature, and also to build up a deep knowledge of nineteenth-century Irish writing in English, he left behind conventional themes and derivative romance.

The Countess Kathleen (1892)[1] bears witness to this change in his style and aims. His falling in love with Maud Gonne in 1889 and his realisation that he would need 'a very public talent' to commend himself to this beautiful, violent, and ruthless revolutionary were reasons for his writing this verse play for her. But he was also deeply impressed by Florence Farr's verse speaking in John Todhunter's *A Sicilian Idyll* (1890), performed at Bedford Park in 1890. He based *The Countess Cathleen* on a story he had found and thought suitable for a poetic drama when he was preparing his *Fairy and Folk Tales of the Irish Peasantry* (1888). He drafted it in prose, beginning work in February or March 1889, and finishing the first version in verse in October 1891.

The play has a simple episodic plot. The Countess leaves her dreams for the reality of life; she opposes the efforts of two demon-merchants to buy the souls of her starving peasants. Finally she sells her own soul to prevent this. Yeats wrote *The Countess Cathleen* out of a general ambition to create a 'great distinctive poetic literature' out of Ireland's pagan and Christian traditions: in contrast to his long poem *The Wanderings of Oisin* (1889), which was concerned with pagan legends, this play was to mingle his personal thought and feeling with the beliefs and customs of Christian Ireland. He regarded the

[1] The original spelling, Kathleen, was altered to Cathleen in 1895; the latter spelling is subsequently used in this edition.

pagan and Christian elements in Irish tradition as a kind of double fountain head of inspiration. His personal feelings are contained in the play, when the poet Kevin vainly attempts to sell his own soul to prevent the Countess from selling hers. He believes that she should leave the ultimate salvation of the peasants to the builder of the heavens, that her concern should be with marriage and children. This was an indirect message for Maud Gonne, which becomes stronger in later versions of the play, when Kevin, altered to Aleel, puts the claims of subjective life (the beautiful life of artists which Yeats dreamed of for Maud Gonne) as opposed to the grey realities of 'the evil of the times'.

Yeats revised the text extensively, in 1895, 1901, 1912, and 1919, making minor alterations at other times. The first of these major revisions[1] was stimulated by the performance in 1894 of *The Land of Heart's Desire* (1894) at the Avenue Theatre. Yeats wrote this slight play at Florence Farr's suggestion, so that her niece Dorothy Paget could play the rôle of a fairy child who tempts a young woman away from a respectable cottage marriage to the timelessness of life with the faery host.

The Shadowy Waters (1900),[2] also a much revised play, on which Yeats worked from 1885 to 1905 or later,[3] explores a different kind of situation: it is a study of the heroic gesture, the union of hearts. More a ritual than a play, according to Yeats, it is a symbolic drama of escape, in which the hero and heroine, lily and rose, seek death and life respectively. The symbols are meant — like those in his poems of the 'nineties — to carry a weight of cryptic meaning. Through their shadows

---

[1] They are described in Peter Ure, *Yeats the Playwright* (1963), pp. 13–15.

[2] First published in the *North American Review*, May 1900.

[3] It was first produced at the Molesworth Hall, Dublin, on 14 January 1904. The acting version was first published in 1907.

they suggest the lovers' contrasting dreams of love and also they symbolise a love beyond this, of superhuman kind.

Yeats's twilight *fin de siècle* weariness changed into a new harsh realism after the turn of the century, and he devoted most of his energy and a great deal of courage to launching, administering, and championing the Irish dramatic movement. He had met Lady Gregory in 1896 and spent subsequent summers in Coole, gathering folk lore with her in the West of Ireland, and finding in her the ally he sought in creating an Irish theatre. Together they established the Irish Literary Theatre, with Edward Martyn and George Moore as co-directors, and in 1899 Martyn's *The Heather Field* and Yeats's *The Countess Cathleen* were performed in Dublin. There was a baptism of fire for *The Countess Cathleen*, which incurred moral, political, and religious opposition on the grounds that the people of Ireland would never sell their souls, and the play was performed with police protection.

The Irish Literary Theatre continued to function until the end of 1902: by then Martyn and Moore dropped out of the movement, but not before Yeats and Moore had quarrelled violently over their joint play *Diarmuid and Grania*[1] and then over a story intended to provide the basis for further collaboration. Yeats hastily wrote *Where There is Nothing* (1902)[2] to stop Moore using the subject. This was an account of an anarchistic country gentleman who, after joining a group of tinkers, marries one of them, disassociates himself from his respectable neighbours, enters a monastery where he becomes heretical, is banished and finally killed by a mob. Nietzsche, whom Yeats began reading in 1902, may well have influenced the superman element in this hero.

[1] The text has been published by W. Becker, *The Dublin Magazine*, April–June 1951.

[2] First published as supplement to the *United Irishman*, 1 November 1902.

The Irish National Dramatic Society, with Yeats as its president, replaced the Irish Literary Theatre; this new group contained the Fay brothers, and it provided Yeats with the Irish actors and actresses he had wanted. He gave it his *Cathleen ni Hoolihan* (1902), and Maud Gonne acted in the title-rôle. The play was almost terrifyingly successful in its revolutionary message, in its portrayal of Ireland as the traditional wronged old woman, calling on her children for help. On the news of the landing of a French force at Killala,[1] she is suddenly seen as a young girl with 'the walk of a queen'. The play is simple and dramatically very effective indeed. In old age Yeats, remembering its startling effect on the audience, wondered

> Did that play of mine send out
> Certain men the English shot?[2]

The Pot of Broth (1904)[3] was an adaptation of a folk tale for which Lady Gregory wrote some dialogue. *The Hour-Glass* (1903), originally a prose morality play, in which a Wise Man humbles himself to a Fool and receives salvation,[4] was rewritten in verse. These plays are due to the aim Yeats and Lady Gregory had formed of bringing the poetical tradition contained in the speech of the countryside to the city. They, along with Synge, thought

> All that we did, all that we said or sang
> Must come from contact with the soil, from that
> Contact everything Antaeus-like grew strong.[5]

[1] The play is based on the *Shan Van Vocht*, a well-known street ballad which celebrated French aid for Irish rebellions. General Humbert landed his men at Killala in 1798.

[2] W. B. Yeats, 'The Man and the Echo', *Collected Poems* (1956), p. 393.

[3] First published in *The Gael*, September 1903; then in *The Hour-Glass and Other Plays* (1904).

[4] It was founded on a story, 'The Priest's Soul', recorded in Lady Wilde, *Ancient Legends of Ireland* (1887), I, ll. 60–67.

[5] W. B. Yeats, 'The Municipal Gallery Revisited', *Collected Poems*, p. 368.

Synge's first plays to be performed in Dublin were *In the Shadow of the Glen* (1903) and *Riders to the Sea* (1904). The melancholia and vitality of Synge's genius (which Yeats felt he had discovered and guided into its right channels) made for a different use of peasant speech and idiom, and Yeats fully realised and wrote enthusiastically of its merits.[1] He and Lady Gregory fought unselfishly for Synge's work, especially *The Playboy of the Western World* (1907), the exuberant yet profound sense of comedy of which aroused vociferous hostility from a section of Irish and later Irish-American public opinion. The poetical quality of Synge's prose drama was, however, *sui generis*, and when, after the success of Yeats's *The Countess Cathleen*, *The Pot of Broth*, and *The Hour-Glass*, and Lady Gregory's *Twenty Five* in London in 1903, the Abbey Theatre was opened in Dublin in 1904 Yeats was writing a very different kind of play.

The King's Threshold (1904) was first performed in 1903. This play was founded upon a middle-Irish story of the demands of the poets at the court of King Guaire at Gort, Co. Galway; it also owed something to Edwin Ellis's play *Sancan the Bard* (1905).[2] It marks, according to S. B. Bushrui,[2] the point at which Yeats abandoned passivity — the idealism of Kevin in *The Countess Cathleen*, the isolation of Forgael in *The Shadowy Waters* — and descended into the world of reality. In this play Seanchan the bard is prepared to become part of the real world and struggle with its trivialities in order to assert his view of the place of poetry in the life of the nation. This is an aristocratic view of poetry. It has moved away from any

---

[1] Cf. W. B. Yeats, *Plays in Prose and Verse* (1922), p. 421: 'The first use of Irish dialect, rich, abundant and correct, for the purposes of creative art, was in J. M. Synge's *Riders to the Sea* and Lady Gregory's *Spreading the News*.'

[2] " 'The King's Threshold": A Defence of Poetry', *A Review of English Literature*, IV, 3, July 1963, p. 83.

desire to become an instrument of nationalistic politics. As
J. I. M. Stewart remarked, 'Yeats was at least as shrewd as he
was mystical,' and must have realised that the forces Maud
Gonne wished to unleash would be as hostile in the end to
Coole Park as to Dublin Castle.[1]

Yeats's romantic dreams were over once Maud Gonne had
married John MacBride in 1903. His new love poetry, now
devoid of decorative trappings, recorded movingly the losses
caused by his barren passion. Maud Gonne had not understood his aims for Ireland and Ireland itself seemed not to want
the new culture he and his friends were creating. Like Seanchan, Yeats was ready to enter the real world; he became
Manager of the Abbey and soon his heartfelt curse lay on plays

> That have to be set up in fifty ways
> On the day's war with knave and dolt, . . .[2]

But despite Yeats's preoccupation with the fascination of
what was difficult his own verse plays were not popular with
the Abbey audience:

> When we are high and airy hundreds say
> That if we hold that flight they'll leave the place.[3]

The audience preferred realism, and Yeats was unselfish
enough to work for the kind of play the younger dramatists
were writing. But his own preoccupation was still with the
heroic.

In 1892 he had written 'The Death of Cuchulain', a poem
based largely on folk-tale sources and on the work of Sir
Samuel Ferguson and Standish O'Grady. Cuchulain continued

[1] *Eight Modern Writers, Oxford History of English Literature* (1963),
p. 326.
[2] W. B. Yeats, 'The Fascination of What's Difficult', *Collected Poems*,
p. 104.
[3] W. B. Yeats, 'At the Abbey Theatre', *Collected Poems*, p. 107.

to occupy his mind as a subject throughout his life, especially at critical periods in it.[1] In 1901 he was working on the play *On Baile's Strand* (1903),[2] which also deals with Cuchulain's unwitting killing of his own son. Birgit Bjersby has shown how Cuchulain grows older in Yeats's work along with Yeats himself; in the revised version of *On Baile's Strand* of 1905 (when Yeats was forty) we are told he is about forty, though, traditionally, he was twenty-seven when he died.[3] This, then, is a play with reflections of Yeats's frustrated love and frustrated desire for a son: in it he is beginning to stylise the form of the play, and to make the characters reflect the abstract ideas that were persecuting him,[4] for the Fool and the Blind Man are shadows of Cuchulain and Conchubar, and are later to become important symbols in *A Vision* (1926; 1937). They affect the play's events and yet are detached from it: they reveal Yeats's increasing interest in extremes and oppositions. The play has a sense of impending doom; its irony and inexorability inevitably remind us of Greek tragedy.

In *Deirdre* (1907) Yeats attempted a more difficult subject, concentrating into one act the treachery and terror which kill Naoise, the pity provoked by Deirdre's suicide. The suspense is skilfully built up, the poetry sensuous and sinister. This is the story of a quarrel which knows no mending, the legend of 'one woman and two men', and the circumstances of Yeats's life gave it imaginative intensity. Naoise plays a self-conscious rôle, but Deirdre triumphs finally over Conchubar; theirs are

---

[1] There were seven main treatments: 'The Death of Cuchulain' (poem, 1892); *On Baile's Strand* (1903); *The Golden Helmet* (1908) and *The Green Helmet* (1910); *At the Hawk's Well* (1917), *The Only Jealousy of Emer* (1919), and *Fighting the Waves* (1934); *The Death of Cuchulain* (1939) and 'Cuchulain Comforted' (poem, 1939).

[2] First published in *The Seven Woods* (1903).

[3] *The Interpretation of the Cuchulain Legend in the Works of W. B. Yeats* (1950), p. 79.

[4] Cf. W. B. Yeats, *Wheels and Butterflies* (1934), p. 102.

'contrasted sorrows'. The attention of the audience, indeed, is meant to centre upon her and her situation. Though the play departs from the simplicity of its sources it has a strange, lofty dignity about it.

Though Yeats returned to the Cuchulain theme in his next play his treatment of the heroic Gaelic material was very different. *The Golden Helmet* (1908), rewritten in verse as *The Green Helmet* (1910), founded on an old Irish tale 'The Feast of Bricriu', was an ironical farce, a farce being for Yeats 'a moment of intense life'. Though the play reflects quarrels and controversies it praises Cuchulain's joyful fighting and powers of reconciliation:

> And I choose the laughing life
> That shall not turn from laughing, whatever rise or fall;
> The heart that grows no bitterer although betrayed by all;
> The hand that loves to scatter; the life like a gambler's throw . . .[1]

The Unicorn from the Stars (1908) was a rewriting of *Where There is Nothing*: it replaces the unsatisfactory episodic activities of the hero of the earlier play with a new concentrated action and a more convincing hero, Martin Hearne. This young coachbuilder has a vision of the unicorns which will destroy the existing order of things; he collects beggars, initiates a drunken revel, and finally realises, before he is shot, that he has been mistaken in giving way to the attraction of destructive violence.

Yeats's concern with the end of one era and the beginning of a new, symbolised by the iron-clawed beast of *Where There is Nothing* and the unicorns of *The Unicorn from the Stars*, was

[1] W. B. Yeats, *The Green Helmet*, *Collected Plays* (1952), p. 243. *The Golden Helmet* was first performed on 19 March 1908; *The Green Helmet* on 10 February 1910, both at the Abbey Theatre, Dublin.

taken up yet again in the unicorn of *The Player Queen* (1922),
the genesis of which is described in a note:

> I began in, I think, 1907, a verse tragedy, but at that time
> the thought I have set forth in *Per Amica Silentia Lunae* was
> coming into my head, and I found examples of it every-
> where. I wasted the best working months of several years
> in an attempt to write a poetical play where every character
> became an example of the finding or not finding of what I
> have called the Antithetical Self; and because passion and
> not thought makes tragedy, what I made had neither sim-
> plicity nor life. I knew precisely what was wrong and yet
> could neither escape from thought nor give up my play.
> At last it came into my head all of a sudden that I could get
> rid of the play if I turned it into a farce; and never did I do
> anything so easily, for I think I wrote the present play in
> about a month . . .[1]

This 'wild comedy' (first performed in 1919) is extremely
effective on the stage. It can be enjoyed as a prose farce as well
as an extension of the theory of the mask which finds expression in *Per Amica Silentia Lunae* (1918).[2] There are other,
obscurer elements of Yeats's 'system' in the play. Decima,
according to Professor Ure, is both harlot and artist seeking
her anti-self, and she can be explained in terms of Yeats's story
The Adoration of the Magi (1897; 1925). F. A. C. Wilson sees
the unicorn as the form in which divinity is to descend to
Decima[3] (as the swan descends to Leda), but Professor Ure
argues against this (since Decima does not marry a unicorn
but the Prime Minister) and suggests that beneath the farce

[1] W. B. Yeats, *Plays in Prose and Verse* (1922), p. 428.
[2] See W. B. Yeats, 'Ego Dominus Tuus', *Collected Poems*, p. 180;
'The Phases of the Moon', *ibid.*, p. 183, is a similar exposition of Yeats's
'system'.
[3] F. A. C. Wilson, *Yeats and Tradition* (1958), p. 182.

lies the tragedy, that Decima finds, instead of death, her anti-self and happiness, but, as a condition of this, has to unite with a buffoon.[1]

There had been much difficulty in getting the right actress for the initial production of *Deirdre*. Miss Darragh (Letitia Marion Dallas) was chosen; this appointment displeased the Abbey actors; and the part was subsequently played by Mrs. Campbell. For the part of Decima, Yeats had Mrs. Patrick Campbell in mind when he began to write the play that became *The Player Queen*. A possible reason for this move from tragedy to the farce of *The Golden Helmet* and *The Player Queen* may have been a desire to provide plays which would suit the Abbey actors. What he wanted, however, was an audience and actors to suit himself, and this situation was achieved in Lady Cunard's drawing-room on 2 April 1916. Here was performed *At the Hawk's Well* (1917),[2] the first of the four *Plays for Dancers* (1921). These were plays written out of his interest in the Japanese Noh drama, to which Ezra Pound had introduced him. This offered him a new, simple technique. He could do without an orthodox theatre — an unpopular one was better since he wanted a mysterious art, a ritual helped into being by music and dancing. This would allow him to make credible strange events and elaborate words.

At the Hawk's Well sums up some personal disillusion and uncertainty. It symbolises man's search for the unobtainable, the hawk suggesting the persecution of the abstract, and Cuchulain the contradictory nature of carnage. *The Only Jealousy of Emer* (1919)[3] is more complicated in structure, and its account of Emer's renunciation of Cuchulain, a solitary act of sacrifice which is unknown to her husband, is encumbered

[1] P. Ure, *Yeats the Playwright* (1963), p. 144.
[2] First published in *Harper's Bazaar*, March 1917.
[3] First published in *Poetry* (Chicago), January 1919.

by the ambiguous temptation offered by Fand, the woman of
the Sidhe. *The Dreaming of the Bones* (1919)[1] is more successful
in its mixture of the supernatural and the political. A revolutionary soldier meets the ghosts of Dermot and Devorgilla
who were responsible for bringing Strongbow and the
Normans into Ireland in the twelfth century. They reveal
their identity; their anguished separation can be ended if
someone of their own race forgives them. But the soldier cannot bring himself to do this, and their remorseful dance of
longing ends the play.

Calvary (1921)[2] possesses the musicians' songs, the dance and
masked actors, the grouped images of the other Noh-style
plays. Its subject, however, marks it off as different, and it
requires some knowledge of *A Vision* for its understanding.
Christ, himself a victim of intellectual despair, can help neither
the Roman soldiers, who are a form of objectivity, nor
Lazarus, nor Judas, nor the heron, eagle, and swan, who are
content with solitude. The play consists in Professor Ure's
words, of 'four variations on the theme of Christ's powerless-
ness to save those who can live without salvation'.

Yeats wrote *The Cat and the Moon* (1926),[3] a brief, curiously
Synge-like exercise,[4] and followed it with his two translations
Sophocles' '*King Oedipus*' (1928) and Sophocles' '*Oedipus at
Colonus*' (1934). *The Resurrection* (1931)[5] occupied him from
1925 to 1930; it develops the static attitudes of *Calvary* into
a far livelier, more effective play which has structure and
development. The plot rests upon Yeats's view of history as

[1] In *Two Plays for Dancers* (1919).

[2] In *Four Plays for Dancers* (1921).

[3] First published in *The Criterion*, July 1924, and in *The Dial*, July 1924.

[4] The play describes the friendship of George Moore and Edward
Martyn. Cf. W. B. Yeats, *Autobiographies* (1956), p. 482.

[5] First published in *Adelphi*, June 1927; then in *Stories of Michael
Robartes and His Friends* (1931).

antithetical; he thought Christianity brought radical thought into the world and with it a new historical period. He makes his abstract system live, first through explanatory dialogue, then through the explosive tension generated out of the situation, an undercurrent of Dionysiac irrational force, beating through the play, contrasting ironically with the talk of the two main characters, the Greek and the Hebrew. This is a masterpiece of dramatic intensity and economy. The stage-craft has a confidence, the dialogue an assurance that reflects the effect that writing *A Vision*, 'getting it all in order', had on Yeats's poetry.

The same superb dramatic skill is at work in *The Words upon the Window-Pane* (1934). Yeats's sense of dialogue and of construction allow him to vary the tension of the play, to make realistic use of a séance to communicate the terror in his sense of Swift's agony of spirit:

> . . . beating on his breast in sibylline frenzy blind
> Because the heart in his blood-sodden breast had dragged
>   him down into mankind.[1]

The King of the Great Clock Tower (1934) was 'the most popular of my dance plays', and *A Full Moon in March* (1935) was a second version of the idea based on Oscar Wilde's *Salomé*. The characters are not convincing as people; they are in fact parts of a ritual. *The Herne's Egg* (1938) — 'the strangest wildest thing I have ever written' — seemed to Yeats to have more tragedy and philosophic depth than *The Player Queen*. The hero, Congal, is at war with the bird-god, the Great Herne: but he does not fully understand what he fights. He is obtuse, he falls into a state of mind where he decides the rape of Attracta will restore the state of disorder which existed before he stole the herne's egg and so began the

[1] W. B. Yeats, 'Blood and the Moon', *Collected Poems*, p. 267.

quarrel which led to his killing of Aedh. The 'first bout' with the God led to disorder, the second to the violation of Attracta, which Corgal fails to understand in its fullest meaning. The third bout leads to his death in terms of the curse at the hands of a fool, and his reincarnation as a donkey. Congal is a tragic hero of the Othello or Coriolanus kind, limited because his virtues are also his flaws; he makes mistakes, and misunderstands the situation into which his mistakes lead him. The Great Herne has an impersonality and mystery which perhaps reinforce the unimportance of Congal's heroic activity, his inability to realise the difference between fighting against men and against the God.

Purgatory (1939)[1] dramatises some elements of a ghost story Yeats told earlier about Castle Dargan, near Sligo; in the play the protagonist is an old pedlar, who tells his bastard son the history of the ruined house and its inhabitants. The ghosts of the house appear to the old man — and then, finally, to the boy, as he and his father grapple together, fighting for the pedlar's money. The murder of the son, however, fails to arrest the haunting of the place, centred upon the pedlar's mother's dream. This is a play, on an Oresteia-like theme, upon the problem of the possible purification of a family and of the sexual act which began it. The irony of the repeated pattern of the murders adds to the horror of the play; the circle cannot be broken by mankind, and the old man prays, finally, to God to appease the misery of the living as well as the remains of the dead.

Yeats wrote *The Death of Cuchulain* (1939)[2] shortly before his death. Here he again returned to the material of Lady Gregory's *Cuchulain of Muirthemne*; he also weighted the play with the intimations of the system of *A Vision*. Cuchulain is

---

[1] In *Last Poems and Two Plays* (1939).
[2] *Ibid.*

given a false message by his mistress Eithne, who is under the spell of the goddess of war, which will lead him into hopeless battle; he faces the prospect of death with his usual bravery, forgiving Eithne with a magnanimity which is ironic. He is mortally wounded, and, though Aoife is about to revenge upon him the death of their son Conlaech, the actual death is ironically administered by a blind man for a paltry reward. This is the Cuchulain, blinded by heroism, butchered by a clown, who is envisaged in the final song of the play as resuming his place in the folk memory of Irish tradition with the occurrence of the Easter Rising of 1916:

> What stood in the Post Office
> With Pearse and Connolly?
> What comes out of the mountain
> Where men first shed their blood?
> Who thought Cuchulain till it seemed
> He stood where they had stood?
>
> No body like his body
> Has modern woman borne,
> But an old man looking on life
> Imagines it in scorn.
> A statue's there to mark the place,
> By Oliver Sheppard done.

Yeats had aimed to 'make the old stories as familiar to Irishmen at any rate as are the stories of King Arthur and his Knights to all readers of books'. In doing so he had helped to bring a regenerated nation into being, and it was fitting that his hero met death with the proud disdain he sought to achieve himself.

NOTE ON THE TEXT

THE copy-text used is that of *Collected Plays* (1952). As the dates given in that edition (in the list of contents and under the title of each play) for the first published versions are not always correct they have been omitted from the body of this text. The notes of this St. Martin's Library edition attempt to establish where possible the dates of the first publication and production of each play included in the selection. The order of the plays in *Collected Plays* (1952) is followed, with one exception. The text of *Cathleen ni Hoolihan* is taken from *Samhain*, 1902, in which it first appeared, in view of the play's immediate effect upon its audience. It is, therefore, placed after those plays which are taken from *Collected Plays* (1952). I am greatly indebted to Mrs. W. B. Yeats for her aid in correcting the text of *Collected Plays* (1952) and for other assistance in annotation. Professor David Greene and Mr. Brendan Kennelly have also helped me greatly with the identification of Gaelic material.

ON BAILE'S STRAND

ON BAILE'S STRAND

PERSONS IN THE PLAY

A Fool
A Blind Man
Cuchulain, *King of Muirthemne*
Conchubar, *High King of Uladh*
A Young Man, *son of Cuchulain*
Kings and Singing Women

*A great hall at Dundealgan, not 'Cuchulain's great ancient house'
but an assembly-house nearer to the sea. A big door at the back, and
through the door misty light as of sea-mist. There are many chairs
and one long bench. One of these chairs, which is towards the front of
the stage, is bigger than the others. Somewhere at the back there is a
table with flagons of ale upon it and drinking-horns. There is a small
door at one side of the hall. A Fool and Blind Man, both ragged,
and their features made grotesque and extravagant by masks, come
in through the door at the back. The Blind Man leans upon a staff.*

Fool. What a clever man you are though you are blind!
There's nobody with two eyes in his head that is as clever
as you are. Who but you could have thought that the hen-
wife sleeps every day a little at noon? I would never be able
to steal anything if you didn't tell me where to look for it.
And what a good cook you are! You take the fowl out of
my hands after I have stolen it and plucked it, and you put
it into the big pot at the fire there, and I can go out and run
races with the witches at the edge of the waves and get an
appetite, and when I've got it, there's the hen waiting inside
for me, done to the turn.

Blind Man [*who is feeling about with his stick*]. Done to the turn.

Fool [*putting his arm round Blind Man's neck*]. Come now, I'll have a leg and you'll have a leg, and we'll draw lots for the wish-bone. I'll be praising you, I'll be praising you while we're eating it, for your good plans and for your good cooking. There's nobody in the world like you, Blind Man. Come, come. Wait a minute. I shouldn't have closed the door. There are some that look for me, and I wouldn't like them not to find me. Don't tell it to anybody, Blind Man. There are some that follow me. Boann herself out of the river and Fand out of the deep sea. Witches they are, and they come by in the wind, and they cry, 'Give a kiss, Fool, give a kiss', that's what they cry. That's wide enough. All the witches can come in now. I wouldn't have them beat at the door and say, 'Where is the Fool? Why has he put a lock on the door?' Maybe they'll hear the bubbling of the pot and come in and sit on the ground. But we won't give them any of the fowl. Let them go back to the sea, let them go back to the sea.

Blind Man [*feeling legs of big chair with his hands*]. Ah! [*Then, in a louder voice as he feels the back of it.*] Ah — ah —

Fool. Why do you say 'Ah-ah'?

Blind Man. I know the big chair. It is to-day the High King Conchubar is coming. They have brought out his chair. He is going to be Cuchulain's master in earnest from this day out. It is that he's coming for.

Fool. He must be a great man to be Cuchulain's master.

Blind Man. So he is. He is a great man. He is over all the rest of the kings of Ireland.

Fool. Cuchulain's master! I thought Cuchulain could do anything he liked.

Blind Man. So he did, so he did. But he ran too wild, and Conchubar is coming to-day to put an oath upon him that will stop his rambling and make him as biddable as a house-dog and keep him always at his hand. He will sit in this chair and put the oath upon him.

Fool. How will he do that?

Blind Man. You have no wits to understand such things. [*The Blind Man has got into the chair.*] He will sit up in this chair and he'll say: 'Take the oath, Cuchulain. I bid you take the oath. Do as I tell you. What are your wits compared with mine, and what are your riches compared with mine? And what sons have you to pay your debts and to put a stone over you when you die? Take the oath, I tell you. Take a strong oath.'

Fool [*crumpling himself up and whining*]. I will not. I'll take no oath. I want my dinner.

Blind Man. Hush, hush! It is not done yet.

Fool. You said it was done to a turn.

Blind Man. Did I, now? Well, it might be done, and not done. The wings might be white, but the legs might be red. The flesh might stick hard to the bones and not come away in the teeth. But, believe me, Fool, it will be well done before you put your teeth in it.

Fool. My teeth are growing long with the hunger.

Blind Man. I'll tell you a story — the kings have story-tellers while they are waiting for their dinner — I will tell you a story with a fight in it, a story with a champion in it, and a ship and a queen's son that has his mind set on killing somebody that you and I know.

Fool. Who is that? Who is he coming to kill?

Blind Man. Wait, now, till you hear. When you were stealing the fowl, I was lying in a hole in the sand, and I heard three men coming with a shuffling sort of noise. They were wounded and groaning.

Fool. Go on. Tell me about the fight.

Blind Man. There had been a fight, a great fight, a tremendous great fight. A young man had landed on the shore, the guardians of the shore had asked his name, and he had refused to tell it, and he had killed one, and others had run away.

Fool. That's enough. Come on now to the fowl. I wish it was bigger. I wish it was as big as a goose.

Blind Man. Hush! I haven't told you all. I know who that young man is. I heard the men who were running away say he had red hair, that he had come from Aoife's country, that he was coming to kill Cuchulain.

Fool. Nobody can do that.

> [*To a tune*]
>> Cuchulain has killed kings,
>> Kings and sons of kings,
>> Dragons out of the water,
>> And witches out of the air,
> Banachas and Bonachas and people of the woods.

Blind Man. Hush! hush!

Fool [*still singing*].

>> Witches that steal the milk,
>> Fomor that steal the children,
>> Hags that have heads like hares,
>> Hares that have claws like witches,
>> All riding a-cock-horse
> [*Spoken*]

Out of the very bottom of the bitter black North.

Blind Man. Hush, I say!

Fool. Does Cuchulain know that he is coming to kill him?

Blind Man. How would he know that with his head in the clouds? He doesn't care for common fighting. Why would he put himself out, and nobody in it but that young man?

Now if it were a white fawn that might turn into a queen
before morning —

Fool. Come to the fowl. I wish it was as big as a pig; a fowl
with goose grease and pig's crackling.

Blind Man. No hurry, no hurry. I know whose son it is. I
wouldn't tell anybody else, but I will tell you, — a secret is
better to you than your dinner. You like being told secrets.

Fool. Tell me the secret.

Blind Man. That young man is Aoife's son. I am sure it is
Aoife's son, it flows in upon me that it is Aoife's son. You
have often heard me talking of Aoife, the great woman-
fighter Cuchulain got the mastery over in the North?

Fool. I know, I know. She is one of those cross queens that live
in hungry Scotland.

Blind Man. I am sure it is her son. I was in Aoife's country for
a long time.

Fool. That was before you were blinded for putting a curse
upon the wind.

Blind Man. There was a boy in her house that had her own
red colour on him, and everybody said he was to be brought
up to kill Cuchulain, that she hated Cuchulain. She used to
put a helmet on a pillar-stone and call it Cuchulain and set
him casting at it. There is a step outside — Cuchulain's step.

[*Cuchulain passes by in the mist outside the big door.*

Fool. Where is Cuchulain going?

Blind Man. He is going to meet Conchubar that has bidden
him to take the oath.

Fool. Ah, an oath, Blind Man. How can I remember so many
things at once? Who is going to take an oath?

Blind Man. Cuchulain is going to take an oath to Conchubar
who is High King.

Fool. What a mix-up you make of everything, Blind Man!
You were telling me one story, and now you are telling me

another story. . . . How can I get the hang of it at the end if you mix everything at the beginning? Wait till I settle it out. There now, there's Cuchulain [*he points to one foot*], and there is the young man [*he points to the other foot*] that is coming to kill him, and Cuchulain doesn't know. But where's Conchubar? [*Takes bag from side.*] That's Conchubar with all his riches — Cuchulain, young man, Conchubar. — And where's Aoife? [*Throws up cap.*] There is Aoife, high up on the mountains in high hungry Scotland. Maybe it is not true after all. Maybe it was your own making up. It's many a time you cheated me before with your lies. Come to the cooking-pot, my stomach is pinched and rusty. Would you have it to be creaking like a gate?

Blind Man. I tell you it's true. And more than that is true. If you listen to what I say, you'll forget your stomach.

Fool. I won't.

Blind Man. Listen. I know who the young man's father is, but I won't say. I would be afraid to say. Ah, Fool, you would forget everything if you could know who the young man's father is.

Fool. Who is it? Tell me now quick, or I'll shake you. Come, out with it, or I'll shake you.

[*A murmur of voices in the distance.*

Blind Man. Wait, wait. There's somebody coming. . . . It is Cuchulain is coming. He's coming back with the High King. Go and ask Cuchulain. He'll tell you. It's little you'll care about the cooking-pot when you have asked Cuchulain, that . . .

[*Blind Man goes out by side door.*

Fool. I'll ask him. Cuchulain will know. He was in Aoife's country. [*Goes up stage.*] I'll ask him. [*Turns and goes down stage.*] But, no, I won't ask him, I would be afraid. [*Going up again.*] Yes, I will ask him. What harm in asking? The

Blind Man said I was to ask him. [*Going down.*] No, no. I'll
not ask him. He might kill me. I have but killed hens and
geese and pigs. He has killed kings. [*Goes up again almost to
big door.*] Who says I'm afraid? I'm not afraid. I'm no
coward. I'll ask him. No, no, Cuchulain, I'm not going to
ask you.

> He has killed kings,
> Kings and the sons of kings,
> Dragons out of the water,
> And witches out of the air,
> Banachas and Bonachas and people of the woods.

[*Fool goes out by side door, the last words being heard outside.
Cuchulain and Conchubar enter through the big door at the
back. While they are still outside, Cuchulain's voice is
heard raised in anger. He is a dark man, something over
forty years of age. Conchubar is much older and carries a
long staff, elaborately carved or with an elaborate gold
handle.*]

Cuchulain. Because I have killed men without your bidding
And have rewarded others at my own pleasure,
Because of half a score of trifling things,
You'd lay this oath upon me, and now — and now
You add another pebble to the heap,
And I must be your man, well-nigh your bondsman,
Because a youngster out of Aoife's country
Has found the shore ill-guarded.
Conchubar. He came to land
While you were somewhere out of sight and hearing,
Hunting or dancing with your wild companions.
Cuchulain. He can be driven out. I'll not be bound.
I'll dance or hunt, or quarrel or make love,
Wherever and whenever I've a mind to.

If time had not put water in your blood,
You never would have thought it.
Conchubar.   I would leave
A strong and settled country to my children.
Cuchulain. And I must be obedient in all things;
Give up my will to yours; go where you please;
Come when you call; sit at the council-board
Among the unshapely bodies of old men;
I whose mere name has kept this country safe,
I that in early days have driven out
Maeve of Cruachan and the northern pirates,
The hundred kings of Sorcha, and the kings
Out of the Garden in the East of the World.
Must I, that held you on the throne when all
Had pulled you from it, swear obedience
As if I were some cattle-raising king?
Are my shins speckled with the heat of the fire,
Or have my hands no skill but to make figures
Upon the ashes with a stick? Am I
So slack and idle that I need a whip
Before I serve you?
Conchubar.   No, no whip, Cuchulain,
But every day my children come and say:
'This man is growing harder to endure.
How can we be at safety with this man
That nobody can buy or bid or bind?
We shall be at his mercy when you are gone;
He burns the earth as if he were a fire,
And time can never touch him.'
Cuchulain.   And so the tale
Grows finer yet; and I am to obey
Whatever child you set upon the throne,
As if it were yourself!

Conchubar.　　　　　Most certainly.
　I am High King, my son shall be High King;
　And you for all the wildness of your blood,
　And though your father came out of the sun,
　Are but a little king and weigh but light
　In anything that touches government,
　If put into the balance with my children.
Cuchulain. It's well that we should speak our minds out plainly,
　For when we die we shall be spoken of
　In many countries. We in our young days
　Have seen the heavens like a burning cloud
　Brooding upon the world, and being more
　Than men can be now that cloud's lifted up,
　We should be the more truthful. Conchubar,
　I do not like your children — they have no pith,
　No marrow in their bones, and will lie soft
　Where you and I lie hard.
Conchubar.　　　　　　You rail at them
　Because you have no children of your own.
Cuchulain. I think myself most lucky that I leave
　No pallid ghost or mockery of a man
　To drift and mutter in the corridors
　Where I have laughed and sung.
Conchubar.　　　　　　　That is not true,
　For all your boasting of the truth between us;
　For there is no man having house and lands,
　That have been in the one family, called
　By that one family's name for centuries,
　But is made miserable if he know
　They are to pass into a stranger's keeping,
　As yours will pass.
Cuchulain.　　　　The most of men feel that,
　But you and I leave names upon the harp.

Conchubar. You play with arguments as lawyers do,
  And put no heart in them. I know your thoughts,
  For we have slept under the one cloak and drunk
  From the one wine-cup. I know you to the bone,
  I have heard you cry, aye, in your very sleep,
  'I have no son', and with such bitterness
  That I have gone upon my knees and prayed
  That it might be amended.

Cuchulain.   For you thought
  That I should be as biddable as others
  Had I their reason for it; but that's not true;
  For I would need a weightier argument
  Than one that marred me in the copying,
  As I have that clean hawk out of the air
  That, as men say, begot this body of mine
  Upon a mortal woman.

Conchubar.   Now as ever
  You mock at every reasonable hope,
  And would have nothing, or impossible things.
  What eye has ever looked upon the child
  Would satisfy a mind like that?

Cuchulain.   I would leave
  My house and name to none that would not face
  Even myself in battle.

Conchubar.   Being swift of foot,
  And making light of every common chance,
  You should have overtaken on the hills
  Some daughter of the air, or on the shore
  A daughter of the Country-under-Wave.

Cuchulain. I am not blasphemous.

Conchubar.   Yet you despise
  Our queens, and would not call a child your own,
  If one of them had borne him.

Cuchulain.   I have not said it.

Conchubar. Ah! I remember I have heard you boast,
When the ale was in your blood, that there was one
In Scotland, where you had learnt the trade of war,
That had a stone-pale cheek and red-brown hair;
And that although you had loved other women,
You'd sooner that fierce woman of the camp
Bore you a son than any queen among them.

Cuchulain. You call her a 'fierce woman of the camp',
For, having lived among the spinning-wheels,
You'd have no woman near that would not say,
'Ah! how wise!' 'What will you have for supper?'
'What shall I wear that I may please you, sir?'
And keep that humming through the day and night
For ever. A fierce woman of the camp!
But I am getting angry about nothing.
You have never seen her. Ah! Conchubar, had you seen
    her
With that high, laughing, turbulent head of hers
Thrown backward, and the bowstring at her ear,
Or sitting at the fire with those grave eyes
Full of good counsel as it were with wine,
Or when love ran through all the lineaments
Of her wild body — although she had no child,
None other had all beauty, queen or lover,
Or was so fitted to give birth to kings.

Conchubar. There's nothing I can say but drifts you farther
From the one weighty matter. That very woman —
For I know well that you are praising Aoife —
Now hates you and will leave no subtlety
Unknotted that might run into a noose
About your throat, no army in idleness
That might bring ruin on this land you serve.

Cuchulain. No wonder in that, no wonder at all in that.
  I never have known love but as a kiss
  In the mid-battle, and a difficult truce
  Of oil and water, candles and dark night,
  Hillside and hollow, the hot-footed sun
  And the cold, sliding, slippery-footed moon —
  A brief forgiveness between opposites
  That have been hatreds for three times the age
  Of this long-'stablished ground.

Conchubar.   Listen to me.
  Aoife makes war on us, and every day
  Our enemies grow greater and beat the walls
  More bitterly, and you within the walls
  Are every day more turbulent; and yet,
  When I would speak about these things, your fancy
  Runs as it were a swallow on the wind.

  [*Outside the door in the blue light of the sea-mist are many old
  and young Kings; among them are three Women, two of
  whom carry a bowl of fire. The third, in what follows, puts
  from time to time fragrant herbs into the fire so that it
  flickers up into brighter flame.*

  Look at the door and what men gather there —
  Old counsellors that steer the land with me,
  And younger kings, the dancers and harp-players
  That follow in your tumults, and all these
  Are held there by the one anxiety.
  Will you be bound into obedience
  And so make this land safe for them and theirs?
  You are but half a king and I but half;
  I need your might of hand and burning heart,
  And you my wisdom.

Cuchulain [*going near to door*]. Nestlings of a high nest,

Hawks that have followed me into the air
And looked upon the sun, we'll out of this
And sail upon the wind once more. This king
Would have me take an oath to do his will,
And having listened to his tune from morning,
I will no more of it. Run to the stable
And set the horses to the chariot-pole,
And send a messenger to the harp-players.
We'll find a level place among the woods,
And dance awhile.

A Young King.   Cuchulain, take the oath.
There is none here that would not have you take it.

Cuchulain. You'd have me take it? Are you of one mind?

The Kings. All, all, all, all!

A Young King.   Do what the High King bids you.

Conchubar. There is not one but dreads this turbulence
Now that they're settled men.

Cuchulain.   Are you so changed,
Or have I grown more dangerous of late?
But that's not it. I understand it all.
It's you that have changed. You've wives and children now,
And for that reason cannot follow one
That lives like a bird's flight from tree to tree. —
It's time the years put water in my blood
And drowned the wildness of it, for all's changed,
But that unchanged. — I'll take what oath you will:
The moon, the sun, the water, light, or air,
I do not care how binding.

Conchubar.   On this fire
That has been lighted from your hearth and mine;
The older men shall be my witnesses,
The younger, yours. The holders of the fire
Shall purify the thresholds of the house

With waving fire, and shut the outer door,
According to the custom; and sing rhyme.
That has come down from the old law-makers
To blow the witches out. Considering
That the wild will of man could be oath-bound,
But that a woman's could not, they bid us sing
Against the will of woman at its wildest
In the Shape-Changers that run upon the wind.

                      [*Conchubar has gone on to his throne.*

The Women. [*They sing in a very low voice after the first few
  words so that the others all but drown their words.*

             May this fire have driven out
             The Shape-Changers that can put
             Ruin on a great king's house
             Until all be ruinous.
             Names whereby a man has known
             The threshold and the hearthstone,
             Gather on the wind and drive
             The women none can kiss and thrive,
             For they are but whirling wind,
             Out of memory and mind.
             They would make a prince decay
             With light images of clay
             Planted in the running wave;
             Or, for many shapes they have,
             They would change them into hounds
             Until he had died of his wounds,
             Though the change were but a whim;
             Or they'd hurl a spell at him,
             That he follow with desire
             Bodies that can never tire
             Or grow kind, for they anoint
             All their bodies, joint by joint,

With a miracle-working juice
That is made out of the grease
Of the ungoverned unicorn.
But the man is thrice forlorn,
Emptied, ruined, wracked, and lost,
That they follow, for at most
They will give him kiss for kiss
While they murmur, 'After this
Hatred may be sweet to the taste'.
Those wild hands that have embraced
All his body can but shove
At the burning wheel of love
Till the side of hate comes up.
Therefore in this ancient cup
May the sword-blades drink their fill
Of the home-brew there, until
They will have for masters none
But the threshold and hearthstone.

Cuchulain [*speaking, while they are singing*]. I'll take and keep
    this oath, and from this day
I shall be what you please, my chicks, my nestlings.
Yet I had thought you were of those that praised
Whatever life could make the pulse run quickly,
Even though it were brief, and that you held
That a free gift was better than a forced. —
But that's all over. — I will keep it, too;
I never gave a gift and took it again.
If the wild horse should break the chariot-pole,
It would be punished. Should that be in the oath?

   [*Two of the Women, still singing, crouch in front of him hold-
      ing the bowl over their heads. He spreads his hands over the
      flame.*

I swear to be obedient in all things

To Conchubar, and to uphold his children.

Conchubar. We are one being, as these flames are one:
I give my wisdom, and I take your strength.
Now thrust the swords into the flame, and pray
That they may serve the threshold and the hearthstone
With faithful service.

> [*The Kings kneel in a semicircle before the two Women and
> Cuchulain, who thrusts his sword into the flame. They all
> put the points of their swords into the flame. The third
> Woman is at the back near the big door.*

Cuchulain.   O pure, glittering ones
That should be more than wife or friend or mistress,
Give us the enduring will, the unquenchable hope,
The friendliness of the sword! —

> [*The song grows louder, and the last words ring out clearly.
> There is a loud knocking at the door, and a cry of* 'Open!
> open!'

Conchubar. Some king that has been loitering on the way.
Open the door, for I would have all know
That the oath's finished and Cuchulain bound,
And that the swords are drinking up the flame.

> [*The door is opened by the third Woman, and a Young Man
> with a drawn sword enters.*

Young Man. I am of Aoife's country.

> [*The Kings rush towards him. Cuchulain throws himself
> between.*

Cuchulain.   Put up your swords.
He is but one. Aoife is far away.

Young Man. I have come alone into the midst of you
To weigh this sword against Cuchulain's sword.

Conchubar. And are you noble? for if of common seed,

You cannot weigh your sword against his sword
But in mixed battle.

Young Man.   I am under bonds
To tell my name to no man; but it's noble.

Conchubar. But I would know your name and not your bonds.
You cannot speak in the Assembly House,
If you are not noble.

First Old King.   Answer the High King!

Young Man. I will give no other proof than the hawk gives
That it's no sparrow!

> [*He is silent for a moment, then speaks to all.*

                    Yet look upon me, kings.
I, too, am of that ancient seed, and carry
The signs about this body and in these bones.

Cuchulain. To have shown the hawk's grey feather is enough,
And you speak highly, too. Give me that helmet.
I'd thought they had grown weary sending champions.
That sword and belt will do. This fighting's welcome.
The High King there has promised me his wisdom;
But the hawk's sleepy till its well-beloved
Cries out amid the acorns, or it has seen
Its enemy like a speck upon the sun.
What's wisdom to the hawk, when that clear eye
Is burning nearer up in the high air?

> [*Looks hard at Young Man; then comes down steps and grasps
> Young Man by shoulder.*

Hither into the light.
[*To Conchubar.*]   The very tint
Of her that I was speaking of but now.
Not a pin's difference.
[*To Young Man.*]   You are from the North,
Where there are many that have that tint of hair —

Red-brown, the light red-brown. Come nearer, boy,
For I would have another look at you.
There's more likeness — a pale, a stone-pale cheek.
What brought you, boy? Have you no fear of death?
Young Man. Whether I live or die is in the gods' hands.
Cuchulain. That is all words, all words; a young man's talk.
I am their plough, their harrow, their very strength;
For he that's in the sun begot this body
Upon a mortal woman, and I have heard tell
It seemed as if he had outrun the moon
That he must follow always through waste heaven,
He loved so happily. He'll be but slow
To break a tree that was so sweetly planted.
Let's see that arm. I'll see it if I choose.
That arm had a good father and a good mother,
But it is not like this.
Young Man. You are mocking me;
You think I am not worthy to be fought.
But I'll not wrangle but with this talkative knife.
Cuchulain. Put up your sword; I am not mocking you.
I'd have you for my friend, but if it's not
Because you have a hot heart and a cold eye,
I cannot tell the reason.
[*To Conchubar.*] He has got her fierceness,
And nobody is as fierce as those pale women.
But I will keep him with me, Conchubar,
That he may set my memory upon her
When the day's fading. — You will stop with us,
And we will hunt the deer and the wild bulls;
And, when we have grown weary, light our fires
Between the wood and water, or on some mountain
Where the Shape-Changers of the morning come.
The High King there would make a mock of me

Because I did not take a wife among them.
Why do you hang your head? It's a good life:
The head grows prouder in the light of the dawn,
And friendship thickens in the murmuring dark
Where the spare hazels meet the wool-white foam.
But I can see there's no more need for words
And that you'll be my friend from this day out.

Conchubar. He has come hither not in his own name
But in Queen Aoife's, and has challenged us
In challenging the foremost man of us all.

Cuchulain. Well, well, what matter?

Conchubar.   You think it does not matter,
And that a fancy lighter than the air,
A whim of the moment, has more matter in it.
For, having none that shall reign after you,
You cannot think as I do, who would leave
A throne too high for insult.

Cuchulain.   Let your children
Re-mortar their inheritance, as we have,
And put more muscle on. — I'll give you gifts,
But I'd have something too — that arm-ring, boy.
We'll have this quarrel out when you are older.

Young Man. There is no man I'd sooner have my friend
Than you, whose name has gone about the world
As if it had been the wind; but Aoife'd say
I had turned coward.

Cuchulain.   I will give you gifts
That Aoife'll know, and all her people know,
To have come from me.   [*Showing cloak.*
                    My father gave me this.
He came to try me, rising up at dawn
Out of the cold dark of the rich sea.
He challenged me to battle, but before

My sword had touched his sword, told me his name,
Gave me this cloak, and vanished. It was woven
By women of the Country-under-Wave
Out of the fleeces of the sea. O! tell her
I was afraid, or tell her what you will.
No; tell her that I heard a raven croak
On the north side of the house, and was afraid.

Conchubar. Some witch of the air has troubled Cuchulain's
    mind.

Cuchulain. No witchcraft. His head is like a woman's head
    I had a fancy for.

Conchubar.   A witch of the air
    Can make a leaf confound us with memories.
    They run upon the wind and hurl the spells
    That make us nothing, out of the invisible wind.
    They have gone to school to learn the trick of it.

Cuchulain. No, no — there's nothing out of common here;
    The winds are innocent. — That arm-ring, boy.

A King. If I've your leave I'll take this challenge up.

Another King. No, give it me, High King, for this wild Aoife
    Has carried off my slaves.

Another King.   No, give it me,
    For she has harried me in house and herd.

Another King. I claim this fight.

Other Kings [*together*].   And I! And I! And I!

Cuchulain. Back! back! Put up your swords! Put up your
    swords!
    There's none alive that shall accept a challenge
    I have refused. Laegaire, put up your sword!

Young Man. No, let them come. If they've a mind for it,
    I'll try it out with any two together.

Cuchulain. That's spoken as I'd have spoken it at your age.
    But you are in my house. Whatever man

Would fight with you shall fight it out with me.
They're dumb, they're dumb. How many of you would
    meet   *[Draws sword.*
This mutterer, this old whistler, this sand-piper,
This edge that's greyer than the tide, this mouse
That's gnawing at the timbers of the world,
This, this — Boy, I would meet them all in arms
If I'd a son like you. He would avenge me
When I have withstood for the last time the men
Whose fathers, brothers, sons, and friends I have killed
Upholding Conchubar, when the four provinces
Have gathered with the ravens over them.
But I'd need no avenger. You and I
Would scatter them like water from a dish.

Young Man. We'll stand by one another from this out.
  Here is the ring.

Cuchulain.   No, turn and turn about.
  But my turn's first because I am the older.
                             [Spreading out cloak.
Nine queens out of the Country-under-Wave
Have woven it with the fleeces of the sea
And they were long embroidering at it. — Boy,
If I had fought my father, he'd have killed me,
As certainly as if I had a son
And fought with him, I should be deadly to him;
For the old fiery fountains are far off
And every day there is less heat o' the blood.

Conchubar [*in a loud voice*]. No more of this. I will not have
    this friendship.
  Cuchulain is my man, and I forbid it.
  He shall not go unfought, for I myself —

Cuchulain. I will not have it.

Conchubar.   You lay commands on me?

Cuchulain [*seizing Conchubar*]. You shall not stir, High King.
  I'll hold you there.

Conchubar. Witchcraft has maddened you.

The Kings [*shouting*].   Yes, witchcraft! witchcraft!

First Old King. Some witch has worked upon your mind,
  Cuchulain.
  The head of that young man seemed like a woman's
  You'd had a fancy for. Then of a sudden
  You laid your hands on the High King himself!

Cuchulain. And laid my hands on the High King himself?

Conchubar. Some witch is floating in the air above us.

Cuchulain. Yes, witchcraft! witchcraft! Witches of the air!
  [*To Young Man.*] Why did you? Who was it set you to this
    work?
  Out, out! I say, for now it's sword on sword!

Young Man. But . . . but I did not.

Cuchulain.   Out, I say, out, out!

  [*Young Man goes out followed by Cuchulain. The Kings
    follow them out with confused cries, and words one can
    hardly hear because of the noise. Some cry, 'Quicker,
    quicker!' 'Why are you so long at the door?' 'We'll
    be too late!' 'Have they begun to fight?' 'Can you see
    if they are fighting?' and so on. Their voices drown each
    other. The three Women are left alone.*

First Woman. I have seen, I have seen!

Second Woman.   What do you cry aloud?

First Woman. The Ever-living have shown me what's to come.

Third Woman. How? Where?

First Woman.   In the ashes of the bowl.

Second Woman. While you were holding it between your
  hands?

Third Woman. Speak quickly!

First Woman. I have seen Cuchulain's roof-tree
  Leap into fire, and the walls split and blacken.

Second Woman. Cuchulain has gone out to die.

Third Woman. O! O!

Second Woman. Who could have thought that one so great
    as he
  Should meet his end at this unnoted sword!

First Woman. Life drifts between a fool and a blind man
  To the end, and nobody can know his end.

Second Woman. Come, look upon the quenching of this great-
    ness.

  [*The other two go to the door, but they stop for a moment upon
    the threshold and wail.*

First Woman. No crying out, for there'll be need of cries
  And rending of the hair when it's all finished.

  [*The Women go out. There is the sound of clashing swords
    from time to time during what follows.*
    Enter the Fool, dragging the Blind Man.

Fool. You have eaten it, you have eaten it! You have left me
  nothing but the bones.

                    [*He throws Blind Man down by big chair.*

Blind Man. O, that I should have to endure such a plague!
  O, I ache all over! O, I am pulled to pieces! This is the way
  you pay me all the good I have done you.

Fool. You have eaten it! You have told me lies. I might have
  known you had eaten it when I saw your slow, sleepy walk.
  Lie there till the kings come. O, I will tell Conchubar and
  Cuchulain and all the kings about you!

Blind Man. What would have happened to you but for me,
  and you without your wits? If I did not take care of you,
  what would you do for food and warmth?

Fool. You take care of me? You stay safe, and send me into every kind of danger. You sent me down the cliff for gulls' eggs while you warmed your blind eyes in the sun; and then you ate all that were good for food. You left me the eggs that were neither egg nor bird. [*Blind Man tries to rise; Fool makes him lie down again.*] Keep quiet now, till I shut the door. There is some noise outside — a high vexing noise, so that I can't be listening to myself. [*Shuts the big door.*] Why can't they be quiet? Why can't they be quiet? [*Blind Man tries to get away.*] Ah! you would get away, would you? [*Follows Blind Man and brings him back.*] Lie there! lie there! No, you won't get away! Lie there till the kings come. I'll tell them all about you. I will tell it all. How you sit warming yourself, when you have made me light a fire of sticks, while I sit blowing it with my mouth. Do you not always make me take the windy side of the bush when it blows, and the rainy side when it rains?

Blind Man. O, good Fool! listen to me. Think of the care I have taken of you. I have brought you to many a warm hearth, where there was a good welcome for you, but you would not stay there; you were always wandering about.

Fool. The last time you brought me in, it was not I who wandered away, but you that got put out because you took the crubeen out of the pot when nobody was looking. Keep quiet, now!

Cuchulain [*rushing in*]. Witchcraft! There is no witchcraft on the earth, or among the witches of the air, that these hands cannot break.

Fool. Listen to me, Cuchulain. I left him turning the fowl at the fire. He ate it all, though I had stolen it. He left me nothing but the feathers.

Cuchulain. Fill me a horn of ale!

Blind Man. I gave him what he likes best. You do not know how vain this Fool is. He likes nothing so well as a feather.

Fool. He left me nothing but the bones and feathers. Nothing but the feathers, though I had stolen it.

Cuchulain. Give me that horn. Quarrels here, too! [*Drinks.*] What is there between you two that is worth a quarrel? Out with it!

Blind Man. Where would he be but for me? I must be always thinking — thinking to get food for the two of us, and when we've got it, if the moon is at the full or the tide on the turn, he'll leave the rabbit in the snare till it is full of maggots, or let the trout slip back through his hands into the stream.

[*The Fool has begun singing while the Blind Man is speaking.*

Fool [*singing*].

> When you were an acorn on the tree-top,
>> Then was I an eagle-cock;
> Now that you are a withered old block,
>> Still am I an eagle-cock.

Blind Man. Listen to him, now. That's the sort of talk I have to put up with day out, day in.

[*The Fool is putting the feathers into his hair. Cuchulain takes a handful of feathers out of a heap the Fool has on the bench beside him, and out of the Fool's hair, and begins to wipe the blood from his sword with them.*

Fool. He has taken my feathers to wipe his sword. It is blood that he is wiping from his sword.

Cuchulain [*goes up to door at back and throws away feathers*]. They are standing about his body. They will not awaken him, for all his witchcraft.

Blind Man. It is that young champion that he has killed. He that came out of Aoife's country.

Cuchulain. He thought to have saved himself with witchcraft.

Fool. That Blind Man there said he would kill you. He came

from Aoife's country to kill you. That Blind Man said they
had taught him every kind of weapon that he might do it.
But I always knew that you would kill him.

Cuchulain [*to the Blind Man*]. You knew him, then?

Blind Man. I saw him, when I had my eyes, in Aoife's country.

Cuchulain. You were in Aoife's country?

Blind Man. I knew him and his mother there.

Cuchulain. He was about to speak of her when he died.

Blind Man. He was a queen's son.

Cuchulain. What queen? what queen? [*Seizes Blind Man, who
is now sitting upon the bench*.] Was it Scathach? There were
many queens. All the rulers there were queens.

Blind Man. No, not Scathach.

Cuchulain. It was Uathach, then? Speak! speak!

Blind Man. I cannot speak; you are clutching me too tightly.
[*Cuchulain lets him go*.] I cannot remember who it was. I am
not certain. It was some queen.

Fool. He said a while ago that the young man was Aoife's son.

Cuchulain. She? No, no! She had no son when I was there.

Fool. That Blind Man there said that she owned him for her
son.

Cuchulain. I had rather he had been some other woman's
son. What father had he? A soldier out of Alba? She was an
amorous woman — a proud, pale, amorous woman.

Blind Man. None knew whose son he was.

Cuchulain. None knew! Did you know, old listener at doors?

Blind Man. No, no; I knew nothing.

Fool. He said a while ago that he heard Aoife boast that she'd
never but the one lover, and he the only man that had
overcome her in battle. [*Pause*.

Blind Man. Somebody is trembling, Fool! The bench is
shaking. Why are you trembling? Is Cuchulain going to
hurt us? It was not I who told you, Cuchulain.

Fool. It is Cuchulain who is trembling. It is Cuchulain who is
   shaking the bench.

Blind Man. It is his own son he has slain.

Cuchulain. 'Twas they that did it, the pale windy people.
   Where? where? where? My sword against the thunder!
   But no, for they have always been my friends;
   And though they love to blow a smoking coal
   Till it's all flame, the wars they blow aflame
   Are full of glory, and heart-uplifting pride,
   And not like this. The wars they love awaken
   Old fingers and the sleepy strings of harps.
   Who did it then? Are you afraid? Speak out!
   For I have put you under my protection,
   And will reward you well. Dubthach the Chafer?
   He'd an old grudge. No, for he is with Maeve.
   Laegaire did it! Why do you not speak?
   What is this house? [*Pause.*] Now I remember all.

   [*Comes before Conchubar's chair, and strikes out with his
      sword, as if Conchubar was sitting upon it.*

   'Twas you who did it — you who sat up there
   With your old rod of kingship, like a magpie
   Nursing a stolen spoon. No, not a magpie,
   A maggot that is eating up the earth!
   Yes, but a magpie, for he's flown away.
   Where did he fly to?

Blind Man.   He is outside the door.

Cuchulain. Outside the door?

Blind Man.   Between the door and the sea.

Cuchulain. Conchubar, Conchubar! the sword into your
   heart!

   [*He rushes out. Pause. Fool creeps up to the big door and looks
      after him.*

Fool. He is going up to King Conchubar. They are all about the young man. No, no, he is standing still. There is a great wave going to break, and he is looking at it. Ah! now he is running down to the sea, but he is holding up his sword as if he were going into a fight. [*Pause.*] Well struck! well struck!

Blind Man. What is he doing now?

Fool. O! he is fighting the waves!

Blind Man. He sees King Conchubar's crown on every one of them.

Fool. There, he has struck at a big one! He has struck the crown off it; he has made the foam fly. There again, another big one!

Blind Man. Where are the kings? What are the kings doing?

Fool. They are shouting and running down to the shore, and the people are running out of the houses. They are all running.

Blind Man. You say they are running out of the houses? There will be nobody left in the houses. Listen, Fool!

Fool. There, he is down! He is up again. He is going out in the deep water. There is a big wave. It has gone over him. I cannot see him now. He has killed kings and giants, but the waves have mastered him, the waves have mastered him!

Blind Man. Come here, Fool!

Fool. The waves have mastered him.

Blind Man. Come here!

Fool. The waves have mastered him.

Blind Man. Come here, I say.

Fool [*coming towards him, but looking backwards towards the door*]. What is it?

Blind Man. There will be nobody in the houses. Come this way; come quickly! The ovens will be full. We will put our hands into the ovens. [*They go out.*

THE END

DEIRDRE

DEIRDRE

PERSONS IN THE PLAY

Musicians

Fergus, *an old man*

Naoise (*pronounced* Neesh-e), *a young king*

Deirdre, *his queen*

A Dark-faced Messenger

Conchubar (*pronounced* Conohar), *the old King of Uladh, who is still strong and vigorous*

A Dark-faced Executioner

A Guest-house in a wood. It is a rough house of timber; through the doors and some of the windows one can see the great spaces of the wood, the sky dimming, night closing in. But a window to the left shows the thick leaves of a coppice; the landscape suggests silence and loneliness. There is a door to right and left, and through the side windows one can see anybody who approaches either door, a moment before he enters. In the centre, a part of the house is curtained off; the curtains are drawn. There are unlighted torches in brackets on the walls. There is, at one side, a small table with a chessboard and chessmen upon it. At the other side of the room there is a brazier with a fire; two women, with musical instruments beside them, crouch about the brazier: they are comely women of about forty. Another woman, who carries a stringed instrument, enters hurriedly; she speaks, at first standing in the doorway.

First Musician. I have a story right, my wanderers,
   That has so mixed with fable in our songs
   That all seemed fabulous. We are come, by chance,
   Into King Conchubar's country, and this house
   Is an old guest-house built for travellers
   From the seashore to Conchubar's royal house,
   And there are certain hills among these woods
   And there Queen Deirdre grew.

49

Second Musician.   That famous queen
  Who has been wandering with her lover Naoise
  Somewhere beyond the edges of the world?
First Musician [*going nearer to the brazier*]. Some dozen years
      ago, King Conchubar found
  A house upon a hillside in this wood,
  And there a child with an old witch to nurse her,
  And nobody to say if she were human,
  Or of the gods, or anything at all
  Of who she was or why she was hidden there,
  But that she'd too much beauty for good luck.
  He went up thither daily, till at last
  She put on womanhood, and he lost peace,
  And Deirdre's tale began. The King was old.
  A month or so before the marriage-day,
  A young man, in the laughing scorn of his youth,
  Naoise, the son of Usna, climbed up there,
  And having wooed, or, as some say, been wooed,
  Carried her off.
Second Musician.   The tale were well enough
  Had it a finish.
First Musician.   Hush! I have more to tell;
  But gather close about that I may whisper
  The secrets of a king.
Second Musician.   There's none to hear!
First Musician. I have been to Conchubar's house and followed
      up
  A crowd of servants going out and in
  With loads upon their heads: embroideries
  To hang upon the walls, or new-mown rushes
  To strew upon the floors, and came at length
  To a great room.
Second Musician.   Be silent; there are steps!

Enter Fergus, an old man, who moves about from door to
window excitedly through what follows.

Fergus. I thought to find a message from the King.
  You are musicians by these instruments,
  And if as seems — for you are comely women —
  You can praise love, you'll have the best of luck,
  For there'll be two, before the night is in,
  That bargained for their love, and paid for it
  All that men value. You have but the time
  To weigh a happy music with a sad,
  To find what is most pleasing to a lover,
  Before the son of Usna and his queen
  Have passed this threshold.

First Musician.   Deirdre and her man!

Fergus. I was to have found a message in this house,
  And ran to meet it. Is there no messenger
  From Conchubar to Fergus, son of Rogh?

First Musician. Are Deirdre and her lover tired of life?

Fergus. You are not of this country, or you'd know
  That they are in my charge and all forgiven.

First Musician. We have no country but the roads of the
  world.

Fergus. Then you should know that all things change in the
  world,
  And hatred turns to love and love to hate,
  And even kings forgive.

First Musician.   An old man's love
  Who casts no second line is hard to cure;
  His jealousy is like his love.

Fergus.   And that's but true.
  You have learned something in your wanderings.
  He was so hard to cure that the whole court,
  But I alone, thought it impossible;

Yet after I had urged it at all seasons,
I had my way, and all's forgiven now;
And you shall speak the welcome and the joy
That I lack tongue for.

First Musician.   Yet old men are jealous.

Fergus [*going to door*]. I am Conchubar's near friend, and that
    weighed somewhat,
And it was policy to pardon them.
The need of some young, famous, popular man
To lead the troops, the murmur of the crowd,
And his own natural impulse, urged him to it.
They have been wandering half a dozen years.

First Musician. And yet old men are jealous.

Fergus [*coming from door*].   Sing the more sweetly
Because, though age is arid as a bone,
This man has flowered. I've need of music, too;
If this grey head would suffer no reproach,
I'd dance and sing —

    [*Dark-faced men with strange, barbaric dress and arms begin to
    pass by the doors and windows. They pass one by one and
    in silence.*

                        and dance till the hour ran out,
Because I have accomplished this good deed.

First Musician. Look there — there at the window, those dark
    men,
With murderous and outlandish-looking arms —
They've been about the house all day.

Fergus [*looking after them*].   What are you?
Where do you come from, who is it sent you here?

First Musician. They will not answer you.

Fergus.   They do not hear.

First Musician. Forgive my open speech, but to these eyes
That have seen many lands they are such men

As kings will gather for a murderous task
    That neither bribes, commands, nor promises
    Can bring their people to.
Fergus.   And that is why
    You harped upon an old man's jealousy.
    A trifle sets you quaking. Conchubar's fame
    Brings merchandise on every wind that blows.
    They may have brought him Libyan dragon-skin,
    Or the ivory of the fierce unicorn.
First Musician. If these be merchants, I have seen the goods
    They have brought to Conchubar, and understood
    His murderous purpose.
Fergus.   Murderous, you say?
    Why, what new gossip of the roads is this?
    But I'll not hear.
First Musician.   It may be life or death.
    There is a room in Conchubar's house, and there —
Fergus. Be silent, or I'll drive you from the door.
    There's many a one that would do more than that,
    And make it prison, or death, or banishment
    To slander the High King.

             [*Suddenly restraining himself and speaking gently*.

                   He is my friend;
    I have his oath, and I am well content.
    I have known his mind as if it were my own
    These many years, and there is none alive
    Shall buzz against him, and I there to stop it.
    I know myself, and him, and your wild thought
    Fed on extravagant poetry, and lit
    By such a dazzle of old fabulous tales
    That common things are lost, and all that's strange
    Is true because 'twere pity if it were not.

                  [*Going to the door again*.

Quick! quick! your instruments! they are coming now.
I hear the hoofs a-clatter. Begin that song!
But what is it to be? I'd have them hear
A music foaming up out of the house
Like wine out of a cup. Come now, a verse
Of some old time not worth remembering,
And all the lovelier because a bubble.
Begin, begin, of some old king and queen,
Of Lugaidh Redstripe or another; no, not him,
He and his lady perished wretchedly.

First Musician [*singing*]

'Why is it', Queen Edain said,
    'If I do but climb the stair . . .'

Fergus. Ah! that is better. . . . They are alighted now.
Shake all your cockscombs, children; these are lovers.

[*Fergus goes out.*

First Musician

'Why is it', Queen Edain said,
    'If I do but climb the stair
To the tower overhead,
    When the winds are calling there,
Or the gannets calling out
    In waste places of the sky,
There's so much to think about
    That I cry, that I cry?'

Second Musician

But her goodman answered her:
    'Love would be a thing of naught
Had not all his limbs a stir
    Born out of immoderate thought;
Were he anything by half,
    Were his measure running dry.

> Lovers, if they may not laugh,
>   Have to cry, have to cry.'

[*Deirdre, Naoise, and Fergus have been seen for a moment through the windows, but now they have entered.*

The Three Musicians [*together*]

> But is Edain worth a song
>   Now the hunt begins anew?
> Praise the beautiful and strong;
>   Praise the redness of the yew;
> Praise the blossoming apple-stem.
>   But our silence had been wise.
> What is all our praise to them
>   That have one another's eyes?

Deirdre. Silence your music, though I thank you for it;
But the wind's blown upon my hair, and I
Must set the jewels on my neck and head
For one that's coming.

Naoise.   Your colour has all gone
As 'twere with fear, and there's no cause for that.

Deirdre. These women have the raddle that they use
To make them brave and confident, although
Dread, toil, or cold may chill the blood o' their cheeks.
You'll help me, women. It is my husband's will
I show my trust in one that may be here
Before the mind can call the colour up.
My husband took these rubies from a king
Of Surracha that was so murderous
He seemed all glittering dragon. Now wearing them
Myself wars on myself, for I myself —
That do my husband's will, yet fear to do it —
Grow dragonish to myself.

[*The women have gathered about her. Naoise has stood looking at her, but Fergus brings him to the chess-table.*

Naoise.   No messenger!
  It's strange that there is none to welcome us.
Fergus. King Conchubar has sent no messenger
  That he may come himself.
Naoise.   And being himself,
  Being High King, he cannot break his faith.
  I have his word and I must take that word,
  Or prove myself unworthy of my nurture
  Under a great man's roof.
Fergus.   We'll play at chess
  Till the King comes. It is but natural
  That she should doubt him, for her house has been
  The hole of the badger and the den of the fox.
Naoise. If I had not King Conchubar's word I'd think
  That chess-board ominous.
Fergus.   How can a board
  That has been lying there these many years
  Be lucky or unlucky?
Naoise.   It is the board
  Where Lugaidh Redstripe and that wife of his,
  Who had a seamew's body half the year,
  Played at the chess upon the night they died.
Fergus. I can remember now, a tale of treachery,
  A broken promise and a journey's end —
  But it were best forgot.

  [*Deirdre has been standing with the women about her. They
   have been helping her to put on her jewels and to put the
   pigment on her cheeks and arrange her hair. She has
   gradually grown attentive to what Fergus is saying.*

Naoise.   If the tale's true,
  When it was plain that they had been betrayed,
  They moved the men and waited for the end

As it were bedtime, and had so quiet minds
They hardly winked their eyes when the sword flashed.
Fergus. She never could have played so, being a woman,
If she had not the cold sea's blood in her.
Deirdre. The gods turn clouds and casual accidents
  Into omens.
Naoise.   It would but ill become us,
  Now that King Conchubar has pledged his word,
  Should we be startled by a cloud or a shadow.
Deirdre. There's none to welcome us.
Naoise.   Being his guest,
  Words that would wrong him can but wrong ourselves.
Deirdre. An empty house upon the journey's end!
  Is that the way a king that means no mischief
  Honours a guest?
Fergus.   He is but making ready
  A welcome in his house, arranging where
  The moorhen and the mallard go, and where
  The speckled heathcock on a golden dish.
Deirdre. Had he no messenger?
Naoise.   Such words and fears
  Wrong this old man who's pledged his word to us.
  We must not speak or think as women do,
  That when the house is all abed sit up
  Marking among the ashes with a stick
  Till they are terrified. — Being what we are
  We must meet all things with an equal mind.
  [*To Fergus.*] Come, let us look if there's a messenger
  From Conchubar. We cannot see from this
  Because we are blinded by the leaves and twigs,
  But it may be the wood will thin again.
  It is but kind that when the lips we love
  Speak words that are unfitting for kings' ears

Our ears be deaf.

Fergus.   But now I had to threaten
These wanderers because they would have weighed
Some crazy fantasy of their own brain
Or gossip of the road with Conchubar's word.
If I had thought so little of mankind
I never could have moved him to this pardon.
I have believed the best of every man,
And find that to believe it is enough
To make a bad man show him at his best,
Or even a good man swing his lantern higher.

> [*Naoise and Fergus go out. The last words are spoken as they
> go through the door. One can see them through part of what
> follows, either through door or window. They move about,
> talking or looking along the road towards Conchubar's
> house.*

First Musician. If anything lies heavy on your heart,
Speak freely of it, knowing it is certain
That you will never see my face again.

Deirdre. You've been in love?

First Musician.   If you would speak of love
Speak freely. There is nothing in the world
That has been friendly to us but the kisses
That were upon our lips, and when we are old
Their memory will be all the life we have.

Deirdre. There was a man that loved me. He was old;
I could not love him. Now I can but fear.
He has made promises, and brought me home;
But though I turn it over in my thoughts,
I cannot tell if they are sound and wholesome,
Or hackles on the hook.

First Musician.   I have heard he loved you

As some old miser loves the dragon-stone
He hides among the cobwebs near the roof.
Deirdre. You mean that when a man who has loved like that
    Is after crossed, love drowns in its own flood,
    And that love drowned and floating is but hate;
    And that a king who hates sleeps ill at night
    Till he has killed; and that, though the day laughs,
    We shall be dead at cock-crow.
First Musician.   You've not my thought.
    When I lost one I loved distractedly,
    I blamed my crafty rival and not him,
    And fancied, till my passion had run out,
    That could I carry him away with me,
    And tell him all my love, I'd keep him yet.
Deirdre. Ah! now I catch your meaning, that this king
    Will murder Naoise, and keep me alive.
First Musician. 'Tis you that put that meaning upon words
    Spoken at random.
Deirdre.   Wanderers like you,
    Who have their wit alone to keep their lives,
    Speak nothing that is bitter to the ear
    At random; if they hint at it at all
    Their eyes and ears have gathered it so lately
    That it is crying out in them for speech.
First Musician. We have little that is certain.
Deirdre.   Certain or not,
    Speak it out quickly, I beseech you to it;
    I never have met any of your kind
    But that I gave them money, food, and fire.
First Musician. There are strange, miracle-working, wicked
      stones,
    Men tear out of the heart and the hot brain
    Of Libyan dragons.

Deirdre.   The hot Istain stone,
　　And the cold stone of Fanes, that have power
　　To stir even those at enmity to love.

First Musician. They have so great an influence, if but sewn
　　In the embroideries that curtain in
　　The bridal bed.

Deirdre.   O Mover of the stars
　　That made this delicate house of ivory,
　　And made my soul its mistress, keep it safe!

First Musician. I have seen a bridal bed, so curtained in,
　　So decked for miracle in Conchubar's house,
　　And learned that a bride's coming.

Deirdre.   And I the bride?
　　Here is worse treachery than the seamew suffered,
　　For she but died and mixed into the dust
　　Of her dear comrade, but I am to live
　　And lie in the one bed with him I hate.
　　Where is Naoise? I was not alone like this
　　When Conchubar first chose me for his wife;
　　I cried in sleeping or waking and he came,
　　But now there is worse need.

Naoise [*entering with Fergus*].   Why have you called?
　　I was but standing there, without the door.

Deirdre. I have heard terrible mysterious things,
　　Magical horrors and the spells of wizards.

Fergus. Why, that's no wonder. You have been listening
　　To singers of the roads that gather up
　　The stories of the world.

Deirdre.   But I have one
　　To make the stories of the world but nothing.

Naoise. Be silent if it is against the King
　　Whose guest you are.

Fergus.   No, let her speak it out.

I know the High King's heart as it were my own,
And can refute a slander, but already
I have warned these women that it may be death.

Naoise. I will not weigh the gossip of the roads
With the King's word. I ask your pardon for her:
She has the heart of the wild birds that fear
The net of the fowler or the wicker cage.

Deirdre. Am I to see the fowler and the cage
And speak no word at all?

Naoise.   You would have known,
Had they not bred you in that mountainous place,
That when we give a word and take a word
Sorrow is put away, past wrong forgotten.

Deirdre. Though death may come of it?

Naoise.   Though death may come.

Deirdre. When first we came into this empty house
You had foreknowledge of our death, and even
When speaking of the paleness of my cheek
Your own cheek blanched.

Naoise.   Listen to this old man.
He can remember all the promises
We trusted to.

Deirdre.   You speak from the lips out,
And I am pleading for your life and mine.

Naoise. Listen to this old man, for many think
He has a golden tongue.

Deirdre.   Then I will say
What it were best to carry to the grave.
Look at my face where the leaf raddled it
And at these rubies on my hair and breast.
It was for him, to stir him to desire,
I put on beauty; yes, for Conchubar.

Naoise. What frenzy put these words into your mouth?

Deirdre. No frenzy, for what need is there for frenzy
   To change what shifts with every change of the wind,
   Or else there is no truth in men's old sayings?
   Was I not born a woman?

Naoise.   You're mocking me.

Deirdre. And is there mockery in this face and eyes,
   Or in this body, in these limbs that brought
   So many mischiefs? Look at me and say
   If that that shakes my limbs be mockery.

Naoise. What woman is there that a man can trust
   But at the moment when he kisses her
   At the first midnight?

Deirdre.   Were it not most strange
   That women should put evil in men's hearts
   And lack it in themselves? And yet I think
   That being half good I might change round again
   Were we aboard our ship and on the sea.

Naoise. We'll to the horses and take ship again.

Fergus. Fool, she but seeks to rouse your jealousy
   With crafty words.

Deirdre.   Were we not born to wander?
   These jewels have been reaped by the innocent sword
   Upon a mountain, and a mountain bred me;
   But who can tell what change can come to love
   Among the valleys? I speak no falsehood now.
   Away to windy summits, and there mock
   The night-jar and the valley-keeping bird!

Fergus. Men blamed you that you stirred a quarrel up
   That has brought death to many. I have made peace,
   Poured water on the fire, but if you fly
   King Conchubar may think that he is mocked
   And the house blaze again: and in what quarter,
   If Conchubar were the treacherous man you think,

Would you find safety now that you have come
Into the very middle of his power,
Under his very eyes?

Deirdre.   Under his eyes
And in the very middle of his power!
Then there is but one way to make all safe:
I'll spoil this beauty that brought misery
And houseless wandering on the man I loved.
These wanderers will show me how to do it;
To clip this hair to baldness, blacken my skin
With walnut juice, and tear my face with briars.
O that the creatures of the woods had torn
My body with their claws!

Fergus.   What, wilder yet!

Deirdre [to Naoise]. Whatever were to happen to my face
I'd be myself, and there's not any way
But this to bring all trouble to an end.

Naoise. Leave the gods' handiwork unblotched, and wait
For their decision, our decision is past.

        [*A Dark-faced Messenger comes to the threshold.*

Fergus. Peace, peace; the messenger is at the door;
He stands upon the threshold; he stands there;
He stands, King Conchubar's purpose on his lips.

Messenger. Supper is on the table. Conchubar
Is waiting for his guests.

Fergus.   All's well again!
All's well! All's well! You cried your doubts so loud
That I had almost doubted.

Naoise.   We doubted him,
And he the while but busy in his house
For the more welcome.

Deirdre.   The message is not finished.

Fergus. Come quickly. Conchubar will laugh, that I —
    Although I held out boldly in my speech —
    That I, even I —

Deirdre.   Wait, wait! He is not done.

Messenger. Deirdre and Fergus, son of Rogh, are summoned;
    But not the traitor that bore off the Queen.
    It is enough that the King pardon her,
    And call her to his table and his bed.

Naoise. So, then, it's treachery.

Fergus.   I'll not believe it.

Naoise. Lead on and I will follow at your heels
    That I may challenge him before his court
    To match me there, or match me in some place
    Where none can come between us but our swords,
    For I have found no truth on any tongue
    That's not of iron.

Messenger.   I am Conchubar's man,
    I am content to serve an iron tongue:
    That Tongue commands that Fergus, son of Rogh,
    And Deirdre come this night into his house,
    And none but they.   [*He goes, followed by Naoise.*

Fergus.   Some rogue, some enemy,
    Has bribed him to embroil us with the King;
    I know that he has lied because I know
    King Conchubar's mind as if it were my own,
    But I'll find out the truth.

       [*He is about to follow Naoise, but Deirdre stops him.*

Deirdre.   No, no, old man.
    You thought the best, and the worst came of it;
    We listened to the counsel of the wise,
    And so turned fools. But ride and bring your friends.
    Go, and go quickly. Conchubar has not seen me;

It may be that his passion is asleep,
And that we may escape.

Fergus. But I'll go first,
And follow up that Libyan heel, and send
Such words to Conchubar that he may know
At how great peril he lays hands upon you.

Naoise enters

Naoise. The Libyan, knowing that a servant's life
Is safe from hands like mine, but turned and mocked.

Fergus. I'll call my friends, and call the reaping-hooks,
And carry you in safety to the ships.
My name has still some power. I will protect,
Or, if that is impossible, revenge.

[*Goes out by other door.*

Naoise [*who is calm, like a man who has passed beyond life*].
The crib has fallen and the birds are in it;
There is not one of the great oaks about us
But shades a hundred men.

Deirdre. Let's out and die,
Or break away, if the chance favour us.

Naoise. They would but drag you from me, stained with blood.
Their barbarous weapons would but mar that beauty,
And I would have you die as a queen should —
In a death-chamber. You are in my charge.
We will wait here, and when they come upon us,
I'll hold them from the doors, and when that's over,
Give you a cleanly death with this grey edge.

Deirdre. I will stay here; but you go out and fight.
Our way of life has brought no friends to us,
And if we do not buy them leaving it,
We shall be ever friendless.

Naoise.   What do they say?
   That Lugaidh Redstripe and that wife of his
   Sat at this chess-board, waiting for their end.
   They knew that there was nothing that could save them,
   And so played chess as they had any night
   For years, and waited for the stroke of sword.
   I never heard a death so out of reach
   Of common hearts, a high and comely end.
   What need have I, that gave up all for love,
   To die like an old king out of a fable,
   Fighting and passionate? What need is there
   For all that ostentation at my setting?
   I have loved truly and betrayed no man.
   I need no lightning at the end, no beating
   In a vain fury at the cage's door.
   [*To Musicians.*] Had you been here when that man and his
      queen
   Played at so high a game, could you have found
   An ancient poem for the praise of it?
   It should have set out plainly that those two,
   Because no man and woman have loved better,
   Might sit on there contentedly, and weigh
   The joy comes after. I have heard the seamew
   Sat there, with all the colour in her cheeks,
   As though she'd say: 'There's nothing happening
   But that a king and queen are playing chess.'
Deirdre. He's in the right, though I have not been born
   Of the cold, haughty waves, my veins being hot,
   And though I have loved better than that queen,
   I'll have as quiet fingers on the board.
   O, singing women, set it down in a book,
   That love is all we need, even though it is
   But the last drops we gather up like this;

And though the drops are all we have known of life,
For we have been most friendless — praise us for it,
And praise the double sunset, for naught's lacking
But a good end to the long, cloudy day.
Naoise. Light torches there and drive the shadows out,
For day's grey end comes up.

[*A Musician lights a torch in the fire and then crosses before
the chess-players, and slowly lights the torches in the sconces.
The light is almost gone from the wood, but there is a clear
evening light in the sky, increasing the sense of solitude and
loneliness.*

Deirdre.   Make no sad music.
What is it but a king and queen at chess?
They need a music that can mix itself
Into imagination, but not break
The steady thinking that the hard game needs.

[*During the chess, the Musicians sing this song*]

Love is an immoderate thing
    And can never be content
Till it dip an ageing wing
    Where some laughing element
Leaps and Time's old lanthorn dims.
    What's the merit in love-play,
In the tumult of the limbs
    That dies out before 'tis day,
Heart on heart, or mouth on mouth,
    All that mingling of our breath,
When love-longing is but drouth
    For the things come after death?

[*During the last verses Deirdre rises from the board and kneels
at Naoise's feet.*

Deirdre. I cannot go on playing like that woman

That had but the cold blood of the sea in her veins.

Naoise. It is your move. Take up your man again.

Deirdre. Do you remember that first night in the woods
We lay all night on leaves, and looking up,
When the first grey of the dawn awoke the birds,
Saw leaves above us? You thought that I still slept,
And bending down to kiss me on the eyes,
Found they were open. Bend and kiss me now,
For it may be the last before our death.
And when that's over, we'll be different;
Imperishable things, a cloud or a fire.
And I know nothing but this body, nothing
But that old vehement, bewildering kiss.

[*Conchubar comes to the door*

First Musician. Children, beware!

Naoise [*laughing*].   He has taken up my challenge;
Whether I am a ghost or living man
When day has broken, I'll forget the rest,
And say that there is kingly stuff in him.

[*Turns to fetch spear and shield, and then sees that Conchubar
has gone.*

First Musician. He came to spy upon you, not to fight.

Naoise. A prudent hunter, therefore, but no king.
He'd find if what has fallen in the pit
Were worth the hunting, but has come too near,
And I turn hunter. You're not man, but beast.
Go scurry in the bushes, now, beast, beast,
For now it's topsy-turvy, I upon you.

[*He rushes out after Conchubar.*

Deirdre. You have a knife there, thrust into your girdle.
I'd have you give it me.

First Musician.   No, but I dare not.

Deirdre. No, but you must.

First Musician. If harm should come to you,
  They'd know I gave it.

Deirdre [*snatching knife*]. There is no mark on this
  To make it different from any other
  Out of a common forge.

                              [*Goes to the door and looks out.*

First Musician. You have taken it,
  I did not give it you; but there are times
  When such a thing is all the friend one has.

Deirdre. The leaves hide all, and there's no way to find
  What path to follow. Why is there no sound?

                              [*She goes from door to window.*

First Musician. Where would you go?

Deirdre. To strike a blow for Naoise,
  If Conchubar call the Libyans to his aid.
  But why is there no clash? They have met by this!

First Musician. Listen. I am called wise. If Conchubar win,
  You have a woman's wile that can do much,
  Even with men in pride of victory.
  He is in love and old. What were one knife
  Among a hundred?

Deirdre [*going towards them*]. Women, if I die,
  If Naoise die this night, how will you praise?
  What words seek out? for that will stand to you;
  For being but dead we shall have many friends.
  All through your wanderings, the doors of kings
  Shall be thrown wider open, the poor man's hearth
  Heaped with new turf, because you are wearing this

                              [*Gives Musician a bracelet.*

  To show that you have Deirdre's story right.

First Musician. Have you not been paid servants in love's house

To sweep the ashes out and keep the doors?
And though you have suffered all for mere love's sake
You'd live your lives again.

Deirdre.   Even this last hour.

        Conchubar enters with dark-faced men

Conchubar. One woman and two men; that is the quarrel
That knows no mending. Bring in the man she chose
Because of his beauty and the strength of his youth.

       [*The dark-faced men drag in Naoise entangled in a net.*

Naoise. I have been taken like a bird or a fish.

Conchubar. He cried 'Beast, beast!' and in a blind-beast rage
He ran at me and fell into the nets,
But we were careful for your sake, and took him
With all the comeliness that woke desire
Unbroken in him. I being old and lenient,
I would not hurt a hair upon his head.

Deirdre. What do you say? Have you forgiven him?

Naoise. He is but mocking us. What's left to say
Now that the seven years' hunt is at an end?

Deirdre. He never doubted you until I made him,
And therefore all the blame for what he says
Should fall on me.

Conchubar.   But his young blood is hot,
And if we're of one mind, he shall go free,
And I ask nothing for it, or, if something,
Nothing I could not take. There is no king
In the wide world that, being so greatly wronged,
Could copy me, and give all vengeance up.
Although her marriage-day had all but come,
You carried her away; but I'll show mercy.
Because you had the insolent strength of youth
You carried her away; but I've had time

To think it out through all these seven years.
I will show mercy.

Naoise.   You have many words.

Conchubar. I will not make a bargain; I but ask
   What is already mine.

   [*Deirdre moves slowly towards Conchubar while he is speak-
       ing, her eyes fixed upon him.*

                              You may go free
If Deirdre will but walk into my house
Before the people's eyes, that they may know,
When I have put the crown upon her head,
I have not taken her by force and guile.
The doors are open, and the floors are strewed
And in the bridal chamber curtains sewn
With all enchantments that give happiness
By races that are germane to the sun,
And nearest him, and have no blood in their veins —
For when they're wounded the wound drips with wine —
Nor speech but singing. At the bridal door
Two fair king's daughters carry in their hands
The crown and robe.

Deirdre.   O no! Not that, not that!
   Ask any other thing but that one thing.
   Leave me with Naoise. We will go away
   Into some country at the ends of the earth.
   We'll trouble you no more; and there is no one
   That will not praise you if you pardon us.
   'He is good, he is good', they'll say to one another;
   'There's nobody like him, for he forgave
   Deirdre and Naoise.'

Conchubar.   Do you think that I
   Shall let you go again, after seven years
   Of longing and of planning here and there,

And trafficking with merchants for the stones
That make all sure, and watching my own face
That none might read it?

Deirdre [*to Naoise*].   It's better to go with him.
Why should you die when one can bear it all?
My life is over; it's better to obey.
Why should you die? I will not live long, Naoise.
I'd not have you believe I'd long stay living;
O no, no, no! You will go far away.
You will forget me. Speak, speak, Naoise, speak,
And say that it is better that I go.
I will not ask it. Do not speak a word,
For I will take it all upon myself.
Conchubar, I will go.

Naoise.   And do you think
That, were I given life at such a price,
I would not cast it from me? O my eagle!
Why do you beat vain wings upon the rock
When hollow night's above?

Deirdre.   It's better, Naoise.
It may be hard for you, but you'll forget.
For what am I, to be remembered always?
And there are other women. There was one,
The daughter of the King of Leodas;
I could not sleep because of her. Speak to him;
Tell it out plain, and make him understand.
And if it be he thinks I shall stay living,
Say that I will not.

Naoise.   Would I had lost life
Among those Scottish kings that sought it of me
Because you were my wife, or that the worst
Had taken you before this bargaining!
O eagle! If you were to do this thing,

And buy my life of Conchubar with your body,
Love's law being broken, I would stand alone
Upon the eternal summits, and call out,
And you could never come there, being banished.

Deirdre [*kneeling to Conchubar*]. I would obey, but cannot.
    Pardon us.
I know that you are good. I have heard you praised
For giving gifts; and you will pardon us,
Although I cannot go into your house.
It was my fault. I only should be punished.

                    [*Unseen by Deirdre, Naoise is gagged.*

The very moment these eyes fell on him,
I told him; I held out my hands to him;
How could he refuse? At first he would not —
I am not lying — he remembered you.
What do I say? My hands? — No, no, my lips —
For I had pressed my lips upon his lips —
I swear it is not false — my breast to his;

    [*Conchubar motions; Naoise, unseen by Deirdre, is taken
        behind the curtain.*

Until I woke the passion that's in all,
And how could he resist? I had my beauty.
You may have need of him, a brave, strong man,
Who is not foolish at the council-board,
Nor does he quarrel by the candle-light
And give hard blows to dogs. A cup of wine
Moves him to mirth, not madness.

                            [*She stands up.*
                    What am I saying?
You may have need of him, for you have none
Who is so good a sword, or so well loved
Among the common people. You may need him,

And what king knows when the hour of need may come?
You dream that you have men enough. You laugh.
Yes; you are laughing to yourself. You say,
'I am Conchubar — I have no need of him.'
You will cry out for him some day and say,
'If Naoise were but living' — [*she misses Naoise*]. Where is
    he?
Where have you sent him? Where is the son of Usna?
Where is he, O, where is he?

> [*She staggers over to the Musicians. The Executioner has
> come out with a sword on which there is blood; Conchubar
> points to it. The Musicians give a wail.*

Conchubar. The traitor who has carried off my wife
No longer lives. Come to my house now, Deirdre,
For he that called himself your husband's dead.

Deirdre. O, do not touch me. Let me go to him.

> [*Pause.*

King Conchubar is right. My husband's dead.
A single woman is of no account,
Lacking array of servants, linen cupboards,
The bacon hanging — and King Conchubar's house
All ready, too — I'll to King Conchubar's house.
It is but wisdom to do willingly
What has to be.

Conchubar.   But why are you so calm?
I thought that you would curse me and cry out,
And fall upon the ground and tear your hair.

Deirdre [*laughing*]. You know too much of women to think so;
Though, if I were less worthy of desire,
I would pretend as much; but, being myself,
It is enough that you were master here.
Although we are so delicately made,
There's something brutal in us, and we are won

By those who can shed blood. It was some woman
That taught you how to woo: but do not touch me:
I shall do all you bid me, but not yet,
Because I have to do what's customary.
We lay the dead out, folding up the hands,
Closing the eyes, and stretching out the feet,
And push a pillow underneath the head,
Till all's in order; and all this I'll do
For Naoise, son of Usna.

Conchubar.   It is not fitting.
You are not now a wanderer, but a queen,
And there are plenty that can do these things.

Deirdre [*motioning Conchubar away*]. No, no. Not yet. I cannot
      be your queen
Till the past's finished, and its debts are paid.
When a man dies, and there are debts unpaid,
He wanders by the debtor's bed and cries,
'There's so much owing.'

Conchubar.   You are deceiving me.
You long to look upon his face again.
Why should I give you now to a dead man
That took you from a living?

                              [*He makes a step towards her.*

Deirdre.   In good time.
You'll stir me to more passion than he could,
And yet, if you are wise, you'll grant me this:
That I go look upon him that was once
So strong and comely and held his head so high
That women envied me. For I will see him
All blood-bedabbled and his beauty gone.
It's better, when you're beside me in your strength,
That the mind's eye should call up the soiled body,
And not the shape I loved. Look at him, women.

He heard me pleading to be given up,
Although my lover was still living, and yet
He doubts my purpose. I will have you tell him
How changeable all women are; how soon
Even the best of lovers is forgot
When his day's finished.

Conchubar. No; but I will trust
The strength that you have praised, and not your purpose.

Deirdre [*almost with a caress*]. It is so small a gift and you will
grant it
Because it is the first that I have asked.
He has refused. There is no sap in him;
Nothing but empty veins. I thought as much.
He has refused me the first thing I have asked —
Me, me, his wife. I understand him now;
I know the sort of life I'll have with him;
But he must drag me to his house by force.
If he refuses [*she laughs*], he shall be mocked of all.
They'll say to one another, 'Look at him
That is so jealous that he lured a man
From over sea, and murdered him, and yet
He trembled at the thought of a dead face!'

[*She has her hand upon the curtain.*

Conchubar. How do I know that you have not some knife,
And go to die upon his body?

Deirdre. Have me searched,
If you would make so little of your queen.
It may be that I have a knife hid here
Under my dress. Bid one of these dark slaves
To search me for it. [*Pause.*

Conchubar. Go to your farewells, Queen.

Deirdre. Now strike the wire, and sing to it a while,

Knowing that all is happy, and that you know
Within what bride-bed I shall lie this night,
And by what man, and lie close up to him,
For the bed's narrow, and there outsleep the cockcrow.

[*She goes behind the curtain.*

First Musician. They are gone, they are gone. The proud may
lie by the proud.
Second Musician. Though we were bidden to sing, cry nothing
loud.
First Musician. They are gone, they are gone.
Second Musician.   Whispering were enough.
First Musician. Into the secret wilderness of their love.
Second Musician. A high, grey cairn. What more is to be
said?
First Musician. Eagles have gone into their cloudy bed.

[*Shouting outside. Fergus enters. Many men with scythes and
    sickles and torches gather about the doors. The house is lit
    with the glare of their torches.*

Fergus. Where's Naoise, son of Usna, and his queen?
I and a thousand reaping-hooks and scythes
Demand him of you.
Conchubar.   You have come too late.
I have accomplished all. Deirdre is mine;
She is my queen, and no man now can rob me.
I had to climb the topmost bough, and pull
This apple among the winds. Open the curtain
That Fergus learn my triumph from her lips.

[*The curtain is drawn back. The Musicians begin to keen with
    low voices.*

No, no; I'll not believe it. She is not dead —
She cannot have escaped a second time!
Fergus. King, she is dead; but lay no hand upon her.

What's this but empty cage and tangled wire,
Now the bird's gone? But I'll not have you touch it.
Conchubar. You are all traitors, all against me — all.
And she has deceived me for a second time;
And every common man can keep his wife,
But not the King.

> [*Loud shouting outside*: 'Death to Conchubar!' 'Where is
> Naoise?' etc. *The dark-faced men gather round Conchubar
> and draw their swords; but he motions them away.*

I have no need of weapons,
There's not a traitor that dare stop my way.
Howl, if you will; but I, being King, did right
In choosing her most fitting to be Queen,
And letting no boy lover take the sway.

THE END

THE PLAYER QUEEN

THE PLAYER QUEEN

PERSONS IN THE PLAY

Decima	The Stage Manager
Septimus	The Tapster
Nona	An Old Beggar
The Queen	Old Men, Old Women, Citizens,
The Prime Minister	Countrymen, Players, etc.
The Bishop.	

SCENE I: *An open space at the meeting of three streets*
SCENE II: *The Throne-Room*

SCENE I

An open space at the meeting of three streets. One can see for some way down one of these streets, and at some little distance it turns, showing a bare piece of wall lighted by a hanging lamp. Against this lighted wall are silhouetted the heads and shoulders of two Old Men. They are leaning from the upper windows, one on either side of the street. They wear grotesque masks. A little to one side of the stage is a great stone for mounting a horse from. The houses have knockers.

First Old Man. Can you see the Queen's castle? You have better sight than I.

Second Old Man. I can just see it rising over the tops of the houses yonder on its great rocky hill.

First Old Man. Is the dawn breaking? Is it touching the tower?

Second Old Man. It is beginning to break upon the tower, but these narrow streets will be dark for a long while. [*A pause.* Do you hear anything? You have better hearing than I.

First Old Man. No, all is quiet.

81

Second Old Man. At least fifty passed by an hour since, a crowd of fifty men walking rapidly.

First Old Man. Last night was very quiet, not a sound, not a breath.

Second Old Man. And not a thing to be seen till the Tapster's old dog came down the street upon this very hour from Cooper Malachi's ash-pit.

First Old Man. Hush, I hear feet, many feet. Perhaps they are coming this way. [*Pause.*] No, they are going the other way, they are gone now.

Second Old Man. The young are at some mischief, — the young and the middle-aged.

First Old Man. Why can't they stay in their beds, and they can sleep too — seven hours, eight hours? I mind the time when I could sleep ten hours. They will know the value of sleep when they are near upon ninety years.

Second Old Man. They will never live so long. They have not the health and strength that we had. They wear themselves out. They are always in a passion about something or other.

First Old Man. Hush! I hear a step now, and it is coming this way. We had best pull in our heads. The world has grown very wicked and there is no knowing what they might do to us or say to us.

Second Old Man. Yes, better shut the windows and pretend to be asleep.

> [*They pull in their heads. One hears a knocker being struck in the distance, then a pause, and a knocker is struck close at hand. Another pause, and Septimus, a handsome man of thirty-five, staggers on to the stage. He is very drunk.*]

Septimus. An uncharitable place, an unchristian place. [*He begins banging at a knocker.*] Open there, open there. I want to come in and sleep.

[A third Old Man puts his head from an upper window.

Third Old Man. Who are you? What do you want?

Septimus. I am Septimus. I have a bad wife. I want to come in and sleep.

Third Old Man. You are drunk.

Septimus. Drunk! So would you be if you had as bad a wife.

Third Old Man. Go away.   *[He shuts the window.*

Septimus. Is there not one Christian in this town? *[He begins hammering the knocker of First Old Man, but there is no answer.]* No one there? All dead or drunk maybe — bad wives! There must be one Christian man.

[He hammers a knocker at the other side of the stage. An Old Woman puts her head out of the window above.

Old Woman [in a shrill voice]. Who's there? What do you want? Has something happened?

Septimus. Yes, that's it. Something has happened. My wife has hid herself, has run away, or has drowned herself.

Old Woman. What do I care about your wife? You are drunk.

Septimus. Not care about my wife! But I tell you that my wife has to play by order of the Prime Minister before all the people in the great hall of the Castle precisely at noon, and she cannot be found.

Old Woman. Go away, go away! I tell you, go away.

[She shuts the window.

Septimus. Treat Septimus, who has played before Kubla Khan, like this! Septimus, dramatist and poet! *[The Old Woman opens the window again and empties a jug of water over him.]* Water! drenched to the skin — must sleep in the street. *[Lies down.]* Bad wife — others have had bad wives, but others were not left to lie down in the open street under the stars, drenched with cold water, a whole jug of cold water, shivering in the pale light of the dawn, to be run over, to be trampled upon, to be eaten by dogs, and all because their wives have hidden themselves.

Enter two Men a little older than Septimus.
They stand still and gaze into the sky

First Man. Ah, my friend, the little fair-haired one is a minx.

Second Man. Never trust fair hair — I will have nothing but brown hair.

First Man. They have kept us too long — brown or fair.

Second Man. What are you staring at?

First Man. At the first streak of the dawn on the Castle tower.

Second Man. I would not have my wife find out for the world.

Septimus [sitting up]. Carry me, support me, drag me, roll me, pull me, or sidle me along, but bring me where I may sleep in comfort. Bring me to a stable — my Saviour was content with a stable.

First Man. Who are you? I don't know your face.

Septimus. I am Septimus, a player, a playwright, and the most famous poet in the world.

Second Man. That name, sir, is unknown to me.

Septimus. Unknown?

Second Man. But my name will not be unknown to you. I am called Peter of the Purple Pelican, after the best known of my poems, and my friend is called Happy Tom. He also is a poet.

Septimus. Bad, popular poets.

Second Man. You would be a popular poet if you could.

Septimus. Bad, popular poets.

First Man. Lie where you are if you can't be civil.

Septimus. What do I care for any one now except Venus and Adonis and the other planets of heaven?

Second Man. You can enjoy their company by yourself.

[*The two Men go out.*

Septimus. Robbed, so to speak; naked, so to speak — bleeding, so
to speak — and they pass by on the other side of the street.

[*A crowd of Citizens and Countrymen enter. At first only a
few, and then more and more till the stage is filled by an
excited crowd.*

First Citizen. There is a man lying here.

Second Citizen. Roll him over.

First Citizen. He is one of those players who are housed at the
Castle. They arrived yesterday.

Second Citizen. Drunk, I suppose. He'll be killed or maimed
by the first milk-cart.

Third Citizen. Better roll him into the corner. If we are in for
a bloody day's business, there is no need for him to be
killed — an unnecessary death might bring a curse upon us.

First Citizen. Give me a hand here.

[*They begin rolling Septimus.*

Septimus [*muttering*]. Not allowed to sleep! Rolled off the
street! Shoved into a stony place! Unchristian town!

[*He is left lying at the foot of the wall to one side of the stage.*

Third Citizen. Are we all friends here, are we all agreed?

First Citizen. These men are from the country. They came in
last night. They know little of the business. They won't be
against the people, but they want to know more.

First Countryman. Yes, that is it. We are with the people,
but we want to know more.

Second Countryman. We want to know all, but we are with the
people.

[*Other voices take up the words,* 'We want to know all, but
we are with the people', *etc. There is a murmur of voices
together.*

Third Citizen. Have you ever seen the Queen, countryman?

First Countryman. No.

Third Citizen. Our Queen is a witch, a bad evil-living witch, and we will have her no longer for Queen.

Third Countryman. I would be slow to believe her father's daughter a witch.

Third Citizen. Have you ever seen the Queen, countryman?

Third Countryman. No.

Third Citizen. Nor has any one else. Not a man here has set eyes on her. For seven years she has been shut up in that great black house on the great rocky hill. From the day her father died she has been there with the doors shut on her, but we know now why she has hidden herself. She has no good companions in the dark night.

Third Countryman. In my district they say that she is a holy woman and prays for us all.

Third Citizen. That story has been spread about by the Prime Minister. He has spies everywhere spreading stories. He is a crafty man.

First Countryman. It is true, they always deceive us country people. We are not educated like the people of the town.

A Big Countryman. The Bible says, Suffer not a witch to live. Last Candlemas twelvemonth I strangled a witch with my own hands.

Third Citizen. When she is dead we will make the Prime Minister King.

Second Citizen. No, no, he is not a king's son.

Second Countryman. I'd send a bellman through the world. There are many kings in Arabia, they say.

Third Countryman. The people must be talking. If you and I were to hide ourselves, or to be someway hard to understand, maybe they would put some bad name on us. I am not against the people, but I want testimony.

Third Citizen. Come, Tapster, stand up there on the stone and tell what you know.

[*The Tapster climbs up on the mounting-stone.*

Tapster. I live in the quarter where her Castle is. The garden of my house and the gardens of all the houses in my row run right up to the rocky hill that has her Castle on the top. There is a lad in my quarter that has a goat in his garden.

First Citizen. That's Strolling Michael — I know him.

Tapster. That goat is always going astray. Strolling Michael got out of his bed early one morning to go snaring birds, and nowhere could he see that goat. So he began climbing up the rock, and up and up he went, till he was close under the wall, and there he found the goat and it shaking and sweating as though something had scared it. Presently he heard a thing neigh like a horse, and after that a something like a white horse ran by, but it was no horse, but a unicorn. He had his pistol, for he had thought to bring down a rabbit, and seeing it rushing at him as he imagined, he fired at the unicorn. It vanished all in a moment, but there was blood on a great stone.

Third Citizen. Seeing what company she keeps in the small hours, what wonder that she never sets foot out of doors!

Third Countryman. I wouldn't believe all that night rambler says — boys are liars. All that we have against her for certain is that she won't put her foot out of doors. I knew a man once that when he was five-and-twenty refused to get out of his bed. He wasn't ill — no, not he, but he said life was a vale of tears, and for forty and four years till they carried him out to the churchyard he never left that bed. All tried him — parson tried him, priest tried him, doctor tried him, and all he'd say was, 'Life is a vale of tears'. It's too snug he was in his bed, and believe me, that ever since she has had no father to rout her out of a morning she has been in her bed, and small blame to her maybe.

The Big Countryman. But that's the very sort that are witches. They know where to find their own friends in the lonely hours of the night. There was a witch in my own district that I strangled last Candlemas twelvemonth. She had an imp in the shape of a red cat, that sucked three drops of blood from her poll every night a little before the cock crew. It's with their blood they feed them; until they have been fed with the blood they are images and shadows; but when they have it drunk they can be for a while stronger than you or me.

Third Countryman. The man I knew was no witch, he was no way active. 'Life is a vale of tears,' he said. Parson tried him, doctor tried him, priest tried him — but that was all he'd say.

First Citizen. We'd have no man go beyond evidence and reason, but hear the Tapster out, and when you have you'll say that we cannot leave her alive this day — no, not for one day longer.

Tapster. It's not a story that I like to be telling, but you are all married men. Another night that boy climbed up after his goat, and it was an hour earlier by his clock and no light in the sky, and when he came to the Castle wall he clambered along the wall among the rocks and bushes till he saw a light from a little window over his head. It was an old wall full of holes, where mortar had fallen out, and he climbed up, putting his toes into the holes, till he could look in through the window; and when he looked in, what did he see but the Queen!

First Countryman. And did he say what she was like?

Tapster. He saw more than that. He saw her coupling with a great white unicorn.

[*Murmurs among the crowd.*

Second Countryman. I will not have the son of the unicorn to reign over us, although you will tell me he would be no more than half a unicorn.

First Countryman. I'll not go against the people, but I'd let her live if the Prime Minister promised to rout her out of bed in the morning and to set a guard to drive off the unicorn.

The Big Countryman. I have strangled an old witch with these two hands, and to-day I will strangle a young witch.

Septimus [*who has slowly got up and climbed up on to the mounting-stone which the Tapster has left*]. Did I hear somebody say that the Unicorn is not chaste? It is a most noble beast, a most religious beast. It has a milk-white skin and a milk-white horn, and milk-white hooves, but a mild blue eye, and it dances in the sun. I will have no one speak against it, not while I am still upon the earth. It is written in 'The Great Beastery of Paris' that it is chaste, that it is the most chaste of all the beasts in the world.

The Big Countryman. Pull him out of that, he's drunk.

Septimus. Yes, I am drunk, I am very drunk, but that is no reason why I should permit any one to speak against the Unicorn.

Second Citizen. Let's hear him out. We can do nothing till the sun's up.

Septimus. Nobody shall speak against the Unicorn. No, my friends and poets, nobody. I will hunt it if you will, though it is a dangerous and cross-grained beast. Much virtue has made it cross-grained. I will go with you to the high table-lands of Africa where it lives, and we will there shoot it through the head, but I will not speak against its character, and if any man declares it is not chaste I will fight him, for I affirm that its chastity is equal to its beauty.

The Big Countryman. He is most monstrously drunk.

Septimus. No longer drunk, but inspired.

Second Citizen. Go on, go on, we'll never hear the like again.

The Big Countryman. Come away. I've enough of this — we have work to do.

Septimus. Go away, did you say, and my breast-feathers thrust out and my white wings buoyed up with divinity? Ah! but I can see it now — you are bent upon going to some lonely place where uninterrupted you can speak against the character of the Unicorn, but you shall not, I tell you that you shall not. [*He comes down off the stone and squares up at the crowd which tries to pass him.*] In the midst of this uncharitable town I will protect that noble, milk-white, flighty beast.

The Big Countryman. Let me pass.

Septimus. No, I will not let you pass.

First Countryman. Leave him alone.

Second Countryman. No violence — it might bring ill-luck upon us.

[*They try to hold back the Big Countryman.*

Septimus. I will oppose your passing to the death. For I will not have it said that there is a smirch, or a blot, upon the most milky whiteness of an heroic brute that bathes by the sound of tabors at the rising of the sun and the rising of the moon, and the rising of the Great Bear, and above all, it shall not be said, whispered, or in any wise published abroad by you that stand there, so to speak, between two washings; for you were doubtless washed when you were born, and, it may be, shall be washed again after you are dead. [*The Big Countryman knocks him down.*

First Citizen. You have killed him.

The Big Countryman. Maybe I have, maybe I have not — let him lie there. A witch I strangled last Candlemas twelve-month, a witch I will strangle to-day. What do I care for the likes of him?

Third Citizen. Come round to the east quarter of the town. The basket-makers and the sieve-makers will be out by this.

Fourth Citizen. It is a short march from there to the Castle gate.

[*They go up one of the side streets, but return quickly in confusion and fear.*

First Citizen. Are you sure that you saw him?

Second Citizen. Who could mistake that horrible old man?

Third Citizen. I was standing by him when the ghost spoke out of him seven years ago.

First Countryman. I never saw him before. He has never been in my district. I don't rightly know what sort he is, but I have heard of him, many a time I have heard of him.

First Citizen. His eyes become glassy, and that is the trance growing upon him, and when he is in the trance his soul slips away and a ghost takes its place and speaks out of him — a strange ghost.

Third Citizen. I was standing by him the last time. 'Get me straw,' said that old man, 'my back itches.' Then all of a sudden he lay down, with his eyes wide open and glassy, and he brayed like a donkey. At that moment the King died and the King's daughter was Queen.

First Countryman. They say it is the donkey that carried Christ into Jerusalem, and that is why it knows its rightful sovereign. He goes begging about the country and there is no man dare refuse him what he asks.

The Big Countryman. Then it is certain nobody will take my hand off her throat. I will make my grip tighter. He will be lying down on the straw and he will bray, and when he brays she will be dead.

First Countryman. Look! There he is coming over the top of the hill, and the mad look upon him.

Second Countryman. I wouldn't face him for the world this
night. Come round to the market-place, we'll be less afraid
in a big place.

The Big Countryman. I'm not afraid, but I'll go with you till
I get my hand on her throat.

[*They all go out but Septimus. Presently Septimus sits up; his
head is bleeding. He rubs with his fingers his broken head
and looks at the blood on his fingers.*

Septimus. Unchristian town! First I am, so to speak, thrown
out into the street, and then I am all but murdered; and I
drunk, and therefore in need of protection. All creatures are
in need of protection at some time or other. Even my wife
was once a frail child in need of milk, of smiles, of love, as
if in the midst of a flood, in danger of drowning, so to
speak.

[*An Old Beggar with long matted hair and beard and in
ragged clothes comes in.*

The Old Beggar. I want straw.

Septimus. Happy Tom and Peter of the Purple Pelican have
done it all. They are bad, popular poets, and being jealous
of my fame, they have stirred up the people. [*He catches
sight of the Old Beggar.*] There is a certain medicine which
is made by distilling camphor, Peruvian bark, spurge and
mandrake, and mixing all with twelve ounces of dissolved
pearls and four ounces of the oil of gold; and this medicine is
infallible to stop the flow of blood. Have you any of it, old
man?

The Old Beggar. I want straw.

Septimus. I can see that you have not got it, but no matter,
we shall be friends.

The Old Beggar. I want straw to lie down on.

Septimus. It is no doubt better that I should bleed to death.

For that way, my friend, I shall disgrace Happy Tom and Peter of the Purple Pelican, but it is necessary that I shall die somewhere where my last words can be taken down. I am therefore in need of your support.

[*Having got up he now staggers over to the Old Beggar and leans upon him.*

The Old Beggar. Don't you know who I am — aren't you afraid? When something comes inside me, my back itches. Then I must lie down and roll, and then I bray and the crown changes.

Septimus. Ah! you are inspired. Then we are indeed brothers. Come, I will rest upon your shoulder and we will mount the hill side by side. I will sleep in the Castle of the Queen.

The Old Beggar. You will give me straw to lie upon?

Septimus. Asphodels! Yet, indeed, the asphodel is a flower much overrated by the classic authors. Still if a man has a preference, I say, for the asphodel —

[*They go out and one hears the voice of Septimus murmuring in the distance about asphodels.*

[*The First Old Man opens his window and taps with his crutch at the opposite window. The Second Old Man opens his window.*

First Old Man. It is all right now. They are all gone. We can have our talk out.

Second Old Man. The whole Castle is lit by the dawn now, and it will begin to grow brighter in the street.

First Old Man. It's time for the Tapster's old dog to come down the street.

Second Old Man. Yesterday he had a bone in his mouth.

Scene II

The Throne-Room in the Castle. Between pillars are gilded open-work doors, except at one side, where there is a large window. The morning light is slanting through the window, making dark shadows among the pillars. As the scene goes on, the light, at first feeble, becomes strong and suffused, and the shadows disappear. Through the openwork doors one can see down long passages, and one of these passages plainly leads into the open air. One can see daylight at the end of it. There is a throne in the centre of the room and a flight of steps that leads to it.

The Prime Minister, an elderly man with an impatient manner and voice, is talking to a group of Players, among whom is Nona, a fair, comely, comfortable-looking young woman of perhaps thirty-five; she seems to take the lead.

Prime Minister. I will not be trifled with. I chose the play myself; I chose 'The Tragical History of Noah's Deluge' because when Noah beats his wife to make her go into the Ark everybody understands, everybody is pleased, everybody recognises the mulish obstinacy of their own wives, sweethearts, sisters. And now, when it is of the greatest importance to the State that everybody should be pleased, the play cannot be given. The leading lady is lost, you say, and there is some unintelligible reason why nobody can take her place; but I know what you are all driving at — you object to the play I have chosen. You want some dull, poetical thing, full of long speeches. I will have that play and no other. The rehearsal must begin at once and the performance take place at noon punctually.

Nona. We have searched all night, sir, and we cannot find her anywhere. She was heard to say that she would drown rather than play a woman older than thirty. Seeing that

Noah's wife is a very old woman, we are afraid that she has drowned herself indeed.

[*Decima, a very pretty woman, puts her head out from under the throne where she has been lying hidden.*

Prime Minister. Nonsense! It is all a conspiracy. Your manager should be here. He is responsible. You can tell him when he does come that if the play is not performed, I will clap him into gaol for a year and pitch the rest of you over the border.

Nona. O, sir, he couldn't help it. She does whatever she likes.

Prime Minister. Does whatever she likes — I know her sort; would pull the world to pieces to spite her husband or her lover. I know her — a bladder full of dried peas for a brain, a brazen, bragging baggage. Of course he couldn't help it, but what do I care? [*Decima pulls in her head.*] To gaol he goes — somebody has got to go to gaol. Go and cry her name everywhere. Away with you! Let me hear you cry it out. Call the baggage. Louder. Louder. [*The Players go out crying,* 'Where are you, Decima?'] O, Adam! why did you fall asleep in the garden? You might have known that, while you were lying there helpless, the Old Man in the Sky would play some prank upon you.

[*The Queen, who is young, with an ascetic timid face, enters in a badly fitting state dress.*

Ah!

Queen. I will show myself to the angry people as you have bidden me. I am almost certain that I am ready for martyrdom. I have prayed all night. Yes, I am almost certain.

Prime Minister. Ah!

Queen. I have now attained to the age of my patroness, Holy Saint Octema, when she was martyred at Antioch. You

will remember that her unicorn was so pleased at the
spectacle of her austerity that he caracoled in his excitement. Thereupon she dropped out of the saddle and was
trampled to death under the feet of the mob. Indeed, but
for the unicorn, the mob would have killed her long before.

Prime Minister. No, you will not be martyred. I have a plan
to settle that. I will stop their anger with a word. Who
made that dress?

Queen. It was my mother's dress. She wore it at her corona-
tion. I would not have a new one made. I do not deserve
new clothes. I am always committing sin.

Prime Minister. Is there sin in an egg that has never been
hatched, that has never been warmed, in a chalk egg?

Queen. I wish I could resemble Holy Saint Octema in every
thing.

Prime Minister. What a dress! It is too late now. Nothing can
be done. It may appear right to those on the edge of the
crowd. The others must be conquered by charm, dignity,
royal manner. As for the dress, I must think of some excuse,
some explanation. Remember that they have never seen
your face, and you will put them in a bad humour if you
hang your head in that dumbfounded way.

Queen. I wish I could return to my prayers.

Prime Minister. Walk! Permit me to see your Majesty walk.
No, no, no. Be more majestic. Ah! If you had known the
queens I have known — they had a way with them. Morals
of a dragoon, but a way, a way! Put on a kind of eagle look,
a vulture look.

Queen. There are cobble-stones — if I might go barefoot it
would be a blessed penance. It was especially the bleeding
feet of Saint Octema that gave pleasure to the unicorn.

Prime Minister. Sleep of Adam! Barefoot — barefoot, did you say? [*A pause.*] There is not time to take off your shoes and stockings. If you were to look out of the window there, you would see the crowd becoming wickeder every minute. Come! [*He gives his arm to the Queen.*]

Queen. You have a plan to stop their anger so that I shall not be martyred?

Prime Minister. My plan will be disclosed before the face of the people and there alone. [*They go out.*

[*Nona comes in with a bottle of wine and a boiled lobster and lays them on the middle of the floor. She puts her finger on her lip and stands in the doorway towards the back of the stage.*

Decima [*comes cautiously out of her hiding-place singing*].

> 'He went away', my mother sang,
> 'When I was brought to bed.'
> And all the while her needle pulled
> The gold and silver thread.
>
> She pulled the thread and bit the thread
> And made a golden gown,
> She wept because she had dreamt that I
> Was born to wear a crown.

[*She is just reaching her hand for the lobster when Nona comes forward holding out towards her the dress and mask of Noah's wife which she has been carrying over her left arm.*

Nona. Thank God you are found! [*Getting between her and the lobster.*] No, not until you have put on this dress and mask. I have caught you now, and you are not going to hide again.

Decima. Very well, when I have had my breakfast.

Nona. Not a mouthful till you are dressed ready for the rehearsal.

Decima. Do you know what song I was singing just now?

Nona. It is that song you're always singing. Septimus made
it up.

Decima. It is the song of the mad singing daughter of a harlot.
The only song she had. Her father was a drunken sailor
waiting for the full tide, and yet she thought her mother
had foretold that she would marry a prince and become a
great queen. [*Singing.*]

> 'When she was got', my mother sang,
> 'I heard a seamew cry,
> I saw a flake of yellow foam
> That dropped upon my thigh.'

> How therefore could she help but braid
> The gold upon my hair,
> And dream that I should carry
> The golden top of care?

The moment ago as I lay here I thought I could play a
queen's part, a great queen's part; the only part in the world
I can play is a great queen's part.

Nona. You play a queen's part? You that were born in a ditch
between two towns and wrapped in a sheet that was stolen
from a hedge.

Decima. The Queen cannot play at all, but I could play so well.
I could bow with my whole body down to my ankles and
could be stern when hard looks were in season. O, I would
know how to put all summer in a look and after that all
winter in a voice.

Nona. Low comedy is what you are fit for.

Decima. I understood all this in a wink of the eye, and then
just when I am saying to myself that I was born to sit up
there with soldiers and courtiers, you come shaking in front
of me that mask and that dress. I am not to eat my breakfast

unless I play an old peaky-chinned, drop-nosed harridan that a foul husband beats with a stick because she won't clamber among the other brutes into his cattle-boat. [*She makes a dart at the lobster.*]

Nona. No, no, not a drop, not a mouthful till you have put these on. Remember that if there is no play Septimus must go to prison.

Decima. Would they give him dry bread to eat?

Nona. They would.

Decima. And water to drink and nothing in the water?

Nona. They would.

Decima. And a straw bed?

Nona. They would, and only a little straw maybe.

Decima. And iron chains that clanked.

Nona. They would.

Decima. And keep him there for a whole week?

Nona. A month maybe.

Decima. And he would say to the turnkey, 'I am here because of my beautiful cruel wife, my beautiful flighty wife'?

Nona. He might not, he'd be sober.

Decima. But he'd think it, and every time he was hungry, every time he was thirsty, every time he felt the hardness of the stone floor, every time he heard the chains clank, he would think it, and every time he thought it I would become more beautiful in his eyes.

Nona. No, he would hate you.

Decima. Little do you know what the love of man is. If that Holy Image of the church where you put all those candles at Easter was pleasant and affable, why did you come home with the skin worn off your two knees?

Nona [in tears]. I understand — you cruel, bad woman! — you won't play the part at all, and all that Septimus may go to prison, and he a great genius that can't take care of himself.

[*Seeing Nona distracted with tears Decima makes a dart and almost gets the lobster.*

Nona. No, no! Not a mouthful, not a drop. I will break the bottle if you go near it. There is not another woman in the world would treat a man like that, and you were sworn to him in church — yes, you were, there is no good denying it. [*Decima makes another dart, but Nona, who is still in tears, puts the lobster in her pocket.*] Leave the food alone; not one mouthful will you get. I have never sworn to a man in church, but if I did swear, I would not treat him like a tinker's donkey — before God I would not — I was properly brought up; my mother always told me it was no light thing to take a man in church.

Decima. You are in love with my husband.

Nona. Because I don't want to see him gaoled you say I am in love with him. Only a woman with no heart would think one can't be sorry for a man without being in love with him — a woman who has never been sorry for anybody! But I won't have him gaoled; if you won't play the part I'll play it myself.

Decima. When I married him, I made him swear never to play with anybody but me, and well you know it.

Nona. Only this once, and in a part nobody can do anything with.

Decima. That is the way it begins, and all the time you would be saying things the audience couldn't hear.

Nona. Septimus will break his oath, and I have learnt the part. Every line of it.

Decima. Septimus would not break his oath for anybody in the world.

Nona. There is one person in the world for whom he will break his oath.

Decima. What have you in your head now?

Nona. He will break it for me.

Decima. You are crazy.

Nona. Maybe I have my secrets.

Decima. What are you keeping back? Have you been sitting in corners with Septimus? giving him sympathy because of the bad wife he has, and all the while he has sat there to have the pleasure of talking about me?

Nona. You think that you have his every thought because you are a devil.

Decima. Because I am a devil I have his every thought.
You know how his own song runs. The man speaks first — [*singing*]

> Put off that mask of burning gold
> With emerald eyes,

and then the woman answers —

> O no, my dear, you make so bold
> To find if hearts be wild and wise
> And yet not cold.

Nona. His every thought — that is a lie. He forgets all about you the moment you're out of his sight.

Decima. Then look what I carry under my bodice. This is a poem praising me, all my beauties one after the other — eyes, hair, complexion, shape, disposition, mind — everything. And there are a great many verses to it. And here is a little one he gave me yesterday morning. I had turned him out of bed and he had to lie alone by himself.

Nona. Alone by himself!

Decima. And as he lay there alone, unable to sleep, he made it up, wishing that he were blind so as not to be troubled by looking at my beauty. Hear how it goes!

[*sings again*]

> O would that I were an old beggar
> Without a friend on this earth
> But a thieving rascally cur,
> A beggar blind from his birth;
> Or anything else but a man
> Lying alone on a bed
> Remembering a woman's beauty,
> Alone with a crazy head.

Nona. Alone in his bed indeed. I know that long poem, that one with all the verses; I know it to my hurt, though I haven't read a word of it. Four lines in every verse, four beats in every line, and fourteen verses — my curse upon it!

Decima [*taking out a manuscript from her bodice*]. Yes, fourteen verses. There are numbers to them.

Nona. You have another there — ten verses all in fours and threes.

Decima [*looking at another manuscript*]. Yes, the verses are in fours and threes. But how do you know all this? I carry them here. They are a secret between him and me, and nobody can see them till they have lain a long while upon my heart.

Nona. They have lain upon your heart, but they were made upon my shoulder. Ay, and down along my spine in the small hours of the morning; so many beats a line, and for every beat a tap of the fingers.

Decima. My God!

Nona. That one with the fourteen verses kept me from my sleep two hours, and when the lines were finished he lay upon his back another hour waving one arm in the air, making up the music. I liked him well enough to seem to be asleep through it all, and many another poem too — but when he made up that short one you sang he was so pleased that he muttered the words all about his lying alone in his bed thinking of you, and that made me mad. So I said to him, 'Am I not beautiful? Turn round and look.' O, I cut it short, for even I can please a man when there is but one candle. [*She takes a pair of scissors that are hanging round her neck and begins snipping at the dress for Noah's wife.*] And now you know why I can play the part in spite of you and not be driven out. Work upon Septimus if you have a mind for it. Little need I care. I will clip this a trifle and re-stitch it again — I have a needle and thread ready.

[*The Stage Manager comes in ringing a bell. He is followed by various players all dressed up in the likeness of various beasts.*

Stage Manager. Put on that mask — get into your clothes. Why are you standing there as if in a trance?

Nona. Decima and I have talked the matter over and we have settled that I am to play the part.

Stage Manager. Do as you please. Thank God it's a part that anybody can play. All you have got to do is to copy an old woman's squeaky voice. We are all here now but Septimus, and we cannot wait for him. I will read the part of Noah. He will be here before we are finished, I daresay. We will suppose that the audience is upon this side, and that the Ark is over there with a gangway for the beasts to climb. All you beasts are to crowd up on the prompt side. Lay down Noah's hat and cloak there till Septimus comes. As the first scene is between Noah and the beasts, you can go on with your sewing.

Decima. No, I must first be heard. My husband has been spending his nights with Nona, and that is why she sits clipping and stitching with that vainglorious air.

Nona. She made him miserable, she knows every trick of breaking a man's heart — he came to me with his troubles — I seemed to be a comfort to him, and now — why should I deny it? — he is my lover.

Decima. I will take the vainglory out of her. I have been a plague to him. O, I have been a badger and a weasel and a hedgehog and pole-cat, and all because I was dead sick of him. And, thank God!, she has got him and I am free. I threw away a part and I threw away a man — she has picked both up.

Stage Manager. It seems to me that it all concerns you two. It's your business and not ours. I don't see why we should delay the rehearsal.

Decima. I will have no rehearsal yet. I'm too happy now that I am free. I must find somebody who will dance with me for a while. Come, we must have music. [*She picks up a lute which has been laid down amongst some properties.*] You can't all be claws and hoofs.

Stage Manager. We've only an hour and the whole play to go through.

Nona. O, she has taken my scissors, she is only pretending not to care. Look at her! She is mad! Take them away from her! Hold her hand! She is going to kill me or to kill herself. [*To Stage Manager.*] Why don't you interfere? My God! She is going to kill me.

Decima. Here, Peter.

[*She begins cutting through the breast-feathers of the Swan.*]

Nona. She is doing it all to stop the rehearsal, out of vengeance; and you stand there and do nothing.

Stage Manager. If you have taken her husband, why didn't you keep the news till the play was over? She is going to make them all mad now, I can see that much in her eyes.

Decima. Now that I have thrown Septimus into her lap, I will choose a new man, Shall it be you, Turkey-cock? or you, Bullhead?

Stage Manager. There is nothing to be done. It is all your fault. If Septimus can't manage his wife, it's certain that I can't. [*He sits down helplessly.*

Decima. Dance, Bullhead, dance — no — no — stop. I will not have you for my man, slow on the feet and heavy of build, and that means jealousy, and there is a sort of melancholy in your voice. What a folly that I should find love nothing, and yet through sympathy with that voice should stretch and yawn as if I loved! Dance, Turkey-cock, dance — no, stop. I cannot have you, for my man must be lively on his feet and have a quick eye. I will not have that round eye fixed upon me now that I have sent my mind asleep. Yet what do I care who it is, so that I choose and get done with it? Dance, all dance, and I will choose the best dancer among you. Quick, quick, begin to dance.

[*All dance round Decima.*

Decima [*singing*].

> Shall I fancy beast or fowl?
> Queen Pasiphae chose a bull,
> While a passion for a swan
> Made Queen Leda stretch and yawn,
> Wherefore spin ye, whirl ye, dance ye,
> Till Queen Decima's found her fancy.

Chorus

> Wherefore spin ye, whirl ye, dance ye,
> Till Queen Decima's found her fancy.

Decima.

> Spring and straddle, stride and strut,
> Shall I chose a bird or brute?

Name the feather or the fur
For my single comforter?

Chorus

Wherefore spin ye, whirl ye, dance ye,
Till Queen Decima's found her fancy.

Decima.

None has found, that found out love,
Single bird or brute enough;
Any bird or brute may rest
An empty head upon my breast.

Chorus

Wherefore spin ye, whirl ye, dance ye,
Till Queen Decima's found her fancy.

Stage Manager. Stop, stop, here is Septimus.

Septimus [*the blood still upon his face, and but little soberer*]
Gather about me, for I announce the end of the Christian
Era, the coming of a New Dispensation, that of the New
Adam, that of the Unicorn; but alas, he is chaste, he
hesitates, he hesitates.

Stage Manager. This is not a time for making up speeches for
your new play.

Septimus. His unborn children are but images; we merely play
with images.

Stage Manager. Let us get on with the rehearsal.

Septimus. No; let us prepare to die. The mob is climbing up
the hill with pitchforks to stick into our vitals and burning
wisps to set the roof on fire.

First Player [*who has gone to the window*]. My God, it's true.
There is a great crowd at the bottom of the hill.

Second Player. But why should they attack us?

Septimus. Because we are the servants of the Unicorn.

Third Player [*at window*]. My God, they have dung-forks
and scythes set on poles and they are coming this way.

[*Many Players gather round the window.*

Septimus [*who has found the bottle and is drinking*]. Some will
die like Cato, some like Cicero, some like Demosthenes,
triumphing over death in sonorous eloquence, or, like
Petronius Arbiter, will tell witty, scandalous tales; but I
will speak, no, I will sing, as if the mob did not exist. I will
rail upon the Unicorn for his chastity. I will bid him
trample mankind to death and beget a new race. I will even
put my railing into rhyme, and all shall run sweetly, sweetly,
for, even if they blow up the floor with gunpowder, they
are merely the mob.

> Upon the round blue eye I rail,
> Damnation on the milk-white horn.

A telling sound, a sound to linger in the ear — hale, tale,
bale, gale — my God, I am even too sober to find a rhyme!
[*He drinks and then picks up a lute*] — a tune that my mur-
derers may remember my last words and croon them to
their grandchildren.

[*For the next few speeches he is busy making his tune.*

First Player. The players of this town are jealous. Have we
not been chosen before them all, because we are the most
famous players in the world? It is they who have stirred up
the mob.

Second Player. It is of me they are jealous. They know what
happened at Xanadu. At the end of that old play 'The Fall
of Troy' Kubla Khan sent for me and said that he would
give his kingdom for such a voice, and for such a presence.
I stood before him dressed as Agamemnon just as when
in a great scene at the end I had reproached Helen for all the
misery she had wrought.

First Player. My God, listen to him! Is it not always the comedian who draws the crowd? Am I dreaming, or was it not I who was called six times before the curtain? Answer me that —

Second Player. What if you were called six dozen times? The players of this town are not jealous because of the crowd's applause. They have that themselves. The unendurable thought, the thought that wrenches their hearts, the thought that puts murder into their minds is that I alone, alone of all the world's players, have looked as an equal into the eyes of Kubla Khan.

Stage Manager. Stop quarrelling with one another and listen to what is happening out there. There is a man making a speech, and the crowd is getting angrier and angrier, and which of you they are jealous of I don't know, but they are all coming this way and maybe they will burn the place down as if it were Troy, and if you will do what I say you will get out of this.

First Player. Must we go dressed like this?

Second Player. There is not time to change, and besides, should the hill be surrounded, we can gather in some cleft of the rocks where we can be seen only from a distance. They will suppose we are a drove of cattle or a flock of birds.

> [*All go out except Septimus, Decima, and Nona. Nona is making a bundle of Noah's hat and cloak and other properties. Decima is watching Septimus.*

Septimus [*while the Players are going out*]. Leave me to die alone? I do not blame you. There is courage in red wine, in white wine, in beer, even in thin beer sold by a blear-eyed pot-boy in a bankrupt tavern, but there is none in the human heart. When my master the Unicorn bathes by the light of the Great Bear, and to the sound of tabors, even the sweet river-water makes him drunk; but it is cold, it is cold, alas! it is cold.

Nona. I'll pile these upon your back. I shall carry the rest myself and so we shall save all.

[*She begins tying a great bundle of properties on Septimus' back.*

Septimus. You are right. I accept the reproach. It is necessary that we who are the last artists — all the rest have gone over to the mob — shall save the images and implements of our art. We must carry into safety the cloak of Noah, the high-crowned hat of Noah, and the mask of the sister of Noah. She was drowned because she thought her brother was telling lies; certainly we must save her rosy cheeks and rosy mouth, that drowned, wicked mouth.

Nona. Thank God you can still stand upright on your legs.

Septimus. Tie all upon my back and I will tell you the great secret that came to me at the second mouthful of the bottle. Man is nothing till he is united to an image. Now the Unicorn is both an image and beast; that is why he alone can be the new Adam. When we have put all in safety we will go to the high tablelands of Africa and find where the Unicorn is stabled and sing a marriage song. I will stand before the terrible blue eye.

Nona. There, now, I have tied them on.

[*She begins making another bundle for herself, but forgets the mask of the sister of Noah. It lies near the throne.*

Septimus. You will make Ionian music — music with its eyes upon that voluptuous Asia — the Dorian scale would but confirm him in his chastity. One Dorian note might undo us, and above all we must be careful not to speak of Delphi. The oracle is chaste.

Nona. Come, let us go.

Septimus. If we cannot fill him with desire he will deserve death. Even unicorns can be killed. What they dread most in the world is a blow from a knife that has been dipped in the blood of a serpent that died gazing upon an emerald.

[*Nona and Septimus are about to go out, Nona leading Septimus.*

Decima. Stand back, do not dare to move a step.

Septimus. Beautiful as the Unicorn, but fierce.

Decima. I have locked the gates that we may have a talk.

[*Nona lets the hat of Noah fall in her alarm.*

Septimus. That is well, very well. You would talk with me because to-day I am extraordinarily wise.

Decima. I will not unlock the gate till I have a promise that I will drive her from the company.

Nona. Do not listen to her; take the key from her.

Septimus. If I were not her husband I would take the key, but because I am her husband she is terrible. The Unicorn will be terrible when it loves.

Nona. You are afraid.

Septimus. Could not you yourself take it? She does not love you, therefore she will not be terrible.

Nona. If you are a man at all you will take it.

Septimus. I am more than a man, I am extraordinarily wise. I will take the key.

Decima. If you come a step nearer I will shove the key through the grating of the door.

Nona [*pulling him back*]. Don't go near her; if she shoves it through the door we shall not be able to escape. The crowd will find us and murder us.

Decima. I will unlock this gate when you have taken an oath to drive her from the company, an oath never to speak with her or look at her again, a terrible oath.

Septimus. You are jealous; it is very wrong to be jealous. An ordinary man would be lost — even I am not yet wise enough. [*Drinks again.*] Now all is plain.

Decima. You have been unfaithful to me.

Septimus. I am only unfaithful when I am sober. Never trust a sober man. All the world over they are unfaithful. Never trust a man who has not bathed by the light of the Great Bear. I warn you against all sober men from the bottom of my heart. I am extraordinarily wise.

Nona. Promise, if it is only an oath she wants. Take whatever oath she bids you. If you delay we shall all be murdered.

Septimus. I can see your meaning. You would explain to me that an oath can be broken, more especially an oath under compulsion, but no, I say to you, no, I say to you, certainly not. Am I a rascally sober man, such a man as I have warned you against? Shall I be forsworn before the very eyes of Delphi, so to speak, before the very eyes of that cold, rocky oracle? What I promise I perform, therefore, my little darling, I will not promise anything at all.

Decima. Then we shall wait here. They will come in through this door, they will carry dung-forks with burning wisps. They will put the burning wisps into the roof and we shall be burnt.

Septimus. I shall die railing upon that beast. The Christian era has come to an end, but because of the machinations of Delphi he will not become the new Adam.

Decima. I shall be avenged. She starved me, but I shall have killed her.

Nona [*who has crept behind Decima and snatched the key*]. I have it, I have it!

[*Decima tries to take the key again, but Septimus holds her.*

Septimus. Because I am an unsworn man I am strong: a

violent virginal creature, that is how it is put in 'The Great
Beastery of Paris'.

Decima. Go, then, I shall stay here and die.

Nona. Let us go. A half hour since she offered herself to every
man in the company.

Decima. If you would be faithful to me, Septimus, I would not
let a man of them touch me.

Septimus. Flighty, but beautiful.

Nona. She is a bad woman.   [*Nona runs out.*

Septimus. A beautiful, bad, flighty woman I will follow, but
follow slowly. I will take with me this noble hat. [*He picks
up Noah's hat with difficulty.*] No, it may lie there, what have
I to do with that drowned, wicked mouth — beautiful,
drowned, flighty mouth? I will have nothing to do with it,
but I will save the noble, high-crowned hat of Noah. I will
carry it thus with dignity. I will go slowly that they may
see I am not afraid.   [*Singing.*

      Upon the round blue eye I rail,
      Damnation on the milk-white horn.

But not one word of Delphi. I am extraordinarily wise.

                                [*He goes.*

Decima. Betrayed, betrayed, and for a nobody. For a woman
that a man can shake and twist like so much tallow. A
woman that till now never looked higher than a prompter
or a property man. [*The Old Beggar comes in.*] Have you
come to kill me, old man?

Old Beggar. I am looking for straw. I must soon lie down and
roll, and where will I get straw to roll on? I went round to
the kitchen, and 'Go away', they said. They made the sign
of the cross as if it were a devil that puts me rolling.

Decima. When will the mob come to kill me?

Old Beggar. Kill you? It is not you they are going to kill. It's

the itching in my back that drags them hither, for when I
bray like a donkey, the crown changes.

Decima. The crown? So it is the Queen they are going to kill.

Old Beggar. But, my dear, she can't die till I roll and bray,
and I will whisper to you what it is that rolls. It is the
donkey that carried Christ into Jerusalem, and that is why
he is so proud; and that is why he knows the hour when
there is to be a new King or a new Queen.

Decima. Are you weary of the world, old man?

Old Beggar. Yes, yes, because when I roll and bray I am
asleep. I know nothing about it, and that is a great pity. I
remember nothing but the itching in my back. But I must
stop talking and find some straw.

Decima [*picking up the scissors*]. Old man, I am going to drive
this into my heart.

Old Beggar. No, no; don't do that. You don't know what you
will be put to when you are dead, into whose gullet you
will be put to sing or to bray. You have a look of a foretelling sort. Who knows but you might be put to foretell
the death of kings; and bear in mind I will have no rivals,
I could not endure a rival.

Decima. I have been betrayed by a man, I have been made a
mockery of. Do those who are dead, old man, make love
and do they find good lovers?

Old Beggar. I will whisper you another secret. People talk,
but I have never known of anything to come from there
but an old jackass. Maybe there is nothing else. Who knows
but he has the whole place to himself? But there, my back is
beginning to itch, and I have not yet found any straw.

   [*He goes out. Decima leans the scissors upon the arm of the
      throne and is about to press herself upon them when the
      Queen enters.*

Queen [*stopping her*]. No, no — that would be a great sin.

Decima. Your Majesty!

Queen. I thought I would like to die a martyr, but that would be different, that would be to die for God's glory. The Holy Saint Octema was a martyr.

Decima. I am very unhappy.

Queen. I, too, am very unhappy. When I saw the great angry crowd and knew that they wished to kill me, though I had wanted to be a martyr, I was afraid and ran away.

Decima. I would not have run away, O no; but it is hard to drive a knife into one's own flesh.

Queen. In a moment they will have come and they will beat in the door, and how shall I escape them?

Decima. If they could mistake me for you, you would escape.

Queen. I could not let another die instead of me. That would be very wrong.

Decima. O, your Majesty, I shall die whatever you do, and if only I could wear that gold brocade and those gold slippers for one moment, it would not be so hard to die.

Queen. They say that those who die to save a rightful sovereign show great virtue.

Decima. Quick! the dress.

Queen. If you killed yourself your soul would be lost, and now you will be sure of Heaven.

Decima. Quick, I hear them coming.

> [*Decima puts on the Queen's robe of state and her slippers. Underneath her robe of state the Queen wears some kind of nun-like dress.*
>
> *The following speech is spoken by the Queen while she is helping Decima to fasten the dress and the slippers.*

Queen. Was it love? [*Decima nods.*] O, that is a great sin. I have never known love. Of all things, that is what I have had most fear of. Saint Octema shut herself up in a tower on a mountain because she was loved by a beautiful prince. I was afraid it would come in at the eye and seize upon me in a moment. I am not naturally good, and they say people will do anything for love, there is so much sweetness in it. Even Saint Octema was afraid of it. But you will escape all that and go up to God as a pure virgin. [*The change is now complete.*] Good-bye, I know how I can slip away. There is a convent that will take me in. It is not a tower, it is only a convent, but I have long wanted to go there to lose my name and disappear. Sit down upon the throne and turn your face away. If you do not turn your face away, you will be afraid. [*The Queen goes out.*

[*Decima is seated upon the throne. A great crowd gathers outside the gates. A Bishop enters.*

Bishop. Your loyal people, your Majesty, offer you their homage. I bow before you in their name. Your royal will has spoken by the mouth of the Prime Minister — has filled them with gratitude. All misunderstandings are at an end, all has been settled by your condescension in bestowing your royal hand upon the Prime Minister. [*To crowd.*] Her Majesty, who has hitherto shut herself away from all men's eyes that she might pray for this kingdom undisturbed, will henceforth show herself to her people. [*To Player Queen.*] So beautiful a Queen need never fear the disobedience of her people [*shouts from crowd of* 'Never'].

Prime Minister [*entering hurriedly*]. I will explain all, your Majesty — there was nothing else to be done — this Bishop has been summoned to unite us [*seeing the Queen*]; but, sleep of Adam! — this — who is this?

Decima. Your emotion is too great for words. Do not try to speak.

Prime Minister. This — this . . .!

Decima [*standing up*]. I am Queen. I know what it is to be

Queen. If I were to say to you I had an enemy you would kill him — you would tear him in pieces, would you not? [*Shouts*: 'We would kill him', 'We would tear him in pieces', *etc.*] But I do not bid you kill any one — I bid you obey my husband when I have raised him to the throne. He is not of royal blood, but I choose to raise him to the throne. That is my will. Show me that you will obey him so long as I bid you to obey.   [*Great cheering.*

[*Septimus, who has been standing among the crowd, comes forward and takes the Prime Minister by the sleeve. Various persons kiss the hand of the supposed Queen.*

Septimus. My lord, that is not the Queen; that is my bad wife.
          [*Decima looks at them.*

Prime Minister. Did you see that? Did you see the devil in her eye? They are mad after her pretty face, and she knows it. They would not believe a word I say; there is nothing to be done till they cool.

Decima. Are all here my faithful servants?

Bishop. All, your Majesty.

Decima. All?

Prime Minister [*bowing low*]. All, your Majesty.

Decima [*singing*].

          She pulled the thread, and bit the thread
          And made a golden gown.

Hand me that plate. While I am eating I will have a good look at my new man.

[*The plate and a bottle of wine are handed to her. The bray of a donkey is heard and the Old Beggar is dragged in.*

Bishop. At last we have found this impostor out. He has been accepted by the whole nation as if he were the Voice of God. As if the crown could not be settled firmly on any head without his help. It's plain that he has been in league

with the conspirators, and believed that your Majesty had
been killed. He is keeping it up still. Look at his glassy eye.
But his madman airs won't help him now.

Prime Minister. Carry him to prison, we will hang him in the
morning. [*Shaking Septimus.*] Do you understand that there
has been a miracle, that God or the Fiend has spoken, and that
the crown is on her head for good, that fate has brayed on
that man's lips? [*Aloud.*] We will hang him in the morning.

Septimus. She is my wife.

Prime Minister. The crown has changed and there is no help
for it. Sleep of Adam, I must have that woman for wife.
The Oracle has settled that.

Septimus. She is my wife, she is my bad, flighty wife.

Prime Minister. Seize this man. He has been whispering
slanders against Her Majesty. Cast him beyond the borders
of the kingdom, and his players after him.

Decima. He must not return upon pain of death. He has
wronged me, and I will never look upon his face again.

Prime Minister. Away with him.

Decima. My good name is dearer than my life, but I will see
the players before they go.

Prime Minister. Sleep of Adam! What has she got into her
head? Fetch the players.

Decima [*picking up the mask of the sister of Noah*]. My loyal
subjects must forgive me if I hide my face — it is not yet
used to the light of day, it is a modest face. I will be much
happier if His Holiness will help me to tie the mask.

Prime Minister. The players come.

Enter Players, who all bow to the new Queen

Decima. They had some play they were to perform, but I will
make them dance instead, and after that they must be richly
rewarded.

Prime Minister. It shall be as you will.

Decima. You are banished and must not return upon pain of death, and yet not one of you shall be poorer because banished. That I promise. But you have lost one thing that I will not restore. A woman player has left you. Do not mourn her. She was a bad, headstrong, cruel woman, and seeks destruction somewhere and with some man she knows nothing of; such a woman they tell me that this mask would well become, this foolish, smiling face! Come, dance.

[*They dance, and at certain moments she cries* 'Good-bye, good-bye' *or else* 'Farewell'. *And she throws them money.*]

THE END

THE ONLY JEALOUSY OF EMER

THE ONLY JEALOUSY OF EMER

PERSONS IN THE PLAY

Three Musicians (*their faces made up to resemble masks*)
The Ghost of Cuchulain (*wearing a mask*)
The Figure of Cuchulain (*wearing a mask*)
Emer
Eithne Inguba } (*masked, or their faces made up to resemble masks*)
Woman of the Sidhe (*wearing a mask*)

Enter Musicians, who are dressed and made up as in 'At the Hawk's Well'. They have the same musical instruments, which can either be already upon the stage or be brought in by the First Musician before he stands in the centre with the cloth between his hands, or by a player when the cloth has been unfolded. The stage as before can be against the wall of any room, and the same black cloth can be used as in 'At the Hawk's Well'.

[*Song for the folding and unfolding of the cloth*]

First Musician.

 A woman's beauty is like a white
 Frail bird, like a white sea-bird alone
 At daybreak after stormy night
 Between two furrows upon the ploughed land:
 A sudden storm, and it was thrown
 Between dark furrows upon the ploughed land.
 How many centuries spent
 The sedentary soul
 In toils of measurement
 Beyond eagle or mole,
 Beyond hearing or seeing,

Or Archimedes' guess,
To raise into being
That loveliness?

A strange, unserviceable thing,
A fragile, exquisite, pale shell,
That the vast troubled waters bring
To the loud sands before day has broken.
The storm arose and suddenly fell
Amid the dark before day had broken.
What death? what discipline?
What bonds no man could unbind,
Being imagined within
The labyrinth of the mind,
What pursuing or fleeing,
What wounds, what bloody press,
Dragged into being
This loveliness?

[*When the cloth is folded again the Musicians take their place against the wall. The folding of the cloth shows on one side of the stage the curtained bed or litter on which lies a man in his grave-clothes. He wears an heroic mask. Another man with exactly similar clothes and mask crouches near the front. Emer is sitting beside the bed.*]

First Musician [*speaking*]. I call before the eyes a roof
With cross-beams darkened by smoke;
A fisher's net hangs from a beam,
A long oar lies against the wall.
I call up a poor fisher's house;
A man lies dead or swooning,
That amorous man,
That amorous, violent man, renowned Cuchulain,
Queen Emer at his side.

At her own bidding all the rest have gone;
But now one comes on hesitating feet,
Young Eithne Inguba, Cuchulain's mistress.
She stands a moment in the open door.
Beyond the open door the bitter sea,
The shining, bitter sea, is crying out,
[*singing*] White shell, white wing!
I will not choose for my friend
A frail, unserviceable thing
That drifts and dreams, and but knows
That waters are without end
And that wind blows.

Emer [*speaking*]. Come hither, come sit down beside the bed;
    You need not be afraid, for I myself
    Sent for you, Eithne Inguba.

Eithne Inguba.   No, Madam,
    I have too deeply wronged you to sit there.

Emer. Of all the people in the world we two,
    And we alone, may watch together here,
    Because we have loved him best.

Eithne Inguba.   And is he dead?

Emer. Although they have dressed him out in his grave-
    clothes
    And stretched his limbs, Cuchulain is not dead;
    The very heavens when that day's at hand,
    So that his death may not lack ceremony,
    Will throw out fires, and the earth grow red with blood.
    There shall not be a scullion but foreknows it
    Like the world's end.

Eithne Inguba.   How did he come to this?

Emer. Towards noon in the assembly of the kings
    He met with one who seemed a while most dear.
    The kings stood round; some quarrel was blown up;

He drove him out and killed him on the shore
At Baile's tree, and he who was so killed
Was his own son begot on some wild woman
When he was young, or so I have heard it said;
And thereupon, knowing what man he had killed,
And being mad with sorrow, he ran out;
And after, to his middle in the foam,
With shield before him and with sword in hand.
He fought the deathless sea. The kings looked on
And not a king dared stretch an arm, or even
Dared call his name, but all stood wondering
In that dumb stupor like cattle in a gale,
Until at last, as though he had fixed his eyes
On a new enemy, he waded out
Until the water had swept over him;
But the waves washed his senseless image up
And laid it at this door.

Eithne Inguba.　　　　　　How pale he looks!

Emer. He is not dead.

Eithne Inguba.　　　　　You have not kissed his lips
Nor laid his head upon your breast.

Emer.　　　　　　　　　　　It may be
An image has been put into his place,
A sea-borne log bewitched into his likeness,
Or some stark horseman grown too old to ride
Among the troops of Manannan, Son of the Sea,
Now that his joints are stiff.

Eithne Inguba.　　　　　Cry out his name.
All that are taken from our sight, they say,
Loiter amid the scenery of their lives
For certain hours or days, and should he hear
He might, being angry, drive the changeling out.

Emer. It is hard to make them hear amid their darkness,

And it is long since I could call him home;
I am but his wife, but if you cry aloud
With the sweet voice that is so dear to him
He cannot help but listen.

Eithne Inguba.   He loves me best,
Being his newest love, but in the end
Will love the woman best who loved him first
And loved him through the years when love seemed lost.

Emer. I have that hope, the hope that some day somewhere
We'll sit together at the hearth again.

Eithne Inguba. Women like me, the violent hour passed over,
Are flung into some corner like old nut-shells.
Cuchulain, listen.

Emer.   No, not yet, for first
I'll cover up his face to hide the sea;
And throw new logs upon the hearth and stir
The half-burnt logs until they break in flame.
Old Manannan's unbridled horses come
Out of the sea, and on their backs his horsemen;
But all the enchantments of the dreaming foam
Dread the hearth-fire.

> [*She pulls the curtains of the bed so as to hide the sick man's face, that the actor may change his mask unseen. She goes to one side of the platform and moves her hand as though putting logs on a fire and stirring it into a blaze. While she makes these movements the Musicians play, marking the movements with drum and flute perhaps.*
>
> *Having finished she stands beside the imaginary fire at a distance from Cuchulain and Eithne Inguba.*

                    Call on Cuchulain now.

Eithne Inguba. Can you not hear my voice?

Emer.   Bend over him;

Call out dear secrets till you have touched his heart,
If he lies there; and if he is not there,
Till you have made him jealous.

Eithne Inguba.   Cuchulain, listen.

Emer. Those words sound timidly; to be afraid
Because his wife is but three paces off,
When there is so great need, were but to prove
The man that chose you made but a poor choice:
We're but two women struggling with the sea.

Eithne Inguba. O my beloved, pardon me, that I
Have been ashamed. I thrust my shame away.
I have never sent a message or called out,
Scarce had a longing for your company
But you have known and come; and if indeed
You are lying there, stretch out your arms and speak;
Open your mouth and speak, for to this hour
My company has made you talkative.
What ails your tongue, or what has closed your ears?
Our passion had not chilled when we were parted
On the pale shore under the breaking dawn.
He cannot speak: or else his ears are closed
And no sound reaches him.

Emer.   Then kiss that image;
The pressure of your mouth upon his mouth
May reach him where he is.

Eithne Inguba [*starting back*].   It is no man.
I felt some evil thing that dried my heart
When my lips touched it.

Emer.   No, his body stirs;
The pressure of your mouth has called him home;
He has thrown the changeling out.

Eithne Inguba [*going further off*].   Look at that arm;
That arm is withered to the very socket.

Emer [*going up to the bed*]. What do you come for; and from
    where?

Figure of Cuchulain.   I have come
    From Manannan's court upon a bridleless horse.

Emer. What one among the Sidhe has dared to lie
    Upon Cuchulain's bed and take his image?

Figure of Cuchulain. I am named Bricriu — not the man — that
    Bricriu,
    Maker of discord among gods and men,
    Called Bricriu of the Sidhe.

Emer.   Come for what purpose?

Figure of Cuchulain [*sitting up, parting curtain and showing its
    distorted face, as Eithne Inguba goes out*]. I show my face,
    and everything he loves
    Must fly away.

Emer.   You people of the wind
    Are full of lying speech and mockery:
    I have not fled your face.

Figure of Cuchulain.   You are not loved.

Emer. And therefore have no dread to meet your eyes
    And to demand him of you.

Figure of Cuchulain.   For that I have come.
    You have but to pay the price and he is free.

Emer. Do the Sidhe bargain?

Figure of Cuchulain.   When they would free a captive
    They take in ransom a less valued thing.
    The fisher, when some knowledgeable man
    Restores to him his wife, or son, or daughter,
    Knows he must lose a boat or a net, or it may be
    The cow that gives his children milk; and some
    Have offered their own lives. I do not ask
    Your life, or any valuable thing;

You spoke but now of the mere chance that some day
You'd be the apple of his eye again
When old and ailing, but renounce that chance
And he shall live again.

Emer.   I do not question
But you have brought ill-luck on all he loves;
And now, because I am thrown beyond your power
Unless your words are lies, you come to bargain.

Figure of Cuchulain. You loved your mastery, when but newly
    married,
And I love mine for all my withered arm;
You have but to put yourself into that power
And he shall live again.

Emer.   No, never, never.

Figure of Cuchulain. You dare not be accursed, yet he has dared.

Emer. I have but two joyous thoughts, two things I prize,
A hope, a memory, and now you claim that hope.

Figure of Cuchulain. He'll never sit beside you at the hearth
Or make old bones, but die of wounds and toil
On some far shore or mountain, a strange woman
Beside his mattress.

Emer.   You ask for my one hope
That you may bring your curse on all about him.

Figure of Cuchulain. You've watched his loves and you have
    not been jealous,
Knowing that he would tire, but do those tire
That love the Sidhe? Come closer to the bed
That I may touch your eyes and give them sight.

   [*He touches her eyes with his left hand, the right being
   withered.*

Emer [*seeing the crouching Ghost of Cuchulain*]. My husband is
   there.

Figure of Cuchulain.   I have dissolved the dark
  That hid him from your eyes, but not that other
  That's hidden you from his.

Emer.   O husband, husband!

Figure of Cuchulain. He cannot hear — being shut off, a
    phantom
  That can neither touch, nor hear, nor see;
  The longing and the cries have drawn him hither.
  He heard no sound, heard no articulate sound;
  They could but banish rest, and make him dream,
  And in that dream, as do all dreaming shades
  Before they are accustomed to their freedom,
  He has taken his familiar form; and yet
  He crouches there not knowing where he is
  Or at whose side he is crouched.

    [*A Woman of the Sidhe has entered and stands a little inside
    the door.*

Emer.   Who is this woman?

Figure of Cuchulain. She has hurried from the Country-under-
    Wave
  And dreamed herself into that shape that he
  May glitter in her basket; for the Sidhe
  Are dexterous fishers and they fish for men
  With dreams upon the hook.

Emer.   And so that woman
  Has hid herself in this disguise and made
  Herself into a lie.

Figure of Cuchulain.   A dream is body;
  The dead move ever towards a dreamless youth
  And when they dream no more return no more;
  And those more holy shades that never lived
  But visit you in dreams.

Emer.   I know her sort.
They find our men asleep, weary with war,
Lap them in cloudy hair or kiss their lips;
Our men awake in ignorance of it all,
But when we take them in our arms at night
We cannot break their solitude.

                         [*She draws a knife from her girdle.*

Figure of Cuchulain.   No knife
Can wound that body of air. Be silent; listen;
I have not given you eyes and ears for nothing.

   [*The Woman of the Sidhe moves round the crouching Ghost of
    Cuchulain at front of stage in a dance that grows gradually
    quicker, as he slowly awakes. At moments she may drop her
    hair upon his head, but she does not kiss him. She is accom-
    panied by string and flute and drum. Her mask and clothes
    must suggest gold or bronze or brass or silver, so that she
    seems more an idol than a human being. This suggestion may
    be repeated in her movements. Her hair, too, must keep the
    metallic suggestion.*

Ghost of Cuchulain. Who is it stands before me there
Shedding such light from limb and hair
As when the moon, complete at last
With every labouring crescent past,
And lonely with extreme delight,
Flings out upon the fifteenth night?

Woman of the Sidhe. Because I long I am not complete.
What pulled your hands about your feet,
Pulled down your head upon your knees,
And hid your face?

Ghost of Cuchulain.   Old memories:
A woman in her happy youth
Before her man had broken troth,

Dead men and women. Memories
Have pulled my head upon my knees.

Woman of the Sidhe. Could you that have loved many a
    woman
  That did not reach beyond the human,
  Lacking a day to be complete,
  Love one that, though her heart can beat,
  Lacks it but by an hour or so?

Ghost of Cuchulain. I know you now, for long ago
  I met you on a cloudy hill
  Beside old thorn-trees and a well.
  A woman danced and a hawk flew,
  I held out arms and hands; but you,
  That now seem friendly, fled away,
  Half woman and half bird of prey.

Woman of the Sidhe. Hold out your arms and hands again;
  You were not so dumbfounded when
  I was that bird of prey, and yet
  I am all woman now.

Ghost of Cuchulain.   I am not
  The young and passionate man I was,
  And though that brilliant light surpass
  All crescent forms, my memories
  Weigh down my hands, abash my eyes.

Woman of the Sidhe. Then kiss my mouth. Though memory
  Be beauty's bitterest enemy
  I have no dread, for at my kiss
  Memory on the moment vanishes:
  Nothing but beauty can remain.

Ghost of Cuchulain. And shall I never know again
  Intricacies of blind remorse?

Woman of the Sidhe. Time shall seem to stay his course;
  When your mouth and my mouth meet

All my round shall be complete
Imagining all its circles run;
And there shall be oblivion
Even to quench Cuchulain's drouth,
Even to still that heart.

Ghost of Cuchulain.   Your mouth!

[*They are about to kiss, he turns away.*

O Emer, Emer!

Woman of the Sidhe. So then it is she
Made you impure with memory.

Ghost of Cuchulain. O Emer, Emer, there we stand;
Side by side and hand in hand
Tread the threshold of the house
As when our parents married us.

Woman of the Sidhe. Being among the dead you love her
That valued every slut above her
While you still lived.

Ghost of Cuchlain.   O my lost Emer!

Woman of the Sidhe. And there is not a loose-tongued schemer
But could draw you, if not dead,
From her table and her bed.
But what could make you fit to wive
With flesh and blood, being born to live
Where no one speaks of broken troth,
For all have washed out of their eyes
Wind-blown dirt of their memories
To improve their sight?

Ghost of Cuchulain.   Your mouth, your mouth!

[*She goes out followed by Ghost of Cuchulain.*

Figure of Cuchulain. Cry out that you renounce his love; make
    haste
And cry that you renounce his love for ever.

Emer. No, never will I give that cry.
Figure of Cuchulain.   Fool, fool!
  I am Fand's enemy come to thwart her will,
  And you stand gaping there. There is still time.
  Hear how the horses trample on the shore,
  Hear how they trample! She has mounted up.
  Cuchulain's not beside her in the chariot.
  There is still a moment left; cry out, cry out!
  Renounce him, and her power is at an end.
  Cuchulain's foot is on the chariot-step.
  Cry —
Emer.   I renounce Cuchulain's love for ever.

> [*The Figure of Cuchulain sinks back upon the bed, half-
> drawing the curtain. Eithne Inguba comes in and kneels by
> bed.*

Eithne Inguba. Come to me, my beloved, it is I.
  I, Eithne Inguba. Look! He is there.
  He has come back and moved upon the bed.
  And it is I that won him from the sea,
  That brought him back to life.
Emer.   Cuchulain wakes.

> [*The figure turns round. It once more wears the heroic mask.*

Cuchulain. Your arms, your arms! O Eithne Inguba,
  I have been in some strange place and am afraid.

> [*The First Musician comes to the front of stage, the others from
> each side, and unfold the cloth singing.*
> [*Song for the unfolding and folding of the cloth*]

The Musicians.
                    Why does your heart beat thus?
                    Plain to be understood,
                    I have met in a man's house
                    A statue of solitude,

Moving there and walking;
Its strange heart beating fast
For all our talking.
O still that heart at last.

O bitter reward
Of many a tragic tomb!
And we though astonished are dumb
Or give but a sigh and a word,
A passing word.

Although the door be shut
And all seem well enough,
Although wide world hold not
A man but will give you his love
The moment he has looked at you,
He that has loved the best
May turn from a statue
His too human breast.

O bitter reward
Of many a tragic tomb!
And we though astonished are dumb
Or give but a sigh and a word,
A passing word.

What makes your heart so beat?
What man is at your side?
When beauty is complete
Your own thought will have died
And danger not be diminished;
Dimmed at three-quarter light,
When moon's round is finished
The stars are out of sight.

O bitter reward
Of many a tragic tomb!
And we though astonished are dumb
Or give but a sigh and a word,
A passing word.

   [*When the cloth is folded again the stage is bare.*

THE END

THE RESURRECTION

TO
JUNZO SATO

THE RESURRECTION

PERSONS IN THE PLAY

The Hebrew   The Syrian

The Greek   Christ

Three Musicians

Before I had finished this play I saw that its subject-matter might make it unsuited for the public stage in England or in Ireland. I had begun it with an ordinary stage scene in the mind's eye, curtained walls, a window and door at back, a curtained door at left. I now changed the stage directions and wrote songs for the unfolding and folding of the curtain that it might be played in a studio or a drawing-room like my dance plays, or at the Peacock Theatre before a specially chosen audience. If it is played at the Peacock Theatre the Musicians may sing the opening and closing songs, as they pull apart or pull together the proscenium curtain; the whole stage may be hung with curtains with an opening at the left. While the play is in progress the Musicians will sit towards the right of the audience; if at the Peacock, on the step which separates the stage from the audience, or one on either side of the proscenium.

[*Song for the unfolding and folding of the curtain*]

I

I saw a staring virgin stand
Where holy Dionysus died,
And tear the heart out of his side,
And lay the heart upon her hand
And bear that beating heart away;
And then did all the Muses sing
Of Magnus Annus at the spring,
As though God's death were but a play.

II

Another Troy must rise and set,
Another lineage feed the crow,
Another Argo's painted prow
Drive to a flashier bauble yet.
The Roman Empire stood appalled:
It dropped the reins of peace and war
When that fierce virgin and her Star
Out of the fabulous darkness called.

[*The Hebrew is discovered alone upon the stage; he has a
sword or spear. The Musicians make faint drum-taps, or
sound a rattle; the Greek enters through the audience from
the left.*

The Hebrew. Did you find out what the noise was?

The Greek. Yes, I asked a Rabbi.

The Hebrew. Were you not afraid?

The Greek. How could he know that I am called a Christian?
I wore the cap I brought from Alexandria. He said the
followers of Dionysus were parading the streets with rattles
and drums; that such a thing had never happened in this
city before; that the Roman authorities were afraid to interfere. The followers of Dionysus have been out among the
fields tearing a goat to pieces and drinking its blood, and
are now wandering through the streets like a pack of
wolves. The mob was so terrified of their frenzy that it left
them alone, or, as seemed more likely, so busy hunting
Christians it had time for nothing else. I turned to go, but
he called me back and asked where I lived. When I said
outside the gates, he asked if it was true that the dead had
broken out of the cemeteries.

The Hebrew. We can keep the mob off for some minutes, long
enough for the Eleven to escape over the roofs. I shall

defend the narrow stair between this and the street until I am killed, then you will take my place. Why is not the Syrian here?

The Greek. I met him at the door and sent him on a message; he will be back before long.

The Hebrew. The three of us will be few enough for the work in hand.

The Greek [*glancing towards the opening at the left*]. What are they doing now?

The Hebrew. While you were down below, James brought a loaf out of a bag, and Nathanael found a skin of wine. They put them on the table. It was a long time since they had eaten anything. Then they began to speak in low voices, and John spoke of the last time they had eaten in that room.

The Greek. They were thirteen then.

The Hebrew. He said that Jesus divided bread and wine among them. When John had spoken they sat still, nobody eating or drinking. If you stand here you will see them. That is Peter close to the window. He has been quite motionless for a long time, his head upon his breast.

The Greek. Is it true that when the soldier asked him if he were a follower of Jesus he denied it?

The Hebrew. Yes, it is true. James told me. Peter told the others what he had done. But when the moment came they were all afraid. I must not blame. I might have been no braver. What are we all but dogs who have lost their master?

The Greek. Yet you and I if the mob come will die rather than let it up that stair.

The Hebrew. Ah! That is different. I am going to draw that curtain; they must not hear what I am going to say. [*He draws curtain.*]

The Greek. I know what is in your mind.

The Hebrew. They are afraid because they do not know what to think. When Jesus was taken they could no longer believe him the Messiah. We can find consolation, but for the Eleven it was always complete light or complete darkness.

The Greek. Because they are so much older.

The Hebrew. No, no. You have only to look into their faces to see they were intended to be saints. They are unfitted for anything else. What makes you laugh?

The Greek. Something I can see through the window. There, where I am pointing. There, at the end of the street. [*They stand together looking out over the heads of the audience.*]

The Hebrew. I cannot see anything.

The Greek. The hill.

The Hebrew. That is Calvary.

The Greek. And the three crosses on the top of it. [*He laughs again.*]

The Hebrew. Be quiet. You do not know what you are doing. You have gone out of your mind. You are laughing at Calvary.

The Greek. No, no. I am laughing because they thought they were nailing the hands of a living man upon the Cross, and all the time there was nothing there but a phantom.

The Hebrew. I saw him buried.

The Greek. We Greeks understand these things. No god has ever been buried; no god has ever suffered. Christ only seemed to be born, only seemed to eat, seemed to sleep, seemed to walk, seemed to die. I did not mean to tell you until I had proof.

The Hebrew. Proof?

The Greek. I shall have proof before nightfall.

The Hebrew. You talk wildly, but a masterless dog can bay the moon.

The Greek. No Jew can understand these things.

The Hebrew. It is you who do not understand. It is I and those men in there, perhaps, who begin to understand at last. He was nothing more than a man, the best man who ever lived. Nobody before him had so pitied human misery. He preached the coming of the Messiah because he thought the Messiah would take it all upon himself. Then some day when he was very tired, after a long journey perhaps, he thought that he himself was the Messiah. He thought it because of all destinies it seemed the most terrible.

The Greek. How could a man think himself the Messiah?

The Hebrew. It was always foretold that he would be born of a woman.

The Greek. To say that a god can be born of a woman, carried in her womb, fed upon her breast, washed as children are washed, is the most terrible blasphemy.

The Hebrew. If the Messiah were not born of a woman he could not take away the sins of man. Every sin starts a stream of suffering, but the Messiah takes it all away.

The Greek. Every man's sins are his property. Nobody else has a right to them.

The Hebrew. The Messiah is able to exhaust human suffering as though it were all gathered together in the spot of a burning-glass.

The Greek. That makes me shudder. The utmost possible suffering as an object of worship! You are morbid because your nation has no statues.

The Hebrew. What I have described is what I thought until three days ago.

The Greek. I say that there is nothing in the tomb.

The Hebrew. I saw him carried up the mountain and the tomb shut upon him.

The Greek. I have sent the Syrian to the tomb to prove that there is nothing there.

The Hebrew. You knew the danger we were all in and yet you weakened our guard?

The Greek. I have risked the apostles' lives and our own. What I have sent the Syrian to find out is more important.

The Hebrew. None of us are in our right mind to-day. I have got something in my own head that shocks me.

The Greek. Something you do not want to speak about?

The Hebrew. I am glad that he was not the Messiah; we might all have been deceived to our lives' end, or learnt the truth too late. One had to sacrifice everything that the divine suffering might, as it were, descend into one's mind and soul and make them pure. [*A sound of rattles and drums, at first in short bursts that come between sentences, but gradually growing continuous.*] One had to give up all worldly knowledge, all ambition, do nothing of one's own will. Only the divine could have any reality. God had to take complete possession. It must be a terrible thing when one is old, and the tomb round the corner, to think of all the ambitions one has put aside; to think, perhaps, a great deal about women. I want to marry and have children.

The Greek [*who is standing facing the audience, and looking out over their heads*]. It is the worshippers of Dionysus. They are under the window now. There is a group of women who carry upon their shoulders a bier with an image of the dead god upon it. No, they are not women. They are men dressed as women. I have seen something like it in Alexandria. They are all silent, as if something were going to happen. My God! What a spectacle! In Alexandria a few men paint their lips vermilion. They imitate women that they may attain in worship a woman's self-abandonment. No great harm comes of it — but here! Come and look for yourself.

The Hebrew. I will not look at such madmen.

The Greek. Though the music has stopped, some men are still dancing, and some of the dancers have gashed themselves with knives, imagining themselves, I suppose, at once the god and the Titans that murdered him. A little further off a man and woman are coupling in the middle of the street. She thinks the surrender to some man the dance threw into her arms may bring her god back to life. All are from the foreign quarter, to judge by face and costume, and are the most ignorant and excitable class of Asiatic Greeks, the dregs of the population. Such people suffer terribly and seek forgetfulness in monstrous ceremonies. Ah, that is what they were waiting for. The crowd has parted to make way for a singer. It is a girl. No, not a girl; a boy from the theatre. I know him. He acts girls' parts. He is dressed as a girl, but his finger-nails are gilded and his wig is made of gilded cords. He looks like a statue out of some temple. I remember something of the kind in Alexandria. Three days after the full moon, a full moon in March, they sing the death of the god and pray for his resurrection.

[*One of the Musicians sings the following song*]
>   Astrea's holy child!
>   A rattle in the wood
>   Where a Titan strode!
>   His rattle drew the child
>   Into that solitude.

Barrum, barrum, barrum [*Drum-taps accompany and follow the words*].

>   We wandering women,
>   Wives for all that come,
>   Tried to draw him home;
>   And every wandering woman
>   Beat upon a drum.

Barrum, barrum, barrum [*Drum-taps as before*].

> But the murderous Titans
> Where the woods grow dim
> Stood and waited him.
> The great hands of those Titans
> Tore limb from limb.

Barrum, barrum, barrum [*Drum-taps as before*].

> On virgin Astrea
> That can succour all
> Wandering women call;
> Call out to Astrea
> That the moon stood at the full.

Barrum, barrum, barrum [*Drum-taps as before*].

The Greek. I cannot think all that self-surrender and self-abasement is Greek, despite the Greek name of its god. When the goddess came to Achilles in the battle she did not interfere with his soul, she took him by his yellow hair. Lucretius thinks that the gods appear in the visions of the day and night but are indifferent to human fate; that, however, is the exaggeration of a Roman rhetorician. They can be discovered by contemplation, in their faces a high keen joy like the cry of a bat, and the man who lives heroically gives them the only earthly body that they covet. He, as it were, copies their gestures and their acts. What seems their indifference is but their eternal possession of themselves. Man, too, remains separate. He does not surrender his soul. He keeps his privacy.

[*Drum-taps to represent knocking at the door*]

The Hebrew. There is someone at the door, but I dare not open with that crowd in the street.

The Greek. You need not be afraid. The crowd has begun to move away. [*The Hebrew goes down into the audience towards the left.*] I deduce from our great philosophers that a god can overwhelm man with disaster, take health and wealth away, but man keeps his privacy. If that is the Syrian he may bring such confirmation that mankind will never forget his words.

The Hebrew [*from among the audience*]. It is the Syrian. There is something wrong. He is ill or drunk. [*He helps the Syrian on to the stage.*]

The Syrian. I am like a drunken man. I can hardly stand upon my feet. Something incredible has happened. I have run all the way.

The Hebrew. Well?

The Syrian. I must tell the Eleven at once. Are they still in there? Everybody must be told.

The Hebrew. What is it? Get your breath and speak.

The Syrian. I was on my way to the tomb. I met the Galilean women, Mary the mother of Jesus, Mary the mother of James, and the other women. The younger women were pale with excitement and began to speak all together. I did not know what they were saying; but Mary the mother of James said that they had been to the tomb at daybreak and found that it was empty.

The Greek. Ah!

The Hebrew. The tomb cannot be empty. I will not believe it.

The Syrian. At the door stood a man all shining, and cried out that Christ had arisen. [*Faint drum-taps and the faint sound of a rattle.*] As they came down the mountain a man stood suddenly at their side; that man was Christ himself. They stooped down and kissed his feet. Now stand out of my way that I may tell Peter and James and John.

The Hebrew [*standing before the curtained entrance of the inner room*]. I will not stand out of the way.

The Syrian. Did you hear what I said? Our master has arisen.

The Hebrew. I will not have the Eleven disturbed for the dreams of women.

The Greek. The women were not dreaming. They told you the truth, and yet this man is in the right. He is in charge here. We must all be convinced before we speak to the Eleven.

The Syrian. The Eleven will be able to judge better than we.

The Greek. Though we are so much younger we know more of the world than they do.

The Hebrew. If you told your story they would no more believe it than I do, but Peter's misery would be increased. I know him longer than you do and I know what would happen. Peter would remember that the women did not flinch; that not one among them denied her master; that the dream proved their love and faith. Then he would remember that he had lacked both, and imagine that John was looking at him. He would turn away and bury his head in his hands.

The Greek. I said that we must all be convinced, but there is another reason why you must not tell them anything. Somebody else is coming. I am certain that Jesus never had a human body; that he is a phantom and can pass through that wall; that he will so pass; that he will pass through this room; that he himself will speak to the apostles.

The Syrian. He is no phantom. We put a great stone over the mouth of the tomb, and the women say that it has been rolled back.

The Hebrew. The Romans heard yesterday that some of our people planned to steal the body, and to put abroad a story that Christ had arisen; and so escape the shame of our defeat. They probably stole it in the night.

The Syrian. The Romans put sentries at the tomb. The women found the sentries asleep. Christ had put them asleep that they might not see him move the stone.

The Greek. A hand without bones, without sinews, cannot move a stone.

The Syrian. What matter if it contradicts all human knowledge? — another Argo seeks another fleece, another Troy is sacked.

The Greek. Why are you laughing?

The Syrian. What is human knowledge?

The Greek. The knowledge that keeps the road from here to Persia free from robbers, that has built the beautiful humane cities, that has made the modern world, that stands between us and the barbarian.

The Syrian. But what if there is something it cannot explain, something more important than anything else?

The Greek. You talk as if you wanted the barbarian back.

The Syrian. What if there is always something that lies outside knowledge, outside order? What if at the moment when knowledge and order seem complete that something appears?   *[He has begun to laugh.*

The Hebrew. Stop laughing.

The Syrian. What if the irrational return? What if the circle begin again?

The Hebrew. Stop! He laughed when he saw Calvary through the window, and now you laugh.

The Greek. He too has lost control of himself.

The Hebrew. Stop, I tell you. *[Drums and rattles.]*

The Syrian. But I am not laughing. It is the people out there who are laughing.

The Hebrew. No, they are shaking rattles and beating drums.

The Syrian. I thought they were laughing. How horrible!

The Greek [looking out over heads of audience]. The worshippers of Dionysus are coming this way again. They have hidden their image of the dead god, and have begun their lunatic cry, 'God has arisen! God has arisen!'

[*The Musicians who have been saying* 'God has arisen!' *fall silent.*

They will cry 'God has arisen!' through all the streets of the city. They can make their god live and die at their pleasure; but why are they silent? They are dancing silently. They are coming nearer and nearer, dancing all the while, using some kind of ancient step unlike anything I have seen in Alexandria. They are almost under the window now.

The Hebrew. They have come back to mock us, because their god arises every year, whereas our god is dead for ever.

The Greek. How they roll their painted eyes as the dance grows quicker and quicker! They are under the window. Why are they all suddenly motionless? Why are all those unseeing eyes turned upon this house? Is there anything strange about this house?

The Hebrew. Somebody has come into the room.

The Greek. Where?

The Hebrew. I do not know; but I thought I heard a step.

The Greek. I knew that he would come.

The Hebrew. There is no one here. I shut the door at the foot of the steps.

The Greek. The curtain over there is moving.

The Hebrew. No, it is quite still, and besides there is nothing behind it but a blank wall.

The Greek. Look, look!

The Hebrew. Yes, it has begun to move. [*During what follows he backs in terror towards the left-hand corner of the stage.*]

The Greek. There is someone coming through it.

[*The figure of Christ wearing a recognisable but stylistic mask enters through the curtain. The Syrian slowly draws back*

*the curtain that shuts off the inner room where the apostles
are. The three young men are towards the left of the stage,
the figure of Christ is at the back towards the right.*

The Greek. It is the phantom of our master. Why are you
afraid? He has been crucified and buried, but only in semblance, and is among us once more. [*The Hebrew kneels.*]
There is nothing here but a phantom, it has no flesh and
blood. Because I know the truth I am not afraid. Look, I will
touch it. It may be hard under my hand like a statue — I have
heard of such things — or my hand may pass through it —
but there is no flesh and blood. [*He goes slowly up to the figure
and passes his hand over its side.*] The heart of a phantom is
beating! The heart of a phantom is beating! [*He screams. The
figure of Christ crosses the stage and passes into the inner room.*]

The Syrian. He is standing in the midst of them. Some are
afraid. He looks at Peter and James and John. He smiles.
He has parted the clothes at his side. He shows them his side.
There is a great wound there. Thomas has put his hand into
the wound. He has put his hand where the heart is.

The Greek. O Athens, Alexandria, Rome, something has come
to destroy you. The heart of a phantom is beating. Man has
begun to die. Your words are clear at last, O Heraclitus.
God and man die each other's life, live each other's death.

[*The Musicians rise, one or more singing the following words.
If the performance is in a private room or studio, they
unfold and fold a curtain as in my dance plays; if at the
Peacock Theatre, they draw the proscenium curtain across.*

I

In pity for man's darkening thought
He walked that room and issued thence
In Galilean turbulence;
The Babylonian starlight brought

A fabulous, formless darkness in;
Odour of blood when Christ was slain
Made all Platonic tolerance vain
And vain all Doric discipline.

II

Everything that man esteems
Endures a moment or a day:
Love's pleasure drives his love away,
The painter's brush consumes his dreams;
The herald's cry, the soldier's tread
Exhaust his glory and his might:
Whatever flames upon the night
Man's own resinous heart has fed.

THE END

THE WORDS UPON THE
WINDOW-PANE

THE WORDS UPON THE WINDOW-PANE

PERSONS IN THE PLAY

Dr. Trench   Cornelius Patterson

Miss Mackenna   Abraham Johnson

John Corbet   Mrs. Mallet

Mrs. Henderson

*A lodging-house room, an armchair, a little table in front of it,
chairs on either side. A fireplace and window. A kettle on the hob
and some tea-things on a dresser. A door to back and towards the
right. Through the door one can see an entrance hall. The sound of a
knocker. Miss Mackenna passes through and then she re-enters hall
together with John Corbet, a man of twenty-two or twenty-three,
and Dr. Trench, a man of between sixty and seventy.*

Dr. Trench [*in hall*]. May I introduce John Corbet, one of the
Corbets of Ballymoney, but at present a Cambridge
student? This is Miss Mackenna, our energetic secretary.

> [*They come into room, take off their coats.*

Miss Mackenna. I thought it better to let you in myself. This
country is still sufficiently medieval to make spiritualism an
undesirable theme for gossip. Give me your coats and hats.
I will put them in my own room. It is just across the hall.
Better sit down; your watches must be fast. Mrs. Henderson is lying down, as she always does before a séance. We
won't begin for ten minutes yet. [*She goes out with hats and
coats.*]

Dr. Trench. Miss Mackenna does all the real work of the
Dublin Spiritualists' Association. She did all the corre-
spondence with Mrs. Henderson, and persuaded the

155

landlady to let her this big room and a small room upstairs. We are a poor society and could not guarantee anything in advance. Mrs. Henderson has come from London at her own risk. She was born in Dublin and wants to spread the movement here. She lives very economically and does not expect a great deal. We all give what we can. A poor woman with the soul of an apostle.

John Corbet. Have there been many séances?

Dr. Trench. Only three so far.

John Corbet. I hope she will not mind my scepticism. I have looked into Myers' *Human Personality* and a wild book by Conan Doyle, but am unconvinced.

Dr. Trench. We all have to find the truth for ourselves. Lord Dunraven, then Lord Adare, introduced my father to the famous David Home. My father often told me that he saw David Home floating in the air in broad daylight, but I did not believe a word of it. I had to investigate for myself, and I was very hard to convince. Mrs. Piper, an American trance medium, not unlike Mrs. Henderson, convinced me.

John Corbet. A state of somnambulism and voices coming through her lips that purport to be those of dead persons?

Dr. Trench. Exactly: quite the best kind of mediumship if you want to establish the identity of a spirit. But do not expect too much. There has been a hostile influence.

John Corbet. You mean an evil spirit?

Dr. Trench. The poet Blake said that he never knew a bad man that had not something very good about him. I say a hostile influence, an influence that disturbed the last séance very seriously. I cannot tell you what happened, for I have not been at any of Mrs. Henderson's séances. Trance mediumship has nothing new to show me — I told the young people when they made me their President that I would probably stay at home, that I could get more out of

Emanuel Swedenborg than out of any séance. [*A knock.*]
That is probably old Cornelius Patterson; he thinks they
race horses and whippets in the other world, and is, so they
tell me, so anxious to find out if he is right that he is always
punctual. Miss Mackenna will keep him to herself for some
minutes. He gives her tips for Harold's Cross.

[*Miss Mackenna crosses to hall door and admits Cornelius
Patterson. She brings him to her room across the hall.*

John Corbet [*who has been wandering about*]. This is a wonderful
room for a lodging-house.

Dr. Trench. It was a private house until about fifty years ago.
It was not so near the town in those days, and there are
large stables at the back. Quite a number of notable people
lived here. Grattan was born upstairs; no, not Grattan,
Curran perhaps — I forget — but I do know that this house
in the early part of the eighteenth century belonged to
friends of Jonathan Swift, or rather of Stella. Swift chaffed
her in the *Journal to Stella* because of certain small sums of
money she lost at cards probably in this very room. That
was before Vanessa appeared upon the scene. It was a
country-house in those days, surrounded by trees and
gardens. Somebody cut some lines from a poem of hers
upon the window-pane — tradition says Stella herself. [*A
knock.*] Here they are, but you will hardly make them out
in this light. [*They stand in the window. Corbet stoops down to
see better. Miss Mackenna and Abraham Johnson enter and stand
near door.*]

Abraham Johnson. Where is Mrs. Henderson?

Miss Mackenna. She is upstairs; she always rests before a
séance.

Abraham Johnson. I must see her before the séance. I know
exactly what to do to get rid of this evil influence.

Miss Mackenna. If you go up to see her there will be no séance at all. She says it is dangerous even to think, much less to speak, of an evil influence.

Abraham Johnson. Then I shall speak to the President.

Miss Mackenna. Better talk the whole thing over first in my room. Mrs. Henderson says that there must be perfect harmony.

Abraham Johnson. Something must be done. The last séance was completely spoiled. [*A knock.*]

Miss Mackenna. That may be Mrs. Mallet; she is a very experienced spiritualist. Come to my room, old Patterson and some others are there already. [*She brings him to the other room and later crosses to hall door to admit Mrs. Mallet.*]

John Corbet. I know those lines well — they are part of a poem Stella wrote for Swift's fifty-fourth birthday. Only three poems of hers — and some lines she added to a poem of Swift's — have come down to us, but they are enough to prove her a better poet than Swift. Even those few words on the window make me think of a seventeenth-century poet, Donne or Crashaw. [*He quotes*]

'You taught how I might youth prolong
By knowing what is right and wrong,
How from my heart to bring supplies
Of lustre to my fading eyes.'

How strange that a celibate scholar, well on in life, should keep the love of two such women! He met Vanessa in London at the height of his political power. She followed him to Dublin. She loved him for nine years, perhaps died of love, but Stella loved him all her life.

Dr. Trench. I have shown that writing to several persons, and you are the first who has recognised the lines.

John Corbet. I am writing an essay on Swift and Stella for my

doctorate at Cambridge. I hope to prove that in Swift's day
men of intellect reached the height of their power — the
greatest position they ever attained in society and the State,
that everything great in Ireland and in our character, in
what remains of our architecture, comes from that day;
that we have kept its seal longer than England.

Dr. Trench. A tragic life: Bolingbroke, Harley, Ormonde, all
those great Ministers that were his friends, banished and
broken.

John Corbet. I do not think you can explain him in that way —
his tragedy had deeper foundations. His ideal order was the
Roman Senate, his ideal men Brutus and Cato. Such an
order and such men had seemed possible once more, but
the movement passed and he foresaw the ruin to come,
Democracy, Rousseau, the French Revolution; that is why
he hated the common run of men, — 'I hate lawyers, I hate
doctors,' he said, 'though I love Dr. So-and-so and Judge
So-and-so' — that is why he wrote *Gulliver*, that is why he
wore out his brain, that is why he felt *saeva indignatio*, that
is why he sleeps under the greatest epitaph in history. You
remember how it goes? It is almost finer in English than in
Latin: 'He has gone where fierce indignation can lacerate
his heart no more.'

   [*Abraham Johnson comes in, followed by Mrs. Mallet and
   Cornelius Patterson.*

Abraham Johnson. Something must be done, Dr. Trench, to
drive away the influence that has destroyed our séances.
I have come here week after week at considerable expense.
I am from Belfast. I am by profession a minister of the
Gospel, I do a great deal of work among the poor and
ignorant. I produce considerable effect by singing and
preaching, but I know that my effect should be much
greater than it is. My hope is that I shall be able to

communicate with the great Evangelist Moody. I want to ask him to stand invisible beside me when I speak or sing, and lay his hands upon my head and give me such a portion of his power that my work may be blessed as the work of Moody and Sankey was blessed.

Mrs. Mallet. What Mr. Johnson says about the hostile influence is quite true. The last two séances were completely spoilt. I am thinking of starting a tea-shop in Folkestone. I followed Mrs. Henderson to Dublin to get my husband's advice, but two spirits kept talking and would not let any other spirit say a word.

Dr. Trench. Did the spirits say the same thing and go through the same drama at both séances?

Mrs. Mallet. Yes — just as if they were characters in some kind of horrible play.

Dr. Trench. That is what I was afraid of.

Mrs. Mallet. My husband was drowned at sea ten years ago, but constantly speaks to me through Mrs. Henderson as if he were still alive. He advises about everything I do, and I am utterly lost if I cannot question him.

Cornelius Patterson. I never did like the Heaven they talk about in churches: but when somebody told me that Mrs. Mallet's husband ate and drank and went about with his favourite dog, I said to myself, 'That is the place for Corney Patterson'. I came here to find out if it was true, and I declare to God I have not heard one word about it.

Abraham Johnson. I ask you, Dr. Trench, as President of the Dublin Spiritualists' Association, to permit me to read the ritual of exorcism appointed for such occasions. After the last séance I copied it out of an old book in the library of Belfast University. I have it here.

[*He takes paper out of his pocket.*

Dr. Trench. The spirits are people like ourselves, we treat them as our guests and protect them from discourtesy and violence, and every exorcism is a curse or a threatened curse. We do not admit that there are evil spirits. Some spirits are earth-bound — they think they are still living and go over and over some action of their past lives, just as we go over and over some painful thought, except that where they are thought is reality. For instance, when a spirit which has died a violent death comes to a medium for the first time, it re-lives all the pains of death.

Mrs. Mallet. When my husband came for the first time the medium gasped and struggled as if she was drowning. It was terrible to watch.

Dr. Trench. Sometimes a spirit re-lives not the pain of death but some passionate or tragic moment of life. Swedenborg describes this and gives the reason for it. There is an incident of the kind in the *Odyssey*, and many in Eastern literature; the murderer repeats his murder, the robber his robbery, the lover his serenade, the soldier hears the trumpet once again. If I were a Catholic I would say that such spirits were in Purgatory. In vain do we write *requiescat in pace* upon the tomb, for they must suffer, and we in our turn must suffer until God gives peace. Such spirits do not often come to séances unless those séances are held in houses where those spirits lived, or where the event took place. This spirit which speaks those incomprehensible words and does not answer when spoken to is of such a nature. The more patient we are, the more quickly will it pass out of its passion and its remorse.

Abraham Johnson. I am still convinced that the spirit which disturbed the last séance is evil. If I may not exorcise it I will certainly pray for protection.

Dr. Trench. Mrs. Henderson's control, Lulu, is able and

experienced and can protect both medium and sitters, but it may help Lulu if you pray that the spirit find rest.

[*Abraham Johnson sits down and prays silently, moving his lips. Mrs. Henderson comes in with Miss Mackenna and others. Miss Mackenna shuts the door.*

Dr. Trench. Mrs. Henderson, may I introduce to you Mr. Corbet, a young man from Cambridge and a sceptic, who hopes that you will be able to convince him?

Mrs. Henderson. We were all sceptics once. He must not expect too much from a first séance. He must persevere.

[*She sits in the armchair, and the others begin to seat themselves. Miss Mackenna goes to John Corbet and they remain standing.*]

Miss Mackenna. I am glad that you are a sceptic.

John Corbet. I thought you were a spiritualist.

Miss Mackenna. I have seen a good many séances, and sometimes think it is all coincidence and thought-transference. [*She says this in a low voice.*] Then at other times I think as Dr. Trench does, and then I feel like Job — you know the quotation — the hair of my head stands up. A spirit passes before my face.

Mrs. Mallet. Turn the key, Dr. Trench, we don't want anybody blundering in here. [*Dr. Trench locks door.*] Come and sit here, Miss Mackenna.

Miss Mackenna. No, I am going to sit beside Mr. Corbet.

[*Corbet and Miss Mackenna sit down.*

John Corbet. You feel like Job to-night?

Miss Mackenna. I feel that something is going to happen, that is why I am glad that you are a sceptic.

John Corbet. You feel safer?

Miss Mackenna. Yes, safer.

Mrs. Henderson. I am glad to meet all my dear friends again and to welcome Mr. Corbet among us. As he is a stranger

I must explain that we do not call up spirits, we make the right conditions and they come. I do not know who is going to come; sometimes there are a great many and the guides choose between them. The guides try to send somebody for everybody but do not always succeed. If you want to speak to some dear friend who has passed over, do not be discouraged. If your friend cannot come this time, maybe he can next time. My control is a dear little girl called Lulu who died when she was five or six years old. She describes the spirits present and tells us what spirit wants to speak. Miss Mackenna, a verse of a hymn, please, the same we had last time, and will everyone join in the singing.

[*They sing the following lines from Hymn 564, Irish Church Hymnal.*

'Sun of my soul, Thou Saviour dear,
    It is not night if Thou be near:
    O may no earth-born cloud arise
    To hide Thee from Thy servant's eyes.'

[*Mrs. Henderson is leaning back in her chair asleep.*

Miss Mackenna [*to John Corbet*]. She always snores like that when she is going off.

Mrs. Henderson [*in a child's voice*]. Lulu so glad to see all her friends.

Mrs. Mallet. And we are glad you have come, Lulu.

Mrs. Henderson [*in a child's voice*]. Lulu glad to see new friend.

Miss Mackenna [*to John Corbet*]. She is speaking to you.

John Corbet. Thank you, Lulu.

Mrs. Henderson [*in a child's voice*]. You mustn't laugh at the way I talk.

John Corbet. I am not laughing, Lulu.

Mrs. Henderson [*in a child's voice*]. Nobody must laugh. Lulu does her best but can't say big long words. Lulu sees a tall man here, lots of hair on face [*Mrs. Henderson passes her hands over her cheeks and chin*], not much on the top of his head [*Mrs. Henderson passes her hand over the top of her head*], red necktie, and such a funny sort of pin.

Mrs. Mallet. Yes. . . . Yes. . . .

Mrs. Henderson [*in a child's voice*]. Pin like a horseshoe.

Mrs. Mallet. It's my husband.

Mrs. Henderson [*in a child's voice*]. He has a message.

Mrs. Mallet. Yes.

Mrs. Henderson [*in a child's voice*]. Lulu cannot hear. He is too far off. He has come near. Lulu can hear now. He says . . . he says, 'Drive that man away!' He is pointing to somebody in the corner, that corner over there. He says it is the bad man who spoilt everything last time. If they won't drive him away, Lulu will scream.

Miss Mackenna. That horrible spirit again.

Abraham Johnson. Last time he monopolised the séance.

Mrs. Mallet. He would not let anybody speak but himself.

Mrs. Henderson [*in a child's voice*]. They have driven that bad man away. Lulu sees a young lady.

Mrs. Mallet. Is not my husband here?

Mrs. Henderson [*in a child's voice*]. Man with funny pin gone away. Young lady here — Lulu thinks she must be at a fancy dress party, such funny clothes, hair all in curls — all bent down on floor near that old man with glasses.

Dr. Trench. No, I do not recognize her.

Mrs. Henderson [*in a child's voice*]. That bad man, that bad old man in the corner, they have let him come back. Lulu is going to scream. O. . . . O. . . . [*In a man's voice.*] How dare you write to her? How dare you ask if we were married? How dare you question her?

Dr. Trench. A soul in its agony — it cannot see us or hear us.

Mrs. Henderson [*upright and rigid, only her lips moving, and still in a man's voice*]. You sit crouching there. Did you not hear what I said? How dared you question her? I found you an ignorant little girl without intellect, without moral ambition. How many times did I not stay away from great men's houses, how many times forsake the Lord Treasurer, how many times neglect the business of the State that we might read Plutarch together!

[*Abraham Johnson half rises. Dr. Trench motions him to remain seated.*

Dr. Trench. Silence!

Abraham Johnson. But, Dr. Trench . . .

Dr. Trench. Hush — we can do nothing.

Mrs. Henderson [*speaking as before*]. I taught you to think in every situation of life not as Hester Vanhomrigh would think in that situation, but as Cato or Brutus would, and now you behave like some common slut with her ear against the keyhole.

John Corbet [*to Miss Mackenna*]. It is Swift, Jonathan Swift, talking to the woman he called Vanessa. She was christened Hester Vanhomrigh.

Mrs. Henderson [*in Vanessa's voice*]. I questioned her, Jonathan, because I love. Why have you let me spend hours in your company if you did not want me to love you? [*In Swift's voice.*] When I rebuilt Rome in your mind it was as though I walked its streets. [*In Vanessa's voice.*] Was that all, Jonathan? Was I nothing but a painter's canvas? [*In Swift's voice.*] My God, do you think it was easy? I was a man of strong passions and I had sworn never to marry. [*In Vanessa's voice.*] If you and she are not married, why should we not marry like other men and women? I loved you from the first moment when you came to my mother's house and began to teach me. I thought it would be enough to look at you, to speak to you, to hear you speak. I followed you to Ireland five years ago and I can bear it no longer. It is not enough to look, to speak, to hear. Jonathan, Jonathan, I am a woman, the women Brutus and Cato loved were not different. [*In Swift's voice.*] I have something in my blood that no child must inherit. I have constant attacks of dizziness; I pretend they come from a surfeit of fruit when I was a child. I had them in London. . . . There was a great doctor there, Dr. Arbuthnot; I told him of those attacks of dizziness, I told him of worse things. It was he who explained. There is a line of Dryden's. . . . [*In Vanessa's voice.*] O, I know — 'Great wits are sure to madness near allied'. If you had children, Jonathan, my blood would make them healthy. I will take your hand, I will lay it upon my heart — upon the Vanhomrigh blood that has been healthy for generations. [*Mrs. Henderson slowly raises her left hand.*] That is the first time you have touched my body, Jonathan. [*Mrs. Henderson stands up and remains rigid. In Swift's voice.*] What do I care if it be healthy? What do I care if it could make mine healthy? Am I to add another to the healthy rascaldom and knavery of the world? [*In Vanessa's voice.*] Look at me, Jonathan. Your arrogant intellect separates us. Give me both your hands. I will put them upon my breast. [*Mrs. Henderson raises her right hand to the level of her left and then raises both to her breast.*] O, it is white — white as the gambler's dice — white ivory dice. Think of the uncertainty. Perhaps a mad child — perhaps a rascal — perhaps a knave — perhaps not, Jonathan. The dice of the intellect are loaded, but I am the common ivory dice. [*Her hands are stretched out as though drawing somebody towards her.*] It is not my hands that draw you back. My hands are weak, they could not draw you back if you did not love as I love. You said that you have strong passions; that is true, Jonathan —

no man in Ireland is so passionate. That is why you need me, that is why you need children, nobody has greater need. You are growing old. An old man without children is very solitary. Even his friends, men as old as he, turn away, they turn towards the young, their children or their children's children. They cannot endure an old man like themselves. [*Mrs. Henderson moves away from the chair, her movements gradually growing convulsive.*] You are not too old for the dice, Jonathan, but a few years if you turn away will make you an old miserable childless man. [*In Swift's voice.*] O God, hear the prayer of Jonathan Swift, that afflicted man, and grant that he may leave to posterity nothing but his intellect that came to him from Heaven. [*In Vanessa's voice.*] Can you face solitude with that mind, Jonathan? [*Mrs. Henderson goes to the door, finds that it is closed.*] Dice, white ivory dice. [*In Swift's voice.*] My God, I am left alone with my enemy. Who locked the door, who locked me in with my enemy? [*Mrs. Henderson beats upon the door, sinks to the floor and then speaks as Lulu.*] Bad old man! Do not let him come back. Bad old man does not know he is dead. Lulu cannot find fathers, mothers, sons that have passed over. Power almost gone. [*Mrs. Mallet leads Mrs. Henderson, who seems very exhausted, back to her chair. She is still asleep. She speaks again as Lulu.*] Another verse of hymn. Everybody sing. Hymn will bring good influence.

[*They sing*]

'If some poor wandering child of Thine
    Have spurned to-day the voice divine,
    Now, Lord, the gracious work begin;
    Let him no more lie down in sin.'

[*During the hymn Mrs. Henderson has been murmuring
    'Stella', but the singing has almost drowned her voice. The*

singers draw one another's attention to the fact that she is
speaking. The singing stops.]

Dr. Trench. I thought she was speaking.

Mrs. Mallet. I saw her lips move.

Dr. Trench. She would be more comfortable with a cushion,
but we might wake her.

Mrs. Mallet. Nothing can wake her out of a trance like that
until she wakes up herself. [*She brings a cushion and she and*
Dr. Trench put Mrs. Henderson into a more comfortable
position.]

Mrs. Henderson [*in Swift's voice*]. Stella.

Miss Mackenna [*to John Corbet*]. Did you hear that? She said
'Stella'.

John Corbet. Vanessa has gone, Stella has taken her place.

Miss Mackenna. Did you notice the change while we were
singing? The new influence in the room?

John Corbet. I thought I did, but it must have been fancy.

Mrs. Mallet. Hush!

Mrs. Henderson [*in Swift's voice*]. Have I wronged you, beloved
Stella? Are you unhappy? You have no children, you have
no lover, you have no husband. A cross and ageing man for
friend — nothing but that. But no, do not answer — you
have answered already in that poem you wrote for my last
birthday. With what scorn you speak of the common lot of
women 'with no endowments but a face —'

> 'Before the thirtieth year of life
> A maid forlorn or hated wife.'

It is the thought of the great Chrysostom who wrote in a
famous passage that women loved according to the soul,
loved as saints can love, keep their beauty longer, have
greater happiness than women loved according to the flesh.
That thought has comforted me, but it is a terrible thing

to be responsible for another's happiness. There are moments when I doubt, when I think Chrysostom may have been wrong. But now I have your poem to drive doubt away. You have addressed me in these noble words:

> 'You taught how I might youth prolong
> By knowing what is right and wrong;
> How from my heart to bring supplies
> Of lustre to my fading eyes;
> How soon a beauteous mind repairs
> The loss of chang'd or falling hairs;
> How wit and virtue from within
> Can spread a smoothness o'er the skin.'

John Corbet. The words upon the window-pane!

Mrs. Henderson [*in Swift's voice*]. Then, because you understand that I am afraid of solitude, afraid of outliving my friends — and myself — you comfort me in that last verse — you overpraise my moral nature when you attribute to it a rich mantle, but O how touching those words which describe your love:

> 'Late dying may you cast a shred
> Of that rich mantle o'er my head;
> To bear with dignity my sorrow,
> One day alone, then die to-morrow.'

Yes, you will close my eyes, Stella. O, you will live long after me, dear Stella, for you are still a young woman, but you will close my eyes. [*Mrs. Henderson sinks back in chair and speaks as Lulu.*] Bad old man gone. Power all used up. Lulu can do no more. Good-bye, friends. [*Mrs. Henderson, speaking in her own voice.*] Go away, go away! [*She wakes.*] I saw him a moment ago, has he spoilt the séance again?

Mrs. Mallet. Yes, Mrs. Henderson, my husband came, but he was driven away.

Dr. Trench. Mrs. Henderson is very tired. We must leave her to rest. [*To Mrs. Henderson.*] You did your best and nobody can do more than that. [*He takes out money.*]

Mrs. Henderson. No. . . . No. . . . I cannot take any money, not after a séance like that.

Dr. Trench. Of course you must take it, Mrs. Henderson' [*He puts money on table, and Mrs. Henderson gives a furtive glance to see how much it is. She does the same as each sitter lays down his or her money.*]

Mrs. Mallet. A bad séance is just as exhausting as a good séance, and you must be paid.

Mrs. Henderson. No. . . . No. . . . Please don't. It is very wrong to take money for such a failure.

[*Mrs. Mallet lays down money.*

Cornelius Patterson. A jockey is paid whether he wins or not. [*He lays down money.*]

Miss Mackenna. That spirit rather thrilled me. [*She lays down money.*]

Mrs. Henderson. If you insist, I must take it.

Abraham Johnson. I shall pray for you to-night. I shall ask God to bless and protect your séances. [*He lays down money.*]

[*All go out except John Corbet and Mrs. Henderson.*

John Corbet. I know you are tired, Mrs. Henderson, but I must speak to you. I have been deeply moved by what I have heard. This is my contribution to prove that I am satisfied, completely satisfied. [*He puts a note on the table.*]

Mrs. Henderson. A pound note — nobody ever gives me more than ten shillings, and yet the séance was a failure.

John Corbet [*sitting down near Mrs. Henderson*]. When I say I am satisfied I do not mean that I am convinced it was the work of spirits. I prefer to think that you created it all, that you are an accomplished actress and scholar. In my essay for my Cambridge doctorate I examine all the explanations of Swift's celibacy offered by his biographers and prove that the explanation you selected was the only plausible one. But there is something I must ask you. Swift was the chief representative of the intellect of his epoch, that arrogant intellect free at last from superstition. He foresaw its collapse. He foresaw Democracy, he must have dreaded the future. Did he refuse to beget children because of that dread? Was Swift mad? Or was it the intellect itself that was mad?

Mrs. Henderson. Who are you talking of, sir?

John Corbet. Swift, of course.

Mrs. Henderson. Swift? I do not know anybody called Swift.

John Corbet. Jonathan Swift, whose spirit seemed to be present to-night.

Mrs. Henderson. What? That dirty old man?

John Corbet. He was neither old nor dirty when Stella and Vanessa loved him.

Mrs. Henderson. I saw him very clearly just as I woke up. His clothes were dirty, his face covered with boils. Some disease had made one of his eyes swell up, it stood out from his face like a hen's egg.

John Corbet. He looked like that in his old age. Stella had been dead a long time. His brain had gone, his friends had deserted him. The man appointed to take care of him beat him to keep him quiet.

Mrs. Henderson. Now they are old, now they are young. They change all in a moment as their thought changes. It is sometimes a terrible thing to be out of the body, God help us all.

Dr. Trench [*at doorway*]. Come along, Corbet, Mrs. Henderson is tired out.

John Corbet. Good-bye, Mrs. Henderson. [*He goes out with*

Dr. Trench. All the sitters except Miss Mackenna, who has returned to her room, pass along the passage on their way to the front door. Mrs. Henderson counts the money, finds her purse, which is in a vase on the mantelpiece, and puts the money in it.]

Mrs. Henderson. How tired I am! I'd be the better of a cup of tea. [*She finds the teapot and puts kettle on fire, and then as she crouches down by the hearth suddenly lifts up her hands and counts her fingers, speaking in Swift's voice.*] Five great Ministers that were my friends are gone, ten great Ministers that were my friends are gone. I have not fingers enough to count the great Ministers that were my friends and that are gone. [*She wakes with a start and speaks in her own voice.*] Where did I put that tea-caddy? Ah! there it is. And there should be a cup and saucer. [*She finds the saucer.*] But where's the cup? [*She moves aimlessly about the stage and then, letting the saucer fall and break, speaks in Swift's voice.*] Perish the day on which I was born!

THE END

A FULL MOON IN MARCH

A FULL MOON IN MARCH

PERSONS IN THE PLAY

First Attendant   The Queen
Second Attendant   The Swineherd

The Swineherd wears a half-savage mask covering the upper part of his face. He is bearded. When the inner curtain rises for the second time the player who has hitherto taken the part of the Queen is replaced by a dancer.

When the stage curtain rises, two Attendants, an elderly woman and a young man, are discovered standing before an inner curtain.

First Attendant. What do we do?
  What part do we take?
  What did he say?
Second Attendant. Join when we like,
  Singing or speaking.
First Attendant. Before the curtain rises on the play?
Second Attendant. Before it rises.
First Attendant. What do we sing?
Second Attendant. 'Sing anything, sing any old thing,' said he.
First Attendant. Come then and sing about the dung of swine.

> [*They slowly part the inner curtain. The Second Attendant sings — the First Attendant may join in the singing at the end of the first or second verse. The First Attendant has a soprano, the Second a bass voice.*

Second Attendant.

> Every loutish lad in love
> Thinks his wisdom great enough,
> *What cares love for this and that?*

175

To make all his parish stare,
As though Pythagoras wandered there.
Crown of gold or dung of swine.

Should old Pythagoras fall in love
Little may he boast thereof.
What cares love for this and that?
Days go by in foolishness.
O how great their sweetness is!
Crown of gold or dung of swine.

Open wide those gleaming eyes,
That can make the loutish wise.
What cares love for this and that?
Make a leader of the schools
Thank the Lord, all men are fools.
Crown of gold or dung of swine.

[*They sit at one side of stage near audience. If they are musicians, they have beside them drum, flute, and zither. The Queen is discovered seated and veiled.*

The Queen [*stretching and yawning*]. What man is at the door?

Second Attendant. Nobody, Queen.

The Queen. Some man has come, some terrifying man,
For I have yawned and stretched myself three times.
Admit him, Captain of the Guard. . . .

Second Attendant [*speaking as Captain of the Guard*]. He comes.

Enter the Swineherd

The Swineherd. The beggars of my country say that he
That sings you best shall take you for a wife.

The Queen. He that best sings his passion.

The Swineherd. And they say
The kingdom is added to the gift.

The Queen.   I swore it.

The Swineherd. But what if some blind aged cripple sing
  Better than wholesome men?

The Queen.   Some I reject.
  Some I have punished for their impudence.
  None I abhor can sing.

The Swineherd.   So that's the catch.
  Queen, look at me, look long at these foul rags,
  At hair more foul and ragged than my rags;
  Look on my scratched foul flesh. Have I not come
  Through dust and mire? There in the dust and mire
  Beasts scratched my flesh; my memory too is gone,
  Because great solitudes have driven me mad.
  But when I look into a stream, the face
  That trembles upon the surface makes me think
  My origin more foul than rag or flesh.

The Queen. But you have passed through perils for my sake;
  Come a great distance. I permit the song.

The Swineherd. Kingdom and lady, if I sing the best?
  But who decides?

The Queen.   I and my heart decide.
  We say that song is best that moves us most.
  No song has moved us yet.

The Swineherd.   You must be won
  At a full moon in March, those beggars say.
  That moon has come, but I am here alone.

The Queen. No other man has come.

The Swineherd.   The moon is full.

The Queen. Remember through what perils you have come;
  That I am crueller than solitude,
  Forest or beast. Some I have killed or maimed
  Because their singing put me in a rage,
  And some because they came at all. Men hold

That woman's beauty is a kindly thing,
But they that call me cruel speak the truth,
Cruel as the winter of virginity.
But for a reason that I cannot guess
I would not harm you. Go before I change.
Why do you stand, your chin upon your breast?

The Swineherd. My mind is running on our marriage night,
Imagining all from the first touch and kiss.

The Queen. What gives you that strange confidence? What makes
You think that you can move my heart and me?

The Swineherd. Because I look upon you without fear.

The Queen. A lover in railing or in flattery said
God only looks upon me without fear.

The Swineherd. Desiring cruelty, he made you cruel.
I shall embrace body and cruelty,
Desiring both as though I had made both.

The Queen. One question more. You bring like all the rest
Some novel simile, some wild hyperbole
Praising my beauty?

The Swineherd.   My memory has returned.
I tended swine, when I first heard your name.
I rolled among the dung of swine and laughed.
What do I know of beauty?

The Queen.   Sing the best
And you are not a swineherd, but a king.

The Swineherd. What do I know of kingdoms?
                   [*Snapping his fingers*] That for kingdoms

The Queen. If trembling of my limbs or sudden tears
Proclaim your song beyond denial best,
I leave these corridors, this ancient house,
A famous throne, the reverence of servants —
What do I gain?

The Swineherd.   A song — the night of love,
  An ignorant forest and the dung of swine.

                        [Queen leaves throne and comes down stage.

The Queen. All here have heard the man and all have judged.
  I led him, that I might not seem unjust,
  From point to point, established in all eyes
  That he came hither not to sing but to heap
  Complexities of insult upon my head.

The Swineherd. She shall bring forth her farrow in the dung.
  But first my song — what nonsense shall I sing?

The Queen. Send for the headsman, Captain of the Guard.

Second Attendant [*speaking as Captain of the Guard*]. I have
  already sent. He stands without.

The Queen. I owe my thanks to God that this foul wretch,
  Foul in his rags, his origin, his speech,
  In spite of all his daring has not dared
  Ask me to drop my veil. Insulted ears
  Have heard and shuddered, but my face is pure.
  Had it but known the insult of his eyes
  I had torn it with these nails.

The Swineherd [*going up stage*]. Why should I ask?
  What do those features matter? When I set out
  I picked a number on the roulette wheel.
  I trust the wheel, as every lover must.

The Queen. Pray, if your savagery has learnt to pray,
  For in a moment they will lead you out
  Then bring your severed head.

The Swineherd.   My severed head.

                                   [Laughs.

There is a story in my country of a woman
That stood all bathed in blood — a drop of blood
Entered her womb and there begat a child.

The Queen. A severed head! She took it in her hands;
  She stood all bathed in blood; the blood begat.
  O foul, foul, foul!

The Swineherd.   She sank in bridal sleep.

The Queen. Her body in that sleep conceived a child.
  Begone! I shall not see your face again.

    [*She turns towards him, her back to the audience, and slowly
        drops her veil.*
    The Attendants close the inner curtain.

Second Attendant. What do we sing?

First Attendant.   An ancient Irish Queen
  That stuck a head upon a stake.

Second Attendant.   Her lover's head;
  But that's a different queen, a different story.

First Attendant.

           He had famished in a wilderness,
           Braved lions for my sake,
           And all men lie that say that I
           Bade that swordsman take
           His head from off his body
           And set it on a stake.

           He swore to sing my beauty
           Though death itself forbade.
           They lie that say, in mockery
           Of all that lovers said,
           Or in mere woman's cruelty
           I bade them fetch his head.

               [*They begin to part the inner curtain.*

           O what innkeeper's daughter
           Shared the Byzantine crown?
           Girls that have governed cities,

        Or burned great cities down,
        Have bedded with their fancy-man
        Whether a king or clown;

        Gave their bodies, emptied purses
        For praise of clown or king,
        Gave all the love that women know!
        O they had their fling,
        But never stood before a stake
        And heard the dead lips sing.

[*The Queen is discovered standing exactly as before, the dropped veil at her side, but she holds above her head the severed head of the Swineherd. Her hands are red. There are red blotches upon her dress, not realistically represented: red gloves, some pattern of red cloth.*

First Attendant. Her lips are moving.
Second Attendant.   She has begun to sing.
First Attendant. I cannot hear what she is singing.
  Ah, now I can hear.

           [*singing as Queen*]
        Child and darling, hear my song,
        Never cry I did you wrong;
        Cry that wrong came not from me
        But my virgin cruelty.
        Great my love before you came,
        Greater when I loved in shame,
        Greatest when there broke from me
        Storm of virgin cruelty.

[*The Queen dances to drum-taps and in the dance lays the head upon the throne.*

Second Attendant. She is waiting.
First Attendant.   She is waiting for his song.

The song he has come so many miles to sing.
She has forgotten that no dead man sings.

Second Attendant [*laughs softly as Head*]. He has begun to laugh.

First Attendant.   No; he has begun to sing.

Second Attendant [*singing as Head*].

> I sing a song of Jack and Jill.
> Jill had murdered Jack;
> *The moon shone brightly;*
> Ran up the hill, and round the hill,
> Round the hill and back.
> *A full moon in March.*
>
> Jack had a hollow heart, for Jill
> Had hung his heart on high;
> *The moon shone brightly;*
> Had hung his heart beyond the hill,
> A-twinkle in the sky.
> *A full moon in March.*

[*The Queen in her dance moves away from the head, alluring and refusing.*

First Attendant [*laughs as Queen*].

Second Attendant. She is laughing. How can she laugh, Loving the dead?

First Attendant. She is crazy. That is why she is laughing.

            [*Laughs again as Queen.*

[*Queen takes up the head and lays it upon the ground. She dances before it — a dance of adoration. She takes the head up and dances with it to drum-taps, which grow quicker and quicker. As the drum-taps approach their climax, she presses her lips to the lips of the head. Her body shivers to very rapid drum-taps. The drum-taps cease. She sinks slowly*

*down, holding the head to her breast. The Attendants close
inner curtain, singing, and then stand one on either side while
the stage curtain descends.*

Second Attendant. Why must those holy, haughty feet descend
  From emblematic niches, and what hand
  Ran that delicate raddle through their white?
  My heart is broken, yet must understand.
  What do they seek for? Why must they descend?

First Attendant. For desecration and the lover's night.

Second Attendant. I cannot face that emblem of the moon
  Nor eyelids that the unmixed heavens dart,
  Nor stand upon my feet, so great a fright
  Descends upon my savage, sunlit heart.
  What can she lack whose emblem is the moon?

First Attendant. But desecration and the lover's night.

Second Attendant. Delight my heart with sound; speak yet
    again.
  But look and look with understanding eyes
  Upon the pitchers that they carry; tight
  Therein all time's completed treasure is:
  What do they lack? O cry it out again.

First Attendant. Their desecration and the lover's night.

THE END

THE HERNE'S EGG

THE HERNE'S EGG

PERSONS IN THE PLAY

Congal, *King of Connacht*
Aedh, *King of Tara*
Corney, *Attracta's servant*
Mike, Pat, Malachi, Mathias, Peter,
  John, *Connacht soldiers*

Attracta, *A Priestess*
Kate, Agnes, Mary, *Friends
  of Attracta*
A Fool
Soldiers of Tara

SCENE I

*Mist and rocks; high up on backcloth a rock, its base hidden in mist;
on this rock stands a great herne. All should be suggested, not painted
realistically. Many men fighting with swords and shields, but sword
and sword, shield and sword, never meet. The men move rhythmic-
ally as if in a dance; when swords approach one another cymbals
clash; when swords and shields approach drums boom. The battle
flows out at one side; two Kings are left fighting in the centre of the
stage; the battle returns and flows out at the other side. The two
Kings remain, but are now face to face and motionless. They are
Congal, King of Connacht, and Aedh, King of Tara.*

Congal. How many men have you lost?
Aedh. Some five-and-twenty men.
Congal. No need to ask my losses.
Aedh. Your losses equal mine.
Congal. They always have and must.
Aedh. Skill, strength, arms matched.
Congal. Where is the wound this time?
Aedh. There, left shoulder-blade.
Congal. Here, right shoulder-blade.
Aedh. Yet we have fought all day.

187

Congal. This is our fiftieth battle.
Aedh. And all were perfect battles.
Congal. Come, sit upon this stone.
  Come and take breath awhile.
Aedh. From daybreak until noon,
  Hopping among these rocks.
Congal. Nothing to eat or drink.
Aedh. A story is running round
  Concerning two rich fleas.
Congal. We hop like fleas, but war
  Has taken all our riches.
Aedh. Rich, and rich, so rich that they
  Retired and bought a dog.
Congal. Finish the tale and say
  What kind of dog they bought.
Aedh. Heaven knows.
Congal.   You must have thought
  What kind of dog they bought.
Aedh. Heaven knows.
Congal.   Unless you say,
  I'll up and fight all day.
Aedh. A fat, square, lazy dog,
  No sort of scratching dog.

SCENE II

The same place as in previous scene. Corney enters, leading a Donkey, a donkey on wheels like a child's toy, but life-size.

Corney. A tough, rough mane, a tougher skin,
  Strong legs though somewhat thin,
  A strong body, a level line
  Up to the neck along the spine.
  All good points, and all are spoilt
  By that rapscallion Clareman's eye!

What if before your present shape
You could slit purses and break hearts,
You are a donkey now, a chattel,
A taker of blows, not a giver of blows.
No tricks, you're not in County Clare,
No, not one kick upon the shin.

   [Congal, Pat, Mike, James, Mathias, Peter, John, enter, in
     the dress and arms of the previous scene but without shields.

Congal. I have learned of a great hernery
  Among these rocks, and that a woman,
  Prophetess or priestess, named Attracta,
  Owns it — take this donkey and man,
  Look for the creels, pack them with eggs.

Mike. Manners!

Congal.   This man is in the right.
  I will ask Attracta for the eggs
  If you will tell how to summon her.

Corney. A flute lies there upon the rock
  Carved out of a herne's thigh.
  Go pick it up and play the tune
  My mother calls 'The Great Herne's Feather'.
  If she has a mind to come, she will come.

Congal. That's a queer way of summoning.

Corney. This is a holy place and queer;
  But if you do not know that tune,
  Custom permits that I should play it,
  But you must cross my hand with silver.

            [Congal gives money, and Corney plays flute.

Congal. Go pack the donkey creels with eggs.

          [All go out except Congal and Mike. Attracta enters.

Attracta. For a thousand or ten thousand years,
  For who can count so many years,

Some woman has lived among these rocks,
The Great Herne's bride, or promised bride,
And when a visitor has played the flute
Has come or not. What would you ask?
Congal. Tara and I have made a peace;
	Our fiftieth battle fought, there is need
	Of preparation for the next;
	He and all his principal men,
	I and all my principal men,
	Take supper at his principal house
	This night, in his principal city, Tara,
	And we have set our minds upon
	A certain novelty or relish.
Mike. Herne's eggs.
Congal.				This man declares our need;
	A donkey, both creels packed with eggs,
	Somebody that knows the mind of a donkey
	For donkey-boy.
Attracta.				Custom forbids:
	Only the women of these rocks,
	Betrothed or married to the Herne,
	The god or ancestor of hernes,
	Can eat, handle, or look upon those eggs.
Congal. Refused! Must old campaigners lack
	The one sole dish that takes their fancy,
	My cooks what might have proved their skill,
	Because a woman thinks that she
	Is promised or married to a bird?
Mike. Mad!
Congal.		Mad! This man is right,
	But you are not to blame for that.
	Women thrown into despair
	By the winter of their virginity

Take its abominable snow,
As boys take common snow, and make
An image of god or bird or beast
To feed their sensuality:
Ovid had a literal mind,
And though he sang it neither knew
What lonely lust dragged down the gold
That crept on Danae's lap, nor knew
What rose against the moony feathers
When Leda lay upon the grass.

Attracta. There is no reality but the Great Herne.

Mike. The cure.

Congal.   Why, that is easy said;
An old campaigner is the cure
For everything that woman dreams —
Even I myself, had I but time.

Mike. Seven men.

Congal.   This man of learning means
That not a weather-stained, war-battered
Old campaigner such as I, —
But seven men packed into a day
Or dawdled out through seven years—
Are needed to melt down the snow
That's fallen among these wintry rocks.

Attracta. There is no happiness but the Great Herne.

Congal. It may be that life is suffering,
But youth that has not yet known pleasure
Has not the right to say so; pick,
Or be picked by seven men,
And we shall talk it out again.

Attracta. Being betrothed to the Great Herne
I know what may be known: I burn
Not in the flesh but in the mind;

Chosen out of all my kind
That I may lie in a blazing bed
And a bird take my maidenhead,
To the unbegotten I return,
All a womb and a funeral urn.

[*Enter Corney, Pat, James, Mathias, etc., with Donkey. A
creel packed with eggs is painted upon the side of the
Donkey.*

Corney. Think of yourself; think of the songs:
Bride of the Herne, and the Great Herne's bride,
Grow terrible: go into a trance.

Attracta. Stop!

Corney.　　　Bring the god out of your gut;
Stand there asleep until the rascals
Wriggle upon his beak like eels.

Attracta. Stop!

Corney.　　　The country calls them rascals,
I, sacrilegious rascals that have taken
Every new-laid egg in the hernery.

Attracta. Stop! When have I permitted you
To say what I may, or may not do?
But you and your donkey must obey
All big men who can say their say.

Congal. And bid him keep a civil tongue.

Attracta. Those eggs are stolen from the god.
It is but right that you hear said
A curse so ancient that no man
Can say who made it, or any thing at all
But that it was nailed upon a post
Before a herne had stood on one leg.

Corney. Hernes must stand on one leg when they fish
In honour of the bird who made it.

'This they nailed upon a post,
On the night my leg was lost,'
Said the old, old herne that had but one leg.

'He that a herne's egg dare steal
Shall be changed into a fool,'
Said the old, old herne that had but one leg.

'And to end his fool breath
At a fool's hand meet his death,'
Said the old, old herne that had but one leg.

I think it was the Great Herne made it,
Pretending that he had but the one leg
To fool us all; but Great Herne or another
It has not failed these thousand years.

Congal. That I shall live and die a fool,
And die upon some battlefield
At some fool's hand, is but natural,
And needs no curse to bring it.

Mike.   Pickled!

Congal. He says that I am an old campaigner,
Robber of sheepfolds and cattle trucks,
So cursed from morning until midnight
There is not a quarter of an inch
To plaster a new curse upon.

Corney.   Luck!

Congal. Adds that your luck begins when you
Recall that though we took those eggs
We paid with good advice; and then
Take to your bosom seven men.

   [*Congal, Mike, Corney, Mathias, James, and Donkey go out.
      Enter timidly three girls, Kate, Agnes, Mary.*

Mary. Have all those fierce men gone?

Attracta. All those fierce men have gone.

Agnes. But they will come again?

Attracta. No, never again.

Kate. We bring three presents.

[*All except Attracta kneel.*

Mary. This is a jug of cream.

Agnes. This is a bowl of butter.

Kate. This is a basket of eggs.

[*They lay jug, bowl, and basket on the ground.*

Attracta. I know what you would ask.
Sit round upon these stones.
Children, why do you fear
A woman but little older,
A child yesterday?
All, when I am married,
Shall have good husbands. Kate
Shall marry a black-headed lad.

Agnes. She swore but yesterday
That she would marry black.

Attracta. But Agnes there shall marry
A honey-coloured lad.

Agnes. O!

Attracta. Mary shall be married
When I myself am married
To the lad that is in her mind.

Mary. Are you not married yet?

Attracta. No. But it is almost come,
May come this very night.

Mary. And must he be all feathers?

Agnes. Have a terrible beak?

Kate. Great terrible claws?

Attracta. Whatever shape he choose,

Though that be terrible,
Will best express his love.

Agnes. When he comes — will he? —

Attracta. Child, ask what you please.

Agnes. Do all that a man does?

Attracta. Strong sinew and soft flesh
    Are foliage round the shaft
    Before the arrowsmith
    Has stripped it, and I pray
    That I, all foliage gone,
    May shoot into my joy —

          [*Sound of a flute, playing 'The Great Herne's Feather'.*

Mary. Who plays upon that flute?

Agnes. Her god is calling her.

Kate. Look, look, she takes
    An egg out of the basket.
    My white hen laid it,
    My favourite white hen.

Mary. Her eyes grow glassy, she moves
    According to the notes of the flute.

Agnes. Her limbs grow rigid, she seems
    A doll upon a wire.

Mary. Her human life is gone
    And that is why she seems
    A doll upon a wire.

Agnes. You mean that when she looks so
    She is but a puppet?

Mary. How do I know? And yet
    Twice have I seen her so,
    She will move for certain minutes
    As though her god were there
    Thinking how best to move

A doll upon a wire.
Then she will move away
In long leaps as though
He had remembered his skill.
She has still my little egg.

Agnes. Who knows but your little egg
Comes into some mystery?

Kate. Some mystery to make
Love-loneliness more sweet.

Agnes. She has moved. She has moved away.

Kate. Travelling fast asleep
In long loops like a dancer.

Mary. Like a dancer, like a hare.

Agnes. The last time she went away
The moon was full — she returned
Before its side had flattened.

Kate. This time she will not return.

Agnes. Because she is called to her marriage?

Kate. Those leaps may carry her where
No woman has gone, and he
Extinguish sun, moon, star.
No bridal torch can burn
When his black midnight is there.

Agnes. I have heard her claim that they couple
In the blazing heart of the sun.

Kate. But you have heard it wrong!
In blue-black midnight they couple.

Agnes. No, in the sun.

Kate.   Blue-black!

Agnes. In the sun!

Kate.   Blue-black, blue-black!

Mary. All I know is that she
Shall lie there in his bed.

Nor shall it end until
She lies there full of his might,
His thunderbolts in her hand.

SCENE III

*Before the gates of Tara, Congal, Mike, Pat, Peter, James,
Mathias, etc., soldiers of Congal, Corney, and the Donkey.*

Congal. This is Tara; in a moment
    Men must come out of the gate
    With a great basket between them
    And we give up our arms;
    No armed man can enter.

Corney. And here is that great bird
    Over our heads again.

Pat. The Great Herne himself
    And he in a red rage.

Mike. Stones.

Congal.   This man is right.
    Beat him to death with stones.

> [*All go through the motion of picking up and throwing stones.
> There are no stones except in so far as their gestures can
> suggest them.*

Pat. All those stones fell wide.

Corney. He has come down so low
    His legs are sweeping the grass.

Mike. Swords.

Congal.   This man is right.
    Cut him up with swords.

Pat. I have him within my reach.

Congal. No, no, he is here at my side.

Corney. His wing has touched my shoulder.

Congal. We missed him again and he
　Rises again and sinks
　Behind the wall of Tara.

> [*Two men come in carrying a large basket slung between two
> poles. One is whistling. All except Corney, who is un-
> armed, drop their swords and helmets into the basket. Each
> soldier when he takes off his helmet shows that he wears a
> skull-cap of soft cloth.*

Congal. Where have I heard that tune?
Mike. This morning.
Congal. 　　　　　　I know it now,
　The tune of 'The Great Herne's Feather'.
　It puts my teeth on edge.

SCENE IV

*Banqueting hall. A throne painted on the backcloth. Enter Congal,
alone, drunk, and shouting.*

Congal. To arms, to arms! Connacht to arms!
　Insulted and betrayed, betrayed and insulted.
　Who has insulted me? Tara has insulted.
　To arms, to arms! Connacht to arms!
　To arms — but if you have not got any
　Take a table-leg or a candlestick,
　A boot or a stool or any odd thing.
　Who has betrayed me? Tara has betrayed!
　To arms, to arms! Connacht to arms!

> [*He goes out to one side. Music, perhaps drum and concertina,
> to suggest breaking of wood. Enter, at the other side, the
> King of Tara, drunk.*

Aedh. Where is that beastly drunken liar
　That says I have insulted him?
　　　　　　Congal enters with two table-legs
Congal. I say it!

Aedh.   What insult?

Congal.   How dare you ask?

When I have had a common egg,
A common hen's egg put before me,
An egg dropped in the dirty straw
And crowed for by a cross-bred gangling cock,
And every other man at the table
A herne's egg.   [*Throws a table-leg on the floor.*
            There is your weapon. Take it!
Take it up, defend yourself.
An egg that some half-witted slattern
Spat upon and wiped on her apron!

Aedh. A servant put the wrong egg there.

Congal. But at whose orders?

Aedh.   At your own.

A murderous drunken plot, a plot
To put a weapon that I do not know
Into my hands.

Congal.   Take up that weapon.

If I am as drunken as you say,
And you as sober as you think,
A coward and a drunkard are well matched.

[*Aedh takes up the table-leg. Connacht and Tara soldiers come
in, they fight, and the fight sways to and fro. The weapons,
table-legs, candlesticks, etc., do not touch. Drum-taps represent blows. All go out fighting. Enter Pat, drunk, with bottle.*

Pat. Herne's egg, hen's egg, great difference.
There's insult in that difference.
What do hens eat? Hens live upon mash,
Upon slop, upon kitchen odds and ends.
What do hernes eat? Hernes live on eels,
On things that must always run about.

Man's a high animal and runs about,
But mash is low, O, very low.
Or, to speak like a philosopher,
When a man expects the movable
But gets the immovable, he is insulted.

Enter Congal, Peter, Malachi, Mathias, etc.

Congal. Tara knew that he was overmatched;
 Knew from the start he had no chance;
 Died of a broken head; died drunk;
 Accused me with his dying breath
 Of secretly practising with a table-leg,
 Practising at midnight until I
 Became a perfect master with the weapon.
 But that is all lies.

Pat. Let all men know
 He was a noble character
 And I must weep at his funeral.

Congal. He insulted me with a hen's egg,
 Said I had practised with a table-leg,
 But I have taken kingdom and throne
 And that has made all level again
 And I can weep at his funeral.
 I would not have had him die that way
 Or die at all, he should have been immortal.
 Our fifty battles had made us friends;
 And there are fifty more to come.
 New weapons, a new leader will be found
 And everything begin again.

Mike. Much bloodier.

Congal. They had, we had
 Forgotten what we fought about,
 So fought like gentlemen, but now

Knowing the truth must fight like the beasts.
Maybe the Great Herne's curse has done it.
Why not? Answer me that; why not?

Mike. Horror henceforth.

Congal.   This wise man means
We fought so long like gentlemen
That we grew blind.

> [*Attracta enters, walking in her sleep, a herne's egg in her
> hand. She stands near the throne and holds her egg towards
> it for a moment.*

Mathias.   Look! Look!
She offers that egg. Who is to take it?

Congal. She walks with open eyes but in her sleep.

Mathias. I can see it all in a flash.
She found that herne's egg on the table
And left the hen's egg there instead.

James. She brought the hen's egg on purpose
Walking in her wicked sleep.

Congal. And if I take that egg, she wakes,
Completes her task, her circle;
We all complete a task or circle,
Want a woman, then all goes — pff.

> [*He goes to take the egg.*

Mike. Not now.

Congal.   This wise man says 'not now'.
There must be something to consider first.

James. By changing one egg for another
She has brought bloodshed on us all.

Pat. He was a noble character,
And I must weep at his funeral.

James. I say that she must die, I say;
According to what my mother said,

All that have done what she did must die,
But, in a manner of speaking, pleasantly,
Because legally, certainly not
By beating with a table-leg
As though she were a mere Tara man,
Nor yet by beating with a stone
As though she were the Great Herne himself.

Mike. The Great Herne's bride.

Congal.   I had forgotten
That all she does he makes her do,
But he is god and out of reach;
Nor stone can bruise, nor a sword pierce him,
And yet through his betrothed, his bride,
I have the power to make him suffer;
His curse has given me the right,
I am to play the fool and die
At a fool's hands.

Mike.   Seven men.

> [*He begins to count, seeming to strike the table with the table-leg, but table and table-leg must not meet, the blow is represented by the sound of the drum.*

One, two, three, four,
Five, six, seven men.

Pat. Seven that are present in this room,
Seven that must weep at his funeral.

Congal. This man who struck those seven blows
Means that we seven in the name of the law
Must handle, penetrate, and possess her,
And do her a great good by that action,
Melting out the virgin snow,
And that snow image, the Great Herne;
For nothing less than seven men
Can melt that snow, but when it melts

She may, being free from all obsession,
Live as every woman should.
I am the Court; judgement has been given.
I name the seven: Congal of Tara,
Patrick, Malachi, Mike, John, James,
And that coarse hulk of clay, Mathias.

Mathias. I dare not lay a hand upon that woman.
  The people say that she is holy
  And carries a great devil in her gut.

Pat. What mischief can a Munster devil
  Do to a man that was born in Connacht?

Malachi. I made a promise to my mother
  When we set out on this campaign
  To keep from women.

John.   I have a wife that's jealous
  If I but look the moon in the face.

James. I am promised to an educated girl.
  Her family are most particular,
  What would they say — O my God!

Congal. Whoever disobeys the Court
  Is an unmannerly, disloyal lout,
  And no good citizen.

Pat.   Here is my bottle.
  Pass it along, a long, long pull;
  Although it's round like a woman carrying,
  No unmannerly, disloyal bottle,
  An affable, most loyal bottle.   *[All drink.*

Mathias. I first.

Congal.   That's for the Court to say.
  A Court of Law is a blessed thing,
  Logic, Mathematics, ground in one,
  And everything out of balance accursed.
  When the Court decides on a decree

Men carry it out with dignity.
Here where I put down my hand
I will put a mark, then all must stand
Over there in a level row.
And all take off their caps and throw.
The nearest cap shall take her first,
The next shall take her next, so on
Till all is in good order done.
I need a mark and so must take
The herne's egg, and let her wake.

[*He takes egg and lays it upon the ground. Attracta stands*
motionless, looking straight in front of her. She sings. The
seven standing in a row throw their caps one after another.

Attracta.

When I take a beast to my joyful breast,
Though beak and claw I must endure,
Sang the bride of the Herne, and the Great Herne's bride,
No lesser life, man, bird or beast,
Can make unblessed what a beast made blessed,
Can make impure what a beast made pure.

Where is he gone, where is that other,
He that shall take my maidenhead?
Sang the bride of the Herne, and the Great Herne's bride,
Out of the moon came my pale brother,
The blue-black midnight is my mother.
Who will turn down the sheets of the bed?

When beak and claw their work begin
Shall horror stir in the roots of my hair?
Sang the bride of the Herne, and the Great Herne's bride,
And who lie there in the cold dawn
When all that terror has come and gone?
Shall I be the woman lying there?

Scene V

Before the Gate of Tara. Corney enters with Donkey.

Corney. You thought to go on sleeping though dawn was up,
  Rapscallion of a beast, old highwayman.
  That light in the eastern sky is dawn,
  You cannot deny it; many a time
  You looked upon it following your trade.
  Cheer up, we shall be home before sunset.

Attracta comes in

Attracta. I have packed all the uneaten or unbroken eggs
  Into the creels. Help carry them
  And hang them on the donkey's back.

Corney. We could boil them hard and keep them in the larder,
  But Congal has had them all boiled soft.

Attracta. Such eggs are holy. Many pure souls,
  Especially among the country-people,
  Would shudder if herne's eggs were left
  For foul-tongued, bloody-minded men.

Congal, Malachi, Mike, etc., enter

Congal. A sensible woman; you gather up what's left,
  Your thoughts upon the cupboard and the larder.
  No more a herne's bride — a crazed loony
  Waiting to be trodden by a bird —
  But all woman, all sensible woman.

Mike. Manners.

Congal.   This man who is always right
  Desires that I should add these words,
  The seven that held you in their arms last night
  Wish you good luck.

Attracta.   What do you say?
  My husband came to me in the night.

Congal. Seven men lay with you in the night.
　Go home desiring and desirable,
　And look for a man.
Attracta.　　　　　　The Herne is my husband.
　I lay beside him, his pure bride.
Congal. Pure in the embrace of seven men?
Mike. She slept.
Congal.　　　　You say that though I thought,
　Because I took the egg out of her hand,
　That she awoke, she did not wake
　Until day broke upon her sleep —
　Her sleep and ours — did she wake pure?
　Seven men can answer that.
Corney. King though you are, I will not hear
　The bride of the Great Herne defamed —
　A king, a king but a Mayo man.
　A Mayo man's lying tongue can beat
　A Clare highwayman's rapscallion eye,
　Seven times a liar.
Mike.　　　　　Seven men.
Congal. I, Congal, lay with her last night.
Mathias. And I, Mathias.
Mike.　　　　　　And I.
James.　　　　　　　　And I.
Peter. And I.
John.　　　And I.
Pat.　　　　　　And I; swear it;
　And not a drop of drink since dawn.
Corney. One plain liar, six men bribed to lie.
Attracta. Great Herne, Great Herne, Great Herne,
　Your darling is crying out,
　Great Herne, declare her pure,
　Pure as that beak and claw,

Great Herne, Great Herne, Great Herne,
Let the round heaven declare it.

[*Silence. Then low thunder growing louder. All except Attracta and Congal kneel.*

James. Great Herne, I swear that she is pure;
I never laid a hand upon her.

Mathias. I was a fool to believe myself
When everybody knows that I am a liar.

Pat. Even when it seemed that I covered her
I swear that I knew it was the drink.

Attracta. I lay in the bride-bed,
His thunderbolts in my hand,
But gave them back, for he,
My lover, the Great Herne,
Knows everything that is said
And every man's intent,
And every man's deed; and he
Shall give these seven that say
That they upon me lay
A most memorable punishment.

[*It thunders. All prostrate themselves except Attracta and Congal. Congal had half knelt, but he has stood up again.*

Attracta. I share his knowledge, and I know
Every punishment decreed.
He will come when you are dead,
Push you down a step or two
Into cat or rat or bat,
Into dog or wolf or goose.
Everybody in his new shape I can see,
But Congal there stands in a cloud
Because his fate is not yet settled.

Speak out, Great Herne, and make it known
That everything I have said is true.

[*Thunder. All now, except Attracta, have prostrated them-*
selves.

Attracta. What has made you kneel?
Congal.   This man
That's prostrate at my side would say,
Could he say anything at all,
That I am terrified by thunder.
Attracta. Why did you stand up so long?
Congal. I held you in my arms last night,
We seven held you in our arms.
Attracta. You were under the curse, in all
You did, in all you seemed to do.
Congal. If I must die at a fool's hand,
When must I die?
Attracta.   When the moon is full.
Congal. And where?
Attracta.   Upon the holy mountain,
Upon Slieve Fuadh, there we meet again
Just as the moon comes round the hill.
There all the gods must visit me,
Acknowledging my marriage to a god;
One man will I have among the gods.
Congal. I know the place and I will come,
Although it be my death, I will come.
Because I am terrified, I will come.

SCENE VI

A mountain-top, the moon has just risen; the moon of comic
tradition, a round smiling face. A cauldron lid, a cooking-pot,
and a spit lie together at one side of the stage. The Fool, a man
in ragged clothes, enters carrying a large stone; he lays it down at

one side and goes out. Congal enters carrying a wineskin, and stands
at the other side of the stage. The Fool re-enters with a second large
stone which he places beside the first.

Congal. What is your name, boy?

Fool.   Poor Tom Fool.
  Everybody knows Tom Fool.

Congal. I saw something in the mist,
  There lower down upon the slope,
  I went up close to it and saw
  A donkey, somebody's stray donkey.
  A donkey and a Fool — I don't like it at all.

Fool. I won't be Tom the Fool after to-night.
  I have made a level patch out there,
  Clearing away the stones, and there
  I shall fight a man and kill a man
  And get great glory.

Congal.   Where did you get
  The cauldron lid, the pot and the spit?

Fool. I sat in Widow Rooney's kitchen,
  Somebody said, 'King Congal's on the mountain
  Cursed to die at the hands of a fool'.
  Somebody else said 'Kill him, Tom'.
  And everybody began to laugh
  And said I should kill him at the full moon,
  And that is to-night.

Congal.   I too have heard
  That Congal is to die to-night.
  Take a drink.

Fool.   I took this lid,
  And all the women screamed at me.
  I took the spit, and all screamed worse.
  A shoulder of lamb stood ready for the roasting —

I put the pot upon my head.
They did not scream but stood and gaped.

[*Fool arms himself with spit, cauldron lid, and pot, whistling
'The Great Herne's Feather'.*

Congal. Hush, that is an unlucky tune!
And why must you kill Congal, Fool?
What harm has he done you?

Fool. None at all.
But there's a Fool called Johnny from Meath,
We are great rivals and we hate each other,
But I can get the pennies if I kill Congal,
And Johnny nothing.

Congal. I am King Congal,
And is not that a thing to laugh at, Fool?

Fool. Very nice, O very nice indeed,
For I can kill you now, and I
Am tired of walking.

Congal. Both need rest.
Another drink apiece — that is done —
Lead to the place you have cleared of stones.

Fool. But where is your sword? You have not got a
sword.

Congal. I lost it, or I never had it,
Or threw it at the strange donkey below,
But that's no matter — I have hands.

[*They go out at one side. Attracta, Corney, and Donkey come
in. Attracta sings.*

Attracta.
When beak and claw their work began
What horror stirred in the roots of my hair?
Sang the bride of the Herne, and the Great Herne's bride.
But who lay there in the cold dawn,

When all that terror had come and gone?
Was I the woman lying there?

[*They go out. Congal and Tom the Fool come. Congal is
carrying the cauldron lid, pot, and spit. He lays them down.*

Congal. I was sent to die at the hands of a Fool.
There must be another Fool on the mountain.

Fool. That must be Johnny from Meath.
But that's a thing I could not endure,
For Johnny would get all the pennies.

Congal. Here, take a drink and have no fear;
All's plain at last; though I shall die
I shall not die at a Fool's hand.
I have thought out a better plan.
I and the Herne have had three bouts,
He won the first, I won the second,
Six men and I possessed his wife.

Fool. I ran after a woman once.
I had seen two donkeys in a field.

Congal. And did you get her, did you get her, Fool?

Fool. I almost had my hand upon her.
She screamed, and somebody came and beat me.
Were you beaten?

Congal.   No, no, Fool.
But she said that nobody had touched her,
And after that the thunder said the same,
Yet I had won that bout, and now
I know that I shall win the third.

Fool. If Johnny from Meath comes, kill him!

Congal. Maybe I will, maybe I will not.

Fool. You let me off, but don't let him off.

Congal. I could not do you any harm,
For you and I are friends.

Fool.   Kill Johnny!

Congal. Because you have asked me to, I will do it,
   For you and I are friends.

Fool.   Kill Johnny!
   Kill with the spear, but give it to me
   That I may see if it is sharp enough.

                                           [*Fool takes spit.*

Congal. And is it, Fool?

Fool.   I spent an hour
   Sharpening it upon a stone.
   Could I kill you now?

Congal.   Maybe you could.

Fool. I will get all the pennies for myself.

   [*He wounds Congal. The wounding is symbolised by a move-
       ment of the spit towards or over Congal's body.*

Congal. It passed out of your mind for a moment
   That we are friends, but that is natural.

Fool [*dropping spit*]. I must see it, I never saw a wound.

Congal. The Herne has got the first blow in;
   A scratch, a scratch, a mere nothing.
   But had it been a little deeper and higher
   It would have gone through the heart, and maybe
   That would have left me better off,
   For the Great Herne may beat me in the end.
   Here I must sit through the full moon,
   And he will send up Fools against me,
   Meandering, roaring, yelling,
   Whispering Fools, then chattering Fools,
   And after that morose, melancholy,
   Sluggish, fat, silent Fools;
   And I, moon-crazed, moon-blind,
   Fighting and wounded, wounded and fighting.

I never thought of such an end.
Never be a soldier, Tom;
Though it begins well, is this a life?
If this is a man's life, is there any life
But a dog's life?

Fool.   That's it, that's it;
Many a time they have put a dog at me.

Congal. If I should give myself a wound,
Let life run away, I'd win the bout.
He said I must die at the hands of a Fool
And sent you hither. Give me that spit!
I put it in this crevice of the rock,
That I may fall upon the point.
These stones will keep it sticking upright.

> [*They arrange stones, he puts the spit in.*

Congal [*almost screaming in his excitement*]. Fool! Am I myself a
    Fool?
For if I am a Fool, he wins the bout.

Fool. You are King of Connacht. If you were a Fool
They would have chased you with their dogs.

Congal. I am King Congal of Connacht and of Tara,
That wise, victorious, voluble, unlucky,
Blasphemous, famous, infamous man.
Fool, take this spit when red with blood,
Show it to the people and get all the pennies;
What does it matter what they think?
The Great Herne knows that I have won.

> [*He falls symbolically upon the spit. It does not touch him.
>   Fool takes the spit and wine-skin and goes out.*

It seems that I am hard to kill,
But the wound is deep. Are you up there?

Your chosen kitchen spit has killed me,
But killed me at my own will, not yours.

Attracta and Corney enter

Attracta. Will the knot hold?

Corney.   There was a look
About the old highwayman's eye of him
That warned me, so I made him fast
To that old stump among the rocks
With a great knot that he can neither
Break, nor pull apart with his teeth.

Congal. Attracta!

Attracta.   I called you to this place,
You came, and now the story is finished.

Congal. You have great powers, even the thunder
Does whatever you bid it do.
Protect me, I have won my bout,
But I am afraid of what the Herne
May do with me when I am dead.
I am afraid that he may put me
Into the shape of a brute beast.

Attracta. I will protect you if, as I think,
Your shape is not yet fixed upon.

Congal. I am slipping now, and you up there
With your long leg and your long beak.
But I have beaten you, Great Herne,
In spite of your kitchen spit — seven men —

                                              [*He dies.*

Attracta. Come lie with me upon the ground,
Come quickly into my arms, come quickly, come
Before his body has had time to cool.

Corney. What? Lie with you?

Attracta.   Lie and beget.

If you are afraid of the Great Herne,
Put that away, for if I do his will,
You are his instrument or himself.
Corney. The thunder has me terrified.
Attracta. I lay with the Great Herne, and he,
    Being all a spirit, but begot
    His image in the mirror of my spirit,
    Being all sufficient to himself
    Begot himself; but there's a work
    That should be done, and that work needs
    No bird's beak nor claw, but a man,
    The imperfection of a man.

                        [*The sound of a donkey braying.*

Corney. The donkey is braying.
    He has some wickedness in his mind.
Attracta. Too late, too late, he broke that knot,
    And there, down there among the rocks
    He couples with another donkey.
    That donkey has conceived. I thought that I
    Could give a human form to Congal,
    But now he must be born a donkey.
Corney. King Congal must be born a donkey!
Attracta. Because we were not quick enough.
Corney. I have heard that a donkey carries its young
    Longer than any other beast,
    Thirteen months it must carry it.

                        [*He laughs.*

    All that trouble and nothing to show for it,
    Nothing but just another donkey.

                    THE END

PURGATORY

PURGATORY

PERSONS IN THE PLAY

A Boy   An Old Man

Scene.—A ruined house and a bare tree in the background.

Boy. Half-door, hall door,
   Hither and thither day and night,
   Hill or hollow, shouldering this pack,
   Hearing you talk.
Old Man.   Study that house.
   I think about its jokes and stories;
   I try to remember what the butler
   Said to a drunken gamekeeper
   In mid-October, but I cannot.
   If I cannot, none living can.
   Where are the jokes and stories of a house,
   Its threshold gone to patch a pig-sty?
Boy. So you have come this path before?
Old Man. The moonlight falls upon the path,
   The shadow of a cloud upon the house,
   And that's symbolical; study that tree,
   What is it like?
Boy.   A silly old man.
Old Man. It's like — no matter what it's like.
   I saw it a year ago stripped bare as now,
   So I chose a better trade.
   I saw it fifty years ago
   Before the thunderbolt had riven it,
   Green leaves, ripe leaves, leaves thick as butter,

219

Fat, greasy life. Stand there and look,
Because there is somebody in that house.

[*The Boy puts down pack and stands in the doorway.*

Boy. There's nobody here.

Old Man.   There's somebody there.

Boy. The floor is gone, the windows gone,
And where there should be roof there's sky,
And here's a bit of an egg-shell thrown
Out of a jackdaw's nest.

Old Man.   But there are some
That do not care what's gone, what's left:
The souls in Purgatory that come back
To habitations and familiar spots.

Boy. Your wits are out again.

Old Man.   Re-live
Their transgressions, and that not once
But many times; they know at last
The consequence of those transgressions
Whether upon others or upon themselves;
Upon others, others may bring help,
For when the consequence is at an end
The dream must end; if upon themselves,
There is no help but in themselves
And in the mercy of God.

Boy.   I have had enough!
Talk to the jackdaws, if talk you must.

Old Man. Stop! Sit there upon that stone.
That is the house where I was born.

Boy. The big old house that was burnt down?

Old Man. My mother that was your grand-dam owned it,
This scenery and this countryside,
Kennel and stable, horse and hound —

She had a horse at the Curragh, and there met
My father, a groom in a training stable,
Looked at him and married him.
Her mother never spoke to her again,
And she did right.

Boy.   What's right and wrong?
My grand-dad got the girl and the money.

Old Man. Looked at him and married him,
And he squandered everything she had.
She never knew the worst, because
She died in giving birth to me,
But now she knows it all, being dead.
Great people lived and died in this house;
Magistrates, colonels, members of Parliament,
Captains and Governors, and long ago
Men that had fought at Aughrim and the Boyne.
Some that had gone on Government work
To London or to India came home to die,
Or came from London every spring
To look at the may-blossom in the park.
They had loved the trees that he cut down
To pay what he had lost at cards
Or spent on horses, drink, and women;
Had loved the house, had loved all
The intricate passages of the house,
But he killed the house; to kill a house
Where great men grew up, married, died,
I here declare a capital offence.

Boy. My God, but you had luck! Grand clothes,
And maybe a grand horse to ride.

Old Man. That he might keep me upon his level
He never sent me to school, but some
Half-loved me for my half of her:

A gamekeeper's wife taught me to read,
A Catholic curate taught me Latin.
There were old books and books made fine
By eighteenth-century French binding, books
Modern and ancient, books by the ton.

Boy. What education have you given me?

Old Man. I gave the education that befits
A bastard that a pedlar got
Upon a tinker's daughter in a ditch.
When I had come to sixteen years old
My father burned down the house when drunk.

Boy. But that is my age, sixteen years old,
At the Puck Fair.

Old Man.   And everything was burnt;
Books, library, all were burnt.

Boy. Is what I have heard upon the road the truth,
That you killed him in the burning house?

Old Man. There's nobody here but our two selves?

Boy. Nobody, Father.

Old Man.   I stuck him with a knife,
That knife that cuts my dinner now,
And after that I left him in the fire.
They dragged him out, somebody saw
The knife-wound but could not be certain
Because the body was all black and charred.
Then some that were his drunken friends
Swore they would put me upon trial,
Spoke of quarrels, a threat I had made.
The gamekeeper gave me some old clothes,
I ran away, worked here and there
Till I became a pedlar on the roads,
No good trade, but good enough
Because I am my father's son,

Because of what I did or may do.
Listen to the hoof-beats! Listen, listen!
Boy. I cannot hear a sound.
Old Man.   Beat! Beat!
   This night is the anniversary
   Of my mother's wedding night,
   Or of the night wherein I was begotten.
   My father is riding from the public-house,
   A whiskey-bottle under his arm.

                      [*A window is lit showing a young girl.*

   Look at the window; she stands there
   Listening, the servants are all in bed,
   She is alone, he has stayed late
   Bragging and drinking in the public-house.
Boy. There's nothing but an empty gap in the wall.
   You have made it up. No, you are mad!
   You are getting madder every day.
Old Man. It's louder now because he rides
   Upon a gravelled avenue
   All grass to-day. The hoof-beat stops,
   He has gone to the other side of the house,
   Gone to the stable, put the horse up.
   She has gone down to open the door.
   This night she is no better than her man
   And does not mind that he is half drunk,
   She is mad about him. They mount the stairs.
   She brings him into her own chamber.
   And that is the marriage-chamber now.
   The window is dimly lit again.

   Do not let him touch you! It is not true
   That drunken men cannot beget,
   And if he touch he must beget

And you must bear his murderer.
Deaf! Both deaf! If I should throw
A stick or a stone they would not hear;
And that's a proof my wits are out.
But there's a problem: she must live
Through everything in exact detail,
Driven to it by remorse, and yet
Can she renew the sexual act
And find no pleasure in it, and if not,
If pleasure and remorse must both be there,
Which is the greater?

                         I lack schooling.

Go fetch Tertullian; he and I
Will ravel all that problem out
Whilst those two lie upon the mattress
Begetting me.

                  Come back! Come back!
And so you thought to slip away,
My bag of money between your fingers,
And that I could not talk and see!
You have been rummaging in the pack.

                   [*The light in the window has faded out.*

Boy. You never gave me my right share.
Old Man. And had I given it, young as you are,
   You would have spent it upon drink.
Boy. What if I did? I had a right
   To get it and spend it as I chose.
Old Man. Give me that bag and no more words.
Boy. I will not.
Old Man.   I will break your fingers.

   [*They struggle for the bag. In the struggle it drops, scattering
      the money. The Old Man staggers but does not fall. They*

stand looking at each other. The window is lit up. A man is
seen pouring whiskey into a glass.

Boy. What if I killed you? You killed my grand-dad,
Because you were young and he was old.
Now I am young and you are old.

Old Man [*staring at window*]. Better-looking, those sixteen
years —

Boy. What are you muttering?

Old Man.   Younger — and yet
She should have known he was not her kind.

Boy. What are you saying? Out with it!

                                [*Old Man points to window.*

My God! The window is lit up
And somebody stands there, although
The floorboards are all burnt away.

Old Man. The window is lit up because my father
Has come to find a glass for his whiskey.
He leans there like some tired beast.

Boy. A dead, living, murdered man!

Old Man. 'Then the bride-sleep fell upon Adam':
Where did I read those words?

                                And yet
There's nothing leaning in the window
But the impression upon my mother's mind;
Being dead she is alone in her remorse.

Boy. A body that was a bundle of old bones
Before I was born. Horrible! Horrible!

                                [*He covers his eyes.*

Old Man. That beast there would know nothing, being
nothing,
If I should kill a man under the window
He would not even turn his head.   [*He stabs the Boy.*

My father and my son on the same jack-knife!
That finishes — there — there — there —

     [He stabs again and again. The window grows dark.

'Hush-a-bye baby, thy father's a knight,
Thy mother a lady, lovely and bright.'
No, that is something that I read in a book,
And if I sing it must be to my mother,
And I lack rhyme.

   *[The stage has grown dark except where the tree stands in white
     light.*

                Study that tree.
It stands there like a purified soul,
All cold, sweet, glistening light.
Dear mother, the window is dark again,
But you are in the light because
I finished all that consequence.
I killed that lad because had he grown up
He would have struck a woman's fancy,
Begot, and passed pollution on.
I am a wretched foul old man
And therefore harmless. When I have stuck
This old jack-knife into a sod
And pulled it out all bright again,
And picked up all the money that he dropped,
I'll to a distant place, and there
Tell my old jokes among new men.

             [He cleans the knife and begins to pick up money.

Hoof-beats! Dear God,
How quickly it returns — beat — beat —!

Her mind cannot hold up that dream.
Twice a murderer and all for nothing,

And she must animate that dead night
Not once but many times!
                    O God,
Release my mother's soul from its dream!
Mankind can do no more. Appease
The misery of the living and the remorse of the dead.

THE END

THE DEATH OF CUCHULAIN

THE DEATH OF CUCHULAIN

PERSONS IN THE PLAY

Cuchulain	An Old Man
Eithne Inguba	A Blind Man
Aoife	A Servant
Emer	A Singer, a Piper, and
The Morrigu, *Goddess of War*	a Drummer

Scene.—A bare stage of any period. A very old man looking like something out of mythology.

Old Man. I have been asked to produce a play called *The Death of Cuchulain*. It is the last of a series of plays which has for theme his life and death. I have been selected because I am out of fashion and out of date like the antiquated romantic stuff the thing is made of. I am so old that I have forgotten the name of my father and mother, unless indeed I am, as I affirm, the son of Talma, and he was so old that his friends and acquaintances still read Virgil and Homer. When they told me that I could have my own way, I wrote certain guiding principles on a bit of newspaper. I wanted an audience of fifty or a hundred, and if there are more, I beg them not to shuffle their feet or talk when the actors are speaking. I am sure that as I am producing a play for people I like, it is not probable, in this vile age, that they will be more in number than those who listened to the first performance of Milton's *Comus*. On the present occasion they must know the old epics and Mr. Yeats' plays about them; such people, however poor, have libraries of their own. If there are more than a hundred I won't be able to escape people who are educating themselves out of the Book Societies and the like,

sciolists all, pickpockets and opinionated bitches. Why
pickpockets? I will explain that, I will make it all quite clear.

[*Drum and pipe behind the scene, then silence.*

That's from the musicians; I asked them to do that if I
was getting excited. If you were as old you would find it
easy to get excited. Before the night ends you will meet the
music. There is a singer, a piper, and a drummer. I have
picked them up here and there about the streets, and I will
teach them, if I live, the music of the beggar-man, Homer's
music. I promise a dance. I wanted a dance because where
there are no words there is less to spoil. Emer must dance,
there must be severed heads — I am old, I belong to mythology — severed heads for her to dance before. I had thought
to have had those heads carved, but no, if the dancer can
dance properly no wood-carving can look as well as a
parallelogram of painted wood. But I was at my wit's end
to find a good dancer; I could have got such a dancer once,
but she has gone; the tragi-comedian dancer, the tragic
dancer, upon the same neck love and loathing, life and
death. I spit three times. I spit upon the dancers painted by
Degas. I spit upon their short bodices, their stiff stays, their
toes whereon they spin like peg-tops, above all upon that
chambermaid face. They might have looked timeless,
Rameses the Great, but not the chambermaid, that old maid
history. I spit! I spit! I spit!

[*The stage is darkened, the curtain falls. Pipe and drum begin
and continue until the curtain rises on a bare stage. Half a
minute later Eithne Inguba enters.*

Eithne. Cuchulain! Cuchulain!

Cuchulain enters from back

                                    I am Emer's messenger,
I am your wife's messenger, she has bid me say

You must not linger here in sloth, for Maeve
With all those Connacht ruffians at her back
Burns barns and houses up at Emain Macha:
Your house at Muirthemne already burns.
No matter what's the odds, no matter though
Your death may come of it, ride out and fight.
The scene is set and you must out and fight.

Cuchulain. You have told me nothing. I am already armed,
I have sent a messenger to gather men,
And wait for his return. What have you there?

Eithne. I have nothing.

Cuchulain.   There is something in your hand.

Eithne. No.

Cuchulain.   Have you a letter in your hand?

Eithne. I do not know how it got into my hand.
I am straight from Emer. We were in some place.
She spoke. She saw.

Cuchulain.   This letter is from Emer,
It tells a different story. I am not to move
Until to-morrow morning, for, if now,
I must face odds no man can face and live.
To-morrow morning Conall Caernach comes
With a great host.

Eithne.   I do not understand.
Who can have put that letter in my hand?

Cuchulain. And there is something more to make it certain
I shall not stir till morning; you are sent
To be my bedfellow, but have no fear,
All that is written, but I much prefer
Your own unwritten words. I am for the fight,
I and my handful are set upon the fight;
We have faced great odds before, a straw decided.

          The Morrigu enters and stands between them

Eithne. I know that somebody or something is there,
    Yet nobody that I can see.

Cuchulain.   There is nobody.

Eithne. Who among the gods of the air and upper air
    Has a bird's head?

Cuchulain.   Morrigu is headed like a crow.

Eithne [*dazed*]. Morrigu, war goddess, stands between.
    Her black wing touched me upon the shoulder, and
    All is intelligible.   [*The Morrigu goes out.*
                Maeve put me in a trance.
    Though when Cuchulain slept with her as a boy
    She seemed as pretty as a bird, she has changed,
    She has an eye in the middle of her forehead.

Cuchulain. A woman that has an eye in the middle of her
    forehead!
    A woman that is headed like a crow!
    But she that put those words into your mouth
    Had nothing monstrous; you put them there yourself;
    You need a younger man, a friendlier man,
    But, fearing what my violence might do,
    Thought out these words to send me to my death,
    And were in such excitement you forgot
    The letter in your hand.

Eithne.   Now that I wake
    I say that Maeve did nothing out of reason;
    What mouth could you believe if not my mouth?

Cuchulain. When I went mad at my son's death and drew
    My sword against the sea, it was my wife
    That brought me back.

Eithne.   Better women than I
    Have served you well, but 'twas to me you turned.

Cuchulain. You thought that if you changed I'd kill you for it,
    When everything sublunary must change,

And if I have not changed that goes to prove
    That I am monstrous.

Eithne.   You're not the man I loved,
    That violent man forgave no treachery.
    If, thinking what you think, you can forgive,
    It is because you are about to die.

Cuchulain. Spoken too loudly and too near the door;
    Speak low if you would speak about my death,
    Or not in that strange voice exulting in it.
    Who knows what ears listen behind the door?

Eithne. Some that would not forgive a traitor, some
    That have the passion necessary to life,
    Some not about to die. When you are gone
    I shall denounce myself to all your cooks,
    Scullions, armourers, bed-makers, and messengers,
    Until they hammer me with a ladle, cut me with a knife,
    Impale me upon a spit, put me to death
    By what foul way best please their fancy,
    So that my shade can stand among the shades
    And greet your shade and prove it is no traitor.

Cuchulain. Women have spoken so, plotting a man's death.

Enter a Servant

Servant. Your great horse is bitted. All wait the word.

Cuchulain. I come to give it, but must ask a question.
    This woman, wild with grief, declares that she
    Out of pure treachery has told me lies
    That should have brought my death. What can I do?
    How can I save her from her own wild words?

Servant. Is her confession true?

Cuchulain.   I make the truth!
    I say she brings a message from my wife.

Servant. What if I make her swallow poppy-juice?

Cuchulain. What herbs seem suitable, but protect her life
   As if it were your own, and should I not return
   Give her to Conall Caernach because the women
   Have called him a good lover.

Eithne.   I might have peace that know
   The Morrigu, the woman like a crow,
   Stands to my defence and cannot lie,
   But that Cuchulain is about to die.

    [*Pipe and drum. The stage grows dark for a moment. When
      it lights up again, it is empty. Cuchulain enters wounded.
      He tries to fasten himself to a pillar-stone with his belt.
      Aoife, an erect white-haired woman, enters.*

Aoife. Am I recognised, Cuchulain?

Cuchulain.   You fought with a sword,
   It seemed that we should kill each other, then
   Your body wearied and I took your sword.

Aoife. But look again, Cuchulain! Look again!

Cuchulain. Your hair is white.

Aoife.   That time was long ago,
   And now it is my time. I have come to kill you.

Cuchulain. Where am I? Why am I here?

Aoife.   You asked their leave,
   When certain that you had six mortal wounds,
   To drink out of the pool.

Cuchulain.   I have put my belt
   About this stone and want to fasten it
   And die upon my feet, but am too weak.
   Fasten this belt.   [*She helps him to do so.*
          And now I know your name,
   Aoife, the mother of my son. We met
   At the Hawk's Well under the withered trees.
   I killed him upon Baile's Strand, that is why

Maeve parted ranks that she might let you through.
You have a right to kill me.

Aoife.   Though I have,
Her army did not part to let me through.
The grey of Macha, that great horse of yours
Killed in the battle, came out of the pool
As though it were alive, and went three times
In a great circle round you and that stone,
Then leaped into the pool; and not a man
Of all that terrified army dare approach,
But I approach.

Cuchulain.   Because you have the right.

Aoife. But I am an old woman now, and that
Your strength may not start up when the time comes
I wind my veil about this ancient stone
And fasten you to it.

Cuchulain.   But do not spoil your veil.
Your veils are beautiful, some with threads of gold.

Aoife. I am too old to care for such things now.

                              [*She has wound the veil about him.*

Cuchulain. There was no reason so to spoil your veil:
I am weak from loss of blood.

Aoife.   I was afraid,
But now that I have wound you in the veil
I am not afraid. But — how did my son fight?

Cuchulain. Age makes more skilful but not better men.

Aoife. I have been told you did not know his name
And wanted, because he had a look of me,
To be his friend, but Conchubar forbade it.

Cuchulain. Forbade it and commanded me to fight;
That very day I had sworn to do his will,
Yet refused him, and spoke about a look;

But somebody spoke of witchcraft and I said
Witchcraft had made the look, and fought and killed him.
Then I went mad, I fought against the sea.

Aoife. I seemed invulnerable; you took my sword,
You threw me on the ground and left me there.
I searched the mountain for your sleeping-place
And laid my virgin body at your side,
And yet, because you had left me, hated you,
And thought that I would kill you in your sleep,
And yet begot a son that night between
Two black thorn-trees.

Cuchulain.   I cannot understand.

Aoife. Because about to die!

                          Somebody comes,
Some countryman, and when he finds you here,
And none to protect him, will be terrified.
I will keep out of his sight, for I have things
That I must ask questions on before I kill you.

[*She goes. The Blind Man of 'On Baile's Strand' comes in.
He moves his stick about until he finds the standing stone; he
lays his stick down, stoops and touches Cuchulain's feet. He
feels the legs.*

Blind Man. Ah! Ah!

Cuchulain.   I think you are a blind old man.

Blind Man. A blind old beggar-man. What is your name?

Cuchulain. Cuchulain.

Blind Man.   They say that you are weak with
wounds.
I stood between a Fool and the sea at Baile's Strand
When you went mad. What's bound about your hands
So that they cannot move? Some womanish stuff.
I have been fumbling with my stick since dawn

And then heard many voices. I began to beg.
Somebody said that I was in Maeve's tent,
And somebody else, a big man by his voice,
That if I brought Cuchulain's head in a bag
I would be given twelve pennies; I had the bag
To carry what I get at kitchen doors,
Somebody told me how to find the place;
I thought it would have taken till the night,
But this has been my lucky day.

Cuchulain.   Twelve pennies!

Blind Man. I would not promise anything until the woman,
The great Queen Maeve herself, repeated the words.

Cuchulain. Twelve pennies! What better reason for killing a
man?
You have a knife, but have you sharpened it?

Blind Man. I keep it sharp because it cuts my food.

[*He lays bag on ground and begins feeling Cuchulain's body,
his hands mounting upward.*

Cuchulain. I think that you know everything, Blind Man.
My mother or my nurse said that the blind
Know everything.

Blind Man.   No, but they have good sense.
How could I have got twelve pennies for your head
If I had not good sense?

Cuchulain.   There floats out there
The shape that I shall take when I am dead,
My soul's first shape, a soft feathery shape,
And is not that a strange shape for the soul
Of a great fighting-man?

Blind Man.   Your shoulder is there,
This is your neck. Ah! Ah! Are you ready, Cuchulain!

Cuchulain. I say it is about to sing.

[*The stage darkens.*

Blind Man. Ah! Ah!

> [*Music of pipe and drum, the curtain falls. The music ceases as the curtain rises upon a bare stage. There is nobody upon the stage except a woman with a crow's head. She is the Morrigu. She stands towards the back. She holds a black parallelogram, the size of a man's head. There are six other parallelograms near the backcloth.*

The Morrigu. The dead can hear me, and to the dead I speak.
This head is great Cuchulain's, those other six
Gave him six mortal wounds. This man came first;
Youth lingered though the years ran on, that season
A woman loves the best. Maeve's latest lover,
This man, had given him the second wound,
He had possessed her once; these were her sons,
Two valiant men that gave the third and fourth:
These other men were men of no account,
They saw that he was weakening and crept in;
One gave him the sixth wound and one the fifth;
Conall avenged him. I arranged the dance.

> [*Emer enters. The Morrigu places the head of Cuchulain upon the ground and goes out. Emer runs in and begins to dance. She so moves that she seems to rage against the heads of those that had wounded Cuchulain, perhaps makes movements as though to strike them, going three times round the circle of the heads. She then moves towards the head of Cuchulain; it may, if need be, be raised above the others on a pedestal. She moves as if in adoration or triumph. She is about to prostrate herself before it, perhaps does so, then rises, looking up as if listening; she seems to hesitate between the head and what she hears. Then she stands motionless. There is silence, and in the silence a few faint bird notes.*

*The stage darkens slowly. Then comes loud music, but now it
is quite different. It is the music of some Irish Fair of our
day. The stage brightens. Emer and the head are gone. . . .
There is no one there but the three musicians. They are in
ragged street-singers' clothes; two of them begin to pipe and
drum. They cease. The Street-Singer begins to sing.*

Singer.

> The harlot sang to the beggar-man.
> I meet them face to face,
> Conall, Cuchulain, Usna's boys,
> All that most ancient race;
> Maeve had three in an hour, they say.
> I adore those clever eyes,
> Those muscular bodies, but can get
> No grip upon their thighs.
> I meet those long pale faces,
> Hear their great horses, then
> Recall what centuries have passed
> Since they were living men.
> That there are still some living
> That do my limbs unclothe,
> But that the flesh my flesh has gripped
> I both adore and loathe.

> > *[Pipe and drum music.*

> Are those things that men adore and loathe
> Their sole reality?
> What stood in the Post Office
> With Pearse and Connolly?
> What comes out of the mountain
> Where men first shed their blood?
> Who thought Cuchulain till it seemed
> He stood where they had stood?

No body like his body
Has modern woman borne,
But an old man looking back on life
Imagines it in scorn.
A statue's there to mark the place,
By Oliver Sheppard done.
So ends the tale that the harlot
Sang to the beggar-man.

[*Music from pipe and drum.*

THE END

CATHLEEN NI HOOLIHAN

CATHLEEN NI HOOLIHAN

PERSONS IN THE PLAY

Peter Gillane
Michael Gillane, *His son, going to be married*
Patrick Gillane, *A lad of twelve, Michael's brother*
Bridget Gillane, *Peter's wife*
Delia Cahel, *Engaged to Michael*
The Poor Old Woman
Neighbours

Interior of a cottage close to Killala, in 1798. Bridget is standing at a table undoing a parcel. Peter is sitting at one side of the fire, Patrick at the other.

Peter. What is that sound I hear?

Patrick. I don't hear anything. [*He listens.*] I hear it now. It's like cheering. [*He goes to the window and looks out.*] I wonder what they are cheering about. I don't see anybody.

Peter. It might be a hurling match.

Patrick. There's no hurling to-day. It must be down in the town the cheering is.

Bridget. I suppose the boys must be having some sport of their own.

Patrick. There is an old woman coming down the road. I don't know is it here she's coming.

Bridget. It will be a neighbour coming to hear about Michael's wedding. Can you see who it is?

Patrick. I think it is a stranger, and she's not coming to the house. She has not turned up the path. She's turned into the gap that goes down where Maurteen and his sons are

shearing sheep [*He turns towards them.*] Do you remember
what Winnie of the Cross Roads was saying the other night
about the strange woman that goes through the country the
time there's war or trouble coming?

Bridget. Don't be bothering us about Winnie's talk, but go and
open the door for your brother. I hear him coming up the
path.

Bridget. Come over here, Peter, and look at Michael's wedding clothes. [*Peters shifts his chair to table.*] Those are grand
clothes, indeed.

Bridget. You hadn't clothes like that when you married me,
and no coat to put on of a Sunday more than any other
day.

Peter. That is true, indeed. We never thought a son of our own
would be wearing a suit of that sort at his wedding, or have
so good a place to bring a wife to.

Patrick [*who is still at the window*]. Here is Michael coming
back, father.

Peter. I hope he has brought Delia's fortune with him safe, for
fear her people might go back of the bargain, and I after
making it. Trouble enough I had making it.

[*Patrick opens the door, and Michael comes in.*

Bridget. What kept you, Michael? We were looking out for
you this long time.

Michael. I went round by the priest's house to bid him be ready
to marry us to-morrow.

Bridget. Did he say anything?

Michael. He said it was a very nice match, and that he was
never better pleased to marry two in his parish than myself
and Delia Cahel.

Peter. Have you got the fortune, Michael?

Michael. Here it is.

[*He puts bag on the table and goes over and leans against chimney jamb. Bridget who has been all this time examining the clothes, pulling the seams and trying the lining of the pockets, etc., puts the clothes on the dresser.*

Peter [*getting up and taking the bag in his hand and turning out the money*]. Yes, I made the bargain well for you, Michael. Old John Cahel would sooner have kept a share of this a while longer. 'Let me keep the half of it till the first boy is born,' says he. 'You will not,' says I. 'Whether there is or is not a boy, the whole hundred pounds must be in Michael's hands before he brings your daughter to the house.' The wife spoke to him then, and he gave in at the end.

Bridget. You seem well pleased to be handling the money, Peter.

Peter. Indeed, I wish I'd had the luck to get a hundred pounds, or twenty pounds itself, with the wife I married.

Bridget. Well, if I didn't bring much I didn't get much. What had you the day I married you but a flock of hens and you feeding them, and a few lambs and you driving them to the market at Ballina. [*She is vexed, and bangs a jug on the dresser.*] If I brought no fortune I worked it out in my bones, laying down the baby — Michael, that is standing there now, on a stook of straw, while I dug the potatoes, and never asking big dresses or anything, but to be working.

Peter. That is true, indeed. [*He pats her arm.*

Bridget. Leave me alone now till I ready the house for the woman that is to come into it.

Peter. You are the best woman in Ireland, but money is good, too. [*He begins handling the money again and sits down.*] I never thought to see so much money within my four walls. We can do great things now we have it. We can take the ten acres of land we have a chance of since Jamsie Dempsey died, and stock it. We will go the fair of Ballina to buy the stock. Did Delia ask any of the money for her own use, Michael?

Michael. She did not, indeed. She did not seem to take much notice of it, or to look at it at all.

Bridget. That's no wonder. Why would she look at it when she had yourself to look at — a fine strong young man; it is proud she must be to get you; a good, steady boy, that will make use of the money, and will not be running through it, or spending it on drink, like another.

Peter. It's likely Michael himself was not thinking much of the fortune either, but of what sort the girl was to look at.

Michael [*coming over towards the table*]. Well, you would like a nice comely girl to be beside you, and to go walking with you. The fortune only lasts for a while, but the woman will be there always.

Patrick [*turning round from the window*]. They are cheering again down in the town. Maybe they are landing horses from Enniscrone. They do be cheering when the horses take the water well.

Michael. There are no horses in it. Where would they be going and no fair at hand! Go down to the town, Patrick, and see what is going on.

Patrick [*opens the door to go out, but stops for a moment on the threshold*]. Will Delia remember, do you think, to bring the greyhound pup she promised me when she would be coming to the house?

Michael. She will surely [*Patrick goes out, leaving the door open.*

Peter. It will be Patrick's turn next to be looking for a fortune, but he won't find it so easy to get it, and he with no place of his own.

Bridget. I do be thinking sometimes, now things are going so well with us, and the Cahels such a good back to us in the district, and Delia's own uncle a priest, we might be put in the way of making Patrick himself a priest some day, and he so good at his books.

Peter. Time enough, time enough; you have always your head full of plans.

Bridget. We will be well able to give him learning, and not to send him tramping the country like a poor scholar that lives on charity.

Michael. They're not done cheering yet.

[*He goes over to the door and stands there for a moment, putting up his hand to shade his eyes.*

Bridget. Do you see anything?

Michael. I see an old woman coming up the path.

Bridget. Who is it, I wonder?

Michael. I don't think it's one of the neighbours, but she has her cloak over her face.

Bridget. Maybe it's the same woman Patrick saw a while ago. It might be some poor woman heard we were making ready for the wedding, and came to look for her share.

Peter. I may as well put the money out of sight. There's no use leaving it out for every stranger to look at.

[*He goes over to a large box by the wall, opens it and puts the bag in, and fumbles with the lock.*

Michael. There she is, father! [*An old woman passes the window slowly. She looks at Michael as she passes.*] I'd sooner a stranger not to come to the house the night before the wedding.

Bridget. Open the door, Michael, don't keep the poor woman waiting.

[*The old woman comes in, Michael stands aside to make way for her.*

Old Woman. God save all here!

Peter. God save you kindly.

Old Woman. You have good shelter here.

Peter. You are welcome to whatever shelter we have.

Bridget. Sit down there by the fire and welcome.

Old Woman [*warming her hands*]. There's a hard wind outside.

> [*Michael watches her curiously from the door. Peter comes over to the table.*

Peter. Have you travelled far to-day?

Old Woman. I have travelled far, very far; there are few have travelled so far as myself.

Peter. It is a pity, indeed, for any person to have no place of their own.

Old Woman. That is true for you, indeed, and it is long I am on the road since I first went wandering. It is seldom I have any rest.

Bridget. It is a wonder you are not worn out with so much wandering.

Old Woman. Sometimes my feet are tired and my hands are quiet, but there is no quiet in my heart. When the people see me quiet they think old age has come on me, and that all the stir has gone out of me.

Bridget. What was it put you astray?

Old Woman. Too many strangers in the house.

Bridget. Indeed you look as if you had had your share of trouble.

Old Woman. I have had trouble indeed.

Bridget. What was it put the trouble on you?

Old Woman. My land that was taken from me.

Peter. Was it much land they took from you?

Old Woman. My four beautiful green fields.

Peter [*aside to Bridget*]. Do you think could she be the Widow Casey that was put out of her holding at Kilglas a while ago?

Bridget. She is not. I saw the Widow Casey one time at the market in Ballina, a stout, fresh woman.

Peter [*to old woman*]. Did you hear a noise of cheering, and you coming up the hill?

Old Woman. I thought I heard the noise I used to hear when my friends came to visit me.

[*She begins singing half to herself.*

> I will go cry with the woman,
> For yellow-haired Donough is dead;
> With a hempen rope for a neckcloth
> And a white cloth on his head.

Michael [*coming from the door*]. What is that you are singing, ma'am?   [*She goes on singing, much louder.*

Old Woman. Singing I am about a man I knew one time, yellow-haired Donough, that was hanged in Galway.

> I am come to cry with you, woman,
> My hair is unwound and unbound;
> I remember him ploughing his field,
> Turning up the red side of the ground.

> And building his barn on the hill
> With the good mortared stone;
> O! we'd have pulled down the gallows
> Had it happened in Enniscrone!

Michael. What was it brought him to his death?

Old Woman. He died for love of me; many a man has died for love of me.

Peter [*aside to Bridget*]. Her trouble has put her wits astray.

Michael. Is it long since that song was made? Is it long since he got his death?

Old Woman. Not long, not long. But there were others that died for love of me a long time ago.

Michael. Were they neighbours of your own, ma'am?

Old Woman. Come here beside me and I'll tell you about them. [*Michael sits down beside her at the hearth.*] There was a red man of the O'Donells from the North, and a man of the O'Sullivans from the South, and there was one Brian that lost his life at Clontarf, by the sea, and there were a great many in the West, some that died hundreds of years ago, and there are some that will die to-morrow.

Michael. Is it in the West that men will die to-morrow?

Old Woman. Come nearer, nearer to me.

Bridget. Is she right, do you think? or is she a woman from the North?

Peter. She doesn't know well what she's talking about, with the want and the trouble she has gone through.

Bridget. The poor thing, we should treat her well.

Peter. Give her a drink of milk, and a bit of the oaten cake.

Bridget. Maybe we should give her something along with that to bring her on her way; a few pence, or a shilling itself, and we with so much money in the house.

Peter. Indeed, I'd not begrudge it to her if we had it to spare, but if we go running through what we have, we'll soon have to break the hundred pounds, and that would be a pity.

Bridget. Shame on you, Peter. Give her the shilling and your blessing with it, or our own luck will go from us.

[*Peter goes to the box and takes out a shilling.*

Bridget [*to the old woman*]. Will you have a drink of milk?

Old Woman. It is not food or drink that I want.

Peter [*offering the shilling*]. Here is something for you.

Old Woman. That is not what I want. It is not silver I want.

Peter. What is it you would be asking for?

Old Woman. If anyone would give me help he must give me himself, he must give me all.

[*Peter goes over to the table staring at the shilling in his hand in a bewildered way and stands whispering to Bridget.*

Michael. Have you no man of your own, ma'am?

Old Woman. I have not. With all the lovers that brought me their love, I never set out the bed for any.

Michael. Are you lonely going the roads, ma'am?

Old Woman. I have my thoughts and I have my hopes.

Michael. What hopes have you to hold to?

Old Woman. The hope of getting my beautiful fields back again; the hope of putting the strangers out of my house.

Michael. What way will you do that, ma'am?

Old Woman. I have good friends that will help me. They are gathering to help me now. I am not afraid. If they are put down to-day, they will get the upper hand to-morrow. [*She gets up.*] I must be going to meet my friends. They are coming to help me, and I must be there to welcome them. I must call the neighbours together to welcome them.

Michael. I will go with you.

Bridget. It is not her friends you have to go and welcome, Michael; it is the girl coming into the house you have to welcome. You have plenty to do; it is food and drink you have to bring to the house. The woman that is coming is not coming with empty hands; you would not have an empty house before her. [*To the old woman.*] Maybe you don't know, ma'am, that my son is going to be married to-morrow.

Old Woman. It is not a man going to his marriage that I look to for help.

Peter [*to Bridget*]. Who is she, do you think, at all?

Bridget. You did not tell us your name yet, ma'am.

Old Woman. Some call me the Poor Old Woman, and there are some that call me Cathleen ny Hoolihan.

Peter. I think I knew some one of that name once. Who was it, I wonder? It must have been someone I knew when I was a boy. No, no, I remember I heard it in a song.

Old Woman [*who is standing in the doorway*]. They are wondering that there were songs made for me; there have been many songs made for me. I heard one on the wind this morning.   [*She sings.*

> Do not make a great keening
> When the graves have been dug to-morrow,
> Do not call the white-scarfed riders
> To the burying that shall be to-morrow.
>
> Do not spread food to call strangers
> To the wakes that shall be to-morrow;
> Do not give money for prayers
> For the dead that shall die to-morrow. . . .

They will have no need of prayers, they will have no need of prayers.

Michael. I do not know what that song means; but tell me something I can do for you.

Peter. Come over to me, Michael.

Michael. Hush, father; listen to her.

Old Woman. It is a hard service they take that help me. Many that are red-cheeked now will be pale-cheeked; many that have been free to walk the hills and the bogs and the rushes will be sent to walk hard streets in far countries; many a good plan will be broken; many that have gathered money

will not stay to spend it; many a child will be born and
there will be no father at its christening to give it a name.
They that had red cheeks will have pale cheeks for my
sake; and for all that they will think they are well paid.

[*She goes out. Her voice is heard outside singing.*

They shall be remembered for ever;
They shall be alive for ever;
They shall be speaking for ever;
The people shall hear them for ever.

Bridget [*to Peter*]. Look at him, Peter; he has the look of a man
that has got the touch. [*Raising her voice.*] Look here,
Michael, at the wedding clothes. [*Taking clothes from dresser.*]
You have a right to fit them on now; it would be a pity
to-morrow if they did not fit; the boys would be laughing
at you. Take them, Michael, and go into the room and fit
them on. [*She puts them on his arm.*

Michael. What wedding are you talking of? What clothes will
I be wearing to-morrow?

Bridget. These are the clothes you are going to wear when you
marry Delia Cahel to-morrow.

Michael. I had forgotten that.

[*He looks at the clothes and turns towards the inner room, but
stops at the sound of cheering outside.*

Peter. There is the shouting come to our own door. What is it
has happened?

[*Neighbours come crowding in, Patrick and Delia with them.*

Patrick. There are ships in the bay; the French are landing at
Killala.

[*Peter takes his pipe from his mouth and his hat off and stands
up. The clothes slip from Michael's arm.*

Delia. Michael! [*He takes no notice.*] Michael! [*He turns towards her.*] Why do you look at me like a stranger?

> [*She drops his arm. Bridget goes over towards her.*]

Patrick. The boys are all hurrying down the hillsides to meet the French.

Delia. Michael won't be going to join the French.

Bridget [*to Peter*]. Tell him not to go, Peter.

Peter. It's no use. He doesn't hear a word we're saying.

Bridget. Try, Delia, and coax him over to the fire.

Delia. Michael, Michael, you won't leave me! You won't join the French and we going to be married to-morrow!

> [*She puts her arms about him. He turns to her as if about to yield.*

> *Old woman's voice outside:*

> They shall be remembered for ever;
> The people shall hear them for ever.

> [*Michael breaks away from Delia and goes towards neighbours at the door.*

Michael. Come, we have no time to lose; we must follow her.

> [*Michael and the neighbours go out.*

Peter [*laying his hand on Patrick's arm*]. Did you see an old woman going down the path?

Patrick. I did not; but I saw a young girl, and she had the walk of a queen.

THE END

NOTES

On Baile's Strand

Yeats began to write this play in 1901, having thought it out while walking in the Seven Woods of Coole Park, Lady Gregory's seat in Galway. It is based on her translation of 'The Only Son of Aoife' in *Cuchulain of Muirthemne* (1902). The original version was first published in 1903; its main revision occurs in the version published in 1906. It was first performed at the opening of the Abbey Theatre, Dublin, on 27 December 1904. It is dedicated to William Fay, an Irish working man who with his brother Frank, an accountant's clerk, had formed a company of actors. They were distinctive actors and were members of the Abbey company until 1907, when they resigned in protest against Miss Horniman's reorganization of the company. See W. G. Fay and Catherine Carswell, *The Fays and the Abbey Theatre* (1935).

p. 18 *William Fay:* (1872–1947), Irish actor.

p. 19 *Cuchulain, King of Muirthemne:* the warrior hero of the *Táin Bó Cuálnge*, or 'The Cattle Raid of Cooley', a Gaelic epic, contained in the Red Branch or Ulster cycle of tales. These were probably transmitted orally in the early Christian period, then written down by monks, and incorporated in late MSS. in the eleventh and fifteenth centuries.

Muirthemne: area ruled by Cuchulain in modern Co. Louth. Early versions of the play show that Conchubar and other kings had come to consult Cuchulain about the re-building of Emain, burned down after the deaths of Deirdre and Naoise, told in tale of 'The Fate of the Sons of Usna', one of the remscéla of the *Táin Bó Cuálnge*.

Conchubar: King of Uladh, or Ulster.

Dundealgan: modern Dundalk, Co. Louth.

p. 20 *Boann* (or *Boand*): Irish goddess, wife of Naada of the Silver Hand, who gave her name to the River Boyne which rose out of a secret well into which Boann looked, though this

was not allowed. The water rose and drowned her. Cf.
Eleanor Hull, *A Text-book of Irish Literature* (Dublin, 1906),
I, pp. 8–9. For derivation of the name, perhaps 'Cow-
white goddess', see T. F. O'Rahilly, *Early Irish History and
Mythology* (Dublin, 1946), p. 3. See also Kuno Meyer, *The
Voyage of Bran* (1895), p. 214.

Fand (or *Fann*): wife of Manannán Mac Lir, god of the sea.
She fell in love with Cuchulain, when her husband forsook
her; but he claimed her again and brought her back to his
realm. Her name may mean a tear, or the moisture of the
eye. Cf. Eleanor Hull, *ibid.*, p. 22.

p. 22 *a young man:* Conlaech, Cuchulain's son by Aoife.

Aoife's country: Aoife was a warrior queen in Scotland, who
was an enemy of Scathach (see note, p. 258). Cuchulain
conquered her, and forced her to grant him three wishes.
She was to become Scathach's vassal, to sleep one night
with him, and to bear him a son.

Banachas and Bonachas: demons of the air, that screamed around
warriors in combat.

Fomor: head of the Fomorians, gods of darkness, finally over-
thrown by the Tuatha de Danaan, gods of life and light.

p. 26 *Maeve of Cruachan:* Queen of Connacht, married to Ailill; she
was an amorous and warlike woman. Cruachan (modern
Rathcrogan, Co. Roscommon) was the capital of Connacht.

the northern pirates: Norse invaders, whose power was finally
crushed by Brian Boru in the Battle of Clontarf, 1014.

Sorcha: part of the Gaelic Otherworld.

p. 27 *your father:* one tradition held that Cuchulain was the son of
Lugh, the god of light. In *At the Hawk's Well* his father is
Sualtam.

p. 28 *Country-under-Wave:* Tir-fa-tonn, Otherworld in Gaelic
mythology.

p. 38 *Laegaire:* or Laeghaire Buadach, Leary the Triumphant, a hero
of the Red Branch.

p. 44 *Scathach:* warrior woman of the Island of Skye who taught
Cuchulain the art of war.

Uathach: daughter of Scathach, who was attracted by Cuchulain's beauty and made him welcome when he visited Scathach; he rewarded her by attacking her and killing the
champion who came to her aid.

Alba: Scotland.

p. 45 *Dubthach the Chafer:* character in *Táin Bó Cuálnge*. He was sent
by Conchubar as an emissary with Fergus (see *Deirdre*,
pp. 49–51) to bring Deirdre, Naoise and his brothers back
from Scotland. After the murder of Naoise and death of
Deirdre he joined Queen Maeve.

DEIRDRE

Yeats probably began to write this play in prose; he was working on
it in 1905 and 1906, largely at Coole Park. He was aware of the story
of 'The Tragical Fate of the Sons of Usna' in many forms (there were
prose translations, by O'Flanagan in the *Transactions of the Iberno-
Celtic Society* and by O'Curry in *Atlantis;* Sir Samuel Ferguson wrote
his version in verse) but based his play on Lady Gregory's *Cuchulain
of Muirthemne* (1902). It was first published in 1907 and first performed
at the Abbey Theatre, Dublin, on 26 November 1906. The dedication
is to Mrs. Patrick Campbell who took the part of Deirdre in 1906,
1907, and 1908.

p. 48 *Mrs. Patrick Campbell:* (1867–1940), famous actress.

Robert Gregory: (1881–1918), son of Lady Gregory, painter and
designer, shot down over Italy in 1918; for praise of his
versatility see Yeats's poem 'In Memory of Major Robert
Gregory'.

p. 49 *Fergus:* MacRoy or Son of Rogh, former king of Ulster who
was tricked out of his crown by Ness, the mother of
Conchubar. He was the poet of the Red Branch cycle of
tales.

Naoise: son of Usna; one of Conchubar's warriors.

Deirdre: formerly Conchubar's ward whom he kept in the hills
in the care of an old nurse Lavarcham, intending to marry
her. Naoise, one of his warriors, saw her, fell in love with
her, and ran away with her to Scotland, accompanied by

his brothers Ainle and Ardan. Deirdre prophesied she
would bring suffering on Ulster.

p. 54 *Lugaidh Redstripe:* a hero of the Red Branch.

Queen Edain: or Etáin, a beautiful woman, wooed, won, and
taken to the Otherworld by King Midir. Here, she is
changed into a fly by Fuamorach, Midir's wife, who blows
her into this world, where she is reborn three times before
Midir, in a game of chess, finally wins her back to the
Otherworld. The account of this forms one of the major
tales in the mythological cycle, *The Wooing of Etáin*.

p. 55 *a king of Surracha:* possibly Sorcha, Gaelic Otherworld.
O'Rahilly explains the name as originally *Syriaca*, Syria,
influenced by the native word *Sorcha*, bright. In later
romantic literature it denotes an exotic country with no
precise geographical position.

p. 60 *The hot Istain stone, And the cold stone of Fanes:* Professor David
Greene suggests that these may come from some medieval
lapidary and have nothing to do with Irish tradition.

p. 61 *a golden tongue:* Fergus was occasionally called 'Honeymouth'.

p. 72 *The daughter of the King of Leodas:* G. B. Saul, *Prolegomena to
to the Study of Yeats's Plays* (1958), p. 46, suggests Leodas
may be 'an imaginary Pictish king? — the "Lord of Dun-
treon"?' Dun Treóin is in Argyll. Leodas is from Leòdhas,
Gaelic name of the Isle of Lewis. Since rhyme in modern
Irish is that of vowels only Treóin and Leòdhais (gen. of
Leòdhas) would be interchangeable in the verse quoted, if
it translated an original. In versions of the Deirdre story the
woman who causes jealousy is the daughter of the Earl of
Dún Treóin. I am indebted to Professor David Greene for
this information.

THE PLAYER QUEEN

Yeats began to write this play in 1907 (cf. *Plays in Prose and Verse*,
1922, p. 429) with the intention of making a verse tragedy of it. He
finished a prose draft in 1908, and was working on a further prose
scenario in 1909. He continued to work on the play in 1914 and 1916.

The first performance was at the King's Hall, Covent Garden, London, on 25 May 1919; the first published version is that of 1922.

p. 83 *Kubla Khan, or Kublai Khan:* founder of Mongol dynasty in the thirteenth century.

p. 86 *the Bible says: Exodus* 22, 18.

Candlemas: celebrated on 2 February.

p. 91 *the donkey:* see *Matthew* 21, 2–10.

p. 94 *'The Tragical History of Noah's Deluge':* probably *Noah and the Flood*, a Chester miracle play.

p. 95 *Saint Octema:* an invented character.

p. 96 *Sleep of Adam: Genesis* 2, 21.

p. 105 *Pasiphae:* in mythology the daughter of Helios, married to Minos of Crete who, in order to secure the throne, prayed to Poseidon to send him a bull from the sea to sacrifice. The bull was so beautiful that Minos would not kill it, whereupon Pasiphae fell in love with it, disguised herself as a cow, and bore the Minotaur, half-man, half-bull, which lived in the labyrinth at Crete.

Leda: in mythology the mother of the Dioscuri and Helen. Zeus approached her in the shape of a swan and begat Helen. Leda was also the mother of Clytemnestra.

p. 107 *Cato:* Marcius Porcius Cato Uticensis (95–46 B.C.) was a Roman stoic who supported Pompey and, after his defeat, joined the Pompeians in Africa. After Caesar's victory at Thapsus, he committed suicide at Pharsalus.

Cicero: Marcius Tullius Cicero (106–43 B.C.), Roman orator, author, politician, led the opposition to Antony and faced death bravely after Octavian took Rome.

Demosthenes: (384–322 B.C.), Athenian orator who, while in exile, tried to organise combined action against Macedon after the death of Alexander. He returned to Athens, which was subsequently occupied by a Macedonian garrison, and a decree for his execution was passed. He took refuge in a temple; being pursued there, sucked poison concealed in his pen and died.

Petronius Arbiter: Roman, author of *Cena Trimalchicius,* a former proconsul and Nero's *arbiter elegantiae,* who, when Nero was turned against him by Tigellinus, committed suicide, writing a document denouncing Nero and his accomplices.

Xanadu: where Kubla Khan decreed a lordly pleasure house, in Coleridge's 'Kubla Khan'; the source is *Purchas his Pilgrimes* (1625).

Agamemnon: husband of Clytemnestra, brother of Menelaus, and leader of Greek armies against Troy. He sacrificed his daughter Iphigenia at Aulis, was murdered on his return to Argos by Clytemnestra and Aegisthus, her paramour.

Helen: wife of Menelaus, who went to Troy with Paris, son of Priam, and was thus the cause of the Trojan war.

p. 109 *Ionian music ... Dorian scale:* Yeats is making the normal distinction here between these modes of Greek music: the Ionic soft and effeminate, the Dorian simple and solemn.

Delphi: situated on slopes of Mount Parnassus, was the seat of a temple of Apollo and of a famous oracle, very influential between the eighth and fifth centuries B.C.

p. 111 *The Christian era ... an end:* an idea expressed by Yeats in *A Vision* and in many poems, that history consists of opposing gyres, one age being the reversal of another.

THE ONLY JEALOUSY OF EMER

Yeats began this play in 1916 and finished it in January 1918. The story probably derives from the legendary tale *The Sickbed* [or *Wasting-away*] *of Cuchulain* which is the basis for Lady Gregory's 'The Only Jealousy of Emer' in *Cuchulain of Muirthemne* (1902). The play was first published in *Poetry* (Chicago), January 1919, then in *Two Plays for Dancers* (1919). There were several revisions, the major ones contained in the version included in *Collected Plays* (1934). The play was first publicly performed in Holland with masks by Hildo van Krop. Cf. W. B. Yeats, *Wheels and Butterflies* (1934), p. 69. A prose version, *Fighting the Waves,* written in 1928, was performed at the Abbey Theatre, Dublin on 13 August 1929.

p. 121 *Cuchulain:* see note, p. 257.

Emer: Cuchulain's wife whom he won after a series of trials.

Eithne Inguba: Cuchulain's young mistress.

Sidhe: the gods of ancient Ireland.

p. 122 *Archimedes:* (287–212 B.C.), of Syracuse, a mathematician and inventor.

p. 124 *Baile's tree:* a reference to the story of Baile and Aillinn, lovers, to each of whom Aengus, the god of love, gave false news of the other's death. They died of broken hearts and were changed into white swans linked by a golden chain. A yew tree grew where Baile's body lay, a wild apple where Aillinn's.

Manannan, son of the sea: Manannán Mac Lir, the god of the sea.

p. 127 *Bricriu:* the figure is here distinguishing itself from Conchobar's poet Bricriu, known for his bitterness.

p. 131 *a hawk flew:* this refers to Yeats's play *At the Hawk's Well*, where Cuchulain is deceived by the guardian of the well, half-hawk, half-woman.

p. 133 *Fand:* wife of Manannán Mac Lir, see note p. 258.

THE RESURRECTION

Yeats drafted this play in 1925. It was first published in June 1927 in the *Adelphi*, then in *Stories of Michael Robartes and His Friends* (1921), and later in *Wheels and Butterflies* (1934). The first performance was at the Abbey Theatre, Dublin, on 30 July 1934.

p. 138 *Junzo Sato:* a Japanese who met Yeats after a lecture in Portland, Oregon, and gave him a sword which is mentioned in 'Meditations in Time of Civil War, III', and in 'A Dialogue of Self and Soul'.

p. 139 *the Peacock Theatre:* a small theatre (sometimes used for rehearsals) attached to the Abbey Theatre, Dublin.

Dionysus: Greek god of an emotional religion which particularly affected women, who seized an animal or a child at the height of their ecstasy and, tearing it apart, ate the pieces, believing they were incorporating the god and his power within themselves in so doing. These lines draw a parallel between the myth of Dionysus and the death and resurrection of Christ. Ellmann (*Identity of Yeats*, 1954, p. 260) draws on Sir James Frazer's *The Golden Bough* (which Yeats read) for this explanation: Dionysus, child of a mortal, Persephone, and an immortal, Zeus, was torn to pieces by the Titans. Athene (the 'staring virgin' of the poems: 'staring' indicating that she acts as if in a trance because the events are preordained) snatched the heart from his body, brought it on her hand to Zeus, who killed the Titans, swallowed the heart, and begat Dionysus again, upon another mortal, Semele.

that beating heart: in his introduction to this play Yeats gives Sir William Crookes's *Studies in Psychical Research* as a source for this image.

Magnus Annus: this passage is explained by a passage in *A Vision* (1926), page 149, where Yeats quotes Virgil's Fourth Eclogue: 'the cycles in their vast array begin anew; virgin Astrea comes, the reign of Saturn comes, and from the heights of Heaven a new generation of mankind descends ... Apollo now is king, and in your consulship, in yours, Pollio, the age of glory shall commence.' The verses state Yeats's idea that Christianity brought a radical violence into the world and ushered in a new historical period. See also *A Vision* (1937), pages 243–54, where he discusses the idea of a Great Year. The Muses sing of Magnus Annus as a play because they regard the ritual death and rebirth of the god as a recurring event, part of the cycles of history. Ellmann points out that 'both Gods had died and been reborn in March when the sun was between the Ram and the Fish, and when the moon was beside the constellation Virgo, who carries the star Spica in her hand'. In these stanzas Yeats is thinking of Virgil, *Eclogue*, IV, 6 'Iam redit et Virgo ...' where Virgo, daughter of Jupiter and Themis, is the last to leave Earth at the end of the golden age; but will return, bringing back the golden age. This Virgilian prophecy was later read as foretelling the coming of Mary (as Virgo) and Christ, the star of Bethlehem (as Spica).

p. 140 *Argo's:* Argo was the ship in which Jason sailed to fetch the Golden Fleece. The idea of a second Argo is in Virgil's Fourth Eclogue and also in Shelley's *Hellas.*

The Roman Empire stood appalled: because though there were but six million Christians in the Roman Empire's sixty million, the world was to become Christian, and the Empire to be destroyed by Christianity (a view Yeats shared with Gibbon).

that fierce virgin: Mary. Here R. Ellmann, *ibid.,* p. 261, remarks that these lines daringly assert a parallelism and even identity between the three pairs, Astraea and Spica, Athene and Dionysus, and Mary and Christ. Cf. Lady Gregory, *Journal,* 263, for an early version reading 'Virgo [the constellation] and the mystic star'.

the fabulous darkness: probably derived from a description of Christianity by Proclus, a fourth-century neo-Platonic philosopher (whom Yeats read in Thomas Taylor's translation of 1816, cf. F. A. C. Wilson, *Yeats and Tradition,* p. 59). Cf. *A Vision* (1937), pp. 277, 278, and *A Vision* (1926), pp. 185 *seq.*:

'... The irrational force that would create confusion and uproar as with the cry "The Babe, the Babe, is born" — the women speaking unknown tongues, the barbers and weavers expounding Divine revelation with all the vulgarity of their servitude, the tables that move or resound with raps — but creates a negligible sect. All about it is an *antithetical* aristocratic civilisation in its completed form, every detail of life hierarchical, every great man's door crowded at dawn by petitioners, great wealth everywhere in few men's hands, all dependent upon a few, up to the Emperor himself who is a God dependent upon a greater God, and, everywhere in court, in the family, an inequality made law, and floating over all the Romanised Gods of Greece in their physical superiority.... The world became

Christian, "that fabulous formless darkness" as it seemed to a philosopher of the fourth century, blotted out "every beautiful thing", not through the conversion of crowds or general change of opinion, or through any pressure from below, for civilisation was *antithetical* still, but by an act of power.'

the Eleven: the disciples, minus Judas.

p. 141 *thirteen:* Christ and the twelve disciples.

Jesus divided bread and wine: see *Matthew* 26, 26–27.

Peter: see *Matthew* 26, 37–75.

p. 143 *born of a woman:* see *Isaiah* 7, 14.

p. 145 *Astrea's:* Astrea, a daughter of Zeus, was said to have lived on earth and been a source of blessing to men during the Golden Age. She is mentioned in the passage from Virgil quoted above. G. B. Saul, *op. cit.,* p. 85, remarks, 'Astræa: goddess of justice, sometimes regarded as the daughter of the Titan Astraeus by Eos; in her heavenly transformation, Virgo.'

p. 146 *the goddess:* Athene. Cf. W. B. Yeats 'The Phases of the Moon', *Collected Poems,* p. 185.

Achilles: son of Peleus and Thetis, bravest of the Greeks in the Trojan war, was wounded in his heel (the only vulnerable part of his body, by which Thetis had held him when plunging him in the Styx) by Paris and died.

Lucretius: Titus Lucretius Carus (*c.* 99–55 B.C.), Roman poet and author of *De Rerum Naturae,* a philosophical poem in which he tries to show that the course of the world can be explained without divine intervention.

p. 151 *the heart of a phantom,* see note p. 264.

Heracleitus: of Ephesus, wrote a work 'Concerning Nature' in which he asserted all things were in a state of flux.

Galilean turbulence: foretold by astronomers in Babylon who reduce man's status by their science; Man is being taught that he is nothing in comparison to the universe; He is becoming featureless: cf. *A Vision* (1937), pp. 273 *seq.*:

'The mind that brought the change, if considered as man

only, is a climax of whatever Greek and Roman thought was most a contradiction to its age; but considered as more than man He controlled what Neo-Pythagorean and Stoic could not — irrational force. He could announce the new age, all that had not been thought of, or touched, or seen, because He could substitute for reason, miracle.'

p. 152 *Everything that man esteems:* a praise of man, who goes on creating heroically despite the fact that all things pass away. Cf. W. B. Yeats, *Autobiographies,* p. 315.

THE WORDS UPON THE WINDOW-PANE

The starting-point for this play, according to Allan Wade, *The Letters of W. B. Yeats* (1954), p. 891 *n.*, was Yeats's finding in 1910 an inscription cut on a window in Oliver St. John Gogarty's Dublin house 'Fairfield'. He wrote the play when he was reading deeply in Swift during 1930; it was finished in October and performed at the Abbey Theatre, Dublin, on 17 November 1930. It was first published in 1934.

p. 154 *Lady Gregory:* Lady Augusta Gregory (1852–1932), Irish playwright, widow of Sir William Gregory; she co-operated with Yeats in establishing the Abbey Theatre.

p. 155 *the Corbets of Ballymoney:* Yeats had Corbet relatives, but this name and that of Ballymoney (there are many villages or towns with this name in Ireland, for instance, in Co. Antrim, Co. Cork, Co. Wexford) are probably taken to indicate a young man of some social and intellectual standing.

p. 156 *Myers' 'Human Personality':* written by F. W. H. Myers (1843–1901) and published in 1903 in two volumes.

a wild book: either *A New Revelation* (1918) or a *History of Spiritualism* (2 vols., 1926) by Sir Arthur Conan Doyle, perhaps more widely known for his Sherlock Holmes detective stories.

Lord Dunraven, then Lord Adare: introduced to 'place' Dr. Trench. The full title of this Irish peerage created for the Quin family was Earl of Dunraven and Viscount Adare.

This reference is probably to the third Earl, Edward Wyndham-Quin, a scholar of literature and archaeology.

David Home: presumably Daniel D. Home (1833–86), Scottish medium and spiritualist.

p. 157 *Emanuel Swedenborg:* (1688–1772), Swedish scientist and mystic philosopher, devoted his life after 1745 to interpreting the scriptures, his being a theosophical system.

Harold's Cross: Dublin suburb and situation of dog-racing track.

Grattan: Henry Grattan (1746–1820), Irish barrister and M.P.; carried an address demanding legislative independence in 1782. The Irish parliament which lasted until 1800 was known as Grattan's parliament.

Curran: John Philpot Curran (1750–1817), Irish barrister and M.P., who defended the prisoners in the 1798 trials and opposed the Union.

Jonathan Swift: (1667–1745), Dean of St. Patrick's Cathedral, Dublin, wrote *Journal to Stella*, a series of letters from 1710 to 1713 to Esther Johnson and Rebecca Dingley, her companion.

Stella: Swift's name for Esther Johnson (1681–1728), whom he met in Sir William Temple's household when he was secretary there; they remained close friends till her death. He was buried by her side in St. Patrick's Cathedral.

Vanessa: Swift's name for Esther Vanhomrigh (1690–1723), whom he met in London in 1708; she fell in love with him, and Swift's poem 'Cadenus and Vanessa' is an account of their unhappy relationship.

p. 159 *Bolingbroke:* Henry St. John Bolingbroke, first Viscount (1678–1751), friend of Swift, author, orator, politician, in charge of the negotiations leading to the Peace of Utrecht in 1710. Dismissed on the accession of George I, he fled to France, but returned in 1723.

Robert Harley: first Earl of Oxford (1661–1724), friend of Swift, a moderate Tory who persuaded his party to pass the Act of Settlement. He remained in a Whig ministry until 1708. In 1710 he and St. John led the Tory Ministry which brought about the Treaty of Utrecht (1713). He was dismissed in 1714 through the Jacobite intrigues of his colleague.

Ormonde: James Butler, Duke of Ormonde (1610–88), born of an ancient Anglo-Irish family, distinguished himself in the Strafford administration and in the rebellions of 1640 was appointed chief commander of the army. James Butler, second Duke of Ormonde (1665–1746), served in the army against Monmouth, at the Battle of the Boyne; Lord Lieutenant of Ireland three times 1703–13; impeached for high treason 1705, retired to Avignon. The Duke was greatly admired by Swift. Benjamin Yeats married into the Butler family in 1773, and the Yeats' family always valued this connection, using 'Butler' frequently as a Christian name.

Brutus: Marcius Junius Brutus (85–42 B.C.) joined Pompey, but was pardoned by Caesar after the battle of Pharsalia. Joined the conspiracy against Caesar; after the latter's murder Brutus and Cassius were defeated at Philippi and Brutus committed suicide.

Jean Jacques Rousseau: (1712–78), born at Geneva, author and philosopher. His *Du Contrat Social* (1762) prepared the way for the French Revolution.

Saeva indignatio: a reference to Swift's epitaph in St. Patrick's Cathedral, Dublin, which runs

> Ubi saeva indignatio
> Ulterius cor lacerare nequit.
> Abi, viator,
> Et imitare, si poteris,
> Strenuum pro virili libertatis vindicem.

Yeats translated it in 'Swift's Epitaph', *Collected Poems*, p. 277.

Cato: see note, p. 261.

p. 162 *the quotation: Job* 4, 13–15: In thoughts from the visions of the night, when deep sleep falleth on men, Fear came upon me, and trembling which made all my bones to shake. Then a spirit passed before my face; the hair of my flesh stood up.

p. 165 *the Lord Treasurer:* Robert Harley, first Earl of Oxford (1661–1724).

Plutarch: (*c.* A.D. 46–120), Greek biographer, wrote parallel lives of twenty-three Greeks and twenty-three Romans.

p. 166 *Dr. Arbuthnot:* Dr. John Arbuthnot (1667–1735) was Queen Anne's doctor, an author, and a friend of Swift and Pope.

a line of Dryden's: 'great wits are sure to madness / Near allied', from Dryden's *Absalom and Achitophel*, I. 163.

p. 168 *Chrysostom:* St. John (*c.* A.D. 345–407), eloquent (Chrysostom = golden-mouthed) Greek Father of the Church, wrote commentaries on the Gospel of St. Matthew and the Epistles to the Romans and Corinthians.

p. 171 *His brain had gone:* probably not correct, but for an expert view of Swift's health see T. G. Wilson, 'Swift's Personality and Death Masks', *A Review of English Literature*, July 1962.

p. 172 *perish the day:* from *Job* 3, 3: Let the day perish wherein I was born.

A FULL MOON IN MARCH

Yeats developed this play, first published in 1935, from *The King of the Great Clock Tower* (1934), which was first written in prose, and on which he was working in 1933. He may have begun to work on the idea about 1929.

p. 176 *Pythagoras:* a Greek philosopher of the sixth century B.C. who thought the universe had a mathematical basis. He believed in the Orphic doctrine of metempsychosis, the purificatory or punishing process in which souls transmigrated from man to man, or man to animal or animal to man.

p. 180 *An ancient Irish Queen:* Queen Maeve of Connacht.

an inkeeper's daughter: the Empress Theophano, married by Romanus II, *c.* A.D. 956.

THE HERNE'S EGG

Yeats began to write this play in 1935. It was first published in 1938 and first performed by Lord Longford's company in 1939; it was later performed at the Abbey Theatre on 29 October and 5 November 1950. Mr. Austin Clarke has suggested that the play is founded on a passage in Sir Samuel Ferguson's *Congal* (1872).

p. 187 *a great herne:* a heron.

    Congal: an Ulster king who rebelled against the High King Domnal in an attempt to reassert paganism; he was defeated at the Battle of Moyra.

    Connacht: one of the five ancient kingdoms of Ireland, its capital being Cruachan.

    Aedh: Irish for Hugh.

    Tara: a hill in Co. Meath, seat of government of the High Kings of Ireland.

p. 191 *Danae's lap:* Danae was the daughter of Acrisius, king of Argos, who shut her in a brazen tower as an oracle foretold he would be killed by his daughter's son. Zeus fell in love with her and visited her in a shower of gold; their son was Perseus, who eventually did kill his grandfather by accident.

p. 203 *Munster:* southern province of Ireland.

p. 208 *Slieve Fuadh:* (modern Sliabh Fuaid) the highest mountain in the Fews range in Armagh. Cuchulain when setting off from Dundalk to Emain Macha as a boy was told by his mother that he would have a hard journey as Slieve Fuadh lay in between.

PURGATORY

Yeats wrote this play between March and May 1938. It was first published in *Last Poems and Two Plays* (1939) and first performed at the Abbey Theatre, Dublin on 10 August 1938.

p. 221 *the Curragh:* district in Co. Kildare, famous for its race-course and as a breeding and training ground for race-horses.

Aughrim and the Boyne: two battles crucial in Irish and European history. At the Boyne on 1 July 1690, William defeated James and thus brought about the triumph of Louis' European opponents. At Aughrim, twelve days later, Ginkle, William's Dutch commander, broke the Irish army, 11,000 men of which left for France after the Siege of Limerick ended in October 1690.

p. 222 *the Puck Fair:* an annual festival lasting three days and nights (Gathering Day, Market or Fair Day and Scattering Day), held at Kilorglin, Co. Kerry. A goat is still crowned king as part of the ceremonies, which are attended by many of the tinkers of Ireland.

p. 224 *Tertullian:* Quintus Septimus Florens Tertullianus (*c.* A.D. 160–225), lawyer and author, native of the Roman province of Africa, was converted to Christianity; his *Apology* rebuts charges against Christianity.

THE DEATH OF CUCHULAIN

Yeats began this play in the autumn of 1938, ending it before Christmas of that year. It was first published in *Last Poems and Two Plays* (1939) and first performed at the Abbey Theatre, Dublin, in 1949.

p. 231 *Cuchulain:* see note, p. 257.

   Eithne Inguba: see note, p. 263.

   Aoife: see note, p. 258.

   Emer: see note, p. 263.

   Talma: François Joseph Talma (1763–1826), French tragedian.

p. 232 *Hilaire Germaine Edgar Degas:* (1834–1917), French painter.

   Rameses the Great: (1311–1245 B.C.), Pharaoh of Egypt.

p. 233 *Maeve:* see note, p. 258.

   Emain Macha: capital of Ulster sited near modern Armagh, said to have been burnt in A.D. 332.

   Conall Caernach: an Ulster hero, greatest in prowess after Culchulain.

p. 236 *The Morrigu:* a crow-headed war goddess.

   At the Hawk's Well: Yeats began *At the Hawk's Well* in 1915; it was first performed in Lady Cunard's drawing-room in

London in March 1916, first published in 1917. This play tells how Cuchulain is lured away by the woman of the well and begets a son on her.

On Baile's Strand: Yeats's play (see pp. 19–46) tells the story of how Cuchulain kills this son.

p. 237 *The grey of Macha:* one of Cuchulain's two chariot horses, a kelpie or lake-horse.

p. 240 *Maeve's latest lover:* the Queen was notoriously amorous.

her sons...these other men: It is likely that Yeats is using poetic licence here. In the oldest version of the legend the hero is killed by Lugaid mac Con Roí and Erc mac Coirbri, by three magic spears prepared by the three sons of Calatín. Later versions add MacNiad mac Finn maic Rosa, to make one man for each spear. The fathers of all six had been killed by Cuchulain; this is the reason given for their combining to kill him.

p. 241 *Usna's boys:* Naoise and his brothers, Ardan and Ainle, who had accompanied him into Scotland when he ran away with Deirdre, King Conchubar's ward.

the Post Office: The General Post Office, Dublin, was held by the insurgents in the Easter Rising 1916, and was the scene of their surrender.

Pearse: Patrick Henry Pearse (1879–1916), Irish poet and leader, shot for taking part in the 1916 Rising, when he was president of the provisional government.

Connolly: James Connolly (1870–1916), Irish trade-union leader and organiser of the Irish Citizen Army, shot for his part in the 1916 Rising.

p. 242 *Oliver Sheppard:* (d. 1941), Irish sculptor.

CATHLEEN NI HOOLIHAN

Yeats, in a note dated 1903 and addressed to Lady Gregory, gives the source of this play (the title is later spelt as Cathleen ni Houlihan) as a dream he had 'almost distinct as a vision, of a cottage where there was well-being and firelight and talk of a marriage and into the midst of that cottage there came an old woman in a long cloak. She was

Ireland herself, that Cathleen ni Hoolihan for whom so many songs have been sung and about whom so many stories have been told and for whose sake so many have gone to their death.' The play was first published in *Samhain*, October 1902, and first performed at St. Teresa's Total Abstinence Association Hall, Dublin, on 2 April 1902, with Maud Gonne in the title-rôle.

p. 245 *Kathleen (or Cathleen) ni Houlihan*: a symbol of Ireland.

        Killala: in Co. Mayo, where a French force under General Humbert landed on 22 August 1798.

p. 247 *Ballina*: town in Co. Mayo.

p. 248 *Enniscrone*: G. B. Saul, *op. cit.*, p. 35, suggests Inchicronan, Co. Clare.

p. 250 *too many strangers*: the English in Ireland.

        four beautiful green fields: the four provinces of Ireland.

p. 251 *Kilglas*: village near Killala, spelt Kilglass in later versions.

p. 252 *a red man*: probably 'Red' Hugh Roe O'Donnell (c. 1571-1602), escaped from prison in Dublin, overran Connacht, shared in victory of Yellow Ford, failed to reduce Kinsale, went to Spain for aid, and was poisoned there.

        a man of the O'Sullivans: probably Donal O'Sullivan Beare (1560-1618), received Spanish garrison in his castle of Dunboy, 1601; Carew demolished it. O'Sullivan fought his way to Ulster, then went to London, but failing to obtain restitution from James, went to Spain, where he was killed by a refugee.

        Brian Boru: (926-1014), High King of Ireland, killed in victorious battle with the Danes at Clontarf, Dublin, 1014.

p. 254 *keening*: Irish form of mourning over the dead.

        white-scarfed riders: white-robed priests at funerals.

SELECT BIBLIOGRAPHY

EDITIONS OF YEATS'S PLAYS

The Collected Works in Verse and Prose of William Butler Yeats (8 vols., 1908)

Volumes II, III, and IV contain the texts of plays and notes.

Plays in Prose and Verse for an Irish Theatre (1922)
Contains brief notes on the plays.

Plays and Controversies (1923)
Contains essays on 'The Irish Dramatic Movement' and 'A People's Theatre'.

Wheels and Butterflies (1934)
Contains very useful introduction.

Collected Plays (1934)

Last Poems and Plays (1940)

Collected Plays (1952)
The best edition, though the dates supplied are misleading. Peter Ure, *Yeats the Playwright* (1963) gives useful information on the dates of composition, publication, and performance; see also Allan Wade, *A Bibliography of the Writings of W. B. Yeats* (1951; rev. ed., 1958).

CRITICISM AND BIOGRAPHY

W. B. Yeats, *Essays and Introductions* (1961); *Explorations* (1962)
These two volumes contain essays by Yeats on the theatre and on particular plays and dramatists. Selections are contained in St. Martin's Library, *Selected Criticism* (1964) and *Selected Prose* (1964).

Birgit Bjersby, *The Interpretation of the Cuchulain Legend in the Works of W. B. Yeats* (1950).

Joseph Hone, *W. B. Yeats 1865–1939* (1943; rev. ed., 1963)

A. Norman Jeffares, *Yeats: Man and Poet* (1949; rev. ed., 1962)

G. B. Saul, *Prolegomena to the Plays of W. B. Yeats* (1958)

Peter Ure, *Yeats the Playwright* (1963)

Helen Vendler, *Yeats's Vision and the Later Plays* (1963)

F. A. C. Wilson, *W. B. Yeats and Tradition* (1958)

F. A. C. Wilson, *Yeats's Iconography* (1960)

*Printed in Great Britain by Richard Clay and Company, Ltd.,
Bungay, Suffolk*

ST MARTIN'S LIBRARY

An attractive and inexpensive paperback series of classics. A complete list of existing titles is given below. Further titles are in the press.

ROLF BOLDREWOOD: Robbery Under Arms

A. C. BRADLEY: Shakespearean Tragedy

LEWIS CARROLL: Alice in Wonderland *and* Through the Looking-Glass. *Illustrated by Sir John Tenniel*

SIR J. G. FRAZER: The Golden Bough

SIR W. S. GILBERT: The Savoy Operas

THOMAS HARDY: Far from the Madding Crowd; Jude the Obscure; The Mayor of Casterbridge; The Return of the Native; Tess of the d'Urbervilles; The Trumpet-Major; Under the Greenwood Tree; The Woodlanders

RICHARD HILLARY: The Last Enemy

THOMAS HUGHES: Tom Brown's School-Days. *Illustrated by Edmund J. Sullivan*

RUDYARD KIPLING: All the Mowgli Stories; Captains Courageous; Just So Stories. *Illustrated by the author;* Kim; Puck of Pook's Hill; The Jungle Book; The Second Jungle Book; Stalky & Co.

A. G. MACDONELL: England, Their England

MARGARET MITCHELL: Gone with the Wind

CHARLES MORGAN: The Fountain; Portrait in a Mirror

SEAN O'CASEY: Autobiographies (in two volumes); Five One-Act Plays; Three Plays

SIR OSBERT SITWELL: Left Hand, Right Hand!; The Scarlet Tree; Great Morning; Laughter in the Next Room

WILLIAM TEMPLE: Readings in St. John's Gospel (1st and 2nd Series)

SIR HUGH WALPOLE: Rogue Herries; Judith Paris; Jeremy

OWEN WISTER: The Virginian

W. B. YEATS: Selected Criticism; Selected Plays; Selected Poetry; Selected Prose

Born in the UK, **Becky Wick**... wanderlust from an early age. ... all over the world, from London to Dubai, Sydney, Bali, NYC and Amsterdam. She's written for the likes of *GQ*, *Hello!*, *Fabulous* and *Time Out*, a host of YA romance, plus three travel memoirs—*Burqalicious*, *Balilicious* and *Latinalicious* (HarperCollins, Australia). Now she blends travel with romance for Mills & Boon and loves every minute! Tweet her @bex_wicks and subscribe at beckywicks.com.

Born and raised on the Wirral Peninsula in England, **Charlotte Hawkes** is mum to two intrepid boys who love her to play building block games with them, and who object loudly to the amount of time she spends on the computer. When she isn't writing—or building with blocks—she is company director for a small Anglo/French construction firm. Charlotte loves to hear from readers, and you can contact her at her website: charlotte-hawkes.com.

HIGHLAND FLING WITH HER BEST FRIEND

BECKY WICKS

NEUROSURGEON, SINGLE DAD… HUSBAND?

CHARLOTTE HAWKES

MILLS & BOON

First published in Great Britain 2023
by Mills & Boon, an imprint of HarperCollins*Publishers* Ltd,
1 London Bridge Street, London, SE1 9GF

www.harpercollins.co.uk

HarperCollins*Publishers*
Macken House, 39/40 Mayor Street Upper,
Dublin 1, D01 C9W8, Ireland

Highland Fling with Her Best Friend © 2023 Becky Wicks

Neurosurgeon, Single Dad...Husband? © 2023 Charlotte Hawkes

ISBN: 978-0-263-30598-2

02/23

HIGHLAND FLING
WITH HER
BEST FRIEND

BECKY WICKS

MILLS & BOON

For the one who got away. You know who you are.

CHAPTER ONE

*Just an hour and a half from Glasgow, the Isle of Bute
is a gorgeous island in the Firth of Clyde, where the
hips and haws and the hum of the bees are all that
interrupts the stillness...'*

A CLATTER FROM the kitchen made Sadie look up from her
laptop. Her good friend of a decade, Owen Penner, was
bent over with his nose in her fridge, looking for something she'd probably forgotten to buy at the supermarket.

She carried on reading the guidebook, grateful it was a
Saturday morning and they had nowhere else to be.

'It says here it's largely ignored by travellers to Scotland,
who arguably miss its abundance of Scottish Isle beauty.
Do you know how quiet it's going to be there, Owen, compared to Chapel Hill…or Boston? Are you sure you're ready
for it?'

'Where's the orange juice?' He was distracted.

'There isn't any.'

'There's always orange juice at your place.'

Sadie tutted. 'Callum bought that, remember? Not me.
Owen, it doesn't sound like you're very excited to be taking this position in literally two weeks' time…'

'Of course I'm serious.' Owen's tone changed abruptly
as he closed the fridge and marched to her dramatically like

a military soldier. 'Checking in with full attention, Commander Mills.' He saluted, sliding his six-foot frame back into the dining chair beside her.

Sadie pulled her newly styled honey-toned waves tighter into their ponytail, biting back a smile as his cologne hit her nostrils, plus that unmistakeable Owen smell—the personalised scent she'd missed the whole time he'd been gone in America, studying the intricacies of functional neurology and adding it to his repertoire. He might be one of London's top neurologists, and undoubtedly had one of the biggest brains she'd ever known, but Owen was still a man. Therefore he sometimes found it tough to multitask.

She'd never admit it, least of all to him, but if you looked beyond the chiselled cheekbones and sculpted nose, and the wicked gleaming brown eyes that drove his female conquests crazy, he was still kind of an adorable kid in a buff adult's body.

His biceps told her he'd spent a lot of his time in Boston working out at an expensive gym with the rest of the fit American colleagues she'd seen on his social media, and now that it was coming on for spring, he probably knew how good he looked in a new green shirt that she'd never seen before.

She'd complimented him on it. Men these days didn't get enough compliments, which she'd read wasn't good for their mental health—an area of huge importance and interest to her since…well, since her brother's death. So she'd been making an effort to change that lately.

Not that it had changed anything with Callum.

It hit her with a jolt of pride that the sound of her ex's name on her lips just now, and the thought of him leaving the flat with her beloved Larry the cactus, wasn't still causing rafts of anger and humiliation and fear to bowl her over—not like it had done before. Thankfully Owen had returned home after his year away just days after the break-up, which had helped things immensely. But…*ugh*. Four years wasted.

Four years of planning a life with Callum McFarley, all for him to tell her, *'It's just not working out. I don't feel a connection any more,'* right before she was due to leave for her coveted placement at Rothesay Recovery.

The high-end facility developed treatment plans to directly address each emotional, physical and psychological issue of its patients. She'd been all set to take a six-month placement in the role of occupational health consultant there, amongst the world's most exclusive clientele, all of whom were paying an absolute fortune to stay at Rothesay. After the break-up, though, she'd almost backed out.

The facility was so remote. She'd had a feeling all that silence would wreck her head, and she wanted to be her very best self for her patients. If it hadn't been for Owen suddenly announcing he wanted to go too, she would have cancelled.

'So, show me more testimonials,' Owen said now, his coffee steaming up his glasses.

She slid the laptop over to him and watched as he used his T-shirt to wipe the lenses before he leaned closer to read the testimonials from satisfied patients against a backdrop of the towering, castle-like mansion that housed the exclusive Rothesay Recovery.

She still couldn't quite believe they were *both* going to be working there. Together. Before he'd left to boost his career in the US, he'd worked at St Thomas's Hospital, while she'd been consulting at various places around London as usual. They'd actually never worked in the same facility before. And heading to this craggy, windswept part of Scotland's west coast would be a world away from his former plan to take a well-earned break from work altogether in Thailand.

'Southeast Asia will still be there later,' he'd told her,

when she'd asked him why he'd give that up to go to Scotland with her.

But hadn't he said that nothing had ever worked him harder than the American health system?

'It's not the kind of island you had in mind when you showed me that resort on Kho Samui,' she said, testing him further now, studying the hilly background to the text alongside him. This page detailed the comprehensive treatments offered in this safe haven for high-profile, high-net-worth individuals who were struggling with various physical and mental health issues.

'It sounds like you don't actually want me to go,' he said, feigning a sorrowful look. 'You don't have to worry, Sadie, I'm committed.'

'That'll be a first.' She couldn't help a sly eye-roll—her way of teasing him, of course, no malicious harm meant.

Owen perched his glasses back onto his nose slowly and played with his phone for a second. For some reason the look that crossed his face at her words sent a spiky shard of ice through her heart.

'I'm teasing you,' she reassured him quickly.

He merely shrugged, and she felt worse.

Now that she thought about it, this notorious playboy who was her best friend in this entire city—OK, maybe in the entire world—hadn't mentioned being with anyone in a while. If he'd met anyone in America, he hadn't said so.

But seriously… Did she need to bring up the stream of women he usually enjoyed hovering around him like dogs in heat? She'd given up trying to meet his girlfriends over the years because they never lasted more than five minutes. He didn't do relationships—which was his prerogative, she reminded herself. Not everyone was like her. Serial monogamy was *her* trademark.

Sadie watched his handsome profile as he clicked

through the website. Then he asked her what she was smiling at.

'You're so paranoid,' she said, nudging him, flushing.

She'd been thinking about how he had arms like a superhero now and wondering—with the strangest twinge of jealousy—how many women must have swooned over his British accent in America.

But she had also been thinking how proud she was to call one of London's most highly rated neurologists her friend. Owen might be a player in his personal life, but he was a hero in his profession. He'd saved more lives than he'd admit—humble as he was, at least when it came to his career.

While conventional neurology was designed to spot diseases and pathology, often it couldn't properly diagnose a problem unless it was already advanced. Owen had come back from Boston one of the most qualified doctors in his profession. He was now equipped to advise and treat people searching for treatments alternative to what traditional neurology might offer them. He could identify which areas of the brain were compromised and figure out how to fix them, and do it all with the same effervescent charm that had always made countless people fall in love with him.

She was probably the only woman in their circle of friends he'd never hit on.

Gosh, it was ten whole years ago now since they'd met at Imperial College, she thought, accepting his offer of a cup of coffee and watching his tall frame as he slunk across the kitchen in his socks to get it for her. He'd accidentally flicked a pen in her direction back then, and had got blue ink all over her white jeans. She'd yelled at him. He'd apologised, bought her lunch, talked her ear off, and made her laugh—and also wonder how it was they'd never spoken to each other before that. They'd been four years into their seven-year course, after all. But then, she'd been a bit of a loner for a long time, grieving for Chris, her brother.

She straightened her back, seeing Owen glancing at her sideways, probably trying to read her mind. He often looked at her the way he was doing now, when she was quiet.

Owen had been instrumental in urging her out of her shell again after they'd become friends aged twenty-two, but even now, ten years later, she still felt like a shadow of the person she'd been before Chris had died.

'Like I said, it's going to be very quiet there,' she reminded him now, pushing thoughts of the past away with a mental broomstick and motioning to the screen before he could ask what was on her mind.

Scotland was exactly what she needed, for many reasons.

'Maybe some quiet will be good for me,' Owen replied with a shrug, but he was still looking at her with interest.

Owen didn't know much about Chris—not all the details anyway. Certainly not the fact that her brother had taken his own life. When the topic of his recent death had come up not long after they'd met she'd let him think it was an accident. Her grief had been all-consuming then, even four years after the event, and talking about it with Owen had been the last thing she'd wanted.

But he'd swept into her life and eased the suffering almost instantly. In fact, Owen Penner was still the friend she called when jokes and light-heartedness were required.

So her brother had loaded up on booze and steered his motorbike into a quarry right before she was due to start her course at Imperial College… So her parents had got a sad, quiet divorce while she was burying herself in her studies… It didn't mean she had to burden other people with her past, or have her issues picked apart and analysed.

She should've been a better sister—yes. She should've noticed sooner that her fun-loving, free-spirited brother had started showing signs of depleting mental health. She should have noticed her own parents slipping further and further apart after his death. But she hadn't seen any of it.

Sometimes she thought that maybe her career choice was an inevitable product of her trying to assuage the guilt she felt over Chris's death. Psychiatry hadn't felt like a great fit—she'd wanted to study something more diverse—but assessing patients' mental health was vital in her consultancy practice now, and she saw a part of herself—and Chris—in every patient.

'Will I need a kilt?' Owen asked now, breaking into her thoughts.

She snorted, imagining it suddenly. He'd look hot in a kilt. Really hot.

Why was she suddenly thinking things like this about Owen?

Because you missed him, she reminded herself, *and you appreciate him, that's all*.

She'd been three seconds away from withdrawing her application for the occupational health consultant placement at Rothesay Recovery the night Owen had offered to apply there too—they'd still had a placement of the same length for a neurologist open at the time.

'Why don't I go with you?'

He'd said it so matter-of-factly, right there and then over the takeaway he'd bought her, as if he didn't even have to think about it.

'Unless you really don't want me jumping in on your dream role?'

'Why would I mind?' she'd replied, quickly. It hadn't even crossed her mind to mind—only that he might not actually mean it.

God, she'd missed him when he'd left for America. Things hadn't been quite the same without him around.

'We've never been anywhere together outside of London,

really, have we?' she said now, sipping her coffee, studying the three-day growth darkening his jawline.

He looked good with a bit of a beard, and a hint of his thirty-two years in the one or two flecks of grey she knew he hated. Owen was, without a doubt, the most physically attractive man she'd ever met. Callum—slimmer, shorter, never quite as successful, though not through lack of trying—had been intimidated by their friendship sometimes.

Make that the whole time, she thought now, remembering one afternoon out on the river in Richmond, when Callum had accused Owen of being in love with her. She and Owen had been having another one of their 'accent competitions', in which they competed to see who could do the best accents from around the world. Callum had called it stupid. Owen had rolled his eyes in her direction and whispered something in a very bad Mancunian accent and Callum had just exploded at both of them. Totally ruined the mood.

Owen had hooked up with some girl from Malaysia that very night in a pub. While she'd been in another corner, saying whatever she could to placate Callum on the subject of what he called her 'blatant flirting' with Owen.

That particular hook-up had been Owen's way of proving to Callum he in no way wanted *her* as another notch on his bedpost. She knew that much. But when he'd ended things, less than a week later, Owen had also been showing everyone—yet again—that he definitely wasn't the relationship type. He was there for all the fun, but Owen Penner just didn't fall in love. He didn't commit to anyone. It wasn't *him*. And that was fine by her. She knew where she stood with Owen and that was all that mattered.

Owen's eyes were still narrowed, as if he was trying to remember somewhere they'd been together that wasn't London. Of course *she* remembered everywhere they'd ever been together. Just as their relationship had never gone beyond the friend zone, their friendship had never gone beyond Zone Five.

They talked on about the clients they might meet, and the fishing they might do in the lake on the Rothesay estate, and as the hours passed, as they always did so easily in his company, she allowed a little bubble of excitement to ripple through her nerves.

'You've never been fishing in your life, Owen!'

'Well, *you've* never hiked up anything higher than Primrose Hill, Sadie.'

He pulled his *Shrek* face at her then, which made his chin curl up into his neck while he bit on his lip, and she sniggered into her cup, thinking, as she always did, that even when he tried to look ugly he couldn't.

She and Owen had fun wherever they went. Why should Scotland be any different? Mind you…they might have more alone time together there, she and Owen. Would their friendship be tested? she wondered suddenly, studying his slender fingers on the laptop keys. Didn't remote living test people?

What about all those wilderness programmes on the telly, about people forced apart by difficult circumstances. She would never do anything to put her friendship with Owen at risk—*ever*. God knew she'd already lost enough important people in her life. To lose him too would be unacceptable.

CHAPTER TWO

OWEN SHRUGGED FURTHER into his jacket and scarf as the seagulls dived and darted at the front of the ferry from Wemyss Bay to Rothesay, the main town on the Isle of Bute. For a moment he imagined himself on a sunny beach in Thailand, cocktail in hand, the shadows of swaying palms playing across his shirtless chest, and wondered if he'd made a huge mistake.

But one look at Sadie huddled into her own scarf reminded him that he'd rather be in cold and rainy Scotland with her than lounging in Thai sunbeams with anyone else. They always had fun.

Besides, it wasn't *actually* raining…yet. It probably would soon enough, despite the current spring vibes. Scotland wasn't exactly renowned for its excellent climate and it was cold even now, in late March. But it was beautiful, and Sadie was beautiful, and everything was working out just fine.

He caught himself. What was he doing, thinking things like *Sadie is beautiful*?

Of course she was beautiful—that was an undisputed, undeniable fact, as pointless to observe as *Scotland is Scottish*.

'Look how gorgeous it is,' Sadie enthused with a slight squeal, looking around from behind her oversized sunglasses.

The smart Victorian buildings lining the seafront in Rothesay were bursting into view now, pretty as the postcard his mother had used to keep on the fridge. The water was as blue as it was in Thailand. He could even see trees that looked suspiciously like palms.

'It's exactly how I imagined,' she said. 'I can't believe we're actually here, Owen. I thought you might at least be *thinking* about changing your mind.'

Owen chewed on his cheek and stared at a strand of honey-brown hair blowing free from her ponytail around her face. He'd thought about it, yes, but his heart would never have let him. The thought of his hard-working, loyal and recently heartbroken friend of ten years missing out on an opportunity like this because of an idiot like Callum made his blood boil. The only choice had been to come with her.

'I had to see the home of whisky and haggis for myself,' he said. 'Otherwise you'd just try to show me on your phone, and we both know you take terrible photos.'

Sadie smiled and told him she was serious, and grateful. Then she looked at her feet, and sniffed self-consciously, as if she didn't know how to handle a man who actually stuck to his word.

So Callum was finally out of the picture. Good riddance. Of course it was only a matter of time before she gave that giant heart of hers away to someone else. She always seemed to be in a long-term thing with someone…almost as if she was afraid to be alone. The opposite of himself, he thought. She didn't exactly *need* a man, either, as far as he was concerned.

Sadie was one of the highest-rated UK-based consultants in occupational medicine. A client had sent 'thank-you' flowers to her door just this morning, right before she'd handed her keys over to the new renter and they caught the train to Glasgow. Proud wasn't the word for what he felt about her. She was winning at life on her own.

Sadie Mills knew how to reach people and make a legitimate, positive difference to their lives, just like he did. He wasn't going to blow his own trumpet, but he knew, professionally, that they were going to do good things where they were going.

They met their driver at the ferry port. A man called Caleb, who helped with their bags. Sadie had somehow packed the world into a sky-blue suitcase almost twice the size of his.

It suddenly occurred to him how remote they were actually going to be, living in a part of the nineteenth-century mansion that housed Rothesay Recovery, treating up to twelve live-in patients. They'd be joining fifteen other specialists who would cater to their wealthy clients' unique needs. The other specialists and staff would be on site, living and working alongside them, but on his days off he planned to explore the forests, take naked dips in idyllic lakes and embark on scenic walks through the Lowlands and Highlands by way of a few whisky distilleries. Alone.

It wasn't as if there would be any options in the hookup department all the way out here. And Sadie was more fun than any of them had ever turned out to be, anyway.

He'd kind of missed her in America. He'd gone to her place the second after he'd ditched his bags at home, and she'd looked at him through her hair all night, eyeing up his new muscles even when she was sniffling over Callum dumping her.

His colleagues in Boston had liked the gym and he'd grown to like it too. Going there had turned out to be a better use of his time than chatting up women—none of them had been Sadie. He'd started to anticipate their weekly Sunday video calls. He'd even turned down a few dates to stay at home and talk to Sadie—especially after she'd hinted that she might be leaving for Rothesay right after he returned. That hadn't sat well with him. He'd been looking forward to spending time with his best friend after being away for so long.

And now here he was. Along for the ride.

A shiver of anticipation tickled his spine as they slid into the back seat of the taxi. This was it. No backing out now. The six-month stint wasn't going to be the holiday he'd planned, for sure. He knew enough about private live-in residencies to know they involved some of the toughest work out there, but he was ready for the challenge…and so was Sadie.

It was a short three-mile drive to Rothesay Recovery.

'Working at Rothesay Recovery, huh?' the driver said. 'I heard a rumour that that actor's in there now. You know the one whose son died in that movie stunt?'

'Conall McCaskill?'

Sadie threw Owen a look that made him direct his smirk out of the window—she was clearly starstruck.

'That's the one.'

She pushed her sunglasses up onto her head and squeezed his knee. Owen cleared his throat, noting her hand on his jeans, her newly trimmed, polish-free manicure. They hadn't been told who the residents were yet. He'd assumed they'd have to sign NDAs when they arrived.

'So sad…what happened,' Caleb muttered, shaking his head. 'I heard he turned to the bottle pretty bad. You pair might have your work cut out with that one.'

Owen listened as Caleb made grand assumptions about the A-list Scottish actor, noting the sunlight in Sadie's hair. *You pair.* Did this guy Caleb think they were a couple? Lots of people did, but it had never happened. Not in this life anyway.

It *could* have happened. At least, he had tried once. He could be back on that dance floor in his mind in seconds if he wanted, but he tried not to think about it too much because... Well, what was the point?

He'd been young and drunk when she'd put him in his place, not long after they'd met. They'd been dancing in that cheesy club, Sylvester's, and she'd kept looking at him strangely, as if she was thinking something wicked. But the second he'd leaned in to act on it she'd sped from the dance floor like a meteor. Neither of them had ever mentioned it again.

It would have ruined their friendship, so it was probably better that nothing had happened. He would have messed it up anyway, if they'd got together. Much as he would now, probably. Getting into something serious was not on his radar—not with anyone, and especially not with a friend like her.

He found his jaw was clicking now, as he pictured that day on the boat in Richmond when Callum had outright accused him of being in love with Sadie. They'd only been having a laugh, like they always did, doing some silly accents or something. He'd laughed off the accusation, just as Sadie had. But that night in the pub he'd overheard them arguing. Sadie had said it over and over again.

'Owen is just a friend! That's all he will ever be, trust me.'

At the time he'd wondered why it had stung so much. It was the truth, after all. But it sounded like something his mother might have encouraged people to think—the woman who'd birthed him and then regretted it. In Josephine Penner's eyes the Penner men were useless, and her rage over his dad's incessant philandering had sealed his own fate, he supposed. He was never going to get himself into anything he couldn't get out of... There would be no wedding bells, no babies, no mortgages and trips to IKEA. No, thanks—not for him. All that couples' stuff only wound up in misery for everyone involved.

Maybe it was best he'd been shut down long ago by Sadie. Now they were purely friends—simple, no complications. Just the way he liked it.

'I've read about that hotel.'

Sadie cut into his thoughts. He realised he'd been staring at her face again, while she'd been looking at a spooky hotel outside. The Scottish sunlight made the blush on her cheekbones even pinker. She rolled down the window. The air smelled sweet and fresh, rolling in over her familiar perfume.

The Glenburn Hotel looked eerily empty.

'Looks like the perfect setting for a ghost story,' he said aloud.

Caleb bobbed his ginger head from behind the wheel. 'Aye, you're not wrong, lad. Plenty of ghosts around here—especially where you're going.'

'Stop it!' Sadie gasped. 'There are no ghosts where we're going... Are there?'

'There's talk of a Lady in White,' the driver replied.

Owen nudged her gently, grinning at the look on her pretty face. 'You don't believe in ghosts, do you?'

'Stop it,' she said again, and nudged him back harder, which prompted an attack of poking fingers on each other and laughter between them.

Sadie cleared her throat as Owen pushed her hand away from his ribcage one last time, registering as he did so just how hard his heart was bucking in his chest. Caleb was rolling his eyes, mouthing the word 'flirts'. But it certainly wasn't flirting. He and Sadie didn't *do* flirting. At least he would never do it. He knew how she viewed him. How could he forget?

He took in the trees and the wildflowers through the car windows as they drove, and found himself thinking, as he often did when it was quiet, about all the things he'd never told Sadie. Or anyone.

Like how, as a kid, he'd got to know the wobble of his mum's chin and what it meant—usually that she was about to spend some time sobbing behind the bolted bathroom door. The meltdowns often came right after his dad had left for some sudden meeting or appointment that they all knew had nothing to do with the business his parents had built together from the ground up.

If it hadn't for him coming along, maybe his mum never would have married his dad and ruined her life. If she hadn't tied herself to the man so irrevocably, in so many ways, maybe she wouldn't have felt obliged to stick around and endure all the lies and belittling put-downs and bitterness. Either way, he'd learned over the years exactly when to leave someone—*before* things had even the remotest chance of becoming serious.

Sometimes he got confused about Sadie—because he was a guy, he supposed, and because she was a beautiful, smart, thoughtful and successful woman, who had to all intents and purposes come to trust him. They'd come to rely on each other through the years. Neither of them was particularly family-orientated—at least she barely ever mentioned her divorced parents, and her brother had died in a motorbike accident the summer before she'd started university. She didn't ever talk about it. He didn't ask.

Sadie was independent, like him. Ambitious, like him. He respected her. Needed her, actually. Her kindness, her insights, her ability to cheer him up without ever being mean. Every other woman came and went. He would never risk losing Sadie's friendship—not for anything. She was irrefutably the best thing in his life.

'Here we are!'

Caleb was steering the taxi up to some giant arched iron gates. He jumped out of the car to press a button and within seconds they were rolling up the long, sweeping driveway. Sadie made that excited squealing noise again and gripped

Owen's arm, and he tried to ignore a sudden lightning bolt that seemed to strike him at her touch. The same one he'd started to feel back in Boston, seeing his screen light up with her face…

'Look at that water feature! Ooh, check out that glass-house—that must be the Victorian fernery… I can't believe these turrets… It looks just like a castle…'

Her being so excited was infectious. Owen smiled to himself. Thailand felt further away than ever, but this was definitely going to be interesting. The house was huge. All fishtail slated turrets and leaded crests, and bay windows with balustraded parapets.

A black-haired lad with a side parting met them in the grand entrance hall. He wore a smart white uniform and his badge read *Fergal: Welcome Host*. Owen watched the way Sadie looked the man up and down, then found himself catching her arm as another guy in the same white uniform wheeled their cases away across the chequered black and white floor. She shot him a look of surprise when he put his hand on her elbow, and he swiftly removed it, wondering why he'd felt the sudden need to have every ounce of her attention.

Stepping into professional mode, Owen made sure he looked suitably impressed as they were given a tour. It wasn't difficult to be impressed.

'The house dates back to about 1844, and the grounds extend to roughly three acres, including our therapeutic Victorian glass-covered fernery,' Fergal said, proudly. 'Our residents like that. In fact, they're all in there now, because it's potting hour. You can see the bay from your suites, I believe, and the golf course. But the best rooms are kept for our paying guests, of course.'

'Of course,' Owen echoed. He cocked an eyebrow at Sadie behind Fergal's back and mouthed *Potting hour?*

incredulously. She frowned at him, as if to say, *'Behave!'* But her lips twitched.

'Your rooms are on the second floor in the right-hand wing,' Fergal explained in his thick Glasgow accent as he led them up a grandiose staircase.

This time it was Sadie's turn to arch an eyebrow. She mouthed the word *Wing?* at him, while pulling a face, and he laughed, then turned it into a cough. Luckily their 'welcome host' was too wrapped up in impressing them to notice.

'I'll show you your rooms later, but first Dr Calhoun would like to meet with you.'

On the landing, Fergal swung open a huge wooden door and ushered them both inside the room onto thick olive-green carpet. Owen felt the tingling heat from Sadie's shoulder creep along his arm and excite his senses as they found themselves standing side by side before Senior Clinical Co-ordinator and CEO, Dr Christine Calhoun. In a setting like this, it felt like coming face to face with the Lady of the Manor.

'Welcome, Dr Penner, Dr Mills.' Dr Calhoun stood and smiled from behind a huge oakwood desk.

Her white teeth gleamed between thin lips as Owen shook the fifty-something doctor's hand.

'We feel lucky to have you both here,' she said in a distinctive Glaswegian accent, glancing between him and Sadie with interest, as if sizing them up in person.

Was she wondering if they were a couple too?

'Let's get to business, shall we? There are a few things you should know now you're here, that we couldn't discuss on the phone.'

'Is this about Conall McCaskill?' Sadie asked, folding her arms in her smart suit jacket. She was almost as tall as Calhoun in her heels.

Dr Calhoun shot her a slightly guarded look as she motioned them to sit. Quickly she produced the expected non-disclosure agreement forms from a creaking drawer, and placed them down in front of them.

'We can't keep a whole lot secret around here—not even with the blacked-out windows on our transport,' she informed them wearily. 'Mr McCaskill is on the premises, yes, you have heard correctly—along with quite an interesting intake. In fact, we're relying on you to help us make the breakthrough Maeve… Mrs McCaskill…is hoping for from him. So far he's refused to speak with anyone, or even acknowledge his own PTSD. The team is excited about your credentials—both of you.'

Sadie turned to Owen, a look of steely determination flashing in her eyes. It fired him up on the spot, as if she'd shot liquid adrenaline into his veins. Then she crossed her legs and turned back to Calhoun, all business.

'You'd better fill us in, Doctor,' she said.

CHAPTER THREE

'MR MCCASKILL?' SADIE tapped her nails on the open door, two steps ahead of Owen.

Conall McCaskill was sitting in silence in a leather arm-chair by the floor-to-ceiling windows of his immaculate modern suite. Maybe it was his grief, or the leaf-brown V-neck sweater and dark army style trousers he wore, but he looked older in person than she'd imagined somehow.

Behind him the bathroom door was ajar, revealing a giant Bird of Paradise plant in a terracotta pot and a French rolltop bath with claw feet. It was luxury compared to their own rooms. Not that hers was bad. She just hadn't slept well, thanks to an old pipe, somewhere she hadn't been able to locate, that just wouldn't stop banging.

Owen pulled two chairs up, one either side of Conall McCaskill's and fixed a smile to his freshly shaven face. 'How are you today, sir?'

Charm personified.

Sadie took the other seat and smirked, remembering catching him taking a selfie earlier, on the staircase. She'd done the same just moments earlier. Their uniforms were vastly different from what they were used to. Nothing like their regular white coats. In her case it was a fitted cream skirt and a sleek white shirt emblazoned with the gold-embroidered *RR* logo. Owen wore a smart white dress shirt and cream dress trousers that hugged his bum just right...

What? She caught herself. Why was she thinking about Owen's bum right now?

There was something about him, she realised suddenly. Something she'd missed while he'd been in America. She couldn't put her finger on it... *And neither should you want to*, she reminded herself. She was simply glad to have him back, and for the chance for them to work together for the first time. Their friendship was going to make them a great team.

Still, he did have an incredibly cute backside...

'We're doing the rounds...introducing ourselves. We're the new recruits. I'm Owen Penner, and this is Sadie Mills.'

Silence. Conall McCaskill still had his gaze fixed on the statue of the mermaid guarding the fountain outside the window. Sadie crossed her legs and adjusted her watch, reining in her thoughts of Owen's...physical attributes.

She'd dealt with this kind of thing before. PTSD developed differently in everyone. But never in her dreams had she imagined she'd see it in the hero of her favourite childhood action movie *Surrender*.

If she'd known Conall McCaskill was on the residents' list before this she would have re-watched that movie. Or maybe that would have made this situation more difficult, she thought, studying his famous sloping nose and square jaw.

She and Owen could have watched it together, she supposed, her with her feet up on his lap, the comfy way they'd watched movies together since their Imperial College days. Well, apart from that time when Callum had caught them and instructed Owen crossly to keep to his own side of the sofa.

Owen started explaining what their roles would be. He was to discover what might be exacerbating Conall Mc-

Caskill's problems and help develop a strategy for calming any overactive areas of the brain. She was to help him regain his purpose in life, so to speak, by helping him with daily life skills and hopefully getting him back to peak performance in society—maybe even in another movie.

It was going to be a challenge. But then, it sounded as if the first psychologist he'd been to hadn't known what to make of his situation at all. Dr Calhoun told them he'd been sent there by someone from the film company's insurance provider. The notes stated that Mr McCaskill was dressed nicely and was well-groomed for his appointments, when in fact, according to Maeve, his wife, he hadn't showered in days and had gone in wearing the same jeans and stained sweater he'd been wearing for a week.

It was Maeve—famous in her own right—who'd insisted he see someone 'professional'. Hence Rothesay Recovery, and them.

The sullen-looking A-list film star looked like a completely different man from the accredited actor she'd grown up watching on screen. And, just as they'd been warned, he didn't seem too warm about the idea of them being there.

'I don't want any help.'

Conall McCaskill's gruff Scottish bark shocked her. This was not the confident, kick-ass, muscled gym addict she'd seen on her TV. He was only in his mid-sixties, but his son's tragic death had clearly aged him in many ways.

'We know you've been through a terrible tragedy—' she started.

'Well, you should—it was all over the Internet. Didn't even take them an hour to get the photos out there after they took Scott's body away.'

Sadie drew a breath. A breeze from the open window ruffled the actor's grey-streaked hair.

'It was a stunt that went wrong,' Owen stated next.

He was looking at the notes, which wasn't entirely necessary—they'd both read all about it when it had happened. Six months later it was still cropping up from time to time on the news—the stunt co-ordinator's legal trial was on-going.

Scott McCaskill, Conall's thirty-two-year-old son, a movie stuntman, had been filling in for his father in a chase scene when the brakes had failed on the car he was driving. The poor guy had collided with a tree and the tree had won. A fake explosion had turned into a real one, which had probably finished him off, although no one really knew. Conall had seen it happen.

'We understand you haven't really had a chance to deal with it all,' Sadie said now, crossing her legs in his direction and noting, just for a millisecond, the actor's liquid blue eyes flash over her knees in the sheer pink tights. 'It must have been difficult to escape and get some privacy...'

'Why do you think they put me in here?' he snapped.

More silence.

Owen stood up and crossed to the window.

Sadie found she was holding her breath again.

Another long pause.

'I remember when I first watched you in *Surrender*,' Owen said.

He crossed his arms in his crisp white shirt, studying the mermaid statue, while Sadie wondered exactly how many hours he'd put into the gym to get biceps like that. How had he even found time for the numerous dates he must have been on while he was in Boston? He still hadn't talked to her about them.

'I knew you were a real hero, even back then.'

'DC Shawn was my *character*—i.e. not me,' snapped Conall.

'Yes. But around the same time you did that commercial to save the dogs in Vietnam. Right after that my friend's mother had to drive her to the cinema to put a bid on a cardboard cut-out of your character. There was a queue there already. Everybody wanted you—the *real* you, the Puppy Ambassador—in their living room.'

'Not any more.'

'Nothing's changed out there,' Owen assured him, and Sadie blinked.

That had been her mum who'd done that for her. She must have told Owen and forgotten. She barely spoke about her family to anyone. It hurt too much to think about how good things had been before Chris died. But the Puppy Ambassador—how could she have forgotten that?

She shuffled closer to Conall McCaskill on her seat, shooting Owen a look. 'I remember donating my pocket money to the cause,' she said. 'If my dad could see me now, he'd tell me to remind you how you made me want to get a dog. Of course we weren't allowed one—not even after my brother begged for one…'

She trailed off, straightening up on the seat. Conall Mc-Caskill was frowning, as if waiting for her to finish. Even worse, Owen was looking at her sympathetically, which rattled her defences instantly. This was not the time or place. Why had she brought up her brother? Conall McCaskill was making her nervous.

'I wasn't allowed to watch *Surrender* unless I'd tidied my room first,' she said quickly, raking a hand through her loose hair. 'That's power, sir. No one else could get me to do that—'

'She's right about that,' Owen interrupted. 'She's the messiest person I've ever met.'

Sadie's mouth fell open. If they'd been anywhere else she would have play-punched him. But to her surprise Conall McCaskill's face softened. Only slightly, but there was an undeniable shift in his mood.

Damn, Owen was good. Buttering up a celeb's ego was probably the only place to start with any kind of treatment, and Owen had realised that immediately. Just the tiniest crack would do to loosen him up—then they could slip into his psyche and start with the real work. And trust Owen to lighten the mood, like he always did.

She'd address his comment about her messiness later, she decided, as Owen continued talking about his friend transporting the DC Shawn cut-out home in her mum's car, how his cardboard head had stuck out through the back window for the whole ride.

Maybe she'd let her standards slip a little since the break-up with Callum. Owen had certainly done her washing up a few times, while she'd been sniffling into a pot of ice-cream on the sofa, feeling sorry for herself. Once, he'd even made her bed for her. She'd stood there, bleary-eyed, watching him from the doorway, while he'd propped up her childhood teddy bear and talked about making her comfy, thinking how even Callum had never made the bed. He'd always waited for her to do it.

'What's the deal with you two anyway?' Conall Mc-Caskill asked now, turning his head back to her.

She realised she'd been looking at Owen in the sunlight, noticing again how good he looked in his uniform. It would have been so different here if he hadn't come too.

'What do you mean?' Owen asked evasively.

'You know what I mean. Are they sending couples here now? I know they've had a few singles who thought it was too remote. They wound up leaving the island.'

'We're not a couple,' she said quickly, as her heart lurched in her chest. 'We're simply colleagues and friends who've known each other a long time.'

Conall McCaskill scanned her from her chin up to her hair, his familiar close-set blue eyes roving her face as if he was looking for a reason to mistrust her. Owen was frowning, seemingly memorising the mermaid's scales in the garden.

She quickly changed the subject to the actor's treatment

plan, explaining her planned series of daily hand-eye co-ordination exercises in addition to a strict dietary regime, which often helped PTSD patients more than it had been previously thought, according to some new research Owen had studied and implemented in the States.

'Colleagues and friends, huh?' mumbled Conall Mc-Caskill, halfway through retying his shoelaces, as if that was better than addressing the difficulties she was observing in his ability to do so without cursing.

'That's correct.' Sadie stood up, allowing him the dignity of continuing without them looking, wondering why his scrutiny had unnerved her. Maybe she was just starstruck. This man was a Hollywood icon. She could think of several people who'd lose their minds if she told them she was caring for this megastar on his road to recovery.

Owen turned. 'We're here for *you*, sir,' he added, although it was Sadie he was looking at now.

In a flash she remembered the look in his eyes that had set her defences on fire before, the sympathy in his gaze after she'd mentioned her brother. If he was here because he felt sorry for her in any way…because of her brother, or Callum, or anything…

No. Surely not. Not Owen. Owen did things for Owen. Always.

Except when he's taking care of me… Then he's the least selfish person I know. Women have come and gone in his life, but he's always been there for me.

Sadie pushed the strange new revelation from her head before it could develop into questions pertaining to their strictly platonic relationship status. Meeting Conall Mc-Caskill was getting to her, that was all.

Next on their rounds was Mr Vivek Kumar, a wealthy businessman who sat wringing his hands, his eyes all over the place.

'I can still hear the sound of the ice cracking under my head,' Mr Kumar explained, making Sadie's heart hurt for the man.

He'd slipped on some icy steps on a business trip to Colorado last winter and hurt his head. He had experienced difficulties in speaking and co-ordination ever since.

Sadie felt Owen's eyes on her the whole time she was assessing his ability to follow instructions, walking in various directions around the room. Every time he turned left instead of right her heart sank further, but Owen was making furious notes, and she knew he was devising a plan of his own that they'd incorporate into a healing schedule.

Again, the thrill of working with him to help a patient through a traumatic brain injury gave her a boost—although unfortunately so did remembering the way he'd put his arm around her shoulders this morning. Just for a second, by way of saying hello on the landing. It had sent a bolt of electric heat through her loins that had taken her quite by surprise. He'd ruffled her hair awkwardly afterwards, as if to turn his affection into something he might also show a puppy dog, and she'd blushed all the way to breakfast.

'How did you sleep last night?'

Owen had caught her up on their way into the fernery for potting hour.

'Why?' she asked him, noting that the patient they'd just assessed, forty-eight-year-old Portia DeMagio, was pressing a hand to her forehead ahead of them in the humid domed glasshouse.

Sadie frowned. She'd suggested Portia stay inside, as she'd mentioned feeling a little unwell, but Portia had insisted on getting some air.

The slight, smartly dressed sexologist, who lived in Edinburgh with her film director husband, was here to get to the bottom of her cluster headaches, which had been diagnosed as 'episodic'. Her illness was characterised by periods of weeks or months of attacks, alternated with pain-free periods. With surgical intervention ruled out already, Sadie was adjusting Portia's existing programme for coping with and hopefully reducing the ferocity of her debilitating headaches.

It really was a diverse list of live-in residents, but only two were here for potting hour. The others were attending a yoga class—with the exception of Conall McCaskill, who'd refused to join in with anything today.

'I just wondered if you'd heard anything in the night,' Owen said now, keeping his eyes on Vivek Kumar, who was settling his large, round, portly self into a seat at the glass table set amongst the ferns and flowers.

'Now that you mention it, there was something banging all night. A door or a pipe or something,' she said.

She noted how Mr Kumar was struggling with sitting too far away from the table, and then too close to Portia for his comfort. They'd concluded by now that his spatial awareness was very much impaired. Sadie helped him with his chair, and luckily Portia just smiled.

'I couldn't find where the noise was coming from.'

'I heard that too.'

Owen scratched his chin thoughtfully. His room was right next to hers, so she wasn't surprised.

'I thought maybe there was a window open in your room.'

'*My* room? Why would I leave a window open?'

'That's what I thought.' He leaned into her and lowered his voice, grinning. His mouth tickled her ear. 'Maybe it was the ghost.'

'Stop it,' she hissed.

Parminder, a trainee care assistant, looked up from her

distribution of shovels and tiny plastic pots of shrubs, which were to be re-planted in peace and quiet.

'Stop what?' she asked, raising her perfect neat brows as they approached.

And Sadie had already caught her looking a little too long and hard at Owen—which annoyed her more than she wanted it to. It was up to Owen what he did and with whom—why should she care? Just because he had possibly come here for her, and not just for 'the challenge', like he'd said, it didn't mean he owed her his full attention all the time. It was probably only a matter of time before she noticed Parminder's crush, if he hadn't already.

Why am I so annoyed by something that hasn't even happened?

'I was saying we think there's a ghost in our wing,' Owen told Parminder.

Vivek rolled his sleepy hooded eyes. 'There's no such thing as ghosts.'

'Exactly,' Sadie replied, taking the heavy iron seat next to Owen's and picking up a small shovel. 'Owen was just messing around.'

She waggled the shovel in his direction, laughing despite her strange mood when he pretended to swipe it from her hand.

Parminder cleared her throat…flicked her gaze between them nervously. 'I saw something in the garden my first night here,' she said, sounding a little embarrassed.

Owen put the shovel down and shot Sadie a sideways glance.

'At first I thought it was one of the residents, but it was after-hours, and they always lock the doors at night.'

'It was probably the caretaker,' Sadie said, nudging Owen's foot under the table.

'In a long white dress?'

Sadie swallowed—just as a bird landed on the glass

dome above her and made her jump. Ghosts weren't real, but still… The thought of encountering anything paranormal here turned her stomach inside out.

'Lots of people wear long white dresses,' she said casually, digging her shovel into a mini plant pot in an attempt to calm her pulse. 'Even Owen here wore one once. Remember that Halloween party at Imperial? When you went as a corpse bride?'

Owen sniggered. Vivek and Parminder looked at them with interest, giving them the same kind of look that Conall McCaskill had given them earlier.

'You guys went to college together?' Parminder asked curiously.

Sadie nodded, chin raised, wondering why she suddenly felt more territorial over Owen than a guard dog on duty.

She was just about to regale them with another funny story about Owen when Portia DeMagio clutched her head again, dropped her shovel to the floor, and promptly fell face-forward into her plant pot.

'Oh, my God! What…? What…?'

Vivek was on his feet before anyone could move, but Owen urged him back into his seat while Sadie and Parminder gently lifted Portia from the soil and readjusted her in the chair. Her mouth was wide open.

'She's out cold.' Owen frowned, coming forward and checking her eyes while Sadie wiped the mud from her cheeks.

If only Portia had listened to her earlier and stayed in the main house when her symptoms had started.

'She told me she can usually tell when an attack this bad is about to happen,' she whispered at Owen.

'She shouldn't be blacking out on the meds she's taking,' he replied.

Parminder was on her radio. In less than a minute someone was rushing down the path towards them with oxygen. Portia was already blinking, coming to on her own, even as they slipped the oxygen mask over her face. She was most apologetic for fainting, but Owen wasn't having any of it.

'We're rescheduling our next one-to-one, Portia,' he told her sternly as Sadie noted a fresh and telling sheen of perspiration on the woman's forehead. 'We need to get you off those meds. They're clearly not working.'

'Nothing's worked so far. That's why my husband sent me here,' she managed through her mask.

Sadie watched the woman grasp Owen's hand and squeeze it with a strength that defied her size and current situation. She'd mentioned her husband 'sending' her here to her too, in an earlier session.

ª'We both will,' Owen replied. 'That's why we're here.'

Sadie stood back with Vivek and Parminder as Owen helped Portia all the way up the gravel path, past the mermaid, till they were out of sight. The poor woman spouted far too many apologies the whole way, and Sadie wondered how she'd been coping with events like this so far. Embarrassing, humiliating, debilitating…

Did her husband think this was his last resort? Sending her to this place? How many times had he scraped Portia off floors and carpets while fearing for his beautiful wife's life?

Cluster headaches weren't life-threatening, but another sufferer had once described them to her as *'Like your brain is being attacked by an angry elf with a machete'*. She wanted to help Portia. She *would* help. She and Owen would work together to make sure of it.

She would also have to work on not noticing Owen's impressive physique as much, she decided. How dare he come back from Boston looking hotter than ever…distracting her like this? Thoughts like that needed to be nipped in the bud pronto, before he caught her and started thinking she *liked* him, or something!

As if.

CHAPTER FOUR

By THE END of the second week Owen had got pretty comfortable with a fishing line in his spare time, but he still felt as if Conall McCaskill was the one who was getting away. No matter how hard he tried to get him to talk in their sessions, the depressed actor used only grunts by way of conversation, and insisted on staring right past him for the most part, officiously offering to tell him the time, as if they needed confirmation that he didn't want to give them any more of his.

It was almost as infuriating as his new attraction to Sadie.

Maybe it was working with her...watching her in action around the patients. The way she'd been with Portia since the incident in the fernery was nothing short of dedicated. She'd sat with her every evening since, when she was reading and journaling in her room, making sure she wasn't alone long enough for another headache to creep up unannounced—which it hadn't, thankfully.

Maybe it was having her close again after so long away from her...or the fact he hadn't had sex in a while...but he'd had a dream about her last night. The kind of dream that would not stop playing on his mind.

Owen cast his line over the side of the little boat while Rothesay Recovery loomed large in the sweeping estate beyond. Only his, Sadie's and Conall's fishing lines were disturbing the ripples of the blue lake. Of course Sadie had to be looking cute as hell in her uniform of a white shirt with a cream jacket and matching fitted skirt—her body was as fine as her brain.

Yes, focus on her brain, he reminded himself in annoyance, frowning into the lake. Her body was off-limits. Unlike the way it had been in that dream. Even thinking about it was torture.

But then, he'd rather think about *anything* other than his father right now. And the way he had casually announced his new engagement at the end of their recent phone call— as if it was more of an afterthought than a big deal.

Owen felt his jaw lock again. It *was* a big deal. *Jay Penner strikes again.* The ink was barely dry on his latest divorce papers. What would this Michaela woman be? His fourth wife? Fifth? He was losing track.

'So, have you done much fishing before?'

Sadie's voice broke into his thoughts. She was trying to make small talk with Conall from the other side of the boat they'd managed to coerce him onto.

'A few times with my co-star on *Ascension 2*,' was McCaskill's simple, bored response.

Owen fought not to intervene. His role this morning was to observe the actor's mood and motor skills in activities like this, now he'd put him on a new anti-inflammatory diet. Conall hadn't had an alcoholic drink in over a month, but Owen suspected his previous diet hadn't helped his PTSD.

Post-traumatic stress was a wicked beast. Sometimes he saw hints of it in his mother—caused by none other than his father, of course. Although she hadn't exactly distanced herself from him, or done anything to try and help her situation. The woman was the very definition of a martyr.

Jay Penner had walked out on the two of them when Owen was eleven, in favour of some woman he'd met on a first-class flight back from Hong Kong—Edwina. Every new relationship and marriage since then had merely put another knife through her wounds.

It didn't help that neither would step down from the business they'd built together. On the surface, everything was about Leap—the ground-breaking web design platform for which they were co-founder and CEO jointly. Underneath... Who knew? His mother seemed to prefer being tortured rather than admit her own stubbornness and pride, and her unadulterated loathing of his father was a mask for a damaging kind of undying love for the man...bordering on the masochistic, in fact.

'Catching any sea monsters over there, Owen?' Sadie called, eliciting another grunt from Conall as she tossed her own line over the side with a yell a lot like a noisy tennis player might emit.

'Not so many,' he replied, momentarily forgetting his annoyance as he noticed her new sunglasses. They suited her. Then again, Sadie looked good in everything.

When he'd mentioned to his dad that he was here in Scotland on a placement with her, he'd heard a low murmur of approval in the back of his throat—Jay Penner's way of ranking a woman highly in the looks department. Dad must have seen photos of them together on his social media over the years, although Owen had managed to keep him away from her in person—more out of embarrassment than anything else.

Owen listened to Sadie and Conall making awkward, stunted small talk while his father crept in and out of his thoughts. The guy could push his buttons, for sure—it was a lost battle for him not to get wound up over the way he treated marriages like throwaway takeout containers.

His mum would probably call any time now, he thought, checking his phone. She'd tell him the same thing she always did: *'Don't you dare do anything to ruin anyone like your father ruined me!'*

She loved to impose her self-righteous opinions on him. The things he'd heard from her over the years still made him cringe. How the Penners—his grandfather and great-grandfather included—were notorious for having too much money and not enough morals…how she'd thought she'd be the one to make his dad into a one-woman guy…how stupid that had been because no one ever would.

His mother was *still* paying for her mistakes…still regretting getting in too deep. Regretting getting serious with his father, walking down the aisle and making babies with him.

Sadie's squeal drew his attention back to her. Her line had bounced back and hooked into her hair. Biting back a smile, he put his line down and crossed the boat to help. He wasn't great at fishing, but she was worse.

'What are you like?' he whispered as his fingers found the hook amongst her thick honey hair and untangled it gently.

'Thank you. I can do it,' she muttered suddenly, catching his fingers just as they went back in to smooth her hair down.

He tried to discern what the new scent was lingering in his nostrils. He sniffed again—lavender. The oil was in every female's room at Rothesay. He'd seen the diffusers in a session with Portia.

Embarrassment flashed in Sadie's eyes as she glanced from him to a smirking Conall and he retracted his hand—*why had he done that?*

'I don't think the fish need to worry with you around,' Owen said, clearing his throat.

'Very funny,' she replied, trying and failing to hide her face behind her hair. Her cheeks were flaming ruby-red in the sunlight.

What the hell was that?

Conall was grinning at them. 'Did I ever tell you how I met my wife?' he asked suddenly.

'No, you didn't,' Sadie replied, flustered, before Owen could say a word. She shuffled back to the side of the boat and resumed her hopeless fishing.

'She was a production assistant on one of my movies. Cutest girl around for miles...wicked sense of humour.'

Conall's eyes found Owen's as he said it, as if they were sharing some kind of moment.

'Maeve was the only one on set who treated me like a human being and not some star who needed special attention. I appreciated that.'

Owen wound out his line. He didn't need to ask why Conall was mentioning his wife here and now. Clearly he was insinuating he and Sadie had some kind of husband-and-wife-type interaction going on—which wasn't entirely untrue, he supposed. They weren't having sex, for a start. Didn't marriage kill that kind of thing?

Wild passion withered. Attraction always faded.

He frowned at the water, remembering how his mother had verbally bashed his 'useless' father even while they were still together...even at the cost of making things deeply uncomfortable for him and any unsuspecting school friend he'd happened to invite to the dinner table.

'I can't believe Maeve sent me here,' Conall said gruffly. 'Of all people...'

'She wants you to get better,' Sadie told him gently.

'She's grieving herself. I told her she should come here too.'

She wasn't drinking herself into a heap every night, Owen wanted to say.

But instead he chose to listen while Sadie asked him more about his early encounters with Maeve. He knew she was dying to know. And they both knew Conall Mc-

Caskill's anhedonia—an inability to express any kind of pleasure—must have been making his wife's life a misery.

Maeve McCaskill had given up 'the biz' years ago, to launch a successful line of luxury cooking items and cookbooks, promoted largely on her YouTube channel. She was a big hit on all social media, apparently, always cooking, and talking about how to use this particular air fryer or that tin for a batch of muffins—not that he paid much attention to things like that.

Unlike Sadie.

Sadie even had one of her aprons.

She'd always looked ridiculously cute in the pink frilly fifties-style thing—like a sexy housewife or something. One time, when they'd both had too much of her girly gin and elderberry mix, she'd danced around her kitchen while she was wearing it, and he'd had to stop himself taking the husband-and-wife game too far by hoisting her up onto the counter.

Owen cursed himself. Now he was imagining what sex with Sadie would be like up against the kitchen counter. It wasn't as if he'd *never* imagined it—even before the dream. He was a guy, after all. She'd just never go there with him— obviously. And he wouldn't initiate it. She'd accuse him of wanting to make her another notch on his bedpost, which he'd never do with someone like her.

If his mother ever met Sadie—which he'd been trying to avoid—she'd only take him aside and remind him of all the things he shouldn't do. Tell him not to ruin her. She might even tell Sadie what she loved to tell anyone else who'd listen—how his father and pretty much all the Penner men were useless. The shame and embarrassment he felt just thinking of her hearing all that caused a fire in his blood. He knew Sadie's approval of him was imperative.

She was professionally perfect to all who encountered her, but behind the scenes she was special—to him, at least—because she made no pretence about who she really was. Not like some of those girls who'd approached him in Boston…the ones he'd wound up going to the gym to avoid…

'Isn't that right, Owen?'

'Huh?' Owen turned. Sadie was scanning his face quizzically.

'I was saying to Mr McCaskill that he should invite his wife here for the annual gala that was coming up. You know…the event they've put up all the posters for?'

Owen vaguely recalled seeing some posters about the place.

'He doesn't think she'd want to come,' she continued.

'Why wouldn't she want to come?' Owen asked, catching Sadie's look. She was letting him know she was fishing for information as much as for the perch that were hiding somewhere in the water below them all.

It was interesting, seeing her studying this troubled man. Every half-smile, every grunt and sigh, was a piece of the actor's story, unscripted. He was telling her how she could help him without even realising it himself.

'Is it that you think she wouldn't want to come? Or do you just not want her to see you in this place?' Sadie asked him carefully. 'There's nothing to be ashamed of, you know. Everyone needs help sometimes.'

Silence.

Tension filled the cool morning air as Conall's face grew tight and sullen. His eyes darkened as he clenched a fist at his side. 'You know nothing about what we've been through,' he growled at them. 'Get me off this boat.'

'Mr Mc—'

Without a beat Owen stepped between Conall and Sadie. The look in the guy's eyes was not unlike the look on his character DC Shawn's face, right before he launched a hand grenade at an approaching battleship.

'Sir, if you'd just—'

'I said, *get me off this boat!*'

McCaskill's lips grew pursed and small, and his eyes went black as a thunderstorm. One look at his dilated pupils told Owen it was obvious their fishing trip was over. They'd pushed him too far.

Owen could almost feel Sadie's disappointment through the light squeeze of her fingers around his wrist.

'OK, we're going back,' he said quickly, reading her signal. 'Sadie, do you want to steer or shall I?'

Half an hour later they'd deposited Conall on the small wooden jetty with Parminder and were back on the boat on the lake—just the two of them. With two hours before their next appointments, Owen had offered to show Sadie a few fishing skills, despite her insisting he had none himself.

She was very quiet, though. Obviously she was still thinking about Conall…or maybe even that weird moment between them earlier…

No, surely not. Sadie had probably forgotten that already.

'He's been off the booze for a while, but the anhedonia is still going strong,' she was saying, with her rod dangled over the side, the sunlight still playing in her hair.

'I know that,' he said, rolling his eyes.

'It's not something *you've* ever had a problem with,' she responded.

Her eyes were twinkling now, but Owen bristled. 'Depends what kind of expression of pleasure we're talking about,' he replied, tossing his own line over the boat a little harder than he'd intended.

Sadie studied his face, eyes narrowed. 'What did I say?'

'You assume too much about me, Sadie Mills,' he answered.

She scoffed. 'I don't assume anything. You're a pleasure-seeker.'

'And what's so wrong with that?'

Sadie opened her mouth to reply, but closed it again, as if she regretted it already, and he bit back the words he was about to say as well. It wasn't worth it.

Or maybe it was. Too many people already assumed he was just like his father, and maybe they were right. At least, they *used* to be right, he corrected himself. When was the last time he'd been with a woman? He couldn't even remember now. His heart hadn't been in it for ages. He'd been too busy missing Sadie from afar.

'If you mean I seek out the good things in life—like spending time with *you*, like being here, trying to make a difference to these people's lives—then, yeah, I'm a pleasure-seeker. But if you mean I just sleep around…'

'But…you do. Don't you?'

'Not any more, if you must know.'

'I'm sorry.' Sadie flung her line out and frowned defensively at the water.

Great. Now he felt like an idiot for making a big deal out of her teasing him—but she might as well have lashed his nerve-endings with a million little whips. Maybe she still saw him the same way she had when they were in their twenties, but he *had* changed. It wasn't that he wanted to settle down, specifically, but he was definitely a lot more discerning about who he gave his time and attention to.

She didn't know that, though, looking at him here, where she'd stuck him years ago, in the friend zone. She didn't know how much he'd missed her. Maybe he hadn't realised the extent of it himself till he'd come home, he realised suddenly.

The silky strands of Sadie's hair blew out on the breeze and tickled his cheek, and he felt the oddest sense of being out of his depth, even with the shoreline right ahead of him.

'I'm sorry,' she said again, softer now. 'Owen, what's really bothering you? You've been weird all morning.'

'My dad's just winding me up,' he said quickly.

No point dissecting these feelings right now…or ever.

'Why?'

'He's getting married. Again.'

Owen was about to elaborate when his phone rang again. His mother.

Sadie's eyes burned into his back the whole time he was talking. As predicted, his mother was furious, but he knew the wobble of her voice by now, and all the things she wasn't saying underneath her irritation. She was heart-broken all over again.

'He'll chew this woman up and spit her out like he did to me—like he did to Edwina, and Abigail. He's like a kid with a shiny new toy. I hope you never treat anyone like that, Owen…'

'Mum, you know what he's like. What do you want me to say?'

Sadie steered the boat back to the jetty after he'd ended the call. They both knew their fishing trip was over for a second time.

'Do you want to talk about it?' she asked, as he tied the boat's ropes to a post on the jetty.

The morning sun showed no sign of disappearing behind the famous Scottish rain clouds, but that conversation had sapped every inch of his own sparkle.

'I don't think there's much to talk about,' he told her tightly. 'He's always been this way. Done with one woman—on to the next. Maybe it runs in the family, huh?'

He said the last part rhetorically, under his breath, but she heard and caught at his arm.

'Owen, I really didn't mean what I said before. I don't know why I even said it. I haven't heard you talk about anyone in a while now. Was there no one in America…?'

Her voice faltered slightly as she asked the question. It

caught him off-guard. Was that a twinge of discomfort at having to ask him such a thing?

'No,' he replied, searching her face.

Something strangely alien hovered between them as she held his gaze, then looked away.

'I know I've never met him, but I'm sure you're nothing like your dad,' she said quickly. 'Is your mum OK?'

'She'll be fine…she's used to it,' he replied, pulling his arm back.

His heart drummed incessantly as he headed up the gravel path.

Sadie followed him. 'How many wives has your dad had, exactly, Owen? You've never actually said.'

'Too many,' he replied, realising that till now he'd been too embarrassed even to talk about it with her.

He exhaled deeply, curling his fists into his pockets for a moment. He shouldn't be venting to Sadie like this…but she'd been unnerving him lately, and the boat had been small, and she'd heard his mother's words just now, even though she hadn't been on speakerphone. Humiliation was encroaching upon his cool, and it was not a nice feeling.

'I don't know why, but it's like Mum's still in love with him. Can you believe that?'

He expected her to laugh—the thought was insane, after all—but Sadie's eyes narrowed as she studied him. Then she shrugged. 'I don't know… I guess being in love is powerful, right?'

'Being in love is a waste of time,' he shot back.

He expected her to roll her eyes, the way she usually did when it came to his opinions on anything regarding romance, but this time she didn't.

'You just don't want anyone to know how wonderful you really are,' she said on a sigh, sending his heart crashing into his ribs. 'I see that, Owen. And love is not a waste of time. Maybe you've just never let yourself feel it.'

'Oh? And you have?' Her nonchalance was infuriating. 'What about Callum? You guys never had anything in common—nothing at all, Sadie. Did you ever even love him for real, or were you just looking for a comfort blanket?'

The hurtful words were out before he'd had time to think. He stepped towards her, cursing himself. 'Sadie, damn it. I'm sorry...'

'Whatever. I haven't got time for this.' Sadie slipped from his reach, put her hands in the air and marched on past him, up towards the house.

Owen let her go, oscillating between annoyance, helplessness and confusion. She'd launched a truth bomb at him out of nowhere and he'd reacted by pushing her away—which was the last thing he really wanted.

What was going on between them lately? Maybe he should give her space, he decided. His father's news was getting to him more than he knew.

CHAPTER FIVE

'So, SPILL IT. What's the deal with you and Owen? You're practically giving off sparks.'

Portia DeMagio was looking down her nose at Sadie over her glasses, and she hoped she'd manage to convey non-comprehension, even as her pulse spiked at the sexologist's keen observation.

'Just now…before he left the room—you should have seen the way he looked at you. But you're ignoring him. Outside of these sessions, I mean. What did he do?'

'This session is about you, not me,' Sadie reminded her, with a smile she was sure hadn't made it to her eyes.

What look had he given her?

'Now, walk me through this week's journal entries,' she told Portia. 'I see you've been noting what you've been eating and drinking before the headaches start?'

'Yes. Owen's plan is already making a noticeable difference. His lovely face always helps, too. Am I right?' Portia shot her a sideways smile and kept her hands on top of the journal, tapping her fingers on the closed book. 'Come on! I see something's going on between you two.'

'We're not going there,' Sadie replied quickly, trying and failing to take the journal from the stubborn woman.

'Don't be offended. Reading people is my job.' Portia

informed her, who was looking radiant in a red shirt and black trousers.

'It's *my* job to focus on you,' Sadie told her patient gently, and finally managed to extract the journal from her hands.

Together they went over her entries for the week, and discussed how Owen's cold laser therapy and new electrical muscle stimulation programme, combined with a plant-based diet, was already helping to reduce the severity of her headaches. Sadie was showing her how to stretch out any tight muscles that might be contributing to her headaches, and advising hot yoga, which Portia was insisting Sadie join in with.

There were regular yoga sessions here at Rothesay Recovery. Maybe they *all* needed some time out in a Zen space, Sadie thought. Her mind would not stop slipping back to that stupid heated encounter by the lake a week ago.

She was still fuming at the way Owen had spoken to her about Callum, saying what he'd obviously been dying to say since the break-up. The person she'd considered her closest ally had accused her of keeping a comfort blanket as a boyfriend!

You're only annoyed because he's right, the voice in her head kept telling her.

'Are you sure you're not going to give me at least a snippet?' Portia wheedled, looking up from her journal. 'If you won't tell me what he's done, start at the start. How did you meet?'

'At college.'

'Have you ever kissed?'

Sadie snorted, feeling her cheeks flame at the question. 'Absolutely not.'

'But you've thought about it. I can tell.'

Sadie sat back in her swivel chair and sighed. Thoughts of kissing Owen raced like poisoned arrows through her brain, faster than she could stop them. But it was no good thinking stuff like this…she'd stopped doing that years ago, after that ill-fated night at Sylvester's.

'You *have*—there's no point denying it!' Portia looked delighted. 'Heck, honey, even *I* have. He's a catch.'

Realising she wasn't going to let it go, and also maybe feeling a little comforted by Portia's profession, Sadie found herself wanting to tell her. What was the harm?

'Actually…there was one time we might have come close…'

They'd not long met. Her group of friends had made plans to hit a cheesy dance club called Sylvester's, and she'd invited Owen along, too. She could still remember the adrenaline, walking into the club with its throbbing music and flickering neon lights, and seeing his handsome face light up, as if he'd been waiting just for her. She'd contemplated that maybe, just maybe, they might take their burgeoning friendship to the next level that night. They'd been dancing around some kind of strange attraction for a couple of months by then, at least.

But, being her, she'd been so nervous about the prospect, and the huge potential for rejection and/or heartbreak, that she'd lost count of exactly how many cocktails she'd poured down her neck. After getting hideously hammered she'd run off to be sick—and woken up the next morning with a severe hangover and even more severe memory loss.

She was glad that she hadn't done anything stupid. It wasn't as if she'd ever had a one-night stand, and she certainly shouldn't have started that night—with Owen, of all people! She'd simply had a momentary lapse of judgement and forgotten he was entirely unsuitable boyfriend material.

Also, she must have been a total idiot when she was drunk, because he'd done a disappearing act for several weeks after that.

A vague recollection of running from the dance floor had sneaked up on her from time to time, and another one of crawling into a taxi alone. She'd been so utterly embarrassed about the whole night that she'd never mentioned it again. Neither had Owen. In fact, the next time she'd seen him after that, she'd simply said sorry. And he'd said the same back. And, while she had never been entirely sure what *he* was sorry for, she'd decided it was far less humiliating to forget about it and stay friends.

'So, you admit you were attracted to him once upon a time?' Portia was twirling one of her artfully designed earrings around her finger, fascinated.

Sadie snapped back to the present. This wasn't very professional, she realised, but then, nobody here much cared for the regular way of doing things, and opening up to her patients often paid dividends when they did the same to her. If only Conall McCaskill would crack just a little more...

'At one time, yes, I suppose I felt some attraction,' she admitted. 'But we were young. It's different now.'

'You're good friends, aren't you?' Portia mused.

'Yes. Exactly. *Friends.*'

'We should always be friends with our lovers.'

'Maybe if we're living in a romcom...sure. Now, can we talk about *you*, please? How did you meet your husband?'

Portia's expression darkened. *Uh-oh.* Sadie had a feeling the husband was still in this woman's bad books, for sending her here.

'We were indeed friends before we were lovers,' she said wistfully, after a moment. 'We had sex as an experiment—can you believe that? To see if we had chemistry. I dared him, thinking he'd turn me down. Don't ever assume a man will turn down sex, even if he *is* just your friend.'

She huffed a laugh as Sadie opened the journal and swivelled her chair closer, trying not to think about having sex with Owen. Although now she was, and her throat had turned into the Sahara Desert. Having his big new-muscled arms locked around her would feel like the ultimate definition of protection, and there was nothing that turned her on more than a guy who could make her feel safe.

'And now you're married,' she said, fanning out her hair and pressing a hand briefly to her hot neck.

'And now he's sent me here,' Portia replied acidly.

'Because he loves you.'

'He does love me...' She sighed, softening slightly, as if she was finally coming to terms with the fact that it might have pained her husband to send her here as much as it had hurt her. 'You know, it's funny. When I'm angry with him I want to have sex with him even more. This is the longest we've ever been apart...and celibate.'

Sadie bit back a laugh. She couldn't imagine experiencing that amount of passion. She'd certainly never had angry sex with anyone, and probably never would. Sex for her was always nice...kind of standard, she supposed. Never particularly passionate or exciting, just something you did in a relationship once or twice a month.

How embarrassing it was that she'd dared to accuse Owen of never letting himself feel real love.

She was used to blocking out the fact that she'd always chosen safety and security over real, burning passion, thanks to losing both after losing Chris. But wouldn't it be nice...wouldn't it be everything...to feel safe as well as sexy, and wanted, and in love. *Really* in love.

Portia was watching her closely. 'When Stan and I fight, we can go at it four, five, even six times a night,' she said. 'Get yourself a man who you can fight with, Dr Mills. Do you and Owen ever fight?'

Sadie cleared her throat. 'Um...not really,' she said, turning back to the journal, her mind spinning.

She and Owen had never had a disagreement at all before coming here. But she did feel that spark between them, if she was totally honest.

She'd felt it when she opened the door to him after he'd

come back from America. He'd pulled her in tight and breathed in her hair on the doorstep, as if the smell of her shampoo was giving him life, and she'd cried in his arms, half over Callum, half in relief at having Owen home and all to herself.

She'd felt it on the lake, when he'd pulled that fish hook out of her hair tenderly, almost lovingly, just like a boyfriend would.

Things had been changing between them ever since he'd come back from America—it was pointless to deny it. But knowing what she knew about him now—how affected he'd been by his parents his whole life—his resistance to relationships made a lot more sense.

He would never give her what she needed.

All the more reason not to let these new feelings marinate, she decided resolutely.

Hours later, alone in her room, Sadie turned another page of her novel and failed, yet again, to take in what was happening in the story.

Owen hadn't come back yet. She'd been listening out for the familiar creak of his door, the sound of the key turning that always told her when he was back in his room. But it was already ten-thirty p.m., and still no sign of him.

Ugh. Maybe he was avoiding her after their altercation by the lake.

Putting her book down, she stared out of the window. Was he really still angry with her for the pleasure-seeker comment? It was clearly her fault they'd argued, but he'd pushed her buttons too.

'Sadie?'

A quiet knock on her door made her leap from the bed so fast she almost tripped over her shoes. Owen's mouth was right up against the door outside—she could see his shadow underneath.

'Are you awake?' he whispered.

Opening the door, she forced herself to look sleepier than she was, having been lying awake, wondering where he was. Seeing him in jeans and his familiar burgundy hoodie sent a warm wave rippling through her, but she crossed her arms over her dress and cardigan to refrain from hugging him.

'Awake,' she confirmed. 'What's up?'

'Are we still in a fight?' he asked, cocking an eyebrow.

She bit back a smile. 'No.'

'Good, because that was boring. I have something to show you.'

Owen took her hand and led her down the corridor, whispering that she'd have to tiptoe so as not to disturb the other staff on their floor. She knew Parminder was in one of the rooms near theirs.

In less than five minutes he was flicking the lights on in the library on the ground floor.

Sadie blinked. The fire in the marble fireplace with its raised slate hearth was crackling. The gardens, which flooded the place with sunlight during the day, were opal-black outside the tall, narrow windows. Without the day-time backdrop, the floor-to-ceiling bookshelves made her feel as if she was back in the seventeenth century.

Owen led her to a soft green couch, motioned for her to sit, and picked up a remote control. Sadie gasped in delight as a huge white screen appeared from the ceiling and a projector high above her head shone the opening titles of Conall McCaskill's movie *Surrender* straight into her eyeline.

'How did you...?'

'I got Fergal to pull a few strings,' he said, and shot her a wink. 'Told him I needed a peace offering.'

He dropped to the couch beside her and reached for a

bag he'd obviously left there earlier. So this was what he'd been doing so late…setting this up!

Producing two wine glasses and a bottle of her favourite Chardonnay, he proceeded to apologise.

She interrupted him. 'Let's forget about it.'

'Deal,' he said with a relieved sigh, pressing 'play' on the movie and scooting to the other end of the couch. She swallowed back a strange disappointment at the distance between them, and studied the lines of his handsome profile in the low light. DC Shawn flashed onto the giant screen. It was the famous scene where the character reeled off a list of curses in French, and it sent Owen's expression to new levels of amusement.

'Check Conall out—he looks so young. You know, I got those tests back tonight… Did I tell you I think his depression is linked to reduced activity in the left frontal lobe? Do you think he still knows any French? We should test him… add some language-related exercises into his programme.'

Sadie couldn't talk about Conall McCaskill's linguistic abilities right now. Reaching for the remote, she paused the movie. Crossing her legs towards Owen on the couch, she studied his face.

'You were right, Owen. What you said about Callum.'

Owen sucked in a breath through his nose and shook his head. Suddenly her heartbeat was loud in her ears.

'Sadie, it's none of my business.'

His face was deadly serious in the firelight, and she gripped her wine glass harder, so as not to lean across and wipe away the tiny black smear of what was probably coal dust across his left cheek.

'I made it your business when I cried on you over him,' she said tightly. 'I came to you because we always have fun. Because I knew my tears wouldn't last long with you around.'

Why was her heart doing that weird fluttery thing again?

'But you were right, Owen. He didn't exactly set my heart on fire. And I'm going to make better choices from now on.'

'Well, don't look to me as a role model,' he shot back, but his eyes narrowed as he searched hers, as if he was wrestling with a need to eject some further self-deprecation. She knew he always cracked jokes when he was nervous.

Owen took their glasses away and scooted a little closer. He reached for her with his big, familiar warm hands and held hers lightly, turning her wrists this way and that contemplatively as he spoke.

'I know I push people away when they get too close. But I'm not... I don't want to...'

'What *do* you want, Owen?'

Sadie felt her breath catch. She forced herself to meet his eyes, even though suddenly it felt like a loaded question that involved her and caused the blood to throb in her veins. What exactly was she wanting him to say, here?

'What I want is...' Owen faltered and went quiet, still turning her hands over in his.

The fire spat and hissed. A cat screeched somewhere outside. The moment felt eternal. A memory flickered to the forefront of her brain and fizzled out before she could catch it. Was it the memory of a moment when they'd been like this before? Close... On a precipice...

She found herself leaning into him slowly, studying the slight stubble across his jawline, then looking back up to his eyes. The gap between their faces grew smaller and smaller. For just a second she honestly thought they were going to...

Owen closed his eyes an inch from her face and dashed both hands through his hair. The moment evaporated. *Poof.* Gone.

'What I really want is popcorn,' he announced, unfurling himself from the cushions with the speed of a cheetah and making for the door. 'I left it in my room. I'll be right back.'

Sadie pressed her palms to her eyes. Her cheeks felt clammy and her toes were numb from sitting cross-legged, frozen in place, waiting…waiting…waiting for what?

Oh. My. God.

What the heck had just happened? Had they almost *kissed*?

Making a steeple of her still-warm fingers, she closed her eyes and caught her breath. That had been a lucky escape. He could have kissed her right then, and she could've kissed him back, and that would've ruined everything! Owen was the only stable thing in her life. Rocking this boat they were on was out of the question. Just because he'd done something nice for her…like a boyfriend would.

You must be out of your mind.

She raked her hands through her hair. Portia had got to her, she reminded herself. He might have been about to bop her on the nose or something equally playful. He would *never* try and kiss her. If Owen felt anything remotely romantic towards her it would have happened years ago, and nothing ever *had* happened. She'd never have let it—not with his reputation.

But, then again, she'd never seen him look at her like that before.

And he hadn't actually been with a woman in ages, if what he'd said about America was true. It was almost as if he'd come back from Boston a different person.

Maybe…

No. She hugged her knees to her chest against the cushions. Owen was off-limits. He'd never give her the commitment, the wedding, the children… He hated all that stuff. All the stuff she wanted. And even if he did decide to want it, who was to say he wouldn't change his mind? Then she'd lose her best friend for ever.

Will you just calm down?

Fanning herself and soothing her hammering heart with

long, deep breaths, she settled into a corner of the couch and did not move—even when he returned with the popcorn and joined her in their silent agreement to act as if nothing had happened.

CHAPTER SIX

'WHAT AN ABSOLUTE BUTE,' Owen quipped, sweeping his arm out over the windswept ocean.

Sadie smirked and huddled further into her coat, which she'd already mumbled about not being quite warm enough. The beach at Ettrick Bay stretched a mile ahead of them, and if he tried hard enough he could *still* picture Thailand.

He went to take his coat off, then paused. Would it be too weird to offer Sadie his jacket after what had happened a few nights ago? The thing they still hadn't talked about.

'*Oui, s'il vous plaît, j'aimerais votre veste,*' she said now in French, which she was pretty good at.

They'd been encouraging Conall McCaskill to remember his French all morning. Sadie's mouth twitched with another smirk below another pair of oversized sunglasses as she held her hand out expectantly.

Shuffling out of his jacket, he settled on handing it over, rather than attempting to do the gentlemanly thing and draping it over her shoulders. For a moment, as she slid her arms into the well-worn leather sleeves and was instantly swamped, the tension that had been there all morning, and for the last few days, lifted.

'Do you think he's making any progress?' she asked him, nodding towards Conall McCaskill. He was squatting on the sand, looking content for maybe the first time ever, tearing bits of bread from a loaf to feed a flock of birds.

'I think so. I think he secretly loves saying lines from *Surrender* in French,' he replied. 'Especially the curse words.'

Thanks to his success in identifying the decreased activity in the actor's left frontal lobe as an antagonist for his ongoing depression, Owen had assigned him a number of rehabilitation exercises to target that area of the brain specifically. Unfortunately, frontal lobe damage often affected an individual's motivation to participate in goal-directed behaviours, like rehabilitation itself, so they hadn't told Conall what they were doing, specifically.

They were being sneaky, but successfully remembering parts of his old screenplay in French whilst casually taking in the sights seemed to be cheering him up.

To their shock, Conall strode over to a dog-walker, who'd stopped to stare in disbelief. He even crouched down to pose for a photo with her huge brown Labrador. Sadie chuckled and shot Owen a look—and *boom!* He was straight back on that couch the other night, closer than close, seconds away from kissing her, and forcing himself not to.

'You talk to him more than I do,' he said to her, clearing his throat, focusing on Conall. 'At least you seem to be getting to him with whatever it is you talk about in your sessions. He only agrees on outings if you come along too.'

'He mentioned his son to me yesterday, actually,' she said, hugging his jacket around her more tightly. 'It was the first time he's brought him up.'

'What did he say?'

'He didn't say much about the accident,' she said, thoughtfully. 'He just talked about the first time Scott said he wanted to be a stuntman. Somehow the kid got up on the roof in a Superman cape and tried to fly off it. He was only five years old. Wound up in hospital with a broken arm.'

'Ouch.' Owen sucked in a breath. 'Who could've predicted his stunts would actually kill him all these years later?'

Sadie looked at him sideways. 'Conall's lost a part of his soul, Owen. Everything is meaningless to him now, which is why he's so angry and cold. I saw myself in him the whole time he was speaking, because it was how *I* felt after Chris died.'

Her chin wobbled slightly, and then she bowed her head. Suddenly Sadie had that look his mum had always used to have when she was trying to stop another tidal wave of emotion from sweeping her away. A stone formed in his stomach.

'Did you talk about Chris to Conall?' he asked now, remembering she hardly ever talked about her brother—not to anyone.

She nodded, biting down on her lip.

'You can talk to me about him if you ever need to,' he heard himself say, reaching for her hand amongst the folds of his jacket.

Why had he never said that before?

'Thank you,' she whispered, squeezing his fingers only slightly before dropping them. 'But this isn't about me.'

They stood together, watching their patient, and he wrestled with the questions he'd never felt permitted to ask her before.

'What happened that made you never want to talk about it?' he ventured eventually, deciding now was as good a time as any. 'If you want to tell me now, I mean. No pressure.'

'Nothing,' she said quickly. 'People die, Owen, and it's horrible, and gut-wrenching, and a million things you can't describe. But that's just a part of it. After that there's nothing. That's the worst. When you can't even think of a reason to breathe.'

Sadie wrapped her arms around herself again and a chill seized his bones, rooting him to the spot. Death's shadow hadn't fallen on him yet. At least, it hadn't taken anyone close to him. He'd always assumed he'd deal with it just fine. Everyone died, like she said, but it was a part of life; it shouldn't necessarily stop you living yours.

But something about her face had him holding his breath. He'd just put up walls…so as not to feel anything. Maybe that was why he'd never pressed Sadie on the details of her brother's death. Deep down he couldn't face what was coming for him. One day that pain would become his, with his mum, even his dad, for all his sins. And, sure, things weren't perfect, but he wasn't ready for *that*. Not by a long shot.

'It took me a long time to get myself out of that and deal with both my parents…'

'They divorced right after he died, didn't they?'

'Not right after. It was more like a slow unravelling. It eventually happened during my first year at Imperial—before we'd even met.'

'But it's not like you never speak to them,' he said.

He'd heard her on the phone with them, separately, a few times.

'I speak to them. But it's never about anything real. They don't talk about Chris…or what was wrong with him. Seventeen-year-old guys don't just decide to die unless there's something really wrong, Owen. He was my younger brother and we were close. I should've noticed it sooner. My parents…' She trailed off, closing her mouth firmly.

'He *killed* himself?'

Owen's heart was skidding under his shirt. How had he never known this? He'd always assumed it had been a terrible accident.

'He said he couldn't "do life" any more,' Sadie said. 'I found the note. He stuck it on the inside of his bedroom door, right before he took his motorbike out. I think he fell in with the wrong crowd…drugs, maybe. He'd started getting moody and secretive…but before that he was the happiest, most laid-back kid you'd ever met.'

'Holy hell…'

Pulling himself together, Owen took her shoulders gently, forcing her to face him, tilting her chin up.

What the hell? I should've known this sooner.

But she'd never said any of this before.

'I'm so sorry you went through all that, but surely you don't blame yourself in any way, do you, Sadie? Your parents don't blame you for what happened?'

'I don't want to think about it, Owen,' she said, avoiding his eyes. 'Your friendship means so much to me. You help me more than you know, even when we don't talk about all that stuff.'

Owen flinched inside at the way she emphasised the word friendship—like a reminder to him not to get too close.

'You wouldn't be you if that "stuff" hadn't happened,' he said. 'And for the record you can *always* talk to me— about whatever you like.'

He almost added something like *That's what friends are for*, but he refrained. He wasn't much of a friend if he hadn't even known all this till now. He'd been too wrapped up in his own family sagas to notice she'd had one of her own—something way, way worse.

'I'm so sorry I never knew about any of this,' he said.

'Why would you? I never told you.'

Dropping his hands from her shoulders, he wrestled with a sudden urge to pull her closer, but he knew nothing would suffice in this moment.

The wind whipped up her hair and the seagulls swooped around them and he couldn't get her words out of his head. How could he not have known? And what else had he totally missed about Sadie? If she blamed herself in any way for not seeing suicide speeding up on her brother—or, worse, if her parents blamed her for not being an attentive enough sister... Well, that was a hell of a lot more than he knew what to do with right now. It needed some serious processing.

'Did you want to kiss me the other night?' she asked him suddenly, out of nowhere.

What?

Sadie was scanning his eyes. He was still reeling from the news about her brother's suicide and now she was bringing this up?

'Because you *have* to be thinking about it, too. It was a bit of a weird moment between us, right? On the couch... before you went to get the popcorn?'

Owen's stomach tied itself into one huge knot as he grappled with how to answer. Her gaze was loaded. He'd assumed they'd both decided to forget it, but here they were. She'd clearly been thinking about it as much as he had.

Before he could stop himself he launched into an award-winning American accent. 'You're pretty as a picture, but you're the last person I'd want to kiss, Sadie Mills.'

Sadie just nodded thoughtfully and was silent for longer than was comfortable. Then she said a very quiet 'Good...' and he kicked himself as she pulled out her phone, signalling the end of their discussion.

Great job, Owen. Way to ruin a serious conversation.

'Hey, you two. *J'ai besoin d'une tasse de café!*'

Conall McCaskill was done with feeding the birds and was strolling purposefully towards them, shouting something about coffee?

'Sure, we'll swing by the tearoom,' Sadie chirped, and then she said it again in French, stepping away from Owen and motioning them all down the beach.

Owen's jaw ticked as he followed after them, watching her in his jacket.

You're the last person I'd want to kiss, Sadie Mills…

Why the hell had he said that—and in such a stupid way, too? Right after she'd dropped the bombshell about her brother.

Sadie knew him. She knew he used humour whenever he felt cornered, or when he wanted to distance himself from something…or someone. He'd said she could always talk to him, and then he'd shown her she actually couldn't.

Idiot.

In the quaint, aquatic-themed white and blue tearoom, Conall wore sunglasses—which, of course, meant more people recognised him than ever. Word was already out that he was staying in the small town, but when Sadie asked if he'd rather leave and go back to Rothesay he was firm in his decision.

'Non, merci.'

Outings like this were imperative when it came to Sadie monitoring his progress in society. And Owen took this new attitude as a sign that the actor was feeling better about being around people than before—thanks to the confidence boost whenever a forgotten word or phrase came back to him, and of course Sadie's constant efforts to coax his grief out into the open, instead of smothering it with rage and alcohol.

His thoughts kept slipping from analysing Conall's movements to Sadie. What she must have gone through, losing her brother to suicide. She'd learned her skills from her own experience as much as from her studies—what to do and what *not* to do when a person's grief overcame them in her presence. He'd pretty much made a habit out of making life a joke around her since they'd met, so it was no wonder she hadn't ever opened up to him properly about the things that actually mattered to her.

But then on his end there had always been an underlying fear of letting her get too close, he supposed. Just in case those feelings ever came back.

Showing his true emotions had brought him nothing but disdain from his mother while he was growing up, and he wasn't very good at showing them now. Not that getting yelled at for being a sniffling and 'useless' person when he was eleven was an excuse any more. That had been years ago!

'Is it OK to get a photo?' A young mother approached, wanting a selfie with Conall.

'No charge for you,' Conall told her, sliding out of his chair and causing the rest of the people in the café to turn and stare.

Owen moved his chair to make more room, and both his arm and knee made contact with Sadie's. She shot him a sideways glance and immediately the tension was back.

Undeniable.

It practically filled the busy bustling tearoom.

She shifted her chair around too, so they weren't touching, and Owen found his foot tapping impatiently under the table. Was it going to be weird between them now?

'We'll have to go if this continues,' she told him, bobbing her head towards the photo session.

For a second he thought she meant if this weirdness between them continued, and he was about to agree. But…

'I know this was his idea,' she went on'. 'But we're not supposed to be encouraging people to—'

'I know when you two are talking about me,' Conall interrupted, as the woman moved off with her daughter. 'I decide what I do with my fans, and when.'

Their surly star was back, grumpy as ever.

Conall slipped on his jacket while someone else sneaked

a photo of him from behind. 'But you're right—we should get going.'

Owen went to hand Sadie his jacket again. It was still pretty chilly outside. But this time she refused.

They spent the ride back in their private car in silence. Both Sadie and Conall stared out of the window from the back seat, seemingly lost in thought. Owen ground his teeth in the passenger seat.

It *was* awkward now. Even if Conall hadn't been in the car it would have been awkward. Confusion spun into irritation. Did she honestly think he would have kissed her that night?

OK, yes, maybe he'd been thinking about it, in another momentary lapse of judgement, but he'd never actually *do* it. That would just be messy. Sadie needed someone who could give her all the things he couldn't offer anyone right now—maybe not ever. Who could blame her after what she'd been through?

He was just contemplating how he could continue to be there for her as a friend, and thinking how much that actually sucked, when Sadie's phone chirped loudly in her pocket. Her face fell as she answered the call.

'What is it?' he asked, instincts primed.

'It's Portia,' she told him, one hand over the phone. 'Driver, please hurry—we need to get back!'

CHAPTER SEVEN

THEY FOUND PORTIA flat on her back in the yoga studio. Dr Calhoun was on her knees, one hand on Portia's clammy forehead, trying to force the poor woman to keep the oxygen flowing. The harrowing howls coming from Portia vibrated in Sadie's ears.

'It started with the usual tingle and escalated faster than usual,' Dr Calhoun explained as Sadie and Owen knelt at her side.

'You were doing so well on the new programme,' Sadie said to Portia as Owen took over with the oxygen. 'It's just a setback. It has made a difference, I promise.'

'I know, but I could feel this coming on when I woke up.' She winced. 'Ooh, I miss Stan… I need my husband.'

'We'll call him soon,' she promised.

The other in-patients were hovering outside the studio, dressed in their activewear. They'd been midway through a blissful yoga-nidra class, apparently, when Portia's cluster headache had caught up with her.

'You can leave me with Owen and Sadie,' Portia managed to tell Dr Calhoun, clutching Owen's wrist as he tried to adjust her mask. 'They know what to do.'

Portia drew a few more sharp consecutive breaths from the apparatus as Dr Calhoun closed the door after her, but her eyes were streaming like waterfalls and Sadie could only imagine the searing red-hot agony she must be experiencing around her skull.

Suicide headaches. That was what they called them.

The name usually sent her mind in a thousand directions, but today she pushed all thoughts of Chris away. It had been bad enough seeing Owen looking at her with pity just now, after what she'd told him. Ever since he'd been looking at her differently, and it made her deeply uncomfortable—especially as she'd brought up their almost-kiss, too.

Well, she couldn't have ignored the giant elephant in the room much longer, even if *he'd* wanted to.

She helped him now, getting Portia to her knees instead of lying on her back.

'Deep breaths from your belly, not your mouth, remember,' he told her. 'Concentrate. Distract your mind. It can only focus on one thing at a time...'

Sadie held Portia's hand, wishing that were true, while Portia did everything Owen asked and had probably instructed her to do before, in case this ever happened.

The yoga studio was small, white and bright. Various ferns in crocheted hanging baskets made living drapes over the floor-to-ceiling windows, and six purple yoga mats sat ominously empty nearby on the hardwood floor. Not a place for this much pain, Sadie observed grimly.

'That's right...in and out...deep and deeper,' Owen instructed—right before Portia emitted another yowl that tore Sadie's heart into shreds.

She squeezed Portia's hand tighter and reminded her that this would pass. Even though the cruel attack seemed to last for ever.

'I ate a bacon sandwich,' Portia told them eventually, squeezing her eyes shut as if it hurt to speak.

Owen's brow crinkled in confusion.

'It's the only thing I ate that was different,' the woman

explained after a moment, courageously swallowing back another stab of pain.

'She's been keeping a journal,' Sadie explained.

'Oh, yes,' Owen replied, without meeting her eyes. 'So it's nitrates…the nitrates in bacon that's one of the triggers. Good to know.'

'It's always the things I love most that cause this,' Portia said next, still wincing although the deep breaths and oxygen finally seemed to be helping somewhat. 'It used to happen after I had sex with my husband. I'm sure he thought I was possessed. He refused to make love to me for months—can you believe it?'

'Well, if sex caused you this much pain, I can,' Sadie replied thoughtfully, imagining for a moment being possessed, her legs locked around some equally wicked demon lover, begging for more. Owen's face flashed onto the image and she swallowed it away.

What?

'We'll get your sex-life back on track, don't worry,' Owen announced.

'Promises, promises,' Portia responded. Her headache was seemingly abating with every breath. 'It's not every day someone like you tells me something like that, Dr Penner.'

'Good to see you've got your sense of humour back,' Sadie interjected, helping her sit up as a stab of something like jealousy surprised her.

The forty-eight-year-old woman was decidedly less pale now, and it hadn't escaped Sadie's attention that she was very attractive for her age. Hmm… Maybe telling Portia about her and Owen's past had ignited Portia's imagination. Maybe she was conjuring up all sorts of thoughts about Owen in the confines of her room, Sadie thought. She was missing her husband, after all.

Irritation tingled around her nerves as Owen waggled

his eyebrows in her direction. He was clearly humouring Portia she was their patient after all.

When Portia announced that she was feeling much better they helped her out of the studio together, supporting her on each side, and took her back to her suite. Sadie stood outside the bathroom while Portia changed out of her yoga clothes, and felt Owen lasering her back with his eyes.

Every time he addressed her about anything at all, she regretted asking if he'd wanted to kiss her. But if she hadn't it would have made things even *more* awkward. He must be thinking about it too—how could he not be?

Asking him about it had been a good way of trying to distract him from asking any more questions about Chris or her estranged family, she supposed. That topic always brought up way too many emotions. More than she had the time or energy to deal with—especially with patients around.

Conall McCaskill was in her head *and* in her heart already. All that pain in his eyes... All she'd seen in the way he'd wrung his hands on his lap when he'd talked about Scott in their last session... It had touched her, and dragged her through Chris's death all over again. It was to be expected, always. It was part of her job. But this time Owen had seen it.

She had no place for vulnerability. It would only set her back on this path she'd forged for herself since all that.

They closed the door on Portia's suite, leaving her to rest, and walked down the photo-lined corridor. Sunlight streamed in through the windows onto Owen's face as they made small talk about how Portia's diet would need even closer monitoring, with the help of Saskia, the resident nutritionist.

Sadie had one foot on the stairs when Owen took her arm and pulled her back up to the landing. Her heart skyrocketed right up to the turrets as he searched her eyes.

'Sadie, how are you?'

'What? I'm fine…'

'I've been thinking about what you told me earlier… about Chris.'

Oh, God.

He paused, and something about his hand on the sleeve of her jumper made sweat break out on the back of her neck.

'Listen, if you ever need to—'

'I don't. I told you,' she said quickly, hating the look of sympathy on his face. Fresh annoyance at herself made her cheeks sting as she removed herself from his concerned grip. 'I shouldn't have told you the details. You didn't need to know.'

Owen stepped back from her, looking slightly wounded. 'I'm just sorry I never asked you about it before.' He lowered his voice, his obvious concern for her making his eyes crease. 'He committed *suicide*, Sadie…that's a little different from dying in a motorcycle accident. You do know that's what I thought happened, all this time?'

'Why wouldn't you have thought that?' she said staunchly. 'I didn't elaborate on the details.'

'I know—but why not?'

Sadie shrugged, wishing her stomach would stop tangling itself into that giant knot. This was exactly what she didn't want to happen. Her best friend looking at her as if she needed to be swaddled in cotton wool, or as if she had some problem he now had to fix, like everyone else in here. It was bad enough that she hadn't seen it coming with Chris. The last thing she wanted was for Owen to start poking around.

'It happened a long time ago, Owen. I'm fine,' she said stiffly, adjusting her wristwatch.

'But you're not, are you? And Conall's getting to you, bringing it all up whenever he talks about losing Scott…'

'It's my job, Owen. And I'll deal with it like I always do. Without your help.'

Owen straightened his shoulders and blew air from his nose, and she knew she wouldn't escape this confrontation. She'd told him something deeply personal and made it his business—like she always seemed to do with Owen lately, despite trying not to.

'I have to go to my next appointment,' she said, hurrying on down the stairs ahead of him.

'Of course you do,' he muttered behind her.

Great—now she'd offended him. And she knew that was grossly unfair. But it was better than feeling torn by his lips being too close again, his eyes being too probing again.

What was she meant to do with all this? It was bad enough that she was even having these weird new feelings for her friend. And he felt the same, she could tell. When he'd said he'd never kiss her this morning…that had been a *blatant* lie. He always did one of those stupid accents whenever he felt put on the spot.

But Owen Penner never wanted more than a good time, and she was not about to let him make *her* his next good time—not for anything.

Sadie continued with her appointments and somehow managed to eat her dinner in the little courtyard outside without Owen interrupting her, like he usually did. As the sun set that evening she still hadn't seen him again.

Good, she thought. For both of them.

She needed to stop treating him like one of her 'comfort blankets' just because there was no one else around who knew her. She'd already decided there would be no more comfort blankets, and here she was, spilling all her issues out to Owen!

That would get her nothing apart from his quick rejection—like he rejected anyone who got too close to him.

* * *

Something woke her at three a.m. Sadie shot up in bed, fresh from a fitful dream about Chris calling out to her from somewhere she couldn't reach. Awful!

Pulling on her white embroidered robe and slippers, she made her way downstairs. Sleep would be impossible now, so she might as well make a cup of tea and get some fresh air.

The spring night was unusually mild and welcoming outside. Sadie found herself strolling by the fernery, breathing in the sweet scent of the jasmine trees that lined its entrance, recalling bits of her dream. Just talking about her parents and Chris so briefly to Owen had brought everything back. No wonder it was creeping into her dreams.

Everything was haunting her now—the fact that she hadn't seen just how much Chris had needed help. The fact that guilt had kept her away from home for so long…long enough that she hadn't even known her parents were getting a divorce until after it had happened. She'd been the worst sister and the worst daughter.

Her stomach knotted again as she sat by the silent mermaid fountain, thinking of Owen, too. He'd looked so hurt that she'd never told him the truth about her brother. All this time she'd let him believe what had happened to him was an accident. All this time. And now he probably thought she didn't trust him with anything serious. That all they had were their laughs, their jokes, their good times.

But it was getting harder not to trust him with *more*… she realised. He was always there for her. He would always be there for her.

As a *friend*, she reminded herself, as soon as her heart started its involuntary fluttering again. All this wandering outside the lines had to stop.

Being in love is a waste of time.

He'd said it himself, the day his mum had called. It

wasn't something he was looking for right now—maybe ever. He'd probably stay single till he reached his fifties and wanted companionship—and if he did, so what? Why should that be *her* problem? Why was she even still *thinking* about all this? Their friendship was too good to risk for anything!

With a sigh at the moon, she decided that maybe it was time to go back inside.

Nearing her room, she heard a whisper in the corridor that made her start. She tiptoed to the end of a towering oak bookcase and peered around a row of old encyclopaedic volumes to see someone standing outside Owen's door.

A barefooted Owen was propped up in the doorway on one muscled arm, his broad naked chest on full display, and wearing a pair of comfy checked pyjama bottoms. Pressing her back to the wall and huddling into her robe, she tried to make out what was going on, but she couldn't hear a thing…except soft laughter between a man and a woman.

At four a.m.?

Hunched in the shadow of the bookcase, Sadie tried her best to slow the sudden pounding of her suspicious heart. Eventually Owen closed his door, with one last soft, telling chuckle. His visitor walked straight past her, oblivious, and Sadie dared a peek just as whoever it was unlocked a nearby door and slipped inside.

Even from the back, the woman's long, black satiny hair and dark exotic grace was a giveaway.

Sadie stood there, fuming in the darkness.

Parminder.

Owen was meeting Parminder in the middle of the night.

CHAPTER EIGHT

Owen carved into a slice of the chicken on his plate, tracking the busy dining room for Sadie. She hadn't stepped foot in here at the usual time for the last five days, and he had a feeling she was afraid he'd probe her about her past again. As if he'd dare!

If she'd wanted to talk about the grief and the guilt she still carried around she would have told him the full story before now, but obviously she didn't trust him with the serious stuff. He was the joker. The stand-in comfort blanket till she found someone more suitable to handle her heart. The *pleasure-seeker*.

'Penny for your thoughts!'

A voice broke into his depressing internal monologue.

'What?'

'You look like you're thinking about something very serious. And you're murdering your peas.'

Parminder slid in next to him, and he realised he'd turned his green peas into tiny explosions, smashed on his plate. He also noticed she'd undone the top three buttons of her shirt, revealing just a hint of cleavage—for his benefit, no doubt.

Parminder had been finding new reasons to talk to him for days—ever since she'd knocked on his door in the middle of the night several days ago in a skimpy nightdress, claiming to be scared after seeing a ghost. It was in his best interests to be polite to her right now, but he'd have preferred to eat in peace or with Sadie.

Where was she, anyway? Avoiding his probing was one thing, taking it to extremes by missing the famous Rothesay Recovery Sunday lunch was not like her at all.

Parminder started telling him about Conall McCaskill's latest spat with a doctor. 'He was only doing a regular check-up, but Mr McCaskill almost got violent. Apparently he only wants to deal with you and Dr Mills going forward.'

Owen frowned at his potatoes. Conall's recent setback was the talk of Rothesay this morning, and it was very disheartening to say the least. He still wouldn't talk about Scott's accident with him, but all healing was a work in progress, after all.

'Might be time to help redirect that anger into something more aggressive than potting plants…like woodwork, or bag punching…' Parminder was still offering advice on Conall, and he forced himself to pay attention.

'Maybe he could learn to play the bagpipes,' he offered. 'Those guys always look like their lungs are about to burst. Could be a good way to tire him out. I'll talk to Sadie about it.'

Speak of the devil.

In walked Sadie—finally. His back tensed all over again as their eyes met.

'Would you mind?' he asked Parminder quickly, and reluctantly she shuffled over and made room for Sadie next to him at the table.

'I knew you wouldn't miss the roast lunch,' he said as Sadie slid into the seat, eyeing him cautiously. Her potatoes were drowning in gravy, as usual. 'Is there chicken under there somewhere too?' he joked, trying to lift the immediate tension between them.

'I like gravy,' she said simply, reaching across him for the pepper.

He caught her arm softly and leaned closer, away from Parminder's hearing. 'Are you OK? You've been…noticeably absent.'

'I've been busy,' she replied curtly, removing her arm and shifting her eyes to Parminder. 'I'm sure you have been too.'

He frowned at her. She knew his schedule the same way he knew hers. She hadn't been *that* busy.

'What were you two talking about just now?' Sadie asked casually.

The way she'd pulled her hair back tight and buttoned her blouse three times higher than Parminder's, right to her throat, made her look like a strict headmistress.

'Parminder and I were discussing how Mr McCaskill should play the bagpipes,' he said, thinking how hot she looked, all prim and proper. 'Maybe we can add it to his rehab regimen, to help him get some anger out.'

Sadie huffed a laugh. 'Just because he's Scottish it doesn't mean he automatically wants to know how to play the bagpipes, Owen. Besides, bagpipes make people angry.'

He chuckled. 'You have a point. But I've come here to Scotland. I want bagpipes.'

A smile teetered on her lips, but it vanished as Parminder cut in enthusiastically.

'Maybe *you* should learn, Owen?' She tossed her veil of long black hair over her shoulder and almost knocked a spoon off the table, too. 'We'll get you a kilt too. I bet you'd look good in one.'

'Now, that I wouldn't mind,' he mused, imagining it for a moment. 'I've heard the fresh Scottish air feels damn fine blowing in under a kilt…'

Sadie stood up again quickly, taking her plate with her. 'I've left my book upstairs. I'll eat in my room.'

Parminder stopped her giggling abruptly and scraped her chair back, looking at Sadie in horror. 'You're not going upstairs on your own, are you?'

Sadie paused. 'What do you mean?'

'Well, aren't you scared you might see the ghost?'

'I don't believe in ghosts.'

'Parminder's eyes grew wide and beseeching. With a lowered voice she said, 'I saw it…*her*. The other night. Ask Owen. I saw the Lady in White.'

Owen pulled a face. How was he supposed to know what she'd seen? He'd been fast asleep till she'd pounded on his door. 'All I know is that you were scared enough by something to wake me at some ungodly hour,' he said.

Slowly, Sadie lowered herself into the chair again, turning to Parminder. 'You saw the Lady in White?'

Parminder bobbed her head, her eyes darting around the room. 'I got up for a wee and I saw her walking in the garden…all around the fernery and the fountain. But she could be anywhere, right? I haven't been anywhere on my own in this place all week.'

Sadie just stared at her plate. A small smile crept over her face before she picked up her cutlery and resumed eating without a word.

'I know you don't believe me,' Parminder continued, glancing vexedly at her.

'I believe you saw *something*,' Sadie said carefully.

Her eyes flashed to his, and for just a second he saw the old Sadie…the Sadie he'd missed since things had started getting weird. Maybe things *could* go back to normal between them, he thought, wondering all of a sudden what her secret was.

Later that afternoon, Sadie caught him just as he was about to start his regular session with Conall McCaskill.

'Apparently he's asked for both of us today,' she said,

smoothing down her shirt and skirt as they took the corridor towards the actor's suite.

'Parminder told me he only wants to deal with us from now on,' he admitted.

Sadie stopped abruptly, arms folded. She had that look on her face, as if she was about to own up to something.

'About Parminder… You know, I've been so annoyed with you for hooking up with a staff member. I thought you were sleeping with her.'

'Why did you think that?' he asked, mimicking her stance while he processed this new information.

So was that why she'd been so cold with him recently? It wasn't just because he'd overstepped some mark and dredged up deep-rooted insecurities she hated to admit to, even to him…it was because she'd deemed him an unprofessional playboy and didn't want to be associated with his behaviour.

Neither was good.

Unless…she'd been *jealous*?

He studied her intently as she spoke, running the possibilities around in his head, noting with some element of concern that he rather enjoyed the thought that she'd been jealous.

'I saw her the other night, after she'd knocked on your door. I was already awake, and coming back to my room. I think it was me she saw down by the fernery, Owen. I was wearing my white robe!'

'The ghost of Sadie walks the grounds at night, tricking the staff?' He smirked.

Sadie pretended to thump him. 'Don't tell her. Then I'd have to admit I saw her that night at your door but didn't say anything, and she'll think I'm weird.'

'You *are* weird,' he confirmed, and she pulled a face at him that made him laugh. 'You didn't tell *me* what you saw, though. That's not like you. Usually I'd get an earful about something like that. Were you jealous?'

'Well, obviously this place is not haunted,' she said thoughtfully, without answering his question. 'Even though there are still those weird banging noises at night. Have you heard them lately?'

'No, but at least now you know it's not *me* who's been doing the banging,' he replied, watching her fiddle with her shirtsleeve buttons, seeing the way she was biting on her lip, the fresh blush of colour on her cheeks. 'For the record, Parminder's crush is all one-sided,' he told her seriously.

'Well, that's good to know,' she replied, talking to the floor. 'Because it wouldn't be very professional to start something up while we're…while you're here.'

'Noted,' he said with a salute, refusing to mention her fumbled Freudian slip as she led the way into Conall Mc-Caskill's suite.

That look. He'd know it a mile off. Women always had that lips pursed, eyes narrowed look when they were jealous. God, if only he could act on his sudden burning urge to grab her, throw her over his shoulder and carry her up to his room. And then throw her on his bed and show her just what her jealousy did to him.

Luckily the A-lister was in a better mood today, but they still had to discuss his recent violent outburst with the other doctor.

'He mentioned Maeve…how I'm upsetting her because I refuse to subject her to this ridiculous gala event, but what did he expect?' he huffed, stretching out on the couch like a cat. 'What if I don't want to attend myself? Did anyone even consider that? It's not like I can be "switched on" all the time. I told you—I decide when I see my fans.'

Owen caught Sadie's look and shut his mouth. OK, so the guy had a giant ego, but it wasn't entirely a bad thing—at least he was getting some of his confidence back, largely thanks to their speech and language sessions that were bringing up things he actually enjoyed remembering and forcing his depression aside in small bursts.

But Conall's wife had been on the phone several times asking for him, and the stubborn man was refusing to speak to her a lot of the time. He blamed her for sending him here, for assuming he needed special help. His pride had taken a kick—that was the real issue here.

'It's not about subjecting anyone to your fans…it's not a public event,' Sadie informed him softly. 'They do it every year. It started as an fundraising event to entertain Rothesay's supporters, and now every year it marks another year since the recovery unit became what it is now: a successful space for healing.'

Owen heard Sadie's voice, laced with empathy.

'It's supposed to be a chance to include people's spouses,' she continued. 'Perhaps Maeve would like to feel more involved with your healing process, seeing as she's still going through her own. It won't help that process if you feel like someone is shutting you out.'

Owen braced himself for another verbal tirade, but Conall just fiddled with the buttons on his stylish tweed jacket and scowled at the ceiling.

'I suppose you would know that,' he said eventually.

He went on to explain how it was the processing of his grief that had caused his violent outburst, something Sadie had encouraged with her sessions, although he regretted lashing out at the doctor the way he had.

Owen prepared his upcoming questions for the actor's weekly analysis, wondering exactly how much Sadie had divulged to him about her own loss. Just by relating to Conall she'd got more out of him than anyone. But she'd never thought to burden *him* with the truth before.

That was still bothering him like a mosquito…the fact

that she didn't trust him with anything serious. But then, it wasn't as if he'd ever given her reason to. She'd always had boyfriends for that. He wasn't settling down…he wasn't cut out for being anyone's rock. Never had he given anyone any indication that he'd stick around for more than a few weeks, and Sadie knew all that. But…

But just now she'd pretty much confirmed a case of the green-eyed Loch Ness monster. That look on her face!

He shook himself, pulling his attention back from dangerous territory. Sadie was not someone he could afford to go there with—not for anything. They'd never had to rely on one another solely for attention before—that was all this was. Even though he'd missed her like hell in America, and was still figuring out what that meant, exactly.

'I asked for you both today because I know I need to talk about the accident itself, and I don't want to say it twice,' Conall was saying now, wringing his hands on the couch. 'I know I've been a little bit of a…well, a *lot* of a grump. But I just miss my boy so much…'

His voice wobbled suddenly. Sadie reached out to place a gentle hand on his.

'I see it every time I close my eyes,' said Conall. 'There isn't a day that goes by when I don't blame myself…'

'It was not your fault,' Owen said, standing up in a primal urge not to upset *anyone* in the room any further.

'But I could have prevented it. If only I'd been watching more closely. It was *my* damn movie set!'

'That doesn't mean anything. It was an accident. Both Dr Mills and I know that—everyone knows that.'

Sadie was silent for a moment, tapping her nails on the arm of her chair, and he wondered again, now he'd learned about Chris's suicide, why she'd chosen a career that must dredge up so many bad memories. And this must feel very close to home for her: Conall McCaskill playing the blame game with himself.

Conall wore the look of a gladiator about to step into an arena with a tiger. Owen half expected him to shut down again and refuse their help entirely, but then Sadie let out a sigh from somewhere deep in her soul.

'The hardest thing is finding a place to start. I know that,' she said into the silence. 'Deep inside, you feel like if you start thinking about it you won't be able stop. But somewhere in between, Conall, there is a place where you can learn to live with it. You have to trust that you will get there.'

Owen felt a lump in his throat like a golf ball. And then, just like that, the stoic, moody, grieving Conall McCaskill broke into a thousand pieces. Their favourite actor literally *surrendered* in a way no one would ever have expected. It was like opening a valve…everything came rushing out.

It was nine a.m.

Scott was late.

Conall yelled at him for holding up the shoot.

The props department said everything was OK.

Usually Scott would check things himself too…go for a test run. But they were on the clock, time was ticking…

Conall was annoyed with his son for wasting everyone's time.

And then the car sped out of control, and that stupid altercation was his last communication with Scott…

Maybe it was witnessing someone so strong expressing his emotions in a way he himself had never quite been able to. Maybe it was the look on Sadie's face. But to his shock, as Conall wiped a hand across his eyes, Owen found he was fighting back a kind of tidal wave of emotion the likes of which he'd never felt before.

Some time later he found himself at the end of the dock, looking over the lake, his eyes on the bobbing fishing boat. Conall's emotional outpouring was still playing on his mind, and his mother would no doubt add to it shortly.

Three missed calls from her, he noted, shoving his phone back into his pocket. He should give her the benefit of the doubt—but then she only ever bombarded him with calls like this when his dad had done something to offend her.

'Thinking of going fishing again?'

Sadie had found him. He made room for her on the wooden jetty beside him.

'Conall has called Maeve and asked her to come to the gala.'

'Good,' he replied as she sat down and drew her knees up.

She'd changed into jeans and a short green linen jacket, and he could smell lavender again. He swallowed back the now familiar pang he felt at her closeness.

'You left that session as soon as you could,' she said. 'Is he getting to you, too?'

Owen grunted. He'd made an excuse to leave without accepting the cup of tea and signed autograph Conall had offered them, and it hadn't all been to do with his next appointment with Vivek Kumar, nor the missed calls on his phone.

'Seeing someone like that, so famous, being so vulnerable... I don't know,' he admitted, tossing a stick out into the water. 'I guess it got to me, yeah. I was more worried about it all affecting *you*, though,' he added quickly. 'After what you've told me lately.'

Sadie's lips twitched. 'That's sweet,' she replied simply, then leaned back on her elbows, as if she were taking in the sky. 'But why do you think I chose this career, Owen? Hearing people work through their grief gives me strength, even after all this time.'

'You're saying helping them helps you, too, in some way?'

She nodded. 'You don't need to worry about me...really.'

Owen thought he would probably always worry about her now, but he understood about her work.

'Do I need to worry about *you*?' she asked him after a moment, sitting back up and touching a hand to his arm.

He felt himself tense and dragged a hand through his hair.

'I know you try to keep your emotions out of things, Owen, and that's just how you are, but…'

'You're right.' He bristled at her blunt observation. 'Maybe I've never got my dad's voice out of my head, telling me Penner men don't cry. Stuff like that stays with you, Sadie.'

'Your dad said what?' Sadie's jaw dropped.

He massaged the back of his neck. Why had he just told her that?

Sadie pressed a warm hand to his arm, as if rooting him to the dock, and he wrestled with what to say now that she was waiting for an explanation of some kind. He'd never told anyone about the day that had probably shaped him more than he'd ever admitted. He couldn't avoid it now, though. The words were spilling out of him before he could think to shut up.

He'd been eleven years old, almost deafened by the row going on in the kitchen. His mother had been yelling at his dad.

'Penner men are useless—all of you. Useless! Your father was the same, and your grandfather too. I don't know why I thought you'd be any different, Jay…

That was when he'd realised his dad had crossed some unthinkable line and his mother was approaching the end of her tether. He'd been sniffling on the stairs, scared the world was crumbling down around him, when his dad had marched right up to him and boomed, *'Penner men don't cry!'*

It had shocked him to the core. But he'd never cried

after that. Not a tear…not a trickle of emotion. Not even after his dad had packed his bags and gone to live with his newest fling. His mum had done enough crying for both of them, anyway, and the last thing he'd wanted was to be useless to her.

Owen paused in his monologue, realising Sadie was staring at him, mouth agape.

'Wow…' she breathed. 'Things are even clearer to me now.'

He felt his eyebrows knit together. 'What do you mean?'

Adrenaline flared in his veins as Sadie's eyes glowed with unexpected affection. Somehow the look on her face riled him up all the more, and he wished he could read her mind. She was probably analysing him…putting him into some box. A guy with daddy issues—*great*.

'It was ages ago. Like I said, I was only eleven,' he reminded her stiffly.

'Like you said, stuff like that stays with you,' she replied, turning him to face her.

She pressed one warm palm to his cheek and stroked her thumb softly to the corner of his mouth. His throat tightened as the lips he knew so well but had never actually tasted hovered tantalisingly close. So close that her breath tickled his nose.

An entire drum kit was going off in his chest now.

For a second longing surged through him, and he braced himself…

Her kiss landed on his forehead, right above his brow. 'You are a special kind of person, Owen,' she said.

Special? Great.

Owen dropped her hand, curling his fists into his sides as her warm smile stretched against his skin. A friendly kiss on the forehead. A compliment on how 'special' he was.

God, Owen, you're an idiot. What else did you expect, anyway?

He pulled away, blew out his cheeks and avoided her eyes, even as heat coursed in his veins. That had been weird.

Resting back on his elbows on the dock, he trained his stare on the water, running over his holiday allowance in his head, feeling his stomach revolt at the pity in her eyes. Humiliation, confusion, the urge to run all made a knot in his insides.

'I have a phone call to make,' he said tightly. The words came out a little more coldly than he'd intended.

Sadie frowned at him. 'What did I do?'

'Nothing,' he said. 'I do have a call to make. And I don't need you to psychoanalyse me.'

'It's a little late for that.' She smirked, getting to her feet.

Owen grunted, not giving her the satisfaction of any ac-knowledgement. He wanted to confide in her and run from her all at the same time. What the hell was that all about?

As she headed for the house without him, he forced himself to stay put.

CHAPTER NINE

Vivek Kumar looked more melancholy than usual when Sadie met him in the music room on the day of the gala. He was staring unseeingly at the piano keys. She closed the door behind her, and crept across the plush red carpet, concerned at his expression. He rested his arms across his portly stomach, then unfolded them, and then folded them again on the piano, frowning at the keys as if he didn't know what to do with them.

'You don't have to do this now,' she said kindly, gesturing to the sheet music on the stand. 'If you're having trouble remembering.'

Vivek was a gifted pianist—at least, he had been before the traumatic head injury that had left a scar inside as large as the one that was displayed on his shaved head, down his neck and across his right shoulder.

He exhaled long and deep through his nose, without looking at her. 'No. I want to,' he said, putting his hands to the keys.

He paused, as if trying to force open some database in his head that he didn't have the password for. Sadie held her breath, staring out through the floor-length windows at the billowing white marquee now dominating the grounds, ready for this afternoon's event. It seemed like people had been talking about it for weeks but she couldn't seem to get excited about it.

Traumatic brain injuries disturbed the delicate chemistry of the brain so its neurons couldn't function normally. Huge changes to Vivek's thinking and behaviour were still taking everyone by surprise—not least him. Sometimes he remembered how to play. Sometimes he didn't. Owen had told him it might take weeks or even months for his brain to resolve the kind of chemical imbalances that could occur with a TBI.

Owen...

She found herself training her eyes on him as he stepped from the marquee and held up a hand to her from the other side of the window. In seconds he was entering the room.

Sadie let free the breath she was holding, then drew in another one. She couldn't help but note that he looked very handsome in his uniform. More so than usual. He'd caught the sun on his face over the past week or so, often fishing alone after his shifts. Now, halfway into May, it was unusually sunny for Scotland at this time of year.

'Are you going to play for us?' he asked Vivek, closing the door behind him and putting a folder down on a plush velvet chair.

Sadie felt their shoulders brush momentarily as he moved to her side behind the piano stool, and she tried not to feel the now-familiar sensation of unease at his closeness.

He regretted telling her about his dad the other day—she could tell. As if she could possibly be repulsed by seeing the real, vulnerable Owen behind the tough-guy facade.

The doctor in her was intrigued. His parents' harsh words back then had most definitely left their mark. And his mother was *still* in his ear about his dad. What she'd overheard on the fishing boat, back when they'd first heard about his dad's new engagement, was making more and more sense now.

What was it she'd said? Something like, '*I hope you never treat anyone like this.*' Almost accusingly. Almost as if she expected him to turn out just like his dad.

Owen just put up a wall whenever she'd tried to talk more about it to him, and that was understandable, she supposed. She knew there was nothing worse than people probing her about *her* parents. But the thought of anyone making him feel less than adequate about anything was infuriating. He was one of the kindest people she knew… and if they hadn't been best friends, and if the example of his parents hadn't made him dread the thought of ever being in a relationship himself, she might just consider…

She caught herself.

Nope. There were no 'ifs' with Owen. His friendship was all she needed.

Wasn't it?

'I wanted to play for my wife later.' Vivek cut into her thoughts. 'She's bringing my niece, Ashanti. I wanted it to be a surprise for them,' he said despondently.

Owen put a comforting hand to his shoulder. 'You've already made so much progress, Vivek! We haven't been working on your gaze stabilisation and eye-tracking exercises for long and you already say you're not feeling dizzy or off-balance any more, right? That's a real mark of success. We can't force these things. It's possible the piano may come back to you…give it time.'

Owen shot her a look that said maybe it would, maybe it wouldn't. People were only just beginning to understand the severity of concussion—people who had been injured decades ago were only just starting to see why they'd been thinking or acting a certain way for so long. So many brain injuries went undiagnosed…but so many were diagnosed properly, thanks to doctors like Owen.

He was kind of an amazing person…

The thought caught her off guard, especially as it came

with a sense of longing to be in his vicinity always...to be cared for by him.

'Sorry I'm late, by the way,' he said now. 'Maeve McCaskill has just arrived. There's a bit of a crowd in the marquee already.'

'Ooh, really? She's here?'

Sadie cleared her throat. That might have come out a little too enthusiastically.

Owen's mouth twitched. 'You're not going to ask her to sign your apron, are you?'

'I would if I'd known to bring it with me,' she admitted.

'My wife has all her stuff,' announced Vivek, turning from the piano as if a light had come on in his mind. 'She's always leafing through this one cook-book...'

'Ah, so you remember that.' Owen grinned. 'Do any specific dishes come to mind?'

Vivek's smile faded. He shook his head, which told them he did not without him saying another word.

Sadie assisted Owen with Vivek's memory-strengthening exercises, sometimes watching the crowds gathering outside the window for the gala. It was their last session of the day, and once they were done it would be time to put her best dress on, as well as her best foot forward, for the event everyone had been looking forward to for weeks.

Just a few hours later she was chatting with Portia and her husband Stan—who was just as fabulous as Portia. Their chemistry was undeniable...

And then Owen approached, with the McCaskills on either side of him, as if he'd been appointed as some kind of celebrity security guard. Sadie tried to keep her squeal confined to her throat as none other than Maeve McCaskill held her hand out.

'I've been looking forward to meeting you,' Maeve said warmly, taking her aside so they could talk in private.

She was the epitome of breezy sophistication. But

through her admiration, it hit Sadie…what this woman—
a mother—had gone through, and how she'd come out the
other side. She felt a rush of empathy that almost brought
tears to her eyes.

'I'm so glad you could make it,' she said, sincerely. 'And
I'm so very sorry for your loss.'

'I wanted to thank you personally for everything you
and Dr Penner have done for my husband,' Maeve replied
coolly. 'Conall talks about you very highly.'

'He's come a long way,' Sadie said, noting the jolt in her
stomach at hearing the words 'you and Dr Penner'.

Owen was looking at her from where the band was setting up, now. He was dressed in a designer jacket and chi-
nos, holding an orange juice, watching her.

She'd expected another smirk from him over her being
starstruck, but he seemed to be appreciating her ocean-
green summer dress and her smart hip-length jacket and
silver sandals. It was one of her favourite outfits, but she'd
never felt so self-conscious under his gaze before.

Ever since he'd opened up to her about his parents she'd
found herself thinking even more about that almost-kiss.
Their relationship felt more honest now…deeper. She'd even
considered lately that perhaps she'd pushed him away all
these years by refusing to talk about her own family, and
he'd responded by doing the same. Now that they were talking about things—serious things—it was clear they had far
more in common than she'd ever realised before.

She *was* psychoanalysing him, in her head. But only because he'd become a hundred times more interesting to her.

And sexy.

How had she failed to notice how sexy he was?

Maybe it had taken coming here to the Western Scottish Highlands, far away from everyone who knew them,
for her to see how she'd been blocking out her attraction to
him ever since that night in Sylvester's. Because of course

nothing had ever happened between them…or would *ever* happen. They'd both kicked down that bridge and set fire to it. Which was good.

Except he looked so damn gorgeous right now, and she couldn't deny she'd been as jealous as hell over Parminder. God, what would it be like to kiss those lips after all this time…?

Suddenly it occurred to her that Maeve McCaskill was still talking to her…and she was zoning out, thinking about Owen again.

The afternoon stretched into sunset. There were games on the lawn, activities in the fernery, a banquet feast complete with a suckling pig, and now this—an organised boat ride around the lake, led by Owen himself.

He looked like the sexiest of sailors at the helm. He'd loosened his shirt at the neck, and his hair in the breeze was cutely dishevelled. Sadie waved off a bee that was buzzing around her face and took in the scene around her from her seat on the wooden boat. For one glorious afternoon Rothesay Recovery had felt more like a country retreat than a luxury medical facility. She couldn't help a huge surge of pride for her patients over everything they'd achieved so far.

Portia nudged her suddenly, waving off the same bee with her other hand. 'Owen looks like he needs some help up there,' she said, winking at her before burrowing her face lovingly in her husband's shoulder.

They seemed so in love, Sadie mused, remembering how Portia had said they were friends first. Friends who'd had sex as an experiment.

Interesting… I would actually love to try that with Owen. I wonder if he'd go for it… Why does he have to look so hot right now?

'How long have you been with Owen?' Maeve asked, catching her off-guard. 'I was just thinking how good you two look together. Conall never told me you were—'

'Oh, no, we're not a couple,' Sadie cut in, fixing her eyes on Ashanti, Vivek Kumar's seven-year-old niece, who was asking Owen if she could steer the boat.

Had these women read her mind? But Owen *was* looking at her with interest. He'd probably overheard what Maeve had said. Sadie felt her face flush, and was just about to change the subject when a cry from the front of the boat rendered everyone silent.

'It stung me!'

The little girl was on her feet now, flapping her hands about. A ruckus ensued. Poor Vivek looked dumbstruck as his wife scrambled to reach the child and pull her down to sit on the bench, almost toppling overboard. Then Owen stopped the boat in the middle of the lake just as Sadie launched forward to help. The jerk sent her flying, but Owen caught her in his arms and righted her before she'd even had a chance to catch her breath.

'Thank you,' she gasped, gripping his forearms, stunned for a moment.

Poor Ashanti was shrieking in agony, and the boat was bobbing vigorously now.

'Everyone stay calm,' came Owen's authoritative voice. 'It's just a bee sting.'

Just as he said that, however, the little girl seemed to droop and fold like a piece of paper, straight into Sadie's arms.

'She's passed out!' she cried, horrified, sliding to the floor with her.

Owen made a shield around them with his body and his arms.

'Is she allergic to bee stings?' she heard him ask the Kumars.

'I don't know…' came the reply.

'Sure seems like she is,' someone else responded.

Vivek's eyes grew wide as saucers, but then the girl

seemed to regain consciousness, and sucked in a breath as if her life depended on it. She panted a little, her cheeks paling further, and in the middle of the chaos Sadie heard Conall McCaskill step in and offer to take the helm.

With concern, Sadie registered the distance to the jetty. There was no doubt about it—the girl was in the early stages of anaphylactic shock and there was nothing they could do without a shot of epinephrine—which no one had. She and Owen were the only medical staff on the boat.

Owen had called the emergency services already, and was radioing Rothesay Recovery. Everyone was flapping about in a panic now, as she cradled the semi-conscious girl in her arms. Conall McCaskill clambered to the front seat and started steering the boat back the way they'd come. They'd travelled pretty far out from the shore on the huge lake.

Sadie felt Owen's steady hand on her shoulder. 'We've got this,' he whispered to her, causing her ear to tingle. 'She's going to be OK.'

Sadie met Owen's piercing eyes. The fact that he was here gave her comfort, in spite of the situation. She trusted him, and so did everyone else. He had this under control.

Just then a judder from the engine sent them both flailing into each other again. Ashanti gasped as the sound of the motor sputtered into nothing. McCaskill tried to get it going again, tugging with all his might, but he failed and another panicked ruckus broke out amongst the passengers.

Owen was peeling off his shirt.

'What are you doing?' she asked, but Owen already had one foot on the side and in seconds was in the water, gripping the boat from the outside.

'Pass her over to me—we don't have much time,' he said.

'Is he insane?' someone muttered behind her.

But Sadie lowered the young girl into his arms and quickly tore her dress over her head before sliding into the lake too, causing Vivek to gasp and avert his eyes, and Portia to clap her hands approvingly.

Together, she and Owen kept Ashanti's head out of the water as they swam back towards the jetty, every stroke feeling as if they were carving through ice, despite the earlier warmth of the day. The little girl's eyes and lips were swollen, as if the bee had injected its venom straight into her face. Sadie was sure her own face must be blue, and already she could barely feel her fingers and toes, but nothing mattered except getting this girl to safety. Untreated anaphylaxis could lead to death within half an hour.

Parminder met them on the jetty, her bright patterned floral sundress a beacon to swim for. They were all shivering wildly, but Owen made a quick job of lifting the girl to the dock, where Parminder wrapped a blanket around her. Fergal handed Sadie a towel to cover herself—but not before making a full body-swipe with his eyes over her bra and knickers.

An ambulance's siren was already adding its own soundtrack to the air and Owen had started CPR. The scene was surreal, and she was sure the cold would have buckled her knees if she hadn't already been on them on the jetty beside him.

They could have died in that freezing cold lake... A life lived with Owen that ended without so much as a kiss...

Why are you thinking about this now? You're clearly in shock.

Just as two paramedics tore down the path through the garden with a stretcher Ashanti spluttered back to consciousness again, and complained of being cold and dizzy. A rush of relief brought tears to Sadie's eyes as Owen wrapped both of his big arms around her shivering body. She leaned into him, letting the paramedics take over with the epinephrine. Their praise for their quick thinking and heroic action washed over her—all she could think, as she huddled into Owen, was it might have been too late for Ashanti.

It had almost been too late.

'She's going to be OK,' Owen told her, as if he was reading her mind.

His eyes were flooded with concern for her and she wondered if her lips were blue. She let him help her to her feet as the ambulance sped away.

'They'll have to keep her in overnight, in case the symptoms recur, but she's fine—you guys made sure of that,' Parminder said.

Sadie realised people were watching them, standing locked together wrapped in towels and blankets. She pulled away from Owen just as a noise behind them made them all spin around. Sadie blinked. There in the distance was the boat, Conall McCaskill at the helm standing tall, steering towards them at speed, like the action hero he'd once been. Everyone on it was cheering.

'How did you get it to go again?' Sadie said when he pulled up at the jetty, windswept but delighted to learn that Ashanti was fine. He was wearing a look of determination on his handsome face that Sadie hadn't seen since the night they'd re-watched his movie, *Surrender*.

'You don't spend years on movie sets without learning a few things,' he said simply, helping his wife back on to safe, solid ground. A glimmer of pride in his eyes twinkled its way through his tough exterior. Even more so when Maeve flung both arms around him and kissed his cheek, as if she knew she was finally getting her husband back.

'We should go and get changed,' Owen said to her, as someone handed them their clothes from the boat.

Vivek's frantic wife was ushered away by Fergal, to follow the ambulance to the hospital.

The adrenaline was wearing off now, and Sadie was starting to shiver even more. Owen's arm slid around her waist again, and this time she didn't shake him off. She needed him and he knew it.

Her heart thumped wildly, both at what had just happened and his closeness, and their dripping wetness left a watery trail all the way back to the house.

CHAPTER TEN

SADIE STUMBLED HALFWAY up the staircase. Owen caught her, pulling her soaking frame against his bare chest.

'Careful,' he said.

'I'm so cold.' She shivered, as if he might be in doubt. 'How are you not freezing?'

'Adrenaline?'

He met her eyes for a second as she drew long, jagged breaths, and then held her close to steady her as they made their way up the rest of the stairs, trying to ignore the way her skin against his was igniting every cell in his body.

The house was eerily quiet everywhere. Most people were still out in the grounds, enjoying the gala. Hopefully that poor little girl would be OK—at least the paramedics had assured them she would be.

He helped Sadie unlock her door and realised her legs were wobbling like a newborn foal's. She'd pulled a towel around her tightly down on the jetty, although Fergal had got a good look before that. In any other situation, seeing some guy's eyes roving her body like that, he would have launched himself at them.

Now, in her room she dropped the towel to the floor and sank onto the bed in exhaustion. Then she gasped, her eyes full of horror. 'Oh, God, sorry!' Grabbing the towel up again, she pulled it back around her and he had to laugh.

'I've seen it all before,' he told her quickly, hoping she hadn't noticed the effect she was having on him, sitting there half naked in her knickers and bra. Her cheeks were flushed, but at least she was getting some colour back.

Sadie stood and crossed to the mirror while he lingered in the doorway. 'No, you haven't,' she replied after a pause. 'Seen all of me before…have you?' She looked wary now, as if she was racking her brains for something she'd forgotten. 'Seeing me in a bikini doesn't count,' she followed. 'Bikinis aren't generally this see-through.'

He bit back another chuckle, picturing the polka dot bikini she'd tottered around in on Hampton Heath that time he'd joined her and Callum and a bunch of other friends for a picnic. London had been so hot that day. Not as hot as Sadie, though. Callum had been watching Owen the whole time that day, as if he was daring him to look at Sadie so he could accuse him of wanting to hit on her or something.

It wasn't the time to tease her now, and definitely not the time to mention the way her nipples were probably the cutest little things he'd ever seen, pushing out against the lace of her wet bra. He should probably get out of here, he thought. But something rooted him to the spot even as she crossed to the bathroom in the towel.

'Need me to help?' he heard himself say, and then he caught himself. 'I mean…in case you fall again or something. I can wait.'

'I'm fine.'

Sadie paused with one hand on the bathroom door and he found himself looking at her feet, then tracing her legs with his eyes from her painted toenails to the rim of the towel, inches above her pale knees.

'I can probably shower on my own,' she added slowly, over her shoulder.

'You probably can. But do you want to?'

The words were out before he could even register he'd

said them out loud. He pulled his eyes away, but not before catching a look on her face that he didn't recognise. She wasn't laughing, but she didn't look offended by his silly quip either. Not so long ago she would have rolled her eyes and told him to stop joking around, but now...

Now he was incredibly turned on, and Sadie had probably noticed.

'What are you implying?' she asked him.

He sucked in a breath, imagining his lips tracing the flesh across her shoulder blades under a steaming gush of water, his hands on slippery tiles, then on her bottom, finally tasting her...

His feet wouldn't move. He started willing his erection to comply with his wishes and not the wishes that would get him in trouble. This was the moment he was supposed to say nothing and walk away.

Just walk away, Owen. Go back to your room, go and get showered alone, and stop being an idiot, thinking things like this about Sadie.

'Owen, are you OK?'

She was looking at him in concern now, maybe reading his silence as distress on his part over what had just happened with Ashanti... And why did she have to look so gorgeous right now?

'What you just did...that was...' Sadie abandoned the bathroom door and walked back towards him, clutching the towel around her. 'That was amazing. I'm really proud of you, you know? That child lived to see another day because of what you did.'

'You did it too,' he said, looking straight into her eyes as her words lit him up and set his heart racing all over again. Genuine praise from Sadie, he realised, was something he lived for. 'Although you couldn't wait to rip your dress off in front of Conall McCaskill.'

She bit her lip and smirked, and instinctively he closed

the gap between them and kicked the door shut behind him. An almost indecipherable moan escaped her mouth as she placed a palm against his bare chest, over his heart.

Her breath was a whisper across his mouth, inches from his lips. 'You're right. It's all about Conall McCaskill,' she said.

They were silent for a moment that felt too long—as something should have been said or done. She seemed to be testing the drumming of his heartbeat in her presence, and he was clearly failing to prove that he saw this half naked woman, beautiful inside and out, as just his friend and colleague.

'Conall thinks you are a hero too,' she told him quietly, clearly choosing to ignore the way he'd just shut himself in her room, and they way his chest was throbbing under her touch. 'I bet you never thought you'd see the day.'

'To be honest, I'm not really thinking about that right now,' he managed.

Sadie didn't move her hand. His heart was a riot, giving him away as much as the bulge in his boxers. Swallowing, he let his mind play out a hundred ways this could go.

Her hand on his torso felt hot as fire, and he knew without a doubt that she was waiting for him to do something now. To kiss her. One kiss. Just to see. Just to see if whatever this was, was real. And definitely not a 'friendly' kiss on the forehead this time. She wanted more. When a woman got that look in her eyes in front of him he was usually ready to give them more.

Her lips hovered close as she studied his gaze, then his mouth, as if she was tracing a prospective pattern. One kiss and he'd have to have another. He knew it. And another, and another.

'This is…' He stopped and let loose the tortured growl that had been building in his throat.

Sadie stepped away instantly. 'You're right,' she said

quickly, flustered, turning her back. 'You're right. It's the adrenaline. I don't know what I was…'

'Get in the shower,' he heard himself say, flinging the bedroom door back open. This was messing with his head. If he didn't leave now he really would ruin everything. She'd regret it too—she was just caught up in the moment, like he was. 'I'll see you downstairs,' he said.

They'd have to talk about this later—there was no way they could avoid it. But right now it was better for both of them if he left and cooled down.

It took everything in his body and soul to turn away from her and go back to his room alone.

Sadie kicked herself internally more than once as she showered the events of the day and the lake water off her body. If only she could shower away the embarrassment and humiliation… What had she been thinking, practically asking him to kiss her…? Well, with her eyes and actions, at least…

He'd been joking when he'd suggested showering with her. Of course it had been a joke—to lighten the tension, probably. That was so Owen. Maybe it had just been his awkward way of making light of the fact he'd seen her in wet, see-through underwear.

She'd been trying to forget all the awkwardness, but the more they opened up and talked, and worked closely like this, the harder it was to ignore her feelings for her friend.

You have to, she reprimanded herself in the mirror. *Even if Owen Penner is no longer a notch on the bedpost kind of person, he is still your* friend!

She pressed her head to the shower tiles and let out a groan. This was all too confusing.

Her throat turned to sandpaper as she remembered the look in his eyes, right before he'd left her room…

The whole time she was drying her hair, a voice in her head was screaming. *If he really doesn't like you like that,*

Sadie, why did he shut the door to your room like that? Why did he look so tortured? And why was his heart freaking out under your hand?

They had a problem. That much was obvious right now. Clearly they were both re-evaluating a few things. But what if she did get the whole package from her best friend and then he realised his mistake and snatched it back? Better not to even go there. God, no… The pain, on top of everything she'd already been through, would finish her off.

She sighed to herself, putting the final touches to her make-up, puckering her lips…imagining Owen's on hers. If she kissed him once she'd want more—she was just that kind of person. So for many, many, *many* reasons she simply couldn't do it, she reminded herself. Ever.

With that decided, she psyched herself up to see him downstairs, reciting a couple of positive affirmations at her reflection in the mirror whilst simultaneously admiring her breasts in the low-cut aubergine-coloured wrap-around dress. It was sophisticated enough for no one to question her professionalism, yet sexy—no one could deny it. At least she had that.

Was she dressing for Owen to find her sexy now?

No, of course you're not—don't be ridiculous.

Outside on the lawn, Owen was the first person she laid eyes on. He was chatting to the CEO, Dr Calhoun, and some of the other staff.

Vivek took her aside and thanked her profusely. Ashanti had made a full recovery already. His wife was on her way back from the hospital, having left the girl to sleep. Sadie told him she was glad, and then made small talk for about an hour with the guests…grazing from the buffet, purposefully avoiding Owen.

He was probably doing the same thing—although every time their eyes met across the lawn goosebumps broke out on her arms. A certain kind of ache, and a longing such as she'd never experienced before was threatening to snatch away all her common sense.

Some time later, the saxophonist on the marquee's stage was doing a fine job of remastering a classic, and she was so absorbed, standing next to Portia, that she was startled when Owen tapped her on the shoulder.

'Good party,' he said.

She crossed her arms. Her feet were already itching to move away. His cologne was too seductive—it made her mentally revisit the way he'd looked earlier, half naked in her bedroom.

'It's OK,' she replied, feeling Portia's eyes on them.

She walked towards the buffet table and busied her hands picking out an olive. Owen did the same, watching her every move, the picture of sophistication in his blue designer suit—an outfit she'd seen him wear on dates. A lot of dates. With different women, none of whom were around any more, she reminded herself.

'Are we good?' he asked, after a moment.

'I don't know what you mean,' she lied, popping the olive into her mouth and vaguely registering Vivek taking to the stage, and talking to the pianist.

'I think you do,' he said, causing a ball of nerves to lodge in her throat. 'Listen, Sadie, we need to talk about—'

He was cut off suddenly by the sound of the piano. They both spun around to face the stage. A beautiful piece of music she recognised was spilling from the instrument under Vivek's hands. His wife, now back from the hospital, was gaping at him from the sidelines in awe, wiping tears from her eyes. Conall McCaskill gave an enthusiastic whoop, and Sadie couldn't help the huge smile that broke out on her face.

'He's remembered how to play,' she whispered to Owen with pride, momentarily forgetting the tension between them.

'Come on!'

Owen grabbed her hand. Before she knew it they were on the dance floor, and Vivek's talents had extended into a slow but moving rendition of *Can't Help Falling in Love*.

They weren't the only ones dancing, so it shouldn't have felt strange at all, but the second Owen's hands landed on her hips the room fell away. She closed her eyes, testing her senses, praying for them all to switch from red alert back to their normal state around him. It was impossible. He pulled her closer, hip to hip, and as they swayed together every inch of her felt magnetised…especially when he lowered his lips to her ear.

'Did you want to kiss me up there in your bedroom before?' he asked her.

She drew a breath, pressed her cheek to his shoulder as her mind whirred. How the tables had turned! Hadn't she said the exact same thing to him after that night in the library? He'd brushed her off then, but the thought of doing the same to him now didn't sit right.

'I think I did, actually,' she admitted after a moment. 'But I know that was stupid. Thrill of the moment kind of thing…after what happened…'

'Whatever it was, I shouldn't have just walked away,' he replied.

'You did the right thing.'

'I bet you want to run right off this dance floor again,' he said, and she felt his smile stretch out like warm honey against the crown of her head.

'Again?' she replied, confused. But he'd caught her chin with one hand, gripped her hand with the other, and she forgot what she'd been going to say.

The way he was looking at her… He wanted her, she could tell. No question. Her blood fizzed like champagne in her veins.

'I don't know what this is, but we can't keep dancing around it, can we?' he said now.

Sadie swallowed. 'We should do exactly that—just keep dancing around it,' she forced herself to say.

Not, *between it, over it*. Not *into it*. But every cell in her body was alive now, as if some new lifeforce had been summoned from the depths of her being, not to be switched off or drowned out. Talking about it was a bad idea. It would only lead to her admitting something she wasn't ready to admit—to him, or to herself. That she had a huge and ever-growing crush on her best friend.

This was bad. Very bad. It could never happen.

'You know what? I'm really tired,' she said, disentangling herself from his arms. Maybe if she excused herself, she could sleep this insanity off.

'No, you're not tired,' he countered, taking her hand again and holding it tightly. 'You just don't want to talk about it.'

'You're right—and I didn't think you wanted to, either,' she said, noting how goosebumps were travelling up her arm, the way his gaze bored into hers.

'We have to.'

Somewhere in the background rapturous applause for Vivek filled the air.

Owen lowered his voice again. 'We *have* to. Sadie, because we both know something's going on here, I can't even think straight around you any more. Something happened when I got back from Boston…'

'Nothing happened, Owen, and nothing *will* ever happen,' she snapped, begging her eyes not to give her raging desire away.

No one had ever looked at her as Owen was looking at her now. Enraged, confounded…consumed by the kind of longing she'd never known he was capable of expressing. Owen never wanted to talk about anything serious, and the fact that he did now, about *them,* fired her up and sent the fear of God rushing through her all at once.

'Fine. Go,' he said coldly, releasing her and turning his back to her.

Shocked, she almost relented. But why open Pandora's box now when it had always been just fine closed?

Quickly, while the crowd was distracted by Vivek taking a bow, she turned on her heel and left before she could make a huge mistake.

CHAPTER ELEVEN

OWEN PACED HIS BEDROOM, dragging both hands through his hair. Midnight had come and gone. He'd helped clear up after the gala—anything to keep Sadie's words from haunting his thoughts.

'Nothing happened, Owen, and nothing will ever happen.'

Weren't women supposed to be the ones who wanted to talk things though? Clear the air and all that? *Never go to bed feeling angry*—wasn't that what they said?

He ripped off his shirt and tossed it to the floor, flopping back on the bed in just his suit trousers, cursing at the ceiling. Admittedly his pride had taken a blow. Sadie Mills had abandoned him on a dance floor for a second time, and this time he'd walked right into it.

But they'd come so close to making out more times than he could count already. She was telling herself not to, just as he was, and he got it. Of course he got it.

There was no point in them hooking up. It would only end in disaster, and more awkwardness than he cared to invite into this precious platonic thing they'd cultivated over the years. But he'd tried to do the right thing: get this blatant attraction between them out in the open so they could at least discuss it and move on, one way or another. He hadn't laughed it off or run away. He'd been trying to give her what he owed her. A chance to get their friendship back on track.

And all she'd done in response was close herself off completely. Was she trying to kill him slowly? It sucked, being the one given the brush-off, he realised with dismay. Maybe this was karma. That was what his mother would say, anyway.

Owen sat up straight. *Screw this.* He wouldn't sleep unless he saw her and cleared the air. This would only drag on into his dreams, into tomorrow. He'd just go and knock on her door, he decided, and demand they talk about it. She would not dismiss him.

Forgetting his shirt, or maybe just not caring enough to bother putting it back on, he felt a brute determination lead him to yank his door open. He was going to march straight to her room. To hell with the time—so what if she was sleeping? This had to end now.

No sooner had he stormed to her room and raised his hand to the door than the wooden panels disappeared in front of him and he almost fell through the doorway.

'What the...?'

'Owen!' Sadie gasped right in front of him. 'I was just coming to...'

'Talk?' he finished, failing to hide the way his eyes had fallen straight to her exposed cleavage in her nightdress.

She bit her lip, shifted on her feet. 'I told you... I don't want to talk about it.'

And before he could even gather his thoughts or protest, she launched herself at him like a rocket.

Her lips were on his now, her hands were in his hair, and she was kissing him as if her life depended on it. They staggered backwards against the banister in the hallway, fraught with passion. He hooked an arm around her waist, aware of the hard wood against his back, her leg around his middle, one hand on her backside.

Then a door creaked somewhere in the corridor. A voice came… 'Hello? Do you know what time it is?'

Who was that? he thought.

Who cares?

Owen pushed Sadie back into her room. Her mouth was red-hot, lips still parted, begging for more of his attention. She didn't want to talk, and neither did he now, as he let his tongue delve into her mouth deeply, then let it linger as they slowed their pace inside the closed room, but only for a moment. Then they crashed together against the dresser, making her hairbrush clatter to the floor.

Lips still locked together, he lifted her nightdress swiftly over her head, lifting her hair with it. The soft, sensual strands floated back down around their faces as his hands stroked her back and hips…new parts of Sadie he'd never thought he'd feel.

He wanted more. He could hardly wait.

Her bare breasts were bouncing in front of him now, teasing him as she started to unbutton his trousers. He shuffled out of them, bent to lock his mouth onto a pert pink nipple, standing up and ready for him. He circled his tongue around it and she arched into him, before staggering backwards again towards the bed, pulling him with her and muffling a cry of pleasure behind her hand before deciding it was pointless.

With a groan that was equally loud and equally telling of his intentions, he released her nipple, placed a hand behind her head, and arched over her on the bed, studying her face for the first time in this new situation. She was utterly breathtaking. A new version of his friend. Hot, messy, begging for him without saying a word.

He should back off. *So what if she started it?* came the voice in his head. But he couldn't stop now—not of his own volition.

He lowered his bulk onto one forearm and pressed a

palm to the front of her knickers—the only thing left between their otherwise naked flesh. He was throbbing for her everywhere.

'Are you sure this what you want?' he asked.

'What do you think?' she gasped, reaching for him again.

As their tongues entwined around each other's he could barely think straight. Had she planned this? Or had she left her room to come and find him on a snap decision, like he had?

Who cares?

She moaned again, softer this time, as he slid his fingers down, circling her navel before going further into the fine, silken hair, stretching out the fabric of her knickers till she scrambled halfway out of them, leaving him to free her of the rest. She responded, exploring him with her hands, fingers, mouth, until they both knew they weren't going to stop.

'I know I have something, Owen…just wait…'

He ran his eyes over her in appreciation as she reached for her purse on the nightstand and scrambled around for a condom. She was everything he'd imagined, maybe even better. He urged her on to her back again when she had the foil packet clenched in her hand. He brushed his fingers lightly, tauntingly, over her mound and she gripped his shoulders hard, in a way he knew would leave circular half-moons in his flesh from her nails. Her eyes shone with new wickedness and a determination that sent an inferno through his blood as she locked on to his gaze.

Suddenly he wanted to possess her completely. He wanted to bind Sadie to him in every single way possible, regardless of the consequences. Maybe she was thinking the same thing. The way she rolled him over and took him in her mouth was nothing short of exquisite, as if she was trying to show him she was the best thing he'd never had.

'You are amazing, Sadie…'

'Shh…don't speak.'

Fine. There were no words anyway. God, he wanted her. If having her lips locked around his shaft was anything to go by, the act of sex itself was going to be something he would have to try very hard to make last for as long as possible.

That was not going to be easy.

Sadie's fingers pulsed hot and urgent against his hardness as they rolled on the condom together. He lifted his head, fighting the urge to ask again if this was what she really wanted. She wasn't backing off. Sadie was doing anything but that. He'd never seen her like this, so determined, so… *So not like Sadie.* He'd never imagined she could be so forceful, or that she could possibly want him. Would she regret this afterwards? Why were they doing this? It was wrong… It would not end well…

'Owen, make love to me.'

How could he refuse?

He positioned himself over her. Sadie was wet and ready for him, and she drew a sharp breath as he slid into her. He took it slowly, went inch by inch, in awe of every second as he went deeper… This was insane! His mind reeled, then went blank. All he felt was bliss, comfort, connection…

She wrapped her legs around him and held him still, clamping her teeth for a moment into his shoulder. Instinctively, he knew she wasn't asking him to stop. He stayed inside her a moment without moving, placing delicate butterfly kisses on her mouth, relishing the way she caressed his face with her fingers, stroked his hair. Their passion built again slowly, gradually, until Sadie was bucking under him, faster and faster, making sounds that made him want to spill into her with every thrust.

What followed was an exercise in mutual pleasure and gymnastics and still no words… They were just exploring and discovering and appreciating every inch of each other. The birds started tweeting outside the windows. The sun threatened to spoil the night and the way she moved in the shadows.

On the edge of her third or fourth climax, Sadie enveloped him with both her arms and her legs. He tried to pull out, to shift position—why end this now? He wanted to prove he was the best she'd ever had too. He could make this last even longer…he had to. The sun was coming up. One-night stands had time limits. Sadie wasn't going to do this again and neither was he.

'Come for me,' she urged, her legs around his waist, gripping him even tighter, begging him not to withdraw.

This time he saw how tired she was, realised how sore she'd be once they released each other and…and what? Went about their friendship as if none of this had ever happened? What could possibly come after this for them? This was a one-night thing only. Wasn't that why they'd made it last all night?

With one final thrust he pressed his hot mouth to hers and heard a husky primal sound echo around the room. He realised it was coming from both of them, and they were coming together yet again.

The contractions made them judder and shudder and gasp, till he rolled from under her, breathless, floating back to reality as if he'd just been lifted up somewhere else and then thrown cruelly back down to earth. That had been like nothing he'd ever experienced—with anyone. That had been something raw and untamed and totally unprecedented. Mind-blowing. He almost didn't know what to think. He had too many thoughts.

He pressed his back to the sheets, finally allowing the softness of the mattress to lull him. His eyes closed. Exhaustion was an understatement. Sadie's fingers curled into his and he heard her emit a laugh of shock, or wonder, maybe both. He wanted to laugh too, suddenly. This was crazy. And reckless. Even now, when he was spent and sticky and tangled in her bedsheets, all he wanted was to hear her say she wanted to do it all over again.

Sadie's breathing slowed and he sensed her succumbing to sleep. As he let himself do the same, common sense crept in and started whispering at him.

What the hell did you just do that for?

Already the moment when he'd been free to touch her and cross any line he wanted was galloping from the present into the past, where it was morphing and twisting into something else. He could feel it already. Tomorrow there wouldn't be kisses and cuddling—not even if he wanted it more than anything. There would only be regret.

He turned away from her, so he wouldn't drape an arm around her sleeping frame and hold her tight for what was left of the night. He wasn't the kind of man Sadie needed in the long run and he never would be. She knew that. She'd just forgotten momentarily, that was all, and he'd gone along with it. If he carried on like this, disrespecting their friendship for the sake of sex, he'd lose her altogether!

Stupid.

Tomorrow he'd make sure they were cool—if that was even possible after he'd given in to her so fast… And he'd definitely make sure she knew that nothing like this would ever happen again.

CHAPTER TWELVE

SADIE SHUFFLED ON her feet in warrior pose, feeling too hot in the glaring sun that was streaming through the roof of the fernery. The yoga instructor had organised another hot session amongst the plants, and while she was glad of a little Zen, admittedly she was a little sore from last night. She could barely remember the last time she'd had so much sex in one night.

'And…let's move into our planks, everyone.'

Sadie followed the instructions, keeping an eye on her patients. She was pleased with Portia's progress. Despite her initial setback, the yoga was helping to strengthen the appropriate muscles around her head, neck, and shoulders. Relaxing facial exercises meant her episodic headaches were now fewer, with far more space between.

As for Vivek's hand-eye co-ordination—he seemed to be a different person after remembering his piano ballads the night of the gala.

The mood around the place was light. It was just Sadie's heart that felt heavy, as if it had suddenly taken on way too much. She kept getting flashbacks of the way she'd pounced on Owen in her bedroom doorway, the way he'd responded, and how it had escalated way beyond what she'd initially intended.

She also had a feeling Parminder knew. She was loitering outside now, on duty in case anything went wrong, but she kept giving her the eye. Parminder had heard them going into her room last night…she was sure of it. *Ugh*, she'd lost all control of her mind!

'And let's meet in our downward dog,' came the next instruction, leading to Vivek's disgruntled groan.

Sadie bit back a smile. 'You can do it,' she encouraged him.

OK, so he'd been happier *before* his therapeutic stretching session in the humid fernery, but soon he'd be Zen again. More Zen than her, anyway.

Her heart gave a little bunny hop as another flashback came for her—Owen's face hovering above hers, the light behind him outlining his strong muscled arms and chest, their perspiration adding to her wetness as they slid and sparked together.

A trickle of sweat dripped from her forehead to her mat. The memories were as persistent as a team of fruit flies around a glass of Pinot Noir. She could recall every single detail of the four times they'd taken each other in rapid succession, stopping only once for Owen to fetch more condoms as discreetly as he could from his own room.

Sadie shifted position on her yoga mat…closed her eyes. Each time her body took on a new shape she was thrown back to her naked gymnastics with Owen. She'd initiated it, yes but she hadn't exactly meant to. She'd been going to apologise for shutting him out. She knew he hated that, maybe as much as she did. She'd been on her way to talk about their obvious attraction, to get it out in the open, maybe even try and laugh about her crush in the hope that it would disappear, but she'd wound up doing none of that.

Just seeing him in her doorway, just as she'd flung open the door, shirtless, looking both furious and full of intent, she had felt something wild overcome her.

There was something to be said for not being the quiet,

shy, serious one, for once. And maybe Portia had got her thinking about experimentation, but she'd been uncharacteristically spontaneous last night. The way Owen had always been. The way she herself had never been.

And it had felt amazing!

Even if she really should *not* have gone there with her best friend.

Portia had been right about a man never turning down sex…but she hadn't exactly given him much choice in the matter, pouncing on him like a jungle cat.

Ugh. Now what?

They'd already had an awkward 'good morning,' after waking up together. And maybe she'd made it more awkward by whispering, 'Thank you for last night' before he'd left her room. But she'd been nervous. They'd crossed some line last night and she didn't want to stick around to hear how he regretted it already. Or worse…that he'd enjoyed it and wanted to do it again.

That could never happen. This was Owen! Even once was one too many times.

'Sadie?'

Her heart pole-vaulted right up into her throat at his voice behind her. She sprang from her yoga mat as the instructor put a finger to her lips to shush him.

Owen grimaced. 'Sorry,' he whispered to the room, getting down on his haunches beside her.

Portia grinned at them from a cat cow position even as his familiar cologne made a knot of Sadie's stomach and sent her back to the way he'd tasted when she'd taken him in her mouth. God, he'd been so hard for her. Such a thrill…

Such a stupid, idiotic thrill to have acted on once, let alone multiple times!

'Ashanti's back from the hospital and has something she wants to give you before she goes,' he whispered. 'She's already said her goodbyes to Vivek, before this session—do you think you can duck out for five minutes?'

Sadie watched his mouth move but didn't hear a word he said. Every nerve-ending was alight again, just from seeing him. She wanted to reach for him suddenly, to reconnect, to feel some sense of reassurance that he hadn't forgotten what had happened, even though she herself had literally just decided to try and forget it and how different it had been from anything she'd experienced before.

'Sorry, what do you want?' she asked him when they were outside.

She gulped the cool air like a goldfish, hiding behind her hair, making a thing of rolling up her mat. Her hands were shaking.

He studied her, a crooked smile on his face. 'Ashanti? She wants to see you before she goes.'

'Oh, yes. Right.' Sadie met his eyes finally. For just a second she felt calm. Then the butterflies started up again.

'Are you OK?' he asked her, searching her face.

He was looking at her too intensely, so she looked at her nails instead. 'Why wouldn't I be?'

He urged her around to the side of the fernery, out of sight and earshot. Then he lowered his voice. 'Last night was… I wasn't exactly expecting that, Sadie…'

'It shouldn't have happened,' she blurted.

Owen straightened up. 'I know.'

What?

OK, she hadn't anticipated he'd agree so quickly. But they were best friends, for God's sake—it really *shouldn't* have happened.

'Sadie, I don't want to ruin what we have…or you.'

'Or me?' She frowned, letting his words sink in.

Was he insinuating he'd break her heart when he moved on—like he always did, at lightning speed? Was one night with her enough to restore his inner playboy?

'Don't worry, I know exactly what last night was about,' she told him, crossing her arms around herself, suddenly feeling smaller. 'We're both tired, and single, and far away from home. It won't go any further.'

'Maybe we just had to…you know…get it out of the way?' he followed up, cocking one eyebrow at her.

Sadie gave an insouciant shrug, but inside his words were scalding her and pouring ice-cold water on her at the same time. She was definitely the one to blame. Her annoyance was only with herself, over starting something that to all intents and purposes was probably the most idiotic thing she'd ever done.

Well done, Sadie.

'It was great sex, though,' he said now, searching her face.

'It was,' she agreed distractedly, swallowing back a sudden urge to blurt out what she'd been thinking all morning.

That it had felt like more than sex—to her anyway. That there had been a couple of moments last night when the pleasure of the physical act had been secondary to the closeness, to the soul connection. That had been something else she'd never felt before. As if she were so crazily intertwined with Owen on every single level.

It was probably all one-sided, though. *He* probably hadn't felt anything like what she had, making love to her. He was Owen, after all. Not only had he had way more sex than her, with more people, but he always kept his emotions out of everything. Why should sex with her be any different?

The gardener walked past and did a double-take. Sadie took a step backwards, realising she'd been standing less than inch from the tips of Owen's shoes.

'Well, now it's out of the way,' she joked, going in to punch his arm lightly for good measure. 'I guess we can go back to being friends?'

'I guess so,' he replied, but his eyes seemed to be making a data log of her innermost thoughts.

She straightened her shoulders, even as her heart bucked and flapped behind her Lycra yoga top. It went haywire as Owen swept her hair gently behind her ear and examined what she knew was his stubble rash on her neck.

A look of dismay and regret crossed his face. 'I'm so sorry,' he growled.

'Don't be,' she told him quickly.

A little scrape or two from Owen's facial hair was not a promise. Right now it felt more like a scar. When would she be able to get *out* of here?

'I don't want things to get complicated...' he said, carefully.

'Mmm...' she replied to his lips, wondering why on earth she was still picturing him naked in her bed and feeling her core throb all over again. It was almost as if her body was completely unwilling to listen to her brain.

Very Important Friendship plus Sex equals Inevitable Disaster.

Catching her eye, he held her gaze and she found her heart thudding wildly as they played a game of who would look away first. What had they gone and done?

She followed him to Reception, where Ashanti was waiting with a bouquet of flowers for them. Sadie accepted the sweet gift and noticed every movement Owen made as he instructed the girl to always carry an epi-pen and told her that bees weren't exactly bad, just bad for *her*. He was good with children, she registered absently. She'd never really seen him with any before.

He kept catching her eye, sending more flashbacks to her frazzled brain. Last night had been so surreal... Had that really been them? Had *they* really done that? Had they really agreed all that hot, sweaty, passionate, frantic, soul-shifting sex was never going to happen again?

Of course it can't happen again. That was what you call a one-night stand, Sadie, and it was fun, but now it's done, so get over it.

Maeve wandered through to Reception with Conall just as Ashanti and Vivek's wife were leaving. She caught Sadie's arm and leaned in, dropped a kiss to her cheek, then reached for Owen's hand.

'Before I go, Sadie, Owen, I want you to know I feel like he's a different man because of you.' She nodded Conall's way and he simply shrugged and sniffed, as if it was no big deal. They all knew it was.

'We'll have some pre-exit evaluations this week,' Owen said. 'All going well, we should have him home with you by next weekend.'

Maeve lowered her voice, drawing them both closer. 'I'm planning a little something in honour of our son. We never had a tribute or a memorial service because Conall couldn't…well, you know. Anyway, I know it would mean a lot to Conall if you were both there. If you could get away? We're in a wee hamlet not far from Loch Ness on the Great Glen Way. If you haven't seen much of Scotland I know Conall would be happy to show you. I dare say he'll be taking some more time off work…'

'Thank you,' Sadie said quickly, wondering how on earth she could refuse such an offer. Their home would be a mansion—the real celebrity deal! She couldn't help the excited look she threw Owen, but he frowned.

'We'll have to see what the schedule is like,' he said—to *her*.

'Of course.' Maeve smiled, squeezing both of their hands.

Sadie chewed on her cheeks, forcing a smile in return. Owen was being realistic. They were busy. A new patient was arriving in less than a week. But already she was panicking that he'd only said that as an excuse not to be around her, and now she'd have to go to the McCaskills' alone, without her best friend there to laugh at her over how star-struck she'd inevitably be the *entire* time.

That would be no fun, she realised. Owen made every-thing more fun. Including sex, now…apparently. Which was annoying. Sure, they'd acted like insatiable teenag-ers most of the night, but that didn't mean laughter hadn't sneaked in occasionally—like the first time she'd seen the hugeness of his shaft and he'd asked her, with a gleam in his eye, 'What did you expect?' She'd told him she'd never thought about it. He'd told her she was lying.

Soon it was just her and Owen standing in Reception.

'I should…um… I should get back to my class,' she said, thrusting the flowers at him. 'Put those in water, will you?'

'Yes, ma'am.'

She hurried back to the fernery, forcing herself not to look back in case he was staring at her bum in her leggings, or in case he wasn't. She didn't know any more which would offend her the most…

Yoga wasn't easy. There was definitely no Zen involved on her part, although her patients seemed totally blissed out. She couldn't get last night or her earlier conversation with Owen out of her head. They'd agreed it was a mis-take, and that it wouldn't happen again, more or less, which should have been totally fine. It had been great sex. Un-disputedly the best of her life—not that she'd tell him that. Why feed his ego?

Owen Penner was everything she'd always steered clear of. Unable to commit, allergic to love, renowned for distancing himself entirely from anything that no longer matched his needs or challenged his emotions. So wrong for her, in so many ways. Why think about it at all?

Forget about it. It was just a bit of sex between friends. It probably happens all the time. Stop making it into such a big deal!

* * *

By the time another night came around Sadie was practically chomping at the bit to go and knock on Owen's door again. She buried her head in her pillow, smelling his now far too familiar scent on her sheets, resisting the urge.

What if she suggested something crazy...like friends with benefits? That way she'd be in full control. She'd know it was just for fun, and she wouldn't be in danger of getting in too deep with someone entirely unsuitable.

Argh! Sadie yanked the covers over her head. What was she even thinking about this for? She wasn't going to be like the other girls he'd brought into his bed and then gone cold on. That wasn't in her plan—no, thanks. No more heartbreak for her. She'd gone through enough after Chris's death...

Owen wouldn't get close enough again to come even halfway towards 'ruining' her—not if she had any say in it. She'd be his friend, he'd be hers...he'd make her laugh, she'd make him laugh—that was what they did. She couldn't lose that. She loved it, needed it—she'd come to rely on it.

Getting their friendship back on track was all that mattered. Tomorrow she'd wash him off her sheets, she decided, and she'd wash that night right out of her brain too.

CHAPTER THIRTEEN

OWEN LOOKED UP as Sadie entered the room and apologised for running late. His instincts were on red alert the second he saw her face—even more so when she whispered that she'd just had to deal with a family emergency.

She took a seat and switched to professional Sadie mode in front of their new patient, a fifty-four-year-old lady from Dundee called Amanda Bond, who'd brought her Siamese cat with her as a therapy animal following a nasty fall down an airport escalator that had affected her in a multitude of unpleasant ways—not least giving her a fear of staircases.

Amanda excused herself to fetch the cat's food before the session, and he took Sadie aside.

'What's going on?' He frowned, realising his hand on her arm was the closest he'd been to her in over a week. Since their night of…whatever they were calling it.

She retracted her arm quickly and adjusted her hair, as if his touch was acid, and told him, 'Nothing of concern.'

She was lying.

'So fill me in,' she said, picking up Amanda's file.

He bit hard on his cheeks, willing himself to stay on topic. So she didn't want to talk to him about it here—fair enough. But she barely spoke to her mum and dad, so whatever the 'emergency' was, it must be something pretty serious.

Maybe she wouldn't want to talk about it anywhere, he realised as she introduced herself officially to their new client—she was Sadie, after all. She was doing her best to go back to normal, like he was, but they both knew things were very far from it.

Every joke between them had fallen kind of flat lately, and as for the serious stuff—well, that had all been swept under the nearest Scottish carpet. Still, they both had a job to do.

'Her last neurologist put her through a four-hour test designed to make her face her weaknesses, then came to the conclusion she was faking the results because she scored too poorly in the memory part,' he told her.

'She said my scores were lower than a patient with dementia,' Amanda cut in, coming back into the room and placing a bowl of food down for the cat. 'I was just telling Dr Penner that I was prescribed Ritalin, anti-depressants and sleep meds. Not all at once, but… I knew none of that would heal me. I went to a cranial sacral therapist next, which helped with the brain fog, but I still wasn't *me*. I didn't know what needed when it came to therapy, apart from Sonny.'

Their patient crouched down to her cat and stroked its soft cream-coloured back. 'I just knew I needed something else. It was a year—a whole year—before someone suggested I come here.'

Sadie turned her gaze to him. Owen could feel it. He could literally sense her looking at him—a gift he'd honed since that night, when he'd tuned in to her and tasted parts of her he was starting to forget already. Which was probably a good thing, he reminded himself.

Focus.

'So here you are,' he said, standing up and crossing to the window, where the gardener was scrubbing something off the stones around the mermaid fountain. Rain was coming…hovering. Probably waiting till they set off later for the McCaskills'.

He turned to look at their patient. 'And you've been extremely patient this morning throughout yet another examination, Mrs Bond. We've concluded that most of your issues are coming from your eyes.'

'I suspected that all along. No one would believe me,' Amanda said incredulously.

He was about to reply but Sadie cut in.

'Dr Penner knows a lot about these things…it's almost like an instinct now, right?'

'Well, we still need to run more tests, of course,' he replied, turning back as his heart surged with pride.

Sadie nodded. 'Of course. But all those other doctors were likely ignoring your concerns about your eyes because they weren't specifically trained in what to look for when related to traumatic brain injuries and concussions. Not like Owen…Dr Penner is.'

She caught his eye and he wondered for the thousandth time why compliments from Sadie made him feel this way. They triggered something in him that made him feel accomplished on a level no one else could reach. It had been the same in the bedroom, he thought reluctantly. More than just proving what he could do with his tongue. It had become an almost instant need for her to want him, to be pleased with him as a whole, mind, body *and* tongue.

'Millions of brain injury survivors are basically disregarded by the medical community and written off as having mental health issues when it's all about the physical. We'll work together on a treatment plan,' Sadie explained. 'You're in the best hands here. For now, just settle in and enjoy some relaxation—it's all part of the process, right?'

Amanda beamed—the first time Owen had seen her look genuinely excited to be here. 'I hear the yoga classes are great.'

'If you don't mind the heat,' said Sadie. 'Did Dr Penner explain how we'll be away for the next few days?'

'I did,' he replied. 'Dr Calhoun is scheduled to oversee everything.'

Sadie tapped a pen to her knee and caught his eyes again. She was probably as apprehensive about this time off as he was. They could hardly back out of taking up Maeve and Conall McCaskill on their offer to attend Scott's memorial, so rather than spending the time off for himself as he'd planned—hiking in the Highlands, clearing his head—he'd now have to spend it in a mansion with a famous film star and his social media star of a wife…and Sadie.

'I bet Sonny here will like this place while we help get you better,' Sadie was saying now, bending to stroke the cat.

He'd bet she'd love a cat, now her ex was out of the picture. Callum had had allergies—how lame. What kind of grown man was allergic to a little cat?

He caught himself. What was his problem, hating Sadie's ex even more than before?

Because you want her in every single way you had her that night, and you know you never will again, while he had her for years.

Talk about the longest week ever. He'd been going to bed at night after satisfying himself in the shower first, just to numb the urge to bang down her door again. His back had burned from her scratch marks the whole of the next day, and the love bite she'd given him on his thigh had been bigger than the patch of stubble rash on her neck. Both had faded now. The last reminder that they'd done anything at all…gone.

God, she was already hard to get over. He'd made her come over and over and over and he'd been exhausted, but completely unable to stop. She was the first woman who'd ever been able to exhaust him to the core, and still he wanted more…

More than sex? It had crossed his mind briefly. She was different. She touched him...parts of him no one else had even got close to reaching.

But no. Why even go there? Relationships ended in misery for the most part, and their friendship was not going to end up like his parents' marriage. No way. It was far too good to watch it crumble into misery and hatred.

Maybe this time away as friends and colleagues would help them get things back to normal, he thought, with a glimmer of hope that lasted just five seconds before morphing into dread.

It would take more than a faded love bite to make him forget that night!

As predicted, it was raining. Owen watched the clouds swallow every other boat in their wake as the ferry bobbed towards Wemyss Bay. On the train across to Glasgow, where they were due to be met by the McCaskills' driver, Sadie was quiet, huddled into another colourful jumper, scrolling on her phone while the evening turned greyer, then blacker, outside the windows. They were alone in the carriage and eventually he couldn't stand the silence.

He tapped the glass front of her phone till she turned it face down on her lap. 'So?' he said.

'So, what?'

'The call with your family earlier on. Everything OK?'

She gave a long, exaggerated sigh and shrugged. 'My mother's in hospital.'

His heart jolted. 'Is that not...concerning you?'

'It's nothing too serious. She's having metatarsal foot surgery. It's just... I offered to go there, and she told me not to.' She held up her phone and showed him the text from her mother.

Owen felt his brow crease—it seemed the woman really was blaming her daughter for something to do with Chris's death. He'd been so sure—that Sadie had just been feeling guilty all this time because she had no one to reassure her otherwise. But here was proof, he supposed.

'Call her,' he said now, anger flaring up on her behalf.

He didn't know the full story, but if she'd offered to go to her mother and been asked to stay away…well, maybe there was more to it.

'I have. She said she has some things to discuss with someone first, and she'll call me back later. She's already decided she doesn't want me there.'

'Don't be ridiculous. It'll be something else—you'll see.'

He reached for her fingers impulsively and she let him hold her hand on her lap. A voice in his head said that he was being a comfort blanket…or a stand-in boyfriend till the next one came along. But to hell with it. That was what friends did.

He forced himself not to say anything that might sound like he was slamming her parents. He didn't know them, and they had their own set of problems after what had happened with her brother, but it sounded a lot as if they had no idea how the whole thing had affected Sadie all these years.

'You know,' he said, tracing a thumb over her knuckles, 'I really hope you don't think that just because we…' Damn, why couldn't he get his words out? 'I hope you know I'm not going to stop being there for you if you need me. I will never stop caring about you.'

A thousand questions flared in the grey of her irises when she looked at him. 'I know,' she replied after a second, before resting her head softly on his shoulder. 'That means a lot to me, Owen. I know you mean those things when you say them. You're a good friend.'

He toyed with how the word 'friend' felt now, coming from her lips. It was all they'd promised to be for each other, all he could offer her…only he'd never given anyone the kind of emotional support he now found himself offering

Sadie. Weirdly, he was wanting to offer it more, even after sleeping with her, which was kind of new.

'Did you hear anything else about your dad's wedding?' she asked now, her head bumping on his shoulder with the train's motion.

'He wants me to go. I said I wouldn't,' he replied, prickling at the thought of it.

The invitation had come via email just a few days ago. He'd declined and had yet to respond to his father's follow-up email, asking him to reconsider. Of course his dad wanted his successful son in attendance, even if their relationship was far from perfect. The rest of their extended family weren't so bad—it would be nice to catch up with them, at least. If it wasn't for…well, *everything* else, he might consider it.

'Your mum doesn't want you to go, right?'

He frowned into the top of Sadie's head. How did she know that? 'I don't do everything she asks me to—' he started, already on the defence.

'You love her,' she interrupted. 'You want to do right by her. That's who you are, Owen, and there's nothing wrong with that. But do you *want* to go?'

She lifted her head to study him and he avoided her eyes, shrugged towards the window. They were supposed to be talking about *her* parents, not his. Just being around his father made him feel like a treacherous son to his mother, yes, but also as if he should have called him out on his lecherous, cruel behaviour years ago, instead of bottling it up inside, letting the effects of it mark his own relationships, or lack thereof. He wasn't an idiot—he knew he probably looked at relationships through a warped lens, or at least a different one from Sadie, because of his parents. But he couldn't exactly unsee what he'd seen, or undo what he'd experienced.

'If you want to go, I'll go with you,' she offered now. 'Maybe if you take a friend with you it'll be easier...'

'No,' he said. 'Thanks, but no.'

Just the thought of it was like dunking his head in an icebox. His mum might not want to be there herself, but that didn't mean she wouldn't be calling everyone else for the gossip. He'd be forced to be a part of that tornado and its wreckage, and so would Sadie if she went with him. Friend or not, she'd also get an earful about the Penner men's playboy ways, how his dad's weddings were now an annual event, how she should watch out in case she was next in line to need a divorce lawyer...blah-blah. All the usual jokes that weren't really jokes. It made him loathe the very notion of marriage and weddings in general... No, thank you. Hell, no.

'I heard your mum on the phone that day, out on the boat,' Sadie said now. 'She's in your ear all the time, Owen, dragging you into things. Doesn't that drive you crazy?'

He stared at her, then dropped her hand, embarrassment making him twitchy.

'Maybe you need to talk to both of them,' she continued. 'You're not a kid any more. They can't keep—'

'We were talking about you calling *your* mother,' he interjected.

Sadie bristled and tutted and took her hand back, slinking back in her seat. 'At least your family involves you, Owen, even if it is too much sometimes.'

He simmered next to her. How had this escalated so fast into another altercation? It was not what he'd intended, but she knew exactly how to rattle his cage—and he hers, apparently.

'Look, I'm sorry,' he offered. 'But I don't need to go to my dad's wedding, and neither do you.'

'Fine,' she huffed. 'I get it. You can be there for me, but

I'm not allowed to be there for you. No one gets close to Owen, huh?'

'I told you not to psychoanalyse me.'

She threw her hands in the air, then picked up her phone again, glowering into the screen. 'I wouldn't dream of it.'

Shame took hold of him instantly. He was hurting people with own stupid attempts at self-preservation. He was hurting Sadie now, by pushing her away again when he'd promised not to! She deserved more.

He ground his teeth at the window. 'No one gets as close as you've got,' he told her reflection suddenly. It was the truth. 'But you have your own issues, Sadie, you don't need to take on any of mine.'

His voice was so low and quiet it was practically a growl, but her head snapped up from her phone. 'I thought that was what friends were for—' she tried.

But this time he couldn't keep his mouth shut. 'Stop it, Sadie. This is verging on insanity now. We can't go back to being *friend*s.'

'What do you mean?'

She looked dubious now, and even more hurt than before. He caught the back of her head and drew her closer, tangling his hand in the hair at the back of her neck.

'You know what I mean,' he said, even as her own hands found the lapels of his jacket.

He wanted to kiss her, to lower his mouth and take hers and show her what his tongue and everything else could do.

She groaned. 'I do know what you mean,' she said, almost regretfully. 'I can't stop thinking about it.'

'Well, that makes two of us.' He drew a deep breath, forced himself to release her. 'But you know I can't give you what you want, Sadie, don't you?'

She clenched his jacket, and unclenched it, and he almost expected her to untangle herself and agree with him. Surely she knew that. This was a warning. He was letting her off the hook right here and now. She knew what she had to do.

'What is it you think I want, exactly?' she asked instead.

'Someone who can give you more than I can.'

'That's such an *Owen* thing to say.'

'But I'm right. I know you, Sadie.'

They'd been inching closer with every word. Her knees were pressed to his now.

'Maybe you do…maybe you don't,' she said, her eyes glimmering with challenge. 'I'm learning some new things about myself lately.'

What?

'I don't want to ruin what we've got already but…maybe we should try being friends with benefits?' she whispered. Then she snorted a laugh and buried her face in his jacket. 'I can't believe I just said that to you. Is that crazy?'

'Yes,' he told her, even as he stiffened in arousal. That was the hottest, most unexpected thing that had ever come from her lips. He released her quickly, balling his fist. 'Don't you think we've made things weird enough already?'

'You're right,' she said with a quiet moan, long and lingering, deep in her throat. 'We probably shouldn't…'

The train rattled on, the rain slammed the windows, and for what felt like for ever he sat there, millimetres apart from her, in what felt like a battle with his own personal angel and demon.

Torture.

Do not go down this road, the angel in his head warned him.

Just do it. She knows it's just a bit of fun…she suggested it herself, said the devil.

He couldn't help it. Hot fire took over as his mouth found hers and in seconds she was straddling him on the seat, kissing him passionately in return, picking up right where they'd left off before.

Even if they hadn't been sitting in an empty train carriage, he didn't think they'd have stopped kissing. Except a train with all manner of filth and grime on its seats was no place to take things further. Besides, anyone could walk in on them.

Regretfully, he pulled back and she sighed in agreement, sliding off his lap.

On the platform at Glasgow he was still wrapping his head around what had just happened when Sadie clutched his hand and pulled him towards a guy with a sign bearing their names.

Halfway there she stopped and pressed her mouth to his, standing high on her tiptoes. He promptly dropped their luggage.

'Are you ready for this?' She grinned. A wicked gleam took over her eyes again.

Who was this woman?

Owen didn't know what 'this' was, exactly, but in that exact second he decided he was done with caring.

CHAPTER FOURTEEN

SADIE GAZED UP at the remains of the crumbled tower, imagining being out there in the middle of Loch Ness in the heavy winds that had taken down this castle's walls in 1715. Their tour of Urquhart Castle had gone ahead despite the rain, and she cuddled into Owen's arm under the umbrella, feeling bad that she wished the tour would be over, so they could get back to the warmth of a quaint pub and a hot chocolate.

She yawned.

Owen nudged her. 'Why are you so tired?'

'Very funny,' she whispered back.

He knew damn well why she was so tired. They'd kept each other busy till four a.m., and then the McCaskill housekeeper had knocked on the door at seven, urging them to get up for their tour.

Conall didn't have time to take them out again today—he was preparing for the memorial service to be held tonight at their home. But yesterday he'd driven them into the majestic Highlands, where the scenery changed dramatically at every turn, and where the pancake-flat terrain of the Lowlands was transformed into glistening lochs, forest-filled glens and craggy mountains.

Scotland was home to some of the most alluring scenery she'd ever seen. She'd almost forgotten it had once been a

battleground for some fiercely territorial Highland clans…
All she knew was that she and Owen were now embroiled
in something so utterly fabulous that put all that gorgeous
scenery to shame.

Sure, it was all spectacular, but she could just have easily admired the contours of his abs all day in bed instead of
these mountains. She wanted it all before they were forced
to get back to the real world, where they'd inevitably have to
stop, and where he'd move on at some point, like he always
did. Had he really changed? She still couldn't be sure…
But last night. *Oh, God.*

She swallowed back the lump in her throat that warned
her how tough he would be to get over. She'd just have to
deal with it. She *would* deal with it—this was the new her!
The new Sadie, who could be just as emotionally detached
as him, and love every second of it.

Every time she'd felt Owen's eyes on her yesterday she'd
had to resist the urge to touch him. They hadn't let on to the
McCaskills that anything was out of the ordinary, although
maybe word would get back to them from the housekeeper
that her bed hadn't been slept in, she mused, once more
zoning out of the tour.

She smiled to herself, tightening her arm on his, as the
tour guide pointed to another crumbling wall and explained
something about the nobles who'd partied there when it had
been the Great Hall.

Talking of great… *What. A. Night.* Last night had possibly been better than the last one they'd spent together.
Behind the closed doors of Owen's room in the McCaskill
mansion she'd lost count of how many times they'd had sex.
Once in the marble-clad shower, twice on the shag pile rug
by the fire, twice this morning in the bed…

In that moment when she'd suggested a 'friends with
benefits' arrangement she'd been trying to channel Portia,

like before. It had felt so freeing, letting herself give in to her desires, knowing she was in full control.

There was also the small issue of her trying to forget the fact that her mother didn't want her in attendance at the hospital and wanted to discuss it with someone else. Whoever that someone else was… Was her mother in a relationship now?

She felt shame flood through her. Was she maybe using Owen a little bit? As a distraction?

The rain blew in on her cheeks and she turned to Owen, who moved the umbrella further to her side to protect her. Maybe she'd thrown herself at him on the train to stop the usual doubts and guilt over her brother from creeping in again. Every time she felt ignored or unwanted she did have a tendency to turn to the closest person for attention. She was probably doing it now, she thought, sniffing into the drizzle.

How many messages had she left her mum and dad so far? Three for her mum, offering to go and visit, and even one for her dad this morning. She'd had nothing in response except a short text message from her mother, saying she'd call later.

It was tearing her up, the way they never reached out to her. She and Chris had been so close. With only a year separating them, she'd sometimes felt they were more like twins. How could she not have known he was thinking about ending his life? He'd always confided in her about everything. Her parents obviously still wondered about that, too. She'd found the suicide note straight away, after all. It had been as if she'd known exactly where to look… It was all too horrid to think about, let alone talk about.

'What's that?'

Owen interrupted her thoughts by pointing at something in the lake.

'Is that the monster?'

She followed his finger, squinting through the rain, just as he nudged her again and laughed. 'My bad—it's another tour boat,' he said. 'You don't honestly think there's a monster down there, do you?'

Sadie shrugged. 'Anything could be down there,' she replied, just as a huge gust of wind snatched the umbrella from Owen's hand and sent it bouncing down the path towards a rocky cliff-edge.

'No! That's Maeve McCaskill's brolly,' she heard herself cry in horror.

Maeve had given it to her this morning—ahead of the forecast for rain. Before she quite knew what she was doing, Sadie was running headfirst after it into the rain, the abandoned tour group far behind her.

'Come back, that's Maeve's umbrella!'

The silly thing bounced and tumbled, a bright red blur against the stony grey castle. It seemed to enjoy leaping from her grasp the second it was within her reach. To her utter horror, it toppled towards a savage clifftop in a dramatic display of somersaults, and just as she took one more step forward, an image of Chris hurtled into her mind from nowhere.

Stop!

'Sadie, what are you doing? Leave it! It's just an umbrella!'

Owen was pulling her backwards against the wind, into him. She felt the breath leave her body in hot, short gasps as he urged her back onto the path with him, still holding her as she spun her head in all directions.

'He was just here, Owen,' she heard herself say through her tears. 'Clear as day.'

'Who?'

'Chris! I heard his voice.'

'No, you didn't—that was me.'

'I heard him!'

Owen's eyes had turned to narrow slits. He was drenched now—they both were. She sniffed in embarrassment, realising several of the other tourists were watching them. Quickly he led her away from all the eyes, hurrying her down the path past the group towards their tour boat, where it was dry. As posters of Loch Ness and the monster closed in on her he sat her down by a heater.

She barely noticed the other people staring as they started boarding and shuffling past. All she could see was Chris. Her brother. That was the clearest image she'd had of him in years. She could have sworn her late brother had just stopped her plunging off a cliff face—the way he had on his motorbike.

'I feel sick,' she told Owen, who bundled her closer and rocked her.

He said nothing as the engine started and they chugged away from the castle.

'You think I'm insane, but I heard him. I heard my brother,' she insisted, halfway back.

Owen still hadn't spoken. He'd just let her cry.

Now he sighed hotly into the top of her head. 'You've just been thinking about him, Sadie, because of all this stuff with your parents…your mum going to hospital… and the memorial service later. It's making you think about him more. You need to talk to them—tell them about all this guilt you carry around with you. I bet they don't even know.'

She buried her head into his shoulder. Maybe he was right.

'Don't ever scare me like that again,' he ordered.

'I'm sorry.'

'You were willing to risk dying over Maeve McCaskill's umbrella? I mean, I know you're a fan, but…'

'Owen.' She turned to him and couldn't help but release a fresh batch of tears as they stung her eyes. 'I was starting to forget him. I was starting to forget what he looked and sounded like till just now. I miss him. I miss him so much.'

'I know you do.'

Owen looked awkward now, as if he didn't know what to do with her, but he held her as she sobbed into him on the boat.

By the time they were in the car, on their way back to the McCaskills' she felt utterly traumatised...but mostly by her own outburst. She hadn't been able to hold it in in front of Owen, whereas usually she'd have kept all that entirely bottled up with a lid on, where it belonged.

Back in her room, she undressed and stepped into the steaming hot shower. She waited for Owen to get in with her. He didn't. In fact, when she exited the bathroom in a towel he'd gone. Back to his own room, probably, to get ready for the service.

She kicked herself.

This friends with benefits thing was meant to be fun, and here she was letting herself get all emotional over her parents and Chris in front of him—what an idiot. He didn't need her laying all that on him. He had his own family dramas going on, what with his dad's wedding—which of course he'd be attending if it wasn't for his mother, always in his ear about what a screw-up the man was.

No wonder Owen kept his emotions at bay, after them *both* telling him that crying was a terrible thing. No wonder he felt awkward and had physically left the room just now, after she'd let Niagara Falls out of her eyeballs.

Well, she'd save him from any more of that.

He was happy to be fun summer fling material while she was enjoying being single and spontaneous for the first time in...*ever*. He wasn't here to console a crying wreck, and she wasn't about to let him think she was after another comfort blanket. From now on there would be no more tears, only fun!

Going for the black satin jumpsuit on its hanger—something she'd been saving without really knowing what she'd wear it for—she wondered absently whether Owen would be wearing a kilt tonight, like all the other men at the service. Did men really wear nothing underneath their kilts?

Yes, focus on that Sadie. That's right. Just one more distraction is perfect—far better than actually facing your problems.

Her reflection seemed to mock her even as she dried her hair poker-straight and applied scarlet lipstick. OK, fine. Maybe hearing Chris's voice earlier, imaginary or not, was yet another sign that she had to initiate a certain kind of talk with her parents when they next opened the door for her to do so, as Owen kept saying she should. Chris would want that.

She should bring the guilt and shame that she and maybe even they still felt out into the open so they could say their pieces and all move on. What would she tell a patient if they told her the biggest block to moving on from something was their own fear?

The Mills family really had to talk this time, she decided, hands on hips in front of the mirror. Not like they usually did, about their cats, and what they were cooking for their respective Sunday dinners, and how the wisteria was blooming early. They had to talk about Chris.

CHAPTER FIFTEEN

Maeve McCaskill looked as solemn as Sadie had ever seen her tonight—which was only to be expected. The ten-foot glass dining table was laid out with her caterer's finest—for once, Maeve hadn't cooked anything herself. Sadie had offered to help in any way she could, and was dutifully helping to distribute little booklets with Scott McCaskill's face and birthdate on them.

She was standing in the doorway on the top step to the house, surrounded by perfectly pruned conifers, welcoming the drove of guests, when Owen came to her side in a green and blue tartan kilt, complete with plaid and knee-high black socks.

She had to do a double take. He quite possibly looked hotter than she had ever seen him look.

'You're giving me serious *Outlander* vibes. You'd better get lost before I ravish you,' she whispered, and he chuckled into his blazer and scarf, taking a pile of booklets from her. 'Have you got a musket under there?' she added cheekily.

'No, I'm just pleased to see you. How are you feeling now?'

'Better,' she said, blinking and shifting uneasily. 'Sorry about before.'

She assumed she'd probably scared him off...made an idiot of herself.

Owen sniffed. 'Don't apologise to me,' he said, turning her throat as dry as paper.

He couldn't meet her eyes now. So he *did* find it uncomfortable, her turning to him with her tears.

'Did you talk to your mum yet?' he asked, his eyes on the driveway, where a girl in leathers had just rolled up on a red Vespa.

She was about to answer, but Conall McCaskill was approaching in a matching kilt. He thanked them both again for being there, and for handing out the booklets. Taking one in his big hands, he sighed at the photo of Scott, running a hand over his tuft of a grey beard.

'Aye, he'd have hated all this,' he said gruffly, handing it back and gesturing around at the guests, some mingling on the driveway, some behind them in the house, others out near the stables—the McCaskills had seven horses. She recognised quite a few of them. There were actors and directors…friends of Maeve's who'd guest-starred on her TV programme. In any other situation she would have been more than star struck, but the excitement was dimmed somewhat by the occasion.

'Did you have a good day today, at the Loch?' asked Conall, his eyes glinting between them. 'Quite a romantic place, that castle, wouldn't you say, lad?'

That famous knowing half-smile was directed at Owen and it threw her off-guard. She compressed her lips, forcing a polite nod.

'We had an interesting time,' Owen said carefully, as someone in the rose garden, where the ceremony was due to take place, fired up the bagpipes.

Conall excused himself, leaving Sadie cringing.

'Don't worry about it,' Owen told her over the sound of the pipes, probably reading her thoughts. 'If they know, they don't care.'

Sadie couldn't read him. Did he care if anyone knew?

Maybe not. Since when did Owen Penner care who knew about his conquests? That was what she was, she supposed. And she'd walked right into it.

'Nice heels,' he said, and smirked, oblivious, his fingers teasing at the gold zipper along the pocket on her hip. 'And that is one sexy one-piece you're wearing.'

'Don't think I wore it for you,' she quipped, seizing back control of her flapping heart, which was starting to feel like a lost bird in her chest.

She wasn't about to start caring that she was just a conquest now—she'd started the whole thing! But this was quite confusing. How *was* she supposed to feel around him now?

Don't be stupid, it's just sex. Feel what he feels about it—nothing, she reminded herself, before her thoughts could take her down a dangerous path.

The ceremony was beautiful. Sadie held her candle close as some of the guests made their speeches in the rose garden. Balloons were launched, candles were floated out on the lily pond, all overlooked by three marble statues of muscled Scotsmen on horseback. She learned a thousand things about Scott, a man of many talents, while she kept her eyes on Conall and Maeve, bowing their heads at the front.

She couldn't help her heart bursting with empathy for Maeve, for how poised she looked when she was probably breaking inside. Her mother hadn't been so strong at Chris's funeral…

It felt like so long ago, but also as if it was yesterday… walking into his room and finding that note. She'd racked her brains for all the things he might have said, the hints at his state of mind she might have missed. How hadn't she even noticed he was suffering?

But then, if it *was* her brother who'd stopped her on that cliff today, and not some perfectly timed memory of him, like Owen said, maybe he'd forgiven her.

If only her parents could, too, she thought, glancing at her phone for a message from her mother, as if one might suddenly appear, like Chris had.

Later, she was talking with one of Scott's friends when she got the call she'd almost been expecting not to come. As nerves consumed her she saw Owen watching her leave the crowd and walk towards the stables. It was quiet there. It smelled like sweet hay and expensive hobbies.

'Hey, Mum, how are you feeling?'

Her mother sounded strangely cheery as she talked about the friendly, encouraging doctors she'd seen after the operation on her foot, and asked about Scotland.

Sadie told her nothing about the developments with Owen—they didn't talk about things like that—but she told her about the film and TV award in the McCaskills' pool room as she psyched herself up to segue into the subject of Chris, wondering how best to do it.

Should she mention she thought he might have saved her today? Or would that sound crazy coming from a medical professional?

She walked through the sweeping stable doors, murmuring at her mother's words, and ran her hands over a smooth leather saddle on a mount on the wooden slat wall. Then, just as she was about to come out and ask why on earth she hadn't wanted Sadie at the hospital with her for her operation, and whether it was because she blamed her in some way for what had happened to Chris, her mother took a deep breath.

Then she blurted something so unexpected Sadie landed flat against the stable wall in shock.

Owen found her several minutes later. He cut a handsome sixteenth-century figure in the stable doorway, where he was devoid of any telling modern landmarks or objects.

'I guessed you were finally talking to your mother,' he said, striding purposefully to where she sat on a wooden bench, tapping her heeled foot against a box of riding crops.

He sat beside her, sending a shock of cologne to her nostrils when she didn't answer. She almost didn't have the words.

'What happened, Sadie?'

'He wants to be there for her,' she said, refocusing on the news she'd just been blasted with out of nowhere.

Owen looked confused.

'My dad... I think he freaked out, hearing how Mum wouldn't be able to walk too well for a while. They've barely spoken in years. She said she didn't quite know how to tell me...she had to talk to him first...but they got to thinking about it and they've decided to give things another shot. He's at the hospital with her.'

She must have looked as perplexed as she felt. Owen folded his arms over his chest, nudged an elbow against hers.

'Well, that's good, isn't it?' he said. 'Maybe he's just realised he needs to start looking out for her again. Do you think they ever really fell out of love, after your brother...?'

'I don't know,' she said, staring at a stray bit of straw at her feet. 'It felt like it to me. But I just don't want him to get all involved with her again, and get into her head, and then decide it's not what he wants. She's been through enough. They both have.'

She looked at him sideways then, realising how maybe it wasn't just her parents' situation she was talking about now. Owen's jaw shifted this way and that, then he stood and pulled her with him, till her arms locked around his broad shoulders.

She toyed with the fabric of his plaid for a second, and then he said, 'Did you tell her how guilty you've felt all this time about what happened? Did you give her a chance to tell you that none of what happened to your brother was your fault?'

Sadie flinched in his arms. She'd meant to start that conversation, of course, but the news about her parents' reunion had kind of cancelled it out. It was obvious they didn't want her around, though, wasn't it? Neither had asked her to visit.

'I will talk to them both together—next time,' she said resolutely.

Maybe she had taken yet another coward's way out of confronting them and her guilt.

You'd rather hide in Owen.

Owen's dark eyes were laced with doubt. She still wanted to hide in him, but that wasn't going to solve anything.

'It's not like you're my boyfriend,' she snapped. 'You don't have to take on all my drama. I wish I'd never told you I heard Chris before either…we're supposed to be having fun.'

His eyes narrowed further and his nostrils flared. 'You're right.'

'I know I'm right!' she said, even as the little white lie came back to taunt her. She'd wanted to tell him about Chris—needed to, in that moment.

She tried to step back from his unnerving, disapproving stare, but he clasped her by the back of her neck, tangling his hand in her hair.

'Then let's have fun,' he said, against her lips.

Sadie gasped, letting him urge her back into an empty stall. He kicked the door shut behind them with one shiny shoe and kissed her with such ferocity and intensity her lips and chin burned with the most delicious heat. She was flat against the wall now, clutching the plaid across his shoulder, her tongue dancing with his, her heels buried in hay.

Somewhere beyond their stall a horse snorted softly. The smell of horses and him mingled in her nose till she was so turned on by the thrill of what they were doing, and where, she could hardly stand it. She had to have him.

Her hands lowered to his kilt. Owen moaned against her mouth as she found his hardness under the folds, throbbing for her. So he hadn't worn anything under it… God, this was the most erotic moment of her life.

She shimmied out of her jumpsuit, noting the way his eyes roved hungrily over her body as she stood naked in front of him. Stepping forward, she was about to help him off with his plaid and claw his shirt undone when something huge and hard that wasn't Owen sprang up between them and thwacked her on the head.

'Sadie!' Owen made a grab for her as she folded like a card to the floor and crumpled onto the hay.

What the…?

Pressing her hands to her forehead, she checked herself. No blood. Thank God.

Owen snatched up the pitchfork that must have been hiding in the hay and tossed it like a poisoned rod to the other side of the stall. She'd just got bopped by a pitchfork.

'Lucky it wasn't the spiky end that got me,' she said, as embarrassment turned her cheeks as hot as flames.

Owen was beside her in the hay now, checking her head all over, his eyes wide and wild. 'Are you hurt?'

'No, just mortified.'

'Would you just stop trying to kill yourself today?' he said in exasperation, before grimacing at his choice of words. 'Sorry, that came out…that's not what I meant.' He lowered himself to his side, checking her face again.

'I'm OK,' she told him, rolling onto her back, catching her breath.

Draping a hand over her forehead, she wanted to laugh, for some reason, but Owen leaned over her on one strong forearm, his eyes searching hers in concern.

'Owen, I'm OK.'

The seriousness of his face made her reach for him. She needed him closer, almost as if she had to console him for getting hurt in front of him—twice! Her fingers found the buttons on his shirt, and soon the kilt was cast aside and they were lying flesh against flesh in the prickly hay. This time he was less ferocious, more tender. She gave soft, encouraging moans as his kisses left a tantalising trail along her collarbone and his fingers traced circles around her nipples, moving down to the softness of her inner thighs, exploring her in the faint beams of moonlight peeking in through the skylight.

Dust from the hay swirled up as they moved and gave him an almost heavenly glow. His intensity turned her skin to goosebumps. Usually she'd be embarrassed, laid out like some wanton object of desire, but she closed her eyes and revelled in the way he made her feel sexy…like a goddess!

She was so absorbed in his touch and how different his tongue felt sweeping hers that she almost missed him unwrapping the condom. He must have been keeping it in his sporran, in case the kilt had to come up—or off, as the case might be. She almost made another *Outlander* joke, but when her eyes flashed open Owen was positioning himself over her and the look in her eyes rendered her silent. They burned into hers, devouring her whole, until she felt as if she was drowning in their depths, completely lost.

There was only them. Only this moment.

Owen rocked deliciously inside her as the hay tickled and scratched her skin, and she found her hands cupping his face, stroking his hair. She never wanted to look away from his eyes. Sadie could have sworn that she was seeing right through to his heart. He was letting her see all the way to the core of the real Owen, and what she saw almost made her cry.

She ran her hands over his bare chest and abs, memorising the coarse, rugged texture of the thick, dark hair around his navel, committing to memory the feeling of having him fully inside her, and what it meant.

She tightened her arms around him, burying her head in his neck, breathing him in. So this was the difference between lust and love…between screwing and creating something sacred. She had never made love to anyone like this—had he?

'Sadie, what are you doing to me?'

His voice was all desire, all awe and need, as he rolled her over on top of him, clasping her backside, begging her with his body and his hands to ride him. She obliged willingly, bringing him to the brink and then slowing down again as he moaned into her mouth and kissed her as she'd never been kissed before.

She couldn't possibly have ever felt closer to him…or anyone. He said her name over and over, and the sound of it coming from his lips while they were connected like this made her feel a thousand things at once—scared, confused, powerful, wanted, *home.*

It was like being on a completely different planet, just the two of them soaring through some heavenly space, and after he'd jolted and convulsed in deep satisfaction she felt a kind of bonding with him such as she'd never known, like two turning into one. He clasped her hand above her head, stayed inside her, working his fingers on her till she bit down hard on her own hand, trying to stop vocalising her orgasm—it was all she could do not to scream the stable down.

'My God, Owen…' Her words came out muffled and full of her aching for him. She was coming so hard her knees were shaking, clenched to his sides like a vice.

Tumbling off him she fell to the hay, breathless, waves of pleasure still shuddering through her. Owen folded around her, his arms and legs like a cage claiming a tiny creature he never wanted to release. She smiled like a cat, curling into the warm hook of his arched pelvis, allowing this new flood of mutual pleasure and bliss to reach her heart.

And then he said, 'You really know how to show a man the benefits of your friendship, Sadie.'

She froze. Owen nuzzled into her neck. The party outside had gone quiet…maybe everyone had gone. How long had they been here? Why did he have to say that after they'd done *that?*

Oh, God. His words were like a blow to her abdomen. She felt as if he'd lifted her soul clean from her body, then slammed it straight into a brick wall. She couldn't help it… water pooled in her eyes even as she squeezed them shut.

Owen's breathing slowed as they lay there glued together, and Sadie was glad her back was pressed to his chest. This way he couldn't see the tears that were clouding her vision, choking her throat.

That hadn't been just sex, or fun between friends—not for her anyway. It had been even more intense than the first time they'd done it. Maybe she'd wanted to hide in him initially, forget the world for a moment, but that had been making love—real, proper, soul-propelling, top-level, out-of-the-blue love stuff—and she couldn't even find the strength to deny it.

What was she doing? This was her all over, she thought helplessly. She couldn't just enjoy sex for what it was—her whole body, mind and soul had to turn it into something more. And now she'd gone and ruined things with Owen.

Blinking her eyes free of tears, she buried herself in his arms, memorising what it felt like to be there, knowing it had to be the last time she allowed herself to do it. She wasn't built the same way he was—what was the point pretending to herself? She was *already* doing what she'd sworn she wouldn't do—she was getting attached.

CHAPTER SIXTEEN

'PENNY FOR YOUR THOUGHTS?'

Owen turned to Portia, who was looking the picture of health now—if a little windswept in her pink down jacket and jeans.

'I'm not really thinking much,' he said, casting his eyes back to the colony of seals lounging in the secluded bay.

They'd taken an afternoon trip to the west coast of the Isle of Bute, where Scalpsie Bay had drawn them in with its resident herd of grey seals, sunning themselves on the rocks just offshore. Sadie was further down, with Amanda Bond, who on this one occasion had been persuaded to leave her therapy cat Sonny at Rothesay.

'Beautiful view,' he commented, watching Sadie as she crouched on a rock, a foot away from a giant seal.

He was talking about her backside in her jeans, which he hadn't seen up close since the night of Scott's memorial in the stable, over a week ago now.

'How's your head today, Portia? I know you had one mild attack while we were away, but nothing since?'

'They're getting easier to handle, thanks to what you and Dr Mills have shown me,' she replied. Then she nudged him with her elbow, nodding towards Sadie. 'Speaking of Dr Mills…what is going on there? You haven't been the same since you got back from Conall and Maeve's.'

Man, this woman was astute. Or maybe he and Sadie were just too obvious. He raised his shoulders, stuck his hands in his pockets and motioned Portia to walk with him up the beach.

The clouds that streaked across the clear blue sky were turning golden at the edges in the afternoon light and the tide was out, for now. It was the best time to take what Dr Calhoun called a 'healing hike' in one of the island's top spots. The undulating green of the hills ahead was therapy in itself—not that it had worked on him. Not on this situation with Sadie.

'Things are complicated,' he heard himself say against his will.

It was funny, but he always felt compelled to open up to Portia on a personal level. Did Sadie feel the same, or was he just slipping up because their patient was a sexologist? She was definitely skilled at reading people.

'Complicated how? Usually it's people who insert complications where there really aren't any.'

He thought how best to respond. 'Well, we went from being friends to colleagues. Now we're...'

'Sleeping together. Is the sex good?'

Portia's grin took him by surprise. In fact, he was so struck by her bluntness he laughed. God, if she only knew the things Sadie could do with those full satin-soft lips... the way she could kiss. A surge of blood tore through his body and made him shuffle awkwardly in the sand.

'It's...well...'

'I knew it!' Portia clapped her hands in glee. 'So, how are you going to overcome these so-called "complications" together?'

'There is no "together".' Owen kicked up a stone, glancing towards Sadie again, who seemed deep in conversation with Amanda Bond. And then she caught his eye.

He had a flashback. Sadie lying down in the hay, her

eyes searching his, taking him inside her slowly, intentionally. He could almost pinpoint the second it had stopped being a frivolous act of sexual gratification and turned into a level of lovemaking he'd never experienced. It had felt as if she'd let him in, admitted a trust in him that was not to be taken lightly.

The intensity of everything that had gone unsaid between them then had blown his mind—even more than their first time, when he'd only felt a taste of it and then pretended it had all just been in his head. So he'd gone and cheapened it by saying something stupid, like he always did.

Either way, it didn't matter any more. She'd put a stop to it that same night. She'd practically run from the stable before he'd even got the kilt back on, citing the need to shower the dust off her. When he'd gone upstairs to her, the door had been locked. It had stayed locked until the next day, when she'd emerged with her bags and the driver had taken them back to the train station.

'She doesn't want to ruin our friendship,' he explained now, still holding Sadie's gaze. 'So there will be no more sex.'

'Rubbish,' Portia scoffed. 'She'll be back—mark my words, lad. You can't turn something like that off so easily once it's been turned on. So to speak! Besides, friends make the very best lovers. Trust me. I know.'

Owen dragged his eyes from Sadie's, wishing he hadn't been quite so open with a patient. It wasn't just unprofessional, it had dredged up that awkward conversation on the train back to Glasgow, when he'd asked why she was acting so weird. Sadie had told him she couldn't do 'this' any more. That 'this' was going to ruin their friendship after all, and she'd made a mistake. She valued having him in her life too much to make things complicated.

She'd done a complete one-eighty on what she'd initiated

on the way there…as if one long weekend with him was all she'd needed for her 'wild woman sex fix' and that was that.

Was she turning into *him?*

If he wasn't so utterly confused he'd probably find it funny.

'She has a point though,' he admitted out loud, watching a speckled baby seal waddle out of the water and tip its head at them in interest. 'I would rather have her as a friend than not at all. She's a pretty special woman. And I'm not exactly her type, anyway.'

Portia smiled. 'You look exactly her type to me.'

Owen shook his head.

'Let me guess—she wants something serious, and you don't think you do?'

'I know I don't.' Owen inhaled the salty sea air as a flash flood struck his brain, sweeping up every argument he'd been subjected to between his parents over the years, all the family engagements they'd ruined with their petty war.

He hadn't told Sadie, but his mother had actually attended his dad's last wedding, at an idyllic winery near Bridport. She'd got drunk on rosé and taken Abigail—his father's last wife—behind a tractor, where she'd proceeded to remind her to hire a cleaner ASAP, because her new husband sure as heck wasn't going to do anything around the house. That had been just one item on her long list of things to expect or *not* to expect from a Penner man.

They'd been out there at least half an hour. Abigail had wound up in tears. His dad had had his mother escorted out of the winery.

'*They used to be so in love…you wouldn't have been able to stand that either,*' someone at the wedding had whispered to him, all while his parents were yelling obscenities at each other in the car park.

He'd stood there in the chaos thinking, *If this is what falling in love amounts to, forget about it.*

'I just can't give Sa…Dr Mills what she deserves,' he told Portia. 'She knows that. Anyway, let's talk about you, shall we? How's the journalling going?'

Portia smirked. She wanted to dig but he wasn't going to let her. Why tell one person about his inability to be in a relationship of any kind? It wasn't as if he was proud of it. But then again…his friendship with Sadie had always come first. Sadie had always been the one person he could count on, the one who wouldn't judge or mock or scorn him for anything. He'd gone to her for light relief from all the others…all the women who'd wanted more than he'd cared to offer.

Sadie had always been there for him.

Had he been a total idiot, denying himself a chance with her all this time? he mused to himself. Maybe he'd always wanted her underneath it all. Even before going to America.

But she'd only told him things because he was there— she'd pretty much said so. *'It's not like you're my boy-friend…you don't have to take on all my drama.'*

His phone rang. *Mum.* Speaking of drama…

Signalling to Portia to meet him further up the beach, he took the call, feeling Sadie's eyes on him again.

'Owen, your dad says you're not going to the wedding. I wanted to say thank you—you know your support means a lot to me. That man is unfathomably selfish sometimes…'

He bristled, stopping on the sand as she ranted about how hurt she was at not even getting an invitation—as if she could have expected one after last time! Usually he'd zone out, like he'd been doing for years… Only Sadie was still lasering him with her stare from afar, as if she knew he was letting his mother go on and on and on—like last time she'd overheard something like this conversation be-tween them on the boat.

Fury made his blood run hotter even in the cool wind. Sadie was right. He could never totally zone out from this.

This feud between his parents was the centre of his world, the reason for everything he'd put himself through over the years.

'Mum—enough,' he snapped, halting her mid-sentence. 'I love you, but this is toxic. Maybe I'll go to the wedding, maybe I won't, but that's *my* decision to make, not yours. I know you're still in love with him. Did you ever consider that's why you're really angry with him?'

Silence.

Then, to his utter shock, his mother started ranting even more. She was livid, practically possessed with her righteous rage. How dared he suggest that? How could he even think she'd still have feelings for someone so hostile and weak? Blah-blah-blah…

He sank to the sand on his haunches, tossed a pebble at the shoreline while she went on and on, and on some more. Why had he thought she'd take his opinions on board?

'That's your mother, isn't it? Give me the phone.'

Owen spun around. Sadie was behind him suddenly, towering over him, hand outstretched, hair flailing in the wind.

'Give me it,' she said again, just as his mother reiterated—loudly—how he was so selfish, just like his father.

He knew they could both hear it.

Amused, he stood and handed Sadie the phone, expecting her to hang up on his behalf. Instead, he watched in shock as she pressed it to her ear.

'Josephine? This is Sadie,' she announced, with an authority he rarely heard, but which turned him on instantly. 'Sadie. Yes, that's right. Owen's best friend. And do you know *why* he's my best friend? Because Owen is the least selfish, most sensitive, most caring man I have ever met. And, with all due respect, he doesn't need you or anyone else to keep telling him otherwise. Now, if you'll excuse us, we have work to do.'

Now she was hanging up, as angrily as anyone could on a smartphone, prodding one finger heavily at the screen in an exaggerated swipe.

She handed it back to him, then crossed her arms. 'You're welcome,' she said as he slid it slowly into his pocket.

'You're my hero,' he said, and smirked, resisting the urge to tell her how aroused he was by her in this moment. She shot him a flicker of a smile, which somehow didn't feel exactly as if it came from her heart. 'I mean it,' he said, but she rolled her eyes.

He followed Sadie's lead, heading back to the slope they'd walked down to reach the bay, thinking how he didn't know whether to be horrified or impressed by what had just happened. He'd bet no one had ever dared confront his mother like that before...no one except him, barely three minutes before Sadie!

Their driver was waiting at the top of the slope, but Sadie stopped just ahead of him, as Amanda let out a sorrowful groan. Their exit was blocked. Since their arrival a couple of workmen in yellow jackets had taken it upon themselves to repaint some lines on the slope. A glaring orange barrier at the bottom told them it was now a no-go zone. *Great.*

Owen strode ahead, waving at the guys. 'We need to get back up!'

'Take the stairs! Just walk around to the right,' came the reply.

'I can't take the stairs.'

Amanda was gripping Sadie's arm now, and Sadie was doing her best to console her. Amanda still had a deathly fear of staircases, thanks to her accident at the airport. Already her face had turned pale, the seals behind them on the rocks forgotten.

Owen tried again. 'Please, if we can just squeeze past you, mate?'

'No can do, lad. There's wet paint everywhere—sorry.'

The man went back to his pot of white paint, but not before Owen caught sight of his name badge: *Peter Forry-Stewart*.

He did a double-take. His godmother was a Forry-Stewart. He vaguely remembered she had some connection to Glasgow, though the two women hadn't spoken in years, to his knowledge…not since he was little. Why, he didn't know.

'Your mother wouldn't be Aisling Forry-Stewart, by chance, would she?' he asked.

Peter looked up in surprise. 'Yes, that's her.'

Owen had to go—poor Amanda was less than happy behind him, and he could hear Sadie soothing her as best she could—but he took a business card from the man, for Aisling Forry-Stewart's Beauty & Botanics shop here on Rothesay, and told Peter he'd pay her a visit for old times' sake. Peter looked touched, but still wouldn't let them use the slope.

At the staircase, Amanda had gone from being slightly pale to apparition-white, and not even Portia's light good-natured banter and jokes would calm her. She sank down to the stony bottom step and at Sadie's instruction took long, deep gulps of sea air.

'I can't do it… I can't do it,' she mumbled.

Amanda was about to have a panic attack, which would be a setback no one had anticipated—least of all today. Owen had already had her on the tilt table this morning, where he'd utilised electric stimulation to calm her startle reflex, but now here she was, startled and shaken by the prospect of climbing some stairs.

She kept putting her palms over her eyes. Taking her hands gently, he crouched in front of her. 'You don't have to climb the stairs if you really don't want to,' he said, catching Sadie's wary glance.

'The tide's coming in pretty fast, though,' Sadie observed. 'There's only one way I can see of solving this situation, Dr Penner.'

She was right.

Owen pulled up his sleeves, not missing the way Portia and Sadie exchanged appreciative glances at his muscular arms in the sunlight. 'Do I have your permission to carry you, Mrs Bond?' he asked.

He felt Sadie watching him the whole way up the stairs, with Amanda Bond's arms looped gratefully around his neck and a crowd of onlookers cheering.

Hero, Sadie mouthed at him, as he helped their patient into the car. He offered a mock salute over the roof, and for a moment it felt as if things were almost normal between them. Being her hero wasn't exactly why he'd done it, but if that was what she thought, he'd take it.

He was quiet on the journey back to Rothesay, thinking how it hadn't exactly been a heroic move risking his friendship with Sadie for sex. He shouldn't have gone there. He might feel as if he wanted more than her friendship sometimes, but he had to remember what was more important. Her confronting his mother like that on his behalf—that had been crazy! It meant more than he could ever express. And she'd done it not because he'd needed her to, but because she *cared* enough to do it.

There weren't many people in his life who cared that much about him—not when he flitted between lovers with barely a thought as to how it might affect them. If he ever did anything to stop Sadie caring about him he'd never forgive himself.

She'd given him a ticket out—freedom, singledom, the chance to move on unjudged, no questions asked. She'd given him what he always wanted after a few weeks of hot sex with someone new.

Yet here was the problem.

The thought of never making love to her again made his

heart physically ache for her closeness, as well as a certain kind of fire start to rage in his belly... All the things he'd missed out on till now, going from one fling to the next, never investing, never allowing himself to get close enough to anyone to really *care* in case...in case he ever had to experience the kind of grief that came from losing someone he cared about, the kind of grief he'd watched consume his mother.

He'd picked up so many pieces over the years he was staggering under the weight of them all. His parents, with or without their acknowledgment of doing so, had rendered him so jaded about love that he'd openly rejected it, time after time, told himself he didn't want it for himself. He'd literally made himself believe he wasn't good enough to be anyone's boyfriend or husband. But he wasn't his father. He'd never let the love of his life turn sour and self-destruct.

He'd never wanted anyone as much as Sadie—never even thought it was possible. Maybe he *should* ask her to his father's wedding, he mused. A date out in the real world, somewhere he could show her off proudly to his family— a chance for her *and* them to see that he'd changed. She'd know she was special to him if he asked her to the wedding. He'd never let anyone meet his family before.

CHAPTER SEVENTEEN

ON THE DOCK beside the lake Sadie sipped her coffee and swiped her tired eyes, trying to wake herself up. She'd barely slept. The banging in the walls was back, and this time it was louder than ever. Knocking on Owen's door had proved fruitless. He'd probably slept through it.

Thinking about it now, though, that was probably for the best. What good would have come from going to his room, to his bed, when she'd put a stop to that kind of thing ten whole days ago, on the train back from the McCaskills'?

Rejection was not something she handled well. There was no way she was about to admit she might be falling for him—not when he'd warned her he couldn't give her what she needed and she'd gone and ignored that warning anyway. They hadn't so much as touched each other since and she'd spent her nights alone, telling herself not to waste so much time thinking about something that was over. Finished. Done.

Her dad's name flashed up on her phone screen, interrupting her thoughts, which were about Owen, as usual. Bringing her knees to her chest, she gathered her strength. He was probably calling to say how he and her mum didn't need her at the hospital, even after she'd offered—*again*.

Picking up the call and casting her eyes to the grey-skyed horizon across the water, she let him talk about the weather, and then asked after her mum and told him again how happy she was that they were giving things another go.

Her father seemed to stall.

'Yes, about that… Sorry I haven't called before. Your mother and I have been busy…and I know how busy you are, especially now you're in Scotland.'

Sadie's heart was pounding in her chest now, the way it always did when she sensed another excuse coming. This was why she'd been stalling on talking about Chris, avoiding calling them as much as she probably should. She couldn't stand to hear the fresh sadness in their voices over something she might've been able to prevent.

'I didn't want to bother you with coming to the hospital—you have enough of all that, what with your day job…'

'If you guys don't want me around you only have to say. It's nothing new,' she cut in, tossing a stone into the water—hard.

Ugh. She had to address this head-on—not dance around it like she'd been doing. Again. Enough was enough, and she was way too tired to care anyway.

'I feel guilty enough, Dad, about what happened to Chris,' she said now. 'I don't need your fabrication…'

'What?'

Something in her father's voice made her swallow back her next words.

'Sadie, I was just going to suggest we all meet, the three of us, somewhere nice…when your mother's in recovery.'

'Oh.'

'We haven't really had any proper family time in a long while. We realise we've both made a few mistakes there. But I can't believe you're telling me you feel guilty about Chris. What happened was no one's fault—least of all yours!'

Sadie blinked at the lake. This wasn't at all what she'd been expecting and she cringed. Her father must think her a raving loon. She listened with an increasingly reddening face as her dad recounted with regret how consumed he'd been by his own grief for Chris, how her mother had shut him out and he her because of it—how they'd never intended her to get caught in the middle or blame herself.

The floodgates had been well and truly opened. They wanted her around…they wanted to talk about Chris together and remember all the things that had made him special. They hadn't meant her to feel this way for so long—just as Owen had said—they'd just thought *she* didn't want to talk about it.

Her dad even suggested she bring someone with her to their family reunion, if she wanted to. 'Maybe that nice man your mother says you're in Scotland with?'

Of course she told him no, that she'd come alone, because she and Owen were just friends.

By the time they hung up, all she wanted to do was go to her parents. This was a chance to make up for lost time, without the threat of self-inflicted guilt hovering above them all like a storm cloud. A thousand memories were ploughing through her mind now—all the times she'd possibly mistaken their wariness to interrupt her or bother her for a lack of caring. She'd seen everything through the perspective of her own guilt when she needn't have done anything of the sort.

Despite her total exhaustion, Sadie found a new spring in her step as she made her way to the morning's peaceful potting session. She was excited to tell Owen what had just happened. He'd roll his eyes, tell her he'd known all along she had nothing to worry about, she knew it. He'd do all the things a good friend would do.

She just needed to stop wanting to sleep with him more than she ever had before, she thought, grimacing at her shoes as she crossed the dewy lawn. Or wondering what it might be like for him to meet her parents. They'd love him. He always made things more interesting.

There was nothing like sexual abstinence to make the heart grow fonder, she thought with a sigh, tossing her coffee cup into the trash on her way into the fernery.

Parminder called Sadie over the second she stepped foot inside the heat-soaked Victorian glasshouse. 'Did you see this?' she asked excitedly, waving what looked like the local newspaper in the air above her head.

Intrigued, Sadie took the paper—then felt her eyes bulge.

Someone at the bay had witnessed their little escapade with the stairs the other day and had sent a photo in. Apparently Owen's actions had started a small quest amongst the locals to determine who the 'hero' was who'd carried the 'sick woman' up the stairs, and now Owen's bulging biceps were a prominent feature on page two.

'Oh, he's going to love this,' she said, smiling to herself at the photo.

Those arms around her had felt so right…like a barrier against the world.

Maybe it wouldn't be such a stupid idea—fessing up to her feelings. Anything that consumed her thoughts like this was worth fighting for, wasn't it?

She took a seat at the round table under the indoor palms. Was he missing her at night too and just didn't know how to say it? She had been the one to end things after all—and rather abruptly at that. What if she just owned up to the fact that she'd been too afraid to like him? *Really* like him. Maybe even love him. In case he ever changed his mind.

Either he felt the same, and they could try and make a go of things, or he didn't. In which case she'd do her very best to keep him as her closest friend. It would be hard. Probably impossible. But if she didn't at least talk to him, take a risk, she'd never know what might've been.

'Going to love what?'

Owen had walked in behind them with Vivek and Portia, ready for this, their last activity. Both were being discharged that afternoon. Sadie groaned internally at how handsome he looked today in his uniform as he pulled out a chair for Portia.

'You're famous,' Parminder said, beaming.

She took the paper from Sadie's hands and placed it on the table so they could all see it. Owen's face was unreadable, but Sadie knew he was secretly loving the acclaim.

'You're the hero of Rothesay now,' Parminder teased him as he took a seat.

The fernery was hot today. The sun was streaming through the roof and windows and Sadie hoped she didn't look as tired as she felt as she fanned her face.

'Is that where you went last night?' Parminder asked Owen. 'Off with one of your new admirers? I saw you coming back late again... What was it? Two a.m.? I couldn't sleep, as usual.'

Sadie balked. *What?*

'I don't have any new admirers,' he answered coyly, swiping a pot from the centre of the table and handing a packet of seeds to Portia.

Something in his voice sent a red flag waving in Sadie's mind. He couldn't even look at her now. He was hiding something.

Oh, my God.

He hadn't been asleep when she'd knocked. He hadn't even been there!

A wave of nausea swept through her belly and lodged in her throat. There she'd been, just seconds ago, fantasising that maybe...just maybe...she could change him. That he might just want to try and be boyfriend material for her. *Idiot.*

Owen's eyes penetrated hers across the table the whole time they were potting plants, but she couldn't look at him.

She'd told him she valued his friendship too much to risk ruining it, and that was true… But now she burned for the other parts of him.

The Owen who comforted her and protected her and gave her the best advice out of all her friends. The Owen who could make her laugh and minutes later make her tremble in awe and wonder at all his previously hidden talents. She physically ached for him, especially now she was picturing him with someone else. *Already.*

Suddenly the shock of Parminder's revelation twisted into fury. Sadie bit hard on her cheeks and tongue, then rammed a seed so hard into a plant pot her finger shot through the bottom of it. He was seeing someone else. *Already.*

Portia's brow was furrowed as she looked in her direction. 'Are you OK, Dr Mills?'

This was no good. Sadie pushed her chair back. 'I just remembered I have some paperwork to attend to. Dr Penner will finish up with you. Please excuse me.'

She couldn't be near him a moment longer. All she could see in her mind's jealous eye was him cosied up with some woman in the town—some admirer he'd turned to the second she'd put a stop to their 'benefits'.

Hurrying back to the house, she busied herself with discharge paperwork she could easily have done after the session, despite her shaky hands. This was always going to happen. He was always going to move on. She knew that. This was Owen! This was what he did.

Let him go, she told herself.

But her bottom lip and her chin insisted on wobbling, and her tears blurred the paperwork. Folding her head onto her arms on the desk, she sobbed as she hadn't sobbed since that day on the loch after she'd thought she'd heard Chris. Deep, soul-crushing, lung-busting, body-shaking sobs.

This was the moment she'd feared most—the reason

she'd been off and on with this arrangement since the start. She was crying over Owen.

God, she'd been a total idiot, falling for the most notorious player she'd ever known, giving him all of herself, knowing deep down she was putting her stupid soft heart in the firing line. She'd fallen harder than she'd even thought, without ever meaning to, and he hadn't even been able to wait five minutes to hook up with someone else!

One cry, she told herself as she sniffed behind the closed study door. *One cry and then you're done. He will never know this happened. You will not waste your tears on him!*

Sadie hoped she was managing to appear unfazed when, a few hours later, Owen took her aside on the front steps.

'It's pretty sad to see them go, isn't it?' he said to her. The driver was here to take Portia and Vivek to the train station with their bags, and they were bidding them a warm farewell with promises of follow-up video calls over the next few weeks.

Just as she was about to descend the steps in her floral shirt and capris, a lipstick-wearing, radiant-looking Portia took Sadie aside. 'I want updates on *you*,' she said, pursing her lips, then glancing sideways at Owen. 'Don't think we're not all rooting for you.'

Even Vivek seemed to be holding back a smile as he looked her way from where he was shaking hands with Owen. Were they all talking about them? she wondered, deciding it was better not to think about it.

'You've helped us more than you know,' Portia said, her kind eyes twinkling. 'I hope you do something nice for yourself where that one is concerned.'

'Owen and I are most definitely just colleagues,' Sadie reminded her, and not for the first time. Although now the words bore a certain heaviness after all the what-ifs and maybes of the past few weeks.

They said their final goodbyes, which was indeed quite emotional for Sadie after all this time of getting to know her patients. She was going to miss Portia's little insights, as invasive as they sometimes were.

Sadie was all set to get back to work on Amanda's new schedule when Owen cornered her in the hallway.

'Sadie?'

His hand on her wrist made all the blood rush to her head and she froze, instantly picturing his hands on someone else.

Quickly, she pulled her hand back. 'I'm pretty busy, Owen…'

'I just wanted to tell you I've decided to go to Dad's wedding,' he said, dashing a hand through his hair.

'Good for you,' she responded, a little more coldly than she'd planned.

He didn't seem to notice.

'I was thinking maybe…' Owen trailed off, shaking his head.

He folded his arms across his chest and stepped aside for Fergal, who was pulling the luggage trolley back towards them from the doorway. Was it her imagination, or did Owen look sheepish? She straightened her back. Of course he probably felt bad for sleeping with someone else so soon, but that was his prerogative, she supposed. He could do what he liked.

'What's wrong?' he asked her now, and she realised she was scowling deeply at the space between his eyes, digging her nails into her palms, imagining him in his tux at the wedding, looking dreamy as hell…checking all the women out, no doubt.

'Nothing's wrong. I told you—I'm busy,' she said, feigning a smile she knew probably hadn't made it to her eyes. 'What were you thinking?'

He looked at her long and hard, as if something heavy was percolating in his brain. She braced herself to hear who he was taking to the wedding—because it sure as heck wasn't going to be her now he'd moved on.

'Forget about it,' he said eventually.

Great. As if she would.

If only her heart wasn't going a million miles an hour. Maybe he wasn't taking anyone at all. Why should she care? Especially now, when there was nothing between them but some vague and twisted form of friendship—what was left of it, that was. It had only ever been going to end this way, with her a mess and him absolutely fine.

'You're angry at me for something,' he accused her now. 'Out with it.'

'Don't be ridiculous,' she shot back.

He huffed a laugh. 'So we're right back here, are we?'

She pulled her eyes away from his challenging stare. That time he'd accused of her being jealous—of Parminder of all people—she'd laughed him off. He knew when she was jealous! He probably knew she was now. But if she voiced her concerns about whoever he was meeting at night, he'd ask her what right she had to question him when *she'd* called things off. Besides, he hadn't made any promises to her. He wasn't exactly in the habit of making promises to anyone—that was why she'd called it off!

Unless... He does look pretty angry. Did you just jump the gun? This is all such a mess!

Owen was still simmering at her. The hallway closed in even further. Even the fountain outside seemed to fall silent.

'You don't want to talk to me?' he asked.

Before she could get her head straight and form a sentence, he threw his hands in the air.

'You know what? If you still don't want to talk to me about

anything real, Sadie, maybe we should think about ending *everything* between us—including this so-called friendship.'

His words left her cold. She was still grappling for speech when he brushed straight past her and stormed up the stairs.

CHAPTER EIGHTEEN

SADIE SQUINTED AT the map app on her phone and took a left, as instructed. For all the time she'd been at Rothesay Recovery, she hadn't exactly spent much time in the town itself, but she needed to post a card to her mother, and it only felt right to do it herself on this Saturday morning instead of handing it to someone at Rothesay.

She'd also seen Owen leave a few minutes before her...

The birds in the trees seemed to be judging her as she took the path towards the row of shops, along the harbour. 'Stop it, birds. It's not like I'm following him,' she said, and tutted at them.

Well, she wasn't. Not really. That would be silly.

OK, fine, she was kind of following him. To see where he'd gone... To see if she was right and he *was* with some new lady friend. Only she'd stopped to check the map and the next thing she knew he'd disappeared. And now she was just feeling silly—and guilty.

The hungry seagulls swirled overhead, squawking into her thoughts and only momentarily blocking the vision of Owen's face...how angry he'd looked yesterday. He'd accused her of not wanting to talk about anything real! But it was *too* real, knowing he'd moved on so fast. How was she supposed to talk about that?

No one had ever made her feel so heartsick, so angry,

so entirely impassioned and…scared. She wanted him… wanted nothing more than to tell him how she felt, which was jealous as hell. But what if…?

What if…?

What if he *did* feel the same, and they got together, and then he changed his mind?

That was the real reason she'd said nothing when he'd challenged her. The real reason she'd tried so hard not to fall for him in the first place.

She sighed long and hard, staring at the mountains ahead. As usual, she'd cut off her own nose to spite her face and that was why she'd followed him. To find him and tell him once and for all how she felt. Madly, jealously, in love with him?

This was what Portia had been talking about, she thought, stopping to rest her arms against the high brick wall around the harbour. Three white boats bobbed in the gentle breeze, while behind them the tops of the rolling hills were swallowed by clouds. It seemed fitting for her clouded brain. She'd found someone who fulfilled every part of her. None of the other men in her life had come close to making her feel like Owen did, which was exactly why she'd felt safe with them. None of them had ever had the capacity to break her the way losing Chris had broken her.

The way losing Owen would break her.

She snapped a photo of a speckled brown bird that had flown onto the wall beside her. A cute young couple had stopped a few feet away and were kissing over their coffee cups.

Callum was back in her head now…their last goodbye and how it had ended. There hadn't even been a row. She'd been stunned by his announcement, and reduced to tears by the sudden rejection—not a thing she'd ever handled well—but she hadn't been broken.

It hadn't been a powerful love with him, she supposed.

Not the kind of love he deserved or *she* deserved. Definitely not the kind she'd tasted with Owen. This was something real... And maybe it was time to trust herself to deal with it and not be so scared by the thought of something else ending that she hadn't even let it begin!

The bird flew away and came to a new perching position on one of the boats. Frowning at the water, and hugging her jacket around herself more tightly, she wondered why on earth she'd let it go this far—pushing away the only person in the whole world she could stand to be around twenty-four-seven. Maybe even pushing him unwittingly towards someone else.

She pressed on, away from the harbour towards the post office, nodding to a passing dog-walker with a German Shepherd. There was still no sign of Owen, but as she rounded the corner something caught her eye. A small shop with a green-and-white-striped frontage: Beauty & Botanics. Something about the name was familiar, but what?

Oh, yes. Owen had a business card from there. She'd seen it sticking out of his back pocket, that day he'd carried Amanda up the stairs. She hadn't thought anything of it at the time, but... Oh, God. Was he with someone else right now?

Someone who worked in this shop?

Owen hadn't exactly meant to burden this woman with the details of his current situation when he'd taken it upon himself to pay her a visit, but he was grateful for someone unbiased to listen. It felt like a long time since he'd spoken to anyone outside of Rothesay Recovery, or anyone who didn't know Sadie, for that matter.

He stood up from one of the two plush green velvet seats by the shop window to accept the cup of mint tea Aisling handed him. This was his second visit. The first, of course, had been the other night, when he'd somehow got so caught in the catch-up and conversation with his godmother that he'd lost all track of time.

'So, tell me, where did we leave off?' she said now, swiping her long grey-blonde hair over one shoulder and lighting a candle.

The smell of lemongrass mingled with the posh soaps and other products dotted amongst the plants. It was as Zen as the fernery in here—like a five-star version

Aisling was a wisp of a woman, the same slender build as his mother. The two had gone to school together and drifted apart after his mum's divorce.

'Did you ask your friend Sadie to your dad's wedding?' she asked.

Owen glowered for a moment into his teacup and forgot his Zen. 'I started to…' He paused, remembering the look on her face, filled with all the accusations she'd been storing up unspoken, her eyes burning into him like red-hot pokers. 'I think she thinks I've moved on from her, but she's too stubborn to ask because *she* ended things and she doesn't want to look jealous. I know her, Aisling. I know her better than she knows herself.'

Aisling nodded slowly, thoughtfully. 'If you know she's jealous, and it's eating you both up, the question is, Owen Penner, what are you going to do about it?'

Owen sat back down, stirred his teabag around by the string. It wasn't as if he hadn't been thinking about that ever since. All of it—everything they'd done over the last few weeks. The times when he'd dissolved into her, let her claim him fully. He'd never done that with anyone—never even dared to let someone that close.

Now he knew he was capable of it, he wanted to do it again and again. But she didn't trust him. Of course she didn't trust him. He hadn't fought for her when he'd had the chance. He'd backed off, as she'd asked. He shouldn't have done that—shouldn't for one second have let her think he was putting her in the same 'been there, done that' category as the other women she'd seen him get bored with.

He'd been trying to be respectful, to keep their friendship alive. But what a joke. He didn't want her at his dad's wedding as his friend—he wanted to show her off and kiss her and dance with her, knowing she wouldn't run from the dance floor this time…knowing she'd stay in his arms where she belonged.

'I want to be with Sadie,' he heard himself say now. 'She doesn't trust me not to hurt her, and I didn't trust myself not to either—not for a long time. But I know I'd never do that…not any more.' He put his cup down on the little dresser by the door. 'I couldn't. I love her, Aisling. I really do. And you have no idea how weird it is to hear myself say that out loud.'

He wrung his hands together on his knees. It felt as if a lead iron weight had been lifted from his shoulders, just knowing he could actually say something like that and mean it.

'She doesn't think I can give her what she needs, and I don't blame her after all this time, but it's different with her.'

Aisling was smiling. 'If she's the one, everything will feel different. You know, your mother tore herself apart over your father. I saw the way that love destroyed her. That was a different kind of love, Owen. It put me off the whole notion of being with someone for a long time…maybe that's why your mother and I drifted apart.'

She cocked an eyebrow, studying him intently as she stroked a finger over a row of fancy-looking lotion bottles. Owen was floored. His own mother had lost her friend because of her issues with his dad? It was just like Sadie said: he'd been preparing himself for the worst in relationships his whole life—never getting into one, telling himself he didn't want one! Choosing to believe love was a waste of time...

But deep down he'd probably always just been waiting for Sadie.

Owen almost laughed as the shock set in. There would never be a time he wouldn't want to laugh with Sadie, make love to her, fight with her! He could live in that cycle his whole life and never get bored.

'I was about to tell her once...how much I liked her,' he said now. 'I almost kissed her. We were twenty-two—can you believe that? She ran off the dance floor before I had the chance. I told myself I was glad, because I would've ruined a good friendship—you don't get drunk and kiss your friends! I hooked up with someone else to get her off my mind, and the next thing I knew I was stuck in the friend zone permanently.'

'You wanted to kiss me that night in the club?'

Sadie's voice behind him sent his stomach plunging to the floor. She'd appeared in the doorway like a ghost, in jeans and a cashmere sweater. Owen got to his feet, stunned. How long had she been there?

He cleared his throat, dashed a hand to his hair. How much had she heard?

'I did,' he admitted. 'Actually, since the moment I flicked ink at you...on purpose.'

'Owen!'

She put her hands over her face, but he took them in his in a second, and Aisling crept into the back of the shop, to give them privacy.

'I can't believe this,' Sadie whispered, swiping at her eyes.

He pulled her closer, scooping her face towards his, close enough to taste her lips again. But she was talking.

'I came to try and find you...to tell you I'm an idiot, that I miss my best friend and I don't want to lose him. But I miss the man who loves me the way you do *more*. I want both, Owen.'

Owen's heart was a riot as he scanned her eyes. 'I want to be both of those things for you,' he said, without looking away.

He knew now, with no trace of uncertainty that he'd do anything for her and go anywhere with her.

'Maybe I was too scared to admit I liked you back then,' Sadie said now, turning his hands in hers. 'Maybe I got stupidly drunk that night, trying to feel brave enough to kiss you first. But I was so drunk that I ran away and threw up. And then…'

She paused, biting on her lip, and he might have laughed, if it hadn't been for the giant lump blocking his throat.

'Owen, we would never be here now if we hadn't been best friends first.'

'Trust me… I know,' he managed, bringing her hand up to kiss her fingers.

Outside, someone reconsidered entering the shop and he swept her away from the doorway, under a line of hanging baskets. He heard Aisling shuffling boxes somewhere in the back room.

'Who *is* that?' Sadie asked now.

'My godmother.'

Sadie's eyes widened, and then she frowned as if she was putting the pieces of a puzzle together.

'I love you,' he whispered, circling her waist, taking her by the hips. She always had fitted against him just perfectly. 'I'm in love with you, Sadie Mills, and it's all your fault for making me miss you so very badly while I was away in America.'

Her eyes clouded over, misty with tears. He attempted to dry them, but it didn't work.

'I thought love was a waste of time…' she said after a moment.

Her voice was broken, but she was looking at him as she'd never looked at him before, and it made his heart expand to the size of a football.

'Not our kind of love,' he said.

He was surprised at the words now falling so effortlessly from his mouth. She was right. If they hadn't been such good friends first, things never would have reached this point of trust…of no going back.

'We will never end. I won't let us. Never. I'm tying you up in chains…'

'To your bed, I hope?' she teased.

'If that's what you'd prefer.'

Owen lowered his lips to hers for a second time, openmouthed. Her tongue was hungry, but soft, like velvet treacle sliding seductively across his, and he responded to her sensuous kisses again and again. Her hands were in his hair now, her fingers caressing the back of his neck, and as he kept on kissing her and kissing her he felt the fire in his veins, the spark of the start of something he knew he would never let die out. He would burn for her until the day he died.

Four months later

Sadie caught Owen's eyes across the garden and he winked at her. He looked amusingly animated, talking with a cousin, and almost as handsome in his tux as he had been in that kilt. But unfortunately there were no hay-strewn barns at the unique waterfront location his dad's new wife had chosen for the wedding.

Nevertheless, the yacht club in Cornwall was a stunning yellow-brick venue, to the right of a half-moon sandy bay. She could not wait to get back to their historic hotel, to lie under the cool sheets with Owen. But that would come later…as would she, many times, if this morning's session was anything to go by.

'Are you glad you let me ask you to come here, finally?' he teased, when he found her moments later, looping his arms around her from behind.

'Oh, absolutely.'

She leaned back against his chest and closed her eyes, smiling at how his being like this with her, doing 'boyfriend' things, made her feel. She felt like a goddess around him, and he wouldn't stop telling her how good she looked in her dress. And out of it.

'I was just wondering if your mother was going to show up,' she said.

Owen smiled into the top of her head. He'd told her about his father's last wedding, how his mother had been escorted out of the venue, but things were different now. For a start, she wasn't at this one.

'Even if she was here, I have a feeling she'd be OK,' he told her. 'She's been making a concerted effort to be happy for him lately. And me, too.'

He dropped a kiss to her head and she turned in his arms. Sadie knew her words to his mother had hit home. Apparently, she'd been quite impressed with her, and had been asking after them as a couple ever since. While Sadie hadn't actually met her yet, it was only because she'd taken herself on a therapeutic trip to Borneo, to relax around orangutans—something she'd always wanted to do.

'She finally admitted she'd never fallen out of love him—can you believe that?' Owen said. 'They actually spoke like civilised beings. My dad apologised…he even asked her here. She said the orangutans were more civilised than the Penner men, but at least she smiled when she said it.'

'Well, if you need me to talk to anyone here, I have a few *nice* things I can say about the Penner men,' she told

Owen now, pulling him closer by the lapels of his jacket and pressing her lips to his.

He smiled under her kiss, which sent a wave of tingles through her belly to her lacy underwear. She would never get enough of this feeling. Her best friend and her boyfriend, all in one unbelievable package.

Of course people here were talking. They'd never seen Owen with a girlfriend before. He'd warned her in advance what people might say. But it wasn't as if that fazed her—not any more. They both knew what they'd built together was unshakable.

It had been strange at first, leaving Scotland and heading back to their normal lives. Only, now 'normal' was so much better. Owen had pretty much moved into her place. They were taking some time out from work to plan their next adventure—potentially spending some time in Thailand, as Owen had planned before—and then a couple's work placement in a medical team on a cruise ship in the Caribbean. Everything was exciting. Anything felt possible.

'I want your best friend benefits to myself…should we get out of here?' he whispered now, as the band started up next to the dance floor.

She frowned up at him. 'You're not even going to ask me to dance?'

'That depends. Will you stay on the dance floor or will you run away?'

'Very funny.'

Surrounded by wedding guests and in front of his rather shocked-looking father, Sadie kissed him in the confetti swirls and made a point to explain—again—how she was sober this time, and was not about to dash away and be sick.

He laughed, of course, sweeping her up in his arms and spinning her around until she told him that, OK, she might be sick after all.

Ugh! To think he'd felt the same back then! And neither of them had followed up on it!

Not that she would have been ready… It had taken all these years for her to be ready for Owen, she thought, letting the music carry her mind elsewhere. It had taken all this time for him to be ready for her, too.

Her parents loved him, of course. They'd all gone away for a weekend, to the Lake District, where they'd laughed and cried and talked openly about Chris. It had felt so freeing, after all this time, not to carry guilt or shame, just to remember her brother as the amazing guy she'd grown up with.

She had to admit it had been nice to see her mother laughing and snuggling against her father again, too. Even nicer that she'd been able to do the same with Owen, knowing she could laugh or cry and he'd be there, like he always was.

She'd never said *I love you* so many times, and she still felt the buzz and the butterflies. Just waking up in his arms was enough to make her start every day with the kind of joy she'd thought belonged only to children's television presenters. It was, as Parminder had joked when she'd video called them last week, *'Quite disgusting to witness.'*

Parminder had thought they might both like to know that they'd finally located the source of the banging in the walls at Rothesay. It was not a horrible haunting, as some people had loved to imagine, but rather a family of squirrels!

Secretly Sadie was glad she hadn't known that before—not because she enjoyed the thought of ghosts, but because seeing Owen with Parminder that night had woken something up in her…some dormant attraction to her best friend and the jealousy that had forced her to address what she really wanted in a partner.

'*Now* can we get out of here?'

Owen's whisper in her ear sent a shiver through her

shoulder blades and she realised she'd zoned out on the dance floor, her head on his shoulder, moving to a slow song. A lazy smile crept over her face. This was her best friend, through and through—impatient, keen to move on to the next good thing. Only this time, and every single time going forward, she was going *with* him.

* * * * *

NEUROSURGEON, SINGLE DAD... HUSBAND?

CHARLOTTE HAWKES

MILLS & BOON

For Z
Forever with us
25/04/2021–02/07/2022

CHAPTER ONE

'THE DAMN THING is a beast. It's wrapped completely around these major vessels.'

'Perhaps,' Seth Mulder mused, peering through the co-observation surgical microscope at his patient's brain tumour to where his fellow surgeon, and friend, was indicating. 'Although, given how well-developed both the post-central and inter-parietal sulci are, they should make particularly good landmarks.'

The clearer those grooves were, the easier it would be for his team to identify the separate functional centres of their patient's brain and avoid cutting into the most essential areas of it.

'I reckon we might be able to take advantage of this in order to achieve a particularly anatomical resection—at least of the most superficial parts of the tumour.'

'And attempt preservation using microsurgical techniques,' his colleague agreed. 'Nice, yes, I like it.'

'Once arterial release is achieved, we should be able to remove the bulk of the tumour in order to create a little more working space in there.'

Seth lifted his head from the microscope and felt some of the tension of the last few weeks began to eek from his body. It felt good to be back in the operating room after the past few, hellish weeks away.

As complex as this surgery was—and as much as he would never wish such a beast of a tumour on anyone—he found he'd missed being in the OR more than he could have imagined.

Brain surgery was his world. It was what drove him on. It was what he was good at—brilliant at, in fact. Complex neurological procedures on patients who had not just paid handsomely to be treated at the state-of-the-art private wing of Baystone Medical Practice but to be treated by him personally.

Up until a month ago, these surgeries had been the sole focus of his highly driven life. They'd been all he lived for. All he wanted to live for. Which was just as well, since he clearly made a lousy excuse for a father. Or surrogate father. Or whatever the hell he was supposed to call himself now.

A wave of something cold and hard seeped into his chest—with an underlying current of something he couldn't quite identify.

The kid deserved better.

He wasn't designed to be a good parent, he thought guiltily. He wasn't designed to be a parent at all. His sister had always had the maternal instincts—generous and patient, just like their beloved grandmother had been. Meanwhile, he was the one who had inherited all the traits from their parents, who had all the parental instincts of cuckoos dumping their young on someone else to look after.

No, he was designed to be a bachelor: free to play the field and love his life as a neurosurgeon. So how was he supposed to help a six-year-old kid who couldn't even stand to look at him, let alone speak a single word to him?

Not for the first time, Seth wondered if he really was the best choice for young, grieving Noah—no matter what his sister's will had instructed. If he was such a good uncle and brother, then he would never have left her to raise her son—his nephew—without any familial help at all.

Another wave of guilt seeped into him, and this time Seth recognised that underlying current for the self-loathing that it was. He was her brother, but he'd been too consumed with his own career, his own life, that he hadn't really acted like a good brother these past years. He'd never meant to let her down. He'd let work, life and Stacey's aggravating insistence that he needed to find a decent woman get in the way. Perhaps, deep down, he'd always thought he'd have time to make it up to her. But now she was gone, and he had Noah to consider.

The irony of it was that he'd begun to tire of that part of himself that played the field a while ago. The parties had started to make his skull pound, the city's most exclusive hotspots looked like tedious carbon copies of each other and the women he dated were certainly beautiful but left him feeling unstimulated. Outside the bedroom, at any rate.

He was only too aware of how shallow that made him sound. A couple of months ago his usually quiet scrubnurse Andrea Perkins had asked directly, curiously but clearly with no agenda, if he ever wearied of being the 'Smoulder' half of the 'Smoulder and Heartstop' duo of fellow surgeon Jack Hart and him. But surely that was better than becoming the kind of deficient father that he'd had the misfortune to call his own?

Lifting his head, Seth steeled himself for that now-familiar punch as Andrea's striking eyes caught his, and in that instant everything stilled unexpectedly around him and he forgot where he was just for a moment.

What was it about this gentle, reserved woman that seemed to get under his skin? That made him feel as though, if he let his guard down even an inch, she would be able to see right through to his very soul? It was not merely because her eyes were the most stunning shade that they reminded him of the pale blue plumbago that his grandmother used to cultivate in her garden.

The memory jolted through Seth's head before coming to a juddering halt.

Where had that sprung from?

He shut the memory down barely a fraction of a second later. But even a fraction of a second was more than he had allowed himself in the past—with anyone, for that matter.

Which wasn't to say that he hadn't noticed Andrea Perkins the moment she'd walked into his very first surgery at Baystone over seven months ago, but he'd quashed the inconvenient attraction instantly.

For all his playboy reputation outside the hospital, Seth had rules—boundaries. He didn't date, or even flirt with, colleagues. It was a line he didn't cross. It was too messy, too complicated. Without his set of carefully constructed rules, he'd be no better than the man who had fathered him—but had never actually been any kind of father.

And perhaps, if that excuse of a man had exerted some similar measure of self-control, then his desperately unhappy wife might not have turned herself inside out trying to be someone she wasn't—so focussed on trying to please her perfidious husband that she didn't have the energy to be any kind of mother to Stacey or himself.

All of which, Seth believed, proved exactly why he wasn't designed to be a husband or father himself. And why he should never cross his own self-imposed line in the sand. Yet if there was one colleague who consistently intrigued him it was the enigmatic Andrea.

He was almost grateful when her soft, professional voice dragged him back to the present.

'So the brain mapping you conducted at the beginning of the craniotomy, when the patient was awake, will help you to avoid eloquent areas of the brain?'

Irked, Seth yanked his gaze away and put the unexpected moment of weakness down to just how upside down his usually ordered life now was. But he needed that line to be there—now more than ever, when everything else seemed to be spiralling so dangerously out of his control.

Besides, he hadn't asked for Andrea to be on this surgery because she had pretty eyes or a way of making him feel oddly more anchored—even though he'd never thought he'd felt *at sea* before; he'd asked for her because she was a damned good scrub nurse. And not because she was the only scrub nurse who'd learned within one single procedure how to set out the instruments exactly the way he preferred, which gloves he favoured for different operations or which sutures he was likely to want in any given circumstance.

Rather, what made her such a good scrub nurse—and, to be fair, Baystone Medical Practice had many good scrub nurses both in the private wing and in the main hospital itself—was how, from the first time that Andrea had been on his team, she'd impressed him with her intuitive approach and her eagerness to learn. Not least as now, when it was the first time she'd been part of a brain tumour resection like this one.

Not for the first time, he thought about the HCP-med course he'd been invited to mentor: a five-year course that would allow a nurse like Andrea to transition to become a doctor. The longer he worked with her, the more she struck him as the ideal candidate—not that he relished the idea of losing such an intuitive scrub nurse.

Little wonder that he found himself specifically selecting her to be part his team whenever he knew she was on duty, and not just today. She'd make up part of the crew he considered to be his dream team whether as a scrub nurse, or if she went on to become a doctor—and wasn't that precisely what each and every one of his patients deserved?

'Yes, the brain mapping will help during the first part of the tumour resection,' Seth confirmed, giving her his attention as he finally answered her question. 'But, once we start to remove more of it and get to sub-cortical levels, there may well be brain shift, so we'll have to stimulate the brain again and look out for abnormal responses.'

'You won't wake the patient up again?'

'Not this time.' Seth shook his head as he lowered his focus back to the patient. 'We'll need to monitor brainwave patterns. Can we irrigate the brain a little more...? Great.'

He'd barely finished the request when she efficiently moved in with the ice-cold saline solution that would help to keep his patient's brain cool and avoid any stroke to the exposed tissue.

He definitely ought to ask her if she'd ever considered retraining as a doctor, with him as her sponsor. At least he could actually do something to help her, which was more than he felt he was capable of doing for his nephew. He might as well be a hated stranger to that six-year-old, and he didn't have a clue what to do about it.

How was it possible for him to be a surgeon so renowned for pushing boundaries in operations, and to achieve results that were gaining him global recognition, yet at the same time be so utterly incapable when it came to being some kind of father to little Noah?

It had always been his darkest fear that he was every bit as heartless, as callous, as his own father had been—which was why he'd always sworn he'd never want marriage or kids. And, with every day that passed with his nephew, that fear was proving more and more astute.

What the hell had his sister been thinking, naming him as Noah's legal guardian? Especially in light of the fact the boy's paternal grandparents wanted to take custody of him.

Something punched Seth in the stomach, but he refused to succumb to it. This was neither the time nor the place to deal with the daunting prospect of becoming a surrogate father to his grief-stricken young nephew. He had a craniotomy to perform, which was something he had no doubt he was the capable of doing.

Setting his mind firmly back on the surgery, Seth began to feel the tension ease a little.

'Okay.' He peered down the microscope and carefully manoeuvred his way around the major vessel that was being swallowed up by the tumour. 'Let's start freeing this one, shall we?'

For the next few hours the team worked steadily, resecting the beast of a tumour using microsurgery where necessary and very anatomical resections where the brain's landmarks allowed it.

They tested the edges of it and stimulated the brain whenever they needed to in order to ensure they wouldn't cause a stroke in the surrounding heathy tissue. And, when they'd removed as much of the tumour as they could without risking damage to the eloquent sub-cortex deeper down, they finally closed up.

Finally he took the suture kit from Andrea, watching as she carefully kept track of the tail and lifted it clear of the sterile field as she passed it across. She had a good career as a specialist nurse and she'd never once mentioned wanting to change it. So why couldn't he shake the impression that beneath her guarded exterior something in her hankered for more?

Was it just her hunger for learning that struck a chord inside him?

A short while later, the surgery finally completed, Seth and Jack finally moved out of the OR to de-gown and scrub out, Andrea following as she noted final instructions for the handover to the ICU team and post-op care.

Seth stepped through the doors and activated the taps with his elbow.

'It's been a nice job,' he heard himself tell her. 'Well done.'

Did he imagine that brief flicker of surprise in her eyes before she carefully schooled her features?

'Thank you.'

Was it really that unusual for him to compliment his team? He really didn't think so. But perhaps he did take it as read that his team would perform well.

'I have another interesting surgery this afternoon, an ependymoma. Do you know anything about them?'

Andrea tilted her head.

'Ependymoma? They're relatively rare tumours. I think they account for less than two percent of all central-nervous-system tumours. I haven't actually seen one performed before.'

'I thought you might benefit from the learning experience.' Seth nodded. 'The scrub nurse who was dealing with this case has been pulled away to an emergency case and I need someone who can get up to speed quickly.'

He ignored the suspicion that he also preferred the idea of Andrea working alongside him.

'Right.'

'This surgery will be on a thirty-eight-year-old female who presented with a ten-week history of neck pain radiating down both arms and numbness in both hands. A neurological examination was relatively normal, but a cervical spinal MRI showed a well-demarcated inter-medullary lesion around the level of C6.'

'I would love to be a part of that surgery,' she admitted regretfully. 'But I don't think I'm scheduled to be on your team this afternoon.'

'Leave it with me, I'll sort it.'

'Thank you...' She hesitated, as though about to say more, but then stopped herself. 'Meanwhile I'll liaise with the ICU team in terms of the brain stimulation responses we had during the surgery.'

'Good.'

He liked how Andrea pulled the conversation neatly back to the patient.

'I'll also advise them of the particular abnormalities you said to look out for as he regains consciousness.'

'I have a few patients to see now, but I'll check in after that,' he confirmed, knocking off the taps as he finished scrubbing and drawing down a few sheets of paper towel to dry his hands.

It was only as Andrea left, the glass doors sliding smoothly closed behind her, that he noticed his friend's curious gaze on him.

'What?'

'I knew you had a soft spot for her.' Jack grinned, amused.

Something odd punched through Seth, but he managed a dismissive snort.

'Because I asked if she was interested in a surgery? Where are we—back in the playground?'

'You like her,' his friend insisted, unperturbed.

'You're the one who dates colleagues.' Seth shook his head. 'Not me.'

Jack laughed.

'Yeah, yeah, your infamous lines not to be crossed. But maybe, just once, you could break your own rules. You're not your old man.'

'I'm well aware,' Seth bit out stiffly. 'But that doesn't necessarily mean, just because I think a colleague might learn from a particular procedure, that I want to sleep with her.'

'It doesn't necessarily mean it, no,' his friend agreed. 'But in this case I believe it does. Either way, I thought you might like to know that Andrea might be leaving Baystone.'

Andrea was leaving?

Seth froze. Only for a moment, but it was enough. And he hated that the revelation upended him in a way it certainly shouldn't have had the power to do. Clearly, he wasn't himself at the moment.

'That's...a shame,' he managed at length when he could be sure his voice sounded vaguely casual. 'She's a good scrub nurse. Do you know why she's leaving?'

And then he kicked himself for sounding so interested.

'No idea. You know Andrea: she doesn't talk to many people.' Jack finished scrubbing his hands and began to dry them. 'But she might tell you. If you decide to ask, that is.'

A hundred different thoughts raced through Seth's head. He pushed them aside.

'Why would I do that?' he demanded crisply. 'If she's leaving, then that's her business and no one else's.'

And then, before he could analyse himself any further, Seth shot the spent paper towel into the bins and left the room.

CHAPTER TWO

'HEY, ANDREA, WHAT did you do to win the OR lottery?'

Lifting her head from the notes on her latest patient she was making, Andrea offered her colleague a bright, if curious, smile.

'Lottery?'

The other nurse, Kate, eyed her with amusement.

'Your surgeries today,' Kate prompted. 'Not least this morning's surgery with a certain Seth.'

Before she knew what was happening, Andrea found herself trying to rein in uncharacteristically errant thoughts about that morning. Not least the inappropriate, wayward things that were still fizzing wildly through her body at... *what*, precisely?

The fact that it had been inexplicably good to be back in a surgery where he was the lead surgeon now that he'd returned from his mysterious, unplanned month-long sabbatical? Or perhaps the fact that she'd thought Seth's gaze had lingered a fraction longer—more intensely—than usual?

Fool.

Most likely she was imagining it. For all his reputation as a playboy outside of the hospital, the sinfully sexy Seth was well-known for maintaining a clear professional distance between himself and his female Baystone colleagues. Why would he suddenly show a personal interest in her?

Even if he had, it shouldn't make any difference to her. Hadn't she always prided herself on her absolute professionalism, never flirting with any of the male surgeons even when other colleagues did?

But, still, she couldn't explain the way her skin prickled deliciously at the memory of Seth's golden-brown eyes holding hers.

As if she hadn't already learned her lesson where men too charming for their own good were concerned. Shouldn't she—of all people—know better than to fall for a handsome face? Not to mention the utterly masculine body accompanying it. His broad shoulders and muscles seemed more fitting for some scorching, sporty, outdoorsy, designer-aftershave model than a neurosurgeon who spent most of his time indoors, in an OR with no natural light.

So much for her valiant attempts to stay professional whenever she was around the man. No matter how fiercely she tried to school her traitorous body, her stomach still twisted itself in knots whenever he was near—as much as she tried to pretend otherwise.

Hating herself for her weakness, Andrea doused the unwanted feelings and pasted a bright smile on her face.

'It was a fascinating surgery, though I'd hardly call it a lottery.'

She hated that she sounded awkward, vaguely stilted, as she always did when the subject veered anywhere near dating male colleagues, so she was hardly surprised when the other nurse waggled her eyebrows and laughed.

'*Pfft!* The procedure isn't the lottery I meant.'

Andrea opened her mouth to deflect, but before she could speak another younger nurse glanced up curiously from her own work station.

'What's going on? Did I hear someone won the lottery?'

'The *OR* lottery,' Kate emphasised. 'Andrea only went

and bagged herself a place on this morning's surgery with Smoulder and Heartstop.'

Andrea wrinkled her nose, thinking how much Seth hated the nickname. Shame for him that his disdain didn't stop it from being electrifyingly apt. Seth 'Smoulder' Mulder and Jack 'Heartstop' Hart: it could hardly have been more perfect.

Strangely, though, she found it so much easier to talk to Jack despite his incessant flirting. Probably because he didn't make her blood heat and her veins pump anything like the way that Seth did. Ironic, really, since both men were notorious for burning the proverbial candle at both ends: boundary-pushing surgeons as well as notorious playboys.

Perhaps it was because, whilst Seth maintained his distance with colleagues, Jack's harem included almost half of Baystone. Maybe her subconscious was allowing her a foolish crush on Seth simply because she knew, deep down, nothing would ever come of it. Even if she hadn't been a colleague, she wasn't the type of beautiful, glamorous woman Seth reportedly dated.

Nothing that described her.

Not for the first time, she cursed herself for her gaucheness. And she condemned herself for allowing her ex to make her feel so insecure. It had taken less than a few months after the end of their lacklustre marriage before she'd wondered how she'd allowed Josh to cow her for all those years.

Why she was letting him influence her decision to leave Baystone, even now? Spotting him walking into the main hospital a few days earlier with his very fresh-faced young wife had hurt, of course. And not just walking into the hospital but the prenatal department. How much more of a scalpel to the heart could he have wielded? How much more of a reminder could there have been of her own horrible, tragic loss?

Andrea had only just made it back into the hospital and to a staff bathroom before she'd been violently sick. She'd barely made it back to her flat to cloister herself in her room and spend the night weeping and grieving into her pillow so that her flatmate didn't hear.

But the shock almost-encounter had also confirmed to her that it wasn't *Josh* who had left a black, aching hole in the middle of her chest when he'd walked out on her. Every single bit of her bereavement was about the precious baby she had lost. The idea of motherhood that was never to be hers.

Even now, a wave of nausea came out of nowhere, threatening to engulf Andrea. But she couldn't let it show. Not here. Not now. Battling to steel herself, she was almost relieved when Dina's swoon rescued her and dragged back to the present.

'Oh, my days!' The young woman sighed. 'You're so lucky. What I wouldn't give for a surgery with even one of the two hottest surgeons in this place. Smoulder, I think. No...wait... Heartstop. No... Smoulder.'

Andrea fought to steel herself a little more.

'Either way, I didn't *bag* anything.' She cut Dina off as lightly as she could manage before the younger woman imploded with her dilemma. 'I didn't even know I'd been assigned to that surgery until I saw it on the board yesterday.'

'Yeah?' Dina grinned eagerly. 'Well, I'd have done all your observations if you'd have traded with me.'

'She can't trade with you,' Kate noted with a wicked grin. 'I've just seen the board and she's on their surgery this afternoon too. Which means one of them is specifically asking for her as their scrub nurse.'

To her astonishment, it was all Andrea could do to quell another rabble of butterflies in her lower belly. But at least that was better than the hollow grief and gnawing regret.

'I don't think so.'

'Well, I do,' Kate retorted. 'We all know that it isn't unusual for a surgeon to favour certain colleagues for their teams, whether it's nurses, anaesthetists or co-surgeons. And didn't I say a month ago that I thought you were on Smoulder's surgeries more than any other scrub nurse?'

Andrea hesitated.

The other nurse had indeed suggested that, but Andrea hadn't believed her. And then Seth had mysteriously gone on sabbatical for several weeks and the topic had been forgotten. Something lurched in Andrea's chest... Now she couldn't help but wonder. Especially after that morning.

And then she hated herself for caring either way.

Andrea measured her tone carefully.

'Well, if it's true, then I admit that I'm delighted to be on the team. Today's brain glioma is one of the most interesting surgeries I've seen.'

And at least that much was true. The surgery had been incredible, as had the teaching opportunity Seth and Jack had created. Both men were more generous with their knowledge and skill than any other surgeons she'd ever known, not just in her time at Baystone but probably in her career.

'And of course it's the surgeries you're interested in!' Kate threw her hands up in mock-despair. 'Rather than either of the surgeons performing them.'

'Of course,' she declared.

She was proud of the way she sounded as though she'd never actually noticed Seth was not only a brilliant surgeon but also a ridiculously hot male. As though she'd never once had the slightest entirely inappropriate and less-than-professional thought about the man.

God help her, she wished she hadn't.

'Maybe I sound old-fashioned, or out of date, but Seth Mulder is a great surgeon and a good teacher: it's good for my career to learn surgeries with him. But, as far as dating goes, I really am not in the slightest bit interested.'

'Good to know.'

As all three nurses spun round, Andrea fought back a sickening sensation as time ground to slow motion. Of all people to overhear her, did it really have to be him?

This was so far from the sharp, professional image she usually took such care to project. And how arrogant was he going to think she was to sound as though she even thought he was interested in her?

'I'm so...' She could feel the heat staining her cheeks as she grappled for words. 'I can only apologise—'

'No need,' Seth cut her off briskly. 'A word about this afternoon's surgery, Andrea.'

And then he was already turning to stride off in the direction of his office, leaving her to hastily save the last of her patient notes and hurry down the sleek, polished corridors of Baystone's luxury private wing. By the time she caught up with him, he was already holding open his office door for her.

'About before...' Andrea muttered, before he held up a hand to stop her.

'There really is no need,' he clipped out. 'Hospital gossip doesn't interest me. I would prefer to discuss this afternoon's patient.'

'Right.' She bobbed her head even as she swallowed uncomfortably.

'But, before that, I would like you to answer a question. Are you planning on leaving?'

Andrea blinked.

'Where did you hear that?'

He at least had the grace to look slightly sheepish.

'Hospital grapevine.'

Something tugged unexpectedly at the corners of her mouth.

'Right.'

'So?' he prompted after a moment. 'Are you?'

'I don't know,' she admitted after another moment. 'It's a consideration.'

'Why?'

No beating around the proverbial bush; no softening of the question: typically straight-to-the-point Seth.

Andrea paused, an image of Josh and his soon-to-be new family in her head. Then she gave an imperceptible shake of her head. That wasn't what had first precipitated the idea of leaving—only what had made it feel as though fate was giving her another nudge.

But Seth didn't need to know any of that. It wasn't his business.

'Personal reasons,' she hedged.

Seth frowned. She might have known he wouldn't be impressed.

'"Personal reasons" don't sound like much of a reason,' he noted sharply. 'I understood your career was important to you.'

'It is,' she bit out quickly.

'Glad to hear it.' He didn't look glad. He looked…irritated…so unlike his usually unemotional self. 'Then you must have a very good reason for leaving Baystone. Our private wing is state-of-the-art, and we work much closer with our main hospital than many other places do, performing procedures some of them can only dream about. You're unlikely to learn as much elsewhere.'

His words unexpectedly scored a direct hit.

Other hospitals might claim that everything in this place screamed money and privilege—a medical clinic to the wealthy and powerful—but Baystone was so much more than that.

True, the place was a symphony of polished limestone, sparkling glass and sleek metal. Staff might speak of Smoulder and Heartstop as though they were akin to medical soap opera stars, but the truth was that both of them were talented, innovative surgeons, who were constantly taking the opportunity that working at a place like Baystone provided. Both, Seth especially, were constantly pushing the surgical envelope and achieving results that their predecessors hadn't even dreamed possible.

Baystone was undoubtedly one of the best places in the country for her to constantly learn and improve. But what choice did she have?

'I'm aware of that.' This time, the regret in her voice was evident. 'But I might not have a choice.'

'Oh?'

She opened her mouth then closed it again.

His irritation seemed to ramp up a notch.

'If I understand what your reasons are then maybe I would know whether Baystone should be fighting a little harder to keep a scrub nurse who makes such a good addition to any team.'

It sounded reasonable enough. So why did she feel almost disappointed—as if she'd hoped he would want her to stay for *his* benefit, not just the hospital's?

Sucking in a breath, Andrea told herself not to be so silly.

'It's complicated. There are several reasons.'

'Such as?' he demanded, unrelenting.

She wrinkled her nose.

'My flatmate is getting married.'

He looked distinctly unmoved and Andrea tried again.

'In truth, she just got engaged, and she'd prefer to live with her new fiancé than a work colleague. I can't really blame her. And it's her name on the lease.'

'And you can't find anywhere else?' Seth frowned. 'There are always flat shares being posted on the hospital employees' bulletin board. It seems nonsense that we should be losing such a good scrub nurse simply because of logistical difficulties.'

'Not where this one was.' She lifted one shoulder in what

she hoped was an eloquent gesture. 'It was close enough to hospital to walk, but it also came with an allocated parking spot.'

'If it's close enough to walk to work, does that matter?'

'Yes, I need a car.'

'What about somewhere a little further out, then?'

'Unlike surgeons, most of us don't get parking spaces at the hospital. The parking charges for staff are ridiculous. I'd be using a significant chunk of my monthly pay just paying them.'

He offered a vexed grunt.

'And there are no private parking garages in town near to your accommodation?'

'Not close enough.' She pulled a face, then hedged again. What could it do any harm to tell him the truth? 'No one else knows this, but my mother...isn't well.'

'Isn't well?'

His instant concern was touching, but that didn't mean she was about tell him all her secrets. No one else at Baystone even knew that much. It was no one else's business.

'It's a long-term illness.' She waved her hand, not prepared to tell him about the unsympathetic disease that was MS that had blighted Maureen Perkins' life for decades. 'It isn't something new—and we've long since learned to deal with it. The point is that I need to be able to get home to her easily and that means a car. It's no good living wonderfully close to work but then not being able to park my car anywhere when I need to get out of the city.'

'I see,' he ground out.

She liked that he was respecting her privacy even if he wasn't entirely satisfied with her answer.

'Thank you,' she heard herself say. 'For saying I'm a good scrub nurse.'

She hadn't realised how much her ex-husband had gradually sapped her self-confidence until she'd found herself so closely guarding compliments from people like Seth. But then, she'd never been the most outgoing of kids. Not since she'd turned ten, anyway.

No wonder her naïve, nineteen-year-old self had let herself get taken in by someone paying her a little attention. She shook her head to empty it of the less than palatable realisation, then caught Seth peering at her curiously.

'You don't think you're a good nurse?'

'Yes, of course,' she lied hastily. 'That is, I work hard, and I'd like to think I am. Still, sometimes it's nice to hear one is doing a good job.'

Or maybe Seth didn't need to hear that. Maybe he was wholly secure and confident in his own skills and abilities. She couldn't imagine him allowing anything or anyone ever to knock his confidence.

She envied him that.

The silence hung around them for a little too long.

'Well, for the record, you *are* a good scrub nurse,' he rasped eventually. 'You're invariably engaged, switched on and able to anticipate the lead surgeon's needs intuitively during surgeries. If there are unexpected bleeds, you're swift to request additional sutures and ties from the circulating staff; if there's a particularly heavy bleed, you're quick to solicit bigger swabs; and you instinctively know when to set up additional diathermy and bipolar.'

She could feel another flush staining her cheeks, but apparently he wasn't finished.

'On top of that, I've always found you quick to remedy any pre- or post-op issues as you liaise between surgical and ward teams, as well as always seeming keen to learn more about the procedures.'

'The more I learn, the more I can anticipate more efficiently,' she confirmed quietly.

'Right.' He dipped his head. 'Hence why you're one of the head scrub-nurses. But have you ever considered retraining?'

'Retraining?' she echoed, taken by surprise.

'As a doctor, say?' he continued, standing up suddenly and moving around the desk, his unexpected proximity sending her body haywire without warning.

'A doctor?' she echoed weakly.

This time she couldn't be sure whether it was his proximity, or the fact that he was actually suggesting her long-abandoned dream was possible. The childhood dream she'd had of being a doctor had faded when her beloved father had died. Josh had scorned it, and she'd given it up as never being within her reach.

'I'm sure you know about the Healthcare Professionals Medical Degree programme?'

'I…' She faltered, still not sure she could believe the turn of conversation.

She wasn't entirely surprised when Seth looked disappointed and took it to be a lack of awareness.

'The HCP-med is a five-year degree that would allow a nurse like you to train to become a doctor whilst still working. It isn't for everyone, but I do think you'd make a good candidate.'

'Yes,' she managed, fighting to gather her thoughts and sound calm and collected. 'I have heard of it. My hesitation was more about the fact that you need good references and money behind you.'

She tried not to blanch at the sharp look Seth cast her.

'Perhaps you are unaware, but there are Nursing Council- and Midwifery-approved programmes now to help with the retraining whilst still allowing you to work.'

Andrea nodded slightly. She almost told him that she avidly read any articles that discussed such programmes, but that the tuition costs had always deterred her. She was aware that Baystone sometimes sponsored conversion courses, especially for staff from its sister hospital in town, but you'd have to sacrifice vestal virgins to give you the power to complete their application forms.

So she stopped herself from speaking. It would reveal

too much to Seth, and he already seemed to be able to read her too easily.

'As for the references, I would be more than happy to provide them for you, Andrea. As I said, I think you're a very good scrub nurse, and you're always keen to learn something more. I believe you could be a very good doctor.'

All at once, heat prickled behind Andrea's eyes. Apart from her incredible, warrior mother—who had always wanted more for her than cruel circumstances had ever allowed them—the last person ever to sound as though they believed in her had been her father. Right before his death, a week after her eighth birthday.

Right before she'd become carer for her mother and her life had changed beyond recognition.

Dr Perkins. She hadn't allowed herself to dream of that in two decades. And now Seth Mulder was the person dusting off that dream and making her feel it could be possible. Making her feel believed-in.

It felt good. And bad.

It made her feel vulnerable in a way she'd sworn she would never let herself be again.

Somehow—Andrea had no idea how—she managed to grab hold of that familiar suit of armour Seth had somehow managed to prise open and clamp it tightly back around herself.

She took a discreet breath. And then another.

'Thank you for the offer,' she managed at last, proud of the crisp note to her voice. 'I shall certainly consider it. Now, I've been going over the notes, but is there anything in particular I need to know about this afternoon's surgery?'

CHAPTER THREE

'BYE, NOAH…' SETH scoured his brain for something else to say as he watched the six-year-old boy being led into Pine Bay's primary school, head down but without a backward glance.

'Have a good day,' he added, no doubt lamely, though he was fairly certain the child wasn't even listening to him. A desperate part of him hoped that the new nanny he'd hired to pick up Noah from school would have more luck, though he feared she wouldn't.

His nephew stepped in through the school entrance to be swallowed up by the efficient slide of the electric doors. Seth stared at the slick metal and glass for a moment before taking half a step towards the building. Then he stopped. The child didn't want him—that much was clear.

How was he ever supposed to do this?

It was incredibly frustrating to realise that they hadn't just failed to make progress but had actually regressed. Today was worse than the day before. Little wonder that now, for the hundredth, thousandth, time, he wondered what had possessed his late sister to designate him as the boy's guardian in her will.

How had she even been able to trust him with her precious son, after the way he'd effectively walked away from her? Sure, he'd seen her, on his own terms and when he could fit it in—and had then made up for it with expensive Christmas and birthday gifts—but that had been no substitute for being there for his sister, offering her real help—even a shoulder to cry on.

Perhaps it really would be better for him to agree to the boy's paternal grandparents having custody after all. The child's father might be a waste of space who had never had anything to do with his son, but it was clear that the little boy's grandparents wanted to be a part of his life.

It was certainly more than could be said for his own parents.

How many times had he pulled up his lawyer's number on his phone to advise them as much—only to terminate the call before it could connect? If Stacey had wanted her ex-boyfriend's parents to have her son then she would have written them into her will rather than him.

He had to honour her wishes no matter how badly he believed she'd handled the entire situation. The child deserved that much at least—hadn't he already been through enough in his short life?

Seth glowered harder at the doors.

Now what?

It took his typically sharp, gifted brain a few moments too long to remember that he still needed to get to work. Another day of surgeries lay ahead of him, surgeries which, up until last month, had been all he lived for. Now he had no idea how to handle it. Since the previous evening, following Seth's first day back at Baystone after a month off trying to bond with Noah, the little boy had refused to communicate with him altogether.

Logically, Seth knew it was to do with the child feeling abandoned again so soon after his mother's death, but that didn't make him feel any less of a failure as his nephew's guardian.

It wasn't a feeling he relished, but what choice was there? He was a surgeon; it was what he did, who he was.

Which brought him right back to why Stacey had given him custody of Noah. What the hell was he supposed to do with a six-year-old kid he didn't even know how to talk to, let alone care for?

Had his own grandmother still been alive, she would certainly have known the right thing to say. And do. She had been the kindest, most caring grandparent that he or his sister could ever have wanted. She'd been there for the pair of them throughout their childhood, taking them on nature walks, teaching them to bake and playing the silliest of games with them whilst their own parents had always been far too wrapped up in their twisted relationship and warped games.

Then again, if his grandmother had still been alive, then Seth had no doubt that Stacey would have made her Noah's legal guardian and the kid would have wanted for nothing. But the old lady was long gone, and resurrecting old memories wasn't going to help anyone. He had to find a way to reach the six-year-old himself.

Jamming one fist into the pocket of his heavily tailored jacket, despite the relatively mild weather, he somehow propelled energy back into his reticent muscles. He should concentrate on things he *could* control—such as the patients who were waiting for him at the private clinic, anxious to be reassured after his absence these past few weeks.

He stalked back to his car, a sleek, muscled beast that had boasted a waiting list of two years but which he'd bought as soon as he could afford to. The kind of car that had been well suited to Seth Mulder, neurosurgeon and bachelor, but was less than ideal for life as a little Noah's replacement father.

Another part of his life that would have to change. Not that he resented it when he tried to imagine what kind of hell this had to be for his young nephew, but how had his sister ever thought that he would make a good legal guardian when he could have been so much more supportive of her? Stacey had never made a fuss about not seeing enough of him, understanding how pressurised his career was. It was only now that she was gone that he was beginning to see that he could have been there for them, even if only a little more.

He might be well on his way to becoming one of the country's most respected neurosurgeons, achieving surgical outcomes that were little short of miraculous, but that certainly didn't make him a potentially good stand-in father figure.

Damn it.

Seth felt wholly out of his depth. It wasn't a sensation he was accustomed to feeling, and he most certainly didn't appreciate it.

With a flick of his key fob, the doors to the supercar unlocked and Seth took a moment to admire the smooth action of the butterfly doors as they moved elegantly up and out via hinges on the A pillar. He realised he was actually looking forward to starting the engine, and hearing it leap into life with its muscular, guttural roar, without having Noah in the seat next to him, shoving his tiny hands over his ears just to muffle the sound.

A last vestige of Seth's former life, but he'd get rid of it today. He could well imagine that his ultra-efficient, no-nonsense PA would be only too happy to pick up the phone and have what she called his *brutish* car spirited away within the hour. Perhaps he could confide in her about the difficulty he was having helping Noah adjust. He imagined she'd only be too willing to help.

No, he couldn't do that. This was his problem to solve—no one else's—for his late sister's sake.

His mind occupied with such thoughts, Seth swung round, only to mow down some innocent bystander.

'*Oof.*'

He summoned a practised smile and suppressed his irritation as he reached out a hand to catch the woman mid-stumble.

'My apologies,' he said smoothly. 'Entirely my fault; wasn't looking where I was going. Are you all right?'

'I'm fine.'

The voice was all too familiar and Seth was wholly unprepared for the frisson of awareness that jolted through him even before his hand made contact with her elbow.

'Andrea?' He breathed in shock as he helped to right her.

She frowned at him, those expressive eyes heading towards a more violet hue that instantly clenched in his belly—and lower, if he were honest. He pushed it back, but it was too late—the damage, it seemed, was already done.

He felt caught off-guard and, no matter how much he tried to scrabble for his customary shield of professional distance, it seemed to be eluding him.

'What are you doing here at a school?' He barely recognised the rasp in his voice let alone the thoughts that were flowing, unchecked, from his brain to his mouth. 'You don't have children, do you?'

He regretted the question the instant it was out. Firstly, it was none of his business. Secondly, he found he loathed the way her eyes darkened without warning, the plumbago replaced by Rich Blue Sun, as if he'd somehow wounded her.

Then the fleeting expression was gone, leaving Seth thinking he had imagined it. He heard her breath catch in her chest when she glanced down at the sight of his hand at her elbow, still steadying her.

She shifted awkwardly, not quite pulling her arm from his hand, yet somehow ending up stumbling against him.

Another shot of pure electricity tore through him, enough to make his heart stop—if only for a split second.

And, when it managed to pump itself back to life, it thumped inside his ribcage hard enough to bruise, an echoing drumbeat like nothing he'd ever experienced before. The strangest sensation, though not unwelcome. It was impossible not to appreciate the body-tingling contact, or to relinquish his hold on her.

Ridiculous!

Somehow—he wasn't sure how—Seth loosened his hold on her elbow and withdrew his hand.

'I apologise. That isn't really any of my business.'

Yet he couldn't bring himself to turn away.

For a moment, she continued simply to stare at him. Then she startled, as though pulling herself back together. Finally, she made a point of brushing herself down and, as his eyes were drawn magnetically to follow the smooth movement of her hands, he found it threw up a whole new set of problems.

Gone were the shapeless scrubs of her hospital attire, replaced instead by a pretty, soft wool jumper that moulded to her feminine curves. It made his palms itch just looking at her. Surprised by his reaction, Seth struggled to pull his gaze away, but when his eyes dropped lower it seemed that was no less of a minefield. Inky-blue jeans clung lovingly to long, lean legs that looked as though they'd been handcrafted to wrap around a man. Around him.

A low growl escaped Seth's throat as the image threatened to topple his brain into all manner of sinful thoughts. It was almost a relief when she finally replied to his initial, arguably brazen, enquiry.

'I'm not in until this afternoon. Sometimes I help out my sister-in-law by bringing her brood to school.'

'I see.'

'Might I wonder what you're doing here?'

This was why he shouldn't have asked about her personal life.

Seth opened his mouth to shut her down.

'I was bringing my nephew to school.'

'Your nephew?' Her eyes widened a fraction before she shook her head. 'Sorry, I didn't even realise you had siblings.'

It was on the tip of Seth's tongue to tell her about Stacey before he bit the words back. He couldn't have said why. Years of being cautious, maybe. Yet it wasn't as though he thought that it would end up on the hospital grapevine if he told this particular woman anything.

'A sister,' he hedged. 'And I was bringing her son to school.'

Her eyes slid curiously to the supercar over his shoulder and then to the building behind her.

'You brought him to school in that?'

A host of different responses jostled in his head. Not least that this was precisely why he feared he was an impostor in Noah's life, a presence that was causing the six-year-old more harm than good.

But why would he want to share that with Andrea—his colleague, his scrub nurse? He hadn't even shared that with Jack—the closest thing he had to a best mate.

'Is there a problem?' he clipped out at length, even as he cursed himself for not simply shutting her down completely. As if the same reservations that he told himself he could read in her expression hadn't just been winding through his own brain.

And then things in his head seemed to upend again as she flashed a smile that was bright yet taut all at the same time. How was that even possible?

'My apologies,' she murmured. 'I guess I never really

thought of you as a family-orientated guy. More just as a surgeon and as...'

'As *Smoulder*?' he suggested when she tailed off hesitantly.

'Sorry.'

She tipped her head at him and a pretty blush stole over her cheeks. Seth found he had to fight back the strangest impulse to reach out and cup her cheek. Or perhaps to lean into her quiet self-assurance and tell her what he was really doing here.

He balled his fist tighter in his pocket whilst cranking his voice to stay breezy.

'Don't worry about it.'

Spilling his guts was the last thing he ought to do, even with Andrea. Especially with Andrea; she was his scrub nurse, not Noah's grief counsellor. Seth was beginning to suspect his atypical need to talk was simply down to the absurdity of him—*him*—suddenly having to step into the role of a father figure. Could anyone be less suited to it?

Suddenly, all he wanted to do was get away—from this place, from this woman and from all the things that had turned his carefully ordered life on its head—and get back into his OR.

Just for the next twelve hours.

He needed just that time to shove the complications of the past few weeks out of his head. Just twelve hours to return to being the dedicated, driven neurosurgeon whose only focus was the next surgery. Back in the OR there would be order, purpose and the work that he loved.

It would be the time he needed to clear his head.

After that, he would throw himself into becoming the kind of uncle, and surrogate father, that the child deserved.

Either way, breaking down in front of his scrub nurse outside his nephew's new school was not part of the plan.

With a muttered grumble, Seth excused himself and

threw himself into his car, flicking the button to hear that longed-for engine roar as the doors slid back into place. Then, spinning the steering wheel, he pulled away from the kerb and out of the school grounds...before the all-too-arresting Andrea could say anything more to him.

And before this strange, slithering thing in his chest could take root.

'More suction,' Seth requested quietly as Andrea leaned in to the patient.

Another day, another procedure. But for once her mind was too busy whirring to appreciate the way she usually would. She couldn't decide whether her thoughts were thrown more from his suggestion the day before that he believed she would make a good doctor, or from their unexpected encounter outside Pine Bay Primary that morning.

There was something about the encounter that had felt... odd. As though she'd been missing a salient detail.

Mentally berating herself, Andrea re-focussed on the procedure—an aneurysmal subarachnoid haemorrhage, or bleeding to the brain, which generally had heterogenous outcomes, but was always interesting to observe with Seth at the lead.

He'd been right the previous day when he'd pointed out that she could learn things at Baystone she was unlikely to learn elsewhere. With a procedure like this, outside of the setting of their private medical unit, around forty percent of patients generally suffered neurological or cognitive defects. However, with surgeons like Seth and Jack always top of their game, Baystone boasted much lower rates. This remained the case whether the procedure being used was open aneurysm clipping—in which Seth would use a metal clip to obstruct blood flow to the weakened area of a blood vessel in the brain—or whether it was endovascular coiling, inserting platinum coils through a microcatheter to induce clotting and prevent blood from getting to the aneurysm.

Even with extensive follow-up, complications such as delayed cerebral ischaemia, where a brain injury occurred due to insufficient blood flow, weren't unusual outside of Baystone. So was she really going to walk away from her dream job without at least trying to find somewhere else nearby to live? As much as she might need Andrea's help, her mother would be devastated to think that her MS had thrown up yet another career obstacle for her daughter.

Andrea hated that she had allowed her shock at seeing her ex entering the prenatal department, with his new wife and her perfect womb, to influence her decision. It was strange how talking to Seth had somehow eased the torment and had made her realise that seeing them had been like scraping a scab off an old wound—it would soon heal again.

It had been fourteen months since her devastating miscarriage. Fourteen months since her marriage had ended. But whilst Josh had been able to walk away to start a new life with someone else—sprint, actually!—she was still left behind, trying to come to terms with everything the doctors had told her. Trying to reimagine her life now that she knew that family, children, weren't going to be a part of it.

And she had reimagined it. Perhaps she wouldn't be a mother, but she could be the best aunt her nieces and nephews could ever hope for. She could be the best scrub nurse. And knowing that someone like Seth believed she could make a great doctor was an unexpected ego boost.

None of which took away the initial shock of seeing Josh walk into that prenatal department. But she'd be fine now that she was beginning to get her head around it.

Perhaps she ought to take a leaf out of Seth's book. Not from the part of the wild and untameable reputation, but from the way he was married to his career.

'I was thinking about your suggestion yesterday,' she

heard herself say before she could bottle it and change her mind. 'Career-wise.'

No need for the entire OR to know the ins and outs—they'd likely assume she simply meant a specialist course or something similar.

'You've given it some thought?' Seth asked approvingly, dropping his eyes back to the surgery.

'I have. Actually, it's an idea I've already contemplated before,' she admitted, though she wasn't about to tell him of her foolish childhood dreams. 'But I've given it more careful consideration since our last conversation and I realise that it isn't possible for me at this time.'

Quiet, assured, final…as if it wasn't like a fist twisting in her chest.

Seth, however, wasn't buying it.

'I believe it's entirely possible, though it will take hard work and dedication. I didn't think you were afraid of that.'

'Of course not.' She scrunched up her face crossly beneath her mask. 'But I'm not in a position to afford the associated costs, not least the part-time element. All the same, I'm grateful for the vote of confidence.'

He was right about the fact she could work for the first three years, but it would only be part-time work to allow for part-time study. The final two years would require her to join a main medical degree course, which meant it simply wasn't feasible.

Seth lifted his head again, frowning.

'It would be an investment in your future,' he pointed out. 'Given you have no family, save for nieces and nephews, what better time to do it?'

She thought about her mother and the money they had been saving to try to move into a new home—one that would be more wheelchair-friendly for the periods when the unpredictable disease that was MS took its toll.

For two decades after the initial diagnosis, her mother

hadn't needed a wheelchair. In fact, she'd abhorred the idea of ever becoming the one in three MS suffers who ended up needing one. But the past six years had been harder, with the bad days having more impact, and Andrea knew her mother now needed a home that was more suited to those periods. A place that had lower light switches, wider doorways, a shower that could take a specialised wheelchair when necessary and maybe a kitchen that had a lower worktop, as well as a regular-height one, for days when her mum couldn't cook standing up,.

Dropping back to part-time work, with a corresponding reduction in pay, simply wasn't possible.

But neither Seth nor anyone else needed to know her private business.

'I have...other demands on my time.'

She fought not to squirm as he lifted his eyes to fix her with a dark, unreadable expression.

'We'll continue this discussion this afternoon,' he asserted in a tone that brooked no argument. 'I have a clinic after this surgery, but I should be finished by four. I'll see you in my consultation room after that.'

Andrea didn't care to analyse what it said about her that she didn't object. She simply nodded once and returned to the surgery.

CHAPTER FOUR

ANDREA SHIFTED UNCOMFORTABLY in the unusually deserted reception area for Seth's clinic, trying to tell herself that she didn't still feel odd, jittery, at speaking to him about her future.

It was as though she'd be letting herself down in his eyes by not being more ambitious. By not grasping with tight fists the opportunity he was offering. She hated the idea that he might begin to think less of her for turning down the chance to become a doctor.

But what could she do, short of telling him about her mum's situation? And that wasn't a secret she was prepared to share—even with Seth. *Especially* with Seth. What was it that was making him get under her skin so much at the moment?

She'd always been aware of him, of course—attracted to him. But lusting after a man—however scorching-hot he might be—was definitely not her style. So why was she sitting here, waiting for him to finish his last consultation in the next room, her hand on her chest, as though that could somehow slow her wildly racing heart?

Andrea was so caught up in her thoughts that she leapt like a scalded cat when the door behind her swished open.

'Joyce.' She greeted Seth's long-time secretary with a

bright smile then stopped at the sight of a little boy being ushered in front of the older woman.

In all the time she'd worked at Baystone, no one had ever even known that Seth had a sister let alone a nephew. Yet today she'd not only bumped into Seth outside the primary school, but the child was here now. The only rational explanation was that Seth's sister was unwell and he was stepping in.

As if the man could get any more noble.

Habit from being with her own extended family made her smile brightly at the boy, who she estimated to be about five or six years old.

'And you must be Noah. Hello.'

The child didn't even look at her, but instead edged around Joyce and made his way to the furthest corner of the room, sitting down and taking a book from his backpack that Andrea recognised as her own nephew's favourite *Space Kids* easy-reading series.

'He's shy,' Joyce informed her quietly with her usual aplomb. 'But I'm afraid Mr Mulder is in with a patient.'

Was it her imagination, or did the secretary look uncharacteristically uncomfortable beneath the practised veneer?

'I know.' Andrea shook off the notion. 'He asked me to stop by after his clinic. It's work-related.'

Of course it was work-related. Why had she felt the need to explain? Joyce, however, didn't appear to notice. Her gaze momentarily slid back to the child.

'Perhaps...today isn't the best day after all.'

She didn't say anything more. She didn't have to. Clearly something was going on with Seth's sister or else Noah wouldn't be here. There was no way Seth would otherwise have allowed his personal life to cross over into his work.

'No problem.' Andrea nodded. 'I'll speak to him tomorrow. You'll tell him I was here, though?'

'Of course.' Joyce offered a half-smile that looked suspiciously like relief.

Bending down to sort out her belongings, Andrea was just packing her bag when the door to Seth's consultation room opened and both he and his last patient emerged. As the patient hurried out of the opposite door into the main reception area, Andrea watched Seth's glance sweep from her to his nephew, then to his secretary.

'I was just leaving,' she managed—somewhat lamely, in her own opinion.

But Seth wasn't listening.

'Did you find out what happened?' he demanded quietly, his voice too low for his apparently absorbed nephew to hear.

'I managed to get through to the agency,' Joyce told him. 'Apparently the new nanny who was to start today and collect him from school had a family emergency.'

'A family emergency?' There was no missing Seth's fury even if he was valiantly restrained. 'You made it clear that he's suffering from trauma-induced selective mutism brought on by the death of his mother? He needs stability, not family emergencies.'

Trauma-induced selective mutism?

Even as she tried desperately not to listen, Andrea couldn't help but pick up the little titbit. It seemed to slam into her head, bringing with it a host of dusty memories. She lowered her bag on the chair and straightened up.

'I made that perfectly clear,' Joyce confirmed, her tone making it clear exactly what she thought about the nanny's behaviour. 'Noah's head teacher was good enough to bring him, given the circumstances, and knowing you would likely be in surgery. I took it upon myself to take us both to the canteen to buy a snack.'

Andrea watched as Joyce laid out a variety of choices

on the table, from an apple and a banana to kids' crisps, little cartons of sugar-free juice and a small bottle of water.

'He couldn't tell me what he wanted so I got a selection,' she continued lightly, though Andrea knew her well enough to hear the hint of concern in her tone.

'Thank you,' Seth murmured before lifting his voice and injecting it with a cheerier note. 'Noah, do you want to choose a snack?'

The two of them smiled kindly at the young boy who raised his head, stared at them for moment then returned his gaze to his book.

Andrea couldn't help noticing the teddy bear practically held in a death grip in his tiny hands.

It was all there—from that shuttered expression to the stance, to the clutched toy. And something else that she couldn't have articulated but which was so familiar to her all the same. To all intents and purposes, he might as well have been her own brother, Daniel, when he had been about the same age.

'Noah, you need to choose now, please.'

Seth picked up the selection and crossed the room to kneel down directly in front of his nephew, his voice gruff but slightly softer than usual, as though he wasn't entirely sure of himself.

It took Andrea by surprise. She'd never thought of Seth Mulder that way before. He was a neurosurgeon, but that didn't mean he had any experience of what it was like to manage a young child who refused to talk.

Then again, just because she'd dealt with her brother two decades ago didn't mean she knew how to do so either. So why did she feel the need to at least try?

Instead, she held her counsel as the boy stared helplessly at the snacks for several paralysed moments. His hand twitched, as though part of him was desperate to reach out for something but he just couldn't bring himself to do so. Then, he looked as his teddy bear, as if for support. Finally, he shifted to the next chair, clutching the soft toy to him and staring at his knees. It was all heartbreakingly familiar to Andrea.

With a deep inhalation of breath, Seth let the boy go and slowly returned to the reception desk.

'Did he ask for anything at all?' he murmured, turning his back to the room so that his nephew wouldn't hear.

Joyce followed suit.

'Not a word,' the older woman confirmed regretfully. 'Just as you said.'

He nodded slowly, though his tight shoulders suggested to Andrea that he felt a lot more frustrated than he was prepared to let on—his infamous control at play, it seemed.

'I'd be grateful if you'd contact the nanny agency and advise them that their services will no longer be required,' he said through gritted teeth. 'I understand there were family circumstances, but Noah is six, his mother has just died and I was in surgery.'

'I already took the liberty of doing so. They couldn't apologise enough and asked me to pass on my assurance that a similar incidence will never occur again.'

'It will not,' Seth bit out. 'As they will not be given the chance to do so. I shall make other arrangements.'

'I assumed as much,'

Another curt dip of the head.

'I can look into after-school care if you like?' offered Joyce.

'Yes,' he answered after a moment. 'Thank you.'

Feeling as though she was eavesdropping, Andrea moved away, not realising she was instinctively travelling in the direction of the little boy until she found herself on the row of chairs next to him. She stayed a couple of seats away, not too close, certainly not crowding him.

She looked around for something that she hoped might

help her to communicate with the little boy—something that would allow for non-verbal communication, which had always been the first step with Daniel. Her gaze settled on a wooden alphabet abacus that sat nestled amongst the small offering of children's toys. It was almost the perfect prop. A final glance across the room assured her that neither Seth nor Joyce was paying attention to her.

Andrea picked up a doll, the perfect toy to mirror Noah's teddy bear, and pretended to stand the toy in front of the abacus, the plastic hand spinning the blocks.

'Hmm,' she murmured, as if to herself or the doll. 'A is for apple, B is for banana, C is for car...but I'd prefer it to be for crisps, wouldn't you, Dolly? And we could pretend that R is for raisins rather than rabbits.'

She spun the B block around a few times until stopping it on the letter rather than the picture.

'I guess you like bananas, huh, Dolly? I wonder what Teddy Bear likes.'

And then Andrea found herself actually holding her breath, just praying that it could work.

For the longest time—which was probably only a minute, but it felt like a century—Noah didn't move. But then, suddenly, a tiny hand gripping the teddy's furry paw reached forward and spun the R block. Her insides flip-flopped and it was all she could do to keep her voice even.

'Raisins, huh, Teddy? That's a great choice.' She deliberately didn't address the little boy but kept her focus on the toys. 'Okay, what do you say, Dolly? J for juice, and W for water?'

The hesitation was shorter this time, and then the furry paw spun the letter J.

'Oh, yes. Another great choice.'

Slowly, carefully, she reached her hand down to push herself back into a standing position to head for the desk.

But, before she could do so, Seth stepped forward and silently passed her the snacks.

For a moment, his eyes locked with hers and her stomach flip-flopped all over again and then he stepped back to the desk. But this time she could feel two pairs of eyes on her. She straightened her shoulders, as if to shake off the additional pressure.

'Raisins and juice for you, Teddy,' she said airily, carefully sliding the snacks to Noah's side. 'And banana and water for you, Dolly.'

The little boy lifted his hand, paused then carefully reached for his snacks. A few moments later he tilted his head so that, whilst he was not exactly looking at her, he could see her. He paused with apparent uncertainty and the cogs in Andrea's brain began to spin. She was all too aware of Seth's gaze still on her, watching her with Noah. Was the little boy hesitating because she wasn't eating her snacks? It certainly seemed like it. Sitting the doll in front of her, she crossed her legs and began to peel a banana.

'Shall we eat, Dolly?' she murmured before taking a bite.

A moment later, Noah took the bag of raisins, opened it, proceeded to take a raisin and offered it to Teddy before putting it in his own mouth. Then another. Then another. Then he took the carton of juice, pulled off the straw and slid them nervously across the floor to her.

Without missing a beat, Andrea unwrapped the straw and pushed it gently through the hole in the carton before gently pushing it back to the little boy.

'Thank you,' he whispered, in a voice so painfully quiet that she had no idea whether Seth had heard.

If he had, would he be pleased or not? She had no way of knowing that. So long as Noah was happier, she would stand up to anything his uncle might have to say to her.

For the next few minutes, Andrea sat in companionable silence with the little boy as they each enjoyed their snacks. Briefly she considered trying to get him to talk again but quickly decided against it. Patience was the key. It had taken months with her brother. For every five steps forward, they had seemed to take two back, and pushing him too far too fast had never seemed to work. Better to stop now whilst Noah was experiencing a confidence boost without feeling under pressure.

A fluttering movement by the desk caught her attention and she looked up to see Seth beckoning her, a grim expression on his face. It was hardly engaging, and she was almost tempted to ignore him. But at the last moment she thought better of it.

'That was lovely, Dolly,' she announced, picking up a banana peel. 'I've really enjoyed spending this time with you, Teddy and Noah but I have to go now. I trust you to look after my new friends.'

With that, she carefully got to her feet and moved across the room, not surprised when Seth inclined his head to summon her to follow him into his consultation room.

She was barely into the room before Seth spoke, closing the door behind them.

'How the hell did you do that?' he demanded, his tone a careful balance of both relief and frustration.

Andrea bit her lip, wondering how little she could get away with telling.

'Luck,' she offered awkwardly. 'And perhaps a little experience.'

'Well, it's experience I don't have,' he ground out angrily. But there was no question that his anger was directed at himself rather than her. 'I've spent the past month trying.'

'It can take months,' she reassured him. 'Sometimes it can take years.'

He shook his head.

'It took you minutes,' he pointed out.

'I got lucky,' she repeated. 'It could easily not have worked at all.'

'But it did. I need you to teach me how you did it.'

Something kicked low in her gut. Seth wanted *her* to teach *him*?

He, who was usually the one teaching everyone else, the one pushing the proverbial envelope, now wanted her help? Suddenly, he was looking to her for guidance?

The tiny hairs on the back of her neck pricked up. What if she couldn't help him? No two children were precisely the same so there was no guarantee that what had worked for her brother would work for Noah. What if she made things worse?

Except that she hadn't made it worse just now, had she? She'd actually managed to help the little boy and that felt ridiculously good—especially when she remembered all the fear and frustration she and her mother had felt when they'd spent months trying to feel their way to helping Daniel.

But it didn't necessarily follow that just because she'd managed to connect with Seth's nephew today she would be able to do so tomorrow. Or the day after. If he suddenly decided he didn't want to communicate through his teddy any longer, then what?

Still, at least she had some kind of idea how this all felt. What she would have given, almost twenty years ago now, to be able to talk things over with someone who had even a little experience with selective mutism. Perhaps she could be that person for Seth, even just acting as his sounding board. The idea made it feel as though the balance was subtly shifting between them.

And Andrea wasn't entirely sure how she felt about that at all.

CHAPTER FIVE

THERE WAS AN incommodious buzzing inside Seth's head that he simply could not get rid of—worse than any bothersome mosquito—and it was stopping him from thinking straight.

Or thinking at all, quite frankly.

How had Andrea achieved in ten minutes what he had been wholly unable to achieve in ten days? More to the point, how had she made it look so damned easy?

He ought to feel more grateful to Andrea, and he did. But he wasn't sure that this thing that sloshed inside him was solely comprised of gratitude. He was supposed to be a neurosurgeon who understood the mechanics of the brain, yet he'd been entirely incapable of making some kind of connection with his own nephew, wheareas his quiet colleague had come along, sat down next to the kid and managed just that.

It was incomprehensible, galling, and humbling. It also felt as though a burden, as heavy as the weight of Atlas carrying the heavens themselves, had just been lifted from his shoulders.

Noah had communicated which, to Seth, meant that his own ineptitude this past month hadn't damaged the little boy the way he'd feared he might have. His gruff ways clearly hadn't encouraged his nephew to want to connect with him. Ironic, since he had often managed to connect with a paediatric patient who had been distancing them self from their own parents.

But now—thanks to Andrea—he knew that Noah was ready to communicate. He just had to learn how. He *would* learn. For his late sister's sake, as well as the boy's.

Yet Seth couldn't help wishing that he could learn from someone less…damned appealing than Andrea Perkins. He'd spent the past few months convincing himself he didn't feel some inexplicable pull of attraction to the scrub nurse.

He would have kicked himself for such misplaced pride, yet even now he could still vividly recall the fizz of chemistry that had arced between them that morning during their unexpected encounter outside the primary school. It was as though being away from the usual environs of the hospital had blurred all his usual lines.

And now, alone in his office, he could practically feel it vibrating around him, inside him. Getting louder and more insistent the longer he remained in such proximity to Andrea. He couldn't even remember having rounded the desk to stand right in front of her, but here he was, blood roaring through him, pooling where it certainly shouldn't be.

With more effort than it rightfully should have required, Seth forced his brain to focus on reminding himself why he had brought her here to his office—or how she had managed to forge that connection with his nephew so quickly.

She'd looked horrified when he'd demanded that she teach him whatever it was she'd just managed to do with his nephew. He wasn't sure he could blame her—he was hardly being gracious about the whole incident. But she still hadn't answered his last question, so Seth gritted his teeth, forced his voice to something less commanding and repeated it.

'Will you teach me how you did that?'

Andrea wrinkled her nose in that awkward yet appealing way of hers.

'I want to help,' she told him. 'I do. But I'm not a speech therapist. They're properly trained allied health and medical care professionals.'

'I know what they are,' he ground out. 'But I've just watched you coax the child into communicating with you, even speaking to you within minutes of meeting him— which is more than the speech and language therapist he's been seeing has managed. I want to understand how.'

Andrea chewed her lip and stared at him. He got the impression she was trying to decide what to say.

'It was just an old trick I once knew,' she hedged. 'I thought it was worth giving it a go, so I tried it. It could have just as easily not worked.'

'But it did work,' he countered, not about to be put off so easily. 'You clearly have some experience in this field, whilst I have none. I need your help.'

Did she have any idea what it cost him to admit that?

Not that in his professional life he'd ever had any problem calling in fellow surgeons to assist in surgeries that included elements from other specialist fields. But Noah was his nephew—not a patient.

'I do want to help.' Andrea dipped her head at last, even as she folded her arms across her chest in a tell-tale defensive response. 'But, like I said, I'm not a speech therapist so I'm not qualified to teach you anything. If I end up making things worse...'

The sheer futility of it all suddenly tumbled through him. Taking a step back, Seth raked his hand through his hair.

'I don't know that it can be any worse; you saw how it is with the child. I shouldn't be putting you under pressure, and I apologise for that, but it has been like that ever since...'

'Ever since his mother died,' she finished when he

stopped abruptly. 'I overheard you talking to Joyce. I'm so sorry for your loss.'

He didn't miss the micro expression that touched her expressive eyes and instantly found himself hungry to understand it.

'You lost someone too?' he asked abruptly. 'That's how you knew what to say and do with my nephew.'

Her expressive violet-blue eyes glinted, but this time he couldn't afford to be distracted by them. He lifted one shoulder.

'I make no apology for wanting to do whatever I can to help that child out there.'

Her expression flickered again.

'Perhaps you should stop calling him "that child" for a start,' she suggested pointedly.

He probably should... Seth dipped his head in acknowledgement.

'You're right,' he acknowledged. *'Noah.'*

'And his mum...?'

'My sister died last month,' he finished for her as something punched deep in his chest. Seth ignored it.

He'd spent his entire career dealing with patients whose lives hung in the balance. But it had taken Stacey's death for him to begin to realise that life might be shorter than he'd ever appreciated.

The irony didn't go over his head.

'Right,' Andrea managed carefully. 'And, given your unexpected sabbatical the past few weeks, I'm guessing you're now Noah's legal guardian?'

Seth thought about the brutal custody hearing he'd attended only a few days before. The next one was due in less than a week. A part of him argued that it wasn't Andrea's business—aside from Jack and his secretary, no one else knew—but instead he heard himself answering.

'Stacey named me as her son's legal guardian in her

will. His father hasn't had anything to do with him since the pregnancy.' He paused again as something new flashed through Andrea's eyes, but the tight expression which swiftly followed deterred him from asking. Seth chose to concentrate on his nephew's story instead.

'However, his paternal grandparents are fighting me for custody.'

'Will they get it, given the history?' Andrea asked.

Seth balled a fist at his side.

'The fact that Noah refuses to talk to anyone—or had been refusing, up until five minutes ago—isn't particularly helping my case.'

Nor was the fact that, save for the obligatory visits at Christmas and birthdays, and the occasional weekends, he hadn't seen as much of his sister or nephew as he should have since Stacey had moved out of his penthouse and into her own modest apartment four-and-a-half years earlier.

Andrea looked unconvinced.

'Surely, if Noah hasn't been talking to anyone, then that would help or hinder both parties in exactly the same way?' she asked, though her tone was gentler now.

'They're claiming that they've never had the opportunity to build a relationship with Noah, whilst I have. And that if the boy trusted me then he wouldn't now be choosing not to communicate.'

Though he tried to keep his tone even and remain factual, it was impossible to keep the regret from threading around his words.

Andrea shook her head.

'It doesn't necessarily work that way. Trauma-related selective mutism is more complex than that. That's assuming that Noah's mutism began as a consequence of his mother's death?'

'Noah is the one who found her. She'd died in her sleep.' Seth clenched his teeth, every word tasting acrid in his mouth. 'An undiagnosed heart condition, of all things. I don't know how, but he had the presence of mind to call 999.'

Andrea made a soft, sympathetic sound.

'That would have certainly been traumatic,' Andrea acknowledged sympathetically, her hand reaching out automatically, as if to touch his arm, before catching herself and dropping it again.

He'd never before realised it was possible to lament the loss of something one had never had. But he shook it off.

'And there hadn't been any problems before that?'

Seth shook his head.

'Noah was a brilliant baby, and my sister was wonderful with him. He was her world. Even the teachers at his former primary school report that he was a bright, friendly, talkative little boy right up until...'

'I understand.' She nodded softly when he didn't finish, though he wondered how it was so hard for him to say words he had to say every day.

It was as though telling Andrea would somehow make him *feel* his sister's death more intensely. As if Andrea somehow made his guard drop a little.

Absurd.

'And I appreciate that bringing Noah here, an hour away from his old home, may not be ideal. But I've been staying in my sister's home for the past few weeks, and Noah didn't communicate there either. Ultimately I'm a surgeon here at Baystone Medical, and I have patients and responsibilities that I can't simply drop.'

'I understand that too,' Andrea said quietly. 'I was eight when my father died in a car crash. My younger brother was seven. Dad had gone out to retrieve Daniel's wooden toy sword and shield that had been left out in the rain. A drugged driver crashed into him. Despite the fact that we were a loving, close family who had always hugged, talked and laughed a lot, Daniel developed selective mutism. We didn't move house, he didn't have to change school and I know he still loved us—but it was just his way of coping.'

'I see.' Her unexpected confession had caught him off-guard, and he was both grateful and surprised that she trusted him enough to tell him. 'Can I ask how long it lasted—the lack of communication?'

'The lack of verbal communication lasted five months but we did manage non-verbal communication. Plus, our situation had additional...complications.'

'Complications?' he echoed, but she was already shaking her hand dismissively.

'My mother wasn't well, but that isn't relevant to your and Noah's situation. The point is, from what I've seen today, and in my limited experience, I think Noah wants to talk. He's just trying to make sense of whatever it is he saw, and I think it's likely he needs you to help him.'

'I have no idea how to do that.' Seth exhaled harshly, angry with himself for his apparent inability to help his nephew.

'You'll learn.' She shrugged. 'You'll feel your way. Though, for what it's worth—and I appreciate you have responsibilities as a surgeon—long days of surgeries aren't going to help Noah right now.'

'I realise that.'

'So can you cut them back?'

Seth eyed her for a moment.

'I don't think I've ever seen you be quite so blunt, Andrea.'

She had the grace to flush a little—a pretty colour that tiptoed over her smooth cheeks and down the elegant line of her neck. Not that he should be noticing.

Even so, she clearly wasn't about to relent.

'So,' she prompted. 'Can you?'

'I've already instructed Joyce to reduce my case load

and try to keep it to more of a seven-to-seven, Monday to Friday. Fortunately, the board are supportive and are bringing in a new surgeon to take up the slack.'

It felt odd, of course. For over a decade, he'd put his career first—ahead of anything or anyone else. But right now his nephew needed him and Seth was prepared to do whatever it took to give Noah what he needed.

Including, he decided in that moment, convincing Andrea to help him reach the little boy.

Whatever it took.

Something had changed. Andrea couldn't be sure what it was, but she felt it. A shift in the room and Seth's shrewd, assessing stare on her, rooting her to the spot. It was so penetrating that she feared he might see through all her bravado—the carefully constructed veil of confidence that she had spent years piecing together, even before her ex's betrayal—to the imperfect individual she'd always felt herself to be, complete with all her shortcomings.

It was the craziest sensation. And beneath it all that current of awareness still lapped around her.

Somehow, *somehow*, she managed to speak.

'So the nanny I heard you mention to Joyce was supposed to cover either side of the day, before and after school?'

The look of disdain was unmistakable.

'Indeed. But after today's shambles I wouldn't ever trust them again,' he bit out, his expression grim. 'Either way, it's being dealt with.'

His protectiveness of his nephew caused a delicious shiver to ripple through Andrea—one she wasn't remotely prepared for. She'd never thought of Seth Mulder as a family man—she doubted many people ever had—but the image was a dangerously seductive one.

She shoved it from her mind.

'You seem to be doing all the right things, although I

don't believe there's any one single solution. You just sort of have to feel your way. Like your surgeries, I guess.'

'Except that in my surgeries I at least have an idea of what I'm doing.' Seth blew out.

'Only because you've learned.' She offered a half-smile. 'And you'll learn with your nephew.'

'And with your help.'

Andrea halted briefly.

'I told you, I'm not qualified in this. And no two individuals are the same. What worked for my brother won't necessarily work for Noah.'

She wished Seth's gaze didn't skewer her quite so much.

'I don't care how unqualified you declare yourself to be,' he answered simply. 'I want you to teach me. Because whatever you did just now worked. Noah talked.'

Andrea wrinkled her nose, hating herself for that swell of pride at Seth's words. She reined herself in.

'I'd hardly say *talk*,' she cautioned. 'And if I'd pushed him to say more then I think he would have clammed up again. But the first thing I tried was talking to him without putting him on the spot. So I didn't ask him anything directly, instead I started up a conversation with a prop— the doll—in order to let him know that I was happy with a one-sided conversation and he didn't have to answer me.'

'Yes, but how did you know that would work?'

'I didn't know for sure.' She shrugged. 'I just saw the way he clutched his teddy bear in front of him, as though he was using it to protect himself. And it was so like what my brother used to do that I took a chance.'

'Okay, but then you still asked him what snack he wanted,' Seth pressed. 'Just like I did.'

She squinted, thinking back to what she'd done. It had all been so instinctive, so organic, that it was hard to remember things precisely. Plus, it was strange, being the one teaching Seth for a change.

But strange in a good way, not a bad one. Or was that her pride again?

'I took a chance using the wooden alphabet abacus as another prop,' she explained. 'Noah might not have liked letters, or he might not have been good at phonics, but I was just showing him that I was happy to accept non-verbal communication. Joyce tried it too, when she laid out the snacks and invited Noah to choose one, or just point at what he liked.'

'He didn't choose anything with her,' Seth pointed out, his frustration evident.

'But he might have. Instead, in this instance, Noah became overwhelmed and took himself off to the corner. I just thought that playing a game by spinning the blocks might introduce a little more fun, or at least enough of a distraction.'

'And you kept talking to the doll, instead of him, so that he didn't feel under pressure.' Seth realised this abruptly. 'But when we put the snacks on the counter all three of us were watching him.'

'Right.'

Seth was beginning to understand already. She really shouldn't be surprised. His ability to learn and adapt was what made him such a good surgeon.

'So what else would you suggest I do to help him feel less overwhelmed?'

'I don't know, I'm not...' she began, catching herself when she saw his expression. 'With Daniel, we tried to give him something fun to focus on whilst we tried to reconnect—taking him to the playground, going on a nature walk. The primary school has a new jungle gym that my nieces and nephew are going crazy over; do you know if Noah likes it?'

'I don't know,' Seth admitted, his jaw locking tightly. 'Why?'

He was so accustomed to having all the answers; this had to be galling for him.

'There's a soft play centre and climbing wall about twenty minutes away,' she told him. 'I thought maybe you could take Noah.'

'I guess.' He looked thoughtful. 'I seem to recall my sister saying he used to love climbing this huge, ten-foot-high sandstone rock in their local park. She used to say her heart was always in her mouth even as she encouraged him to be bold and confident.'

'Well, there you go.' Relief pulsed through Andrea. 'Just like my nieces and my nephew. And they all love going to the local play centre. I could ask my sister-in-law if she wants me to give her a few hours' break tonight.'

'Tonight?' Seth hardly looked eager.

She thought about the little boy in the room down the hall and steeled herself.

'No time like the present, surely?' she pressed, reminding herself that this wasn't about her inconvenient attraction to this man. It was about helping a young boy who was going through the same thing her brother had once gone through. 'I was heading to their house tonight anyway for a couple of hours; I'm fairly confident she'll say yes. Though, if it's too far out of your comfort zone...?'

'It isn't exactly appealing,' he admitted wryly.

All at once, unwanted images of Seth on hot dates assailed her.

'No, I imagine it's nothing like your usual nights of glamorous dates at exclusive restaurants.'

She could tell he didn't like that, though he didn't deny it. Still, why she was deliberately goading him was anybody's guess. Apparently she'd developed some kind of death wish.

'I just don't want them to think Noah is too much hard work and ignore him,' Seth ground out at length. 'Won't that isolate him all the more?'

Laughter instantly bubbled up inside her as she thought of Daniel's and Julia's wonderfully crazy brood.

'That lot play with everyone!' She chuckled. 'They couldn't ignore someone if they tried. They're full of confidence—*swagger,* my brother and his wife call it. And I'll make a point of telling them that Noah needs them to look out for him.'

Seth still looked dubious.

'You're sure that will help Noah?'

'No, I'm not sure.' She shook her head, determined to be honest. 'It's just an idea. It might work, it might not. So it's up to you.'

'Right.'

Andrea waited a moment as he seemed to weigh things up; she couldn't have said why she was holding her breath. This was about a six-year-old boy, not about Seth choosing to spend an evening with her instead of on a date with some model.

'Have you ever been to anything like it before?' she asked curiously, though she was fairly sure that she already knew the answer.

But, a moment later, he surprised her.

'Once,' he said. 'Three or four years ago, with Noah and my sister. It was full of screaming kids.'

She couldn't stop herself from laughing at his unimpressed expression.

'Yes, well, that's sort of the point.'

At least he had the grace to look abashed.

'I suppose that's true.'

She didn't know why this chagrined, uncertain Uncle Seth was just as damned sexy as the self-assured surgeon Seth who had caught her from stumbling outside the school that morning.

'So you know where it is?'

'I think I can remember.'

She couldn't work out if he was being genuine or if

there'd been a little bit of sarcasm in his voice. She erred on the side of genuine, though she suspected the latter.

'If you give me your mobile, I'll input my number, just in case you get lost.'

'You're too kind.'

This time there was definite dryness. She resolutely ignored it.

'Do you want to ask Noah if he wants to go?'

'Ask Noah?' His brows knitted and once again Andrea found herself trying to ignore her body's sudden reaction as his gaze washed over her, just like before.

'Tell him where you're thinking of going and give him the choice of whether he wants to do that or not.'

Seth blew out another breath.

'I don't know how to give him the choice. If I ask him what he wants to do, he doesn't answer me. But if I tell him where we're going, he just obeys.'

'Right.' She nodded slowly.

'I'd ask him if he would answer.'

There was a hint of uncharacteristic defensiveness in his tone, which was perhaps understandable, but Andrea decided the best way to deal with that was simply to ignore it.

'Well, you could just tell him where we're going and bring him along, then allow him to join in or not when he's there. Or we could try asking him.'

She stopped abruptly. There was an idea in the back of her head but it wasn't fully formed.

Seth eyed her curiously.

'What would you have done had it been your brother?' he demanded, as though reading her thoughts.

She pursed her lips, wondering at the wisdom of treating Noah exactly as she might have treated her brother.

'It's worth a try, you said,' Seth reminded her quietly, and she nodded slowly.

'Sometimes Mum and I would come up with a plan together and then we'd deliberately discuss it in front of Daniel. He'd usually find a way of conveying to us whether he wanted to go or not.'

'How?'

She offered an apologetic shrug.

'It varied. But he'd find a way if it mattered to him.'

Seth bobbed his head, his brain clearly working overtime. For several long moments they stood in silence, the only sounds coming from the sprawling park beyond his office window.

'Okay, let's give it a try,' he decided at last. 'I'll follow your lead.'

She was reminded again how somehow they seemed to have switched roles, with her the teacher and Seth the student. And Andrea wondered what she was to make of the fact that his quiet vote of confidence had done more to boost her self-esteem than anything else in a long time.

CHAPTER SIX

RELAX, SETH TOLD himself less than forty minutes later as he watched the play area from his chipped, once-glossy table—his back ramrod-straight in the uncomfortable, plastic bucket-chair.

Relaxing was easy to say, not nearly as easy to do.

He gripped the off-white mug, more for something to hold than actually wanting the drink. A glance around the other parents, all happy and at ease, should have helped, but it didn't. He wasn't exactly a *parent*, and he just felt tense and out of his depth. Certainly not sensations he was accustomed to.

He ought to be able to take comfort from the fact that Andrea had been right about Noah communicating his desire to come. They'd been talking to Joyce—Andrea had done most of the talking, of course, casually but deliberately discussing her nieces and nephews and how much they loved this place. Then she'd appeared to speculate as to whether Noah might want to join and the little boy had stood up and walked over. Without a word, he'd handed the doll to Andrea then slipped his hand into hers—his teddy bear clutched tightly in his other hand.

It was all Seth had needed to convince himself that Andrea was one person he needed—no, his young nephew needed—right now.

So here they were at the local kids' soft play centre, his muscular supercar surprisingly not incongruous, parked amongst some expensive saloon cars and four-by-fours out in the car park. Noah, Andrea, her five-year-old twin nieces and her seven-year-old nephew were all somewhere in the mayhem of climbing frames, rope ladders and clear plastic tunnels, with a four-metre-wide and two-storey-high bumpy slide running through the middle.

The smell of cooking chips and freeze-dried coffee assailed his olfactory senses, whilst his ears were ringing from the ceaseless shouts and screams. It should have felt like hell to him.

It *did* feel like hell.

'Wishing you were somewhere else?' Andrea's amused voice cut into his thoughts. 'Like on some dazzling date?'

He turned his head to deny it, then caught her eye and felt a wry smile tug at his mouth.

'A date? No,' he heard himself admit. 'Though maybe a surgery.'

'I should have known!' She laughed and rolled her eyes, and something startling tiptoed warmly through him. 'I told you that you should have had a go on the long slide. It's quite good fun.'

'I'm not sure the equipment could take my weight,' he replied evenly, as if that was the only thing that would stop him.

Andrea glanced around the vast space.

'You're probably right, this place is built for kids. Or for adults like me who have never grown up.'

But, though she tried to hide it, there was an edge to her tone that he thought was revealing. It made him think back over things she'd already told him, his brain trying to piece it together, wanting to understand her better.

He was no longer able to squash his curiosity the way he'd been able to when they'd been merely colleagues.

Though did that mean that they were more than colleagues now? Could one evening of her helping him with his nephew constitute a friendship?

More to the point, why did he want it to do so?

And still his mind whirred. Now he knew about her father's death when she'd been eight, and her brother's time suffering from selective mutism, Seth couldn't help but wonder if that had made her grow up too soon. It would explain that deeply serious side to Andrea which didn't quite match most of her Baystone colleagues.

Yet tonight he realised she had a surprisingly fun side too, which the women he dated usually didn't. At least, not in this pure, uncorrupted way. Their kind of fun was usually had in bed.

Too late, Seth realised his mistake. Putting together images of Andrea and thoughts of sex was a huge blunder. It set off a chain reaction in his body that he felt was wholly inappropriate. Yet, even as he castigated himself for his lack of self-control—reminding himself that she was his *scrub nurse*, for pity's sake—he found his gaze being drawn back across the table. Drawn to those expressive eyes and that all-too-inviting mouth; to the long, blonde curl of ponytail that danced on her shoulder, and the hint of a swell of flesh that disappeared beneath her simple tee.

A far cry from the bland tunic uniform she wore for work. Even now, her legs, encased in plain blue jeans, she seemed to speak to him in a way that was far more primitive than the women he'd known who dressed in the shortest skirts or poured themselves into the most plunging, figure-hugging evening gowns.

He needed to regain control. Damn it but this wasn't about him or the greed that this woman awakened in him, licking at his sex.

'Seth?'

Snapping back to the present, he realised the object of

his unseemly thoughts had been speaking to him and was now eyeing him strangely.

'Sorry?' he rasped.

'I was saying that there is a climbing wall for adults over that barrier behind you, if that's more your speed. It's designed for older children, or for parents and guardians to have something to do whilst their kids are playing.'

Blinking, he turned his chair to look.

'I do enjoy climbing,' he managed.

'I know. Jack has often mentioned the two of you going in the past. I've tried a little wall, but not roped up, and not one that high.'

'It's good fun,' he admitted, not mentioning that, at about twenty metres, the wall didn't look that high to him—not compared to the rock faces he usually scaled. 'It's rewarding, reaching the top after a challenging climb. I've missed it this past month.'

'Come on, then.' She stood abruptly. 'Let's have a go instead of sitting around here being ignored by our lot. We'll tell them where we are and we'll go right there, just over the barrier, so no more than four metres from where we are now. They can easily get our attention if they need us. I know that's what my brother does when he comes, hence why they picked this table.'

Her grin was infectious and Seth was almost tempted. When had any date of his ever wanted to do something more exciting than be taken to the latest hotspot in the city?

Not that this was a *date*, of course.

'And it's safe?'

She waggled her wrist in front of him, complete with electronic tag.

'That's what these are for. The gate is manually operated and no kid is allowed to leave the area without the adult with the corresponding tag.'

It was incredibly tempting, though Seth told himself

it was more about the climb—however tame—than the woman who was currently jiggling her hand in front of him like a big kid herself.

A lot like his sister had been, he realised with a jolt.

Stacey would have liked Andrea.

Seth pulled up short. Not for the first time during these last few weeks, he wished he and his sister hadn't drifted so far apart in the last four years.

Dimly, in the back of his mind, he could recall a conversation he'd with his sister where Stacey had teased him for not knowing much about his date, and he'd shrugged and told her that he knew all he needed to—namely that she'd liked red wine, didn't eat anything apart from salad and was hot in bed.

An unexpected stab of grief pierced him as he recalled the way his sister had rolled her eyes, told him that he was shallow and declared that she couldn't wait for the day when some woman finally cut him off at the knees—or some other, more apt, part of his anatomy.

He'd dismissed her, of course, since that would never have happened. Still, he could imagine Stacey's amusement now if she could see the knack that Andrea Perkins had for getting under his skin.

It was bizarre. Andrea was pretty enough, but nowhere near as glamorous as any of the women he dated. Yet she seemed to get to him in a way that no one ever had before.

Had it always been that way, back in his OR, where he'd smothered the inconvenient attraction beneath all those professional lines he'd always maintained he never crossed?

Now he allowed himself to consider it, it occurred to him that she'd always had a way of making those perfectly groomed, expensively dressed, socially rich women seem plastic and superficial. He'd begun to wonder how he hadn't seen it for himself before.

Thrusting the image aside, Seth strode across to where

Andrea had tracked down the quartet, watching Noah's unconcerned response as she suggested what they were thinking of doing.

It struck him that the little boy actually looked at ease. The closest to happy that Seth had seen ever since that awful moment when Seth had collected him from the solicitor's office.

Another thing that was all down to the ever-surprising Andrea.

This had been a terrible idea.

The realisation crashed through Andrea as she stood stiffly, acutely aware of Seth kneeling down in front of her. Her entirely body felt hot, crackling, *needy.* And all the man was doing was untying the harness around her body and preparing to slide it down her legs and off.

It all felt ludicrously intimate.

He'd been wearing his usual bespoke waistcoat when he'd arrived, which always clung so lovingly to him over his crisp white shirt. It should have made him look ridiculous and out of place, given the location. But of course it didn't. Andrea had even noticed more than a handful of women sending flirtatious looks their way.

The attention had only increased when Seth had decided to give her an impromptu climbing lesson and the waistcoat had come off. He'd even untucked the shirt and rolled up the sleeves to reveal perfect tanned, muscular forearms which had the oddest effect on the butterflies in Andrea's stomach.

'Relax.' His low voice slid through her. 'You did fine. I told you I wouldn't let you fall.'

Except that she feared she had. Not from the wall, but into lust, with a man who was as good as her boss, for pity's sake.

His hand brushed her hip and it was all she could do not

to react visibly. Her humiliation would reach new depths if he realised her reaction was more about him than her nervousness about climbing the wall.

She could feel his hand on her ankle and his touch at her waist, guiding her from hand-holds to foot-holds, catching her so easily when she lost her grip and swung from the vertical face, making sure she never dropped on the rope.

And then the harness was off and he was standing back up, right in front of her. So close that it stole the very breath from her lungs as she lifted her head to look up at him.

'You did really well,' he murmured, his eyes meeting hers and holding them.

Something roared through her, even as she pretended not to be aware of it.

'Thanks. Though not as well as you did when you had to give staff a demonstration that we could climb under our own supervision—suit trousers included. I think they were about to offer you a job here.'

He laughed. But even that sounded like a low, intimate sound.

'I usually climb in jeans,' he rasped. 'And I can't say this would be a bad place to work.'

'You'd miss your surgeries.' She laughed shakily.

'That's true.'

'And your galas and super-yacht parties,' she heard herself tease. 'Your glamorous dates.'

His face grew sombre...more intense...and a sensual shiver rippled through her.

'I've had more fun with you today than I have with anyone in a long time,' he answered suddenly, and she wondered which of them was more shocked at the revelation.

Yet should she really be so taken aback? Hadn't there been brief moments when they'd both seemed to forget where they were and why they were there? And, in those moments, hadn't he'd looked at her in a way that made her feel eaten alive?

A hot flame licked over her at the idea as a deliciously wicked part of her wished that he would do just that. And, once the image was in her brain, she couldn't quite get it to leave. So she stood scant millimetres from him, with her breath lodged somewhere in her chest, feeling utterly hollowed out.

'I'm not sure I can believe that,' she answered at length, in a voice that sounded so husky, so raw, that it took her moments to realise it was her own.

The black, hungry look in Seth's gaze only made the flame burn that little hotter.

'Andrea...' he croaked, his hands lifting to cup her shoulders.

'Andrea... Aunt Andrea.'

With a jolt, Andrea registered the chorus of little voices calling her name. Later, she would wonder how she'd managed to break the delicious contact of Seth's hands on her, but she found herself hurrying to the barrier.

'What is it, is anything wrong?'

'We've lost Bear,' her twin nieces chorused with a level of excitement that only a child could manage.

Automatically, her eyes slid to Seth's, the question in those blue-grey depths mirroring her own.

'Bear?' she asked calmly. 'Do you mean Noah's teddy bear?'

Then, to her shock, a white-faced Noah nodded his head faintly, before speaking quietly but firmly.

'Bearosaurus,'

'You know...like Tyrannosaurus or Stegosaurus?' her nephew piped up enthusiastically. 'It's such a cool name. And it's Bear for short.'

'Bearosaurus...' Seth echoed neutrally, and Andrea

knew only she could read the myriad emotions that tumbled beneath his controlled exterior.

No doubt he was processing the fact that his verbally non-communicative nephew had apparently spoken to her nieces and nephew. Even if only a single name.

But then, her nephew spoke again.

'Noah said that Bear looks after him, so we have to find him. *Now*.'

Andrea didn't think Seth could have looked any more stunned if the ground had shifted sideways and tipped up. But there was no time to dwell on and absorb the revelation, as the two of them shed the rest of their climbing equipment and hurried to the gate into the play area.

A grim expression had pulled Seth's features taut and she didn't need him to tell her he was worried about how it would affect Noah if they couldn't find the teddy bear, the thing that had become the little boy's security blanket since his mother's death.

For the next ten minutes, the group checked every inch of the soft play area, Seth's expression growing ever more ominous as they remained empty-handed. And then, just as it seemed hopeless, Andrea spotted a member of staff walking to the reception desk with the teddy—with *Bear*— in hand.

Ten minutes later, as she gathered up her nieces' coats, Andrea watched as Billy dodged around her to walk next to Noah and proceeded to talk about his own polar bear teddy which he'd made himself at a Build a Bear party a year or so ago.

'Are you okay?' she whispered quietly to Seth as they followed behind.

The disconcerted look he shot her made her wonder if anyone had asked him that in some time. Her stomach flip-flopped for no apparent reason.

'I'm fine,' he replied automatically, before pausing.

'Actually, averted disaster aside, I feel good. Better than good. Today feels like completing a successful, complex surgery—you know the patient might have months of recovery and rehab ahead of them, but the surgery has gone well, and that's the best start you can hope for.'

Her stomach flip-flopped again, but this time for a less agreeable reason.

'I don't want to rain on your parade,' she murmured as he stepped forward to open the door to outside, the early evening-air hitting them. 'But don't be surprised if Noah regresses.'

'He only said a few words.' Seth frowned. 'How can he regress?'

'Daniel did.' Andrea remembered as they stopped beside his unmistakeable car. 'Many times. Mum and I used to feel that, for every two steps forward that we took, he always took one step back.'

'I see.'

If it had been anyone else, Andrea thought they would have looked almost defeated. But this was Seth, the surgeon who carried out extraordinary operations on a weekly basis. If anyone had the patience and determination to succeed, it was Seth.

She only hoped he knew that being a surrogate dad to his six-year-old nephew was going to be a heck of a lot harder than any of the impossible neurosurgeries.

CHAPTER SEVEN

THIS WAS WHERE Seth lived?

Stepping into lift, Andrea managed a weak smile at the concierge and tried not to grip the side rail too tightly. The last thing she'd expected when she'd dropped her nieces and nephew back with her sister-in-law was to receive a text from Seth summoning her to his home and sending her the address.

Already nervous, it was now proving even harder to stop her nerves from jangling riotously. Not least because it transpired that Seth lived in one of the most sought-after buildings in the city, in a sprawling penthouse which occupied the top two floors. And one which required the elderly concierge to accompany her up in the private lift as if she were some kind of impostor who he didn't really trust to be there.

Or perhaps that was just her overactive imagination. The older gentleman had been nothing but courteous from the moment she'd walked through the pristine glass doors, advising her that Mr Mulder was expecting her.

Now, the higher the lift rose to the penthouse, the more elevated her sense of disquiet became.

'Here we are, Miss Perkins.' The concierge smiled warmly as the lift glided to a stop and the doors slid smoothly open.

And of course Seth had to be waiting by his open door, watching her step out stiffly as she thanked the older man.

'Thank you, Stan, I'll take it from here,' Seth murmured pleasantly before turning to her with an arch expression. 'Are you coming in, Andrea? Or do you intend to ride the lift back down like a fairground attraction?'

She wasn't prepared for the way his words rippled deliciously over her. She told herself to move away, but couldn't. Not when he was pinning her in place with that killer gaze.

'I was just making a coffee.' He stepped back into the apartment, breaking the spell. Or perhaps that was just fanciful.

'I don't...' She began to step forward before faltering. 'Why am I here, Seth?'

'For what it's worth, you were right to warn me about regression with Noah.'

If she'd been looking for an excuse, then this was it. Straightening her shoulders, Andrea took a breath and forced herself to follow.

'Is that why you sent the text SOS?'

'I wouldn't call it an SOS.' He pulled a grim smile. 'But I did hope you might have some advice for me.'

'What happened?'

Seth busied himself making coffee from a machine that wouldn't have looked out of place in a coffee house. His sleek, neat kitchen area was tastefully decked in burnished steel appliances, white granite surfaces and sleek dark-chocolate-coloured wall tiles.

She didn't dare turn round to look at the space behind her, but that meant concentrating on Seth.

'Did he stop communicating with you entirely?' she asked.

He'd still been wearing a suit jacket at the play centre—

not that it had stopped a decent number of women from staring at him. Not that she'd cared, of course. Not one bit.

'Actually, not entirely,' Seth replied. 'I was able to ask him direct questions without him retreating into his room, and he indicated he wanted a bath with bubbles.'

'Well, that's good.'

'It is,' he agreed. 'I just...suppose I was hoping he might actually say something to me. Even just one word.'

'Give him a chance; he's doing well.' She looked around the room suddenly. 'I take it he's in bed now?'

'He's in bed, yes. In fact, he was pretty much asleep the moment his head hit the pillow.'

'Apparently, the twins do that.' Andrea grinned. 'Or so I'm told. That's the beauty of being the aunt—I get to take them out and have fun and if that tires them out, then, great. But, if it over-tires them, it's Daniel and Julia's problem, not mine.'

'You're particularly good with them.'

'Thanks.'

'Do you want any of your own?'

She blinked, momentarily thrown off-balance, despite the fact it wasn't an uncommon topic of conversation between colleagues. Nonetheless, it took her a moment to regroup.

How was Seth to know that it was a subject she always avoided as carefully as she could? The last thing she wanted to start talking about with her Baystone colleagues was her past. Not about her husband, nor her miscarriage and certainly not her septate uterus—the anomaly which meant a membrane ran through her uterus, dividing it into two parts. And even though she knew she'd done nothing to cause it, that it was something she'd been born with, it had still been the reason for her miscarriage, and it was what made her feel less than a woman every time the subject of children came up.

That cruel twist of fate meant her chances of getting pregnant were low—her chances of actually carrying a baby to term, even lower.

It was impossible to describe to anyone quite how... defective that made her feel. Especially when she'd once dreamed of becoming a mother and giving her children the kind of childhood she wished she'd been able to enjoy.

Little wonder that she doted on her brother's brood, even if neither Daniel nor Julia knew her secret. She'd decided long ago not to burden her family with her problems, though whether because she thought her family had dealt with enough, or because she didn't want to say the words out loud, she couldn't be sure.

'I haven't really considered kids,' she lied stiffly.

She might have known Seth wouldn't be fooled. He lifted his hands instantly.

'My apologies, I was merely curious. You seem so natural.'

Handing her what had to be a designer coffee-mug, he made his way round the kitchen island and indicated for her to follow, the subject apparently dropped. And finally she had a chance to see Seth's incredible penthouse.

The sheer dizzying scale of the place was all too evident. The stunning, two-storey area, with the vaulted ceiling of the main area painted a sharp, clean white to give the place a spacious, light feel, walloped her with its soaring height. All further helped by the wide expanse of sparkling glass that ran the entire length of the building.

On one side, the side she was on now, an oval glass dining table with designer, metal-framed chairs sat boldly in front of the view.

The other side of the main space boasted the living area. It contained a dark, plaid couch sitting opposite two dark leather easy chairs, the coffee table in between looking like another expensive designer piece in crystal-clear glass. A staircase just off to the side and rear appeared to float out of the side of the main wall, with its glass railing almost invisible from this angle.

Finally, her eyes were pulled from one expensive piece of artwork or sculpture to another, and then another, each more stunning than the last.

The place screamed out that it was the residence of a successful, wealthy, confirmed bachelor. The kind of aspirational apartment that looked as though it had come straight out of the pages of a slick architectural magazine, pristine and minimalist. She could barely have afforded a square foot in a place like this. Seth's life was so far removed from her own that, for the first time in a very long time, Andrea actually felt intimidated enough to make her wonder what on earth she'd been thinking in coming here at all tonight.

'You don't like it?' He sounded amused as he unfolded himself onto the couch with all the grace of a predatory hunter.

'Actually, I do like it,' she told him sincerely.

'The frown lines on your face seem to say otherwise.'

She wrinkled her nose, considering.

'It's spectacular,' she told him at last. 'But—and this is just my opinion—it isn't homely. There's nothing soft in here; nothing that suggests it would be home to a six-year-old child.'

'That's pretty much what Stacey would have said,' he murmured softly.

'Your sister? You mentioned that she and Noah lived with you for the first eighteen months of his life. She didn't try to...?'

She stopped, not wanting to offend, but Seth's smile held a tint of regret rather than affront.

'Make it more *homely*?' he finished for her. 'She did.'

She should leave it there; she knew that. But she found herself still speaking.

'But *you* didn't like that?'

He didn't exactly shrug—he was too *male* for that.

'It looked quite nice, as it happened. But after she left I got rid of some things. The cushions, the pictures…things like that.'

Another shadow passed over him; a sadness which she could do nothing about. Suddenly all she wanted to do was lighten the mood and see that striking smile of his again.

'Hence the dark wood, the glass and the sleek metal.' She forced a grin. 'Remarkably unblemished by sticky fingers—though, give it time. This place is masculine and bachelor to a tee.'

'I suspect that isn't the compliment that it sounds.' His voice rumbled over her—*doing* things to her—but he still didn't sound offended.

'That bookcase, by contrast, tells a different story about its owner.'

He followed the direction of her gaze.

'Is that so?' He arched one eyebrow. 'And what, I might wonder, does it tell you about me, Andrea?'

The sound of her voice on his tongue sent a lick of pure lust straight through her, and it didn't matter if she tried to remember why she was here. Or who she was with. She might as well be drowning in the deepest, darkest well with no way to get out.

So instead Andrea focussed her attention on the shelves. She regarded the battered, leather-bound books, the antique globe with tiny holes here and there and the unusual pieces of art which she couldn't categorise but looked original.

It was almost thrilling, trying to piece together this man from his personal belongings that she suspected not every woman got to see. Or, perhaps, not every woman who'd come to this penthouse had bothered to look.

'I'd say you travel a fair amount.'

'A fair assumption.' He lifted one shoulder. 'You'll have to do better that that.'

'Okay,' she mused. 'How about the fact that the tiny pinpricks in that old globe tell me that you don't spend months, or even weeks, deliberating on your trips? You close your eyes and stick something in at random. Then you just pack a bag and leave, like some kind of adventurer.'

He looked discernibly more impressed.

'Observant.'

'I take it that *is* a compliment?'

'Do you want it to be?' he asked heavily.

Another lick moved though her.

'I don't suppose it matters,' she lied.

Why did she care what he thought?

'What *does* matter?' Seth murmured quietly, taking a very deliberate step towards her.

Heat rolled between them. She ought to move away, but she was powerless to. Least of all when he lifted his hand and grazed the tips of his fingers down one side of her jaw, his expression so intensely hot that it licked through her chest.

She silenced the voice inside screaming at her that, for all intents and purposes, this was her boss. That he didn't date colleagues. That she certainly didn't.

But then suddenly he was kissing her. A kiss like nothing she'd ever known before. A kiss that breathed life into something deep inside her that had been dormant for so long.

Had it ever existed like this before?

Without even realising what she was doing, her hands splayed themselves out on Seth's chest, resting on the angular muscles beneath and letting the heat seep from his body to hers as his mouth moved, unhurried, over hers. As though he had all the time in the world.

It was a heady experience and it made her melt.

Everywhere.

'And this?' he muttered dryly against her mouth. 'Does this matter?'

Andrea had no idea how she broke the contact long enough to reply, let alone to murmur to him.

'Should it?'

It was as though she wasn't the inexperienced, frigid woman that her ex-husband had always accused her of being. As if she was versed in seductive ways, the way so many of her acquaintances and colleagues seemed to be. As if her previous experience, as limited as it was, had been hurried, perfunctory and almost always unsatisfactory.

Any minute, she thought to herself, *he's going to see me for the fraud that I am.*

But Seth didn't appear to see anything of the sort. Instead, he simply angled his mouth against hers to deepen the kiss, sending her further and further away from anything she considered to be sane, with every deliciously wicked slide of his tongue.

Again and again he kissed her, stoking up that fire inside until it was so high that the heat was practically scorching her from the inside out.

She wasn't aware of moving, yet Andrea became aware of the fact that her back was against the same bookcase that she'd been avidly studying what felt like a lifetime ago. Worse—or maybe *better*—that her legs had parted and Seth was settled between them, steel against molten softness.

Shifting her hips, she revelled in the low, primal sound that slid from him. The way his hands seemed to glide down her back with such restrained leisure only made her feel all the more desirable. All the more precious.

The way her body was responding to Seth's skilled touch, in a way she'd never known it was capable of doing, was a revelation.

With your boss, a muffled voice tried to remind her.

But she wasn't listening She wanted more. So much more.

As if reading her thoughts, Seth lifted his mouth from hers, moving to trail hot, sensual kisses right along the jawline that he'd caressed minutes before. When he dipped further to kiss down the long column of her neck, she couldn't stop her gasp of pleasure as she tipped her head back to grant him better access.

She felt raw, exposed, and she was loving every moment of it.

When he hooked one finger on the buttons at the front of her top, pausing as if to give her a chance to stop him, she merely met his gaze. The dark hunger mirrored her own.

'Do you have a particular attachment to these buttons?' he growled, and the sheer desire in his voice made her tremble.

'Attachment?' she echoed dully.

'Too late.' He grinned wickedly, snagging his finger so the buttons popped off.

One.

The sound was deliciously rude.

Two.

It echoed sinfully around the space.

Three.

Four.

Had there ever been such a decadent sound?

Five.

Then she didn't have time to think anything, because his hand was hooking the lace of her bra, exposing the taut, dark nipple and taking it into his mouth.

Like fireworks.

Andrea gasped as his tongue, his teeth, grazed over her. Without realising what she was doing, she found herself arching into him, wanting more. *Aching* for more.

And Seth gave it. He lavished attention on her breast,

sending sensation rushing through her that had her crying out. And, when he'd finished on one side, he turned his attention to the other. Andrea couldn't think straight. All she could do was let him.

Let him lead her wherever he wanted to go.

When he removed first his top, then hers, she took the opportunity to lower her head and trace the taut lines of his chest with her hands, then her mouth, in much the same way that he'd done for her.

Almost as though he was giving her a kind of power over him, lower and lower as she followed the sharp contours, until her hands were on the belt buckle of his trousers. She almost protested when he uttered a low curse and caught her wrists in his hand.

But the next thing she was on her back on the deep rug and her trousers were discarded, thrown somewhere—she didn't care where—his almost-black eyes snaring hers and daring her to look away as his hand grazed up the inside of her thigh.

Higher.

And higher still.

Until her pulse was leaping around erratically and her breath was sawing in and out of her.

And then as he reached the apex of her legs—the part of her that ached for him the most—he skimmed the back of his hand over her heat and trailed his fingers down the inside of her other leg.

Andrea heard a primal groan, but it took a moment to realise that the low sound came from her.

'Patience,' he commanded, his mouth crooked up into an indecorous smile.

Then he lowered his head and allowed his mouth to take over from his hand, working back the other way now, his warm breath making her skin shiver with anticipation.

'Seth,' she managed, her voice glutted with lust.

His eyes burned blacker, as though the sound of his name on her voice was almost too much for him to stand.

And then, just as she expected him to tease her once again, he lowered his head between her legs and pressed his mouth to the very heart of her need.

Andrea fractured.

There was nothing but the feel of Seth between her legs, licking her, tasting her, *feasting* on her as though he'd been waiting to do for centuries. But it wasn't just his tongue that he wielded against her so expertly, but his fingers too, sliding inside her, in and out, until she was writhing against his touch, seeking out more. Then more again.

With every slide he was sending her higher and higher, spiralling upwards until her body didn't even feel like her own. It had never, *never,* been like this.

And then he did something—a twist, perhaps, or an added bit of pressure—and Andrea was gone, splintering apart in the inky night sky.

Andrea had no idea how much longer she stayed there, soaring in the nothingness, but by the time she came back to herself Seth was stretched out languorously next to her. But he was betrayed by the hungry expression on his face, and the unyielding lines of his hard, ready body.

'I... I didn't know,' she faltered. 'That is, I've never...'

But, whatever it was she was struggling to say, it didn't matter. A muffled cry came from upstairs—the unmistakeable sound of Noah caught in a bad dream.

She'd barely moved before Seth was already up, pulling his clothes back on without missing a beat.

'I have to go,' he muttered.

She was eminently grateful that they were out of sight on the other side of the bookcase from the stairs and gallery.

'He won't tumble on the stairs, will he?' she asked hazily. Her brain, it seemed, was still trying to process what had just happened between Seth and her.

'I doubt he's even out of bed. He'll still be asleep; it happens most nights,' Seth assured her before rounding the bookcase away from her. 'He just needs someone to sit with him and talk softly. Wait here.'

The worst of it was that there was a part of her that desperately, desperately wanted to obey. As if she hadn't already learned the worst lesson of all when it came to men who wanted something from her.

Pushing herself shakily up onto her surprising wobbly legs, Andrea pulled her clothes back on as quickly as she could.

What kind of an idiot was she, anyway?

Because it was one thing to decide that maybe this was her time to let loose a little and have some fun. But it was another thing entirely to be foolish enough to think that having fun meant rushing headlong into heartbreak with a man like Seth.

CHAPTER EIGHT

'DRILL, PLEASE.'

Seth checked the vitals on the monitors that were connected up to his patient—an eighteen-year-old girl who had been hit by a truck when she'd stepped out from behind a waiting bus. She'd been flown straight in by helicopter, having been found to be deeply unconscious with a blown pupil at the scene, and scans had confirmed an acute subdural haematoma.

Now it was a race against time for Seth to evacuate via a craniotomy, and he'd already made his first incisions and removed the temporal muscle to gain access to his patient's skull. Taking the medical tool, Seth concentrated on drilling the burr holes that would allow him to remove the necessary area of bone to access the leathery, tough dura. Once he could get to the bleed beneath that, he could finally start to remove the blood which was compressing his patient's brain.

It was a process he'd successfully carried out hundreds of times in the past and, whilst he never allowed himself to become complacent, he was nonetheless grateful for the distraction. As well as for the fact that Andrea Perkins wasn't his scrub nurse for this procedure today. Fortunate, really, considering what had happened between them the last time they'd met.

What had he been thinking? He didn't date work colleagues. He sure as hell didn't have feverish sex with them. He had rules, and no other woman had ever come close to making him break them the way that Andrea had.

'Hold that a little more to the right, please,' he instructed. 'And a little more irrigation. Better.'

He suppressed his irritation as the scrub nurse, whilst solid, didn't act quite as intuitively as he felt Andrea would have. He tried to eject the thought from his head but it refused to go.

Last night had thrown him. Heck, the woman herself had thrown him. He'd acted instinctively, and he never did that. Not where women were concerned, and definitely not since his nephew had entered his life.

But with Andrea he'd thrown out the damned rule book. Seth couldn't understand what it was that was so different about her compared to any of the women that he had dated—not that he was dating her, he reminded himself hastily. Yet nonetheless she seemed to have sneaked under his skin. He had no idea what he was supposed to do about that.

If it hadn't been for Noah calling out, then Seth was fairly sure that Andrea would have ended up in his bed. And, despite all his professional lines and boundaries, he couldn't say he'd been remotely unhappy at the prospect. Despite the *very* cold shower that he'd taken last night, he'd lain awake for a long time, staring at the ceiling as he'd tried to work out exactly what it was about this one woman that had him so easily casting aside all his previous rules— and since when had he ever lost sleep over a woman before?

Invisible lines and rubric set him apart from the man whom he had called a father, but who had never actually *been* any kind of father. He'd been a man who had spent his entire life taking what he wanted, and doing as he pleased, with no heed for the consequences for anybody else. Especially not for his and Stacey's desperate mother.

With deep distaste, Seth thrust any memory of his so-called father out of his head. He refused to compare himself to that man. He might be the son, cut from the same damaged cloth, but he would not live the same life.

He might have the same playboy reputation that his father had, but the difference was that Seth wasn't married. He wasn't cheating, flaunting all his indiscretions in his frantic wife's face.

By contrast, Seth had always prided himself on never so much as flirting even in the direction of one of his colleagues.

Those were his rules—whatever they might be worth.

Was it the disconcerting experience of having had his life turned upside down that had caused this unusual state of affairs? It would be easy enough to use his sister's death and his nephew's presence to explain away this inexplicable attraction to Andrea Perkins—his damned scrub nurse.

Besides, he tried to argue to himself, it didn't even make sense to be so ridiculously drawn to her. The woman was certainly pretty, but by no means displayed the kind of glamour and glitz of the women he was accustomed to dating. Part of him had been growing weary of that kind of woman for some time, anyway.

It would be easier still to tell himself that the attraction was borne out of gratitude for her help around the situation with Noah. He recalled his relief at seeing his nephew begin to come alive—if only for an hour or so—at that play centre the day before.

But an *easy* excuse didn't mean an accurate one. And Seth suspected that the reasons for his attraction to Andrea Perkins went beyond any excuses he could conjure up by way of explanation.

'A little suction here,' he instructed as the small incision he was making in the scalp began to provide the excess blood with an escape, somewhat obscuring the field.

He worked quickly and meticulously, making a series of incisions to ensure as much of the bleed as possible had a route out.

'Yep, that's looking good,' he declared at length.

'Ready to put the dura back in place?' his resident asked, peering at the site.

'Yeah, I think so,' Seth confirmed.

Though he wouldn't close up one of the layers of connective tissue that completely covered and protected the brain and spinal cord in case his patient's brain began to swell and needed room to expand.

'Scalp on or off?'

'I would say it's safe to put the scalp back in place—we've left enough room. Now it's down to the intensive care team.'

And Baystone had a great ICU unit; his patient would be in good hands.

Efficiently but flawlessly, Seth completed the surgical procedure, scrubbing out and heading through the doors back to his office—where Joyce was waiting for him.

'Noah's school called.'

His stomach lurched instantly.

'Is he okay?'

'He isn't injured,' Joyce assured him straight away. 'Though he was apparently involved in an altercation with another boy.'

Seth frowned.

'Noah was? What happened?'

'They wouldn't give me all the details,' Joyce apologised. 'But, since they understand you're in and out of surgeries all day, they asked me to pass on that another boy was teasing Noah about not being able to talk and was threatening him with some old football net that he'd found. It seems

Noah decided that wasn't happening, and did something with the net and the boy first.'

'I see,' Seth remarked grimly.

'If you ask me, Noah did well to stand up for himself if he was being bullied. But the school would like you to call in for a conversation as soon as you are able.'

Seth grunted. Joyce's allegiances were clear, and heartening. He tried to not wonder what Andrea's opinion on the matter might be. In many ways, it was moot—she was only an aunt, the way that he was an uncle. Yet he couldn't shake the feeling that, in the same situation, she would be handling all this so much better than he currently was.

What would her advice be if she knew all the circumstances? The school was only too aware of the custody dispute involving Noah's paternal grandparents and their own views might come into play. Anything that suggested Noah was struggling emotionally could be used down the line to prove that, as Noah's uncle, Seth was less suited to being the boy's new caregiver than the grandparents.

No doubt Andrea would know the right way to react.

'Is there anything I can do to help?' Joyce asked kindly.

He imagined she made a wonderful grandmother to her five young grandchildren—just as wonderful as his own beloved grandmother had been to Stacey and him—and would be only too happy to offer sage advice.

'Thank you, Joyce. I shall deal with it,' he declared, striding back up the hallway and to his office.

But saying he could deal with it and actually having a plan were, it turned out, two very different things. Stumped, he moved to the window and stared out at the park beyond.

An image of Andrea slid, unbidden, into his brain. He tried to eject but it just squatted down lower, reminding him that he still had her phone number. He could still call her outside the hospital—if that allowed him to keep some semblance of maintaining his lines in the sand.

Glowering at the freshly mown lawn, he strode back to his desk and sat down again. He was a neurosurgeon, top of his field. People came to him from across the country—across the world. He didn't need a stranger to help him resolve an issue concerning his own nephew.

Determinedly, he flipped up his Internet browser and typed in a search. A few moments later, he shut the page down, picked up his phone and swung his chair back to the window.

This, he told himself resolutely, was not about his own ego but about what was the best solution for Noah.

Nothing more.

Andrea circled the large play area in the country park for the third time and wondered if inviting Seth and Noah to her family's picnic had been her best idea.

She wasn't sure why she had. Obviously she wanted to help Noah, especially when Seth had told her about the altercation in school, but there was still the issue of what had happened between her and Seth the other night.

Self-consciously, she lifted her fingers to touch her lips. They still felt as though they were tingling, just as her body still seemed to be fizzing with something inexplicable.

Fool.

That was why she'd suggested the huge public park. Not only was it a public space, but her family would be around. She couldn't make a fool of herself here, surely?

Striding down the path, her eyes still alert for Seth, Andrea rounded the little bend to take in the beauty of the miniature lake and felt her chest ease a little. It didn't matter how many times she saw it, the pretty sight always seemed to make her smile, complete as it usually was with ducks and their ducklings. Today, a handful of couples also dotted the view, out on the water in little punts, cocooned in their romantic bubbles, and she felt a strangely unexpected pang of envy. She struggled to catch herself.

Hadn't she got over the idea of false romance a long time ago?

Even her mother had noticed her odd frame of mind when they'd been doing the daily physio that Maureen Perkins needed to help her MS. Today had been a harder day—the last few months things had been getting progressively harder, if she was honest—and it was clear that her mum really needed more help.

Perhaps being evicted by her current flatmate, however nicely, was the push she needed to find somewhere a little bigger which she could share with her mother. A place that would allow her to be on hand more for her, even if that meant being further away from Baystone and work.

Maybe fate would smile on them and she would find a new place that would make it easier for her mum to manoeuvre herself, instead of the tight corners she was trying to negotiate now. Somewhere with wider hallways and doors, lower light fittings and an accessible shower.

But all that took money, and they didn't have enough. Love might always have been plentiful in the Perkins household, before and after her father's death, but after his death money had become an issue.

Her mother had always worked—she still worked now—because she was a fighter and because she'd always insisted on it, despite her illness. But, with only one income and two growing kids to feed, one income hadn't stretched far. When her brother had grown up and moved out, it had eased the strain; and when Andrea had grown up, and begun her nursing career, her second income had been a life saver.

If she decided to leave her job, and didn't simply walk into a new one, they might have to survive on her mother's income alone. At least her brother's work meant that he was now back in Baystone full-time, with his family. It was all additional help that made Andrea feel like the responsibility wasn't hers alone.

'Andrea.'

Seth's rich voice halted her in her path as she jerked her head up to see him heading towards her, looking as sinfully handsome as ever—and she felt instantly wrecked. Though, she derived a modicum of satisfaction that he faltered when he saw her, just for a split second.

So much for her idea about coming here to remind herself of the easy, professional relationship they'd once had. Rather, all she could think about was the other night. The way he'd felt and tasted. The way he'd tasted her.

'Hello, Seth,' she managed.

Seeing him at work had been one thing, but meeting him here was something altogether more nerve-racking. He affected her far too much.

Instead, she concentrated on the little boy walking next to him.

'Hi, Noah, I'm really happy you're here. Billy and the twins can't wait to see you again.'

She smiled, relieved when Noah glanced up at her and offered a shy smile.

'Come on, I'll introduce you to my family.'

'That sounds great, right, buddy?' Seth encouraged cheerfully, falling into step as she made her way back to where they'd set up their picnic.

For the next half hour or so, Andrea watched as Seth easily charmed her sister-in-law, before launching into a game of quasi-football with all four children, as well as her delighted brother.

She wasn't sure what she'd expected but it hadn't been for Seth to fit into her extended family's dynamics so seamlessly. Andrea had to school herself not to feel that punch of delight that he'd achieved in thirty minutes what Josh had never managed during multiple family events.

And then, at last, Seth excused himself from the game and made his way over to her.

'I was thinking that we could maybe take a walk?' He lowered his voice, though no one was around. 'Talk about Noah?'

'Sure.' She nodded, trying valiantly to ignore her sister-in-law's conspicuous thumbs-up.

'Perhaps we could walk around the lake I saw on the way in, if the path continues all the way?'

'You've never been here before!' she exclaimed before she could help herself.

'I haven't.'

'It's literally between your penthouse and the hospital, which is why I suggested it.'

He offered her a grim look.

'Which no doubt makes it all the more pitiable that I haven't been here, but no less true, I'm afraid.'

'Right. Sorry. I just thought maybe you'd been here in the early days, with Stacey and Noah?'

The muscles in his face pulled taut.

'Not even then,' he confessed uncomfortably. 'Clearly I was a pretty lousy uncle and brother.'

'That wasn't what I was implying.' Andrea felt instantly guilty. 'It doesn't matter. I was just...surprised, that's all. It's a popular place.'

'So I can see,' he agreed. 'Although, I can't say I can imagine you being one of those people to take a romantic row out on some lake.'

She never had been, as it happened. Yet for some reason she found herself bristling uncharacteristically at the dryness in his tone.

'You're saying you don't think anyone would want to do something romantic with me?'

She could have kicked herself, especially when Seth emitted a less than amused laugh.

'That isn't what I'm saying, no,' he clarified. 'I'm just not a fan of romance, personally. I find it gets in the way of practicality. You always gave the impression you felt the same.'

She probably had, Andrea realised, thinking about the few romantic gestures Josh had ever made, and how hollow they seemed when she thought about the way he had treated her the rest of the time.

'I guess,' she answered flatly. 'I used to think I would love to be romanced. Now I realise it can just be a way of getting away with treating the other person like dirt. Like doing something wonderful for them on their birthday yet treating them badly for the rest of the year.'

She regretted her words the instant she felt his piercing gaze on her. She had no intention of revealing her pitiful past to anyone, least of all Seth.

'Personal experience?'

'No, of course not.' It was all she could do to feign nonchalance as they fell into step alongside each other and began an easy walk around the shimmering water. She reached around for something more positive to say. 'I was four when we moved to the area. My parents were always doing fun, romantic things.'

'Like rowing out on that lake?'

'Actually, that was one thing they missed. My father promised my mother they would on their tenth anniversary, but then he died and…' She tailed off, shaking her head.

Seth was watching her very carefully and she was scared he could read too much.

'So she hasn't ever been?'

'My brother has been trying to take her out ever since— I know he'll try again today—but she always politely declines. She says it's a lovely idea but that it isn't the same.'

'Your mum isn't here yet, though?'

'No.' Andrea bit her lip as though to keep in the truth

that she had never told anyone at Baystone before. She hesitated. 'Mum was meant to be here earlier, but today's...a bad day. Hopefully she'll make it later.'

His gaze raked over her again.

'Bad days from what? Is that why you think you have to walk away from the conversion degree?'

Whether it was the fact that she knew so many of Seth's secrets, or whether it was the simple fact that it was Seth himself, she found the words slipping out anyway.

'My mum has MS. I've been helping to care for her ever since I was eight years old.'

CHAPTER NINE

'YOUR MUM HAS MS?'

Andrea nodded stiffly, wondering what on earth had possessed her to utter the words. It wasn't something she told that many people. She certainly couldn't believe she'd told Seth.

Turning awkwardly, she moved jerkily along the path, resuming their lake walk as though it was no big deal. But everything was still tumbling around her head.

'So you're still her carer.'

'We pay someone to come in a couple of times a week, when she needs it. She's a warrior, and you'll never hear her complain, but we both know that MS is an unsympathetic disease.'

He nodded, but his too-shrewd gaze bored into her all the same, locking her in place. She was suddenly afraid that he was able to read a whole raft of secrets that she'd always hugged so close to herself.

'When you were telling me about your brother's selective mutism, you said it happened after your father had died in a car crash,' he continued when she didn't answer, and she realised that he was racing back through all those tiny snippets of personal information she'd reluctantly dropped in the past week.

'Yes,' she muttered, because what else could she do but confirm what he already knew?

She could practically see him piecing a jigsaw together, slotting all the scraps together with his super-speedy brain.

It was impressive and terrifying all at once. Not least because the last time he'd looked at her so intensely had been that night in his penthouse. And look what that had led to...

At the memory, her body gave a delicious, involuntary shiver, as if it had simply been waiting for the chance to relive the experience.

God help her, was that why she'd so readily invited him to her family picnic—just for the excuse to spend more time with him outside the hospital, lines and boundaries be damned?

'You also mentioned that the reason it lasted six months in your brother's case was because there were additional complications.' Seth dragged her back to the less than thrilling conversation. And, despite everything, she couldn't help feeling surprised he remembered. 'By which you meant your mother's MS?'

Did she answer, or did she shut the conversation down?

'Yes,' she admitted a beat later.

'So her MS has always been quite severe?'

Andrea opened her mouth then closed it again. She needed to weigh up exactly what she was going to say next.

'Not always.' She inhaled deeply. 'Before Daniel's birth, she didn't even know.'

'Daniel's older than you?'

'Younger. When she was pregnant with me, she suffered a little with fatigue and discomfort, but nothing that really threw up red flags, and no one was looking for MS. After I was born, apart from a difficult couple of months, the symptoms subsided again.'

'Ah. So it went back to some semblance of normal until the second pregnancy?'

'Pretty much. With Daniel, her symptoms were more pronounced. The pain was more intense, and she suffered a lot with weakness of limbs and dizziness.' She only had vague memories of this time. 'By the time Daniel was born, she was showing more signs of muscle spasticity.'

'And this time they made the MS diagnosis?'

She nodded.

'Yes, there was more to go on by then. Mum has always been very strong and determined. She refused to let it control her life and she kept her job going. She still had flare-ups, but Dad was her main carer, and they worked together to try to ensure it didn't affect Daniel or I.' She closed her eyes for a split second. 'Then Dad died in the crash.'

'I'm sorry.' Seth's low voice rumbled through the air. She couldn't have said why, but she felt that he would have given anything to spare her that memory.

It was enough to steel her again.

'After he died, everything changed,' she continued. 'More for me than for Daniel. I was eight, but I had to become Mum's carer whenever she was having a relapse. I started being late for school, or missing days altogether when Mum needed help to get up and showered. Or I had to take care of my younger brother, either because he'd stopped talking and the school wanted Mum to go in and explain what was happening, or simply because someone needed to cook the family meal. Mum hated that she had to rely on me, but what else could she do?'

'I'm sorry you had to go through that.'

He sounded touchingly sincere.

'Thank you.'

'It certainly explains some things,' he murmured.

She wasn't sure whether it was more for himself than her, but it piqued her curiosity all the same.

'Things like what?'

He eyed her for a moment.

'Like why someone as bright, as ambitious and as keen as you never tried to become a surgeon yourself, or even a doctor.'

'That's how you see me?'

The question was out before she could stop herself. Being a doctor had always been her secret dream, but she'd never, ever voiced it to anyone. The idea that someone like Seth could imagine her achieving it was ridiculously gratifying.

'That isn't how you see yourself?' he challenged quietly.

She couldn't bring herself to tell him about her marriage. About how she'd allowed her egotistical ex to slowly squeeze every ounce of self-confidence she'd ever had.

It was too shameful.

'As a young kid, I used to want to be a doctor,' she admitted. 'I thought I could be the kind who fixed people like my mum. Dad always encouraged me and I got good grades. But when I became Mum's sole carer it was enough to look after my younger brother and the house. Homework fell by the wayside and my grades suffered. After that, it was never an option.'

'You still did well for yourself. I can't think of many people who could carve out a career as a head scrub nurse, having had to sacrifice so much of their childhood and education to be a child-carer,' he pointed out, as though it was obvious.

But it wasn't obvious. She'd spent most of her life feeling as though she'd fallen short. And Josh's disdain for her job had only further damaged her self-confidence. As though he'd had any kind of measure of success. What a fool she'd been for allowing him that power over her.

'And, as you grew older, your brother couldn't help? Allow you to go back to school and get the grades you needed?'

'Daniel got a job on an oil refinery. He was away for

months at a time, but his job paid very well, and he sent much of it back home to help with Mum.'

'Even when he got married?'

'Yes.'

She didn't add that her own ill-conceived marriage had cost her money, bailing Josh out from his many gambling debts as she had over the years they'd been together.

Nor did she allow a voice to that tiny part of her that had always wondered if part of her brother's monthly offerings had been guilt money to salve his conscience over leaving her alone to help their mother all these years.

Not that she didn't love her fierce, determined mum with all of her heart. But, even though she didn't say any of this to Seth, she couldn't shake the suspicion that when he looked at her he could read all too much of it for himself.

'I did try once. Along with my wages and Mum's, Daniel's money gave us enough to get someone in once every week or two and let me go back to an adult learning college when I was about twenty.' Andrea forced a smile. 'But after the first month Mum woke up one morning to find she was having a relapse, and that was it; I couldn't go. I couldn't leave her.'

'And that's also why you can't do the conversion degree now.'

Regret washed through her.

'Exactly. It would demand so much time and money. I simply can't guarantee either. But you didn't come here to talk about my mum.' She gave herself a mental shake. 'You came to talk about Noah.'

She thought that Seth might have grunted a little but at least they were off difficult conversations and onto the point of why he'd asked to meet her.

'I'm asking if there's anything else you know of to help speed things up with getting Noah back to talking. After what happened in school this week, it's clear that his refusal to communicate is causing issues and stopping him from making friends.'

Andrea raked her hand through her hair. Her heart went out to both the little boy and the man walking alongside her.

'I wish I could help speed things up, but I can't. Noah just needs to go at his own pace and you're going to have to find a way to make him feel comfortable communicating with you.'

'He doesn't want to talk to me. Yet he talked to you within minutes of meeting you,' Seth pointed out, his frustration palpable. 'He talked to your nieces and nephews, too. He even told them the name of his bear.'

'Because he felt comfortable and happy. As ironic as it may be, since he doesn't talk to you, he probably felt more secure talking to us simply because he knew you were there.'

'I'm afraid that *secure* is the last thing I seem to make him feel.'

'Not necessarily.' She shook her head. 'You're the one person who has been stable in his life since his mother's death, but at the same time maybe you're the one he has come to associate with her loss. Even so, it's still possible that he feels safer simply by you being there.'

'I wish I knew that.'

'It is possible. You just have to give it time.'

'I don't have time,' Seth bit out before shaking his head in apology. 'I told you about his paternal grandparents fighting me for custody.'

Andrea nodded as it began to slip into place.

'You said that he doesn't talk to them either.' She nodded. 'And that they're arguing that's only due to them not having had any contact before now, hence why Noah would ultimately be better with them.'

She couldn't put her finger on why, but she was certain that, if Noah had connected easily with his paternal grandparents, and if he was happy to be with them, then Seth would have agreed to them having care of Noah after all. She'd never known Seth to have a false ego.

'I worry that they're right,' he confided. 'Yet, though I feel compelled to honour my sister's will, it concerns me that Noah hasn't spoken to anyone in almost a month—until your family.' A shadow skittered through his golden-brown eyes but otherwise Seth kept his voice even, low, like a surgeon delivering the worst kind of news to a patient's family. 'When my sister was alive, I remember him being a bright, confident kid; he always seemed to do well in school and he had plenty of friends.'

'This was when they lived with you?'

'No, afterwards. He was always a happy baby, though they left my apartment when Noah was eighteen months. Even so, Stacey brought him for a week at Christmas and a week or two in the summer.' Seth lifted his shoulder in self-censure. 'I was often working, but we did spend some time together, and they always looked to be having a good time. Noah adored his mother, and she adored him.'

Andrea's heart twisted. She had been so close to her own father before his death, so it was only too easy to imagine what was going on in Noah's head right now. But at least she'd had her mother. And her brother—however badly he'd taken it. They'd still been a unit. A family.

Noah had lost the only parent he'd known, shipped off to an uncle he'd not seen very much and might not even really remember well. No wonder he wasn't talking.

'I really think you need a proper medical professional, and qualified speech and language therapist.' She felt oddly helpless.

'He has one. He saw her again yesterday and he didn't say a word to her,' Seth told her. 'For whatever reason, he trusts you. And your family. I could hand-pick the best professionals in the country, but it's you who he wants. Who *I* want.'

She told herself it was the gravelly timbre of his voice that was causing all that strange sloshing inside her—and not the fact that those words could be interpreted so differently.

'The other night...' she began, but Seth cut her off.

'We crossed a line the other night—*I* crossed a line—and for that I can only apologise. And assure you that it won't happen again. I just want you to help Noah.'

'All right,' she answered softly, automatically; not at all sure what she was agreeing to. 'I'll try to help, but I can't guarantee anything.'

'I'm not asking for guarantees. I just want you to try.'

'Right.'

She thought of the little boy in question. Seth was right—this was about Noah, not about them. No matter that her thoughts—and her body—seemed to go haywire whenever Seth was around.

She simply couldn't fail to connect with him. Seth might have assured her that he wasn't looking for a guarantee, but she knew so much riding on it that the prospect was almost daunting.

'And when you say you don't have much time, how much time are we talking?'

Seth's expression pulled tight.

'We're due for another court assessment next week. If I could just show them we've made some progress, even the tiniest bit, then it would buy me another week or two. I just want to see my nephew somewhere like back to his old self. He'll still process his mum's death in his own way, but at least he'll be able to talk to people. And at least he won't have the additional weight of being bullied because other kids can't understand why he won't speak.'

She understood that—more than Seth could know.

The question was, how could she best connect with Noah?

'We could try more places like the other day.'

At least they would be public places and not back at his penthouse. Anything to keep her mind from what had happened the other night. More to the point, how much more she'd *wanted* to happen, had they not been interrupted.

'Like the play centre?' He grimaced.

'I thought you half-enjoyed that in the end!' She hadn't meant to laugh. It just bubbled out of her at the memory.

He offered a half-sheepish look.

'I did. In the end.'

But the look he sent—however fleeting—made her breath catch in her chest.

Then he blinked and it was gone.

'Public places, then,' he agreed tightly.

For the little boy's sake, she had to set aside her private feelings for Seth, and complications with this particular man was something that she didn't have the time or energy for. Especially not now.

Yet, every time she thought about what had happened between them the other night, she worried that she couldn't trust herself around him at all. Since when had she ever acted so impulsively?

This was why, whatever else happened, she was determined that she wasn't going to set foot in Seth Mulder's penthouse ever again.

She is astonishing.

That was the only thing Seth could think as he watched Andrea move elegantly down the stairs in his penthouse from where she'd been wishing Noah goodnight.

As if she belonged.

Irritably, he chased the errant thought from his brain and wondered what was wrong with him.

Of course she didn't *belong* here; she shouldn't even be

here. She was a work colleague, not a date. Aside from fellow surgeon and friend, Jack, no other colleague had ever been invited into his home.

True, his life had been completely turned on its head with Noah's arrival. Also true, the lines between professional and personal were a little blurred at the moment as he attempted to navigate this new situation, but he really shouldn't keep losing sight of the fact that Andrea wasn't even here for him.

Rather, she was here for that little boy upstairs who she'd clearly been tucking into bed. And he was grateful for her presence—not least after his fear back at the park that she had no intention of visiting his apartment again after the other night. But somehow, after offering to drop her mum home, it was where she'd ended up.

'Did he go to sleep okay?'

'Seth, I didn't hear you come in.' What did it say about him that he got a kick out of the way she startled? Then her urvilleana eyes momentarily darkened before she pulled down those shutters. 'Yes, I think he was asleep before his head even hit the pillow.'

Seth nodded, relieved. Though he shouldn't be surprised; he got the impression Noah would happily take Andrea over him any time.

He watched as she descended the rest of the stairs and crossed the room, stopping a safe distance from him. It was as though she was afraid to get too close for fear of a repeat of the last time she'd been in his penthouse.

He couldn't say he blamed her. Not when the very air seemed to crackle in the room around them.

'Thank you for driving my mum home this evening,' she managed, her voice cracking slightly with the tension. 'You didn't have to.'

He didn't point out that, with Daniel's car full with his family, and Andrea's mother clearly unable to fold herself easily into her daughter's little car, it had seemed like the only sensible solution. He certainly hadn't liked the idea of her waiting for a wheelchair-friendly taxi, as she'd arrived in.

'I wanted the excuse to test out my new car anyway.' He tried to play it down. 'It's a different feel, being in a four-by-four to my previous car.'

'I can imagine.' A wry smile tugged at her soft mouth and his eyes followed the movement. 'But you still didn't have do it, just like you didn't have to row her across the lake.'

'It was nothing.' This time he dismissed Andrea's gratitude, feeling oddly embarrassed.

'Actually, it wasn't,' she continued softly. 'You made her laugh more than I've seen her laugh in a long time. Consequently, I think my sister-in-law is about ready to divorce my brother to marry you, and my brother is more than happy to let her. You made my whole family happy.'

'I'm glad they're happy,' Seth replied. 'Though I have to say that I didn't do it for them. I didn't even think about them, really. I did it for you.'

Her mouth opened into a perfect O, but she didn't speak. Instead, that now-familiar, pretty blush started in her cheeks and stole down over her neck…and lower.

He wondered how much lower before he was hastily forced to shut down the deliciously naughty image that had instantly invaded his brain.

It was ridiculous how easily she made him feel like some hormone-fuelled teen.

Boundaries.

He shouldn't have to keep reminding himself that Andrea Perkins was his colleague just to keep those sinfully sexy images from assailing his brain. What was it about her that kept making him forget his rules, his code? Did he really have to keep reminding himself that perhaps if his father had believed in that same code then his childhood, and Stacey's, would have been so very different?

They would have felt wanted, loved and safe—the way that his sister had been determined her son should always feel. The way he now owed it to Stacey to ensure Noah always would. The way that Andrea made the little boy feel.... He was beginning to understand that.

The reason Noah talked when Andrea was around because he felt safe with her there. Therefore, the more Andrea was around, the more secure the little boy would be.

Which meant...what?

'Did he say anything?' Seth couldn't keep the gruffness out of his voice as his brain whirred with only half-formed ideas.

Hardly a state of mind he was accustomed to.

'He whispered that he had a good time and asked me to tell you goodnight,' she murmured softly, crossing the room to where he stood in the kitchen area, only to hover there, as though uncertain whether to sit or leave.

He ought to encourage her to do the latter.

'Coffee?' He found himself reaching for his eye-wateringly expensive machine before she shook her head.

'Thanks, but I try to avoid it after seven p.m.'

Which they both knew was an excuse—if a sensible one.

'Probably wise,' he acknowledged, and then poured himself a mug anyway—possibly more for something to occupy his hands than anything else.

Because, despite his own private self-admonishment earlier, whenever he looked into those incredible eyes, each time he was drawn to that sensuous mouth—or, worse, every time he let his gaze slip to the lushness of her mouth-watering body—it belied every word he managed to utter.

It was getting harder and harder to keep all his boundaries straight in his head. Especially today, when he hadn't seemed to be able to take his eyes off her. It could have been the carefree, fun way she'd played and interacted with her family, or it could have been those endless legs that lay beneath the summery dress.

He suspected it was a little of both—and he should probably be more ashamed of his apparent inability to control his lust. But every time he saw Andrea a tautness wrapped itself around him and began to tug, slowly but surely, until he believed he might fracture and shatter if he moved to be with her.

It was nonsensical, really. Since when had he ever lusted after any woman like this? She wasn't even his usual type.

She wasn't lithe-like, as were most of the women he'd dated recently. Yet, despite the fact she was clearly toned, she boasted soft, subtle curves in all the best places. Curves that made his hands itch with the desire to reach out and touch her. To trace every glorious contour.

Every time she'd laughed with her nieces, he'd had to pretend that he didn't feel the sound winding right through him, curling sensually around his insides.

It was nonsensical the way she had him reacting like some kind of untrained schoolboy. His body was hard and ready before he could even turn round. He'd never felt so out of control before. *Never.*

And then, as if to prove his point, Andrea slid elegantly onto the stool at the breakfast bar and his mouth instantly went dry. He couldn't have said what it was about the movement that affected him, but he couldn't seem to drag his eyes from her long, lean legs. A far cry from her in the shapeless scrubs that she usually wore in his company.

He fought valiantly to regroup but his tightening body apparently had other ideas. And maybe he would have acted on it under other circumstances. The worst of it was that he knew the attraction certainly wasn't one-sided.

She might have her own set of lines that she didn't cross, but Seth could read her desire for him in every hot glance she cast his way when she caught herself off-guard. Could read it in the way her pulse beat that little bit too wildly when he stood close to her, and the way each time she swayed instinctively into him before reining herself back.

As it was, he kept reminding himself that she was here because he'd asked her to help him with Noah. And he couldn't do anything to jeopardise that.

Noah, he reminded himself quickly. The reason she was even here.

She splayed her hands on the granite countertop as though she was also trying to pull herself back in check. 'I think the most significant part, though, is that he is now talking to you again.'

'It is.' Seth bowed his head in acknowledgement.

That had come like a punch to the chest, knocking all the air out and leaving him paralysed for what had felt like a lifetime. His nephew had finally talked to him at the picnic. Right *to* him, looking him straight in the eye and speaking a full sentence.

It was almost too good to be true. And he had this woman to thank for it.

But what would happen if she left Baystone the way she'd said she might have to? Would his nephew regress again, like yesterday?

So don't let her go.

The thought slammed into his brain, harder than a racquetball and just as impactful—a wild idea that perhaps there was a way they could help each other. He slid his hands into his pockets as if that could somehow silence himself.

The force of the attraction was crazy. And thrilling. And entirely inappropriate. Which was precisely why it would be a good thing for his haywire libido if she were to leave Baystone Medical. The thoughts flip-flopped in his head.

What was best for him versus what was best for Noah.

He might value his standards and rules, but Andrea was the first person to whom Noah had opened up. It was clear that the lad was beginning to blossom due to her presence, like a sapling reaching for the sun.

Would his little nephew wilt again if she suddenly disappeared?

He couldn't risk it, Seth told himself.

'How's the flat hunt going?' His mouth seemed to formulate the words all on their own.

She scrunched her nose.

'It isn't,' she admitted.

Reluctantly, he thought.

Because she didn't want to leave? Or because she thought this was none of his business?

'Now I know that you declined my suggestion of your HCP-med degree more out of familial obligation than out of *time and money,* as you suggested, I believe I have a workable solution.'

What did it say that he liked the flash of fire in her eyes that reminded him that Andrea wasn't at all intimidated by him. Far from it.

'You don't understand the situation,' she bit out.

'Having seen where your mum is currently living, I can see that it might have been okay at one time, but that her needs have changed since her MS has progressed.'

'Then you'll understand that I can't afford to drop back to part-time work to allow for all the studying that the degree requires.' Evidently she was trying to appear logical rather than frustrated, but she didn't quite succeed, and it was clear how much she secretly wanted that degree. 'I need to work full-time and use that income—as well as anything Daniel can spare—to get my mum into a better place. Somewhere that has a wheelchair-accessible shower and lower kitchen counter-tops, for starters.'

'Which is why I propose your mum moves into my late

sister's apartment on the other side of town,' he suggested calmly—though with a surprising undercurrent of triumph. 'My name was on the lease, so it has come to me now, and I was going to keep it as an investment for Noah. It a spacious ground-floor apartment with dedicated parking.'

'Well, yes, that's great. But I don't think...'

'It has a pretty, low-maintenance garden.' He deliberately ignored her interruption. 'And it would easily lend itself to being modified for your mum with the accessible shower and countertops that you mentioned. Whatever she needs.'

'I don't have the money for that!' Andrea exclaimed.

'You don't need to. I'll cover the costs. Plus, it's three-bed, so enough room for your mum, for a carer whenever they need to stay and for you when you eventually move back in.'

'When I *eventually* move back in?' Andrea peered at him. 'Where will I be until then?'

It shouldn't have felt like trump card—but somehow it did.

'Until then,' he told her calmly, confidently, 'You could move in here.'

CHAPTER TEN

'OKAY, LET'S START the cortical stimulation, starting at two-point-zero milli-amps, please.'

Andrea observed, fascinated as always, as Seth worked on a low-grade glioma in their patient's right parietal lobe. Her own mind was grateful for something tangible to concentrate on, if only to stop her from dwelling on Seth's shocking offer.

Had it really only been twelve hours ago? It felt like a lifetime.

He wanted her to move in with him.

Well, not *with him* per se, more with Noah. But the entire notion was preposterous.

Wasn't it?

Every time she replayed it in her mind, the sheer shock of it walloped into her. For the longest time, she hadn't answered. She'd waited for him to make a joke. To take it back. He'd almost looked appalled. But he'd looked something else, too. Something that she couldn't name, but that had set off detonations inside her chest. No matter that Seth had made it all sound so rational, so logical—a quid pro quo, with her helping him with Noah, and him giving her a temporary accommodation reprieve.

It all made perfect sense despite the part of her brain still attempting to rationalise what he was suggesting. And, even though she wasn't sure she'd quite processed it, there was a strange, reckless part of her that wanted to agree.

That wanted to leap at the offer.

Though not, she suspected, for the right reasons.

'Andrea.' Seth's voice pulled her up from her thoughts. 'Want to tell us why we're doing this?'

Her face hot, Andrea snapped back to attention.

They'd already been operating for some time, working meticulously from their first incision in the man's front temporal lobe and removing the section of scalp and the dura, to localising all the significant structures inside the brain.

And, as much as she knew they were fighting to save a patient's life, there was an undeniable beauty in what Seth was doing that was almost mesmerising to watch. It made learning from him something like a joy.

So far, she'd already seen how he'd used neural navigation to identify the tumour limits, and now he was mapping the motor cortex and sub-cortex to try to reduce the risk of post-operative neurological deficits.

Guilt weaved through her at allowing herself to be distracted, as well as something else she pretended not to understand.

Steeling herself, Andrea stepped forward and answered his question. 'The location of this particular tumour is near the eloquent tissue, so neurological deficits could include loss of sensory or motor functions in the patient's face, arms, legs or even cause speech deficits. You've already established the limits of the tumour, as we saw before, and now you're going to map motor functions over multiple assessments using the asleep-awake-asleep method of anaesthesia.'

Whilst they were mapping the involuntary motor functions, the patient would remain under light anaesthesia, but once Seth was ready to map the language centre he would need voluntary functions, so they would wake up the patient.

She already felt more a part of it than she'd ever felt before, so how would it actually feel if she were on a nurse-to-doctor conversion course? Not that she fooled herself that she would ever become a neurosurgeon like Seth, but that had never been her dream. And it was Seth who had given her this new lease of life.

Was she really going to turn down his offer just because she was afraid she was too attracted to him?

Seth wasn't her ex, saying one thing but doing another—he'd been more than clear about the terms of the proposed agreement. It would be somewhere convenient for her to live whilst she found a new flat share, at the same time as helping him to bond with his nephew.

It was that simple. A win-win.

He'd made it abundantly clear that sponsoring her for the HCP-med degree wasn't at all contingent on her decision, assuring her that both Jack and him would provide the references and sponsors. It was like an answer to the prayers she hadn't even dared to say. Like a lottery win... only better.

Because it meant that Seth was so confident in her ability to achieve her long-abandoned dreams that he was actually prepared to put himself out there for her. And just knowing that fact somehow revived a sense of worth in herself that she had thought had been killed off years ago.

If only her insides weren't rioting or aching for something even remotely non-practical about everything he was suggesting... The tiniest hint that a traitorous part of him wanted her there because he still sensed that pull of attraction that had walloped them both that first night.

But of course he didn't want her around for his own personal reasons—something about which she should be pleased.

Something about which she *was* pleased, she silently berated herself.

Seth had been clear on what he wanted from her, and what he was prepared to offer in return. He had set out clear terms. He had end dates. As long as she went into it with her eyes wide open, then how could he ever have the power to make her feel as small, as inconsequential, as Josh had made her feel?

What a time to be learning such hard truths about herself. What a time to realise that she'd let her ex-husband steal more than the money out of her purse. She'd let him steal her trust in anyone—but especially in herself.

Shaking her head to empty it of the wayward thoughts, Andrea dragged her focus back to the patient on the table. She watched Seth meticulously map his patient's brain, increasing the milliamps until the cortical stimulation could be recorded, and keeping the exposed stimulated cortex constantly irrigated with ice-cold saline solution to minimise the risk of stimulation-induced seizures. Once he had localised the motor and sensory areas of the cortex, he turned his focus on the spatial awareness mapping.

'Okay, Andrea, you're up.'

Her heart pounded with adrenalin as she picked up the clipboard she'd prepared with a series of vertical lines drawn on an A4 sheet.

She handed the pen to the patient and waited whilst Seth's team explained to the man that he would carry out a line bisection test whilst they stimulated the inferior parietal lobule cortex. She felt almost proud when no disturbances were detected and the man's strike-throughs remained smooth and steady.

And then he began the tumour resection itself.

'We're using microsurgical technique in an attempt to preserve all major vessels, since it's the best way to avoid stroke in the normal brain tissue surrounding the tumour,' he advised the room before turning his attention to his resident. 'You can use the sulci as landmarks to ensure a more precise resection of the more superficial areas of the tumour. Just be aware that the tumour can distort these landmarks at a deeper level, hence the importance of through mapping.'

For several hours, they continued to work on their patient, stopping where normal tissue was encountered or where the neural deficits would have been too significant. This, Seth had warned her in advance, would be the difference between a gross total resection, where he would be able to remove the tumour in its entirety, and a subtotal resection where he would concentrate on removing only the necessary parts of the tumour to alleviate his patient's motor symptoms without creating even greater deficits.

He'd described it as the most delicate balancing act and, being in the OR with him now, she could clearly see why.

But his passion and dedication were inspiring to watch. When she thought about the sheer complexity of the neurosurgery that he did, and coupled it with the way he was more than happy to set his own ego aside and ask her for help with his nephew, it only made her admire him all the more.

And, more treacherously, it would have made her fall for him all the harder—had she been falling for him at all, of course.

Which she wasn't.

She would control that.

She just needed to remember the parameters of their agreement, in the same way that he'd established the parameters of this awful tumour, and not allow herself to get too comfortable, too complacent, living with Seth.

How hard could that be? It wasn't neurosurgery, after all.

Perhaps not, a voice murmured insidiously inside her head.

Because, no matter how piously she tried to claim otherwise, the fact remained that she was ridiculously, undeniably attracted to the man. Consequently, she was horribly afraid that she was letting her heart influence her decision. And surely that made agreeing to his terms—however generous they may be—all the more dangerous?

On the other hand, unless she wanted to leave Baystone and start afresh all over again—which she definitely didn't—then how could she possibly afford to turn him down?

Andrea rode the private lift up to Seth's penthouse two days later. But this time it felt different, and it wasn't just the fact that neither Seth nor his efficient concierge were accompanying her.

She patted the key card in her pocket, as though for reassurance, and clutched her small bag to her. She still wasn't sure that moving into Seth's home was a good idea. Aside from the financial and career aspects, or the fact that she wanted to do everything she could to help little Noah, it was the tell-tale, thrilling tingle that excited her the most. As if, despite all her brain's logical and practical arguments, her heart was entertaining illicit fantasies all of its own.

Well, that stops now, she commanded herself silently, and lifted her chin pugnaciously.

It felt like perfect timing when the lift chose that moment to come to a smooth halt and its doors slid quietly open to face the penthouse's main door.

Throwing her shoulders back and swinging her bag up, Andrea stepped across the floor before swiping her card at the door. The lock turned with an obliging sound, allowing her to push the door open. Even so, it took her another two or three steadying breaths before she could galvanise her legs into action and walk inside.

It felt...different.

The place felt should have felt less intimate in Seth's

absence, less intimidating. And perhaps it did indeed feel the former, but it certainly didn't feel less intimidating.

Seth had suggested she take the time to take a proper tour and orientate herself without the pressure of anyone else being there. She realised now that it was probably a good idea.

She knew the way to Noah's room upstairs, and understood that her guest room was the door opposite his. Seth's master suite was apparently at the other end of the apartment, so that was good—there would be no need to venture down his way.

Ever.

The kitchen, dining area and living space downstairs were all as she remembered but, now that she looked around, she noticed a set of double doors on the other side of the front door. Seth's study, as it turned out. And, though he hadn't said that it was off-limits, she resolutely turned her back and refused to give in to some uncharacteristically curious part of herself that seemed to be itching to take a peek. As though the private space might reveal something about its often enigmatic owner… A treacherous part of her was desperate to learn more about Seth.

Determinedly, she turned her back on the doors and took a step back towards the kitchen area, her eyes honing in on two laundry bags behind the front door that she'd missed when she'd first entered, one marked with Seth's name, the other with Noah's.

Was he having the laundry sent out?

Andrea almost laughed aloud. It was so fitting. She couldn't imagine Seth even owning a washing machine, and she certainly couldn't imagine him using it. Then again, why would he need to, when he lived in a place like this? No doubt it was a complimentary service that was all taken care of by the infinitely capable Stan.

A far cry from her own life.

The closest her family had ever got to having their laundry done for them was when she'd been nine and her mum had been going through a particularly difficult period with her MS. The lady at the local laundrette had told her that, if Andrea put the clothes in the dryer before she left for school, then she would fold them into a bag to collect on her way home again that afternoon.

Andrea crossed the room and picked up the bag containing the little boy's clothes, her hand hovering momentarily over Seth's bag before deciding against touching it. Then she headed upstairs, her low heels echoing loudly in a way she hadn't noticed before, making her feel all the more self-conscious.

On the landing, to the left of the stairs, was a kind of open mini-gallery, and on the right was a chess table which she hadn't noticed the other evening in the low light. Now, she couldn't help but imagine Seth sitting up here and playing a game—perhaps even teaching his nephew. It was surprisingly easy to picture him in this space. It was so *Seth.*

Andrea turned into the short hallway heading straight for Noah's room, but she couldn't prevent her gaze from sneaking to the set of double heavy doors that she knew to be Seth's master suite.

She didn't know why the sight of it now sent a little something rolling along her spine. Or, rather, she didn't want to admit why that happened.

Stuffing the unwelcome emotions back down, she placed her hand on the handle to the little boy's room and stepped inside. The room was more spacious than it had seemed the other night—arguably bigger than both her bedroom and her mother's put together—and spotlessly clean, with what was clearly a red, blue and white designer nautical theme.

It looked straight out of a catalogue but lacked anything that made it seem personal. Sure, there was a small toy box in one corner, and a few books on a bookshelf, but there were no personal items such as drawings or crafts. And there were no photos—not even of Noah's mother.

Andrea thought of the little home where she'd grown up. It had invariably been full of pictures that she and her brother had drawn, or crafts that they'd made for Mum. Everything had gone proudly onto the fridge, or the walls, or had been propped on dressers.

Her mother's pride in her children had been so unwavering that the rest of it—their father's death, the fact that she needed them to help care for her—hadn't seemed so bad.

Irritation rolled through her. Seth was clearly neat and tidy, with very few knick-knacks and no clutter around his home. But that didn't mean Noah ought to live according to those standards. It was a conversation she intended to have with Seth as soon as possible, she decided as she busied herself with putting the fresh laundry away.

A few minutes later, quietly closing the doors behind her, Andrea made her way back out to the hallway, deliberately not looking towards Seth's master suite. It was as though she was frightened of the fantasises that would assail her if she did. Such as the memories of what had happened between them both only a few nights before: the image that filled her head every night, right before she fell asleep.

But, in those fantasies, it never stopped at just that.

So instead she headed for a wide single door back down the hall, which Seth had mentioned to her, and edged tentatively inside.

It was like a mirror image of Seth's room, except white sheets covered this queen-sized bed, and there were paintings on the wall. The modern splashes of colour brightened the space and made it feel a little more welcoming, even if they weren't precisely her taste.

Moving across her new room, Andrea peered through another door to reveal a generous *en suite*, complete with gorgeous roll-top bath which begged to be filled with hot, bubble-laden water.

Yet another door led her into a walk-in closet that had to be bigger than the bedroom she'd had in her last flat share.

She defiantly ignored the snide voice in her head warning her not to get used to it; reminding her that in less than two months she would be out of Seth's apartment and into her new flat share.

Back to real life.

But, for now, she was here. The first thing she would do would be to cook her new charge something from scratch— if Seth was sending his laundry out, she imagined he was feeding his nephew on the most expensive takeout in the city—and then she would tackle Seth about the bedroom décor.

Andrea hurried down to the kitchen, already mentally preparing a shopping list as she opened the fridge to check its presumably scant contents.

She stopped abruptly, staring in surprise, just as Seth came through the penthouse door with Noah in tow.

'Andrea!'

The little boy's cry of delight had her closing the fridge door and swinging round quickly, hoping that Seth wouldn't see her guilty expression as she levelled a bright smile at the little boy.

'Hey Noah, I hope you had a great day in school.'

Nodding vigorously, the six-year-old held up a poster for her to admire.

'Wow, "the life cycle of penguins",' she read aloud. 'This is excellent; did you do this?'

Another enthusiastic nod.

'Well, I think it's brilliant, Noah. I wonder if we should perhaps hang it on the fridge? Or on the wall in your bedroom? Show it off a little?'

'Yes,' Seth agreed loudly, making them both jump.

Was it her imagination or was this a chink in his usually calm, unflappable demeanour? Did she see relief chasing through those impossibly handsome features?

'Yes?' she echoed before she could stop herself.

'I think hanging it is a great idea. I think I might have some tacks in my office. Noah, why don't you get changed out of your school uniform whilst I go and find them?'

And then, before she could say anything, Noah gambolled off up to his room whilst Seth turned quickly for his study. For a split second, Andrea hesitated, and then she followed Seth across the hallway.

'Was that eagerness because you want to see him hang the work in his room?' she asked as soon as she was sure Noah was out of hearing. 'Or because you didn't want to see him hang the work on the fridge?'

Seth looked up at her.

'I thought it would be good to begin to make his bedroom his own,' he answered simply.

'Right.'

She thought of the empty room and the questions only pushed harder against her brain. She couldn't have said why she bit them back.

'If you want to know why there are no pictures on the walls, you can just ask,' Seth suggested mildly.

Perhaps a little too mildly.

She couldn't help feeling wrong-footed. It was a strange feeling when she was normally so careful never to say anything that could offend.

'Right.' She licked her lips. 'Why is Noah's room relatively empty?'

Carefully, he indicated a couple of large crates in the corner of the office behind the door.

'Both are full of the personal belongings I had packed up from my sister's apartment. They contain Noah's toys, artwork, anything Stacey had which I thought he might like.'

'Oh.'

'I hung up pictures from his old bedroom and I set up photos of him with Stacey that had been around her apartment. But when I went in the next morning he'd taken them all down and put them into the bottom of his toy box.'

'And you couldn't ask him why because he wasn't talking to you,' she realised with a thud.

He twisted his wrist upwards in acknowledgement.

'My best guess was that the pictures I chose reminded him too much of his life with Stacey. I figured he wasn't quite ready, and I didn't want to upset him further by pushing the subject.'

'You've been allowing him space to adjust to his new life in his own time.' She exhaled heavily. 'And you didn't put those crates into storage because you want them on hand the moment Noah might decide he wants something from them.'

'I might be a confirmed bachelor with a certain reputation...' He eyed her with something approaching tight-lipped amusement. 'But I'm not quite as inept with my nephew as you seem to think I am.'

'I didn't...' She could feel the heat rush into her cheeks. Seth continued as though she hadn't spoken.

'I also enjoy cooking. My grandmother taught me when I was a kid, before she died, and I find it relaxing after long days in surgery. So, contrary to whatever you might have been thinking when you opened my fridge earlier, I have not been feeding my young nephew take-out morning, noon and evening.'

Andrea didn't answer. She didn't think she needed to; she felt her guilt was all too evident in her blooming cheeks. So, instead, she watched as Seth moved around the desk in the middle of the room, searching for the tacks he'd said he had, and took a moment to gaze around the space.

Like the rest of the penthouse, it was every inch what

a confirmed bachelor might have—all dark wood and angular lines. The desk itself was a solidly built piece, fit for
a man who looked stronger and more solid every time she
saw him. The groaning bookcases boasted works that were
clearly well-thumbed and there because they were wanted,
rather than simply being there to impress anyone who cared
to enter the space.

Her eyes slid to the worn leather chair in one corner of
the space. It was a soft, yet utterly masculine affair which
made it only too easy to imagine Seth sitting in this room,
reading, learning.

As if he wasn't already the most educated man in almost
any room he walked into. She could well believe that he
would do everything he could to ensure that he learned all
he required to do the best for his young nephew. So much
for the notorious playboy.

Yes, Seth Mulder was definitely everything that she'd
expected him to be.

Yet nothing like she'd expected.

'You do know that you're doing a great job, don't you?'
She blew out a low breath.

A fresh jolt of awareness sliced through her at the expression that momentarily crossed his features. And then
it was gone, replaced by one that was far harsher.

'I think my nephew might beg to differ,' he bit out.

'Kids are more resilient than parents often give them
credit for.' Even to her own ears it sounded trite.

Seth's disdainful expression confirmed it.

'I'm well aware of that fact; I see it every day with my
patients. But this is my nephew I'm talking about. I need
to be there for him. Like I should have been there for my
sister. If I had been...'

The sheer pain in his expression sharply cut into her,
sucking the air from her lungs.

She knew that pain, that sense of loss, only too well.

'You can't go down that path.' She waved her hand, as though she could magic all that hurt away for him. 'Those arguments aren't relevant. The point is, you're here for Noah now.'

He looked as if he wanted to argue, but instead he dipped his head curtly.

'I am,' he ground out. 'But I still need your help.'

The bleak expression on his face had turned his usually animated eyes to a dull grey, as though the life and light had dimmed. It wasn't, Andrea realised abruptly, a look that she wanted to see on this usually dynamic man.

He was more complex, more wounded, than she had ever known.

All these years she'd thought she was seeing the real Seth, but she hadn't known him at all. And now she realised she would give almost anything so be the one to heal him.

'Come on,' she called out with deliberate cheerfulness. 'Let's get Noah and get out of here for a few hours.'

'Where are we going?'

Seth sounded dubious but she was gratified to note that he was obeying her.

'I've no idea.' She grinned at him suddenly. 'But somewhere fun.'

CHAPTER ELEVEN

THE FOLLOWING DAYS bled into weeks as Seth—still adjusting to living with his nephew—also began to adjust to having Andrea there.

He'd been prepared for the transition to be difficult, expecting to stay at the hospital more often than not, if only to give the two of them space. It was more than clear to him that Noah found Andrea's presence far easier to deal with than his own.

But, in the end, that didn't happen.

Andrea dragged them out on an almost a nightly basis, making it clear that she thought they would bond better on neutral ground rather than in Seth's apartment. And she was right: Noah was beginning to communicate more and more easily with every passing day. From swimming lessons to football in the park, and from racing remote-control boats on the lake to visiting the local petting farm, Andrea constantly engineered ways to help Noah and him get to know each other better.

To help the three of them get to know each other better.

Because, the more time they spent together, the more Seth found himself actually looking forward to getting home and seeing what exciting ideas Andrea had in mind for them that day. Though he was beginning to wish he could talk to her in work as freely as he talked to her back at the apartment.

He didn't care to examine what it might mean that the secretive nature of their situation was beginning to grate on him.

Perhaps that was why, tonight, he was taking advantage of Noah's much-demanded first sleepover with the twins and Billy in order to take Andrea out on a child-free date.

No, not *date*, he corrected himself hastily. Just two friends enjoying a meal out a restaurant together. Michelin-starred, of course, since Andrea had once told him she'd never eaten anywhere like that before.

He conveniently ignored the fact that he'd deliberately selected a restaurant that he'd never taken any woman to before—even if that meant having to drive an hour or so out of the city. And the fact that he'd been to his preferred barber for a cut-throat shave and a hair trim two weeks ahead of schedule.

Seth waited until the waiter had left with their orders, then turned to the Andrea. Her eyes were almost violet in the light of the restaurant.

'How is your mum doing?'

As though staying close to neutral topics could stop this dark, hungry thing that had been stalking through him ever since she'd emerged from her room looking like some kind of Hollywood star, in a deceptively simple little black dress that skimmed lightly over her body yet moved with her deliciously.

'Good.' Andrea nodded. 'Excited. The alterations you had carried out will be completed by the end of the week and she'll be moving in after that. So, thank you.'

He lifted his hand dismissively. He didn't want her thanks; he just wanted her to enjoy her degree course, secure in the knowledge that her mum was okay.

'Have you received your HCP-med schedule yet?'

'Not yet,' she answered, the happiness in her soft voice dancing over his skin. 'Next week, I'm told.'

One more week and then he'd lose her from his OR for many of his surgeries. He wasn't relishing it, though he wasn't sure since when he'd come to look forward to working alongside her as often as possible.

'Then we'll call this a pre-emptive, celebratory dinner,' he told her gravely.

She tilted her head, her gaze direct—and the blood quickened within his veins.

'Is that really why we're here?'

He wanted to brush off the question. Instead he heard himself answering, 'We're here because I think you deserve an outing that isn't geared towards a six-year-old for once.'

He was satisfied that 'outing' was a more appropriate term than 'date'. If only he could make his wandering mind remember that. 'And I wanted to thank you for everything you've done and continue to do. Without you, I fear that I would have already lost Noah to his grandparents.'

He didn't add he feared that he still could lose his nephew. That they were still waiting for final decisions with regard to custody.

'No thanks are necessary,' Andrea answered quietly. 'I told you a month ago that you were doing a great job, and I still think that's the case.'

You're doing a great job.

The uncomplicated declaration echoed around Seth's brain, bouncing off the inflexible walls of his skull. Andrea's words meant more to him than they had any right to—if only he could even half-believe them.

'A month ago I felt as though I was drowning in the responsibility of playing father—and mother—to my worryingly stoic little nephew,' he confessed. 'I told myself it was nonsense, since I'd never shied away from my responsibilities to any of my patients as a neurosurgeon. Not even once, no matter how hopeless the operation threatened to be. Yet the role of being a parent was terrifying me in a way that I would never have believed possible.'

'I can't help but wonder if part of being terrified was because you hated the idea of something you weren't good at,' she suggested softly. 'You're so used to being the best in your class—in Baystone, in your field—that the idea of not knowing what you were doing must have been an anathema to you.'

A few weeks ago he would have instantly denied it. Now, he couldn't help wondering if there wasn't at least a grain of truth to it.

'It's possible.' He dipped his head, taking a sip of his wine. It had a delicate flavour that seemed to complement the food and cleanse the palate, just as the sommelier had claimed. 'It has certainly given me a newfound appreciation for everything my sister achieved, all those years as a single parent.'

And it made him feel guiltier than ever that he hadn't helped her out more.

'If Noah gets through this—mind and soul intact,' he managed gruffly, 'It will be despite me, not because of me.'

It was an admission that he would never have expected to hear himself make—not even to his best mate, Jack. But there was a quality about Andrea that had a way of reaching into his very being and drawing the truth out of him.

Even if—right now—she was shaking her head.

'I think we both know that isn't true.'

'Do we?' His voice sounded harsh even to his own ears. 'Because all I know is that, without you around, he wouldn't even be communicating with me right now. The courts may well have already decided that he would be better off with his paternal grandparents, I would have failed Stacey.'

'His reaction to his mother's tragic death isn't a reflection on you. My brother stopped communicating with me—

with my mother—and we were in his life every single day. It was simply his way of coping, just as it was Noah's way of coping. I suspect that, if he had been given to grandparents he didn't even know, then the problem would have only manifested even more severely—not less.'

Seth couldn't answer that. But he wanted so much to think that she was right. The more time she spent living at the apartment with them, the more evident it became that she made everything feel...not *lighter* or *brighter*, exactly, but less...dark? Less *heavy*.

Her outlook was more like Stacey's than his.

'You're still doing a great job,' she repeated firmly as his mouth tugged into a rueful smile.

'I think we have different definitions of *great*.'

'Whilst I think you have unrealistically high expectations of yourself,' Andrea countered gently. 'I suspect your sister left Noah in your custody, not because she knew you would instantly be the perfect parent to the person who was clearly the most precious thing in her life, but because she knew she could trust you to do everything you could to learn to be the best version that you could be.'

'Is that why, that first night you'd moved in, you wondered if my fridge contained anything other than beer? And if my nephew's bedroom was supposed to look like some kind of bare prison cell?'

'And I apologise again for that. They were my prejudices rather than yours.' Andrea grinned. 'Consider me re-educated now.'

He still wanted too much to believe her.

'Don't be so quick to vindicate me. There wouldn't even have been photos of Stacey around the place if not for you.'

Even now, he could still remember with vivid clarity how she had challenged him over that, looking incredulous when he'd told her he didn't have any.

'Not even from your childhood together?' she'd pressed

several times, until he'd replied darkly how neither he nor Stacey had wanted to remember a lot from that time.

But Andrea hadn't let it go, and ultimately she'd reminded him of several happy memories he'd hidden away, of times he and his sister had spent with their grandmother. And then Andrea and Noah had found a way to access Stacey's old digital photo albums to uncover a pile of childhood pictures of the silvery-haired woman he remembered.

Now his nephew had photos of his mother and great-grandmother to look at whenever he wanted to.

Yet, as grateful as Seth was, it wasn't that which affected him the most. Instead, it was how unperturbed she appeared by everything. As if it wasn't so shocking. As if he wasn't the heartless monster he had felt himself to be since Stacey had died; the one who hadn't done more for his sister when she'd been alive.

Even when she and Noah had lived with him, he'd managed five minutes or so of listening to her during the evenings he'd bothered to return to the apartment, before sequestering himself in his study in order to watch video after video of surgeries in order to perfect his own techniques. Why had it taken her death for him to regret just how much he'd allowed his work to keep himself too busy for either of them?

How had he ever thought that his career was more important than family? And why had it taken someone like Andrea to make him realise how much of a mistake that had been?

Not someone like Andrea, a whisper floated through him. *Only Andrea.*

Shame punched through him.

'Stop it.'

Her soft voice had him jerking his head up.

'Pardon?'

'Whatever that was.' She circled her hand in the vicinity of his face. 'Whatever you were just thinking. Stop. It won't help you, and it certainly won't help Noah.'

It unsettled him that she seemed to read him so easily— though he suspected not quite for the reasons it ought to. He was accustomed to people deferring to him, both in the hospital and out of it. Patients revered him, staff obeyed him, even dates conceded to him. But Andrea—though always respectful—had never been intimidated by him.

And, since she'd moved into his apartment, there had never been any veneration or genuflection. She was refreshingly honest—to the point of disapproval.

'Anyway, I have something I want to talk to you about.' She swallowed, looking unexpectedly uncomfortable.

Sliding his hand across the table, he lifted his wine glass and took another sip, wishing it were a crystal brandy balloon containing a couple of fingers of his favourite cognac.

'If you have something to say, Andrea, then say it,' he prompted.

'I was considering brightening the place. Maybe. If you don't object. Perhaps reintroduce a few of those homely touches that your sister used to have?'

'Fine.'

She opened her mouth, as though to further her argument, then stopped.

'Fine?' she echoed. 'It isn't an issue at all for you?'

'I don't know that I'd say *at all*.' He supressed a grin. 'I mean, Stacey had taste. You might not.'

'I have taste!' she exclaimed, reaching across the table to bat her hand against his forearm before she realised what she was doing. 'As for the consequences, I believe your bark is far worse than your bite, you know.'

The electricity crackled straight through him. And, by the way Andrea's muscles froze, her fingers still against the skin of his arm, it crackled through her too.

Move, he commanded himself silently. *Move*.

But he didn't. He couldn't. And it felt as if they both stayed in place for an eternity, their eyes locked, neither of them speaking. Playing the gentleman with this woman was exhausting. He'd far rather play the big, bad wolf that she was pretending she didn't think he was.

He'd far rather show her that his bite could definitely be worse than his bark... With teeth...preferably all over her delectable body.

It was getting harder and harder to remember his rules about not blurring lines. Breaking rules—even his own— was something he'd never done. He'd seen how destructive that could be—watching his mother waste her entire adult life trying to make a selfish, egocentric man into something he could never become. Watching her ignore his sister and him because she hadn't had energy enough for them as well as the man who had fathered them—though had never been any kind of father to them.

That man had been too busy trying to nail anything in a skirt. He certainly wasn't the man that Seth had ever aspired to be. It wasn't part of the deal he'd made with Andrea.

He'd promised not to lay a finger on her. And he didn't break his promises.

Finally, *finally,* he broke the moment and slid his arm back.

'Ah, here comes our waiter...' His voice was more of a rasp than before.

'Oh. Good.' She pulled her own arm back, sounding as dazed as he felt.

For a moment, they both launched into thanking the waiter, as though desperate for something to break the sudden tension. And then the man was gone and they were plunged back into a taut silence.

Seth scrabbled for more prosaic conversation.

'You remember that you're shadowing me on an awake

craniotomy the day after tomorrow? It's a surgery I think you'll really enjoy.'

And, when she lifted her cutlery and turned her attention to the exquisite food on her plate, he told himself that he welcomed it.

Andrea wasn't entirely certain how she got through the meal, though it was heavenly.

But somehow the evening seemed to have blurred into two halves—before that white-hot, blindingly bright flame had flared up between her and Seth, and after.

No matter how they'd tried to direct the conversation back to more banal topics, they somehow kept finding their way back to gentle teasing. And if she wasn't mistaken, given her pitted history in the art, flirting.

She suspected it had been happening more and more over the past few weeks, but she'd told herself she was imagining it. Tonight, whether it was the wine or the fact that they were out without Noah as a buffer, Andrea couldn't tell herself again that it was only in her head. No matter how much she tried to pretend otherwise, she was terribly afraid that she was coming to enjoy living with Noah and him that little bit too much.

How many times had she caught herself thinking that the three of them were like a ready-made family? How many times had she berated herself for imagining they could ever be the family she'd thought she would never have?

Without warning, when they rose to go, his hand slid to the small of her back as he escorted her from their table and to the cloakroom. And in a heartbeat her mouth ran dry, though she pretended not to notice.

It was harder to pretend when he ushered her into the buttery leather back seat of the luxurious car that he had ordered to collect them, then moved in alongside her, so deliciously close that his solid, muscular thigh pressed so tightly to her.

The action sent all sorts of dangerously illicit images hurtling through her brain. It felt as though he were the deepest, richest well of every single temptation she'd never before experienced in her life and she was teetering precariously on the edge.

And, if she toppled over it, then she was terribly afraid that she would fall for an eternity.

'I hope you aren't going to go so quiet at the gala this weekend.'

His rich, amused voice snapped her back to the present as she twisted her head to stare at him, her brain still processing the words.

'The gala?' She shook her head, as if that would get it to work faster.

'The medical ball,' Seth clarified. 'The fundraiser for the main hospital.'

'Oh. Right.' It began to click into place. Then she shook her head. 'No, I'm not attending.'

Seth frowned at her.

'No choice—it's a three-line whip. We might be the private wing but we're expected to support all the same. Don't tell me you haven't attended before? You've been at Baystone for years.'

'I must have always been on shift,' she lied easily.

No reason for him to know that had been because she'd been only too happy to swap her shifts. The idea of attending a gala like that had always been a daunting one. Not least when it came to trying to find a dress that she could afford but that wouldn't make her stand out when she had to rub shoulders with some obscenely wealthy patrons.

She didn't imagine any of them would buy a cocktail

dress from a charity shop, like the one she was wearing tonight. She was only grateful that Seth had been so complimentary.

'Besides, three-line whip or not, no one really cares whether a scrub nurse attends.'

'Well, this year I care.' He growled abruptly, sending her into freefall, spiralling downward.

'Don't be silly,' she managed, barely recognising her own voice.

'Whatever traits I may have,' he rasped, 'I don't believe *silly* is one of them.'

She felt flummoxed.

'No. But... I imagine you'll be far too in demand to care who is there,' she hedged.

'So, you imagine me?' His all-male voice wove around her, heating her blood from the inside.

'Sorry? No-no...' she sputtered, horrified, as he seemed closer to her without even moving. 'No, that isn't at all what I said.'

That was *horror, wasn't it?*

His quirky smile fizzled though her, making her feel all the more feverish.

'On the contrary, it's precisely what you said.'

He was definitely closer. Only she couldn't be sure whether Seth had moved, or her. Possibly both.

'I—'

'Perhaps it might interest you to know what I think when I imagine you?' He cut her with a gravelly sound that was like a feather-light stroke in all the places where she was beginning to ache most.

She stared at him for what felt like a lifetime.

'You imagine *me*?'

Was that really her own voice? It was difficult to tell. Difficult even to recognise herself when she felt as though she was being overwhelmed by the raw, unadulterated masculinity that emanated from this man.

Heady and gloriously decadent.

Not least when he reached out and twirled a lock of her hair around his finger, almost lazily, making her breath hitch right there in her chest.

'All too often,' he muttered as she twisted in her seat to face him.

But, no matter how loudly that voice inside her tried to shout that this was a conversation more dangerous than any stunt an adrenalin-junkie could undertake, there was no way to stop all those...emotions within herself from skittering off.

She lifted her hands without even being aware of the movement, compelled by something she didn't fully understand—or want to understand. By the feel of that powerfully built chest beneath her palms, and the faintest hint of his warm breath on her cheek.

So much for telling herself that she could handle tonight and a meal at a Michelin-starred restaurant with Seth Mulder. She'd warned herself against treating it like a date, and yet here she was, practically throwing herself at him in the hope that the evening might turn into something more.

Why?

It was almost a relief when the shrill sound of her phone broke the consuming silence in the car.

Fumbling in her clutch bag, she snatched up her mobile and checked the screen.

The moment between Seth and her disappeared in a flash.

'It's my mother.' Andrea bit her lip.

Her mum knew their restaurant plans, so she wouldn't have called unless there was a problem.

It was ridiculously gratifying when, without needing

any further explanation, Seth instantly hit the intercom between the driver and them.

'Change of plan.' He spoke efficiently, before giving her mother's address.

And she tried not to read too much into the fact that he knew it by heart.

CHAPTER TWELVE

'THE MAN WASHED his wife's car,' Andrea read out.

'The man washed his wife's car,' echoed Seth's craniotomy patient, as Andrea noted the results whilst Seth mapped the speech centre of his patient's brain. She worked in harmony with him, as she had always done, without giving any of their hawk-eyed colleagues any reason to know about their new living arrangements.

Or the fact that he'd been the one to take charge the other night when her mum had taken a fall, offering support and a shoulder to cry on.

When was the last time she'd had someone do that for her?

It felt bizarre, and illicit, and unexpectedly thrilling—especially for someone who had spent her life trying to do the right thing.

'Okay.' On Seth's signal, Andrea turned back to her patient. 'Let's try another sentence: "the cat slept in front of the fire".'

'The cat slept in front of the fire.'

'Good, that's great,' she encouraged, pausing for the next signal.

'The rooster crowed at dawn every day.'

'The rooster crowed...day.'

'Great, you're doing well.' Andrea kept her smile bright,

even as she knew Seth would be responding on the other side of the curtain.

It was the warning they needed that he was now entering the dangerous, eloquent areas of the brain. If the tumour was here, then he would need to leave it.

'The boy slid down the long, blue slide.'

'The boy…slide.'

'Good,' Andrea repeated, because it wasn't about the patient getting it right. It was about allowing Seth to understand where all the major structures of his patient's brain were located, particularly all the eloquent tissue. She watched as Seth marked out the areas of his patient's brain with a sterile marker.

The amount she'd learned already from Seth was incredible. She'd always found him to be generous with his time as well as with his expertise but, since his promise to sponsor her to undertake the nurse-to-doctor conversion course, he wasn't stinting on the time he afforded her.

'Shall we begin the comprehension section of the test?' she murmured quietly over the curtain.

'Go ahead.' Seth dipped his head as she selected the next set of sheets for the patient.

'All right, you're doing very well.' She smiled another bright smile. 'Could you now try to answer these questions for me?

'Do fish swim?'

The patient hesitated, and Andrea found herself almost willing the woman on.

'Yes.'

With a smile, Andrea noted it on her paper, then waited for her signal.

'Do cars have wheels?'

Another pause, and then the patient uttered a nonsense

word. Clearly, Seth was back to a treacherous area of the patient's brain.

For the next half-hour, Andrea continued the tests, meticulously noting the results the way she'd been taught, knowing that, the more complete the map of the patient's brain, the more chance Seth could have of staying out of the danger zones when he went in to resect the tumour.

So far, she'd seen Seth perform these awake craniotomies on musicians as they'd played an instrument, on an opera singer as they'd sang arias and on a radio presenter who'd given them an almost impromptu radio show.

She knew that he had another operation scheduled to help an epilepsy sufferer to try to reduce the number of episodes he was having, once he completed this surgery. Whilst she, for her sins, would be heading off for the gala ball after all.

For no apparent reason, something zapped through her at the prospect of the evening to come, and she couldn't work out if it was fear or apprehension.

At least she'd finally found a dress. Dragged out by her sister-in-law, they'd traipsed into the city to the charity shops that so often offered a stunning find of vintage designer-style dresses which could hardly have been worn more than once, if at all.

Even now, she smiled beneath her surgical mask as she remembered how, she and her sister-in-law had both been drawn to the same rack of striking gowns the moment they'd walked into a particular shop. Clearly a collection donated by someone who had an eye for beautiful designs.

Andrea had gone straight for a stunning burgundy dress with an intricate gold-leaf overlay, whilst Julia had gone for a rose-gold one.

'I might not have a posh gala evening to wear it to,' she'd

laughed as she'd swirled it round. 'But I have a feeling Daniel would like to see me in it all the same.'

Andrea had scrunched up her face and feigned an objection.

'That's my brother you're talking about. Too much information.'

But, even as she and her sister-in-law had laughed, Andrea had found it impossible not to wonder what Seth might make of her in such a striking-looking gown. If he would like it. If it would make him forget all his rules and see her the way he had that first night at his penthouse. Not that she wanted a repeat performance, of course, but it would be nice to think he still felt that attraction, the way that she did.

And Andrea might even have managed to convince herself that she really meant that—if only it hadn't been for her perfidious heart tattooing out its very own agitated beat.

Seth knew Andrea had arrived even before he turned to see her at the top of the sweeping stone staircase that led down to the triple-height, vaulting ballroom. He couldn't explain how he felt this growing awareness of her—even before that thorny night—save for the fact it was something about the way his skin suddenly prickled and he felt compelled to turn and look at the double-door entrance on the mezzanine level.

And in that one moment all the air seemed to get sucked out of his lungs. So much for all his stern lectures to himself about maintaining those carefully erected barriers.

Andrea stood at the top of the wide balcony looking more polished, more beautiful, than in any of the dreams he hadn't realised he'd been having.

Her hair was piled on her head and pinned with some intricate gold hair clip, whilst long, glamorous curls tumbled down from one side and tumbled over one semi-bare shoulder, given the way the straps were positioned to fall deliberately half-on, half-off.

He'd spent the past few weeks keeping his distance from her, throwing all his focus into Noah and his patients, and wresting his mind from thoughts of Andrea every time it had threatened to wander. But right now he couldn't seem to drag his eyes or focus away from the vision above him.

He'd had weeks of schooling himself whenever she was around, of finding a way to maintain distance between them even though she was living in his home, yet right now he couldn't find a solitary grain of self-restraint.

Excusing himself from the small group he'd been chatting with, he moved on dazed autopilot to the bottom of the staircase. And then, as she turned her head and bestowed the most dazzling smile to someone he couldn't see, something detonated in Seth's chest.

Something that felt ridiculously like jealousy.

Crazy.

He tried to move away but found himself rooted to the spot. It was surely going to take a damned sight longer for him to compose himself than the time it was going to take her to descend the stairs? If he could have turned, gone back up to the main doors and taken her home so that they could be alone, he would have done.

He wanted nothing more than to wrap her around him and swim in her until he drowned. No matter that he could never be capable of offering a woman like Andrea the kind of family life that he knew she wanted deep down.

Yet, still, he stood there waiting for her to descend the garland-festooned stone stairs.

'Seth.'

His name slid out of her mouth on a whisper, which in turn threaded itself right through him. It weaved through his ribs and spiralled perfectly through his core. And the way her eyes widened only put deliciously wicked ideas in his head of other ways he could make those violet-blue eyes darken in surprise and delight.

'I didn't think you'd manage to get away tonight,' she murmured quietly as she finally reached him.

He liked it too much that her thoughts about the evening had included his presence.

'I'm here,' he replied redundantly. His tongue didn't quite feel as if it was his own at that moment. 'You look… incredible.'

He hadn't thought her face could light up any more until that moment, even as her breath hitched. Something he could only describe as…a hint of possessiveness punched through him.

Mine.

'You think?' she began, then caught herself. 'Thank you.'

It was true enough, of course. Her dress looked like something from the most exclusive designer houses. It was a stunning affair that clung lovingly to her mouth-watering curves before fanning slightly at the knees. It made his arms—and, frankly, other more primitive parts of him—ache with the urge to reach out and test those glorious contours for himself.

'People are staring,' Andrea muttered to him after a moment. 'Are you sure the dress is okay?'

'The dress is stunning.' He lowered his head to her ear as they moved seamlessly together. 'But it isn't the dress they're staring at. It's you. You look radiant.'

And that was what was truly mesmerising about this incredible woman tonight—light seemed to sparkle around her, catching on the gold embellishments of the gown. Yet it was the light that seemed to be pouring out from her very core that was really drawing him in.

But he was already aware that he wasn't the only one who had noticed the vision standing with him. He found he was clenching his teeth so hard that he was shocked his jaw didn't shatter.

'This place is amazing!' Andrea breathed as her eyes darted left and right, up and down, from the sixteenth-century chequered tile floor at their feet, up the sixteen-feet-high columns which stood to attention around the space and to the barrel-vaulted ceiling above their heads.

'It was inspired by the Baths of Caracalla in Rome, though the history is a little potted. Architecture aside, however, let me introduce you to the people you should get to know.'

For the next hour or so, he threw himself into guiding her around the room. He told himself that he was playing the good sponsor, introducing her to those who could help her career as she studied to go from nurse to doctor.

The reality, he suspected, was far less altruistic. He simply wanted to spend time with her, to be close to her. But it wasn't enough and, the more he had of her, the more he wanted.

'Would you care to dance?'

Her eyes instantly snapped to his, but Seth didn't wait for a reply. Instead, he tucked her arm through his and led her through the throng, and her body pressed so close to his that it was all the answer he needed.

The heat of it seemed to sear into his own.

One dance. It wasn't part of their agreement, but he couldn't bring himself to care. One dance. Then he'd walk away.

He had to.

Because, if he'd found it hard to resist her at the penthouse these past few weeks, how in hell was he ever supposed to resist her tonight? It felt like an impossible task.

Or maybe it was just that he didn't want it to be possible. Maybe he'd had enough of denying the fire that had been smouldering between them ever since that first night.

Stepping out onto the ballroom floor, Seth swept her around and straight into his arms. She fitted against him as if they'd been hand-crafted for each other.

'I should probably have warned you,' Andrea muttered belatedly. 'I'm not the best dancer. I'm not sure I'll know what to do.'

'You don't need to.' He lowered his head again, so close that this time he could feel her delicious shiver as he spoke softly in her ear. 'I'll lead; you just have to follow.'

And then, before she could voice any more objections, he gathered her closer and swirled them around the dance floor, up one side, then back down the other, holding her so very close the entire time.

It was possibly the most thrilling, intimate thing he could remember doing. He could feel Andrea's body pressed to his, hear the sound of her shallow, choppy breaths in his ear and feel the rhythm as it moved through him like some slow, sensuous drumbeat. He'd dreamed of her night after night after night, yet his wildest fantasies seemed to pale against the reality of having her in his arms.

Her delicate perfume seemed to fill his nostrils, the graze of her cheek against his doing such things to his body, whilst that searing heat scorched every part of him that she touched.

'Today's surgery was good,' she managed after a few silent, loaded moments.

It was true, but he hadn't asked her to dance in order to talk about the surgery.

'It was.' He was aware that his voice sounded thicker than usual. 'But that isn't what I'm interested in right now.'

'No?'

He liked the way her breath caught against his neck.

'No,' he confirmed.

And he didn't imagine the way her body moulded itself to his that fraction closer, or the electricity that arced between the two of them. Surely he could allow himself a turn around the floor...just that much?

As the band played, they danced and swirled. That first song led into another, then another and another. Seth didn't care that he was supposed to mingle, or network, or whatever else it was that he'd been instructed to do. He only knew that he wanted to stay here with Andrea.

Or be somewhere else with her.

Spinning her to an abrupt halt, Seth lifted a finger and slid it into the curl of her hair, unable to help himself.

'I think there's something we need to discuss.'

Her face pulled taut, that familiar red flush creeping instantly over her cheeks.

'If it's about the last time we—'

'Or we can keep pretending.' He cut her off, unable to bear seeing that embarrassment spread further. As though what coursed between them was something to feel ashamed about. 'We can continue tiptoeing around each other at my apartment.'

When she gave an almost imperceptible shake of her head as she breathed his name again, he took her hand tightly in his and led them both off the dance floor, weaving through the throng.

He was dimly aware of her asking him where they were going, but he didn't answer. To do so would mean stopping, and he was fiercely aware that if he stopped he might start kissing her. Right there, in front of the wealthiest in the country. Not that he cared who saw them—but he had a feeling Andrea might. Even if she did, she left her hand in his and was keeping satisfyingly close to him.

Moving this way and that, he dodged any number of patients or potential donors who were keen to catch his attention, with a cleverly dropped word here and there to ensure that they didn't feel snubbed, but the reality of the situation was that all he wanted was to be alone with Andrea.

To bury himself in her molten heat. And to hell with whatever agreement they'd made weeks ago because he knew, without a shadow of doubt, that it was what she wanted too.

They'd spent over a month trying to pretend otherwise, trying to hold to the agreement they'd made, but neither of them had been particularly convincing.

They needed a new agreement.

For the first time in his career, Seth found himself cursing his rule against blurring the lines. Yet still he didn't stop. He didn't turn round.

A glut of... *feelings* he couldn't quite fathom swirled around him.

'You can walk away any time,' he ground out. 'Right now, if you want to.'

'And...if I don't want to?' she asked in a voice so unlike her own. 'If I want to stay? Right here?'

A fresh punch of desire slammed though him.

'Then I guarantee I won't be able to keep my hands off you, as per our agreement, any longer.'

She watched him, unblinking.

Slowly, painstakingly, he lifted his liquid-heavy limbs to pull her to him. And as she splayed her hands over the front of his chest his muscles beneath bunched and tightened under her touch.

'Then,' she muttered thickly, 'I'd ask what you were waiting for.'

Seth didn't try to fight it a moment longer.

His mouth was on hers, the way it had been aching to do for what felt like a thousand years, and every graze of their lips and slide of their tongues felt like a benediction.

Seth poured everything into it and she went straight to his head.

All the nights he'd spend hot, restless and alone in his bed, fantasising about being with her even as he'd chastised himself for such inappropriate thoughts, as if he was some kind of monk… And, before he'd even thought about the wisdom—or not—of all the self-imposed rules they were breaking, he had her with her back up against the stone pillar, covering all her glorious heat with his own body.

No fantasy could possibly have lived up to the reality of kissing this one woman. Or of being kissed by her. His mouth assaulted her with all the skill he'd ever honed, because she deserved nothing less.

And still he kissed her, his palms cupped around her face as if she was something infinitely precious. It was a heady sensation.

When the phone went off, slicing through the silent air with its demanding tone, it took Seth far too long to register where the wholly unwanted cacophony was coming from.

Half-dazed, he lifted his mouth from her soft, warm lips and tried to work out what he was supposed to be doing.

Not, he realised with a start, *kissing Andrea*.

Seth stared in dismay at the woman whose silken skin he was still caressing.

So much for his promises to maintain that distance between them. His assurances that he wouldn't lay his hands on her again. One sight of her in that flowing ball gown and he'd lost his head. Again.

To his chagrin, Seth realised that his damned phone was still ringing. No doubt the hospital—yet here he was, barely registering it over this rushing thing that crashed over him and made him ache simply to shut the world out for once and give himself up to this moment with Andrea.

But that was the last thing he could do.

'I have to take this,' he clipped out, ignoring the thing which roared within him. 'I asked them to contact me if anything happened with my patient overnight.'

And it shouldn't have taken him even that second's hesitation to remind himself that his career was his priority. It always had been.

'Of course,' Andrea managed. But she sounded thrown. Bewildered.

'This...now...' Seth halted and wrenched his stare up to meet hers. 'It was a mistake. It shouldn't have happened.'

Except that it didn't feel like a mistake. It felt like the best thing he'd done in a long time.

'A mistake,' Andrea echoed weakly, making him feel even more of a heel.

He opened his mouth to apologise. Or, at the very least, qualify what he'd said. But the phone seemed to sense his vacillation and rang all the louder.

Or could that have been his own guilt?

In that instant, Seth decided he would have liked nothing more than to throw the phone into the fountains outside and erase everything else from her brain. Instead, he slid the phone out of his pocket and moved his finger over the 'accept call' button.

But it wasn't Baystone Medical calling. It was his lawyer.

For the second time in ten minutes, his entire world receded from view. His finger pressed 'accept call' even as his mind was racing through the ramifications.

'I apologise again,' he bit out to Andrea. 'You should get back to the gala before anyone sees you're missing.'

And then, before he could second-guess himself, he instructed the caller to wait a moment before pacing further down the chequerboard-patterned floor, heading for the library he knew was down the hall, and grasping the phone tightly in his palms.

'Go ahead,' he commanded, hitting the mute button and thrusting open the library door.

It took all he had to get himself inside and stride over to one of the gargantuan windows, glaring into the black beyond as though his entire future depended on this singularly important call.

Perhaps the truth was that it did. He already knew that

if it hadn't been for that timely interruption then he would surely have crossed the invisible line and given into the temptation that was uniquely Andrea Perkins.

He would have been no better than the man he'd always sworn he wouldn't be—a man who couldn't abide by the rules he'd chosen to life his life by.

Admittedly, he wasn't married, as his father had been, overtly cheating with every woman who had taken his fancy whilst his wife had driven herself literally insane back at home with two small children. But staying away from colleagues had been Seth's own private rubric nonetheless.

Andrea Perkins was the only one who had ever made him forget all of that. And he had to put an end to it tonight. Now. Whatever this phone call was about, he had to cut Andrea from his life—free her. If he didn't, he was afraid that he'd never, ever be able to let her go—which was certainly against all his rules.

And, without those self-imposed guidelines that he had spent so many years pulling around himself like some kind of permanent shroud—then what would he even have left?

CHAPTER THIRTEEN

ANDREA DIDN'T KNOW why she was waiting outside the small library. Perhaps because she'd been jittery and electrified ever since Seth had met her so unexpectedly at the bottom of the staircase, never leaving her side as he'd walked her round that room, introducing her to prominent guests to whom she alone would never have had the courage to speak. It was as if he thought she was that important.

She'd been swept up in the magic of the evening, right up until that phone call had brought him crashing back to reality. She ought to return to the gala, as he'd rather harshly instructed. Instead, she dwelt on the expression that had crossed Seth's face the moment he'd seen the caller's ID.

An expression that had sent a tight band of tension winding around her chest. Though she couldn't put her finger on how she'd known, a sixth sense had warned her that the phone call wasn't about a patient.

She suspected it was about Noah. Her heart lurched. They'd decided that the best place for him to spend the night would be with her brother's family, especially since his friendship with Billy had only become stronger and stronger over the past month. But Andrea didn't think it had been her brother calling. If it had been, she was pretty sure that Julia would have called her at the same time. And her phone had remained defiantly silent, no matter how many times she'd checked it.

Which meant it surely had to be the lawyers?

Forcing herself to lean back casually—the coolness of the stone pillar offering her a strange sort of comfort— Andrea tried to keep her breathing even, heart steady and her eyes locked onto the bookcase that she could just about see through the sliver where Seth had left open the door.

He hadn't wanted her to follow but how could she have done anything less, given the circumstances? Still, that didn't mean she felt confident enough to follow him into the room. Instead, she'd just have to content herself with waiting for Seth to emerge—her stomach feeling as though it was now lodged somewhere in the vicinity of her throat.

It didn't help that she'd spent the entire evening feeling as though her belly was full of nerves, knotted tighter than a tangle of coiled ropes. Only up until now her jumpiness had been squarely down to Seth's proximity, and the way he'd been looking at her, touching her, making her feel.

Love.

The word snuck inside her brain before she could shut it out. But she refused to accept it, telling herself instead that it was mere *lust.*

Lust from several hours of glorious tiny touches—a guiding hand on the small of her back, an encouraging squeeze of her palm, or a lingering moment as their eyes had caught—but thrilling enough to keep her senses jolting deliciously.

And then the dancing. Oh, how she'd loved that dancing. She, who almost never danced.

The way he'd held her. It had felt as though he had threaded a ribbon of intimacy around them, and somehow she felt more exposed and aware of him here than she had in all the nights they'd been alone just with Noah at his penthouse.

And, just like that, she knew what she wanted. What she was ready for.

It felt inconceivable that the judge would award custody of Noah to the little boy's grandparents. He had already carved such a space for himself in their lives—in Seth's life. And now Andrea knew that she wanted to be in their lives—permanently.

She pushed herself off the pillar, desperate to go inside and find out what was going on, but not quite sure enough of herself to take that step. She had no idea how long she stood, paralysed, as she stared at the space between where she was standing and the library door.

'Andrea?'

She practically cracked her neck spinning round.

'What did they say?' The question was out before she'd even had time to think.

He strode out of the room and, for a split second, she thought he was heading towards her to scoop her in his arms to swirl her around.

He stopped abruptly.

'The judge awarded custody of Noah to me. The decision came in late, and my lawyer was on another case so just picked it up, but she wanted me to know as soon as possible.'

Heat instantly pricked the back of her eyes. She was sure she could practically feel all the fears and worries seeping right out of her body and puddling on the chequered floor beneath them.

'That's fantastic.'

'Yes.'

Somewhere, in the back of her head, alarm bells were going off. Andrea ignored them.

'What did the judge say?'

She told herself she was imagining the beat of hesitation before Seth answered.

'Apparently Noah was very talkative with her and told her that he misses his mummy but that he loves his new life in Baystone. That he...loves me.'

Seth's voice actually cracked at this last part and Andrea took a half-step forward to reach out to him. But something stopped her. That unfamiliar, brooding expression almost warned her off without him even saying a word.

'That's good news.'

'Yes,' he agreed, unsmiling. Then, 'Thank you for all you did with Noah.'

And there it was again—that strange edge to his voice that shuddered through her.

'All I did?' She echoed the use of his past tense.

'You helped my nephew and I find a way to communicate with each other. Without you, I wouldn't be celebrating this news now.'

Except he didn't look as though he was celebrating. He looked relieved, admittedly, but he also looked tense in a way she hadn't seen before.

'You don't have thank me,' she managed hoarsely, because his proximity was sending her entire body haywire. 'It was a pleasure to do.'

All she could think of—all she could *feel*—was the heat of his body near her. But no longer pouring into her the way it had been when they'd been dancing. No longer making her feel as though she was being burned alive—only far more intense and far more pleasant.

Now it was different. Peculiar.

'Seth...' She breathed his name, not at all certain what else she even intended to say.

'You are officially released from your agreement with

me,' he rasped, as though it was taking him far more effort than it should to say the words.

'Released?' She felt numb.

He continued as if she hadn't spoken. His voice sounded so intensely raw and harsh.

'You can walk away any time,' he ground out. 'Now, if you want to.'

The moment swirled around her. She felt as though she was in freefall, hurtling to the ground.

'And…if I don't want to?' She wasn't sure how she managed to speak. 'If I want to stay? Right here?'

He stared at her wordlessly for a moment.

'That wasn't the agreement.'

A hundred thoughts seemed to crowd into Andrea's mind at once. No, that wasn't the agreement. The agreement was that she would use her experience with her brother in order to help Seth communicate with Noah. But now Noah was speaking again. He was happy—in so far as a child who had lost their beloved mother could be—and she was surplus to requirements.

No longer useful, so easily discarded.

Just as she'd been to Josh.

The pain burst through her so brightly that she wasn't sure how she managed to stay standing.

What a fool she'd been.

Miraculously, she heard herself talking in a voice that actually sounded remarkably composed.

'I understand completely.' She dipped her head. 'I'm pleased that it all worked out as planned. Now you and Noah can get on with becoming a family and I can get back to my own life.'

Whatever hope she might have had about what he would say was dashed when he stared at her for a beat before nodding.

'Yes,' he agreed steadily. 'I believe that's for the best.'

* * *

Seth stared up at the ceiling, unable to sleep.

Andrea was planning to leave and it should be everything he wanted to hear.

It was for the best.

She'd helped Noah and him to communicate. She'd helped them to bond and the court had determined that he should be one to take care of his nephew, as per Stacey's will.

He should have been the one initiating Andrea's departure. She had fulfilled her end of their bargain and he had secured her place on the nurse-to-doctor conversion course.

Yet, despite all the earlier reminders about his rules and about keeping his distance, he realised that he was wholly unprepared for her to leave. No matter what he tried to pretend, or how logical he tried to be, there was logic in his body. It burned for her and ached for her in equal measure. Her delicate scent still haunted him as much as the way she'd felt in his arms all evening.

And there was no way that he was going to be able to sleep like this.

He threw the sheet off his body and swung himself out of bed; he couldn't stay in bed stewing about it. Better to do some work, or watch a surgical video. Throwing on a pair of low-rise joggers, he padded softly through the penthouse.

Someone had left the floor lamp on, so he used the soft glow to navigate to the kitchen without bothering to turn on the other lights. Flicking the tap, he poured himself a glass of water, as if that could douse the fire roiling inside him.

'You can't sleep either?'

Seth jerked up his head to see Andrea peering round the side of an easy chair.

He tried not to think about what it meant that neither of them was feeling settled tonight.

'I didn't realise you were down here,' he forced himself to answer. 'Do you want some water?'

'No.' She shook her head. 'Thank you.'

But she didn't retreat behind the chair either—her gaze held his. He picked up his glass and wandered past her to the chair opposite, where he sank down and eyed the book she was holding. Little wonder he hadn't noticed her, nestled as she was in the over-sized chair, her legs tucked beneath her, reading silently beneath the lamp. She wore soft yoga pants with a camisole vest-top, and he couldn't seem to drag his eyes from the thin ribbon straps that dropped over her silken tanned shoulders.

It revealed nothing, yet he found his mouth watering at the hidden promise. Irritated—and feeling something rather more carnal—he fought to drag his wayward glance away.

'Something on your mind?' he rasped, barely recognising his own voice.

It sounded different in the dark, somehow—raw.

'I was thinking when the best time to leave would be.'

He hated that an invisible fist tightened in his chest. It took far more than it should have done to keep his voice even.

'Are you in a particular hurry?'

'No,' she answered quickly. Perhaps too quickly…?

'Then…?'

'I just don't want to out-stay my welcome.'

A hundred responses crowded Seth's mouth at that moment. He swallowed back every one of them then took a mouthful of water, as though to wash them down.

The longer he was around her, the less sense all his objections and his rules seemed to make. He needed a moment to regroup.

'When you leave is up to you. I'd simply ask that you give Noah some warning. I appreciate he already knows the basic idea, but I don't want him to wake up one day and you're gone, like—'

'Of course not!' she cut in, looking horrified. 'I understand exactly what he went through with his mother. I would never do that to him.'

Good; at least he wouldn't come home from work one night to find that she'd packed her bags. Though Seth felt ashamed that the relief he felt wasn't merely on behalf of his young nephew.

'I'm not sure I know what we would have done these past weeks without you,' he admitted after a moment. 'I really do want to thank you.'

She watched him for a moment, clearly choosing her words.

'No problem,' she settled on in the end. 'I've enjoyed it. A lot.'

'Then perhaps there's no rush to leave after all?' he couldn't help asking.

And all of a sudden the flush in her cheeks revealed everything she was trying so desperately hard not to let him see.

She wanted him. Every bit as much as he wanted her.

His breath caught as surely as if she'd punched him in the chest—hard. No, not a punch, so much as a caress. And it was moving decidedly lower.

He clenched his teeth. It was enough of a challenge to ignore his attraction to her during the bright hours of day time. But here, in the quiet dead of night, everything felt softer. More out of focus. As though anything that happened between them could be theirs. A secret they could lock away as soon as morning came.

But he suspected it wouldn't be that easy.

'So, where will you go once you leave here?' He forced a light note into his voice, even if he didn't really feel it.

She blinked at him.

'I don't know, actually.'

As far as confessions went, it was an unexpected one.

'What about getting the apartment on your own that you talked about?' he asked, pressing on when she frowned at him. 'You mentioned it that day back at the play centre.'

'I remember the conversation.' Andrea seemed to catch herself at last. 'I was just surprised that you do.'

He couldn't blame her. No doubt it revealed a little too much about how arresting he'd found her, even from that first day. He could probably bluff it, but why bother?

The air in the room seemed to thicken and grow heavier.

'So…our agreement is officially over.'

Not a question, but a statement. This time he knew he didn't imagine how loaded it was.

'It is.'

And, if that prospect made his heart actually stop for a beat or two, then no one else needed to know it but him.

'I'm free to walk out that door any time I like?' she clarified. 'Barring what we've said about Noah, of course.'

'You are.' Seth barely recognised his own voice. It held a hoarse quality that he wasn't accustomed to. 'The latter being a request rather than a demand,' Seth confirmed.

Although, would he have made it a demand if he hadn't already known that this woman would never deliberately hurt the young boy? Possibly. But, if that had been the kind of person she was, then he wouldn't still have been here, beginning to lose the battle with his self-control.

The atmosphere shifted again this time, the kind of suffocating heat that was growing more overwhelming, and at the same time intoxicating, by the second. Had he ever wanted any woman the way he wanted Andrea?

He knew the answer, of course—it was why he needed her to leave. If he stayed here any longer he wasn't entire certain what he might say next, what he might do. Four strides and he could be in his study.

Standing abruptly and taking a step, he realised too late that Andrea had had the same idea. They each jerked to a standstill, scant inches from the other.

'Sorry... I...'

'No,' he growled, more to himself than to her.

The shallow, rapid rise and fall of her chest definitely wasn't helping matters. He knew the woman well enough to read the desire in her body language, the lust. Hell, it matched his own. But they shouldn't. They couldn't.

His arms lifted instinctively, his hands reaching for her shoulders of their own volition.

It was fatal.

Rather than moving her gently to one side, as he was sure he intended to do, he found his fingers curling around the bare skin that had snared his gaze only minutes before.

It was every bit as silken as he'd imagined.

Her mouth trembled.

'Seth... I...'

'You should go back to bed,' he rasped. 'Before...'

He didn't finish. Nor did he move.

'Before...what?' she whispered, her voice almost wickedly thick, wanton.

'Our deal is done,' he muttered. 'Which includes the part about me not kissing you.'

But he wanted to. And he wanted so much more than just a kiss.

'It does.' She dipped her head a fraction in agreement.

She still did not move even an inch.

She didn't add that it left them free of obligation. She didn't need to; it was in every line of her sinfully sexy body.

'Last chance to leave,' he ground out.

She exhaled, a shaky, choppy sound.

'Do stop being so chivalrous.'

Then, before he even had time to process her words, she rose up on tiptoe and pressed her mouth to his.

And any last vestiges of his resolve crumbled to dust.

He was kissing her.

Finally.

Thrillingly.

Andrea didn't think she'd ever felt quite so deliciously light-headed.

His mouth was on hers, and every graze of his lips and slide of his tongue felt like a benediction. It was over a month since he'd last kissed her, but it might as well have been a lifetime. And she poured everything into it. All the nights she'd spent hot, restless and alone in her bed, fantasising about being with him even as she'd chastised herself for such inappropriate thoughts, as if she was some kind of nun.

Besides, no fantasy could possibly have lived up to the reality of kissing Seth. Or of being kissed by him. Not when his mouth assaulted her with devastating skill, even whilst his hands were cupped around her face, as though she was something infinitely precious.

It was a heady sensation and one she might have said was every bit as glorious as she remembered from that last time, only it turned out that her gloriously irreligious fantasies about this man hadn't even come close to the real thing.

Slowly, painstakingly, she found the strength to lift her own liquid-heavy limbs and splay her hands over the front of his chest. The muscles beneath bunched and tightened under her touch, causing delicious heat to lick down the length of her spine.

His kisses were soft, intense, careful and demanding. It was as if he'd been waiting for ever to taste her again, and now he couldn't stop himself drinking her in. It was perfect. *He* was perfect.

She revelled in the feel of his palms against her cheeks, holding her there for what felt like an eternity as he deepened the kiss, angling her head for a better, deeper, marvellous fit. It could have lasted a lifetime, maybe two, and all the while myriad sensations cascaded through her. And, when he slid his hands down the long line of her neck, or gently into her hair, she revelled in all those sensations too.

This was what she'd been waiting for, *yearning for,* these past few weeks. This was what had kept her heart ticking up a beat whenever he'd walked through the door. Or first thing in the morning when she'd woken up and remembered where she was.

'Animal attraction', her brother used to call it. But she'd never experienced it—not even with Josh—so she'd never understood it.

Not until now.

How could she have missed feeling this incredibly *alive*?

Over, over and over again, Seth kissed her. And each time felt more magical than the last. He tasted her this way, and angled his head that way, and each slide of his tongue sent bolts of white-hot need straight through her. Straight to *there*—where she ached for him most.

Still, she wasn't prepared when he dropped his hands to her hips and used the contact to pull her against him to where he was hardest for her. A low sound escaped her lips and she found herself moving against him before she could help it.

'Careful.' He growled against her mouth, the sound rumbling over her lips.

It was meant to be a warning, but instead it fired up a devilish part of Andrea that she had long since forgotten existed.

'Or what?' she pulled her head back long enough to mutter. And then repeated the movement.

His groan of response only made her that much more needy, that much more molten.

'Or, so help me, I'll take you on that couch.'

'Is that supposed to offend me?' she whispered, pressing herself to him all the more and shivering with the unmistakeable promise. 'Only, as deterrents go, I have to tell you that it isn't really that effective.'

'Is that so?' he ground out, pulling back his head.

'We were on that couch the last time we…'

'I recall the event with perfect clarity, thank you,' he shot back, pulling his head from hers. His eyes glittered with heat, and something else she wasn't sure she could identify but liked the look of all the same. 'This time, I have no intention of it ending so abruptly. This time I want more—for both of us.'

And then, before she could offer any kind of response, he swung her up high against the solid wall of his chest and gave her little time to throw her arms around his neck before carrying her off. He crossed the living area within a couple of easy strides, taking the stairs two at a time before shouldering open the door to his room and depositing her with infinite care on his bed.

Seth took his time moving over her, lowering his head to hers and kissing her: her lips, her jaw, her neck. He took his time—though it damned near killed him—sampling her, claiming her, revelling in her.

And with every touch she wove some kind of glorious magic around them both. Again and again and again.

He couldn't possibly get enough.

The thought should have terrified him, but it didn't. Instead, it thrilled him. Slowly, almost reverently, he divested her of each layer of clothing—his gaze more possessive the flimsier and lacier they got—until, at last, she lay before him. Sprawled out on his bed like the most delectable feast laid out just for him.

Insatiable hunger and greed roared inside him.

Mine.

With a guttural sound he didn't think he'd made before,

Seth lowered his head and took one proud, straining nipple into his mouth.

Andrea's response was instant, and he thought he could have lost himself for days in her low cry of desire, in the way she arched her body in blissful response, as though she was his for the taking.

And so he took.

He feasted on her. First one breast, then the other. He traced whorls on her breasts with his tongue, toying with her fingers with his teeth. Never hard, just enough to elicit those low moans which cascaded through him and into his very sex.

But he wouldn't indulge himself.

Not yet. Not when there was so much more he wanted to do to his captivating Andrea.

Instead, Seth contented himself with trailing kisses over the soft swell of her breasts, inching his way down over every delicious curve and contour until he reached her navel. He licked it before meandering down over her lower abdomen as if they had all the time in the world.

As if his body wasn't hard and aching with the need that had been thundering through him ever since that first night when he'd tasted her. As if he'd been hiding it from himself all these years, pretending he'd never dreamed of crossing that invisible line he'd always maintained for himself in work.

But he wasn't pretending any longer.

No. Right now he was taking, claiming everything she wanted to give him. Not least when he curved his tongue down to the inside of her thigh, his hands curling around her hips to hold her still as her sensitive body anticipated what was to come next.

'Seth... I don't...'

'I do.' He growled, lowering his head and pressing his lips to where she was hottest for him.

She tasted of cream and honey, of all things rich and smoky. It was a heady, intoxicating taste that he thought would make him drunk for days—delirious, perhaps. And as for those low cries of need she was making…

All for him.

It was incredible how possessive it made him feel. How savage.

Gripping her hips a little tighter in his palms, Seth licked, teased and sucked, triumphing in that carnal dance his tongue could make her perform. A dance that was as old as time. Over and over, until her shivers grew lighter and her shudders more intense.

And when she called out his name and raised her hips to meet him, he took the greatest of delight in sucking harder on the very core of her need and catapulting her right over the edge.

And then he kept going.

By the time Andrea had come back to herself, Seth was lying on the bed next to her, propped on one elbow and watching her breathing return to something more approaching normal. Her eyes blinked back into focus slowly, and the expression in them was little short of wondrous as she turned her head to look at him.

That aching need gripped his body once again, reminding him how very badly he wanted her—as if he'd been likely to forget.

As she reached for him, he barely had enough time to reach for protection from the bedside drawer before sliding his body over hers, liking too much the way he fitted perfectly between her legs, his hard length sliding sensually against her wet heat. He thought perhaps that he'd forgotten to breathe as he held himself above her when she grazed her fingertips over his chest, apparently delighting in acquainting herself with the angular ridges that she encountered.

And then he couldn't restrain himself any longer. The

need to bury himself inside her was too overwhelming. With a shift of his hips, Seth nudged against her entrance, a surge of victory racing through him as she instinctively wrapped her legs around him. Another guttural groan and he was thrusting inside her, in and out, so gloriously deep that he had no idea where he ended and she began.

He'd planned to take his time, but there was something about Andrea that had him losing his usual control. She drove him wild in a way that he couldn't quite fathom. He slammed into her with all the need and desire he'd been quashing for all this time. And, with every thrust, she lifted her hips to meet him as if they were hand-crafted for each other.

Finally, when he didn't think he could take it any longer, Seth reached down between them and pressed his fingers to her core, hearing her cry out his name just as she shattered all around him.

And then, at last, he thrust into her and shattered too.

CHAPTER FOURTEEN

IT WAS THE early hours when Andrea woke up in the unfamiliar, all too decadently comfortable bed.

Seth was gone.

She sat up quickly, hugging her knees to her chest. Of course he was gone; what else had she expected? Because hadn't he said too many times that anything happening between them wasn't part of the agreement? Hadn't she agreed? Yet hadn't she gone ahead and slept with him anyway?

Tossing her head as if that could shake out the unwanted questions, Andrea slid to the edge of the bed and began to get up.

The sound of the door opening had her scurrying back under the safety of the covers.

'Suddenly shy?' Seth cocked an eyebrow at her as he entered the room carrying a large wooden tray.

The fact that he was wearing little more than a pair of charcoal joggers slung mouth-wateringly low around his hips really made her insides dip and spin in the most thrilling way.

'I thought you'd gone,' she stated before she could check herself.

He cast her an odd look.

'I thought maybe you'd decided it was another mistake,' she continued a little awkwardly. 'Not part of the agreement.'

At least he had the decency to look a little wry.

'It isn't at all in the agreement,' he conceded. 'Only I can't seem to regret one single second of what happened between us last night. Several times.'

She flushed, as she suspected he'd intended.

'As you can see, however—' he indicated the tray that was laden with two glasses of orange juice, bowls full of strawberries and melons and natural yoghurt '—I simply went for breakfast.'

Andrea glanced at the window.

'What time is it? It must be early.'

'Relatively. But I imagine Noah will be back here early enough, and I thought we should make the most of the few hours left.'

He paused, as if about to say more, but decided against it.

'That sounds...nice.' She lowered the sheet tentatively. 'And the breakfast?'

'I thought it might be nice to eat together.' His lips twitched. 'Call me crazy.'

Screwing up her courage, Andrea allowed the sheet to drop as she reached for her night top and briefs, and she forced herself not to rush to pull them on. This time Seth didn't comment, for which she was grateful. Perhaps his usual conquests weren't quite so bashful; but, whilst she might not have body image issues, she was acutely aware that she wasn't his usual brand of whippet-thin bedfellow.

'I don't make it a habit to prepare breakfast for women I sleep with.'

She jumped so easily, he could read her.

'Just the select few, then.' It wasn't easy to paste a non-chalant smile on her lips, but she managed it all the same. 'I'm honoured.'

He gave a low growl.

'You should be. You're the only one.'

This time, there was no concealing her reaction. She spun round to face him.

'The only one? I must say, I find that hard to believe.'

'That, I'm afraid, is your choice.' He shrugged. 'But that doesn't make it any the less true.'

She wanted to pretend she didn't care. That it didn't matter to her one way or the other.

'You haven't prepared breakfast for anyone else but me?' She was sceptical. 'Ever?'

'Not breakfast in bed, no,' he confirmed. 'Certainly not my bed. And not like this. Though, sometimes when I was heading out for an early work shift when Noah was a baby, my sister would creep down to the kitchen and I might make her scrambled eggs or a goat's cheese omelette.'

'I think I like her style.' Andrea grinned, as she dipped a forkful of juicy melon into her yoghurt, and this time it was a genuine one. 'Not that I'm not enjoying this offering, because I am.'

'You would have liked her style.' Seth nodded, before looking unexpectedly serious. 'You would have liked *her*. And she would definitely have liked you.'

Andrea rebuked herself for the way her heart lurched.

'Why do you say that?' she asked as casually as she could.

'Because you are the kind of woman she was always trying to push me towards. Stacey always hated the women I dated, and she made no bones about that fact.'

'You liked them, though,' she couldn't help pointing out.

'I was attracted to them physically, not mentally,' Seth countered with a momentary expression that suggested he was as surprised at his admission as she was. 'I can't say I *liked* them, precisely.'

Even as she was about to ask why he'd dated them if

he didn't like them, she bit her lip. The answer was obvious, wasn't it?

'Sex.'

After the night they'd just shared, she could hardly complain.

'It wasn't just the sex,' he refuted, almost thoughtfully.

She was almost afraid to ask, afraid that he would shoot her down and tell her that it wasn't any of her business. And it wasn't. So she'd enjoyed one glorious night with him; it didn't now make them a couple. That wasn't Seth's way, and it wasn't what she wanted either. No matter how her heart pounded.

Still she found herself holding her breath.

'Then what?'

He hesitated.

'I don't know,' he ground out, though she could see that he was lying. 'Maybe because I don't think any woman has done anything to deserve being stuck with the real me.'

'The real you?' she prompted.

Seth didn't know whether it was the stillness of the hour or the night he'd just shared with Andrea that had him reaching inside himself for words he'd never dared voice aloud before.

'It's uglier than you think.'

She blinked at him.

'Ah, yes. And remind me—is that the ugliness of the brother who took in his sister when she was pregnant and alone, or the ugliness of a brother who fought for custody of his young nephew when the worst thing that could ever happen to a child happened? Or perhaps it's the ugliness of the surgeon who dedicates himself to saving his patients' lives every single day.'

'You think you know me, but you don't.' He laughed, but there was no humour in it, and he could feel its razor-sharp edges in his chest. He wanted to stop—why ruin the night they'd had?—but he couldn't. It was as if this long-buried truth had somehow been uncovered and now wanted a voice.

It was *demanding* a voice.

Because he wanted something else too. Last night had been like the wake-up call he hadn't known he'd needed. Not long ago he'd been living a life he'd thought was enough. Now, in the space of a couple of months, he had a ready-made family. A child and a woman.

Noah and Andrea.

Neither of whom he could ever imagine having wanted back then but now couldn't imagine living without.

How the hell had that happened?

But somehow, against all the odds, it had. Yet, if he wanted Andrea to want him, then she deserved to know the real him. Everything about him.

But would that scare her away? A part of him didn't want to take the risk. He wished he could be a better man, a different man—the kind of man that would be worthy of a woman like Andrea—but he wasn't.

Still, if he could give nothing else, then he could at least give her the truth.

'You deserve better than me,' he muttered. If she agreed, then he'd have his answer.

'You're going to have to explain that to me.' She breathed softly.

He was barely aware of crossing the floor to close the distance between them. Then, without knowing what he was doing, Seth found himself reaching out and sliding his hand against the side of her neck to cup it, as if compelled by some desperate need.

Her pulse beat wildly against his palm, as if they were connected by some invisible thread.

'Set me right,' she whispered, and he didn't miss the tremble in her voice, as though she felt the same thread.

'But you'd better make it good, because I think it's you who doesn't know yourself as well as you think you do.'

Perhaps it was the words, or maybe it was the way she was looking at him, but Seth felt himself fold then crumble.

'The truth is that I was never really a good brother even before I found out that Stacey was pregnant,' he began. 'My father was never the best role model—an egocentric man, a compulsive cheat and a distant father. He drove my mother to an early grave with his selfish ways. And I was becoming more and more like him every day.'

'I find that hard to believe,' she countered. She looked at him as though he was so much better than he knew he was.

'Did I tell you that, when he discovered Stacey was pregnant, he called her a whore and told her she ought to *deal* with her situation?'

Andrea shook her head, as he'd known she would.

'So she came to me for support. And I didn't offer it immediately.'

He hated how the words sounded, almost as much as he hated the way this incredible woman was looking at him now. As if she simply didn't believe him, because she expected more.

'You took her in, did you not?' Andrea challenged softly. 'You told me that you gave Stacey a home whilst she was pregnant, and then both her and Noah a home for the first eighteen months or so of his life.'

'And then I paid her off. Just like I was ready to pay you off last night.'

And his lovely Andrea simply looked at him head-on.

'How did you pay your sister off?'

Guilt and grief chased through him. If he could have avoided answering, he would have.

'I found it tough the year or so the two of them lived with me,' he admitted, though it was an effort to force each word out. 'I knew she wanted company but, instead of going

home when I could, I happily took on extra rounds, or studies, or surgeries. I deliberately worked longer hours, happy
to have an excuse not to have to return home.'

'Perhaps.' Andrea shrugged. 'But you were still a new
surgeon, learning your craft and building your career.' She
shook her head. 'I imagine you would have worked long
hours, whether your sister was back home or not. You're
career-driven and—newsflash—surgeons don't make it if
they don't work obscene hours, Seth. You certainly aren't
the only surgeon to dedicate themselves to their craft like
that even if—unlike you—not all surgeons have the talent
that they need to accompany that hard work.'

'You're seeing what you want to see.' Was that really
his voice? He didn't even recognise it. 'I could have given
her more—my time, my care—as her brother, as well as
Noah's uncle.'

'Are you forgetting that I've seen the photos of you with
them both?' She shook her head at him. 'When we were
looking for those photos Stacey had uploaded for you both,
I saw the trips you went on together, the holidays you took
them on. You made her laugh and—'

'Guilt,' he cut in, the word tasting acrid in his mouth.
'For not being around more. For not doing more.'

'Then you need to make up your mind, Seth. Did you
avoid spending time with your sister? Or did you only spend
time with her out of guilt? Because, hearing what you're
telling me now, I suspect that the real guilt came from your
fear that you're too much like your father.'

'I am like that man!' His voice was getting louder and
he fought to control it, so unlike his usual composed self.
'I don't want to be. I've spent years creating rules for myself to keep me from being like him.'

'Rules?' Her brows knitted together instantly. 'You mean
like never dating your colleagues? Like not breaching the
parameters of the agreement we had?'

'Rules!' he threw back at her angrily, though his frustration was more with himself than with her. 'Yet there I was, doing all the same things as he would do. I threw money at the problem, just like he always used to. Paying her to leave my penthouse and take her infant son with her.'

'I thought Stacey asked for the deposit,' Andrea said gently.

He hated that she still refused to see him for what he was.

'She did ask for a deposit,' he heard himself saying. 'She said she wanted somewhere of her own. And maybe she did. But I didn't even ask her to stay. I was only too happy to throw more money at her and help her out of the door. I never intended us to drift so far apart, but then again I never did anything to stop it from happening.'

'You were—what?—thirty-two, thirty-three? An eligible bachelor who was focussed on your career as a surgeon. Yet you took your sister and her baby in for over a year. No one could really blame you for preferring the idea of having your home to yourself. I can't imagine you ever said anything to her about not wanting her there.'

'Perhaps not.' He raked his hand through his hair. 'But Stacey wasn't a fool; she must have known a part of me resented it.'

'Just as a part of me resented missing out on my childhood to care for my mother, perhaps?' she suggested. 'We're human, Seth, we aren't without our flaws. We aren't supposed to be. But it doesn't stop us from loving them.'

His chest ached with the desire to see himself through her eyes, even for a moment. To be the kind of man that she was describing. But he knew it wasn't who he really was.

His thumb caressed the line of her jaw and, as her eyelids momentarily shuttered closed, he had to battle the urge to bend down and kiss her. To pour out everything he felt—

which wasn't love, it couldn't possibly be, but felt as close as his broken, damaged self could ever get to it.

'You always see the good in people,' he rasped. 'But you're wrong about me. I'm not a good man, but I want to be. I can be. With your help.'

For the longest time, she held his gaze. Then, without warning, she wrenched her head away.

'You don't need my help. I'm not wrong about you, Seth. Because, trust me, I know what *not a good man* looks like. Spoiler alert—it's nothing like you!'

He couldn't have said what it was about her tone that snared him but there was a bleak expression in her eyes that he'd never seen before. When she jerked her head, making it clear that she regretted the outburst, he found himself balling his fists.

As the word 'love' bounced frenetically around his head once again, the idea of anybody hurting this incredible, unique woman slammed though him with an intensity that shook him to his core.

'Who was he, Andrea? What did he do to you?'

Andrea tossed her head.

How could she even begin to answer that? She cursed herself for even bringing up her worthless ex. Perhaps it was the shock of Seth's unexpected confession that had reminded her that she had secrets of her own, prodding her to share with him. As if there was an explanation for why she should suddenly feel the urge to open up to this man and make herself vulnerable in a way she'd never been inclined to with anyone in the past.

Not even her mother knew the full details of her past.

Because you care for him, that voice whispered in her brain. Just as it had last night. Just as it had been doing for some time, even though she'd pretended not to hear it. Andrea steeled herself.

'This isn't about me,' she dodged. 'This is about you not feeling like the *real* you. Why are you telling me all of this?'

His penetrating gaze warned her that he knew what she was doing, and she found herself holding her breath until he gave an almost imperceptible nod.

'Because last night, when I went to drop Noah off at your brother's, he asked me if we were going to get married.'

Her heart stumbled, regained its footing and then began to gallop.

'You told him that it wasn't like that between us?' she asked. 'That I might not be in his life much longer?'

Seth paused, but when he spoke it wasn't an answer, rather a startled realisation.

'I told him that we'd talk about it when he came home today. And that was what I planned to say. But...'

He stopped, raking his hand through his hair again. She realised she'd never seen him look so at odds with himself before.

'But?' Her voice was little more than a breath, yet it fizzed with anticipation.

How could she be so desperate to know what he meant to say yet so terrified to hear it?

'But then last night happened...and I realise that I love you.' His voice cracked, as though he could hardly believe it. As though he was grappling with the reality of what he'd just said.

Andrea wasn't sure how long they both stood there—a lifetime perhaps, maybe two—but, the longer she watched him, his eyes snaring hers, the clearer his expression became, the calmer. As if, now the shock was over, he was seeing things for the first time.

And then he repeated, more firmly this time, 'I love you, Andrea.'

As if he truly meant it.

Shock, and something far more potent, shot through

her limbs, rooting her to the spot. A jumble of emotions tumbled through her.

With a jolt, she realised it was exactly how she felt too. All those *things* she'd been feeling these past couple of months suddenly made sense—thrilling, terrifying sense. She didn't just *care for* Seth. She loved him.

She *loved* him.

She'd thought she wasn't capable of love any more—not that kind, anyway. That losing her baby had robbed her of that capacity. Now she realised that wasn't true at all.

But she had to know Seth meant it. That it was *real*.

'You…love me?' She could hear the wonder in her voice but that didn't matter.

This was a moment she'd never thought would happen. Not for her. She was more than happy to drink in every single, extraordinary moment of it.

'I love you,' he repeated quietly. 'I want a future with you. A family.'

This time her heart screeched to a painful halt right there in her chest.

'A…family,' she echoed, not quite sure how she'd managed to speak.

Her tongue felt too big for her mouth, her skin too tight for her body.

How was she even still able to breathe?

Seth, by contrast, was continuing as though nothing was amiss.

'Noah also asked that, if we were going to have any babies, we have a baby sister for him, not a brother, because Billy could teach him how to be a good big brother to a sister.'

Slowly, so slowly, her heart began to thump again. It did so quietly at first, but got louder and stronger until it was hammering in her ears, deafening her.

'He asked you for siblings?'

'He did. And it made me realise that I want it all with you, Andrea.'

'No…' she whispered, but her throat was so dry and so constricted that she wasn't surprised he didn't hear her.

'I want a marriage, a family, a future,' Seth continued, his eyes shining with something she'd never seen in him before.

It should have made her heart sing. Instead, it made it plummet. And that glorious sensation inside her that had begun to blossom and grow instead started to wither and die—right in front of her eyes.

Family.

The sound echoed in her head, taunting her. Slamming her from the inside, as though it wanted to burst its way out of her body and rain down her shame for all to see. Her deficient body with its deformed womb.

The irony of ironies.

Family was the one thing she couldn't give him.

'You don't want a family,' she countered in a voice that was so taut that she kept waiting for it to fracture. 'You don't even want second dates.'

'I didn't,' he agreed. 'Until Noah came along. Until you came along. You both made me realise what I've been hiding from all these years, with my rules and my lines in the sand. You brought me back to life, Andrea. You made my heart beat again in a way I don't think it has done since my grandmother died.'

'No,' she managed, wondering if that strangled voice was really hers. 'You don't mean that. You don't love me.'

Yet all she could think was that he was right there. So close that she could reach out to touch him. But she couldn't move. Her eyes locked defiantly with his and she wasn't sure she'd ever seen him look so fierce, so passionate.

'I do love you,' he confirmed simply. 'And you can fight it, but I know you feel the same way.'

And she did. There was no denying it. But neither was there any denying that she couldn't promise him all the things he'd told her he wanted.

Family.

The word was like a noose around her neck, killing her.

'No,' she choked out, hating the very feel of the word in her mouth.

'Yes,' Seth countered. 'Everything we've shared these last few months shows it.

She wanted so, so much to believe him—perhaps she wanted it too much. Something unfurled in her belly but she couldn't put a name to it.

'You're confusing sex with love. Which makes you an even bigger fool than I am.'

'As hot as the sex may be between us, I am not foolish or inexperienced enough to confuse it with love,' he rasped, and she could have sworn she felt the words move over her skin. 'And perhaps I should have said it sooner, but I didn't realise it before. Or, if I did, then I didn't allow myself to believe it.'

'Then think again.' She shook with the pressure of the emotions. 'Because, whatever you're feeling, it isn't love.'

'It's love,' he repeated quietly.

'I didn't intend to do any of this.' She shook her head miserably.

He could never know how much it was killing her not to tell him she loved him too. But the woman he thought he loved didn't exist. She was too damaged, too imperfect—too incapable of giving Seth what he wanted. He just didn't know it.

But she did. Which meant that she was going to have to make the hardest decision for both of them.

'I don't know what you feel, or why you're saying this, Seth.' She mustered up every inch of strength she had. 'But I don't love you, and I certainly don't want a family with you. In fact, I think the best thing all round would be for me to leave, as we discussed last night.'

Then, before he could say anything to make her already fragile resolve splinter and break, Andrea rose from her seat and strode out through the bedroom door.

And out of the life of the only man she realised she had ever loved.

CHAPTER FIFTEEN

'OKAY, WE'LL FILL the cavity with physiological saline and then we can go ahead and close up,' Seth directed coolly, professionally. Giving no one else on the team any clue of the storm that had been raging around his head since Andrea had walked away from him.

He'd told himself it was a good thing. He'd told himself just how right he'd been to do it then and there, before anyone became invested. He'd shown her the real him and she'd turned away. Just as he'd feared she would.

But the hard part had been having to admit it out loud to his nephew. Andrea had barely been gone two nights when Noah had demanded to know where she was. He'd tried to explain. He'd taken his time, sat Noah down and assured the little boy he'd answer any questions that Noah might want to ask him.

Even so, he'd shocked himself at just how difficult it had been to find the words. As though his tongue hadn't wanted to speak them because his brain hadn't yet accepted that she wasn't coming back.

It was ironic—laughably so, really—that the only woman with whom he could ever, *ever* have imagined spending the rest of his life couldn't imagine spending her life with him.

It wasn't a situation in which he could have ever imagined himself before.

And, now that he'd had time to think, he realised how foolish it was to believe anyone could love him. Foolish to believe he was capable of being a family man. Foolish to believe that he deserved more.

But there was still a surgery to do. Still a patient to help. It was the first time they'd been scheduled onto a surgery together all week. Ever since the conversation that had resulted in Andrea walking out of his penthouse—and out of Noah's and his lives.

It didn't matter how many times he'd reminded himself that her walking away was the best—the only—course of action. He'd still spent the past seven days trying in vain to quell the sickening tumult that had tossed through him at the most unexpected moments.

He still fought the sensation in his chest that pulled so very, painfully taut that if it pulled any tighter then it would have nowhere else to go and would suddenly, violently, implode.

And he still acted, as he always did, as though there was nothing in his head at all but the surgery and the patient on that table in front of him.

As Andrea passed him the equipment he needed with her usual impressive instinct, he silently congratulated himself on the fact that neither of them had allowed their personal turmoil to adversely affect the surgery at all.

He wouldn't have expected them to. If anything, it had made him sharper and more focussed—grateful to have something tangible that he could solve as he'd spent the last five hours performing a resection of the spinal tumour, slowly and meticulously removing all final signs of the mass whilst ensuring he didn't damage the patient's spine.

The last part had been particularly painstaking. He'd cut away at the interloper little by little as it moved up across the anterior epidural space, whilst trying to keep far away from the anterior spinal artery—it was always such a delicate balance between not damaging the spine yet trying to cut away as much of the tumour as they possibly could.

Seth had been quietly confident about the operation. Constant monitoring of brain activity during the operation had suggested that signals in the patient had improved. Stimulation on the left side of her scalp had produced some very good results, and even though her left side was weaker there had still been improvements.

The more of the tumour they'd managed to resect, the more neurological activity had been evident in the legs. With any luck the patient should wake up with minimal to no deficit.

'You want to use a non-absorbable silk suture to enclose the dura in a watertight fashion using a running locking suture,' he advised Andrea.

And he told himself that it wasn't a sense of loss that was making him avoid looking into those violet-blue eyes.

'Watertight closure will ensure there is no spinal fluid leaking,' she agreed, her head bent so close to his that the faintest hint of her favourite vanilla shower gel wafted towards him.

Under the operating microscope, he concentrated on tying off the distal end.

'Good,' Seth managed curtly. 'Now we place some ties on top, and some haemostatic agents into the cavity. Okay, now what?'

'Irrigate the wound with saline?' Andrea suggested, and he knew it was only him who heard that tiniest hint of a tremor in her voice. 'Re-approximate the muscle layer, then close up the fascia.'

'Right.'

All in all, he told himself, it had been a good afternoon. Never mind the jumble inside him that made him feel turned inside out.

It had been a good afternoon, he repeated silently to himself, because he needed it to be a good afternoon.

'Congratulations on your baby.'

Andrea was proud of how composed and how at ease she sounded. Even if deep down she felt as though she was being ripped apart at the seams.

This past week had been a fresh hell. But, if she could find the courage to walk away from Seth and Noah when the only thing she'd really wanted to do was to stay right there with them for ever, then she could certainly gather the strength to congratulate her ex-husband and his girlfriend who had just stepped through the doors in front of her, barring her way. Giving her no passage unless she pushed past them whilst they took their time manoeuvring their baby seat through it.

And Andrea refused to do that. She simply would not give them that power over her. Instead, she would show them that she was a bigger person than the two of them combined could ever be.

She might have known they'd have a way of making her feel small again. Or that Josh would. The new mum looked so entranced with her baby that she barely seemed to notice Andrea, the love in her eyes utterly pure and unfettered.

Andrea's heart twisted anew with the pain of what she would never be able to experience for herself.

'Have you ever seen a more beautiful baby?' The new mother sighed, besotted.

She clearly had no idea who Andrea was, and somehow that made it easier for Andrea to bear. How many times had she seen new mothers so cocooned in their magical bubbles that they were convinced that the rest of the entire world must surely be able to share in their sense of wonder? with no malice intended in their comments.

The girl seemed so naïve and innocent that Andrea was suddenly struck by how similar they were. The girl might as well have been her, a few years ago. Was that how Josh's so-called charm worked? He just chose the most gullible and gentle of females?

Her eyes slid to her ex-husband, the smirk on his face as he threw his arm around the young woman's shoulders almost making her feel sick.

That could have been her. Despite all her pain, she thanked goodness it wasn't. New baby aside, she actually felt a rush of utter sympathy for the girl. She had no idea what she'd let herself in for with a man like Josh.

'And a boy too!' He grinned triumphantly. 'You did so well, babe.'

Andrea hated herself for allowing the aimed barb to hit its target.

In Josh's wildest fantasies, he could never even be a fraction of the man that Seth Mulder was. *That* was a man worthy of love, worthy of happiness. Worthy of a family.

And a family was the one thing she couldn't give him. Losing her baby had been the most painful experience of her life. She'd spent so long in a black hole, wishing she could stay there and never come out. If it hadn't been for her mother needing her, or seeing patients face death every day, then she wasn't sure if she would have ever come out.

But she couldn't go through that pain again. Not even for Seth. Not even for Noah.

Andrea fixed her eyes on the steel doors in front of her and willed them to move the car seat faster.

'Well, congratulations again,' she managed. 'Anyway, I have work to get to, so…'

'Yeah, good job you've got something, eh, Andi?' Josh shot back, his grin overtly gloating as he used the nickname she'd always hated. 'Nice for old spinsters to have a little job to occupy their time.'

Then, before Andrea could catch her breath, he swept his puzzled new girlfriend away, practically pasting her to the wall as he pushed past. For several long moments, she leaned against the cold plaster—not sure whether her suddenly unsteady legs could hold her upright on their own. Finally, not knowing where it came from, she found the strength to push herself off and woodenly move through the still-open door.

Right into the furiously scowling Seth.

'What,' he began quietly, precisely, 'Was that?'

Her mind scrambled. He couldn't have heard, could he? But he was asking her what that had been about... Could she brazen it out?

'Oh, that!' She tried to wave her hand airily but snatched it down as soon as she saw the tremor in it. Hopefully, he wouldn't have heard the quiver in her voice. 'I was just congratulating a set of new parents.'

'You were being verbally mauled by that...excuse of a man,' Seth ground out, his hand sliding to her elbow as he began to smoothly steer her away.

She hated the way that the heat from his body seemed to sweep over her, warming up her icy body again and making her ache to lean into him. To take advantage of the support he was silently offering her.

She wasn't sure how she stopped herself from doing so. Instead, she forced herself to move forward, one stiff step at a time, and tried to ease her ramrod-straight back into something vaguely less uncomfortable.

'How much did you hear?' she managed to rasp out.

'All of it.' His tone was grim. 'Why didn't you tell me?'

The question wound its way through her and she was terribly afraid she would crumple right there in front of him, even as she offered a shrug of feigned nonchalance.

'It isn't something I particularly want to revisit.'

Was she ready to face up to how much a failure it made her feel, rightly or wrongly, knowing that her body hadn't been able to carry her own baby to term?

'Anyway, I have an emergency surgery to prepare for.'

But he was still ushering her the opposite way down the long, pristine corridors in the direction of his office. And she was still letting him.

'The surgery was cancelled,' he told her.

'Cancelled?' She frowned, not sure she believed him. 'Are you trying to stop me from going into surgery?'

His face pulled into something inscrutable.

'The heli-med called in,' he told her softly as he opened the door to his office and eased her gently inside. 'The patient didn't make it.'

Andrea stared at him.

The patient had died, and she'd assumed Seth's actions had been about her. What kind of a person—of a future doctor—did that make her?

The patient hadn't made it. Just like her precious baby. All of a sudden, the enormity of it hit her and she felt her legs buckle. Vaguely, she was aware of a cabinet digging uncomfortably into her back as she slid to the floor, but the stinging was nothing compared to the pain in her chest as it cleaved open.

She had no idea how long she sat there, sobbing, but when she came back to herself Seth was sitting on the floor right beside, his arms wrapped tightly around her.

'You told me the other week that you know what *not a good man* looks like. You meant him, didn't you?'

Somehow, Andrea ignored the deafening pounding of her heart. 'Yes,' she managed, barely even recognising her own voice.

'You lost a baby?' he pressed as gently and as kindly as he could.

As if he truly cared.

Still, Andrea couldn't bring herself to answer immediately. The silence seemed to swirl around the room, growing thicker with every passing moment.

'You don't have to carry this burden alone.' He lifted his arms around her. 'I'm here. You can share it with me.'

The silence grew more taut.

'Tell me again how you aren't a good man,' she murmured shakily as she watched the fierce protectiveness in his eyes.

Shame and grief sloshed around inside her. And something else, too.

Relief.

Because, even if the truth wouldn't change the fact that she couldn't be with Seth, or give him the family he wanted, she knew it was time to talk. Time to share the load she hadn't wanted to burden her mother with.

If she couldn't admit it to Seth, the man she loved— whom she had probably loved from that first day and had loved even more when she'd realised what he'd sacrificed to take on his nephew—then she would never be able to admit it to anyone.

Because, for her, no one else but he would ever count. Even though it wouldn't change anything, at least giving him the truth would mean he could understand.

Drawing a breath, she summoned every ounce of courage she had.

'Josh wasn't just my boyfriend...he was my husband.' Her temples throbbed with pressure, but she kept her hands tightly pressed against her sides. 'We were married just over a year, but together a few years longer than that.'

Seth squeezed her shoulder gently. Not talking, just listening.

'The day he actually left me,' she continued in a stilted voice, 'I was in hospital and the doctor had just told me that there wasn't a heartbeat. I'd had a miscarriage at eleven weeks.'

'He left you just after you'd lost your baby?' Seth rasped furiously, unable to contain himself.

She squeezed her eyes shut at the memory, but that didn't keep the pain out. A familiar band pulled tight around her chest. That sense of loss that she'd tried to put behind her had never quite gone away. Yet there was something almost…heartening about the expression on Seth's face.

'No decent human being would ever do that.' His voice vibrated with disgust.

She shrugged, as though it hadn't once scraped away inside her. As though it didn't still have the power to leave her with that yawning, gaping hollowness.

'Perhaps. But he isn't the first man to ever do that to his wife. He won't be the last.'

'Why?' Seth demanded. 'Why would you even be with a man like that? Why would you marry him?'

It was a question she'd demanded of herself a hundred times over. She supposed this was the really shameful part of her confession.

'I was young; naïve, really,' she ventured, hating how weak that sounded. 'I was eight when my father died, and I was so busy caring for my mother that I kind of missed out on normal stuff. I had a few dates, but the minute they found out about my family situation, and the fact that I wasn't your usual carefree, responsibility-free single girl, they ran a mile. I suppose I was just grateful that he showed any interest in me.'

'So was he your first boyfriend and he took advantage?'

How pathetic that must sound to a man like Seth Mulder. But then, that was who he was, wasn't it?

'Looking back, I can see that our relationship wasn't a good one, though I didn't realise it at the time since I had nothing to compare it to. He was just after someone biddable and quiet who he could control,' Andrea forced herself to admit.

'Quite a man,' Seth said scornfully and getting up slowly, ostensibly to retrieve a box of tissues for her.

She couldn't help wondering if it was his way of putting some space between them.

'I later learned he had a bit of a gambling habit, and the fact that I saved money and spent so much time with my mother instead of going out meant that he had a cushion to fall back on when he lost. Which he did rather a lot.'

'Yet presumably you *loved* this man at some point?'

The blood roared in her ears.

'I thought I did once. Now I realise I was just seduced by his flattery. He knew how to turn on the charm, but if I could turn back time I would never be so gullible or foolish.'

'Don't ever take on the blame for someone else's failings.' Seth growled. 'He was the one who treated you abhorrently. You are not the one at fault.'

'I know that now,' she managed. She knew it logically, anyway. 'I never really understood what love was supposed to look like.'

It was odd how much easier it was becoming to share her story with Seth now that she'd started. As if she had nothing to lose by telling him about her hateful, sordid past. She had to keep reminding herself that it wouldn't change anything between the two of them, but it felt strangely freeing finally to be able to face up to her life.

'I can't imagine how deeply his betrayal must have run. How badly he must have hurt you,' Seth ground out, as though the words were bitter in his mouth. 'How much he still hurts you now.'

'He doesn't hurt me now,' she said suddenly, fiercely. 'The situation hurt me, but *he* can't hurt me, because he no longer has that power over me. He doesn't have my love, and he never really did. The whole time we were divorc-ing—which, to be fair was relatively straightforward, given that we had no children or property to split between us—I kept waiting for the pain to hit. But all my hurt was centred around the baby that I'd lost. And, yes, I felt isolated—I didn't want to admit what had happened to anyone. But, as far as thinking about Josh went, there was just a slowly building sense of relief to finally be getting free of him.'

Seth scrutinised her with a gaze that was so intense she wasn't sure how she didn't dissolve beneath it.

'That's good.' He gritted his teeth. 'Healthy, even.'

Andrea jerkily shook her head.

'Not that healthy. You were right last week when you said I was scared,' Her temples throbbed, but she forced herself to continue. 'When you told me you loved me, I wanted to say it back. I wanted to show you. But I couldn't because I was too scared of my feelings. And I was also ashamed.'

'Ashamed?'

'You said you wanted children, Seth, that Noah wanted siblings. I was too ashamed that my body had failed me, and I couldn't stand the idea that it might do so again.'

'Say that again?' There was no mistaking the incredu-lity in his tone.

'What if I can't ever have children, Seth?' The words crashed out of her like an avalanche, weighty, unstoppable and suffocating. 'What if I can't give Noah siblings? What if I can never be…enough of a woman for you?'

Neither of them moved even a millimetre. Had she stopped breathing? She couldn't be sure. But, however much her brain flailed for words, none came.

So instead there was silence, and she didn't think any-thing could ever fill it.

CHAPTER SIXTEEN

A WHOLE LIFETIME might have passed but they still hadn't moved.

'You think you aren't enough of a woman for me?' Seth demanded at last, as odd things twisted and pulled inside his gut.

Was this what it had all been about? Was this why she'd run away? She'd been trying to spare him—spare herself—what she felt was the inevitable pain of him leaving her later if she couldn't give him the family he deserved.

'So, in your mind, I said I love you just because I think you'd be perfect for carrying my babies?'

'That can't happen.' Her breath juddered out.

'You think you can't have children?' he demanded slowly as Andrea swallowed hard. 'One miscarriage doesn't mean you can't have children.'

'It wasn't just the miscarriage,' she managed, each strangled word coming out after the next. 'I have a septate uterus—severely so. Corrective surgery would be a long shot, and the doctors told me that my chances of carrying a baby to term are less than fifty percent. I can't go through that again. I can't lose another baby...'

She stopped abruptly, shaking her head.

In that moment, if he could have taken her pain away from her, he would have done.

'Even if that's the case, I don't need you to carry my child for me to feel the way about you that I do.'

He could tell by her expression that she didn't believe him—her eyes shifting between despair to hardness then back again. Or that she wouldn't allow herself to believe him.

Seth silently cursed her ex-husband for the way he had treated his beautiful Andrea. And she was *his*—just as he was hers. Even if she was too scared to admit it right now.

'I don't need your pity, Seth,' she choked out. 'I told you the other day that I have enough going on in my life right now without additional complications.'

'You were scared,' he countered tersely. Was that really what she thought of him? 'You still are. Only now I understand why.'

She was so close he could smell that soft, faint cocoa-butter scent that had become so achingly familiar to him. His body ached simply to reach out—to reach for her. But it would be yet another mistake—and hadn't they already accumulated a litany of them?

'You pity me,' she ground out, forcing herself to step back from him. 'That isn't the same thing. I'm a means to an end for you.'

It sounded jagged and dangerous, and it lacerated him with every syllable.

'You're comparing me to your contemptible ex. Who, let's face it, is the epitome of an oxygen thief.'

And, though he hadn't intended it as a joke, she snorted gently with laughter. The sound took the heat straight out of him. He would far rather spend a lifetime making this strong, intelligent, beautiful woman laugh than cry.

He'd moved away from her, not wanting to crowd her or suffocate her, but now he edged closer again, trying to show how sincere his words were.

'What happened to you must have been horrific; I won't

presume to know,' he began. 'But it doesn't diminish you as a woman, Andrea. Nothing could. You're unique and incredible, and the only woman I've ever wanted to be worthy of.'

'What are you talking about?' Andrea shook her head desperately. 'Of course you're worthy of me. More than worthy. It's me who can't promise you the family you want.'

A hundred things pounded through his brain but he didn't voice a single one of them, and soon the air swirled around them, thick and heavy with the things they were struggling to say.

He had to make her understand.

Suddenly he found himself cupping her face in his hands. Moreover, she was letting him.

'A few months ago I would have said that *family* was the last thing I ever wanted,' he confessed slowly. 'Then you and Noah came along and I realised what it was to share my life with people who matter to me. You helped me to remember what it was like for my sister and I to be a family with our grandmother before she died.'

An expression of pure pain skittered over Andrea's face.

'And now you've remembered what it's like to have a family, you want one of your own,' she managed jerkily.

He had no idea how to chase it away. He just knew he wanted to do so more than anything else.

'You're missing the point,' he rasped. 'You have become my family, Andrea. You and Noah. You two are enough—more than I ever thought I would get. The truth is that I don't know how to be the man *you* deserve.'

Andrea gazed at him for a long moment before shaking her head in confusion. Then, abruptly, she lifted her arms to place her palms over the back of his hands. But, instead of peeling them away as he'd thought she was going to do, she simply left them there, warm and almost comforting.

'So you don't want a family?' Her voice sounded strangled.

'I want you, Andrea. I love *you*. And I love Noah.'

'I love Noah too.' She smiled automatically, in spite of everything else.

'The three of us are already a family—or could be. And that's perfect enough for me. But if we want more then we can do that any way we want to—by birth, by adoption, whatever. It won't make those children any less ours. We won't love them any less, and we could offer them a life that they need.'

'Seth…'

He slid his thumbs along her jawline, repeating himself as if to ensure she'd really, truly heard him.

'As long as you and I are together, we can make our family any way we choose to.'

'I don't… What if…?' She tailed off, her voice that little too high, her eyes that little too bright.

'It's you that made the family for Noah and me,' he told her ferociously. 'We love you. *I* love you. I think I have done from the moment I met you, though I never let myself consider it. And, when Noah appeared, and I finally had an excuse to let my guard down with you, you slotted straight into our lives as though there was a cut-out there made perfectly for you. You made us whole.'

'You could have any woman. One who could give you a real family.'

'You and Noah are my real family. It has always been you, Andrea. There has never been anyone else for me but you. I couldn't imagine sharing my life with any other woman. I never thought I would want this.'

He tilted her head up, knowing from that look in her eyes that she wanted so desperately to believe him.

'I love you, Andrea,' he told her again with all the certainty he felt coursing through every inch of him.

And he knew she was finally hearing him when her body started to tremble with the weight of his stare. Because this was it. This was where she either believed him enough, and loved him back enough to stop being scared, or she didn't. He didn't know how he could bear it if it was to be the latter.

Andrea stared intently into his eyes, and if felt as though he was stripping her bare. Yet then, somehow, building her up anew with his words.

She loved him—she was in no doubt about that. It had been coursing through her for weeks now, for months. But it felt too much to believe that he, Seth Mulder, could love her back, even when he'd told her.

Except he did. He'd said so again. She could read it in every sweep of his eyes and in every line of his body. And this time she believed him.

She'd known Seth the surgeon far, far longer than she'd known Seth the man, and never, not once, had he lied. He was tough, exacting and incredibly focussed. But he was also fair. And honest.

He was nothing like her ex whatsoever. To pretend otherwise would only do Seth and herself a disservice.

The simple truth was that she was scared, and that was why she was fighting against the very thing she wanted most. All the while telling herself that being strong and resisting love was the brave thing to do.

It wasn't.

It was time she learned to make the truly brave decisions. And, as Seth edged another inch closer to her, something fresh lurched through her.

Hope.

Reaching out, she took hold of his hand, forcing her eyes up to his.

'I do love you, Seth Mulder.'

More than she'd ever known possible.

This man and his nephew were the family she'd never thought she'd have. Or had been afraid to have. Whatever the reason, the result had been the same when her fears meant she'd almost lost them.

'I'll never walk away from you again,' she managed.

She didn't know which of them moved first but suddenly his mouth was on hers and her body was moulding itself to him. And the last vestiges of that dark hollowness within her began to fracture and crack apart as new light started to spill out.

Andrea poured everything into that kiss. All the fears she had, all the doubts and finally all the promises that she wasn't yet sure she could voice but that she wanted to make to this incredible man all the same.

Finally, when Seth lifted her up against his deliciously hard body and she wrapped her legs around his waist as he carried her to his desk, they made a new set of vows and rules to each other—over and over again.

Rubrics of love and commitment that Andrea knew in her bursting heart would last for ever.

EPILOGUE

THEY BECAME MR and Mrs Mulder in a gorgeous private ceremony a year later, with a proud Noah in attendance. Their daughter was born a year after that, crashing into the world with a lungful of air that made her big brother grin with delight. A baby brother followed, with the same quiet certainty as his father, two years after that.

'I'm glad, Mrs Mulder,' Seth told her, with an indulgent smile at his contented little brood, 'That you broke though all my foolish barriers on love, marriage and family. Without you, I would never have known how it feels to be made whole.'

'That's because,' she whispered, taking her husband's arm and slipping it around her waist as she lifted her head to kiss him, 'Some rules were made to be broken.'

* * * * *